Italian Industrial Literature and Film

PANORAMAS • ITALIAN MODERNITIES

VOL. 2

Edited by
Pierpaolo Antonello and Robert Gordon,
University of Cambridge

PETER LANG
Oxford · Bern · Berlin · Bruxelles · New York · Wien

Italian Industrial Literature and Film

Perspectives on the Representation of Postwar Labor

Edited by
Carlo Baghetti, Jim Carter
and Lorenzo Marmo

PETER LANG
Oxford · Bern · Berlin · Bruxelles · New York · Wien

Bibliographic information published by Die Deutsche Nationalbibliothek
Die Deutsche Nationalbibliothek lists this publication in the Deutsche Nationalbibliografie;
detailed bibliographic data is available on the Internet at http://dnb.d-nb.de.

A catalogue record for this book is available from the British Library.

Library of Congress Cataloging-in-Publication Data

Names: Baghetti, Carlo, 1987- editor of compilation. | Carter, Jim, 1990-
   editor of compilation. | Marmo, Lorenzo, editor of compilation.
Title: Italian industrial literature and film : perspectives on the
   representation of postwar labor / Carlo Baghetti, Jim Carter, Lorenzo
   Marmo, (eds.)
Description: Oxford ; New York : Peter Lang, 2021. | Series: Panoramas,
   2297-8410 ; volume 2 | Includes bibliographical references and index.
Identifiers: LCCN 2020029531 (print) | LCCN 2020029532 (ebook) | ISBN
   9781788745987 (paperback) | ISBN 9781788745994 (ebook) | ISBN
   9781788746007 (epub) | ISBN 9781788746014 (mobi)
Subjects: LCSH: Italian literature--20th century--History and criticism. |
   Labor in literature. | Motion pictures--Italy--History. | Labor in
   motion pictures.
Classification: LCC PQ4088 .I84 2021 (print) | LCC PQ4088 (ebook) | DDC
   850.9/3553--dc23
LC record available at https://lccn.loc.gov/2020029531
LC ebook record available at https://lccn.loc.gov/2020029532

Cover image: Workers in Fiat factories, Turin, Italy. Originally published in *Epoca*, 16 February
1961, year XII, no. 69, page 32. In the public domain.

Cover design by Peter Lang Ltd.

ISSN PAN: 2297-8410 / SIMIC: 1662-9108
ISBN 978-1-78874-598-7 (print) • ISBN 978-1-78874-599-4 (eBook)
ISBN 978-1-78874-600-7 (ePub) • ISBN 978-1-78874-601-4 (mobi)

© Peter Lang Group AG 2021
Published by Peter Lang Ltd, International Academic Publishers,
52 St Giles, Oxford, OX1 3LU, United Kingdom
oxford@peterlang.com, www.peterlang.com

Carlo Baghetti, Jim Carter and Lorenzo Marmo have asserted their right under the Copyright,
Designs and Patents Act, 1988, to be identified as Editors of this Work.

All rights reserved.
All parts of this publication are protected by copyright.
Any utilisation outside the strict limits of the copyright law, without
the permission of the publisher, is forbidden and liable to prosecution.
This applies in particular to reproductions, translations, microfilming,
and storage and processing in electronic retrieval systems.

This publication has been peer reviewed.

Contents

List of Figures   xi

CARLO BAGHETTI, JIM CARTER AND LORENZO MARMO
Italian Industrial Literature and Film: A Brief Introduction   1

Part I – History, Method, Legacy   23

CLAUDIO PANELLA
1 Industrial Labor in Italian Literature and Film before Neorealism   25

LORENZO MARMO
2 Spaces and Bodies of Industrial Labor in Italian Cinema, 1945–1975   41

PAOLA BONIFAZIO
3 A Short History of Sponsored Film in Italy   59

JIM CARTER
4 For a New Humanism: Literary and Cultural Debate in *Il Menabò di letteratura*   77

EMANUELE ZINATO
5 The Factory as Cultural Center   91

SERGIO FERRARESE
6 Alienation and Class Struggle in Italian Literature   105

ALESSANDRA DIAZZI
7 Care or Control? Psychology and Psychoanalysis in Italian Factories		119

ANDREA SARTORI
8 Class Struggle and Its Metamorphoses: A Path through Postwar Italian Political Thought		137

AMBRA ZORAT
9 Women and/in the Factory		151

PIERGIORGIO MORI
10 Ecocritical Approaches to Factory Life		165

PAOLO CHIRUMBOLO
11 The City, the Countryside and the 'Great Transformation' in Italian Industrial Literature		177

FRANCESCA CANTORE AND ANDREA MINUZ
12 Against Working-Class Idols: Thieves, *Vitelloni*, Hunks and the *Dolce Vita* in 1950s Italian Cinema		193

CARLO BAGHETTI
13 Contemporary Returns to Questions of Industry and Labor		207

MALVINA GIORDANA
14 Italian Cinema in the Twenty-First Century: Representing the Precarious Subject		219

Contents vii

Part II – Italian Industrial Literature 237

UGO FRACASSA
15 Luigi Davì: The Caliber of a Working-Class Writer 239

FABRIZIO DI MAIO
16 Mechanization and Exploitation in Ottiero Ottieri: *Tempi stretti* (1957) and *Donnarumma all'assalto* (1959) 251

TIZIANO TORACCA
17 Giovanni Arpino's Industrial Novels: *Gli anni del giudizio* (1958) and *Una nuvola d'ira* (1962) 261

SILVIA CAVALLI
18 Industrial Absurdities and Utopia in Giancarlo Buzzi's *Il senatore* (1958) and *L'amore mio italiano* (1963) 273

GIOVANNI CAPECCHI
19 Failure and Solitude in the Boom Years: The Vigevano Stories of Lucio Mastronardi 283

MARK PIETRALUNGA
20 Luciano Bianciardi and the New Frenetic Era of Labor 295

DANIELE FIORETTI
21 Writing the Factory: Paolo Volponi's Industrial Novels 307

RICCIARDA RICORDA
22 Reversing the Coming-of-Age Story in Industrial Society: *Il padrone* (1965) by Goffredo Parise 315

PASQUALE VERDICCHIO
23 When Nothing Meets the Needs of Everything: Nanni
    Balestrini's *Vogliamo tutto* (1971)   327

PIERPAOLO ANTONELLO
24 *La chiave a stella* (1978): Labor *sub specie* Faussone   337

ERICA BELLIA
25 Tommaso Di Ciaula's *Tuta blu* (1978): The Voice and Body
    of the Working Class   349

Part III – Italian Industrial Film   359

PAOLA D'AMORA
26 "Casa e lavoro": Southern Labor and the Housing Problem
    in Eduardo De Filippo's *Napoletani a Milano* (1953)   361

ANNA MASECCHIA
27 *Giovanna* (1955) and the Others: Factory Women in
    Reconstruction Italy   371

FEDERICO VITELLA
28 Love Is Not a Many Splendored Thing: Pietro Germi's
    L'uomo di paglia (1958)   381

VALERIO COLADONATO AND DALILA MISSERO
29 *Rocco e i suoi fratelli* (1960): Patterns of Labor, Space and
    Integration   391

VERONICA PRAVADELLI
30 *Il posto* (1961) and the Gender of Italian Modernity   401

LUCIA CARDONE
31 Earth and Water: The Market of Bodies in *La ragazza in vetrina* (1961) — 415

ANDREA MARIANI
32 The Working Class in Post-Neorealist Italian Cinema: Times and Politics of Mario Monicelli's *I compagni* (1963) — 427

ELEONORA LIMA
33 The Factory as a Work of Art and an Alienating Force in Michelangelo Antonioni's *Deserto rosso* (1964) — 439

LUCA PERETTI
34 *Italiani nel mondo* (1965): The Glorification of Italian Labor Abroad — 449

LOUIS BAYMAN
35 A Spanner in the Works: Elio Petri from *Il maestro di Vigevano* (1963) to *La classe operaia va in paradiso* (1971) — 459

ILARIA A. DE PASCALIS
36 The Seduction of a Worker in Lina Wertmüller's *Mimì metallurgico ferito nell'onore* (1972) — 469

MATTIA LENTO
37 Migration, Industry and Class Struggle in *Trevico-Torino: Viaggio nel Fiat-Nam* (1973) — 479

Appendix: Italian Industrial Literature and Film – A Tentative Canon — 491

Bibliography 497

Author Affiliations 525

Index 529

Figures

Figure 1	Maciste disperses the strikers and saves the honest industrialist Thompson in *Maciste innamorato* (*Maciste in Love*, Romano Luigi Borgnetto, 1919).	28
Figure 2	The Terni steelworks in Walter Ruttmann's *Acciaio* (Steel, 1933).	33
Figure 3	The industrial worker as a gearwheel in the mysterious mechanisms of international crime and capital. Alberto Sordi (the small figure in white at the center of the frame) in *Mafioso* (Alberto Lattuada, 1962).	51
Figure 4	The negative impact of industrial labor on women's bodies: Stefania Sandrelli in Luigi Comencini's *Delitto d'amore* (Somewhere Beyond Love, 1974).	56
Figure 5	Alberto Sordi's 'Italian salute' to a group of highway laborers in Federico Fellini's *I vitelloni* (1953).	198
Figure 6	Marcello Mastroianni, Renato Salvatori, Carlo Pisacane, Vittorio Gassman and Totò (left to right) in *I soliti ignoti* (Big Deal on Madonna Street, Mario Monicelli, 1958).	201
Figure 7	Poster for the theatrical release of Paolo Virzì's *Tutta la vita davanti* (Your Whole Life Ahead of You, 2008). The pose of the mass of characters clearly replicates and parodies the famous early-1900s painting *Il quarto stato* (The Fourth Estate) by Giuseppe Pellizza da Volpedo, representing a workers' strike.	230

Figure 8	Marta (Isabella Ragonese) works as a telephone operator in the hyper-transparent workspace of precarity in *Tutta la vita davanti* (Your Whole Life Ahead of You, Paolo Virzì, 2008).	233
Figure 9	Eduardo De Filippo as Don Salvatore, the unofficial mayor of the *borgata* in *Napoletani a Milano* (Neapolitans in Milan, Eduardo De Filippo, 1953).	362
Figure 10	Don Salvatore (Eduardo De Filippo) mediates between the sub-proletarian mass and the ILAR management team in *Napoletani a Milano* (Neapolitans in Milan, Eduardo De Filippo, 1953).	365
Figure 11	Ciro (Max Cartier) in his professional context, at the Alfa Romeo assembly line in *Rocco e i suoi fratelli* (Rocco and His Brothers, Luchino Visconti, 1960).	394
Figure 12	Nadia (Annie Girardot) at the Parondi family home in *Rocco e i suoi fratelli* (Rocco and His Brothers, Luchino Visconti, 1960).	397
Figures 13–14	Domenico and Antonietta (Sandro Panseri and Loredana Detto) look through the window shop, look at the city and look at themselves, and the look becomes the active agent fueling desire in *Il posto* (Ermanno Olmi, 1961).	410
Figure 15	Vincenzo (Bernard Fresson) is plunged in the dark, narrow, infernal dimension of the mine in *La ragazza in vetrina* (Girl in the Window, Luciano Emmer, 1961).	419
Figure 16	Vincenzo (Bernard Fresson) and Else (Marina Vlady) on the beach in *La ragazza in vetrina* (Girl in the Window, Luciano Emmer, 1961).	425

Figures xiii

Figure 17	Prodromes of the strike in the factory in *I compagni* (The organizers, Mario Monicelli, 1963)	430
Figure 18	Professor Sinigaglia (Marcello Mastroianni, far right), leader and inspirer of the strike's organization, makes room for a plural protagonist in *I compagni* (The organizers, Mario Monicelli, 1963).	437
Figure 19	Giuliana (Monica Vitti) and her son walk by the factory's chimneys, and in the background a row of steaming smokestacks paint yellow stripes against the gray sky in *Deserto rosso* (Red Desert, Michelangelo Antonioni, 1964).	440
Figure 20	Giuliana's son (Valerio Bartoleschi) sleeps as his toy robot watches over him in *Deserto rosso* (Red Desert, Michelangelo Antonioni, 1964).	443
Figure 21	Antonio Mombelli (Alberto Sordi) in his classroom in *Il maestro di Vigevano* (The Teacher from Vigevano, Elio Petri, 1963).	461
Figure 22	Lulù Massa (Gian Maria Volonté) in the factory, as the white cleansing liquid from the mechanism forms ejaculatory droplets on his face in *La classe operaia va in paradiso* (The Working Class Goes to Heaven, Elio Petri, 1971).	464
Figure 23	In *Mimì metallurgico ferito nell'onore* (*The Seduction of Mimì*, Lina Wertmüller, 1972), the refinery is a metal Moloch, a dark entanglement of tubes and knobs towering against the pale sky.	475
Figure 24	The Fiat factory appears almost as a mirage in *Trevico-Torino: Viaggio nel Fiat-Nam* (Trevico-Turin: Voyage in Fiatnam, Ettore Scola, 1973).	484

| Figure 25 | In some scenes of *Trevico-Torino: Viaggio nel Fiat-Nam* (Trevico-Turin: Voyage in Fiatnam, Ettore Scola, 1973), Ettore Scola's style is close to social documentary or *cinéma vérité*, thanks to the synchronous sound of voices, uncontrolled camera movements and the proximity of the camera to the subjects represented. | 487 |

CARLO BAGHETTI, JIM CARTER AND LORENZO MARMO

Italian Industrial Literature and Film: A Brief Introduction

Among the "invisible cities" described by Italo Calvino in his eponymous 1972 novel is the city of Valdrada. Valdrada is a perfectly picturesque place, the type of hilltop hamlet that is often associated, in the international imagination, with the Amalfi Coast or the Ligurian seaside above Sanremo, where the author grew up. "Gli antichi costruirono Valdrada" (The ancients built Valdrada), Calvino writes, "sulle rive d'un lago con case tutte verande una sopra l'altra e vie alte che affacciano sull'acqua i parapetti a balaustra" (on the shores of a lake, with houses all verandas one above the other, and high streets whose railed parapets look out over the water).[1] But because it sits "on the shores of a lake," there are arguably not one, but two Valdradas. As if poised atop a giant mirror, Valdrada sees its own image reflected and inverted in the waters below: "ad ogni viso e gesto rispondono dallo specchio un viso o gesto inverso punto per punto" (every face and gesture is answered, from the mirror, by a face and gesture inverted, point by point).[2]

Is the relationship between these two Valdradas one of sameness or difference? At first glance, they are perfectly reciprocal: all events on top cause – even coincide with – their match below. But at second glance, they could not be more dissimilar: a smile requires a frown, height needs

---

1 Calvino, I. 2002. *Le città invisibili*. Milan: Mondadori. 51. Calvino, I. 1974. *Invisible Cities*. Translated by William Weaver. San Diego, New York and London: Harcourt Brace Jovanovich. 53. Wherever possible, published translations are referenced throughout this book. Wherever published translations are not available, the chapter author(s) or chapter translator has provided an original English translation.
2 Calvino, I. 2002. *Le città invisibili*. 52. Calvino, I. 1974. *Invisible Cities*. Translated by William Weaver. 54.

depth, language demands illegibility – Valdrada is a paradox of mimesis and alterity.

Valdrada could stand in for the Italy of the 'economic boom' – that period of rapid industrial expansion which began in the late 1950s – which usually appears to us, by force of habit, only in its constructed half. We overlook that 'other' economic boom, where all phenomena are plunged into their opposites: the Rome of the *paparazzi*, with its public fountains, trendy nightlife, Vespa rides and *dolce far niente* philosophy becomes a metropolis of industrial factories, with its migrant workers, labor unions, mass strikes and workplace injuries. Regardless of one's position in the accelerating cycle of production and consumption, the Italy of the economic boom was a world in transition that required negotiating new practices related to urban living and new values related to self and society.

This essay collection intends to show how the *dolce vita* (sweet life) portrayed by Federico Fellini coexisted with the *vita agra* (hard life) evoked by Luciano Bianciardi (and adapted from literature to film by Carlo Lizzani). It seeks to address the full complexity of economic boom Italy by exploring how industrialization was narrated, celebrated, challenged and even influenced by literary and cinematic texts. Those readers with access to Italian-language scholarship will already be aware that industrial literature and industrial film constituted, if not genres, certainly movements that were as visionary as they were popular, especially between the mid-1950s and the late 1970s. This was the period of Italy's 'late' and short modernity, and it left an indelible mark on the cultural imaginary of the first post-Second World War generation.

But if for the Italian reader 'letteratura industriale' and 'cinema industriale' conjure up a definite tradition of creative production (even a vague canon of well-known texts), for the Anglophone reader 'Italian industrial literature and film' does not. This is due in part to the proximity of these texts to the intricacies of contemporary Italian cultural politics: it is difficult to narrate such a specific historical conjuncture without recourse to excessive footnotes or explanatory titles, and indeed very few Italian industrial short stories, novels and films were ever released in English (for a list of literature in translation, see the Appendix to this collection).

Moreover, industrial literature is chronologically hedged between two strong movements, neorealism and the neo-avantgarde, and English-language survey histories have tended to jump from strength to strength while scarcely remarking on the spaces in between. For example, Peter Brand and Lino Pertile's monumental *Cambridge History of Italian Literature* (1996) masterfully synthesizes more than eight centuries of writing in Italian, but it reserves only two pages for a section by Michael Caesar titled "Industrial Novels." Citing some acclaimed authors like Ottiero Ottieri and Paolo Volponi, Caesar rightly emphasizes how, starting in the late 1950s, literature engaged "the economic boom and the vast social transformations taking place in its wake," before listing fourteen texts, including only eight of the twenty-one short stories and novels covered in this collection.[3] Nevertheless, more recent scholarship, like Norma Bouchard and Valerio Ferme's special issue of *Annali d'Italianistica* titled "From *Otium* and *Occupatio* to Work and Labor in Italian Culture" (2014), has started to drive English-language interest in Italian industrial literature, and many of the essays collected here are in active dialogue with their issue.

Industrial film has been difficult to see for methodological reasons. The influence of the French critic André Bazin's auteurist approach to studying Italian cinema from an international perspective has meant that texts like *Il posto* (1961) and *Deserto rosso* (Red Desert, 1964) were initially seen not as products of the economic boom, but rather inventions of directors like Ermanno Olmi and Michelangelo Antonioni. With the publication of P. Adams Sitney's *Vital Crises in Italian Cinema* (1995), postwar labor was treated as a comprehensive concern of the Italian cinema industry as such: a major theme through which a national visual culture anxiously negotiated its new, post-Fascist identity. But it was not until Jeremy Parzen translated Gian Piero Brunetta's book *The History of Italian Cinema* (2009) that English-language Italian Film Studies took a decisive turn toward social history. One of Italy's foremost film historians, Brunetta, stresses that filmmaking and film spectatorship during the economic boom were

---

[3] Ceasar lists works by: Calvino, Bianciardi, Lucio Mastronardi, Ottiero Ottieri, Goffredo Parise and Paolo Volponi. Caesar, M. 1996. "Industrial Novels." *The Cambridge History of Italian Literature*. Edited by Peter Brand and Lino Pertile. Cambridge: Cambridge University Press. 568–569.

crucial practices through which a particularly anti-modern national culture confronted and attempted to make sense of the changing world of industrialization. But he discusses only six of the thirteen films covered in this collection, while acknowledging that "this now historic window on the world of the workers has yet to be fully analyzed."[4] While this is particularly true of feature films, in the meantime, entirely new fields of inquiry have begun to appear. The most recent scholarship, namely Paola Bonifazio's book *Schooling in Modernity* (2014) and Luca Peretti's PhD dissertation *Neocapitalist Realism* (2018), has opened the question of Italian industrial film to the history of sponsored productions by government agencies and private companies – a tremendously fruitful direction that some essays collected here follow.

In the process of composing this essay collection, which began in 2017 and involved fruitful exchanges with a vast international community of professional researchers, we have always tried to keep three different audiences in mind. First, we have thought about scholars of Italian industrial literature and film, and we have thus attempted to offer new and global perspectives on an articulated and plural artistic movement. Second, we have considered scholars of twentieth-century Italy who have not studied the particular tradition of cultural production covered here, which is often considered marginal or minor but which, upon close inspection, involved some of the most famous Italian writers and directors, who sought to analyze the industrial motor of the economic boom: the factory. And third, we have endeavored to furnish a set of historical and critical tools for scholars of other disciplines, students and general readers who are interested in understanding the story of Italian industrial development and its cultural representation. Our challenge was to compose a collection that speaks to multiple simultaneous audiences, and in a way that is not too complex for some and not too generic for others.

---

4   Brunetta discusses works by: Luchino Visconti, Ermanno Olmi, Lizzani, Ugo Gregoretti, Mario Monicelli, Elio Petri, Lina Wertmüller, Ettore Scola and Luigi Comencini. Brunetta, G P. 2009. *The History of Italian Cinema: A Guide to Italian Film from Its Origins to the Twenty-first Century*. Translated by Jeremy Parzen. Princeton: Princeton University Press. 175–176.

An Italian Industrial Revolution?

The industrialization of Italy, which began slowly during the second half of the nineteenth century and picked up between 1890 and 1914, was at the center of the Fascist regime's rhetoric of corporativism and modernization starting in the mid-1920s. In particular, the policy of autarchy, which was adopted in response to the League of Nation's sanctions against the 1935 Fascist invasion of Ethiopia, was a real turning point in the history of Italy's image as an industrial nation. The Partito Nazionale Fascista (National Fascist Party, PNF)-sponsored Istituto Luce (Educational Film Unit) cranked out propaganda documentaries about the mechanization of agricultural and factory production. The state holding company Istituto per la Ricostruzione Industriale (Institute for Industrial Reconstruction, IRI) absorbed countless private firms, thus extending the influence of the state in economic affairs. Synthetic dyes, pharmaceuticals and fertilizers all boomed; the railways were electrified; telephone and radio service developed quickly; and machine manufacturing flourished, with important technical advances in clothing, leather and wood products.[5] Yet this was mainly confined to the North West, leaving most of the peninsula and islands overwhelmingly rural. As one popular textbook puts it, "Fascist Italy remained a relatively poor and backward country where the image of strength and action was more important than reality."[6]

The years immediately following the Second World War were filled with economic and social distress, as powerfully rendered in neorealist literature and film. But by 1965, about half of all Italian families owned a television and more than half of all homes had a refrigerator.[7] The words 'Italian design' had become international shorthand for sleek, colorful and even technologically advanced products. Olivetti typewriters, Necchi sewing machines, Zanussi washing machines and Vespa motor scooters were

---

5   Duggan, C. 2014. *A Concise History of Italy*. 222.
6   Frankforter, A and Spellman, W. 2009. *The West: A Narrative History, Vol. 2 – 1400 to the Present*. Upper Saddle River: Pearson Education. 643.
7   Ginsborg, P. 2003. *A History of Contemporary Italy: Society and Politics 1943–1988*. New York: Palgrave Macmillan. 432.

being touted in global cities like Milan, Paris, London, New York and Tokyo. What historians call the Italian 'economic boom' or 'economic miracle' was a series of upward-sloping graphs: between 1951 and 1963, GDP doubled, per capita income grew an average of more than 5% per year and about half of the total workforce became employed in industrial production.[8]

How did a country of farmers making grain, olive oil and wine, whose storied landscape lay in shambles after the West's most violent war, become an industrial powerhouse capable of competing with the major European nations – and all in the space of scarcely twenty years? The 'miracle' has many explanations, only some of which can truly be considered 'miraculous.' One obvious catalyst was foreign aid: between 1943 and 1948, Italy received more than $2 billion in food, fuel and loans, then another $1.5 billion under the American government's Marshall Plan. At the same time, the national economy came out of isolation, rejoining the world market and creating new opportunities for global trade. People put their money in banks, which funneled savings into loans for industry. The mix of public holding companies and private firms set up under Fascism remained largely intact, and IRI doubled down on steel production with new facilities at Cornigliano (Liguria), Piombino (Tuscany) and Bagnoli (Campania). The demand for urban labor (especially in the North) was met by a supply of rural migration (especially from the South). Between 1955 and 1961, more than 800,000 southerners arrived in northern cities, often with no industrial skills, no place to sleep and little understanding of the Italian language.[9] Thus, one major driver of the economic 'miracle' – one that historians often overlook – was low wages (while middle-class salaries improved, factory workers were often unable to afford the products they themselves made). Most importantly, Italy discovered new sources of energy. As early as 1944, the state-sponsored oil company Agip found deposits of natural gas in the Po Valley. Then in 1953, the newly formed conglomerate ENI found oil in southern Sicily. From the foothills of the Alps to the tip of the island,

---

8 Zamagni, V. 1993. *The Economic History of Italy, 1860–1990*. Oxford: Oxford University Press. 37, 38.
9 Ginsborg, P. 2003. *A History of Contemporary Italy*. 439.

Italy suddenly had a reserve of domestic power – the cheapest in Western Europe – which was complemented by imports from the Soviet Union.

Thus, the economic 'miracle' was the result of foreign aid, liberalization, investment, exploitation and discovery. It produced a consumer society organized around the café television, the family automobile and the carefully ordered modern home. Religion trended down as building prices trended up until much of the rural landscape had been covered with hastily constructed apartment blocks. Industrial workers rushed into factories, which quickly reached an unspoken consensus that Italian identity could add value to exportable products via an aesthetic of sleek forms, bright colors and dynamic tactility. Italian design quickly spread to institutions like Manchester's City Art Gallery and New York's Museum of Modern Art. These showcased objects like La Pavoni espresso machines, Cassina chairs, Flos area lamps and Solari alarm clocks made by superstar architects like Gio Ponti, Pier Giacomo Castiglioni, Achille Castiglioni and Gino Valle. By 1965, Italy had fashioned for itself a brand-new image, which was also a self-image because it began to influence how Italians pictured themselves in the world.

Historians usually reserve the language of 'industrial revolution' for late eighteenth-century Britain or its close neighbors in nineteenth-century Europe, describing a process of socioeconomic transformation that had very little impact in Italy. But if by definition 'revolutions' must occur quickly, then in a very real sense, what happened in postwar Italy was the epitome of – and not the exception to – industrial revolution. Changes took place in every sphere of social life, from the household, where new objects improved the living conditions of middle-class families, to the more public contexts of work and politics. Many Italians, especially those from the South, abandoned the countryside and moved to the northern cities, where they learned to wear blue overalls, work in factories and measure their labor, but also to understand their dissatisfactions, resentments, desires for transformation, for stability and for the wealth and welfare they saw circulating in the clothes of bourgeois individuals, stores and advertisements.

One important feature of this historical period was the gradual development of working-class consciousness. In this regard, the labor unions and the Partito Comunista Italiano (Italian Communist Party, PCI) were fundamental, but also the dialectic between these more 'institutionalized' forms of dissent and the wave of profound contestation represented by extra-parliamentary groups. From the protests of 1967–1968 to the 'hot autumn' of 1969, the demands of workers and students posed a formidable challenge to the Italian sociopolitical system and achieved a remarkable result with the Statuto dei Lavoratori (Workers' Charter) in 1970. This momentum rolled to a halt for both political and economic reasons (the rise of terrorist groups and the energy crisis of the mid-1970s), the complexities of which we cannot hope to exhaust here.

Nevertheless, such cultural and political movements are important reference points for the essays in this collection, which reflect on the ways in which literature and cinema recounted, mediated and engaged these transformations. Economic and social progress, for all its contradictions and violence, was always accompanied by intellectual reflection that attempted to offer cultural representations, to articulate direct or indirect perspectives on the changes underway. As the essays of this collection show, the aesthetic and narrative strategies employed were quite diverse, but they shared a desire to restore the complexity of reality, which was often simplified in schematic or triumphalist visions of development. The authors of these essays have each provided an original and in-depth analysis of this historical and cultural juncture, a perspective on peculiar theoretical questions or an exploration of the work of a certain writer or filmmaker. It was our task as editors to arrange the material in a coherent way, to give the reader an opportunity to see intersections, exchanges, reciprocal influences and the circulation of ideas and poetics.

Genealogies of Italian Industrial Literature and Film

Some scholars have argued that industrial labor has always been a part of Italian literature. They point to Dante Alighieri who, in Canto XXI of the *Inferno*, wrote about this most important aspect of everyday life, which he defined "divin'arte" (God's art).[10] In their 2007 *Dizionario di*

10 Alighieri, D. 1996. *The Divine Comedy of Dante Alighieri*. Translated by Robert M. Durling. New York and Oxford: Oxford University Press. 318–319.

temi letterari (Dictionary of Literary Themes), Remo Ceserani, Mario Domenichelli and Pino Fasano gloss Dante's passage as follows:

> Dante Alighieri fa riferimento ai gesti frenetici dei lavoratori delle fabbriche dell'arsenale di Venezia. L'ampia similitudine dell'"Arzanà de' Veneziani" esprime una realtà vista e osservata nei suoi particolari tecnici. In particolare, la "pece" o "pegola" spessa e vischiosa e ardente è immagine tratta dalle grandi caldaie di pece che bollivano giorno e notte nell'arsenale.
>
> (Dante Alighieri refers to the workers' frenetic gestures at the factory of Venice's arsenal. The broad verisimilitude of the "Venetians' arsenal" expresses a reality seen and observed in its technical details. In particular, the thick and viscous and burning "pitch" or "resin" is an image of the big furnaces of pitch that boiled night and day at the arsenal.)[11]

Dante's condensed and effective description of industrial labor is, of course, not the only example from the Italian literary tradition. One particularity of the theme is that it lends itself to description, reflection and digression across genres, even when it does not occupy the narrative focus. In Medieval literature, representations of labor were somewhat rare, even if laborers – characters whose identities were tied to their profession – were sometimes present (for example, Cristi the baker or Chichibio the cook, both from Giovanni Boccaccio's fourteenth-century *Decameron*). During the fifteenth and sixteenth centuries, labor became an important topic of intellectual treatises in both Latin and the vernacular, some of which drew connections between human activity and military preparation, agriculture or horseback riding.[12] Labor animated the pages of Jacopo Sannazaro's *Arcadia* (1504),[13] passing to seventeenth-century melodrama and the reflections of Alessandro Verri. But it was not until the nineteenth century that the topic of industrial labor made its way into the center of Italian literature.

---

11   Cesarani, R. and M. Domenichelli and P. Fasano. 2007. *Dizionario dei temi letterari*. Milan: Garzanti. 778.
12   For an overview of these connections, see: Cerchi, P. 2014. "Lavoro e letteratura dall'antichità al Rinascimento." *Annali d'Italianistica*, vol. 32. 31–52.
13   See: Caracciolo Aricò, A. 1997. "L'industria dei pastori d'Arcadia da Virgilio a Jacopo Sannazaro." *Letteratura e industria: Atti del 15° Congresso AISLLI*. Edited by Giorgio Bàrberi Squarotti and Carlo Ossola. Florence: Olschki. 109–116.

This was not restricted to what Carlo Ossola and Adriana Chemello have called "letteratura per operai" (literature for workers) – that expanding genre with which a part of the political class attempted to give workers models of good behavior and ethical conduct – but rather included even the most canonical Italian texts.[14] Alessandro Manzoni, Giovanni Verga, Cesare Cantù and Edmondo De Amicis all offered, in different ways, representations of labor that influenced literary models for years to come. Since the turn of the twentieth century, the topic of labor has remained a fixed presence in Italian literature: in 1909, Filippo Tommaso Marinetti wrote in the *Manifesto del Futurismo* (Manifesto of Futurism) that the Futurists were intent on praising "le grandi folle agitate dal lavoro, dal piacere o dalla sommossa" (the great crowds excited by work, by pleasure and by riot) and "il vibrante fervore notturno degli arsenali e dei cantieri incendiati da violente lune elettriche" (the vibrant nightly fervor of arsenals and shipyards blazing with violent electric moons).[15] In the same years, just before Fascism imposed its heavy hand of censorship, labor occupied a primary space in the writings of Carlo Bernari, Luigi Pirandello, Romano Bilenchi, Massimo Bontempelli and many others. This brief introduction to the theme of industrial labor in Italian literature before the 1950s is intended as a backdrop for the short stories and novels discussed in this collection, all of which are in conversation with this history.

Industrial film too has some claim to the origin story of motion pictures: the first public projection, which took place in Paris in 1895, opened with Louis Lumière's *Workers Leaving the Lumière Factory*, a short documentary that depicts the industrial world. As a technology of mechanical reproduction, film itself was a product of industrial processes, which spliced together modern advances in chemistry, mechanics and optics. But as the title of Lumière's film anticipates, early filmmakers were more concerned

14   Ossola, C. 1984. "Introduzione." In Cantù, C. *Portafoglio di un'operaio*. Milan: Bompiani. 7–68. Chemello, A. 1991. *La biblioteca del buon operaio*. Milan: Unicopli.
15   Marinetti, F. T. 2008. "Fondazione e manifesto del futurismo." *Manifesti del futurismo*. Edited by Viviana Birolli. Milan: Abscondita. 14. Marinetti, F. T. 1973. "The Founding and Manifesto of Futurism." *Futurist Manifestos*. Edited by Umbro Apollonio. New York: Viking Press. 22.

with providing entertainment after work than they were with showcasing production at work. In Fascist Italy, images of industry became practically a monopoly of the Istituto Luce, and postwar neorealism was remarkably lacking in terms of the representation of industry. It was not until the mid-1950s that a more expansive Italian 'visual culture of labor'[16] began to take center stage in the public arena. Italian industrial film, in particular, was diversified across modes and genres: sponsored films promoted the reputations of companies, documentaries registered the gains and losses of the economic boom and narrative features – both highbrow projects by respected directors such as Antonioni and Elio Petri and more genre-oriented fare like melodramas and comedies – added social commentary to a world turned upside down.[17] Such representations of labor also intersected with the formal aspects of mise-en-scène. For example, a filmic fascination with ironworks emerges across several decades: Walter Ruttmann's Fascist-era *Acciaio* (1933), Eduardo De Filippo's postwar social comedy *Napoletani a Milano* (Neapolitans in Milan, 1953), Giuseppe Fina's unjustly forgotten *Pelle viva* (Scorched Skin, 1962) and Francesco Rosi's political film *Il caso Mattei* (The Mattei Affair, 1972) all belong to this tradition. While these films are all very different, they all employ high key cinematography to give spectators a sense of the processes taking place inside factories and the astounding atmosphere created by the elemental forces involved. The spectacular force of iron, whose light emerges from the darkness and invades the frame, produces a remarkable form of the technological sublime, and seems to represent the cinematic concretization of Marinetti's aforementioned electric moons. The continuity and constant hybridization between

---

16   This 'culture of labor' included television and photography, complex and layered in their own right, but beyond the scope of this collection. See: Sangiovanni, A. 2006. *Tute blu: La parabola operaia nell'Italia repubblicana*. Turin: Donzelli.

17   On popular Italian cinema, see: Bayman, L. and S. Rigoletto (eds). 2013. *Popular Italian Cinema*. Basingstoke: Palgrave Macmillan. In the years considered here, cinema was tremendously popular in Italy. While in most European countries, cinema began losing spectators to television in the 1960s, in Italy, this process was delayed, for a number of reasons, until the mid-1970s. Cinema's economic relevance and cultural influence then gave way to a period of deep crisis, just around the time when industrial culture was fading from view.

different facets of the cinematic reflection on labor gave rise to an intertextual conversation that was crucial for negotiating a national identity well into the 1960s and 1970s.

Organization and Contents

This essay collection is organized in three parts. Part I, "History, Method, Legacy," introduces a variety of critical approaches to the study of Italian industrial literature and film, and each essay addresses itself to multiple literary and/or cinematic texts. Some of these essays trace the genealogy of industrial culture before the economic boom, some evaluate the usefulness in this context of scholarly traditions like Marxism, feminism and ecocriticism, and others consider the enduring relevance of labor stories today. Part II, "Italian Industrial Literature," presents what are considered the most canonical literary texts. Each essay focuses on one author, treating one or more work from a diversity of perspectives. Part III, "Italian Industrial Film," mirrors Part II, but it takes up cinematic texts. Here too, each essay focuses on one canonical filmmaker, providing distinct critical analysis of one or more works.

The collection opens with some historical background. Claudio Panella's "Industrial Labor in Italian Literature and Film before Neorealism" identifies in late nineteenth-century literature a tradition of representing factory laborers as 'good workers' that, as Panella argues, served the purpose of discouraging revolt. Moving through the advent of cinema to Fascism, Panella evidences a link between the growth of the working class and the production of films about revolt that in some cases required censorship.

Lorenzo Marmo's "Spaces and Bodies of Industrial Labor in Italian Cinema, 1945–1975" picks up chronologically where Panella leaves off, concentrating on 'the body of the worker' as a cinematic site of tension between Italy's old agricultural and new industrial identity. Marmo follows the body's slow materialization during the years of migration to its extreme visibility during the hot autumn, where, in a wide variety of texts and genres, it became not only a reflection of social struggles, but also a medium for performing social crisis.

Paola Bonifazio's "A Short History of Sponsored Film in Italy" provides a foundational overview of documentaries financed by government agencies, public corporations and private companies, which became very popular after the Second World War. Bonifazio highlights the educational intentions of these films, which appealed to widespread desires for prosperity and happiness in order to promote democratic, capitalistic and modern ways of life.

Jim Carter's "For a New Humanism: Literary and Cultural Debate in *Il Menabò di letteratura*" glosses Elio Vittorini's 1961 charge that writers are incapable of dealing with industrial society as a call to rescue literary language from the realm of consolation and to point it toward emancipation. Carter reviews the contributions of poets and novelists to *Il Menabò*'s special issue on industrial culture, mapping a discursive space that became a point of reference for a generation of literary and cinematic production.

Emanuele Zinato's "The Factory as Cultural Center" explores the merging, during the economic boom, of humanistic and social scientific cultures. This process was visible in glossy magazines financed by companies like Pirelli and IRI, where many intellectuals who were trained in the humanities went to work in sociology roles. But as Zinato notes, when employers began to demand that culture directly serve profit, these intellectuals started to critique the new sciences as tools of exploitation.

Sergio Ferrarese's "Alienation and Class Struggle in Italian Literature" asks how Marx's two concepts were addressed in industrial literature during the economic boom. While alienation is constantly present, Ferrarese finds that class struggle is not, a disparity that can be partially explained by the reformist positions of the PCI and Partito Socialista Italiano (Italian Socialist Party) during this period.

Alessandra Diazzi's "Care or Control? Psychology and Psychoanalysis in Italian Factories" narrates the history of industrial psychology, which became an important social lubricant for production in the 1950s. Diazzi considers both the positive and negative aspects of applying psychological methods to human resource management, namely that it helped workers adapt to difficult jobs but also medicalized discontent. She then assesses what impact this had on literature and film, where the factory space was frequently represented as a sort of asylum.

Andrea Sartori's "Class Struggle and Its Metamorphoses: A Path through Postwar Italian Political Thought" illuminates the political-theoretical backdrop against which industrial writers and filmmakers created their stories. Sartori introduces and comments on contributions from multiple generations of political theorists while charting what he sees as the broad migration of the notion of struggle from its origin in class politics to various destinations within and beyond neoliberal capitalism.

Ambra Zorat's "Women and/in the Factory" poses a direct challenge to scholarship on Italian industrial culture, this essay collection included. Zorat points out that scholars have almost entirely overlooked the contributions of female industrial writers, including Teresa Noce, Anna Maria Ortese, Elsa Morante, Dacia Maraini and Nella Nobili. This is especially unfortunate, because not only do their stories offer different perspectives on the industrial world, they also directly contest the male-dominated canon, for example, by exposing the disconnect between masculinist intellectual culture and working-class life. We might respond by noting that this collection, which is organized around the canon, also reflects its deficiencies: one priority for future research in English (and Italian) should be to re-inscribe these and other female writers in the historical record.

Piergiorgio Mori's "Ecocritical Approaches to Factory Life" mines the literary tradition for a specifically Italian way of thinking about the landscape in relation to humanity. Mori finds that the idea of nature as an uncorrupted sphere, set off from the degradation of urban civilization, is omnipresent in the works of poets and novelists since the Renaissance, but also that it is variously treated by twentieth-century industrial writers, some of whom even expose 'mother nature' as an unprotective fantasy of shelter.

Paolo Chirumbolo's "The City, the Countryside and the 'Great Transformation' in Italian Industrial Literature" takes a similar spatial approach to the question of humanity in nature, but it also meditates on the ties, internal to literary form, between space itself and time. Recalling Mikhail Bakhtin's chronotope of the 'idyllic novel,' which is founded on a double correspondence between, on the one hand, humanity and nature and, on the other hand, space and time, Chirumbolo demonstrates how industrial writers registered the breakdown of such a harmonious model in the age of mass production.

Francesca Cantore and Andrea Minuz's "Against Working-Class Idols: Thieves, *Vitelloni*, Hunks and the *Dolce vita* in 1950s Italian Cinema" reviews a set of films that gave the lie to leftist culture's celebration of the selfless Italian worker. Cantore and Minuz look beyond the well-known Marxist discourses of Stakanovite sacrifice to see the ways in which many directors, leftists included, constructed alternative characters defined by supposed national vices like laziness, laxity and incompetence.

Carlo Baghetti's "Contemporary Returns to Questions of Industry and Labor" calls attention to a new generation of writers in the age of neoliberalism. Pausing to consider both their continuities and discontinuities with respect to economic boom literature, Baghetti concludes that these contemporary returns must be read together with their historical antecedents, a practice that reveals, above all, today's dwindling faith in labor as a motor for social progress.

Malvina Giordana's "Italian Cinema in the Twenty-First Century: Representing the Precarious Subject" also inquires into the most recent period of labor narratives, this time by focusing on film. According to Giordana, Italian directors have successfully depicted the 'precarious subject,' an underemployed worker who must cobble together various short-term contracts to make ends meet, but they have not yet been capable of posing the problem in collective (political) terms, which also seems to be the case for public debate at large.

Part II opens with an essay on one of the most understudied Italian industrial writers. Ugo Fracassa's "Luigi Davì: The Caliber of a Working-Class Writer" presents what is certainly a rarity in industrial literature: an author of working-class extraction. Narrating Davì's fraught yet productive relationship with what he considered an elitist literary establishment, Fracassa shows how the worker-writer complicated intellectuals' understanding of the industrial world but also developed his own inferiority complex as a supposedly unrefined writer.

Fabrizio Di Maio's "Mechanization and Exploitation in Ottiero Ottieri's *Tempi stretti* (1957) and *Donnarumma all'assalto* (1959)" investigates instead one of the most well-known Italian industrial writers, but from an innovative perspective that delves into Ottieri's intellectual biography. After discussing the writer's early encounter with the works of Marx and Simone Weil, Di Maio provides an analysis of two novels that denounce alienation as the result of mechanization plus exploitation.

Tiziano Toracca's "Giovanni Arpino's Industrial Novels: *Gli anni del giudizio* (1958) and *Una nuvola d'ira* (1962)" draws out from two influential texts a structuring tension between the individual and the collective. Toracca shows how in both novels, Arpino constructs a sort of industrial paradox whereby individual action is politically futile while collective solutions require a sterile conformism, especially to the directives of the PCI.

Silvia Cavalli's "Industrial Absurdities and Utopia in Giancarlo Buzzi's *Il senatore* (1958) and *L'amore mio italiano* (1963)" furnishes an intertextual reading of two novels, with special reference to modernist literature and biblical metaphors. Touching on topics like the demise of family-based corporate authority and the rise of consumer capitalism during the economic boom, Cavalli presents Buzzi's work as a search for 'third way' alternatives between apocalyptic denunciations and integrated celebrations of industrial society.

Giovanni Capecchi's "Failure and Solitude in the Boom Years: The Vigevano Stories of Lucio Mastronardi" covers three novels set in Mastronardi's hometown (Vigevano, Lombardy), the capital of Italian shoemaking from the 1930s through the 1960s. By highlighting the author's excruciating depictions of moneymaking as psychological compulsion and nihilistic performance, Capecchi makes clear that Mastronardi is among the most uncompromising vilifiers of the economic boom and its claim to unfettered progress.

Mark Pietralunga's "Luciano Bianciardi and the New Frenetic Era of Labor" identifies in Bianciardi's private correspondence and published novels an early critique of 'the culture industry.' Such a critique, Pietralunga shows, was articulated from a position of interiority with respect to the emerging ecosystem of mass communications: Bianciardi worked at the Feltrinelli publishing house, an experience that had a definite effect on his analyses of, for example, the role of the intellectuals in commodifying leisure.

Daniele Fioretti's "Writing the Factory: Paolo Volponi's Industrial Novels" treats the work of Italy's most famous industrial author while chronicling the evolution of his position from hopeful participant in the project of modernity during the 1960s to despondent lamenter of its unsustainable turn during the 1970s. Fioretti reads Volponi's stories in parallel to the author's friendship with Adriano Olivetti, demonstrating how after Olivetti's death, Volponi slowly lost faith in the idea of a democratically organized industrial society.

Ricciarda Ricorda's "Reversing the Coming-of-Age Story in Industrial Society: *Il padrone* (1965) by Goffredo Parise" begins by noting that Parise's novel opens as a traditional Bildungsroman, with a young protagonist from the countryside who moves to the city in search of work. But as Ricorda's close reading goes on to reveal, *Il padrone* flips the archetype by defining success in industrial society as the renunciation of subjectivity and the adoption of an animalesque materiality.

Pasquale Verdicchio's "When Nothing Meets the Needs of Everything: Nanni Balestrini's *Vogliamo tutto* (1971)" analyses the most memorable novel of the hot autumn within the context of the social, literary and political movements that produced it. Verdicchio carefully illustrates Balestrini's triple rejection of trade unions, conventional language and interclass cooperation in favor of the emerging new left cultures of workerism, the neo-avantgarde and autonomism.

Pierpaolo Antonello's "*La chiave a stella* (1978): Labor *sub specie* Faussone" distinguishes Primo Levi's book from the rest of industrial literature on a number of grounds: it comes well after the economic boom, is a collection of short stories, is set outside Italy and follows a privileged worker, but most importantly it cuts against the dominant Marxist culture that associated labor with alienation. Antonello demonstrates how for Levi, one's occupation is integral to their identity, implying a series of moral and ethical choices, but not for this reason an acritical acceptance of industrial society.

Erica Bellia's "Tommaso Di Ciaula's *Tuta blu* (1978): The Voice and Body of the Working Class" addresses another 'late' writer and one who is, like Davì, of working-class extraction. Bellia contemplates the terminal chronology of Di Ciaula's contribution as a chance to reflect on, and reject, the established tradition of industrial literature, and she reveals how the author castigated, for example, the institutionalization of 'savage literature' written from the factory floor.

Part III opens with an essay on a topic that was more prevalent in film than in literature: migration. Paola D'Amora's "'Casa e lavoro': Southern Labor and the Housing Problem in Eduardo De Filippo's *Napoletani a Milano* (1953)" shows how De Filippo's film overturns the stereotype of southern Italians as unproductive idlers by casting them as the prolific saviors of a northern industrial factory. Because *Napoletani a Milano* was filmed at the real Dalmine steel factory, D'Amora's decision to read the film against Dalmine-sponsored productions is as justified as it is enlightening, uncovering some understudied aspects of the dialog between fiction and corporate filmmaking.

Anna Masecchia's "*Giovanna* (1955) and the Others: Factory Women in Reconstruction Italy" analyzes the Italian portion of an international episode film that fully adhered to neorealism by recreating the true events of a textile strike with a cast of real female workers. Just as De Filippo emphasized the positive agency of a group of outsiders (southern workers), so too did Pontecorvo: as Masecchia points out, *Giovanna* challenged dominant ideas about gender by showcasing politically active women who shun the domestic sphere and end up outperforming their male counterparts in both conceptual analysis and practical struggle.

Federico Vitella's "Love is Not a Many Splendored Thing: Pietro Germi's *L'uomo di paglia* (1958)" covers a film that, on the other hand, can be effectively defined as a 'male weepie.' Germi's film was criticized for portraying a blue-collar character uninterested in class struggle, with a bourgeois mindset and lifestyle. Here, Vitella's formal analysis uncovers the melodramatic techniques through which the film encourages the audience to identify with the flawed yet redeemable protagonist, in spite of his adulterous conduct.

Valerio Coladonato and Dalila Missero's "*Rocco e i suoi fratelli* (1960): Patterns of Labor, Space and Integration" also emphasizes how director Luchino Visconti mobilized the narrative and stylistic registers of melodrama. In Visconti's hands, however, melodrama becomes an analytical tool for offering a layered account of the transformational process that made southern peasants into northern factory workers. Coladonato and Missero suggest that the purpose of the film's family structure is to allow for multiple migratory outcomes, including one brother's successful integration into industrial society and the others' melodramatic failures.

Veronica Pravadelli's "*Il posto* (1961) and the Gender of Italian Modernity" inquires into a similar ambiguity at the heart of director Ermanno Olmi's approach to the metropolis. Making recourse to the trope of 'modernity', which combines positive and negative views of industrial society, Pravadelli argues that Olmi ultimately differentiates between the skills of versatile, assimilating women and the struggles of rigid, maladapted men.

Lucia Cardone's "Earth and Water: The Market of Bodies in *La ragazza in vetrina* (1961)" provides a close reading of Luciano Emmer's film, which is notable for its setting in non-Italian industrial and commercial locations in Belgium and the Netherlands. By homing in on the complex cinematography, Cardone is able to expose how the film is designed to provoke in the audience a bodily reaction: a carnal and gender-differentiated experience of modernity.

Andrea Mariani's "The Working Class in Post-Neorealist Italian Cinema: Times and Politics of Mario Monicelli's *I compagni* (1963)" points out that Monicelli's ostensibly historical film about the birth of the socialist movement in the nineteenth century also deals with a set of contemporary issues that were increasingly urgent in the mid-1960s. Commenting on neorealism's political impasse and the Italian film industry's turn to genre films, Mariani argues that *I compagni* was able to anticipate some concerns of the late 1960s, including the transformation of the family, the importance of women as harbingers of emancipation and the renegotiation of individual and collective subjectivities.

Eleonora Lima's "The Factory as a Work of Art and an Alienating Force in Michelangelo Antonioni's *Deserto rosso* (1964)" takes up the tension, central to Antonioni's film and its reception, between aesthetic appreciation and social critique. Reviewing the director's ultimately agnostic approach to the factory environment, Lima also calls upon his previous work on sponsored films for the SNIA chemical company, suggesting that sponsored filmmaking was a sort of training ground where directors – not only Antonioni – developed new cinematic languages capable of dealing with the impact of industrial society on human perception.

Luca Peretti's "*Italiani nel mondo* (1965): The Glorification of Italian Labor Abroad" treats an understudied documentary film about Italians in Argentina, the United States and elsewhere that registers a curious rhetorical shift in the construction of international Italian labor from unskilled manpower to creative genius. After considering the film's status as an ephemeral archival object and reviewing some key scenes, Peretti concludes by arguing that the insistence on labor migration as a temporary and exceptional phenomenon allowed *Italiani nel mondo* to allay any domestic anxieties about the availability of good jobs in economic boom Italy.

Louis Bayman's "A Spanner in the Works: Elio Petri from *Il maestro di Vigevano* (1963) to *La classe operaia va in paradiso* (1971)" investigates two films by Elio Petri: an adaptation of Mastronardi's 1962 novel and one of Petri's most famous and political films, a striking story about the detrimental effects of the assembly line on the body and mind of a model worker. In Bayman's view, what Petri's two films share is a concern for Italian identity as a product of social belonging and a force with potentially destructive power, here illustrated with the examples of a teacher stripped of his dignity and a factory worker stripped of his humanity.

Ilaria A. De Pascalis' "The Seduction of a Worker in Lina Wertmüller's *Mimì metallurgico ferito nell'onore* (1972)" addresses the work of one of the most controversial Italian directors, especially with respect to the representation of gender. Articulating a wide-ranging analysis that touches on Wertmüller's critique of feminism, her treatment of adulterous lovers and the relationship between personal and political spaces, De Pascalis emphasizes the rituals of social power that come to determine male and female behavior, especially the organization and visualization of gendered regimes of labor.

The collection closes with Mattia Lento's "Migration, Industry and Class Struggle in *Trevico-Torino: Viaggio nel Fiat-Nam* (1973)," which provides a formal antidote to the usual political readings of Ettore Scola's PCI-sponsored film, a hybrid between documentary and fiction. This is not to say that Lento disregards questions of politics; on the contrary, he uses details from the screen to engage historical topics that are sociopolitical in a broad sense. Lento notes, for example, that Scola employs photographs depicting the exterior of the Fiat factory because he was denied entry to the building and thus had to make do with an outsider's point of view.

Such an anecdote is a fitting way to end this introduction, because it reminds us of the slidable distance between industrial society and its representations. In the words of Ottiero Ottieri, one of industrial modernity's most perceptive interpreters, the factory space is ultimately "un mondo chiuso. Non si entra – e non si esce – facilmente. Chi può descriverlo?" (a closed world. One does not enter or exit easily. Who can describe it?)[18] Italian industrial literature and film was often aware of its problematic distance from working-class life and always determined to engage with it.

---

18 Ottieri, O. 2004. *La linea gotica*. Parma: Guanda. 183.

PART I

History, Method, Legacy

CLAUDIO PANELLA

1 Industrial Labor in Italian Literature and Film before Neorealism

The Representation of 'Good Workers'

Italy was a latecomer to industry, and it should come as no surprise that representations of the industrial world in mid-nineteenth-century Italian literature were limited to serial novels: these stories were set in the slums of cities like Turin, Milan and Naples, made to look like the Paris of Eugène Sue and Émile Zola or the London of Charles Dickens by popular authors like Carolina Invernizio and Luigi Mastriani. Considering the low literacy rate in the year of the proclamation of the Italian Kingdom (1861) – 26% for males, 16% for females – these serial novels initially had a prevalently bourgeois readership. A character lineup of marginal and sensational laborers played to this readership's prudishness and prejudices: on the one hand, there was the woman or man of the people, directed only by their base instincts; on the other hand, there was the honest woman or the noble worker, a new configuration of the noble savage myth.

In the second half of the nineteenth century, this last typology became the protagonist of a literary movement that spread through Italy and was modelled on a conspicuous British literary production intended to instill in the masses an active work ethic and the Victorian age's puritan values. Edifying literature for Italian laborers[1] was part of a broader pedagogical trend that was inaugurated in the 1770s with the translation of Benjamin

---

1 For more on this literature see Chemello, A. 1991. *La biblioteca del buon operaio*. Milan: Unicopli.

Franklin's autobiographical texts.[2] These included *La maniera di farsi ricco* (The Way to Wealth, 1758), which was reissued many times during the nineteenth century, and continued with the paternalistic literature of Samuel Smiles, whose *Self-Help* (1859) was released in Italy with the title *Chi si aiuta Dio l'aiuta* (God Helps Those Who Help Themselves, 1865).

Such models were taken up by the textile entrepreneur and industrial author Alessandro Rossi, and by writers like Michele Lessona in his bestseller *Volere è potere* (Will is Power, 1869) and Cesare Cantù in his *Portafoglio d'un operaio* (Worker's Wallet, 1871). The idea was to write a book inspired by the moral universe of Alessandro Manzoni's *I promessi sposi* (The Betrothed, 1827), but also to update that image of sixteenth-century artisanal society with the new reality of large Lombard factories. *Portafoglio d'un operaio* also borrowed Manzoni's 'found manuscript' framing device, enriching it with empirical data and concrete precepts to recount the biography of a southern migrant worker in North Italy. In refusing to drink or smoke (vices that killed his father), Cantù's protagonist confronts labor as a means of moral elevation, comprehends the importance of education, distances himself from the materialist and socialist ideas that have contaminated even one of the factory's managers, and finally meets the 'good *padrone*' Pensabene, a figure reminiscent of Alessando Rossi (who himself appears in the novel).

One of the most read authors of the nineteenth century, Edmondo De Amicis invoked interclass solidarity and a love for one's country in his novel *Cuore* (Heart, 1886). But when he turned to the contradictions of the new Italian State, adhering to a broadly socialist humanitarianism, De Amicis had less success. His novel *Primo Maggio* (May First), completed in 1900 but published posthumously in 1980, denounces social inequalities and the lack of unity among various currents of socialism, something that strains the workers' ability to make demands. In the end, De Amicis' teacher-protagonist, who has already been fired for his ideas, is killed by the police during a demonstration.

2   Pace, A. 1958. *Benjamin Franklin and Italy*. Philadelphia: The American Philosophical Society. 208–209.

In reaction to the spread of socialist ideas, especially among the subaltern classes, the doctrines of self-help and hard work transmitted in the most popular books became more and more conservative during the second half of the nineteenth century. Rather than inciting individual enterprise or promoting the cults of moral hygiene and parsimony, such books tended more and more toward achieving greater social control over the popular masses.

Something similar was happening in the cinema. The protagonists of the first Lumière brothers' films were workers, but even in *La Sortie de l'Usine Lumière à Lyon* (Workers Leaving the Lumière Factory in Lyon, 1895), we do not see the workers' point of view. After the pioneering age of 'documentary' views, silent cinema plundered serial novels and reproduced their models, re-proposing the most stereotypical representations. Such was the case in Italy, where most films were shot between the two cinema capitals of the 1910s and 1920s: Turin and Naples. *Il fascino della violenza* (The Seduction of Violence, 1912), for example, was shot in Naples with the diva Francesca Bertini, whose character marries a worker, then is harassed by a watchman named Salvatore. Salvatore's attempts to organize a strike are merely a pretext to develop his romantic relationship with the female lead. In Eduardo Bencivenga's *Il fischio della sirena* (The Siren's Call to Duty, 1912), written by the Turin-based author Arrigo Frusta, workers strike to defend a man who has been unjustly fired, but the strike is broken, in an ode to interclass solidarity, by the intervention of the boss' daughter.

The same paternalistic ideology comes through in the anonymous film *La giustizia dell'abisso* (The Justice of the Abyss, 1912) and in Oreste Gherardini's *Il domani della coscienza* (Consciousness' Future, 1914).[3] In both films, a 'good *padrone*' on his deathbed names a 'good worker' as his successor. But in the first case, the worker repudiates his factory darling (and thus his class), while in the second case he fails to live up to the challenge and returns to his subaltern role. In the beginning of Eugenio Perego's *Il padrone delle ferriere* (The Owner of the Ironworks, 1919), adapted from Georges Ohnet's serial novel *Le Maître des Forges* (The Iron Master, 1882),

3 Thank you to Silvio Alovisio (University of Turin) and Cristina Jandelli (University of Florence) for this and other suggestions on silent Italian cinema. For on overview of this period see Alovisio, S. and G. Carluccio (eds). 2014. *Introduzione al cinema muto italiano*. Turin: UTET.

the protagonist receives a gift and an important message: "A Filippo Derblay / al padrone delle ferriere / come ad un padre e ad un fratello / gli operai / nel suo giorno onomastico" (To Filippo Derblay / the owner of the ironworks / like a father and a brother / the workers [present this gift in recognition] / on his name day). Shortly thereafter, part of Derblay's iron mine collapses onto some of the workers, and it is Derblay himself who runs to assist the first victims. In Romano Luigi Borgnetto's *Maciste innamorato* (Maciste in Love, 1919), the honest industrialist Thompson – another 'good *padrone*' – must weather a violent strike provoked by a few employees in the payment of an aggressive competitor. Thompson is saved by Maciste, a popular character inaugurated by Bartolomeo Pagano in *Cabiria* (1914), who disperses the strikers and, after having been recognized as the star he is, encourages everybody back to work (see Figure 1). The film was shot in Turin, an industrial city boiling with class antagonism, exacerbated by the sacrifices of the First World War and by the first large-scale monopolies that gave rise to the 'biennio rosso' (red years) of 1919–1920.

Figure 1. Maciste disperses the strikers and saves the honest industrialist Thompson in *Maciste innamorato* (Maciste in Love, Romano Luigi Borgnetto, 1919).

Adelardo Fernández Arias' two-part film *Il delitto della piccina* (The Child's Crime, 1920) reflected a similar historical climate. Unlike all the previous examples, the first part of this film actually shows factory labor, especially female labor. La Piccina (The Child) is the name of a very young female worker at a factory managed by two brothers: personifications of good and evil bosses. La Piccina is fired for refusing the advances of the one brother, so she kills him and – in classical melodramatic fashion – is absolved of her crime. The second part of the film was released in a moment of intensifying workplace conflict, and it shows La Piccina exhorting a group of strikers back to work in order to overcome the post-First World War economic crisis.

The cruel reality of child labor was the focus of another successful film, Ubaldo Maria Del Colle's *I figli di nessuno* (Nobody's Children, 1921). The first part of the film is set in the 'white inferno' of a Tuscan quarry. After a fatal accident, the laborers accuse the manager Anselmo of skimping on safety in order to steal money from the latter. The quarry owner is a count with a big heart, but his mother and Anselmo do all they can to impede his every move. When the film was released, the censors pushed back against certain scenes where the workers seemed too organized, and the extant version still contains intertitles to gloss the protest scenes with careful appeals to non-violence and selfless dedication to labor.

This brief overview has provided a catalog of novels and films designed to educate workers, and to introduce especially female workers to the dangers that waited outside the traditional control of the family. It has also hinted at a series of narrative *topoi* present from the earliest labor stories: exhausting routines, workplace accidents, strikes and layoffs.

Infernal Machines and Machinic Workers

One of the oldest *topoi* of industrial literature (and not only literature, but also other media) is the representation of the factory as an inferno, a tradition that was renewed between the nineteenth and twentieth centuries to address the frightful reality of new factories. The growing ubiquity and size of industrial machinery regularly caused poets of all stripes to treat the 'infernal' environment of workers fashioning materials and struggling against the elements with Dantesque overtones. This was the case for Italy's first truly proletarian authors, like Ada Negri, whose *pathos*-rich verses described the heroic labor and suffering of the workers. It was also the case for men like Giovanni Pascoli and Giosuè Carducci, *letterati* from a pre-industrial world who confronted modernity by passing from a total refusal to a tenuous hope in working-class emancipation via the progress of technology.[4]

Even the refined aesthete and self-designated "Vate" (Poet) Gabriele D'Annunzio scornfully condemned the massification of society in *Il Piacere* (The Child of Pleasure, 1889) as "il grigio diluvio democratico" (the gray deluge of democratic mud).[5] Nevertheless, in the poem *Maia* (1903), he sang the praises of labor with infernal overtones, then in later works celebrated the sublime of new and grandiose industrial companies, expanding metropolises and Western imperial conquests. In this way, D'Annunzio reaffirmed his own aristocratic convictions, representing not workers, but rather entrepreneurs and financers, the Nietzschean 'supermen' of a new capitalist era.

The Futurists were slightly less elitist in their transformation of machines (automobiles, airplanes, et cetera) and industrially produced items and goods into aesthetic objects. The movement began in 1909, reaching its peak in the figurative arts, thanks to the formal experimentation of Giacomo Balla, Umberto Boccioni and Fortunato Depero. The poetic form of the *Manifesto del Futurismo* (Manifesto of Futurism, 1909) – something that distinguishes this avantgarde movement from the rest – aimed to revolutionize the old classicizing approach to Italian poetry by forging verses with a factory rhythm while contaminating verbal and visual languages with the help of new typographic technologies.

Even the founder of the Partito Comunista Italiano (Italian Communist Party) Antonio Gramsci looked favorably upon Futurism. After the Second

---

4   For a good account of these positions, see Tessari, R. 1973. *Il mito della macchina: Letteratura e industria nel primo novecento italiano*. Milan: Mursia.
5   D'Annunzio, G. 1995. *Il piacere*. Milan: Mondadori. 34. D'Annunzio. 1991. *The Child of Pleasure*. Translated by Georgina Harding. Sawtry, Cambs: Dedalus. 22.

World War, Gramsci would become a major political and philosophical point of reference, thanks to the many notebooks he wrote while imprisoned by the Fascist regime. But already in the 1920s, when the Italian working class was beginning to impose itself as a new political subject, recognized even by liberal intellectuals like Piero Gobetti, Gramsci defended the revolutionary character of the Turin-based Futurists, who officially endorsed Moscow's Proletkult and were composed in part of poets with factory experience. Nevertheless, the anti-conformism of the Futurists quickly degenerated from a cult of speed and the aesthetic novelty of industrial products to a cult of the nation, its wars and Fascist politics, enthusiastically supported by the movement's founder, Filippo Tommaso Marinetti.[6]

By crowning industrial progress with an epic and revolutionary halo, D'Annunzio, the Futurists and other poets of the nineteenth and twentieth centuries intended to exorcise a whole series of social and psychological consequences that were generating as much apprehension as expectation. To this end, twentieth-century Italian literature gradually abandoned its reliance on Dantesque imagery, adopting new means to convey the infernal character of human-machine relations and the mechanization of humanity.

Perhaps the best example in this regard is Luigi Pirandello. The Sicilian writer narrated the anguish of reification and alienation in modern society across three media: theater, literature and cinema. Already in 1904 – just after finishing his masterpiece *Il fu Mattia Pascal* (The Late Mattia Pascal, 1904) – Pirandello drafted the first Italian novel with a meta-cinematic theme. *Si gira ...* (Shoot!, 1915) was revised with the title *Quaderni di Serafino Gubbio operatore* (The Notebooks of Serafino Gubbio, Cinematograph Operator) and published in 1925. The protagonist is a movie camera operator who becomes a slave to his machine. P. Adams Sitney has called Pirandello's novel the "autobiography of a metonymy" whereby Serafino is condemned "to be nothing more than a hand that turns a handle," a figure of metonymy for the movie camera itself.[7]

---

6   Vené, G. 1963. *Letteratura e capitalismo in Italia dal '700 ad oggi*. Milan: Sugar. 404–411. Tessari, R. 1973. *Il mito della macchina*. 209–275. Golino, E. 1976. *Letteratura e classi sociali*. Rome and Bari: Laterza. Part 1.

7   Sitney, P. 2005. "The Autobiography of a Metonymy." *Shoot! The Notebooks of Serafino Gubbio, Cinematograph Operator*. Chicago: The University of Chicago

The alienation generated by powerful machines was naturally central to all representations of labor in nineteenth- and twentieth-century art and philosophy. But Pirandello was among the first to give comprehensive literary form to the "loss of aura" mentioned by Walter Benjamin, who cited *Si gira ...* to describe the end of a time-space identity for art in his famous essay "The Work of Art in the Age of Mechanical Reproduction" (1936).[8] Indeed, with respect to the dwindling aura of the artist as creator, Pirandello's relationship with cinema was exemplary of the tensions of attraction and suspicion that characterized the work of many early twentieth-century *letterati*. The culture industry demanded that artists adapt themselves to the realities of mass production.

Pirandello: Between the Film Industry and Fascist Propaganda

Just as D'Annunzio sold his name to Giovanni Pastrone for the film *Cabiria* (1914) – Pastrone's intertitles were only partially inspired by the poet's suggestions[9] – so too Pirandello, who in his public life was highly critical of cinema, regularly sold his own stories to the industry and even signed other writers' scripts, as long as he approved of them.

This was the case for the most important labor film realized under the Fascist regime, titled *Acciaio* (Steel, 1933), set in Terni and commissioned to Pirandello in 1928 at the personal request of Mussolini.[10] The need for a film that would celebrate labor in Fascist Italy was becoming more and

---

Press. 230. For more on the figure of the movie camera operator in Pirandello, Buster Keaton and Dziga Vertov, see Casetti, F. 2008. *Eye of the Century: Film, Experience, Modernity*. New York: Columbia University Press. 83–87.

8 Benjamin, W. 1968. "The Work of Art in the Age of Mechanical Reproduction." *Illuminations*. New York: Schocken Books. 229.

9 Alovisio, S. 2020. "'In verità le sue didascalie furono una palla di piombo'. La collaborazione tra d'Annunzio e Pastrone alla luce di una nuova fonte d'archivio." *Fotogrammi a parole*. Avellino: Edizioni Sinestesie. 49–65.

10 The film's production is also recounted in a popular novel: Soldati, M. 1964. *Le due città*. Milan: Garzanti. 277–312.

more evident, and pressure built on Pirandello, especially after the interwar economic crisis. Between 1929 and 1932, industrial production fell by 27%, and the number of unemployed rose from 300,000 to over one million workers. It was not a coincidence that the production company, Cines-Pittaluga, was controlled by the same Banca Commerciale Italiana (Italian Commercial Bank) that subsidized the Terni Steelworks (see Figure 2).

Figure 2. The Terni steelworks in Walter Ruttmann's *Acciaio* (Steel, 1933).

Moreover, the first Italian sound film was inspired by one of Pirandello's short stories. *La canzone dell'amore* (The Song of Love, 1930) was adapted from the Sicilian writer's *In silenzio* (In Silence, 1905), and made in two other versions with different directors and actors for the French (*La dernière berceuse*, 1930) and German markets (*Das Liebeslied*, 1930). In the United States, Metro-Goldwyn-Mayer made *As You Desire Me* (1932), inspired by Pirandello's comedy *Come tu mi vuoi* (1930) and starring the diva Greta Garbo. The regime's goal was to exploit Pirandello's international stature to its own benefit, an opportunity that culminated in 1934 when he won the Nobel Prize in Literature. However, the writer also knew how to play his cards right. When it came to *Acciaio*, Pirandello really could not afford to refuse Mussolini's orders, so he asked his son Stefano Pirandello to draft a story that recalled Giovanni Verga's *Cavalleria rusticana* (Rustic Chivalry, 1880). In the resulting text, two workers named Mario and Pietro fall in love with Gina, who dates Mario first, then Pietro when Mario leaves for military service. Pirandello's interlocutors, the writers Emilio Cecchi and Mario Soldati, who worked for Cines at that time, showed no particular respect, let alone deference, for the text of the great author who, in an effort to distance himself from the screenplay developed by Soldati and Walter Ruttmann,[11] subsequently published his own version of the story, titled *Gioca, Pietro!* (Play, Pietro!) in 1933.

It was the choice of the German documentarian Ruttmann, author of *Berlin: Symphony of a Great City* (1927), that really moved Pirandello to castigate his colleagues:

> Che vogliamo fare una specie di documentario su quella misera baracca di ferri vecchi che è una fonderia italiana? Tutto il mio sforzo è stato di cavare dalla stupidità meccanica un po' di dramma umano […] sento dire che Ruttmann non dispera di trovare gli attori tra gli stessi operai. […] Ma non scherziamo.
>
> (Do we really want to make a sort of documentary about that miserable shack of old metal that is the Italian iron industry? I have spent all my effort trying to extract from that mechanical stupidity a bit of human drama […] I hear that Ruttmann thinks he can find actors among the workers themselves. […] Now, let's not horse around.)[12]

The part of Mario was given to the famous soccer player Piero Pastore, while those of Pietro and his father were given to real factory workers. If for Pirandello, the core of the story was supposed to be the dynamic between the characters, for the formalist Ruttmann, it was virtually the opposite. The German director orchestrated the many scenes into a proper 'symphony of machines,' fusing the din of the factory to the music composed by Gian Francesco Malipiero. He filmed the entire process of steel production in

---

11   Claudio Camerini has collected and published Pirandello's original story, Soldati and Ruttmann's screenplay and a shot-by-shot analysis of the film. Camerini, C. 1990. *Acciaio. Un film degli anni Trenta*. Turin: Nuova Eri.
12   Letter from Luigi Pirandello to Emilio Cecchi, 5 August 1932. Cited in Camerini, C. 1990. *Acciaio*. 242.

a continuous association of movements, intending to create some sort of dialogical continuity between the factory interior and exterior which in fact were actually in deep contrast: Marmore Falls and the natural world surrounding Terni versus the dark factory reddened with casting materials, the town carousels versus workers breathlessly forging hot metal ingots without any breaks. When one of these ingots strikes and kills Pietro, Mario must overcome the suspicions of the townspeople, who accuse him of purposefully distracting his friend/rival. In the end, the working masses return to the factory in a scene that reverses the Lumière brothers' paradigm while associating the modern laborer with the bicycle, an indispensable means of transportation that will grow in importance during neorealism. Mario abandons his desire to become a professional cyclist, revives his love for Gina and returns to work beside his deceased friend's father.

The film garnered some positive reviews, but its commercial failure was difficult to hide, especially for the Fascist regime, whose hopes of a celebrative masterpiece were undercut by the struggle between Pirandello and Ruttmann. The only effect was to reinforce the ties between Italy and Germany, where national socialism was beginning to assert itself, and where *Acciaio* was distributed with the title *Arbeit macht glücklich* (Work Makes You Happy) Pirandello himself was present at the German premiere, amid a "jubilation of Italian and Nazi flags."[13]

Fascist Censorship and Precursors to Neorealism

Acciaio was marked by the formalist aesthetics of the 1920s avantgardes, but it also anticipated elements of neorealism in its use of non-professional actors and on-location shooting, both in the countryside and in the factory. Such elements were also present in Alessandro Blasetti's *La tavola dei poveri* (The Table of the Poor), made by the same Cines production company in 1932. The film's screenplay was adapted by Soldati and Cecchi from a theatrical piece by Raffaele Viviani. Though it presents itself as a

---

13   Camerini, C. 1990. *Acciaio*. 49.

comedy, *La tavola dei poveri* also shows the grinding misery of a large Neapolitan population, including the protagonist, who is a disgraced aristocrat. In a celebrated scene, the protagonist enters the real Officine Ferroviarie Meridionali di Napoli (Southern Railway Factory of Naples), passing among tram cars and motors still under construction. A long tracking shot through the workstations was accomplished by placing the camera on the same rails used during factory production.

Nevertheless, starting with *Sole* (Sun, 1929) and *Terra madre* (Mother Earth, 1931) and continuing through *Quattro passi fra le nuvole* (A Walk in the Clouds, 1942), Blasetti's variety of realism was more interested in rurality. Such a poetics corresponded in literature to the 'Strapaese' (super-country) current, which shared the Fascist regime's defense of peasant values and autarchy. This was set off against the 'Stracittà' (super-city) current, represented by Massimo Bontempelli's magazine *900*.[14]

At the intersection of these two currents, but also somewhat beyond them, was the most important proletarian novel before neorealism: Carlo Bernari's *Tre operai* (Three Workers, 1934). This too was set in a Naples poised between the reality of underdevelopment and a desire to industrialize, and it was the first title in the Rizzoli publishing house's series 'I Giovani' (The Young Ones), directed by the future neorealist screenwriter Cesare Zavattini. Bernari was a self-taught writer who had lived in France, encountered literature and surrealist films, and even began using cinematic and polemical objectivist techniques to undermine the authority of art prose, including D'Annunzian and Futurist rhetoric. The protagonists of *Tre operai* are Teodoro, Marco and Anna, three workers in search of fortune around the First World War years. Like Bernari himself, Teodoro has a father who owns an industrial laundromat and drycleaner. Teodoro

---

14   Massimo Bontempelli also wrote industrial novels like *522. Racconto di una giornata* (522: Story of a Day, 1932), commissioned by Fiat to celebrate the release of a new automobile. Fiat's promotion of industrial literature also produced Pietro Maria Bardi's novel *La strada e il volante* (The Road and the Steering Wheel, 1935). Moreover, during the 1930s, Italy's first industrial intellectuals began to recount their experiences. Leonardo Sinisgalli published *Ritratti di macchine* (Portraits of Machines) in 1937, then was hired by the Olivetti company together with many other writers.

cultivates socialist ideas, but fails to fully apply them in any southern industrial context, from Taranto (Apulia) to Crotone (Calabria). With the help of Marco, Teodoro finally succeeds in occupying a factory, but Anna – who is sick at home – dies, the strike fails and Teodoro is arrested. The protagonist incarnates the immaturity and impotence of the Italian proletariat during the regime years, putting on display a sort of *ménage à trois* that Giovanni Arpino will take up in *Una nuvola d'ira* (A Cloud of Rage, 1962).

The release of *Tre operai* was met with a Fascist censorship campaign – Mussolini himself called the novel "communist"[15] – and even after significant cuts to the original text (subsequently restored by Bernari for 1951 and 1965 editions), the volume enjoyed only partial distribution. Romano Bilenchi's *Il Capofabbrica* (The Foreman, 1935) met a similar fate. Like Bernari, Bilenchi was the son of an entrepreneur, and he grew up among workers. The protagonist of *Il Capofabbrica* is Marco, a fascist laborer who befriends the communist Andrea. Marco's political conversion is not quite explicated in the novel, but Bilenchi narrates the long arc of a journey toward self-consciousness through labor and interclass communication. The original ending was deemed too 'subversive' (it was published in full only after the Second World War), but at any rate, the novel circulated widely and had a notable influence on Italian literature in the 1940s.

The lives of Bilenchi and Bernari illustrate the contradictions of what some historians have labelled 'imperfect totalitarianism':[16] Bernari was prevented from leaving the country, yet despite the regime's hostility, he continued to win prizes, write for journals and magazines and work as a screenwriter. Not only did official Fascist dogma attempt to conjugate rural values with a modernization process that was imagined as a military industrialism; it also cared less than one might think about controlling and censoring either literature or cinema. This is partially due to the fact that Italian cultural geography has always been polycentric, both in terms of literary and – at least during the first decades of the twentieth century – cinematic

15 Franchini, A. 2011. "Prefazione." in Bernari C. *Tre operai*. Venice: Marsilio, 7.
16 For more on the concept of imperfect totalitarianism, see Aquarone, A. 1995. *L'organizzazione dello Stato totalitario*. Turin: Einaudi. 290–311. It should be borne in mind that this thesis has been criticized, for example, in Gentile, E. 2008. *La via italiana al totalitarismo*. Rome: Carocci.

production. For example, many industrial documentaries slipped easily by the censors: Giuseppe Ceccarelli and Eugenio Fontana made *Col ferro e col fuoco* (With Iron and Fire, 1926) for the Italsider steelworks company, showing the entire steelmaking process without concessions to the official rhetoric of labor; Umberto Barbaro made *Cantieri dell'Adriatico* (Adriatic Construction Sites, 1932–1933) for the Cines production company, including an unglossed shot from Monfalcone (Venezia Giulia) of a banner reading "Viva Lenin." If in Mario Camerini's 1930 film *Rotaie* (Rails), the adventurous protagonist becomes a worker in order to support his wife, in Francesco Pasinetti's 1934 film *Il canale degli angeli* (The Canal of the Angels), a story of proletarian adultery is presented from the point of view of a child, and in a Venice that is anything but picturesque. *Il canale degli angeli* did not have a wide national distribution, but it anticipated proto-neorealist films like *I bambini ci guardano* (The Children Are Watching Us, 1942) by Vittorio De Sica and *Ossessione* (Obsession, 1943) by Luchino Visconti.

With respect to cinema, Fascist cultural paternalism concentrated on the production of propaganda documentaries used to indoctrinate the adult population through the Opera Nazionale Dopolavoro (National Afterwork Recreational Club). The production of 'cinegiornali' (newsreels) was gradually monopolized by the Istituto Luce – an acronym for L'Unione Cinematografica Educativa (Educational Film Union) – inaugurated by Mussolini in 1924 and dubbed "il megafono del governo" (the megaphone of the government).[17] Starting in 1926–1927, commercial cinemas were obliged to show these reports, which usually concentrated on domestic goals or Italian imperial wars in Africa. It was only in 1937, with the inauguration of Cinecittà (Cinema City) studios, that the cinema industry was definitively centralized in Rome, enabling a more autarkic coordination of fiction filmmaking.

Until that moment, Italian commercial cinemas were regularly filled with Hollywood productions. These were pure entertainment films, though Maria Casalini has called them "trasgressioni a lieto fine" (transgressions

---

17 Zagarrio, V. 2004. *Cinema e fascismo*. Venice: Marsilio. 157–186. Lussana, F. 2019. *Cinema Educatore: L'Istituto Luca dal fascismo alla Liberazione (1924–1945)*. Rome: Carocci.

with a happy ending) because they nourished the audience's escapist aspirations with calculated risk.[18] Screenings of Soviet films were reduced to a minimum, and European auteur cinema was turned over to the Fascist censors. Among the films deemed most dangerous were Fritz Lang's *Metropolis* (1927), which saw significant cuts to the scenes of workers arriving slowly on the job, and René Clair's *À nous la liberté* (Freedom for Us, 1931), whose title was changed to *A me la libertà* (Freedom for Me). The scenes of workers having fun while machines automatically perform their labor were censored in Clair's film. As regards censored Italian cinema, the release of Ivo Perilli's *Ragazzo* (1934) was blocked on account of its antirhetorical depiction of the Roman peripheries, unacceptable for a regime that had baptized Rome the new *Caput Mundi*.

After the fall of Mussolini in 1943, the Second World War and the Liberation definitively removed the veil from the miseries of the Italian proletariat. Writers and directors were given the chance to gain immediate experience of the working world – to develop stories and films for the postwar years – and more and more laborers took up to narrate their own lives.

Translated by Jim Carter

18   Casalini, M. 2016. "Tra Hollywood e Cinecittà: modelli di genere nell'Italia fascista." *Donne e cinema*. Edited by Maria Casalini. Rome: Viella. 28.

LORENZO MARMO

2 Spaces and Bodies of Industrial Labor in Italian Cinema, 1945–1975

In this chapter, I explore the ways Italian narrative cinema has dealt with the theme of industrial labor in a period ranging from the postwar moment to the mid-1970s.[1] In such a timeframe, the figure of the factory worker slowly came into focus through a wide variety of different narratives, styles and genres. In order to account for these heterogeneous representations, the following discussion is divided into three sections, ordered chronologically yet also organized around some thematic specificities and narrative tropes: the emphasis on landscape, the relationship between labor and movement across space, and the attention to the workers' embodied experience.

The Postwar, Reconstruction and the Loss of Landscape

Industrial labor is largely absent from immediate postwar narrative cinema. The most important film movement of this period, neorealism, depicted the postwar scenario as one of wide-ranging lack and despair.[2]

---

1   Andrea Sangiovanni has written an important analysis of the perceptions and representations of industrial workers between 1950 and 1980, employing many visual and audiovisual materials to support his historiographical argument. See: Sangiovanni, A. 2006. *Tute blu: La parabola operaia nell'Italia repubblicana*. Turin: Donzelli. For a wider historical discussion of the period, see: Crainz, G. 2003. *Il paese mancato. Dal miracolo economico agli anni Ottanta*. Rome: Donzelli.

2   A different case can be made for a lesser-known melodrama like Max Neufeld's *Un uomo ritorna* (Revenge, 1946), a film recounting the struggle of patriarch Gino Cervi's efforts to reactivate his family's hydroelectric mill after his return from the

The protagonists of the core group of neorealist films are usually portrayed in their struggle for survival through menial jobs, such as shoeshines or bill stickers. Lamberto Maggiorani, the non-professional actor chosen by Vittorio De Sica and Cesare Zavattini to play the lead in *Ladri di biciclette* (Bicycle Thieves, 1948), was in fact a worker at the mechanical manufacturing company Breda. Yet the character he plays in the film is the symbol of the high unemployment rates plaguing the country in the 1940s. Wary of any discourse on progress – perceived as tainted by its complicity with the triumphalist rhetoric of the Fascist regime – neorealism preferred to chronicle the dramatic plight faced by the Italian people during and after the war through the tropes of suffering and victimhood.[3]

When they did deal with the dynamics of labor, the films of this era focused on the rural or maritime rather than the industrial complex, coherently with the predominantly agrarian economy of the country: see, for example, the Marxist-informed representations offered by Aldo Vergano's *Il sole sorge ancora* (Outcry, 1946), Giuseppe De Santis' trilogy *Caccia tragica* (Tragic Hunt, 1947), *Riso amaro* (Bitter Rice, 1949) and *Non c'è pace tra gli ulivi* (No Peace Under the Olive Tree, 1950) or Luchino Visconti's *La terra trema* (1948). Another important film of the time, Pietro Germi's *Il cammino della speranza* (Path of Hope, 1950), confirmed the crucial role played by the rural landscape in the postwar imaginary. It described the whole country as a hostile environment, the only chance for survival left to its southern Italian miner protagonists being migration abroad.

A rare direct representation of the factory in postwar Italian cinema is to be found in Carlo Lizzani's *Achtung! Banditi!* (Attention! Bandits!,

---

war. The film's anachronistic praise of the strong man in command was probably the cause for its decades-long disappearance, before a recent rediscovery by film scholars. See: O'Rawe, C. 2017. "Back for Good: Melodrama and the Returning Soldier in Post-war Italian cinema." *Modern Italy*, vol. 22. 123–142.

[3] On the troubled relationship between neorealism and modernity, see: Forgacs, D. 2008. "Neorealismo, identità nazionale, modernità." *Incontro al neorealismo. Luoghi e visioni di un cinema pensato al presente*. Edited by Luca Venzi. Rome: Fondazione Ente dello Spettacolo. 41–47. On the themes of suffering and victimhood in neorealism, see: Schoonover, K. 2012. *Brutal Vision: The Neorealist Body in Postwar Italian Cinema*. Minneapolis: University of Minnesota Press.

1951): the film describes the resistance to Nazi-fascism in the Liguria region, focusing on the alliance between the partisans operating in the mountains around Genoa and the industrial laborers active in the city. Aiming at renewing the celebration of the combined efforts of all strata of society in the fight for freedom that had characterized earlier neorealist films – like Roberto Rossellini's *Roma città aperta* (Rome, Open City, 1945) – the film confirms the role played by industrial workers in the collective struggle[4] evoking a thoroughly powerful image: refusing any collaboration with the German invaders, the workers bravely meet their deaths by hanging on the same steam crane that was the instrument of their labor. The originality of such an account, in the context of postwar Italian cinema, derives from the rather unique initiative the film originated from: the project was financed by a cooperative of local industrial laborers through the promotion of a crowdfunding campaign. The film thus represents an interesting attempt at bypassing the hesitancy of mainstream studios to back more independent-minded projects (the director, Carlo Lizzani, had been a partisan himself and was a member of the Communist Party) and rebutting the industrial mode of film production.

And yet, even in such a politically conscious film, the mass of laborers is shown to be guided in its heroic effort by a leader higher in rank: an engineer played by Andrea Checchi, who refers to the mass of laborers as "i miei operai" (my workers). Such an element of paternalism in the class dynamics was also present, and predictably far stronger, in other, more mainstream, narratives of the time: see, for example, one of Raffaello Matarazzo's highly popular melodramas, *I figli di nessuno* (Nobody's Children, 1951).[5] The film's male protagonist, played by Amedeo Nazzari, owns a marble quarry, and his relationship with the workers is at once authoritative and friendly, respectful and protective, perpetuating the fantasy of the owner as a good father. Such a metaphorical structure is literalized when, through the convolutions of the melodramatic plot, the illegitimate son of the industrialist

---

4   On the historical importance of workers in the resistance against Fascism and Nazism, see: Musso, S. 2011. *Storia del lavoro in Italia. Dall'Unità a oggi.* Venice: Marsilio. 176–181.
5   This was the remake of a successful silent film. See Claudio Panella's chapter in this volume.

(a lineage both of them are unaware of at this point) is employed in the quarry. The young man is instrumental to channel the workers' growing discontent towards a revolt. The elements of class struggle the narrative introduces are, however, completely displaced onto the oedipal structure: in the end, the conflict is only solved at the familial level, any potential strand of actual class consciousness swept off by the melodramatic anagnorisis between father and son, and the consequent inter-generational reconciliation. Essential to the cathartic ending is a spectacular collapse in the marble cave: the film thus reaches its conclusion through an enhancement of its already strong elemental imaginary (the plot also involves an arson and a suicidal fantasy by a waterfall), firmly locating the narrative's heart in the realm of nature (and passion), rather than in any actual reflection on the dynamics of labor.

The negotiation between such an emphasis on ruralism, landscape and the environment,[6] on the one hand, and the fashioning of an alternative, innovative version of industrial modernity, on the other, emerged as an issue of ever increasing import as the 1950s progressed. The debate grew more contentious in the years leading up to the economic boom, and the divisions in the public sphere are rather evident when looked at through the filter of audiovisual production. While sponsored films became a crucial instrument to advocate the positivistic perspectives of institutional culture,[7] narrative cinema, albeit sparsely tackling the theme of industrial labor, rather assumed a demystifying attitude towards official, pompous statements on the topic.[8]

Some of the most influential directors of the decade emancipated themselves from the precepts of neorealism to produce more patently

---

6   See: Steimatsky, N. 2008. *Italian Locations. Reinhabiting the Past in Postwar Cinema*. Minneapolis: University of Minnesota Press.

7   On sponsored films, see: Bonifazio, P. 2014. *Schooling in Modernity: The Politics of Sponsored Films in Postwar Italy*. Toronto: University of Toronto Press. See also Bonifazio's chapter in this volume.

8   *Napoletani a Milano* (Neapolitans in Milan, Eduardo De Filippo, 1953) and *Giovanna* (Gillo Pontecorvo, 1955) constitute two important exceptions to this trend. For an analysis of these films' more nuanced take on industrial modernity, see Paola D'Amora and Anna Masecchia's chapters in this volume.

modernist[9] reflections on the bewilderment of humankind in the age of industrial labor. With *Europa '51* (Europe '51, 1952), Roberto Rossellini explicitly condemned the shortcomings of both communism and Catholicism, the two main ideologies of 1950s Italian culture, for their inability to interpret contemporary concerns. A few years later, Michelangelo Antonioni proceeded along the same path with *Il grido* (The Outcry, 1957). The film is the story of an industrial worker whose life plunges into a state of disarray after the end of a love affair: heartbroken, Aldo (Steve Cochran) decides to quit his job and wander aimlessly through the peripheral, exasperatingly flat and empty landscapes along the river Po, in the company of his young daughter. Masterfully exploiting the misty atmospheres of the region, Gianni Di Venanzo's cinematography has been effectively described as "una sinfonia del grigio" (a symphony of gray):[10] the unsparingly monotonous shade of the world around the protagonist becomes a perfect aesthetic correlate to his depression. Aldo is a proletarian whose deep-seated alienation cannot be canalized towards the usual forms of class struggle (he is extraneous to his colleagues' strike) because it has a deeper existential origin. This does not mean that his malaise is unrelated to industrial society: Aldo's melancholy is clearly also the effect of humankind having lost a more harmonious relationship with the natural landscape. The peripheral spaces he travels are studded with industrial architecture and symbols of progress (factories, gas pumps, construction works) whose positive connotations are, however, extrinsic to his individual experience. The film is thus animated by a pronounced environmental sensibility: Antonioni's film mourns the detachment from nature as a sign of the catastrophe of the times.[11] The protagonist's wandering becomes a painful going around in circles, and the film's modernist, lagging narration intentionally hinders the spectator's perception of the exact amount of time transpiring between the different sequences. Aldo

9   On cinematic modernism, see: Kovács, A. B. 2007. *Screening Modernism: European Art Cinema, 1950–1980*. Chicago and London: The University of Chicago Press.
10 Bernardi, S. 2002. *Il paesaggio nel cinema italiano*. Venice: Marsilio. 149.
11 For an examination of Antonioni's previous and subsequent cinematic investigations on labor, see Eleonora Lima's chapter on his later film *Il deserto rosso* (Red Desert, 1964) in this volume.

eventually gives up any hope to get back in synch with his epoch: in the film's last scene he kills himself by jumping off the tower of the factory where he used to work. Once again, as in the case of *Achtung! Banditi!*, the factory's very structures are associated with death: where Lizzani's characters confronted a heroic sacrifice, though, Antonioni's protagonist proclaims his ultimate defeat. *Il grido* thus ends its reflection on a note of radical negativity. Such a tragic ending, as well as the film's structuring of the narrative around the trope of the journey, makes it a pivotal text to understand later representations of labor subjectivity, as we shall see. At the same time, it must also be recognized that the film's focus, while not devoid of sociological and political implications, still concerns something wider and more philosophical than any concrete preoccupation with the experience of the 1950s Italian individual *qua* industrial worker.[12]

The Economic Boom: Trajectories of Discovery and Alienation

A keener, more specific interest in the themes of industrial labor emerged in the 1960s. The decade saw intense political mobilization, and with the advancement of the political struggle, industrial workers started to become more visible figures in the public arena. Most of the portrayals of industrial era subjectivity proposed by the films of the time are strongly linked to the issue of movement and migration, focusing on one of the three types of relocation propelled by work opportunities (the commute

---

12 It is not my intention, of course, to reiterate the criticism aimed at the time at Antonioni's film by left-wing commenters for its preferred focus on the private, inner life of the working-class protagonist, rather than his political struggle. Similar criticisms were also aimed at Pietro Germi's important depictions of industrial era masculinity, *Il ferroviere* (The Railroad Man, 1956) and *L'uomo di paglia* (A Man of Straw, 1958, analysed by Federico Vitella in the present volume). While Antonioni's film and Germi's diptych are radically different films, such criticisms sound myopic and unfair in both instances today.

between dwelling and workplace, the movement internal to Italy, usually describing a trajectory from South to North, and the migration abroad). From Lizzani's adaptation of Luciano Bianciardi's *La vita agra* (It's a Hard Life, 1964) to Luciano Emmer's *La ragazza in vetrina* (Girl in the Window, 1961), many films of the time successfully exploit cinema's intrinsic link to travel to reflect on the superimposition of different spatial perceptions and experiences characterizing the life of the worker.[13] The results of such movements range from integration to alienation.

The director who reflected most constantly on such themes was perhaps Ermanno Olmi. The earlier phase of his directorial career (after debuting with a series of sponsored films and documentaries while working in the film department of the electric utility company Edison-Volta) invariably deals with work-related movements in space that become a coming of age experience for the protagonists.[14] In his first and second feature-length films, *Il tempo si è fermato* (Time Stood Still, 1959) and *Il posto* (1961), Olmi associates employment with the acquiring of new knowledge and becoming attuned to a new atmosphere, and such a process is brought to even more interesting results in his third film, *I fidanzati* (1963). The film deals with quite an original trajectory, recounting the relocation of a Milanese skilled worker to Sicily. Giovanni (Carlo Cabrini)'s experience of the world that surrounds him involves both the acknowledgment of the imposing effect of the industrial factory on the southern landscape and the exploration of the environments hosting older working practices, such as saltworks and mills. The expanding of the horizon that such a process entails is aptly rendered through the recourse to the widescreen and frequent horizontal pans. Giovanni's encounter with Sicily is also intertwined with flashbacks, flashforwards and mental images, in order to suggest some parallelisms with his life in Milan. Through such an elliptical narrative style we also witness the effects of the migration on the protagonist's relationship with his girlfriend, who has stayed up north: their love affair, which has

13 On cinema's intrinsic link to travel, see: Bruno, G. 2002. *Atlas of Emotions: Journeys in Art, Architecture, and Film*, London and New York: Verso.
14 On early Olmi, see: Sitney, P. 1995. *Vital Crises in Italian Cinema: Iconography, Stylistics, Politics*. Austin: University of Texas Press. 163-194.

entered a stalemate, paradoxically benefits from the distance, as each of the two lovers has a chance to reflect on their longing, misgivings and desires. All in all, the film, just like Olmi's previous features, does not offer a clear-cut interpretation of the character's path, rather opting for a multilayered account of the worker's experience. In stark contrast to Antonioni and his protagonists' meandering in a landscape of negativity, Olmi's reflections try to balance the losses and the gains of modernity. The dimension of melancholy and disorientation and that of discovery and growth are inextricably intertwined in his account of the intimate and affective dimensions of migration.

The focus on the connection between labor and migration that characterized the 1960s often worked in tandem with another important feature of Italian cinema of the decade: its pervasive aesthetic hybridity. Rather than coalescing into a specific genre, the theme of labor emerges during this decade across a range of widely different films, and is recounted through the registers of melodrama, comedy, political social drama, even sci-fi and also – most importantly – through a combination of several of the above. The prime example of this is Luchino Visconti's celebrated *Rocco e i suoi fratelli* (Rocco and His Brothers, 1960), where the commingling of different narrative and visual modes accounts for the different outcomes of the process of migration of the individual characters. As noted by Veronica Pravadelli, the film dedicates its melodramatic core narrative to the two maladjusted brothers Rocco and Simone (Alain Delon and Renato Salvatori), yet still offers the model of a new, positive, integrated worker of southern origin through the character of the younger brother Ciro (Max Cartier), who is associated with a plainer, less flamboyantly excessive style.[15]

A similar, productive stylistic eclecticism also characterizes the lesser-known, yet staggering *Pelle viva* (Scorched Skin, 1962), the only feature film ever directed by journalist Giuseppe Fina. The protagonist, Andrea (Raoul Grassilli), is employed at an ironworks on the outskirts of Milan, while living in his family's original rural village at approximately one hour

---

15   Pravadelli, V. 2006. "Visconti's 'Rocco and His Brothers': Identity, Melodrama, and the National-Popular." *Annali d'Italianistica*, vol. 24.

distance by train. The film devotes large portions of its narrative to the description of such a long and tiresome commute that Andrea shares with a large group of fellow workers and friends. The director dedicates a number of close-ups and splendidly lit shots to the faces of the laborers, emphasizing both their fatigue and their strong collective bond and mutual support. The style of the film appears to be indebted to both the tradition of neorealism and to aesthetic options of 1930s and 1940s American cinema (the names of John Ford and Elia Kazan come to mind), which indeed represented, according to Vincenzo Buccheri, a kind of "seconda paternità" (second paternity) for 1960s Italian cinema.[16] Also crucial in this respect is the film's portrayal of Andrea's love affair with Rosaria, a southern single mother (Elsa Martinelli): their romance is filmed through a markedly noirish cinematography (by Antonio Macasoli), whose high contrasts give the film an utterly romantic look (further enhanced by Carlo Rustichelli's jazzy score). The same lighting style is also employed in a few remarkable scenes describing the protagonist's activity, in order to account for the deeply elemental fascination involved in working with iron: the spectacle of the incandescent, white iron casts handled by the workers manifests the concrete materiality at the roots of the industrial technological sublime. The commingling of realism and lyricism in the film's style does not diminish, however, its whipping social critique: Andrea's attempt to better his social position, moving to the city and getting a more petite bourgeois job as a building superintendent, is destined to fail because of the prejudices manifested against Rosaria by the local priest. The film's bleak ending represents one of the most uncompromisingly negative depictions of labor conditions and workers' rights in the cinema of this era. *Pelle viva* is hence particularly riveting in that it succeeds perfectly in conciliating aesthetic research with a clear-minded political perspective.

While Fina's film emphasizes the insurmountable distance between the spaces the worker has to traverse (and the eventual clash of his attempt to move up the social ladder), other films propose rather different takes on the same narrative trope. Alberto Lattuada's *Mafioso* (1962),

---

16 Buccheri, V. 2010. *Lo stile cinematografico*. Rome: Carocci. 125.

for example, uses the idea of the worker's travel for a reflection on the very opposite concept: the uncanny proximity, in industrial modernity, of far-away spaces. The film's protagonist, Antonio (Alberto Sordi) is a Sicilian-born model employee and chronometer in an automobile factory in Milan, and the narrative recounts his return (with his northern wife and two daughters in tow) to his hometown for a holiday. Once there, he is dragged into a complex plan by the local mob boss (who is shown to have ties with Antonio's industrialist employer in Milan): always the obedient underling, Antonio agrees to pretend to leave for a weekend of hunting in the countryside, but he is actually transported illegally to New York. There, he carries out his duty as a one-shot contract killer and then returns to Italy and to his daily life as if nothing ever happened. The 'normal' modernity of industrial Milan is thus relegated to the margins of the story, while most of the narrative focuses on the two 'other' spaces of Sicily and the United States. Apparently at the antipodes from one another, in terms of archaism and modernization, these spaces are shown to actually be interconnected, both representing two different aspects of the dark side of the Italian economic boom. Antonio's American experience, stemming from his Sicilian vacation, feels just like a dream, a twisting of all usual spatio-temporal coordinates, and the film also mirrors this in terms of tone and style. While Sicily is portrayed according to the rules of baroque excess typical of *commedia all'italiana* (comedy Italian style), the US scenes are shot with an attention to urban space, and accompanied by a jazz soundtrack, so as to resemble the cool and detached tone of late film noirs such as Irving Lerner's *Murder by Contract* (1958) or Stanley Kubrick's *The Killing* (1956). The narrative register thus involves different degrees of the surreal, through which the film proposes a most chilling depiction of a worker's subservience. Sordi's naïve and bewildered protagonist makes for a perfectly functional gearwheel in the shocking mechanisms of international crime: significantly, the image of the assembly line, working with utmost precision and tirelessness, opens and closes the film, fittingly alluding to the transformation of the protagonist himself into an emotionless automaton in service of the mysterious mechanisms of international crime and capital (see Figure 3).

Industrial Labor in Italian Cinema

Figure 3. The industrial worker as a gearwheel in the mysterious mechanisms of international crime and capital. Alberto Sordi (the small figure in white at the center of the frame) in *Mafioso* (Alberto Lattuada, 1962).

An extreme reimagining of this trope connecting work and migration is offered by Ugo Gregoretti's *Omicron* (1963). In the film, a factory worker's dead body (Renato Salvatori) is re-appropriated by an alien entity, sent to earth to set up the imminent invasion of the whole planet by its species. Through its commingling of physical comedy, social critique and sci-fi imagination, the film reflects on the theme of alienation. While such superimposition of alienhood and alienation could sound like nothing more than a pun, on the contrary the film uses it to lucidly spell out the dynamics of class exploitation and the cost of the labor experience on the very body of the worker: possessed by the alien intelligence, whose sole aim is to learn how to move and use the human body to the highest effect, the worker becomes a super-efficient machine, dispossessed of free will and only directed toward increasing the level of production. Through the metaphor of the inter-galactic journey, *Omicron* shows how industrial labor can represent a trip outside the usual, healthy corporeal experience, as the worker finds himself deprived of his own humanity and transported onto another realm: that of a hybrid between subject and object.

The film thus anticipates the post-1968 turn to a more specific attention to the body of the worker, which will find in Gregoretti one of its most attentive observers.[17]

Post-1968: Working Bodies to a Halt

In 1968 and the 'hot autumn' of 1969, the theme of industrial labor enjoyed an unwonted centrality in the public sphere: the widespread diffusion of discourses on labor rights translated to a new attention to the concrete physical experience of the worker. Such an attention is best exemplified by one of the most topical films of the time, Elio Petri's *La classe operaia va in paradiso* (Lulù the Tool, 1972). The film gives a stunning account of the toll taken on the body of the worker by the inhuman and repetitive rhythms of the factory. The film's protagonist, Lulù Massa (Gian Maria Volonté) is initially shown to identify with his role as a producer of goods so completely that he suffers a transformation of his bodily functions accordingly. Having irremediably compromised his digestion as well as his sexual appetite, Lulù is ill, yet painstakingly aware of the ideological implications of his condition: in one of the film's earlier scenes he expresses a clear comparison between the functioning of the plant he works at and that of his body, defining both of them as "una fabbrica di merda" (a shitty factory, but also a factory producing shit). After a workplace accident, Lulù changes his attitude, and puts his acute intelligence at the service of workers' rights. He is played with immense neurotic energy (before and after his transformation) by Volonté, a performer whose histrionic expressivity aptly communicates the character's feverish physicality. At the same time, the film's tone of grotesque excess is

17 Gregoretti will chronicle the different phases of the worker's struggle in the years 1968 and 1969 through two documentaries, *Apollon, una fabbrica occupata* (Apollon, An Occupied Factory, 1969) and *Il contratto* (1970), offering "una perfetta rappresentazione dell'operaio dal punto di vista sindacale e comunista" (a perfect representation of the industrial laborer from the unionist and communist standpoint). Sangiovanni, A. 2006. *Tute blu*. 215.

actually functional to a clear-headed analysis of the complex interactions between workers, the unions and the student movement, where cultural distances and dynamics of idealization seem to get in the way of a fruitful collaboration in the fight for rights. The film thus concludes with the image of a dead end: reinstated after being fired, Lulù finds himself demoted to the assembly line, and in the last scene – amidst the deafening noise of the machines – he recounts to his fellow workers a dream he had of overcoming a high wall and entering paradise. The narrative trajectory, centered around the idea of movement we have explored above, encounters here a definitive halt: the only possible form of relocation available to Lulù and his colleagues is an illusorily transcendental one. In the very years when the fight for workers' rights inflamed the public debate and the industrial laborer emerged as the crucial figure for "una modernizzazione conflittuale della società" (a conflictual modernization of society),[18] the film unflinchingly portrayed the struggle as doomed.

The film's representation is hence rooted in pessimism, and such a trait is common to many other filmic representations of these years. In these films, the worker's body emerges as a sort of battlefield for an impossible struggle; it becomes the site for the symptomatic expression of an aborted emancipation. Such a structure may be found in several quite different films, depicting altogether different situations and classes. One can think, for example, of Ettore Scola's hybrid between documentary and narrative cinema, *Trevico-Torino: Viaggio nel Fiat-Nam* (Trevico-Turin: Voyage in Fiatnam, 1973), recounting the experiences of Fortunato (Paolo Turco), a southern youth who migrates to Turin to work at Fiat. While the film describes the young man's gradual acknowledgement of the dramatic realities of the working class, such a process of awareness does not produce any significant betterment of his conditions. And in the end, the film finds its climax in an act of physical desperation: while running to catch the train that will bring him to work, Fortunato is overcome by exhaustion and the negativity of his living and working conditions, and erupts into crisis in the middle of the street. Letting go of his belongings and dropping them on the street, he explodes in a melodramatic cry with which the film ends. The body becomes here the only possible outlet for the expression of a subject

18   Sangiovanni, A. 2006. *Tute blu*. 143.

whose feelings the society seems incapable of integrating in its structure through language.

On the other end of the social spectrum, one can think of the industrialist played by Massimo Girotti in Pier Paolo Pasolini's *Teorema* (1968), whose dissatisfaction with life induces him to an even more radical gesture. He completely abandons his lifestyle and his wealth, literally stripping naked and donating his factory to the workers.[19] Class mobility, social justice and the end of paternalism are mostly articulated then, in the Italian narrative cinema of the time, in terms of an extreme act of defiance and defeat, rather than through any indication of concrete options for social change.

Melodrama, as a narrative mode thoroughly centered on the struggle between the subject and an incommensurable and unbeatable force, is therefore a preferred mode for the depiction of the dynamic we are outlining.[20] And yet, the impossibility of fully articulating one's point of view through language, and the consequent need to resort to the body, might also be thematized effectively through comedy.[21] In Luciano Salce's *Il sindacalista* (1972) the worker (Lando Buzzanca)'s protest against the (admittedly amiable) owner of the factory (Renzo Montagnani) consists of 'blowing him a raspberry' (making an offensive flatulence noise) over the phone, signaling the utter impossibility and an actual fear of direct confrontation, degrading the dialogue to the purely physical level of the apotropaic gesture.[22]

---

19 Girotti's figure is the exact reverse of the many figures of wealthy, evil industrialists populating Italian cinema at the time, both in the genre of political cinema and in that of comedy, from *Le mani sulla città* (Hands Over the City, Francesco Rosi, 1963) to *In nome del popolo italiano* (In the Name of the Italian People, Dino Risi, 1971), from *C'eravamo tanto amati* (We All Loved Each Other So Much, Ettore Scola, 1974) to *Todo Modo* (Elio Petri, 1976).

20 On melodrama, see: Kovács, A. B. 2007. *Screening Modernism*. 84–90.

21 On Italian comedy, see: Bayman, L. 2017. "The Popularity of Italian Film Comedy." *Wiley-Blackwell Companion to Italian Cinema*. Edited by Frank Burke. Oxford: Wiley-Blackwell. 180–197.

22 Other comedic titles partaking to the same comedic depiction of the dynamics of class struggle are Steno's *Il padrone e l'operaio* (The Boss and the Worker, 1975) and *La patata bollente* (1979). See: Zaccagnini, E. 2009. *I mostri al lavoro. Contadini, commendatori ed impiegati all'italiana*. Rome: Sovera. 95–99.

Another aspect of the centrality of the worker's body in post-1968 Italian cinema resides in its sexualization, in accordance with the general social trends of the time. The male proletarian body in particular becomes an object of lust and desire: see, for example, Massimo Ranieri in Mauro Bolognini's *Metello* (1970) or Giancarlo Giannini in Lina Wertmüller's *Mimì metallurgico ferito nell'onore* (The Seduction of Mimì, 1972). The female body is also involved in such a dynamic, of course (see Romy Schneider in Alberto Bevilacqua's adaptation of his own novel, *La califfa*, The Calif, 1970). And yet it also becomes a preferred site for the symbolization and condensation of a larger array of discourses related to the trope of the body as a symptom.

Most especially, the body of the woman emerges as the locus for reflecting on the newly acquired awareness of the damages of pollution and chemical poisoning in the work environment. The ecological debate that started to develop in the early 1970s features prominently in a group of melodramas and comedies of the decade focusing on female protagonists. Vittorio De Sica tackled the topic in two of his last films: first comedically (*Lo chiameremo Andrea*, 1972), then melodramatically (*Una breve vacanza*, A Brief Vacation, 1973). The first film, centered on a married couple (Nino Manfredi and Mariangela Melato) that is trying to conceive a child, is particularly interesting. Both the protagonists are teachers in a school located in the vicinity of a cement factory, and the devastating amount of dust polluting the air is said to be the cause of the wife's inability to become pregnant. The whole situation is treated through a series of (rather sexist) gags, yet it is in this film that we find the ultimate depiction of the body as a medium for the expression of the illnesses of society, with the hysterical pregnancy developed by the female protagonist representing a further variation of the melodramatic nervous breakdowns mentioned above.

A similarly negative portrayal of the impact on industrial labor on women's bodies can be found in Luigi Comencini's *Delitto d'amore* (Somewhere Beyond Love, 1974). The film recounts the love affair between two factory workers hailing from rather opposite backgrounds: Nullo (Giuliano Gemma) is a northerner, coming from a proletarian family of workers with a strong anarchic tradition; Carmela (Stefania Sandrelli) is a southerner still embroiled in the atavistic mores of her region of origin and a rather superstitious Catholicism. While the film seems to point to the possibility for the two lovers to overcome both the factory restrictions (the maze-like structure of the plant is re-appropriated by the two flirting youths, and the machinery used as a means to transmit love messages) and the abysmal difference between their cultural attitudes, the two are eventually unable to find common ground and they break up. The film then opts for a fatalistic turn as Carmela, already condensing on herself several conventional markers of 'weakness' (femininity, southern origin), falls ill due to the chemicals she is forced to work with (see Figure 4). The film offers a description of the polluted landscape of the Milanese periphery as unforgettable as insufferably mawkish (we even witness the burial of dead birds on the plastic-invaded riverbank), and its melodramatic conclusion once again proposes death as the only solution to a seemingly unavailable integration in modernity.

Figure 4. The negative impact of industrial labor on women's bodies: Stefania Sandrelli in Luigi Comencini's *Delitto d'amore* (Somewhere Beyond Love, 1974).

In the thirty years we have dealt with in this chapter, the worker gradually became a central figure in Italian cinema. At first, they emerged very sporadically, mostly presented as a marker of existential negativity. Consequently, they were narrativized more widely through the trope of movement (or impossibility thereof). Finally, they were accounted for in their full-fledged physicality. And yet, the prevalence of negative trajectories of defeat in the narrativization of industrial subjectivity seems to portend the rather sudden obsolescence they would face soon thereafter. Swept away by the socioeconomic changes that ushered in the postindustrial era, industrial laborers soon disappeared from Italian screens. By the mid-1970s, the central figure of the Italian labor imaginary had already shifted: from the blue to the white collar worker, aptly represented by Paolo Villaggio's comedic rendition of the stereotypically unlucky and submissive Italian office clerk, *Fantozzi* (Luciano Salce, 1975).[23]

---

23   For an examination of the trends of popular Italian cinema leading up to *Fantozzi*'s success, see: Manzoli. G. 2012. *Da Ercole a Fantozzi. Cinema popolare e società italiana dal boom economico alla neotelevisione (1958–1976)*. Rome: Carocci.

PAOLA BONIFAZIO

3 A Short History of Sponsored Film in Italy

What is a 'sponsored' film? To answer this question, we need to look beside the world of spectacular entertainment and beyond its beauty. In this chapter, and in the Film Studies literature within which the term was generated, 'sponsored' indicates a kind of cinema that exploits, in the words of Charles Acland and Haidee Wasson, film's ability "to transform unlikely spaces, convey ideas, convince individuals and produce subjects in the service of public and private aims."[1] In other words, when using the attribute 'sponsored,' we mean to identify a particular category of film productions (non-commercial), but also to approach the medium from the point of view of its utility (for example, as an educational tool or a persuasive means) rather than its aesthetics (though questions of style are still relevant to understand how films function, for example, as instruments of propaganda). Short in length and usually shot in 16mm, often labeled as documentaries even though they frequently employ fictional narratives, sponsored films are free products of both entertainment and instruction, presented in conjunction with featured presentations in regular movie theaters or screened in other locations such as schools, factories and public squares.[2] In the broader context of 'useful cinema,' sponsored films also specifically point to the agencies (private or public) that fund their production. In this sense, sponsored films are 'ephemerals' insofar as, once their

---

1   Acland, C. R. and Massoon, H. (eds). 2011. *Useful Cinema*. Durham: Duke University Press. 2. See also Prelinger, R. 2007. *The Field Guide to Sponsored Films*. National Film Preservation Foundation. See also the online resource "Prelinger Archive." <www.archive.org/details/prelinger>
2   Most sponsored films are around ten to fifteen minutes, and never longer than thirty minutes. They can be either in black and white or in color.

temporary function is fulfilled – be that one of advertising a particular governmental program or instructing employees in a factory – they are often discarded, either in storage at inaccessible archives or even in dumpsters. Occasionally, archives hold reels that are missing part of the footage, lack any information about producers and directors or cannot be identified by means of catalogues. Usually, archives hold only positive prints, and the negative cannot be found. In this sense, sponsored films can also be 'orphans,' a term used by archivists and preservation scholars to address the issue of neglected moving images left behind in the depository/orphanage. These films are often missing their 'mother' (the negative), or their 'father' (someone holding and claiming the copyright).[3]

The history of sponsored films in Italy that I will sketch in this chapter is informed by the theoretical framework briefly delineated above. It is short because of space limits, but also because in Italy national and international private and public agencies funded short film productions in large numbers only during a limited period of time: roughly from the immediate postwar period to the early 1960s. Corporate films have existed since the first decade of the twentieth century, and state sponsored documentaries spread under the Fascist regime thanks to the creation of the Istituto Luce (1924–1947) and the successful business of the Industria Cinematografica (Incom), a private competitor in making film propaganda.[4] But it was only

3   For a general introduction to 'orphan' films, see the University of South Carolina's website "Orphanage: A Home for Orphan Film" <http://www.sc.edu/orphanfilm/definition.html>. This page provides information about film symposia regularly organized on the topic, including Paolo Cherchi Usai's presentation "What is an Orphan Film? Definition, Rationale and Controversy," delivered at the University of South Carolina in September 1999. I must also specify that the term 'orphan' addresses the material existence of a reel apart from its content/style or usage; 'orphans' can also be forgotten silent films and theatrical features whose negatives are lost.

4   See Luca Comerio's recording of Fiat industries of July 6, 1911 and other examples available online on the YouTube channel of the Archivio Nazionale Cinema d'Impresa in Ivrea (Italy): <https://www.youtube.com/watch?v=oVHrd9TdLo&t=215s> The Istituto Luce closed in 1947 and then reopened in 1948, continuing to produce films for the Italian democratic state. For a history of Istituto Luce that surveys both its Fascist and its postwar activities, see Laura, E. 2004. *Le*

in the transition from Fascism to democracy (1946–1948), during the country's reconstruction (1948–1958) and up to the spread of televised entertainment after the economic boom (1958–1963), that companies, state and multiple foreign organizations (particularly American) aligned in their greatest effort to educate the Italian citizenry by means of short films about the practices, duties and perks of modernity, and on their own role as both welfare providers and educators.[5] In addition to showing how sponsoring agencies could help Italy (and Western Europe at large) move towards progress and betterment, sponsored film narratives explained to Italian citizens how their individual involvement has made or could make a difference. In many cases, the fictional story of a worker or a working-class family was inserted and connected to the history of Italy, editing together dramatizations and newsreel footage, so that the master narrative of national development and the private events of individual prosperity were tied along the same teleology of progress.

In the early 1950s, several Italian companies including Fiat (automobiles and appliances), Olivetti (typewriters), Edisonvolta (electricity) and ENI (oil and gas) opened their own cinema units to produce educational and informational films depicting the role played by industry in the social environment, and in the private lives of employees.[6] In 1951, the executive

---

stagioni dell'aquila: Storia dell'Istituto Luce. Rome: Istituto Luce. Incom was created in 1938 by Sandro Pallavicini and continued to produce films for the regime after the armistice in 1943, during the Italian Social Republic (RSI). See Laura, E. 2004. *Le stagioni dell'aquila*. 145–156, 180–186, 212–213, 228–240.

5   For a 'longer' (in length, not in timeframe) history of sponsored film in postwar Italy, see Bonifazio, P. 2014. *Schooling in Modernity: The Politics of Sponsored Films in Postwar Italy*. Toronto: University of Toronto Press.

6   For an introduction to Fiat's film unit Cinefiat, see Torchio, M. 2003. "Cinefiat e l'egemonia possibile." *Cinemambiente 2003: Enviromental Film Festival*. Turin: Associazione Cinambiente. 141. On the Edisonvolta Film Unit, see 2005. *Il mestiere dell'uomo: Ermanno Olmi regista per la Edison*. Milan: Motta. On Olivetti films, see Bellotto, A. 1994. *La memoria del futuro: film d'arte, film e video industriali Olivetti: 1949–1992*. Ivrea: Fondazione Adriano Olivetti and Archivio Storico del Gruppo Olivetti. Director Ermanno Olmi was responsible for creating the Sezione Cinema Edisonvolta. His personal views and style affected the way in which it represented the company and its business in the 1950s.

branch of the Italian government created the Centro di Documentazione (Documentation Center), an information agency that eventually commissioned private producers and the Istituto Luce to produce about two hundred shorts (the practice of showing short films before theatrical features ceased in the early 1960s).[7] In addition to being screened in Italian movie theatres, the shorts of the Centro were translated for foreign audiences and the Italian agency held copyright over international distribution. From 1948 to 1951, both the private Italian companies that worked for the Centro (Astra Cinematografica and Documento Film) and others that did not (Phoenix Films, Wessex Film Productions and Telefilm) collaborated with the Economic Cooperation Administration (ECA), the American agency that implemented the Marshall Plan on the peninsula. They also collaborated with the Mutual Security Agency (MSA), which replaced the ECA for a couple years after the end of the Plan in 1951.[8] These films were dubbed in several languages and shown in all the countries participating in the Marshall Plan. They were screened in public squares, schools and factories. The United States Information Services continued to distribute ECA and MSA films, as well as other American short films until the mid-1960s.[9]

7 The complete archive of the 'Centro di documentazione' is housed in Rome at the Dipartimento dell'informazione e dell'editoria, Presidenza del Consiglio dei Ministri. For a catalog of these films, and some discussion of their contents, see the following sources: Frabotta, M A. 2002. *Il governo filma l'Italia*. Rome: Bulzoni. Orabona, A and Bellumori, C. 1978. *25 Anni di documentari della Presidenza del Consiglio dei Ministri*. Rome: Tipografia Artistica. Presidenza del Consiglio dei ministri and Dipartimento per l'informazione e l'editoria, 1995. *Per immagini: gli audiovisivi prodotti dalla Presidenza del Consiglio dei Ministri: 1952–1995*. Rome: Ufficio per l'informazione e la documentazione istituzionale. Several films are available online at the Archivio Storico Istituto Luce website: <www.archivioluce.com/archivio/>
8 The European Recovery Program, known as the Marshall Plan (named for its creator, General George C. Marshall) provided economic support to European countries for reconstruction after the Second World War (1948–1951). Financial aid was delivered as a combination of loans and counterpart funds: the United States sent goods to European countries (cotton, wheat, coal, etc.) and the proceedings from the sale of these goods were used by local governments for projects of reconstruction and economic recovery. The Marshall Plan involved seventeen countries.
9 The United States Information Service Trieste collection at the Archivio Centrale dello Stato in Rome contains most of the films produced for ECA Italy and MSA

A Short History of Sponsored Film in Italy

These are only some examples of private and public film units that used cinematography with similar goals: that is, to construct economic, political and social citizens within and beyond industry.[10] Corporate films engaged in the very same national issues as those films funded by the Italian government through the Centro and by the American State Department through the ECA and MSA, which represented industrial companies in their pivotal role in the country's progress. For example, Edisonvolta's *Piccoli calabresi sul Lago Maggiore: Nuovi ospiti alla colonia di Suna* (Little Calabrians on Lake Maggiore: New Guests at Suna's Summer Camp, 1951) explained how the company took care of displaced children after an earthquake in southern Italy, while *La diga del ghiacciaio* (The Dam of the Glacier, 1955) conveyed some attention and concerns about how rural environments and their social groups were transformed by the arrival of the electrical company.[11] Respect for and attachment to the rural environment are also features of the films representing work at Olivetti, whose president Adriano Olivetti's interests

  Italy, as well as several other films produced and distributed by the United States Information Services. For a complete listing of the films in the collection see Barbera, G and Tosatti, G (eds). 2007. *United States Information Service di Trieste. Catalogo del fondo cinematografico 1941–1966*. Rome: Pubblicazione degli Archivi di Stato.

10 Non-governmental commissioners were also involved: for example, philanthropic associations such as the Italian Unione per la Lotta contro l'Analfabetismo (Union for the Fight Against Illiteracy), an organization funded by the "Friends of America," the Centro Cattolico Cinematografico (Catholic Center for Cinematography), supported by the Vatican and collaborating with the Catholic producer Orbis and the Comitato Civico, sustained by Azione Cattolica (Catholic Action) and affiliated with the Christian Democrat Party. Companies like Pirelli and Peroni were also involved; their films are available online at the Archivio Nazionale Cinema d'Impresa's YouTube channel.

11 Titles of sponsored films can be either in Italian or in a foreign language, depending on production and distribution. When a film was first release in Italian, and then dubbed in other languages, I will provide the Italian and the English titles at the beginning, and then use the original one throughout the chapter, for example: *Cristo non si è fermato a Eboli/Christ Did Not Stopped at Eboli*. Vice versa, for films produced in other countries, I will use the Italian official translation only at the beginning, for example: *Men and Machines/Uomini e machine*. Whenever an Italian short film did not have an official English version of the title, translations will be mine and will be placed between parenthesis, for example: *La diga del ghiacciaio* (The Dam of the Glacier).

in architecture, politics and humanist culture influenced the future development of the company.¹² *Incontro alla Olivetti* (Welcome to Olivetti, Giorgio Ferroni, 1950), *Infermeria di fabbrica* (The Factory Infirmary, Aristide Bosio, 1951) and *Una fabbrica e il suo ambiente* (A Factory and Its Environment, Michele Gandin, 1957) all represented the factory in this harmonious relationship to nature, showing how it had improved the quality of life for individuals and also how it coexisted respectfully with agricultural activities, social practices and cultural habits. None of the films failed to show the modern glass windows and luminous buildings that hosted workers during the day, nor the equally modern and 'people-friendly' housing projects built by Olivetti for employees and their families.

In sum, the coincidence between government and corporate narratives confirms Vinzenz Hediger and Patrick Vonderau's theory that industrial cinema is not a genre, but rather "a strategically weak and parasitic form," whose conventions are "pliable to whatever organizational purpose the filmmaker has to meet."¹³ As Mario Minardi argued in the late 1960s about Olivetti, all that remained of the films' industrial character was the sponsors' signatures that they displayed.¹⁴ In many cases, private companies were actually "sneaky sponsors;"¹⁵ appropriate adjustments were made in order to avoid accusations of commercial purposes and it was considered

12   Most of the films were produced internally by company employees, including leftist intellectual Franco Fortini, working for the Direzione Pubblicità e Stampa, where the Sezione Cinematografica opened in 1952. Adriano Olivetti was convinced that the company needed to employ people with an education in the humanities, and not only in the cultural divisions (library, publicity and the press), but also in social services (for example, psychologists) and even at the managerial level (one third of the managers had a humanities background). Adriano Olivetti was also the founder of a political movement (Movimento Comunità) supported by the United States government, an alternative to the more prominent mass-based parties.
13   Hediger, V. and Vonderau, P. (eds). 2009. "Introduction." *Films that Work: Industrial Film and the Productivity of Media*. Amsterdam: Amsterdam University Press. 46.
14   Minardi, M. 1966. "Cinema e industria." *Notizie Olivetti*, vol. 14, no. 88. 57.
15   Ken Smith uses this expression to characterize American businesses that made educational films for the classroom in the 1950s and 1960s. See Smith, K. 1999. *Mental Hygiene: Better Living Through Classroom Films 1945–1970*. New York: Blast Books. 55.

likely that the general public would not distinguish governmental from industrial reels, especially when shown in regular movie theaters. At their core, sponsored films showed how the Italian government shared industry's goal of transforming a mostly rural country into an industrial economy and to homogenize blue- and white-collar workers into a modern middle class of consumers.

To a certain extent, the postwar legislation favored the production of sponsored films, and it can thus explain what seems to be a unique event in the history of Italian cinema. Both article 18 in 1947 and article 15 in 1949 assigned 3% of the tax on revenues to documentary films. These had to be passed by a Government Commission that considered 'documentary' any film shorter than thirty minutes and containing some realistic content as well as some treatment of cultural or social values.[16] The proportion of funds was lowered in 1956 to 1.75%, after which the number of short film productions fell drastically: from 1149 in 1955 to 157 in 1956. In conjunction with state funding, the law provided for the obligatory release of documentary films in movie theaters before features. It was therefore profitable to make sponsored films that could be easily approved by the Commission (independent documentary filmmakers were often rejected). Private companies such as Documento Film and Astra Cinematografica (as well as Incom) took advantage of the law by financing films at a low cost on particular subjects, like reconstruction programs. The choice of topics was usually made for political reasons, since reels that provided a favorable image of the country and positive inspiration for the citizenry were most certain to meet the Commission's selection standards for funding.

However, economic profit and legislative support are only one side of the story. The process that transformed the country from a mostly rural to an industrial economy and the continuities that shaped its transition from the Fascist dictatorship to the democratic state in the midst of the Cold War are crucial historical contexts that frame how useful cinema was to corporate, state and foreign interests. The Cineteca Scolastica Italiana

---

16 Law 379, Article 18 (May 16, 1947). <http://www.edizionieuropee.it/LAW/HTML/50/zn88_02_006.html> and Law 958, Article 15 (December 29, 1949). <http://www.edizionieuropee.it/LAW/HTML/50/zn88_02_009.html>

(CSI) is a case in point. The CSI opened on the remnants of the Cineteca Autonoma per la Cinematografia Scolastica (Independent Film Library for Educational Cinema), created in 1938 as part of the Istituto Luce to produce and distribute films for use as audiovisual aids in the classroom.[17] It was directed by Remo Branca, a Fascist supporter who had accepted a position at the Gioventù Italiana del Littorio (GIL) as an expert in charge of organizing youth film services. After the war, the Minister of Public Education Antonio Segni asked Branca to create a film unit at the Ministry of Agriculture. Then, as director of the CSI, Branca actively participated in the debate on educational cinema, and he even traveled to Chicago and Boston, thanks to an exchange program organized by the American State Department, in order to study American educational film libraries and producers.[18] Almost mirroring the personal trajectory of its director, the 1952 and 1954 catalogues of the CSI listed about 50% Fascist films from the 1930s and 1940s, a couple of CSI productions, some corporate films such as Olivetti's *Un millesimo di millimetro* (A Thousandth of a Millimeter, Virgilio Sabel, 1949) and reels donated by the British Embassy and by the United States Information Services.[19] Remnants of Fascist rhetoric can

17   The CSI is also a great example of an orphan collection: it was saved by Gaetano Martino, director of the Cineteca Lucana (in Basilicata) in 1991. Martino found twelve thousand reels, twenty thousand volumes and five hundred projectors still in their boxes in an abandoned warehouse attached to a primary school in the San Lorenzo neighborhood in Rome that was set to be demolishment. See Sassi, E. 2009. "Il duce di spalle e altre scene proibite," *Corriere della Sera*. December 7. 39. See also, for example, 2011. "C'erano una volta nelle scuole i documentari della Cineteca," *Corriere della Sera*. December 14. 57.
18   Branca, R. 1952. *Curva di fatica del bambino nella visione del film a colori e in bianconero*. Rome: Ministero della Pubblica Istruzione. See also Branca's historical essays: Branca, R. 1952. *Funzioni e limiti cineteca scolastica italiana*. Rome: Edizioni Ministero Della Pubblica Istruzione. Branca, R. 1956. *Società e scuola negli Stati Uniti*. Rome: Edizioni Ministero Della Pubblica Istruzione.
19   I must thank Pier Luigi Raffaelli for giving me copies of these catalogues, collected at the Cineteca Lucana. It should be noted that films in the catalogues are undated, but I was able to find this information by consulting the online collection of the Istituto Luce, where these films can also be found. Films inherited from the Fascist Cineteca Autonoma include 37 films on surgery, directed by Francesco Pasinetti in the late 1930s.

be found in certain biopics that exploit the lives of famous scientists or artists to exalt the Italian race, such as *Galileo Galilei* (Giovanni Paolucci, 1942) and *Armonie Pucciniane* (Puccini's Harmonies, Giorgio Ferroni, 1938). More interesting for their visual and verbal rhetoric are the films representing labor. For example, in *Vele e prore* (Sails and Bows, 1939), directed by Fernando Cerchio and produced by the Istituto Luce, the physical strength of muscular male bodies, triumphant music and monumental crane shots depict Italian industry as national pride and industrial labor as superhuman effort. Representations of labor determine the most interesting contradictions within the collection, since labor and productivity were also staples of postwar culture, marking the transition from Fascism to democracy as a conversion from warfare to workfare. On the one hand, in a film like *Vele e prore*, industry and labor constitute the epitome of the virile power that the Italian nation at its best had demonstrated (or should have demonstrated) on the battlefield. On the other hand, in the American-sponsored productions showing industrial development in Europe after the Second World War, Italy is depicted as pre-modern and backward in comparison with northern European countries, where the transition from the first (British) to the second (American) industrial revolution is already taking place. I am referring in particular to the series titled "Changing Faces of Europe." Shot originally in 35 mm Technicolor Mopac, the series was produced by the British company Wessex Film for the MSA, and it was subsequently dubbed and distributed in all the countries participating in the Marshall Plan.[20] In comparison to the films inherited from the Cineteca Autonoma and the few produced by the CSI, the series represents Italy (and Greece) as the South of Europe, the backward and pre-modern 'other.' Each film seems to describe European progress towards economic recovery from a northern perspective. The role played by the

---

20   Each film in the series focused on one of the following areas (in chronological order): energy (*Power for All/Carbone Bianco*, Graham Wallace and Anthony Squire, 1950), agriculture (*300 Million Mouths/Nostro pane quotidiano*, 1950), the housing industry (*A Place to Live/Case per tutti*, Jacques Brunius, 1951), serial production (*Men and Machines/Uomini e macchine*, Diane Pine, 1951), communication (*Clearing the Lines/Via libera*, Kay Mander, 1951), health services (*A Good Life/Vivere sani*, Humphrey Jennings and Graham Wallace, 1951).

Italian economy in Europe's postwar renaissance is radically different in this series from what is conveyed in *Vele e prore*. On the other hand, a film like *Dalla lana al tessuto* (From Wool to Fabric, Edmondo Cancellieri), commissioned by the CSI in the 1950s, can be read as a practical example of the lesson that Branca must have learned during his trip to the United States. Though ostensibly representing the stages of production in a textile factory, Cancellieri's documentary promoted the latest fabrics by Ermenegildo Zegna. Product promotion, however, does not come until the end, after the film has established a much more important message: that the personal engagement of the owner ensures the company's integrity and social awareness. As they watch the film, viewers learn the details of mass production in the age of the second industrial revolution: images of workers attending to machinery that seems to do all the labor go hand in hand with the idea of technologically advanced systems making high-quality products in the tradition of craftsmanship. At the same time, *Dalla lana al tessuto* teaches about the positive values of capitalist enterprise and family business, where economic profits seem to be secondary to (if not absent from) the benefits that the factory brings to the community. In sum, viewers are taught to appreciate business and, in a larger sense, Italy's transformation into an industrially advanced economy.

By comparison to the Fascist example, where the state was idolized, postwar sponsored films showed achievements in industrial development in order to prove that the sponsoring agency of power cared for the welfare of its citizens/employees. Instead of indoctrinating viewers, sponsored films excited and emotionally charged the popular audience with lures of prosperity and happiness. The fact that many people involved in filmmaking for democratic agencies had previously been involved with the Fascist regime should not come as a surprise, and it should not necessarily make us conclude that there are no differences between Fascist prewar propaganda and democratic postwar sponsored films. As historian Christopher Duggan pointed out,

> when combined with the uncertainties over who or what exactly a 'Fascist' was, [the] idea of the essential neutrality of the administration was a major reason why attempts

to conduct a political purge after the war ran aground, and why there was such a marked level of continuity with the Fascist state in the new Republic.[21]

A collective pardon took place across the political spectrum and extended into the world of cinematography, from the amnesty of Fascist criminals promulgated by Palmiro Togliatti, Minister of Justice in 1946 and secretary of the Communist Party, to the narratives of neorealist films, which also contributed to the "collective tendency to externalize responsibility for fascism."[22] In this light, the fact that many directors and leading figures of short film productions were previously involved with the Istituto Luce is not as important for proving that they were 'Fascists' as it is for showing the extent to which their involvement in the Republic was tainted by the desire for redemption and by the claim of victimization, for themselves and for all other Italian citizens who lived under Fascist rule. In 1948, when the democratic constitution had already been signed and the first national elections were taking place, Fascism was meant to be a thing of the past, never to be mentioned in the narratives of modernization. The Second World War, purged of the uncomfortable political question of the armed resistance, represented the traumatic experience that turned Italians from a country of perpetrators into one of victims and supporters of the Allies. In sponsored films, Italy's history was a progressive movement towards a future of prosperity and happiness, where each event demonstrated the country's bright future.[23]

21 Duggan, C. 1995. "Italy in The Cold War Years and The Legacy of Fascism." *Italy in the Cold War: Politics, Culture and Society 1948–1958*. Edited by Christopher Duggan and Christopher Wagstaff. Oxford: Berg. 3.

22 Ben-Ghiat, R. 1999. "Liberation: Italian Cinema and the Fascist Past, 1945–50." *Italian Fascism: History, Memory, and Representation*. Edited by Patrizia Dogliani and Richard J. B. Bosworth. New York: Palgrave. 84.

23 Such a teleological interpretation of history was common to all sponsored films, and possibly connected to Benedetto Croce's idealist/liberal philosophy, still the most influential in Italy. For a study on Croce's influence on postwar Italian cinema, particularly on film criticism, see Caminati, L. 2012. "The Role of Documentary Film in

The Cold War of sponsored films did not play out in open political confrontation. In many cases, the dichotomy between democracy and communism articulated the opposition between rationality and irrationality and linked democracy to anything that was considered 'human,' especially the ideas of freedom and knowledge.[24] It was as much a "struggle for men's minds," to quote the title of one ECA film, as a project to govern people's conduct.[25] Sponsored films joined the US fight against communism (and the Soviet Union) by displaying the economic prosperity brought by democracy. In the words of ECA official Vincent Barnett, "economic improvement and rising living standards [...] can halt the rise of communism."[26]

The imperative behind sponsored film narratives was that of making Italian citizens fit in the modern world. Viewers received instructions on how to adapt to the changing lifestyle and landscapes brought by industrialization. In particular, many sponsored films represented the industrialization of southern Italy, highlighting the social and economic changes already in place and the new hope ingrained in the population. In this context, 'work' meant not only prosperity and social stability, but also political unity, for it represented the solution to the Southern Question: the old divide between the North and the South of Italy that troubled Italian politicians and

---

the Formation of Neorealist Cinema." *Global Neorealism: The Transational History of a Film Style*. Edited by Saverio Giovacchini and Robert Sklar. Jackson: University Press of Mississippi. 52–67.

24   In his 1949 "Inaugural Address," Harry Truman spoke in similar terms, opposing democracy to communism. He argued that democracy was "based on the conviction that man has the moral and intellectual capacity, as well as the inalienable right, to govern himself with reason and justice." See the speech at the Harry S. Truman Library and Museum here: <http://www.trumanlibrary.org/whistle-stop/50yr_archive/inagural20jan1949.htm>

25   *Struggle for Men's Minds* was an ECA film set in Italy and revolving around the struggle between communists and non-communists. It was part of the "Strength for the Free World," series, produced in 1952 by the ECA (Paris) at the request of the MSA in Washington, and consisting of twenty-four half-hour documentaries for American audiences. These were shown nationally on the ABC-TV network in 1952–1953.

26   Barnett, V. 1955. "Competitive Coexistence and the Communist Challenge in Italy." *Political Science Quarterly*, vol. 70, no. 2. 230. Vincent Barnett was Program Chief of the Italian Mission of ECA.

intellectuals alike since Unification. In American-sponsored films, 'work' indicated the solution to the North/South divide in the larger European context, assimilating Italy to countries such as France and Germany, towards the creation of a so-called 'United States of Europe.' In both cases, the narratives of modernization publicized the assimilation of the rural and underdeveloped South to the industrial and progressive North. However, while national governmental agencies were interested in showing complete homogenization, both within the country and vis-à-vis Western Europe, American-sponsored films focused more on how the Marshall Plan brought civilization to the entire nation, including the rural South. The Centro strived to demonstrate to foreign audiences that Italy was finally unified in the name of economic recovery, social welfare and political change, as well as on 'the moral basis of a modern society' (to paraphrase the title of a well-known essay by American sociologist Edward Banfield).[27] At the same time, the ECA and the MSA treated modernization and the spread of democracy as a form of enlightenment that made technical knowledge accessible to viewers, educating them on rational and scientific thought and helping them to leave behind a pre-modern and uncivilized state of existence. All sponsors agreed that by means of education, even southern Italians would eventually learn the rules of modern living. Michele Gandin's film *Cristo non si è fermato a Eboli* (Christ Did Not Stop at Eboli, 1949) is a very good example in this sense. Produced for the non-governmental organization Unione nazionale per la lotta contro l'analfabetismo (National Union for the Fight Against Illiteracy, UNLA), and translated into English for American viewers, *Cristo non si è fermato a Eboli* is a docu-fiction about the successful opening of a school in the southern Lucania region (in other words, it is a documentary about the work of UNLA, told by means of a fictional narrative, in which a single experience represents a common situation). The title of the film refers to novelist Carlo Levi's recently published

---

27   Banfield, E. 1958. *The Moral Basis of a Backward Society*. Glencoe: Free Press. Banfield's thesis on the fundamental inability of Southern Italians to modernize has been criticized by many. However, at the time of publication, similar ideas permeated the American discourse on the economic recovery of the Italian south. See, for example, Allason, B. *Unrra-Casas: contributo alla ricostruzione*. 1950. Rome: Istituto Grafico Tiberino.

memoir of internal exile in Lucania during the 1930s, titled *Cristo si è fermato a Eboli* (Christ Stopped at Eboli, 1945). In his Introduction, Levi described the region in these words: "Cristo non è mai arrivato qui, né vi è arrivato il tempo, né l'anima individuale, né la speranza, né il legame tra le cause e gli effetti, la ragione e la Storia" (Christ never came this far, nor did time, nor the individual soul, nor hope, nor the relation of cause to effect, nor reason nor history).[28] Epitomizing the postwar response to Levi's argument, the film *Cristo non si è fermato a Eboli* explains how the democratic regime and the Friends of America association brought hope and progress even beyond Eboli, to Lucania. Gandin's film also shows that, judging by their moral and social conduct, southern Italians are eager to fit in to the modern world. In the final sequence, the Lucanian peasants who attend the school showcase what they have learned to the viewers. Looking straight up at the camera, these men and women, young and elderly, take turns reciting the values of social solidarity, the importance of religion and the advantages of education.

The case of ENI is also very interesting, particularly for a discussion of the stakes shared by government and corporate bodies in the representation of industrial work.[29] Similar to private companies, and particularly Olivetti, ENI supported various cultural activities, especially between 1955 and 1958, from publishing to architecture: new design for plants, modern housing for employees, a factory magazine and, of course, film. ENI sponsored filmmaking as early as 1949 (*3000 metri sotto il suolo* (3000 Meters Below the Surface), produced by Edelweiss Film and directed by Giulio Briani), and later opened its own film unit. People working for ENI before the opening of the film unit included seasoned directors such as Virgilio

---

28   Levi, C. 1945. *Cristo si è fermato a Eboli*. Turin: Einaudi. 3. Levi, C. 1947. *Christ Stopped at Eboli*. Translated by France Frenaye. New York: Farrar, Strauss and Co. 2.
29   For further readings of ENI films, see the following sources: Bonifazio, P. 2014. "United We Drill: ENI, Films, and the Culture of Work." *Annali d'Italianistica*, vol. 32. 329–350. Latini, G. 2011. *L'energia e lo sguardo. Il cinema dell'Eni e i documentari di Gilbert Bovay*. Rome: Donzelli. Peretti, L. 2019. "Between Auteurism and Sponsored Cinema: Joris Ivens, Bernardo Bertolucci, and ENI." *Journal of Italian Cinema and Media Studies*. vol. 7, no. 2. 199–215.

Sabel (who also directed films at Olivetti), editors like Pino Giomini and musicians like Virgilio Chiti (who worked for ECA). Producers of ENI films included the Istituto Luce and Incom. ENI productions showcase a variety of genres, which was typical of sponsored filmmaking at the time. In addition to more traditional documentaries such as *Le ricerche del metano e del petrolio* (Research in Gas and Oil, Virgilio Sabel, 1951), ENI's collection includes animated cartoons such as *Servizio nelle stazioni di rifornimento* (Service at Gas Stations, 1955), anthropological inquiries like *Gela 1959: Pozzi a mare* (Gela 1959: Drilling at Sea, Vittorio De Seta and Franco Dodi, 1960), as well as many films combining fictional stories with newsreel footage: for example, *Una fiammella si è accesa* (A Flame is On, Enzo Trovatelli, 1960) and *Le vie del metano* (The Methane Way, Ubaldo Magnaghi, 1951). Similar to Olivetti, ENI had major plants both in northern Italy (in Caviago-Ripalta, Cortemaggiore and Ravenna) and in southern Italy (in Sicily and Lucania), and the company represented them both in films. In those set in Sicily, the modern drilling platforms become symbols of a reborn economy based on the collaboration of northern technicians with southern workers. In fact, ENI not only employed local unskilled laborers, but also endeavored to educate qualified workers, thus hoping to homogenize the national workforce and improve economic conditions in the South. For these reasons, ENI films are particularly interesting for studying how cinematography functioned as a tool to educate Italian citizens in political unity as much as social conformity. They are also appropriate to explaining how the rhetoric of education exploited the language of warfare while representing the conversion to workfare. In this respect, there are strong similarities between Cinefiat and ENI productions, for example, between *Scuola allievi Giovanni Agnelli* (Fiat Vocational School, 1962) and *I prigionieri del sottosuolo* (The Prisoners of the Underground, Ubaldo Magnaghi, 1956). At the same time, the kind of work men perform on the platform, fighting against extreme living conditions, assimilates ENI's films to Edisonvolta's. The characteristics of loneliness and courage belong just as much to the men stationing on ENI's platform in the Mediterranean, shown in *Gela 1959*, as they do to those climbing mountains to repair electric cables in the ice and cold weather, portrayed in *La diga del ghiacciaio*. Different from other companies involved in filmmaking, ENI was the only one "a partecipazione statale" (with partial state ownership).[30] Starting in 1953, it had a monopoly on the oil and gas resources available in northern Italy, and by 1958 it also controlled drilling throughout the nation, when a state law made private investments in the sector quite difficult, resulting in very limited margins of profit. ENI was built on the ex-Fascist oil company Agip, which united with other smaller companies to form the postwar public company, which included petrochemical manufacturing. The political discussion of the socialization or privatization of the country's economy on which the law was created constituted a case of both national and international conflict. Under the leadership of the anti-Fascist partisan Enrico Mattei (1953–1962), ENI engaged in a controversial relationship with the so-called 'seven sisters' (the major companies in the oil business) as well as with the factions of the Christian Democrat Party that were in power and opposed to any public interference in the economy. This historical context is relevant to filmmaking, for it established the background against which many cinematic narratives appraised national methane and petroleum. For example, *Pozzo 18: Profondità 1650* (Well Number 18: Depth 1650), a short film sponsored by ENI and produced by Scientia Film in 1955, positively emphasized Mattei's entrepreneurial skills and the narrow-mindedness of a press that was frequently critical of his actions. As much as any ENI film, *Pozzo 18* defined the oil industry in terms of the ideals of national pride, excellence and independence. Here, the development of national oil and gas productions was seen as a process that had the potential to liberate Italy from foreign domination.

30   In this sense, ENI was closer to the Ferrovie dello Stato (Italian State Railway), also involved at this time in making films that showed the reconstruction of the railways system and the building of new and modern trains that travelled from North to South. Indeed, the Ferrovie dello Stato also offers examples of a curious mixture between private and public interests. For example, when a new high-speed route opened, one film was made to publicize the novelty, and another (sponsored by the Breda mechanical manufacturing company) to explore the construction of the train's engine.

Conclusions

In 1962, the release of *Deserto Rosso* (Red Desert, Michelangelo Antonioni) delivered to national and foreign audiences a fictional representation of the Italian petroleum industry and the wealthy bourgeoisie responsible for its management. Set in the industrial area of chemical plants and refineries in the countryside around Ravenna, the film was a commentary on and contribution to the cultural discourses of modernization dominating the period that runs, roughly, from the aftermath of the Second World War to the mid-1960s. Such commentary contrasts with the message delivered by the many sponsored films that portrayed the same industrial landscape and that advertised the positive effects of industry vis-à-vis the national economic recovery and social progress. The protagonists of these sponsored postwar narratives of industrialization were not the middle-class managers but rather, the male workers (unskilled, qualified or specialized) attending to factory machines or stationed on the drilling platforms. Italian women co-starred in the same reels as wives or fiancées, enjoying the products of male labor or nurturing their partners after work. Whereas Antonioni's middle-class characters showed a bourgeois and intellectual audience the impossibility of moving forward, the protagonists of sponsored films demonstrated to a popular audience that industrialization was the only possible solution to poverty. Thanks to aerial shots and enthusiastic voice-over commentaries, industrial plants in sponsored films appeared just as fascinating as the images in Antonioni's mind. However, while *Deserto Rosso* conveyed the cracks in the relentless motion of progress through the inadaptability of its main female character, sponsored films cast their male workers as shining champions of adaptability. The malaise of an unfit bourgeoisie against the mindless embracement of the working class is the starting point of a dialogue between art film and sponsored filmmaking – beyond the barriers of one or the 'other' cinema – that I have sought to open in this chapter. The history of sponsored filmmaking has important theoretical implications, vis-à-vis our understanding of film as an industry, an art and an educational tool.

Moreover, it allows us to reconstruct more accurately the discourses of modernization, industry and work that originated in the postwar period and that are still relevant today. The goal, in my view, is to create a more nuanced understanding of the role of filmmaking in the manufacturing of postwar subjectivities in the Italian society of welfare and consumption.

JIM CARTER

4 For a New Humanism: Literary and Cultural Debate in *Il Menabò di letteratura*

Founded in 1959 by the writers Elio Vittorini and Italo Calvino, the journal *Il Menabò di letteratura* was at the forefront of Italian literary and cultural debates during a period of intense economic and social transformation. Its pages gathered poetry, prose, criticism and letters on a vast sweep of developing topics like dialect literature, war narratives, poetics, the Italian South, new avantgarde movements and more. But even though *Il Menabò* took up such a varied set of important concerns, it has been memorialized by Italian scholars as a journal with one main focus: industrial culture. The literary historian Emanuele Zinato has rightly remarked that this narrow focus has prevented a greater appreciation of the full scope and dynamism of *Il Menabò*, and he has gone to some length to restore to the journal's memory a more inclusive and nuanced picture.[1]

In the English-language scholarship things are slightly different, as *Il Menabò* is little known to literary and cultural historians with specializations outside of twentieth-century Italy. That the journal should make an appearance here, in a volume on Italian industrial culture, must raise concerns that we make the same mistakes of emphasis as scholars in Italy. The best way around this is to plainly recognize that *Il Menabò* was much more than a forum for debate on industrial culture. It was a virtual meeting point for a new generation of writers and critics whose interests were as many as the pages they published.

Why, then, has *Il Menabò* been remembered as a journal of industrial culture? Certainly because that topic, as it was addressed by Vittorini,

---

1   Zinato, E. 1990. "'Il Menabò di letteratura': La ricerca letteraria come riflessione razionale." *Studi Novecenteschi*, vol. 17, no 39. 131–132.

Calvino and their colleagues, had some sort of staying power. This was a first chance for Italian culture to measure itself against the intense economic and social transformations of the postwar period, and it came away profoundly shaken. Of the ten issues published between 1959 and 1967, only one of them focused exclusively on industrial culture. Nevertheless, the topic resonated across all issues, and it gives us a snapshot of the developing literary and cultural debate.

My goal in this chapter is to explore the main theoretical questions surrounding the rise of industrial culture in postwar Italy. These questions can all be approached through a close study of *Il Menabò*, especially issue number four (1961), dedicated to "Industry and Literature." This is something that the Italian-language scholarship has long made a priority, and it is a necessary basis for understanding the novels and films covered in the rest of this book. We are therefore interested in questions of literary and cultural theory: How does *Il Menabò* develop a theory of literary and cultural production, and why is that important? These questions are fairly easy to handle when the journal provides sustained critical analysis, but when it gives us creative works like short stories and poetry, the job becomes more difficult. Since *Il Menabò* famously dismisses the traditional boundary between non-fiction and fiction writing, we must investigate how narrative relates to critique, and how both make contributions to theoretical debates.

There is no good English-language equivalent to the Italian word *menabò*, but it can be translated approximately as 'model,' 'plan' or 'arrangement,' especially with regard to the publishing process. More specifically, it refers to the proposed visual layout of a newspaper, magazine, journal or book, a spatial guide that establishes a relationship among elements of text and image. It thus communicates both structure and freedom, law and improvisation, limitation and possibility. It conjures up visions of industrial society and processes of machine production that can set and modify a world design independent of the human hand. According to the journal's opening proclamation (1959), the word *menabò* is "legato a un'idea di funzionalità, e rapido e allegro di suono" (tied to an idea of functionality, with a rapid and pleasing sound).[2]

---

2 Anon. 1959. *Il Menabò di letteratura*, no. 1. 4.

Though on paper Vittorini and Calvino shared all editorial responsibilities, in practice *Il Menabò* was, from the start, a Vittorini publication. By issue number five (1962) Calvino's interests had diverged so far from the journal's line that he could admit, in private correspondence, that he no longer read anything: "lascio che mettano il mio nome [sul frontespizio] per amicizia verso Vittorini, che è una delle poche persone che stimo nella letteratura" (I let them put my name [on the title page] as a sign of friendship towards Vittorini, who is one of the few people in Italian literature whom I admire).[3] But already in 1959 the reigns of *Il Menabò* were firmly in the hands of Vittorini, and he went about contacting authors, commissioning contributions and managing the editorial process.

This was not Vittorini's first foray into the business of publishing, and *Il Menabò* was largely the culmination of his work on two previous ventures. The first was the political and cultural journal *Il Politecnico*, founded in Milan in 1945, which came to advocate a sharp rupture from the history of anti-fascist cultural production in Italy. During Fascism, Vittorini had championed the anticapitalist aspects of authoritarian rule, then he joined the Partito Comunista Italiano (Italian Communist Party, PCI) in 1942. In the pages of *Il Politecnico*, Vittorini accused his comrades of having failed to prevent both dictatorship and world war. In his view, the culture of antifascism – whether Marxist, idealist, Catholic or mystic – had developed the foolish goal of consoling the Italian people with pursuits that were purely intellectual. What it really needed to do was translate that theory into practice: to provide protection, and indeed liberation.[4]

This was an abstract distinction whose elaboration would have to wait for *Il Menabò*, but it put Vittorini on a collision course with the PCI leader, Palmiro Togliatti. Anti-fascist culture was determined, to a

---

3   Calvino, I. 1991. "A Gerda Niedieck, Frankfurt am Main." December 19, 1963. *I libri degli altri: lettere, 1947–1981*. Turin: Einaudi. 442.

4   Vittorini outlined this critique in his article "Una nuova cultura" (A New Culture), published in 1945: "Questa cultura [italiana e europea] non ha avuto che scarsa, forse nessuna, influenza civile sugli uomini" (This [Italian and European] culture has had nothing but a scarce influence – perhaps none at all – on the lives of men). Vittorini, E. 1960. "Una nuova cultura." *Il Politecnico. Antologia critica*. Edited by Marco Forti and Sergio Pautasso. Milan: Lerici. 44.

large extent, by the top-down centralized policy of Togliatti and his team, and the party line was that all creative production must be subservient to political decisions.[5] Vittorini's journal objected to this, calling for a new anti-fascist culture that could challenge and even reject the politics of the Party. By the time *Il Politecnico* ceased publication in 1947, Vittorini had broken with the official communist world.

The second venture that predates *Il Menabò* was the book series *I Gettoni*, which Vittorini edited for the Turin-based Einaudi publishing house from 1951 to 1958. The series became known for printing low-cost paperbacks of contemporary Italian fiction, including works by three authors covered in this book (Luigi Davì, Ottiero Ottieri and Giovanni Arpino). Like *Il Politecnico*, so too *I Gettoni* challenged the cultural policy of the PCI, introducing to the tradition of socialist realism innovative elements of linguistic and genre experimentation. These were the same elements that would subsequently find full expression in *Il Menabò*, and there is a high degree of continuity running from the book series to the journal.

When in 1956 the secretary of the Communist Party of the Soviet Union Nikita Khrushchev delivered his address to the Party's twentieth congress, the Italian left went into a state of shock. Khrushchev railed against former Party secretary Joseph Stalin for creating around himself a cult of personality antithetical to egalitarian society and for ordering that the Party's membership be periodically, systematically and violently purged of 'traitors.' This ground-shaking revelation was quickly followed by the Soviet invasion of Hungary and the brutal suppression there of a people's movement seeking greater independence from Moscow. Western Marxists were horrified, and the PCI, which was somewhat subservient to the Soviets, lost more than one tenth of its membership.

The effect of 1956 was to open up a new space for experimentation in Italian leftist culture. If the politics of the PCI were no longer sacrosanct, then culture no longer needed to serve those politics. This was precisely what Vittorini had pushed for ever since the days of *Il Politecnico*, and he

---

5 The faceoff between Togliatti and Vittorini was started by the following article: Alicata, M. 1946. "La corrente *Politecnico*." *Rinascita*, vol. 3, no.s 5–6. 116. Find the main debate anthologized here: Lupetti, F et al. 1974. *La polemica Vittorini-Togliatti e la linea culturale del PCI nel 1945–47*. Milan: Lavoro Liberato. 16–51.

now found himself in a good position to lead the way forward. It was in this context that he and Calvino conceived *Il Menabò*. Their idea was to create a journal that could inherit the literary and cultural legacy of *I Gettoni*, and to this end they decided to stick with the Einaudi publishing house. This had some effect on the content and form of *Il Menabò*, which aimed, in its opening proclamation (1959), to bring together "i caratteri insieme di una rivista e di una collana letteraria" (the features of both a magazine and a book series).[6] In reality, *Il Menabò* never enjoyed a large and popular readership. It was too philosophical, academic, even pedantic to become anything but a specialized journal.

While most journals combined articles on all sorts of topics, *Il Menabò* tended to organize each of its issues around one single and overarching theme. This allowed Vittorini and Calvino to illuminate different sides of the same object, and it gave readers not specific pieces of knowledge, but rather a general sense of how the relevant intellectual conversation was developing. Issue number one (1959) focused on the use of dialect in war narratives, followed by issues on poetry (1960), the Italian South (1960), industrial culture (1961), linguistic experimentation (1962) and so on. As regards form, *Il Menabò* was much less methodical, purposefully mixing all sorts of languages and genres that most journals kept strictly separated. In its pages, we find Italian and dialect, poetry and prose, narrative and critique, history and letters. This was all part of a plan to democratize culture by providing not only a plurality of perspectives, but also (something that is closely related) a diversity of expressive means.

For the literary historian Silvia Cavalli, what unites all the issues of *Il Menabò* is a common search to understand the transforming relationship between literature and society.[7] What Cavalli means by 'society' is itself always in transformation, taking on the guise of history first, then industry and eventually reality. These conceptual waypoints help us to map the winding path of *Il Menabò* as it travelled from the Cold War through the economic boom and into the information age.

6 Anon. 1959. *Il Menabò di letteratura*, no. 1. 1.
7 Cavalli, S. 2017. *Progetto «Menabò» (1959–1967)*. Venice: Marsilio. 205.

When issue number four (1961) of *Il Menabò* hit Italian newsstands, bookshops, libraries and classrooms, it ignited a passionate discussion about industrial culture that would influence an entire generation of writers and filmmakers. The issue included two intellectual *tours de force* from Vittorini and the literary critic Gianni Scalia, both of whom criticized Italian culture for being unable to deal with the transformations of industrial society. Vittorini's contribution had the added bite of being placed as the issue's editorial, and it has become a sort of stand-in for the whole developing critique of contemporary factory culture.

Like many powerful ideas, the editorial's main charge is surprisingly simple: "Chiunque racconti di fabbriche e aziende lo faccia sempre entro dei limiti letterariamente 'preindustriali' " (Whoever tells stories about factories and companies always does so within literary limits that are 'pre-industrial').[8] In other words, the only way for Italian writers and filmmakers to narrate the world of industry was by forcing it through a culture that was developed to express other things. Vittorini's is clearly more than a jab at individual novels and films; it is a total indictment of the Italian humanistic tradition that has failed to 'keep up with the times.' Since the Renaissance, writes Vittorini, it had been the priority of that tradition to represent 'man-in-nature' by giving us rolling hills and gushing streams, wild forests and violent seas. This focus on 'nature-as-content' had been compounded, in his eyes, by the rise of natural*ism*, a mode of expression developed in nineteenth-century France and imported to Italy by writers like Giovanni Verga and Luigi Capuana. Philosophically, naturalism is founded on the belief that reality is separated from consciousness, and that humans come to know the world objectively through experimentation, observation and discovery. Naturalist literature and film are governed by a detached approach to storytelling, full of thick description and apersonal forces that run right up to *Il Menabò* in the guise of postwar neorealism.

With respect to other European countries like England, France and Germany, Italy had a late industrial revolution that completely transformed everyday life, at least in the North, and very quickly. For Vittorini, this process had been so profound that it had created a new human: no longer

---

8 Vittorini, E. 1961. "Industria e letteratura." *Il Menabò di letteratura*, no. 4. 15.

at home in a knowable natural world, this new human was adrift on a confusing but ultimately changeable sea of factory machines and consumer goods. Only a culture that was equally 'industrial' would be able to plot the way to safety, but what exactly did 'industrial culture' mean? It certainly had nothing to do with the Italian humanistic tradition, whose attitude toward capitalist modernity had usually been one of refusal. And despite many important attempts by Italian writers and filmmakers to engage with industrial society in its own terms, Vittorini insisted that they always fell back on inadequate models: "I narrativi [...] si comportano dinanzi a [la società industriale] come se fosse un semplice settore nuovo d'una più vasta realtà già risaputa, [...] riducendosi con ciò a darne degli squarci pateticamente (o pittorescamente) descrittivi che risultano di sostanza naturalistica" (These stories [...] behave as if [industrial society] were just a new and simple part of a larger reality we already know, [...] reducing themselves to giving pathetically (or picturesquely) descriptive slices of it that turn out to be the stuff of naturalism).[9]

Industrial culture would not be accomplished by making factories the object of literary and cinematic representation (though many successful industrial novels and films are factory stories). Most Italians did not work in factories, and yet their daily lives were transformed by the impact of industry on consumer practices, sexual mores, family life, leisure activities, language and so on. Industrial culture needed to focus on these ramifications, to explore what Vittorini called "la catena di effetti che il mondo delle fabbriche mette in moto" (the chain of effects that the factory world sets in motion).[10] One might write an industrial novel on just about any topic: education, travel, commerce, even farming or woodworking. The important thing was that it take account of the social transformations brought on by mass production, and that it propose some sort of literary solution to the alienation of modern humanity. When we say 'industrial culture' with Vittorini, it must be clear that we mean a broad culture of industrial society, not one of industrial production in the narrow sense.

9   Vittorini, E. 1961. "Industria e letteratura." 14.
10 Vittorini, E. 1961. "Industria e letteratura." 20.

Vittorini's editorial has overshadowed all other contributions to issue number four of *Il Menabò*, but in my opinion it is only second in importance to Scalia's condemnation of Italian culture during the economic boom. Both critics share the general sense that the Italian humanistic tradition is unprepared for the machine age, but only Scalia is shrewd enough to suggest that the Renaissance and Enlightenment concept 'human' has lost all currency. Reason, liberty and individuality were central to the rhetoric of post-Medieval humanism, but as a rule humanity remained subject to the external forces of providence, fate, necessity and so on. It is only with the development of mass production and the rise of industrial society that humanity finds itself in full possession of the world, able to make and remake civilization as it pleases.[11] "L'industria è il mondo dell'assenza di futuro" (Industry is the world of no future), Scalia proclaims, by which he does not mean that there is no hope, but rather that there is infinite opportunity.[12] While the old human had limited control over nature's course, the new human has total power over the direction of industry.

With great power comes great responsibility, and Scalia understands perfectly well that industry might be developed to destroy humanity as it might be developed to enrich it. It is the job of culture to explore the effects of industry on humanity, to approve its achievements, denounce its crimes and prescribe their remediation. In short, culture must be the conscience of industry. It must build a common-sense morality that can hitch the proverbial industrial locomotive to the winding tracks of social progress. Like Vittorini, Scalia believes that Italian writers and filmmakers have so far failed in this mission, and not least because they defend outdated ideas, with so many anti-modern prejudices.

Against the Italian humanistic tradition, Scalia advocates a culture that accepts and even celebrates the transformation of humanity into technology. The human is no longer a purely biological entity; it has been fitted out with the great tools of capitalist modernity. From a twenty-first-century perspective, this might conjure up dystopian images of manipulative robots,

---

[11] One must remember that Scalia's article predates any widespread awareness of the ecological consequences of consumer capitalism.

[12] Scalia, G. 1961. "Dalla natura all'industria." *Il Menabò di letteratura*, no. 4. 101.

menacing cyborgs and artificial intelligence. But Scalia means nothing of the sort. In fact, his view of technological humanity is overwhelmingly positive: technology frees humanity from the limits of biology, providing the raw materials needed to build a more, not less, humane society. It is the job of culture, and more specifically of the modern writer, to "costruire una antropologia trans-industriale che conosca, comprenda e trasformi l'industria industriale nell'industria umana" (construct a trans-industrial anthropology that recognizes, comprehends and transforms industrial industry into human industry).[13]

Thus while it is true that both Vittorini and Scalia take aim at the Italian humanistic tradition, it would be a mistake to call them antihumanists, transhumanists or even posthumanists. On the contrary, theirs is a new humanism, one that accepts industrial society as a condition of art and politics, but only to the extent that its methods can be bent toward the needs of humanity. Their claim to humanism is perhaps stronger than all those who refuse the modern world, because they seek to drag a runaway economy back down to the ground, back down to the level of the human.

What about those contributions to issue number four of *Il Menabò* that make no explicit argument? How do poetry and prose develop theories of literary and cultural production that support, complicate or even challenge the perspectives of Vittorini and Scalia? Issue number four includes three collections of poetry and two short stories on industrial society, but we cannot possibly do them all justice in a short chapter of this sort. The best remedy is to focus our attention very closely on one example of poetry and one example of prose, keeping in mind that while these are more or less representative of the literary and cultural debate developed in the issue, they certainly do not exhaust the material.

The writer Vittorio Sereni's five-part poem "Una visita in fabbrica" (A Visit to the Factory) appears, perhaps provocatively, before Vittorini's opening editorial. This gives the poem the air of a creative overture, raising important questions about its relationship to the rest of the journal issue: is Sereni's poem supposed to be a good example of 'industrial culture' or a bad one? Does it exemplify the arguments developed by Vittorini and Scalia or

13   Scalia, G. 1961. "Dalla natura all'industria." 113.

does it propose its own ideas? "Una visita in fabbrica" is the story of two intellectuals who tour the production lines of a large industrial company. They are the narrator and the reader, and at a certain point they (that is, we) become interested in understanding and representing the labor regime operating there. The workers pass tools back and forth, they move to and fro, but all of this somehow resists translation into the language of the intellectuals:

> le macchine, le tarfile e calandre,
> questi nomi per me presto di solo suono nel buio della mente,
> rumore che si somma a rumore e presto spavento per me,
> straniero al grande moto e da questo agganciato.
> (the machines, the dies and calender rollers,
> these names for me are merely sound in the darkness of my mind,
> noise that adds to noise and then fright for me,
> a stranger to the great motor and by this grasped.)[14]

As the new industrial environment confounds the old humanistic culture of these intellectuals, so too do the lives of the workers who must become the center of their attention:

> Ma anche di costoro che ne sappiamo tu e io,
> tu che tanto bene ne discorri, io con parole
> buone a scovare larve di passato
> dall'ombra di quei muri.
> (And of these people what do we know, you and I,
> you who discourse on them so well, I with good
> words unearthing old larvae
> from the shadows of those walls.)[15]

Sereni's poem anticipates an important aspect of Vittorini's argument: that it is not individual writers and filmmakers who have failed to create an industrial culture in Italy; it is their language that cannot express the things of industrial society. Even when intellectuals like those in Sereni's poem consciously want to represent industry, they cannot help

---

14   Sereni, V. 1961. "Una visita in fabbrica." *Il Menabò di letteratura*, no. 4. 8.
15   Sereni, V. 1961. "Una visita in fabbrica." 9.

but falter on the rigid structures of a humanistic tradition that was developed in a context by now superseded. What is needed is a revolution in language to match the revolution in economy, something that would allow these intellectuals to represent the factory, and to bring industrial development into line with human development.

If for Sereni a properly industrial culture is a suitable and realizable goal, the same cannot be said for the writer Ottiero Ottieri. Starting in 1955, Ottieri worked in southern Italy for the Olivetti typewriter company, where he gained valuable experience of the production lines at Pozzuoli, the factory workforce there and daily life in the surrounding community. Between 1954 and 1957, Ottieri kept a personal diary, which was redacted, partially fictionalized and published as the short story "Taccuino industriale" (Industrial Notebook) in issue number four of *Il Menabò*. The premise of the story is strikingly similar to that of Sereni's poem: an intellectual struggling to describe the factory environment wonders if it might not be indescribable after all. Ottieri's narrator takes a rigorously rational approach to this problem by asking who, specifically, can be expected to represent the industrial factory: "Que[i operai] che ci stanno dentro possono darci dei documenti, ma non la loro elaborazione [...]. Gli artisti che vivono fuori, come possono penetrare in una industria?" (Those [workers] on the inside can give us documents, but not their elaboration [...]. Those artists living on the outside, how can they penetrate into an industry?)[16] His response is patently pessimistic: they cannot, "l'industria è inespressiva" (industry is inexpressive), industrial culture is a contradiction in terms, it is a structural impossibility.[17]

At seventy-five pages, "Industrial Notebook" is the longest contribution to issue number four of *Il Menabò*. True to its origins as a personal diary, it is a fragmented, discontinuous, and often erratic piece that mixes workplace memories with philosophical musings about the development of consumer society and much more. As regards literary and cultural theory, it is peppered with undeveloped ideas for industrial novels: "*I traditori*, romanzo. I socialisti che, in un'azienda, finiscono pian piano dalla parte

---

16 Ottieri, O. 1961. "Taccuino industriale." *Il Menabò di letteratura*, no. 4. 21.
17 Ottieri, O. 1961. "Taccuino industriale." 21.

del padrone" (*The Traitors*, a novel. A group of socialists who, at a certain company, slowly end up on the side of the boss).[18] "Un nuovo romanzo su Milano, intorno a una grande azienda (*Lotte a Milano*)" (A new novel about Milan, centered on a big company (*Struggles in Milan*)).[19] "*Il tradimento*. [...] La storia lineare di un operaio che non crede più nel socialismo" (*The Betrayal*. [...] The linear narrative of a worker who no longer believes in socialism).[20] Though scholars have never taken these notes very seriously, they may help to explain Ottieri's maturation as an author of real industrial novels during the late 1950s (see Fabrizio di Maio's chapter on Ottieri in this book).

Other contributions to issue number four of *Il Menabò* include literary criticism and history from Agostino Pirella and Marco Forti, poetry from Lamberto Pignotti and Giovanni Giudici, plus a short story from Luigi Davì. Together, they lent intellectual weight to the arguments of Vittorini and Scalia, provoking a vehement backlash from the greater Italian literary establishment. In fact, Vittorini and Calvino received so much mail about issue number four, that they decided to open issue number five (1962) of *Il Menabò* by publishing a selection of critical responses. These tended to attack Vittorini's thesis from one of two angles: it either exaggerated the real extent of Italy's slow industrialization or it asked Italian culture to compromise itself with industrial capitalism.

Il Menabò di letteratura remained dedicated to exploring the relationship between economy and culture, only abandoning the question of industry when the economic boom gave way to the information age. The journal became a formative publication for new avantgarde movements, and Calvino drifted into the background, leaving behind only his name. In 1966, Vittorini died of stomach cancer, and Calvino reappeared, publishing one last issue, number ten (1967), in memory of his beloved friend. In the opening editorial – a sort of eulogy – Calvino had the difficult task of summing up a life's work. He chose

---

18   Ottieri, O. 1961. "Taccuino industriale." 67.
19   Ottieri, O. 1961. "Taccuino industriale." 67.
20   Ottieri, O. 1961. "Taccuino industriale." 74.

these words: "poco conta la modernità della tematica se la letteratura non istaura, nei suoi mezzi specifici, un nuovo rapporto di conocenza del mondo" (modern themes do not count for much as long as literature does not use its own methods to found a new epistemological relationship with the world).[21]

---

[21] Calvino, I. 1967. *Il menabò di letteratura*, vol. 10. 8.

EMANUELE ZINATO

5 The Factory as Cultural Center

New Disciplines, New Magazines

The field of Italian industrial culture was extremely varied during the economic boom, but it was characterized above all by the activity of cultural magazines, the interdisciplinary quality of the so-called 'human sciences' and the rise of factory literature.

Some magazines were directly linked to public or private companies, like *Pirelli* and *Civiltà delle macchine* (Machine Civilization). *Pirelli* was published from 1948 to 1972, with the aim of uniting the culture of science and technology to the culture of the humanities. Articles on industrial production and technology were published alongside articles on topics ranging from art to architecture, sociology to economics, town planning to literature. The magazine counted among its collaborators Giulio Carlo Argan, Dino Buzzati, Italo Calvino, Gillo Dorfles, Umberto Eco, Eugenio Montale and Elio Vittorini. *Civiltà delle macchine* was directed from 1953 to 1958 by the poet Leonardo Sinisgalli. One of Sinisgalli's closest collaborators was Giuseppe Eugenio Luraghi, the Finmeccanica manager whose company – along with the magazine – would later join the Istituto per la Ricostruzione Industriale (Institute for Industrial Reconstruction, IRI). In a 1965 interview with Ferdinando Camon, Sinisgalli recounted the birth of *Civiltà delle macchine* in legendary terms:

> L'inverno del 1953, a Roma in un ufficio di Piazza del Popolo, quando io misi a fuoco il progetto di *Civiltà delle macchine*, […] la cultura dell'Occidente era rimasta incredibilmente arretrata e scettica nei confronti della tecnica, dell'ingegneria. Voglio dire che erano sfuggite alla cultura le scoperte di Archimede e di Leonardo, di Cardano e di Galilei, di Newton e di Einstein. Io volevo sfondare le porte dei laboratori, delle specole, delle celle. Mi ero convinto che c'è una simbiosi tra intelletto e istinto, tra

ragione e passione, tra reale e immaginario. Ch'era urgente tentare una commistione, un innesto, anche a costo di sacrificare la purezza.

(In the winter of 1953, in an office in Rome's Piazza del Popolo, when I started focusing on the *Civiltà delle macchine* project, […] Western culture was still incredibly backward and skeptical with regards to technology and engineering. I mean, even the discoveries of Archimedes and Leonardo had escaped the attention of culture; even those of Cardano and Galilei, Newton and Einstein. I wanted to break down the doors of the laboratories, observatories and cells. I was convinced of a symbiosis between the intellect and the instincts, between reason and passion, between the real and the imaginary. I was convinced of the need to urgently attempt a mixture or a graft, even if it meant sacrificing purity.)[1]

One of the most original results of the encounter between humanists and industrial culture was the acceptance, in a context still strongly influenced by Benedetto Croce's idealism, of sociology, psychology and psychoanalysis: disciplines that would become the specialties of Luciano Anceschi's neo-avantgarde journal *Il Verri*. On the one hand, the Fordist imperatives of human resource organization acted in instrumental ways on sociology and psychology, but on the other hand, a series of tensions and experiments around psychoanalysis enabled critical research to coexist, for about a decade, with goals that were strictly production-driven. At the beginning of the twentieth century, the center of psychoanalysis on the Italian peninsula was Trieste (technically part of the Austrian Empire), but by the mid-twentieth century it had shifted to the Olivetti company. Already before the end of the Second World War, the enlightened industrialist Adriano Olivetti was convinced that the fall of Fascism would facilitate the introduction of psychoanalysis' most dynamic currents. Olivetti laid the foundations for a publishing house – the Nuove Edizioni Ivrea (New Editions Ivrea), which became the Edizioni di Comunità (Community Editions) – and acquired the rights to publish some works, like Carl Jung's *Psychological Types*. Olivetti also hired Cesare Musatti, one of the first Italian psychologists, to set up a 'Centro di psicologia del lavoro' (Center of Industrial Psychology).[2] The writings of Paolo Volponi and Ottiero

---

1   Cited in Camon, F. 1965. *Il mestiere del poeta*. Milan: Lerici. 96.
2   Musatti, C et al. 1980. *Psicologi in fabbrica. La psicologia del lavoro negli stabilimenti Olivetti*. Turin: Einaudi. XV–XVII.

Ottieri, both Olivetti employees, presented such a high concentration of psychic themes that their works have been indexed under the heading "follia" (madness).[3] Moreover, Volponi invented poetic-narrative forms with which to work through the trauma of displacement and the processes of personality dissolution integral to sociocultural transformations. In their consistency, Volponi's writings presented themselves as both realist and visionary, while the distress of the characters was always represented in relation to collective contradictions.

Starting with *Memoriale* (My Troubles Began, 1962), Volponi used his own factory experience to build a reserve of images and psychoanalytic situations. When Olivetti hired Ottieri and Volponi (the first in 1953 as human resources manager, the second in 1956 as director of social services) the company was enjoying a period of intense expansion that allowed for the presence, alongside technicians and engineers, of intellectuals like psychologists, poets, architects and sociologists. Every minute, the company's ten factories – in Ivrea (Piedmont), Agliè (Piedmont), Turin (Piedmont), Massa (Tuscany), Pozzuoli (Campania), Barcelona, Glasgow, Buenos Aires, São Paulo and Johannesburg – produced six typewriters or calculators, and in 1957 it became the first in Italy to adopt a forty-five hour workweek. Nevertheless, there were problems: with the introduction of new electromechanical typewriters, Olivetti abandoned the individual piecework system and adopted the collective piecework system, a move that workerist critics like Raniero Panzieri judged paternalistic and a sign of the rising neo-capitalist "corte feudale" (feudal court).[4] These tensions were reflected in the circumstances leading to Volponi's hiring: in February 1956, Olivetti fired the psychoanalyst, Auschwitz survivor and director of social services Luciana Nissim, together with her husband, the head of internal relations Franco Momigliano. Further tensions were reflected in marketing contexts, where the neo-Marxist poet and essayist Franco Fortini had the job

---

3   Santato, G. 1988. "Follia e utopia nella narrativa di Volponi." *Studi Novecenteschi*, vol. 25, no. 55. 29–66.
4   Cited in Zinato, E. 2018. "Ciclostilati in proprio. La critica dei *'Quaderni piacentini.'*" *Sistema periodico. Il secolo interminabile delle riviste*. Edited by Francesco Bortolotto et al. Bologna: Pendragon. 173–174.

of naming the most famous Olivetti machines: *Lexicon*, *Lettera 33* and *Divisumma*, among others.

After Adriano Olivetti's death in 1960, factory psychology (and, to a lesser extent, sociology and marketing) was exposed to the suspicions of 'scientific reason.' Olivetti engineers saw psychologists as mere instruments for the selection and adaptation of employees, in line with the dictates of scientific management, whose mathematical criteria were gaining ground. As a result, Olivetti psychoanalysts who worked in medicine and factory sociology were faced with a difficult choice: adopt the rationalizing ideology of industrial psychology or leave the company.[5] In a similar way, those writers and poets who had discovered at Olivetti a hospitable 'court' with an encouraging patron found it arduous to carry the utopian alliance of industry and literature beyond the 1960s.

Factory Culture and the Culture Industry

Scholars have usually approached this period of Italian literary production with an eye toward two moments: Vittorini's discussion of industry and literature in issue number four of *Il Menabò di letteratura* (1961) and the writings of Olivetti intellectuals. But what is of equal importance is that in these same years, Italian society was developing a feature already known to advanced capitalist countries: a culture industry. Thanks to his experience at Olivetti, Fortini mercilessly predicted this development in his celebrated 1960 essay "Verifica dei poteri":

> I luoghi dell'opinione e del gusto letterario sono stati sorpresi nel giro di pochi anni dall'insorgere ed estendersi di forme per noi nuove di industria della cultura che hanno mutato aspetto e funzione ai tradizionali organi di mediazione fra scrittori e pubblico, come l'editoria, le librerie, i giornali, le riviste, i gruppi politici e d'opinione. Alla motorizzazione la società letteraria ha resistito anche meno dei nostri storici centri urbani.

5   Novara, F. 1980. "Organizzazione del lavoro: gli equivoci della ragione scientifica." in Musatti et al. *Psicologi in fabbrica*. 405.

(In just a few years, the role of opinion and literary taste has been surprised by the rise and spread of culture industries that are for us new. These industries have changed the appearance and function of the traditional organs of mediation between writers and the public, like publishing houses, bookstores, journals, magazines, political and opinion groups. Literary society has resisted motorization even less than our historic urban centers have.)[6]

Fortini's essays were polemically designed to demystify the idealistic illusions of *Il Menabò*. He wrote against a certain neopositivist ideology that foresaw a process of permanent cultural updating necessary to raise traditional humanism to the level of new technologies imposed by the industrial world. Nevertheless, in the opening proclamation to issue number six of *Il Menabò* (1963), Vittorini showed a precocious awareness of the cultural consequences of industrialization. In fact, Vittorini impatiently liquidated what he called the "solfa" (same old story)[7] about industry and literature that was quickly becoming an intellectual fad:

> Quello che [la questione industria e letteratura] nascondeva era molto semplicemente solo di essere il modo più aggiornato di tornare a porre il problema 'letteratura e realtà' […]. Per intanto possiamo contentarci di riconstatare che la materia della letteratura come disciplina è almeno di stabilire 'nessi.' Cioè verificare che ci sono [i nessi]. Accorgersene. E istituirli letterariamente. Non ha nessun compito proprio, la letteratura, appena si ripeta che il suo compito sia di rappresentare il mondo; quasi che non ne faccia anche parte, del mondo; quasi cioè ch'essa sia parte solo dell'altro, il cosiddetto altro del vecchio linguaggio diviso tra 'catene' e 'spirito,' 'materia' e 'sospiro ardente,' 'valle di lagrime' e 'paso doble,' 'soldato morto' e 'bandiera,' 'peccato' e 'redenzione,' 'carne' e 'caro ideal,' 'elettrodomestici' e 'missa est,' 'esistere' ed 'essere,' 'Coca' e 'Cola,' eccetera, eccetera.

> ([The question of industry and literature] was very simply hiding the fact that it was only the most updated way of retuning to pose the problem of 'literature and reality' […]. For now, we can be satisfied with verifying that the goal of literature as a discipline is at a minimum to establish 'nexuses.' That is, to verify that [nexuses] exist. To notice them. And to institute them in a literary way. Literature has no job, as

---

6   Fortini, F. 1969. "Verifica dei poteri." *Verifica dei poteri. Scritti di critica e di istituzioni letterarie.* Milan: Il Saggiatore. 41.
7   Vittorini, E. 2008. "Premessa al Menabò 6." *Letteratura arte società. Articoli e interventi 1938–1965.* Edited by Raffaella Redondi. Turin: Einaudi. 1031.

soon as we say that the job of literature is to represent the world; almost as if it were not already part of the world; that is, almost as if it were only part of the other, the so-called other from an old language divided between 'chain' and 'spirit', 'material' and 'ardent breath,' 'valleys of tears' and *'pasodoble,'* 'dead soldier' and 'flag', 'sin' and 'redemption,' 'flesh' and 'beloved ideals,' 'household appliances' and *'missa est,'* 'Coca' and 'Cola,' etcetera, etcetera.)[8]

Vittorini's unscrupulous and anti-idealistic reasoning uses irony to unmask a long cultural heritage of dualisms. This results in a drive to overstep disciplinary boundaries and contaminate the most distant semantic fields, from consumer culture ("household appliances" and "Coca Cola") to patriotism ("flag" and "dead soldier"), from philosophy ("material" and "spirit") to the popular imagination ("ardent breath"). If even the most important promoter of the debate around Italian industrial literature in the 1960s was aware of the developing contamination of humanistic culture with the omnipresent hegemony of neo-capitalist forms of life, then any consideration of a literary genre devoted to representing industrial conditions during the economic boom must examine two interconnected and conflicting aspects. On the one hand is a more plainly literary aspect, regarding the forms with which the novel represented factory labor. On the other hand is a more sociological aspect, regarding the relations of force in the field of intellectual labor, including the labor of writers. Here, it is useful to reference Pierre Bourdieu's concepts:

> One could ask whether the division into two markets characteristic of the fields of cultural production since the middle of the nineteenth century, with on one side the narrow field of producers for producers, and on the other side the field of mass production and 'industrial literature,' is not now threatening to disappear, since the logic of commercial production tends more and more to assert itself over avant-garde production (notably, in the case of literature, through the constraints of the book market).[9]

---

8   Vittorini, E. 2008. "Premessa al Menabò 6." *Letteratura arte società. Articoli e interventi 1938–1965*. Edited by Raffaella Redondi. 1031.
9   Bourdieu, P. *The Rules of Art: Genesis and Structure of the Literary Field*. Translated by Susan Emanuel. Cambridge: Polity Press, 1996. 345.

If we want to get a full critical understanding of the field, then we must contrast those magazines directly connected to factory culture, like *Civiltà delle macchine*, with more peripheral publications like *Quaderni piacentini* (1962–1984). Under the direction of Piergiorgio Bellocchio and Grazia Cherchi, *Quaderni piacentini*'s many articles on culture, art, factory life and social conflicts served to illuminate and contradict each other in turn, according to a method of cultural investigation and power critique derived from the Frankfort School and, in Italy, from the writings of Fortini. *Quaderni piacentini* also traversed the student-worker protests of 1968, becoming a veritable laboratory of politics and culture by mixing different disciplinary approaches and offering diverse ways of interpreting them politically. This is clear from the magazine's rubric 'Libri da leggere, libri da non leggere' (Books to Read, Books to Not Read), which recommended the novels of Beppe Fenoglio, Luigi Meneghello, Lucio Mastronardi and Paolo Volponi, but warned against those of Giovanni Arpino, Giorgio Bassani, Carlo Cassola, Dacia Maraini, Mario Soldati, Edoardo Sanguineti, Nanni Balestrini and Alberto Arbasino. Bellocchio used *Quaderni piacentini* to attack the Viareggio Prize jurors Pier Paolo Pasolini and Alberto Moravia, calling them "servi" (servants) of the culture industry. Roberto Roversi also labelled the writers of the Gruppo 63 (Group of 63) "funamboli leggiadri" (graceful tightrope walkers) who "giungono sorridendo sul palco dei vincitori" (arrive smiling on the winners' podium).[10] The neo-avantgarde had opposed the traditional Italian literary establishment with a managerial dynamism. But the young intellectuals of the *Quaderni piacentini* met the neo-avantgarde with a powerful critique of ideology and with an idea of literature as an instrument of freedom. This was very different from the neo-avantgarde's technical and linguistic understanding of literature, which implied a renewal of poetic forms absorbed by industrial (and profit) production.

---

10   Cited in Zinato, E. 2018. "Ciclostilati in proprio. La critica dei '*Quaderni piacentini*.'" *Sistema periodico. Il secolo interminabile delle riviste.* Edited by Francesco Bortolotto et al. 173–174.

The Factory Novel

From a strict literary history perspective, the term 'Italian factory novel' refers to a group of narrative texts that took as their object of study the world of industrial production, from Ottieri's *Tempi stretti* (Tight Times, 1957) to Primo Levi's *La chiave a stella* (The Wrench, 1978) and Volponi's *Le mosche del capitale* (The Flies of Capital, published in 1989 but begun during the second half of the 1970s).

The Italian factory novel drew its formal features from documentary autobiography, naturalism and modernist experimentalism. All three of these traditions were concerns of Vittorini's, whose Einaudi book series *I Gettoni* published one industrial novel (Ottieri's *Tempi stretti*) and a collection of factory short stories (Luigi Davì's *Gymkhana-Cross*, 1957). Vittorini carried this commitment forward with the journal *Il Menabò di letteratura*, which he founded together with Calvino in 1959. *Il Menabò* published authors close to the journal *Officina* (Workshop), like Francesco Leonetti, Volponi and Roversi, but it also looked with favor upon some neo-avantgarde writers like Elio Pagliarani.[11] In 1961, Vittorini opened the debate on the relationship between literature and industry with a surprising move: he distanced himself from the same authors he had published. Vittorini lambasted the traditional literary opposition between content and form: in his opinion, the Italian industrial novel had so far failed to move beyond the models of realism and naturalism presented by Charles Dickens and Émile Zola. Instead, it simply narrated the "novità" (novelty) of the industrial world with the outdated language of tradition.[12] For Vittorini, the translation of industrial reality into literature was not a question of objectively describing the themes and settings of the factory; it was a question of inventing new literary forms that could communicate

---

11   Zinato, E. 2009. "L'esperienza del *Menabò*." *Il demone dell'anticipazione. Cultura, letteratura, editoria in Elio Vittorini*. Edited by Edoardo Esposito. Milan: Il Saggiatore. 163–176.

12   Vittorini, E. 2008. "Industria e letteratura." *Letteratura arte società. Articoli e interventi 1938–1965*. Edited by Raffaella Redondi. 956.

the "catena di effetti che il mondo delle fabbriche mette in moto" (the chain of effects that the factory world sets in motion).[13] As he wrote:

> I prodotti della cosiddetta 'école du regard,' il cui contenuto sembra ignorare che esistano delle fabbriche, dei tecnici e degli operai, sono in effetti molto più a livello industriale, per il nuovo rapporto con la realtà che si configura nel loro linguaggio, di tutta la letteratura cosiddetta d'industria che prende le fabbriche per argomento.
>
> (The products of the so-called 'école du regard,' whose content seems to ignore the existence of factories, technicians and workers, are in effect, because of the new relationship with reality configured in their language, on a level much more industrial than all of the so-called industrial literature that takes factories as its argument.)[14]

The Italian industrial novel was thus inaugurated in the context of a polarization between old and new, and of the resulting avantgardist and technological idea of a literature that transcends itself *ad infinitum* thanks to a commitment to experimentation. It is not a coincidence that the neo-avantgardist critic Renato Barilli spoke in these same years of breaking the "barriera del naturalismo" (barrier of naturalism), alluding to the breaking of the sound barrier by the newest jet airplanes.[15]

Vittorini's merit consisted in having identified the formal problems of a literary genre that, starting from its name, presented itself as the mere documentation of a specific productive reality. Nevertheless, the opposition between formal and thematic aspects imposed by his analysis glossed over the existence, in twentieth-century Italian literature, of a vast and fertile gray zone between avantgardist innovation and traditional conservation, represented first and foremost by the modernist novel.[16] It is therefore legitimate to ask, in rewriting the history of the Italian industrial novel, what sort of debt this narrative form might owe to authors like Luigi Pirandello, Italo Svevo and Carlo Emilio Gadda. Faced with Vittorini's provocation, it is also necessary to establish the borders of the genre: not by opposing content to form, but rather by conjugating the two. One could reasonably count as

---

13   Vittorini, E. 2008. "Industria e letteratura." 960.
14   Vittorini, E. 2008. "Industria e letteratura." 959.
15   Barilli, R. 1964. *La barriera del naturalismo. Studi sulla narrativa italiana contemporanea*. Milan: Il Saggiatore.
16   Luperini, R and Tortora, M (eds). 2012. *Sul modernismo italiano*. Naples: Liguori.

industrial novels – in the strict sense – only those narrative texts that refer to settings, characters and situations pertinent to industrial production. But such an approach would exclude, for example, stories of the new intellectual condition, unthinkable without the processes of modernization, yet void of direct references to industrial labor (see Luciano Bianciardi's *La vita agra* (It's a Hard Life, 1962) and Goffredo Parise's *Il Padrone* (The Boss, 1964)). We can thus distinguish between two models: the first concerned with documentary or testimonial forms, styles and narrative structures that includes autobiographical notes, *reportage* and neorealist stories, and the second defined by neo-modernist experimentation, especially with regard to the narrator's voice and point of view. Examples of the first model are Ottieri's *Tempi stretti* and *Donnarumma all'assalto* (The Men at the Gate, 1959), of the second Volponi's *Memoriale*. Novels like Mastronardi's *Il calzolaio di Vigevano* (The Shoemaker from Vigevano, 1962) mix elements of both.

The first Italian industrial novel of the economic miracle was Ottieri's *Tempi stretti*. Published in 1957, the book presents a traditional narrative structure, founded on the naturalistic assumption of impersonal representation and with typical characters. These include the hesitant intellectual who is optimistic about industrial development (Giovanni), the worker who is fired for striking (Aldo), the female laborer fallen victim to the intense factory rhythms (Emma) and the paternalistic boss (Alessandri). *Tempi stretti* is situated at the intersection of autobiographical experience and realist fiction: just like Ottieri (who worked for Olivetti as a human resources manager), the protagonist Giovanni is a technician active in working-class politics but also attracted to the cultural milieu of the capitalist managers. Mastonardi's *Il calzolaio di Vigevano* is, on the contrary, perched between the literary reflection of reality and its deformation. Following the realist tradition, it is one part of a three-part series that also includes *Il maestro di Vigevano* (The Teacher from Vigevano, 1962) and *Il meridionale di Vigevano* (The Southerner from Vigevano, 1964). The book narrates the aspirations of social mobility of a generation of shoemakers who make tremendous sacrifices in an attempt to become wealthy entrepreneurs. After a long life of forbearance, the indebted protagonist Mario Sala is forced to close his small factory and return to work as a common laborer. But Mastonardi's messy language relentlessly contaminates the free indirect discourse with neurotic and painful caricatures of Lombard dialect, something that associates his writing with that of Gadda. Moreover, the corporeal, grotesque and deforming aspects of the text render an exclusively realistic reading impossible. *Il calzolaio* is marked off from the tradition of naturalism by "la nera, atroce carica distruttrice, quasi la voglia di sporcare tutto, di indurre nausea di tutto: la vita privata, quella pubblica, l'universo borghese e operaio, il linguaggio stesso" (the black, atrocious destructive drive, practically the desire to dirty everything, to inspire a nausea of everything: private and public life, the bourgeois and working-class universe, language itself).[17] Mastronardi's hyperbolic and aggressive language is not the sign of amateurism; it is the twisted and apocalyptic representation of a provincial setting where shoemakers live out their days.[18]

In *Memoriale*, Volponi veers closer to neo-modernist experimentation with a story told retrospectively by the insane factory worker and farmer Albino Saluggia. Recalling Svevo's delirious conscience of illness and impasse, Volponi builds his text on the practice of introspective self-analysis. Albino lacks the irony and mendacity of Svevo's protagonist Zeno, but his tendency to transform reality and his pathological attachment to his mother are of unmistakably modernist inspiration. The introspective nature of *Memoriale* serves to challenge the mimetic horizon of industrial literature: the genre is confronted by the point of view of an unreliable narrator, and by the insertion in the narrative universe of unfamiliar poetic techniques.

On the whole, the dilemma of 'industrial' writers was to develop narrative forms that could account for the anthropological processes integral to Fordist organization and for the constant oscillation between productive life and the 'free time' of mass consumption. The co-presence in their texts of *topoi* like the descent to the underworld and the factory/

---

17 Rinaldi, R. 1985. *Il romanzo come deformazione. Autonomia ed eredità gaddiana in Mastronardi, Bianciardi, Testori, Arbasino*. Milan: Mursia. 9.
18 Jacomuzzi, A. 1983. "*Il maestro di Vigevano.*" *Per Mastronardi. Atti del Convegno di studi su Lucio Mastronardi*. Edited by Maria Antonietta Grignani. Florence: La Nuova Italia. 68.

church[19] evidences the ambivalence of undertaking a Fordist organization of time and space across factory departments in the 1950s and 1960s. The environment of industrial labor was simultaneously perceived as infernal and sacred because it implied, in all of its spatial segments, the dialectic between exploitation and emancipation, between the capitalistic coercion and the servile self-awareness typical of modernity. During the 1970s, with the development of post-Fordist working conditions, such a space-time relation began to disintegrate. One could ask: Is Levi's 1978 book *La chiave a stella* an industrial novel, or does it signal instead the crisis of the genre? *La chiave a stella* does not represent factory life: the factory worker Libertino Faussone is a freelancer who travels regularly, thanks to his specific knowledge of the metal structures required by the global labor market. Starting with his name – 'Libertino' for libertine suggests an unwillingness to suffer any sort of restrictions – the protagonist refuses to be confined, obeying only his own creative temperament in a way that would make it impossible to take on Albino Saluggia's job. Faussone signals the triumph of *homo faber* and the gesture of labor: "la fabbrica è scomparsa, e così la segregazione ma anche la dimensione collettiva. [...] Scomparsa dunque l'alienazione, ma anche qualunque idea di conflittualità: Faussone trova il suo riscatto nella professionalità, non nella lotta di classe" (the factory has disappeared, and with it segregation, but also the dimension of the collective. Thus alienation has disappeared, but also any idea of conflict: Faussone finds his redemption in professionalism, not in class struggle).[20] The last fruits of the season of Italian industrial literature might be represented by Volponi's 1989 book *Le mosche del capitale*. The novel recovers the genre's main features, but it also transforms and exacerbates them, bitterly liquidating the 'democratic' experience of Olivetti and celebrating the tragedy of working-class defeat. *Le mosche del capitale* thus inserts itself into the neo-modernist tradition

---

19   Lupo, G. 2013. "Orfeo tra le macchine." *Fabbrica di carta. I libri che raccontano l'Italia industriale*. Edited by Giorgio Bigatti and Giuseppe Lupo. Rome and Bari: Laterza. 16–17.

20   Meneghelli, D. 2010. "Gli operai hanno ancora pochi anni di tempo? Morte e vitalità della fabbrica." *Letteratura e azienda. Rappresentazioni letterarie dell'economia e del lavoro nell'Italia degli anni 2000*. Edited by Silvia Contarini. Special issues of *Narrativa*, no.s 31–32. 64.

inaugurated by *Memoriale*.[21] By juxtaposing the company story of a factory manager (Saraccini) with the industrial story of a worker (Tecraso), *Le mosche del capitale* seems to measure, in hyperrealist forms, the high price paid by the most combative European working class in the transition from the critique of capitalism to a more supine and euphoric acceptance of its rules and compatibility.

Translated by Jim Carter

21 Fioretti, D. 2013. *Carte di fabbrica. La narrativa industriale in Italia (1934–1989)*. Pescara: Edizioni Tracce. 211.

SERGIO FERRARESE

6 Alienation and Class Struggle in Italian Literature

Karl Marx articulated his theory of class struggle in his best-known work, *The Communist Manifesto* (1848), co-written with Frederick Engels. He developed his concept of alienation, on the other hand, in some less accessible works, like the *1844 Manuscripts* (1844) and the first volume of *Capital* (1859). Of the two concepts, however, it seems only alienation has survived in present-day discussions of Marx's work, at least within the context of work in the digital era and the exploitation of human intellectual, verbal and affective skills. Class struggle has instead been relegated to the past, where it was seemingly meaningful only while it played a key role in the daily fight of the industrial working class against the factory bosses. This chapter will illustrate the theoretical evolution of both ideas and their instrumentality to Italian literature during the economic boom.

Even before Marx, the concept of alienation had been at the center of many philosophical systems. The Swiss-born French philosopher, Jean-Jacques Rousseau, argued in the eighteenth century that human beings become alienated when they subscribe to the social contract. By coming together in societies, he wrote, people relinquish their inherent individual rights to the "general will," a social organism formed from the association of all individual wills.

> To renounce your liberty is to renounce being man, to surrender the rights of humanity and even its duties. For him who renounces everything no indemnity is possible. Such a renunciation is incompatible with man's nature; to remove liberty from his will is to remove all morality from his acts. Finally, it is an empty and contradictory convention that sets up, on the one hand absolute authority, and on the other, unlimited obedience.[1]

1 Rousseau, J.-J. 2008. *The Social Contract*. New York: Cosimo Books.18.

Alienation, in Rousseau's view, deprives people of certain qualities that render them human. In a similar fashion, the German philosopher Georg Wilhelm Frederick Hegel, in his *Phenomenology of the Spirit* (1807), theorized that the spirit animating each individual becomes something different from itself when it materializes itself in the world: the more social structures we create, the more we become alienated from our true and natural self. Hegel calls this true self the "spirit," something quite abstract, but once this spirit materializes into something concrete in the world, like the aforementioned institutions, it loses its ethereal essence. The subject feels therefore separated from the world, and nature appears as an original and autonomous reality, totally independent from human intellect. Ludwig Feuerbach further elaborated the concept of alienation in his book on *The Essence of Christianity* (1841), where the German philosopher argued that alienation is typical of organized religions, in particular Christianity. Human beings are alienated, he insisted, because they project their highest moral values onto God, worshipping Him as if He were a mighty and superior entity, or as Feuerbach calls it, "the realized idea."[2]

Marx was in part inspired by Hegel's and Feuerbach's theories of alienation. However, in elaborating his own take on the concept, he placed humanity's alienation at the center of modern capitalism and class society. While previous studies of alienation had focused on humanity's spiritual estrangement from itself, Marx emphasized the material nature of this phenomenon. One can say that Marx transformed a philosophical problem into a socioeconomic category.

According to Marx, human labor – that is the satisfaction derived from making an artifact – determines ontology, or rather an individual's very being. Humans are happy, we could say, when each one of them takes pleasure in creating and seeing the end product of their creativity. In the 1844 *Manuscripts*, Marx's essay on "Estranged Labor" argued that capitalism eliminates the possibility of that pleasure by alienating the worker in four distinct but closely related ways. First, workers are alienated from the product of their labor. Everything the worker produces is "someone

---

2   Feuerbach, L. 2008. *The Essence of Christianity*. Mineola, New York: Dover Philosophical Classics. 40.

else's," that is, it belongs to the capitalist.[3] Second, the worker is alienated from the very act of production, since they produce only for the capitalist and not for themselves.[4] What's more, the production process consists of a never-ending repetitive and mechanical rhythm that offers the worker no psychological gratification. Devoid of pleasure, labor thus seems to be coerced because the worker undertakes it as a means for survival, forced to sell their labor power as if it were any other market commodity. Third, the worker is alienated from their "species-essence" – the term Marx uses, "gattungswesen," is difficult to translate from the German, but includes all the innate potential of a worker who loses their own identity and the possibility of self-development in the capitalist mode of production.[5] Fourth, the worker is alienated from other workers.[6] The reduction of labor to the status of a mere market commodity translates into the birth and development of a labor market in which one worker is pitted in a competitive fashion against other workers.

Moreover, once a commodity enters the market, it is outside of anyone's control: it seems on the contrary to be governed by some sort of divine power. Marx says that the commodity

> is nothing but a definite social relation between men themselves which assumes here, for them, the fantastic form of a relation between things. In order, therefore, to find an analogy, we must take flight into the misty realm of religion. There the products of the human brain appear as autonomous figures endowed with a life of their own, which enter into relations both with each other and with the human race. So it is in the world of commodities with the products of men's hands. I call this the fetishism which attaches itself to the products of labor as soon as they are produced as commodities, and which is therefore inseparable from the production of commodities. [...] this fetishism of the world of commodities arises from the peculiar social character of the labor which produces them.[7]

---

3   Marx, K. 1975. "Estranged Labor." *Economic and Philosophic Manuscripts of 1844. Collected works of Karl Marx and Frederick Engels*, vol. 3. New York: International Publishers. 274.
4   Marx, K. 1975. "Estranged Labor." 275.
5   Marx, K. 1975. "Estranged Labor." 277.
6   Marx, K. 1975. "Estranged Labor." 277–278.
7   Marx, K. 1990. *Capital, volume 1*. London and New York: Penguin Books. 165.

For Marx, then, it is as though human beings consistently confer unto commodities a sort of divine power without realizing that commodities are in reality the result of relations of production. In such a context, the commodity becomes all powerful and as a result humanity is fundamentally unhappy. Under industrial capitalism the social relationships among individuals, once involved in production, lose their human traits and are perceived as economic relationships between money and the commodities that are bought and sold on the market.

This process is called reification – literally 'to become a thing' – and it was amply discussed by György Lukács, in his seminal work *History and Class Consciousness* (1923). According to the Hungarian philosopher, the depersonalization of labor typical of capitalism is compounded by a growing rational and abstract organization of all sectors of society (similar to the rationalization and organization of labor in a factory). Human beings are estranged from this system, incapable as they are of understanding and controlling an ever-growing complex reality that seems to follow its own laws. For Lukács, this complex reality is embodied in the commodity, as he eloquently explains:

> [The] development of the commodity to the point where it becomes the dominant form in society did not take place until the advent of modern capitalism. Hence it is not to be wondered at that the personal nature of economic relations was still understood clearly on occasion at the start of capitalist development, but that as the process advanced and forms became more complex and less direct, it became increasingly difficult and rare to find anyone penetrating the veil of reification.[8]

The commodity is also key to understanding the concept of alienation for another Marxist thinker, Herbert Marcuse. Known for his association with the Frankfurt School from 1932 until his death in 1970, and championed by students worldwide during the rebellions of 1968, Marcuse argued that alienation derives from the imperative imposed on humanity to produce commodities that need to be made at all costs. Modern societies, with the expansion of technological rationalization, have integrated into

---

[8] Lukács, G. 1968. *History and Class Consciousness*. Cambridge, Massachusetts: The MIT Press. 86.

the industrial system every aspect of human existence, demanding from human beings passivity, submission and conformism. In Marcuse's view, industrial society is an enormous control apparatus with human beings as its cogs, dominated by overriding laws. Such an apparatus, Marcuse writes, "becomes the more alien the more specialized the division of labor becomes. Men do not live their own lives but perform pre-established functions. While they work, they do not fulfill their own needs and faculties but work in *alienation*."[9]

How can we overcome alienation in modern industrial society? The earliest answer came from Marx himself. In his 1847 book *The Poverty of Philosophy*, the German philosopher presented the factory as the ideal locus for the working class to overcome the barriers of isolation from their labor and themselves. Marx writes:

> Large-scale industry concentrates in one place a crowd of people unknown to one another. Competition divides their interests. But the maintenance of wages, this common interest which they have against their boss, unites them in a common thought of resistance – *combination*. Thus combination always has a double aim, that of stopping competition among the workers, so that they can carry on general competition with the capitalist. If the first aim of resistance was merely the maintenance of wages, combinations, at first isolated, constitute themselves into groups as the capitalists in their turn unite for the purpose of repression, and in the face of always united capital, the maintenance of the association becomes more necessary to them than that of wages. Once it has reached this point, association takes on a political character.[10]

In these lines, Marx emphasizes the role of "combination" as the true motor of factory workers' united resistance. The working class becomes one entity and develops self-awareness about its alienated condition, its exploitation and the possibility of initiating a class struggle against the industrialists. Marx points out:

---

9   Marcuse, H. 1955. *Eros and Civilization: A Philosophical Inquiry into Freud.* Boston: Beacon Press. 45. Italics mine.
10 Marx, K. 1976. *The Poverty of Philosophy: Collected Works of Karl Marx and Frederick Engels*, vol. 6. New York: International Publishers. 210–211. Italics mine.

> Economic conditions have in the first place transformed the mass of the people of the country into wage workers. The domination of capital has created for this mass of people a common situation, common interests. Thus this mass is already a class, as opposed to capital, but not yet for itself. In the struggle, of which we have only noted some phases, this mass unites, it is constituted as a class for itself. The interests which it defends are the interests of this class. But the struggle of class against class is a political struggle.[11]

These words anticipate by one year the publication of *The Communist Manifesto* (1848), in which the rallying cry "Workers of the world, unite!" disseminated the idea of class struggle to the masses worldwide. For Marx, class consciousness was the preliminary and necessary phase that sets the ground for class struggle. The latter is conducted in the name of common interests of the proletarian class against those of the bourgeoisie.

In a similar fashion, Lukács argues that class consciousness is the result of the awareness of the proletariat of its historical condition. While the bourgeoisie falls victim to a false consciousness and remains incapable of feeling and viewing itself as a class, the industrial working class strives to be united under the leadership of the party towards the ultimate goal of a classless society.

All these groundbreaking studies on the phenomenon of alienation, along with theories that attempted to instill in the proletariat class self-awareness and revolutionary objectives, found an echo in postwar Italian literature. Starting in the 1950s, Italy experienced rapid industrialization in the North. Many factories adopted the methods of rationalization and organization of factory work devised by Fredrick Winslow Taylor and Henry Ford at the beginning of the century. Taylor proposed a scientific approach to the management of human labor, one that optimized production time and output by selecting the right type of worker to perform preset movements. Henry Ford introduced Taylor's method in his factories, at whose center was the assembly line. The factory assumed an unprecedented presence in the lives of many Italians, who as a result of their daily work in the plants of the industrial triangle started experiencing psychological and physical discomforts. This new reality is portrayed most notably in

---

11 Marx, K. 1976. *The Poverty of Philosophy*. 211.

the works of Ottiero Ottieri, Paolo Volponi, Goffredo Parise and Nanni Balestrini.

Ottiero Ottieri's *Tempi stretti* (Tight Times) was the first of such portrayals, written while the author was working in the human resources office of the Olivetti typewriter factory in Pozzuoli. Published in 1957, in the middle of the economic boom, the strength of the novel lies in the author's ability to describe the desire of industrialists to organize and rationalize factory labor, affecting the private lives of workers until they become totally dependent on the rhythm of the industrial plants.

The book centers on two young wage workers in Milan: Giovanni is a specialized worker in a typography shop and Emma is an unskilled worker at a large machine parts factory named Zanini. Emma complains about the psychological and physical hardships resulting from her work on the assembly line: the repetitive and mechanical tasks render her working experience alienating. Ottieri presents her mechanized gestures with precision:

> Depose un pezzo a rovescio. L'attrezzo si incantò. Colpa dell'attrezzo vecchio che funzionava male; ma aveva paura di denunciarlo al caposquadra, che si arrabbiava. Del resto il caposquadra cronometrista se n'era andato. Con la sinistra trasse giù dalla cassetta verso il banco una manciata di pezzi. Riprese la corsa, raggomitolata nel guscio del rumore. Le ritornò la lena, il ritmo giusto: prendere il pezzo con la sinistra, deporlo nell'attrezzo aperto, chiudere l'attrezzo. Con la sinistra che lo tiene fermo sotto l'utensile, la destra aziona la leva, fa scendere l'utensile nel punto giusto, trapana, si rialza l'utensile, si riapre l'attrezzo, si leva il pezzo fatto e si butta via a destra. A non sbagliare, sono sei tempi. Un getto d'olio bianco, emulsionato, inonda l'attrezzo, le mani, schizza addosso. Ma, col ritmo giusto, quasi Emma non faticava più: sei tempi, sei tempi, sei tempi e il sesto e il primo si rincorrevano.

> (She inserted a piece upside-down into the machinery. It stalled. It was the old machinery's fault, but she was afraid of reporting this to the foreman, who would get upset. And anyway he had already left. With her left hand she grabbed a handful of pieces from the box and put them on the workbench. She started working again, hunched up within the shell of factory noise. She found the energy, the right rhythm: take one piece with the left hand, insert it into the open machinery and close it. With the left hand she keeps the piece steady under the machine, the right hand activates the lever, lowers the drill in the right place, drills, the tool moves up, the machinery is opened again, the finished piece is pulled out and thrown way to the right. If done right, it takes six steps. A gush of white emulsified oil floods the machinery, her hands and splashes on her. But with the right pace, Emma didn't

even feel tired anymore: six steps, six steps, six steps and steps six and one follow each other closely.)[12]

In the factory, nothing counts more than the blind observance of the administration's imposed production times, which are gradually shortened over the course of several months and therefore become harder and harder for the worker to meet. Whence, the 'tight times' of the title, which alludes among other things to the increasing brevity of each motion the worker is required to make during production. Because of the intense demands of this mechanized labor, Gianni and Emma's human relationship becomes troubled and eventually ends.

In Ottieri, Marx's theory of alienation is further elaborated with clear reference to Antonio Gramsci's analysis of the assembly line as it was devised by Taylor and Ford. In his notebook *Americanismo e fordismo* (Americanism and Fordism, 1934), the Marxist thinker discusses, among other things, the totalitarian aspects of factory labor. The rational organization of labor, the total subjection of the worker to the movements of the machine and the control of the industrialists over the private lives of factory workers all conspire to transform human beings into automatons, whose only aspiration is productivity.

Alienation also dominates Paolo Volponi's *Memoriale* (My Troubles Began, 1962). Set in postwar Italy, between the reconstruction years and the economic boom, the novel explores the mental state of Albino Saluggia, a tubercular ex-soldier and prisoner of war who now works for an industrial company. Once Saluggia is confronted with the depersonalizing reality of factory work, he becomes increasingly paranoid. Like Ottieri, Volponi based his fiction on his own personal experiences at work in the industrial world: he was an assistant and the director of social services at the Olivetti factory in Ivrea. While at Olivetti, Volponi received a letter from a worker complaining that the company medical staff had falsely claimed that the worker suffered from tuberculosis, issuing false medical reports so that the company could lay him off. In reality, the worker was delusional, and indeed suffered from tuberculosis. *Memoriale*'s main character is based on

---

12   Ottieri, O. 1964. *Tempi stretti*. Turin: Einuadi. 43.

this worker and is, like him, delusional; he is simultaneously attracted to and repulsed by the factory in which he works. Albino states: "Nel corso di tanti anni, qualche volta mi è sembrata bellissima; ma ero io a giudicare dentro di me quasi senza vederla" (There were times during the course of many years, when the factory did seem beautiful, but it was I who judged it so, inside myself, without really seeing it).[13]

As in Ottieri's *Tempi stretti*, the rational organization of the factory and the repetitiveness of the same gestures transforms Volponi's individuals into isolated monads who are competitive and suspicious of each other, incapable of communicating among themselves:

> La gente non esisteva più ed io pensavo che per quanto nella fabbrica si lavori tutti insieme, stretti nei reparti, con le fresatrici su tre file ad intervalli regolari, e così coi torni e le presse, o tutt'in fila nelle catene di montaggio o nei controlli, o si mangi tutti alla mensa insieme e si viaggi tutti sulle corriere, è difficile poter avere delle compagnie e degli aiuti dagli altri.
>
> (People ceased to exist, and I thought that even though we worked together, squeezed into different departments, with the power saws and the vises and steam presses lined up three rows deep, even though we worked in long assembly lines, ate together in the cafeteria, travelling together on busses, even though we did all these things – it was difficult to find a friend or someone who would help you.)[14]

The "species-essence" of each worker – to reference Marx – is destroyed by the seemingly perfect organization of the factory environment. Moreover, in the story of Albino Saluggia lies hidden another layer of the alienation he experiences in his monotonous factory routine. Of rural roots, Albino, like many industrial literature characters, feels the contrast between his prewar life – in contact with nature and its cycles – and the new industrial and urban civilization with its rhythms of factory production.

This theme of the countryside versus the city/factory reappears in Goffredo Parise's 1965 novel *Il padrone* (The Boss). *Il padrone* is the story of a provincial young man who moves to an unspecified city to work at a

13 Volponi, P. 2012. *Romanzi e prose*, vol. 1. Turin: Einaudi. 14. Volponi, P. 1964. *My Troubles Began*. Translated by Belén Sevareid. New York: Grossman. 12–13.
14 Volponi, P. 2012. *Romanzi e prose*, vol. 1. 47. Volponi, P. 1964. *My Troubles Began*. 43–44.

trading company. The company boss, Dr. Max, is a neurotic man who rules as a dictator with total control over the lives of his employees. As the protagonist of the story remarks: "[Il dottor Max] è padrone del mio tempo, dei miei atti, dei miei pensieri, dei miei sentimenti e del tempo libero che è interamente occupato dalla sua presenza" ([Dr. Max] is the owner of my time, my actions, my thoughts, my feelings and my leisure, which is entirely occupied by his presence).[15] In the words of the protagonist, Dr. Max's company is a "[luogo] razionale, luminoso, asettico e quasi meccanico, dove tutto funziona regolarmente appunto come un meccanismo" (rational, luminous, aseptic, and almost mechanical place, where everything functions like a mechanism) and has become the locus "dove anche gli uomini, a lungo andare, si confondono con le cose" (where even men, in time, become confused with objects).[16] These words seem to reference Lukács' theory of reification, whereby the subject, separated from its true self, views itself as a commodity among other commodities, ruled by the same laws that regulate what it produces.

In 1962, the Italian industrial working class underwent a significant transformation. Tired of poor representation from both unions (at the bargaining table) and the Communist Party (in parliament), a group of workers gathered spontaneously in Turin's Piazza Statuto to launch a violent protest. This event did not go unnoticed by Marxist intellectuals and activists who were already weary of the Communist Party (PCI)'s reformist approach to politics, and they decided to organize a movement around two magazines: *Quaderni rossi* (1961–1963) and *Classe operaia* (1964–1965). The pages of these magazines became the laboratory of 'operaismo' (workerism), a political philosophy that contributed to the birth of a workers' movement autonomous from the PCI and Socialist Party (PSI) and by 1969 a mass political force. In October 1969, during the 'autunno caldo' (hot autumn), the autonomous workers' movement partially but significantly satisfied their demands with a long streak of unannounced strikes and large street protests. The theory born from this experience claimed that the working

---

15   Parise, G. 1999. *Il padrone*. Milan: Rizzoli. 194. Parise, G. 1966. *The Boss*. Translated by William Weaver. New York: Alfred A. Knopf. 178.
16   Parise, G. 1999. *Il padrone*. 141. Parise, G. 1966. *The Boss*. 129.

class must place itself in a position of dominance over capitalism. If factories deprive workers of their identity, assigning them anonymous roles as unskilled laborers on the assembly line, then workers should claim a new combative identity based on reconnecting with the fruits of their labor, themselves and society.

The tenets of 'operaismo' informed Nanni Balestrini's *Vogliamo tutto* (We Want Everything, 1971). A prominent member of the Italian literary neo-avantgarde in the late 1960s, Balestrini decided to join the autonomous workers' movement and write an epic novel about the real-life experiences of Alfonso Natella, a nonspecialized factory worker at Fiat. This experimental novel is the only representation of all three of our concepts – alienation, class consciousness and class struggle – in a single work of Italian literature.

In *Vogliamo tutto*, the country/city divide is embodied in the economic and social division between a vastly unemployed South and a production-centered North. When Alfonso migrates to Milan and then to Turin, he possess little work ethic, a result of the endemic and historical lack of employment in southern Italy. Alfonso is uninterested in politics, and set apart from his coworkers by a rebellious nature against any form of discipline and hierarchy. But when faced with the harshness of factory labor and its debilitating psychological effects, Alfonso embraces the politics of rebellion against the oppressive Fordist system. When Alfonso intentionally hurts himself at work and is given a period of sick leave, he does not know what to do with the free time. He tries to distract himself in Turin – going to bars, the movies and parks only to realize that he feels restless all the time. In Alfonso's words: "Stavo così mi riposavo della stanchezza di un lavoro di merda. Una cosa abbastanza assurda cioè assurda veramente. E in quei dodici giorni di mutua pagata me ne accorgevo che non sapevo neanche come riposarmi del lavoro e non sapevo che cazzo fare a Torino" (I was like that, resting up, tired out by that shit work. It's a crazy thing, really absurd. In those twelve days of sick leave I realized that I didn't even know how to relax, away from work, and that I didn't know what the fuck to do in Torino).[17]

---

17   Balestrini, N. 1988. *Vogliamo tutto*. Milan: Mondadori. 85. Balestrini, N. 2016. *We Want Everything*. Translation by Matt Holden. London: Verso. 82.

The entire city depends on the factory and its rhythms, and Alfonso is unable to separate his leisure time from that spent working on the assembly line:

> Io ho fatto tutti i lavori il muratore il lavapiatti lo scaricatore. Tutti li ho fatti ma il più schifoso è proprio la Fiat. Io quando sono venuto alla Fiat credevo che mi sarei salvato. Questo mito della Fiat del lavoro Fiat. Invece è una schifezza come tutti quanti i lavori anzi peggio. Qua ogni giorno ci aumentano i ritmi. Molto lavoro e pochi soldi. Qua pian piano si muore senza accorgersene.
>
> (I've done all kinds of work, bricklayer, dishwasher, loading and unloading. I've done it all, but the most disgusting is Fiat. When I came to Fiat I believed I'd be saved. This myth of Fiat, of work at Fiat. In reality it's shit, like all work, in fact it's worse. Every day here they speed up the line. A lot of work and not much money. Here, little by little, you die without noticing.)[18]

One day, Alfonso is approached by a student who invites him to join a meeting of other factory workers. During this meeting, the workers discover that they share the same problems, the same type of alienation: alienation from the products of their labor, from the very act of production, from their species-being and ultimately from each other. Alfonso remembers:

> Allora vado a quella riunione li al bar di fianco a Mirafiori. Conosco Mario e degli studenti e gli dico in che officina stavo quello che facevo. Conosco anche altri operai e Raffaele uno della 124 che vedevo che veniva tutte le sere alle riunioni. Lui diceva che conosceva un'ottantina di compagni che erano disposti a fermarsi quando diceva lui.
>
> (I go to the meeting at the bar near Mirafiori. I meet Mario and some other students, and I tell him which workshop I'm in, what I do. I also meet some other workers and Raffaele, from the 124 line, who I had seen going to the meetings every evening. He said he knew about eighty comrades who were ready to stop work when he said.)[19]

By recognizing their common exploitation and alienation, the workers decide to join forces, and Alfonso, now politically motivated, carries out the factory struggle together with his comrades.

---

18   Balestrini, N. 1988. *Vogliamo tutto*. 91. Balestrini, N. 2016. *We Want Everything*. 82.
19   Balestrini, N. 1988. *Vogliamo tutto*. 89. Balestrini, N. 2016. *We Want Everything*. 79–80.

Alienation and Class Struggle in Italian Literature

In the 1950s and 1960s, Italian intellectuals focused on the experiences of single workers in contact with factory labor, spurring a debate about alienation that touched only tangentially on the problem of class struggle. The cases of Ottieri and Volponi are paradigmatic of this tendency. Their adherence to the official lines of the PSI (Ottieri) and the PCI (Volponi) helps to explain this omission: these parties had long abandoned revolutionary goals in favor of reformist agendas. As Riccardo De Gennaro has noted, writing of Ottieri (but in a way that applies to Volponi as well):

> Ottieri non è un irregolare, un ribelle, un indisciplinato [...]. Ha lavorato pur sempre in un'azienda, la punta più avanzata dell'industria manifatturiera, che ha addirittura un suo progetto di società, basata sulla solidarietà tra le classi, non sul superamento delle classi, sulla ricerca della terza via tra socialismo e capitalismo, non sulla rivoluzione sociale.
>
> (Ottieri is not an irregular, a rebel, an undisciplined individual [...]. He has worked after all in a company, the most advanced point of the manufacturing industry, which has its own project for a society, based on solidarity between classes, and not on the elimination of class itself, based on the search for a third way between socialism and capitalism, and not on a social revolution.)[20]

In the late 1960s and 1970s, Italian writers came to view class struggle not so much as a literary trope, but rather as the representation of a specific historical moment. With Balestrini, the traditional man of letters became involved in the workers' movement, and at the same time, wrote a novel representing the evolution of an unemployed southerner and his transformation into a collective revolutionary subject. Alienation and class struggle did appear in literature after *Vogliamo tutto*, but the perspective on these two issues mutated. In Vincenzo Guerrazzi's *Le ferie di un operiao* (A Worker's Vacation, 1974) and Tommaso Di Ciaula's *Tuta blu. Ire, ricordi e sogni di un operaio del sud* (Blue Overalls: Rages, Memories and Dreams of a Worker from the South, 1978), the writers are themselves factory workers. While *Le ferie di un operaio* bears witness to the combativeness of the working class, *Tuta blu* laments the failure to bring about the revolutionary project that had been illustrated so poignantly in *Vogliamo*

---

20   De Gennaro, R. 2012. "Tra fabbrica e clinica, in preda al plusdolore." *Il manifesto*. August 3.

tutto. The alienation experienced by both Guerrazzi and Di Ciaula is described as an estrangement from themselves and from the products of their labor. Their presentation also carries forward the concerns of earlier works, especially the contrast between the prison of industrial society and the freedom of the southern Italian countryside.

ALESSANDRA DIAZZI

7 Care or Control? Psychology and Psychoanalysis in Italian Factories

This chapter sets out to examine the intersections between the industrial world and the psychological disciplines in Italy, discussing the crucial role that psychology and psychoanalysis played in factories.[1] After a brief outline of the history of industrial psychology in Italy, the chronological framework of my analysis will span from the late 1950s to the early 1970s. In this way, we will focus on the period that radically changed and even revolutionized factory labor in the country.

In addition to providing an historical overview of the encounters between the psychological disciplines and Italian industry, this chapter will also cast light on the influence this synergic relationship had on fictional representations of factory life. The chapter is divided into two main parts: the first examines the set of socioeconomic motives that turned psychology into a fundamental tool to assess and improve industrial work. In this section, I will mostly discuss Adriano Olivetti's approach to the factory, which stands out as one of the most innovative and revolutionary ways of putting the psychological disciplines at the service of industry. The second part looks at how industrial psychology affected the representation of industrial labor in literature and cinema. In particular, this analysis is aimed to show that the adoption of a psychological framework to narrate

1 Fascism jeopardized the development of psychoanalytic and psychological studies in Italy. As a result, in the early postwar years, Italian practitioners had to reestablish their schools and societies. It is therefore difficult to make a clear distinction between the two trends of cure in postwar years. In fact, many psychologists were also trained in psychoanalysis and they combined different approaches in their practice. For this reason, in what follows I will refer to both psychoanalysis and psychology, starting from the assumption that the development of industrial psychology was influenced by the two disciplines.

the factory conceals a crucial political significance. In fact, writers and filmmakers frequently employed a psychological and psychoanalytical outlook in order to denounce the alienation of exploited workers, as well as to reveal the ambiguous aspects of Olivetti's utopian dream of a 'good' and 'human' factory.

Psicotecnica in Italy: Development, Innovations and Limits

The application of psychological and psychoanalytic knowledge to industry is called industrial psychology or organizational psychology. In Italy, the discipline of 'psicologia del lavoro' was also referred to as 'psicotecnica,' a term that combines the ancient Greek words 'psyche' (ψυχή), meaning psyche, soul, or mind, and 'techne' (τέχνη), meaning technique. The definition of the new discipline clearly reveals the twofold objective of its employment in factories. On the one hand, attention was paid to the (traumatic) effects of industrial work on the psyche; on the other hand, the use of psychology was aimed to assess workers' technical and attitudinal skills.

In Italy, industrial psychology became popular in the 1950s, when factories began to employ a considerable number of psychologists and the discipline became a fundamental aid for making Italian industries competitive on a worldwide scale. However, the history of Italian 'psicotecnica' must be dated back to the first decade of the twentieth century, in coincidence with the development of Italian industry, the consequent emergence of a working-class consciousness and the rise of syndicalism. As early as 1910, Milan saw the birth of the first 'clinica del lavoro' (labor clinic) with a center for industrial psychology. With the outbreak of the First World War, the discipline (at least apparently) came to a halt when psychology shifted its field of application from industrial labor to military life: "si scrive della stanchezza mentale delle vedette sulla linea del fuoco, delle reazioni psicologiche dei feriti, dei vari disturbi psichici delle truppe; vi sono contributi specifici sull'anima del soldato sul campo di battaglia, sul problema del pelandronismo, sulla psicologia dei fucilandi" (one wrote of the mental exhaustion of the front lines, of the psychological reactions of the wounded, of the troops' various disturbances; there were specific contributions on the soldier's soul on the battlefield, on the problem of idleness, on the psychology of shooting a rifle).[2] However, this temporary diversion did not jeopardize the development of industrial psychology. Rather, it helped the discipline to remain relevant. In 1922, Milan hosted the second 'Convegno di psicotecnica' (Congress of Industrial Psychology), an event that confirmed the vitality of industrial psychology in Italy and helped to promote recognition of national developments in the discipline.

Despite Fascism's controversial relationship with the psychological disciplines, not even the regime stopped the diffusion of 'psicotecnica.'[3] On the contrary, Fascism considered industrial psychology a fundamental tool for the development of industry and a means to control workers. Accordingly, the Ente Nazionale Prevenzione Infortuni (National Agency for the Prevention of Workplace Injuries, ENPI), founded in 1938, devoted particular attention to the introduction of industrial psychology specialists into factories and even founded a center for industrial psychology. As the psychologist Agostino Gemelli contended, during the Fascist years "l'industria italiana grazie al[l'] [...] ordinamento corporativo dello stato presenta un'occasione singolarmente favorevole alle applicazioni della psicotecnica nella razionalizzazione del lavoro" (Italian industry, thanks to the corporatist state, presented a singularly favorable occasion for the application of industrial psychology to the rationalization of labor).[4]

But Italian workers would have to wait for the fall of Fascism and the end of the Second World War to experience the most revolutionary application of psychology to industrial labor: the employment of psychoanalysts in factories. As Ian Parker has argued, "psychoanalysis came into being as a psychological practice to address the particular forms of alienation that capitalism produced." In other words, "psychoanalysis and capitalism are

---

2   Rozzi, R. 1977. *Psicologi e operai: Soggettività e lavoro nell'industria italiana*. Milan: Feltrinelli. 16.
3   For a detailed account of the history of psychoanalysis under the Fascist regime see Zapperi, R. 2013. *Freud e Mussolini: La psicoanalisi in Italia durante il periodo fascista*. Milan: Franco Angeli.
4   Cited in Rozzi, R. 1977. *Psicologi e operai*. 25.

twins," and Italy is no exception in this respect.[5] In the postwar years and, more precisely, in the years of the economic miracle, when the country grew into a neo-capitalist power, psychoanalysis and industry enjoyed a concurrent 'boom.' As Paul Ginsborg has observed,

> the years 1958–1963 saw the beginning of a social revolution which was to turn the world of [rural laborers] upside down. In less than two decades Italy ceased to be a peasant country and became one of the major industrial nations of the West. The very landscape of the country as well as its inhabitants' places of abode and ways of life changed profoundly.[6]

Such a radical "social revolution," the profound change in lifestyles and growing factory employment triggered an unparalleled demand for psychological and psychoanalytic aid. Far from being a time of mere collective excitement and euphoria, the miracle years brought along a profound discomfort and a widespread sentiment of alienation. In this context, psychoanalysis became a fashionable therapy for relieving "il disagio psicologico e [i]l malessere sociale che accompagnavano il boom economico, l'industrializzazione e i sempre più rapidi cambiamenti di costume" (the psychological distress and the social discontent that accompanied the economic boom, industrialization and the increasingly rapid changes of custom).[7] But psychoanalysis was not only a luxury cure for upper-class Italians who, suffering from the new neuroses of consumerist society, could afford such an expensive treatment to mitigate their discomfort. The economic miracle also saw psychoanalysis enter the factory to become a working-class, rather than an exclusively bourgeois, matter. Psychological disciplines were in fact seen as innovative therapies and fundamental tools to deal with "il propagarsi delle nevrosi – la nuova malattia che sta diventando una vera e propria epidemia in chi lavora in fabbrica [e che] si rivela una sconfitta della medicina tradizionale" (the propagation of neuroses – the new sickness that was becoming a real

---

5   Parker, I. 2007. *Revolution in Psychology: Alienation to Emancipation*. London and Ann Arbor: Pluto Press. 178.
6   Ginsborg, P. 1990. *A History of Contemporary Italy: Society and Politics, 1943–1988*. London: Penguin Books. 212.
7   Muzzarelli, A. 2014. *Il guaritore ferito*. Rome: Armando. 82.

epidemic in those who worked in the factory, and that could not be defeated with traditional medicine).[8]

Adriano Olivetti, the president of the Olivetti typewriter company, stood out as the protagonist of the factory revolution by means of psychology and, in particular, of psychoanalysis. The Olivetti company was not the only one in Italy to make use of 'psicotecnica,' but Adriano Olivetti was certainly "l'unico presidente, e uno dei pochi ingegneri in Italia, che credesse nell'inconscio" (the only president, and one of the few engineers in Italy, who believed in the unconscious).[9] Adriano Olivetti's view of a new and more human factory was based on the ideal of collaboration between industrial technicians and intellectuals like writers and artists: "politica, cultura, architettura sono i vertici di un grande triangolo entro cui si situa il percorso dell'utopia olivettiana: un luogo di convivenza dialettica in cui sono convocati operai e urbanisti, intellettuali e amministratori" (politics, culture architecture – these are the corners of a great triangle within which the development of Olivetti's utopia was situated: a place of dialectical cohabitation, where workers and urban planners, intellectuals and administers all converged).[10] It is not surprising that psychoanalysts – seen as being halfway between medicine's scientific approach to the individual and philosophy's humanist approach to the psyche – were key to Adriano Olivetti's project. The company employed psychoanalysis and psychology as tools to radically rethink the organization of labor, which played a crucial role in the dream of revolutionizing industrial work for the good of workers. Accordingly,

> l'obiettivo di Olivetti non era quello di creare un semplice laboratorio di psicotecnica, sul modello dei pochi già esistenti in Italia (un laboratorio cioè diretto alla selezione psicomotoria del personale mediante l'impiego di test attitudinali), ma quello di avviare una vera e propria attività di psicologia industriale, intesa come applicazione della psicologia sperimentale e clinica allo studio delle condizioni oggettive del lavoro e della situazione soggettiva del lavoratore.

---

8   Lupo, G. 2016. *La letteratura al tempo di Adriano Olivetti*. Rome and Ivrea: Edizioni di Comunità. 247.
9   Ottieri, O. 1963. *Donnarumma all'assalto*. Milan: Bompiani. 117.
10 Lupo, G. 2016. *La letteratura al tempo di Adriano Olivetti*. 63.

(Olivetti's objective was not to create a simple laboratory for industrial psychology on the model of the few already existing ones in Italy (that is, a laboratory using aptitude tests to select psychologically and physically fit personnel), but to set in motion a full-scale practice of industrial psychology, intended as the application of experimental and clinical psychology to the study of the objective conditions of labor and the subjective situation of the laborer.)[11]

Thus, the psychoanalytic approach to industrial work promoted by Adriano Olivetti had two major goals. First, psychologists and psychoanalysts were supposed to help design the factory to reorganize industrial work in a way that could contribute to the utopian project of de-alienating the workers.[12] By radically rethinking factory work through psychological lenses, Olivetti was able to acknowledge that "il sistema usato dall'azienda per la determinazione dei tempi e dei metodi di lavorazione fosse astratto e arbitrario, in quanto non considerava i caratteri concreti del lavoro umano, cioè i fattori psicologici e fisiologici che condizionano le modalità e i tempi di esecuzione delle varie operazioni lavorative" (the company's system for determining the pace and methods of labor was abstract and arbitrary insofar as it did not consider the concrete characters of human labor: that is, the psychological and physiological factors that condition the manner and pace of execution of various labor-related operations).[13] The intent of the new factory was to give each individual the opportunity to fully develop their skills and ambitions, while remaining fully aware of the active role played in the good functioning of the company as a whole:

> gli psicologi dell'Olivetti misero in rilievo la centralità del colloquio clinico: le prove psicotecniche tradizionali dovevano essere completate da colloqui individuali,

[11] Università degli Studi di Milano Bicocca, Archivio storico della psicologia italiana, Centro di psicologia del lavoro di Ivrea. <https://www.aspi.unimib.it/collections/entity/detail/173/>.

[12] Adriano Olivetti claimed that one of his main goals was "evitare l'alienazione prodotta dalle fabbriche gigantesche, e dal distacco opprimente dalla natura" (to avoid the alienation produced by gigantic factories and by the oppressive detachment from nature). Olivetti, A. 1960. *Città dell'uomo*. Milan: Edizioni di Comunità. 108.

[13] Università degli Studi di Milano Bicocca, Archivio storico della psicologia italiana, Centro di psicologia del lavoro di Ivrea. <https://www.aspi.unimib.it/collections/entity/detail/173/>.

finalizzati a conoscere l'immagine del mondo aziendale e le aspettative che i soggetti avevano maturato; l'operaio doveva essere interpellato sul proprio lavoro e sulla propria storia.

(the Olivetti psychologists underscored the importance of the clinical interview: the aptitude tests of traditional organizational psychology needed to be completed by individual interviews intended to understand the subjects' image of the business world and the expectations that they had built up. The worker needed to be asked about their own work and about their own history.)[14]

'Psicotecnica' can thus be seen as a progressive and revolutionary instrument intended to create a more favorable environment for workers by attempting to reduce the phenomenon of exploitation, thereby mitigating distress and alienation:

La razionalizzazione e parcellizzazione del lavoro andava comportando rischi di precoce deterioramento psicofisico anche per i nuovi assunti. Il criterio per destinarli ai lavori più razionalizzati come le linee di montaggio non poteva consistere tanto in una specifica idoneità attitudinale [...] quanto nella capacità di sopportare lo stress prolungato di detti lavori.

(Rationalizing and parceling out labor involved risks of precocious psycho-physical deterioration, even in new hires. The criteria for sending a worker on to more rationalized labor like the assembly line needed to depend less on some specific aptitudinal suitability [...] and more on their ability to stand the prolonged stress of those jobs.)[15]

The introduction into factories of psychological interviews – based on talking and listening, rather than on mere assessment and evaluation – effectively broke "il muro di silenzio che in un'azienda si erge tra i piani alti, dove domina il 'puro verbo' e i reparti in cui trascorrono le giornate coloro i quali appartengono al mondo dell'operare e del 'non verbale'" (the wall of silence raised in every business between the upper levels, dominated by the 'pure word,' and the departments where those who belong to the working

---

14 Università degli Studi di Milano Bicocca, Archivio storico della psicologia italiana, Centro di psicologia del lavoro di Ivrea. <https://www.aspi.unimib.it/collections/entity/detail/173/>.

15 Novara, F. 1997. "Psicologia del lavoro: vita, opere, e morte di un'esperienza." *Per una storiografia italiana della prevenzione occupazionale ed ambientale*. Edited by Antonio Grieco and Pier Alberto Albertazzi. Milan: Franco Angeli. 231.

world, to the 'non-verbal' pass their days).[16] For the first time, psychologists gave workers the possibility to speak out, and to do so through a legitimate and institutional channel of expression. By participating in such innovations, psychoanalysts contributed to the development and growth of industrial production, insofar as 'happier' individuals were supposed to be better workers. The synergic relationship between the psychological disciplines and industry seemed therefore to positively revolutionize the organization of the factory as a whole.

However, the presence of psychologists in factories also presented quite a few problematic aspects. Commenting on Adriano Olivetti's "utopia urbanistico/industriale" (urban planning/industrial utopia), Giuseppe Lupo has noted that the project risked "[di] scivolare su un terreno vischioso" (misstepping on a slippery slope). Even if the project was animated by "il bisogno di migliorare le condizioni di vita degli individui" (the need to improve the living conditions of individuals), it also "nasconde[va] [...] diversi pericoli, il più rilevante dei quali [era] il rischio che [...] [potesse] mutare i suoi presupposti umanitari in aspetti distopici e degenerare in un vero e proprio ordine totalitario" ([hid] [...] many dangers, the most significant of which [was] the risk of [...] changing its humanitarian premises into dystopic aspects and degenerating into a real totalitarian order).[17] The same can be said of the application of psychology to industrial work.

The Italian psychoanalyst Cesare Musatti, who was employed in 1942 to direct the Olivetti company 'Centro di psicologia del lavoro' (Center of Industrial Psychology) in Ivrea, acknowledged himself the issues related to making the psychological disciplines serve Olivetti's project of corporate welfare. Commenting on his own experience as an industrial psychologist, he contended:

> Qualunque sia la sua posizione ideologica, lo psicologo deve parlare il linguaggio dell'azienda, che – nel nostro mondo – è per forza il linguaggio del profitto. [...] Per migliorare le condizioni dell'operaio lo psicologo non può che rivolgersi alla direzione aziendale, e se vuole ottenere qualcosa da questa deve dimostrare, col linguaggio dei costi, che un tale miglioramento può significare: una flessione dell'assenteismo,

---

16 Lupo, G. 2016. *La letteratura al tempo di Adriano Olivetti*. 150–151.
17 Lupo, G. 2016. *La letteratura al tempo di Adriano Olivetti*. 101.

un allungamento del tempo di permanenza nell'azienda, una minore incidenza dei tempi di apprendimento del lavoro, una riduzione della morbilità, sia nei confronti di malattie organiche che di disturbi nevrotici.

(Whatever their ideological position, the psychologist must speak the language of the company, which – in our world – is necessarily the language of profit. [...] In order to improve the workers' conditions, the psychologist cannot avoid turning to the company management, and if he wants to obtain something from them, then he must demonstrate, with the language of costs, what such an improvement could mean: a fall in absenteeism, a rise in lifetime employment at the company, a shorter training period, a reduced rate of sickness, both with respect to organic diseases and neurotic disturbances.)[18]

As Musatti's reflection makes clear, the psychological disciplines lose their freedom in the approach to patients/workers as soon as they enter the factory because any form of therapy must respond to the logic of profit. Psychological aids thus became a mere instrument, intended to "stillare olio fra gli ingranaggi" (grease the wheels) of workers' minds and psyches in order to boost their performance.[19]

In other words, improvements in working conditions and interventions in workers' health were not made for the sake of wellbeing itself. Rather, because the system of cure was inextricably interwoven with the factory system, psychological approaches to working life were shaped mostly around principles of productivity and performance. As Lupo has put it, "questa nuova scienza [era] adottata dalle aziende come panacea dei mali (e in alcuni casi diventava perfino motivo di vanto, fiore all'occhiello dell'organizzazione aziendale), tuttavia piegata ai fini della produttività" (this new science [was] adopted by companies as a panacea for all evils (and in some cases, it even became a point of pride, the feather in the cap of the corporate structure), but nevertheless, it was oriented toward the goals of productivity). Psychoanalysis was, in sum, "ridotta a semplice lubrificante del taylorismo" (reduced to a mere lubricant of Taylorism)[20] to the extent that

---

18   Musatti, C. 1976. *Riflessioni sul pensiero psicoanalitico*. Turin: Boringhieri. 327.
19   Ottieri, O. 2012. *Tempi stretti*. Matelica: Hacca. 245–246.
20   Lupo, G. 2016. *La letteratura al tempo di Adriano Olivetti*. 247.

> ci si chiede [...] se davvero l'applicazione della psicologia in campo industriale non sia semplicemente una maniera mascherata per obbedire ai bisogni dell'organizzazione aziendale (alla sua efficienza, al suo esasperato funzionamento anche se a danno dei dipendenti), piegando il tentativo di soccorrere gli individui affetti da nevrosi alle esigenze della produzione.
>
> (one must ask [...] if in reality the application of psychology to industry is not simply a masked way of obeying the needs of the company (its efficiency, its exacerbating mode of operation, even at the cost of harming employees), orienting all attempts at providing individual aid to the needs of production.)[21]

Adapting psychology and psychoanalysis to the needs of capitalism also involved the medicalization of workers' demands and claims. As Renato Rozzi has argued, the industrial history of Italy is characterized by "un'enorme quantità di colloqui, pari soltanto a quelli esercitati *sull'altra devianza* dagli psichiatri" (an enormous quantity of interviews, equaled only by those administered by psychiatrists *with respect to the other form of deviance*).[22] Workers were approached and treated as patients because of their subaltern position, and as a result, psychological assessments and therapies often became means of control and repression or, in some instances, exclusion from the possibility of employment. Where psychological interviews were employed to assess and select prospective workers, the consulting room was a symbolic threshold: a space in which the destiny of the unemployed masses was determined. In Michel Foucault's terms, psychological assessment marked the nature of the factory as a heterotopia: a separate space, perceived from the outside as 'other,' and characterized by strict rules of exclusion/inclusion:

> Heterotopias always presuppose a system of opening and closing that both isolates them and makes them penetrable. In general, the heterotopic site is not freely accessible like a public place. Either the entry is compulsory [...] or else the individual has to submit to rites and purifications. To get in one must have a certain permission and make certain gestures.[23]

---

21 Lupo, G. 2016. *La letteratura al tempo di Adriano Olivetti*. 249.
22 Rozzi, R. 1977. *Psicologi e operai*. 54.
23 Foucault, M. 1986. "Of Other Spaces." *Diacritics*, no. 16. 26.

Furthermore, entrusting care procedures to factory-employed psychologists and psychoanalysts meant silencing all those symptoms that were the expression of a sociopolitical – and not exclusively pathological – discomfort. As Rozzi has observed:

> riducendo tutto ciò che il soggetto considera il sé a qualcosa di privato, astraendolo con ciò dal suo corpo sociale, quella clinica a cui viene permesso di funzionare diviene solo curativa a posteriori, e così di nuovo adattativa ad un potere immodificabile, e perde la sua capacità di trasformazione sociale.
>
> (by reducing everything that the subject considers its self to the sphere of the private, by abstracting it in this way from the social, an authorized clinic becomes therapeutic only a posteriori. It becomes adaptable to an unchangeable power, and it loses its capacity for social transformation.)[24]

Thus, bringing psychoanalysis into the factory also had the effect of producing integrated and docile workers, unable to understand their psychological sufferance as a social malady and to identify their neuroses with the symptoms of exploitation. As Parker has put it, the major risk of making psychology an instrument of industrial companies is that "even the moments of unhappiness that could lead us to reflect on what is wrong with the world are turned into signs of pathology that must be blotted out; alienation in psychological culture is thus reinforced and any awareness of it is suppressed."[25]

---

24   Rozzi, R. 1977. *Psicologi e operai*. 70.
25   Parker, I. 2007. *Revolution in Psychology: Alienation to Emancipation*. 111. It is worth mentioning that, in the late 1960s, the Italian psychoanalyst and psychiatrist Enzo Morpurgo attempted to offer workers a form of psychological therapy entirely devoted to principles of care and freed from any aspect of control. In 1969, Morpurgo inaugurated the first 'consultorio popolare' (popular counseling service) in Niguarda, a periphery north of Milan. Whereas the other centers for industrial psychology carried out projects of assistance and support in collaboration with industry, Morpurgo's center was independent. The Niguarda center could therefore offer free analytical sessions to workers and their families, without complying with companies' requests. Despite the center's short life, Morpurgo's project was a significant experiment of working-class psychoanalysis with no financial support from companies.

The 'Good' Factory in Literature and Cinema: Fictional Representations of Industrial Psychology

The introduction of psychology and psychoanalysis into factories affected the ways in which 'scrittori olivettiani' (Olivetti writers) represented industrial reality in two main ways.[26] At the level of content, it meant that they represented 'psicotecnica' itself. The presence of psychologists, psychoanalysts and 'psicotecnici' in factories became a recurrent theme and, in some instances, a narrative device informing the plot of industrial novels. The most paradigmatic example of this tendency is Ottiero Ottieri, who himself worked as a psychologist for Olivetti, portraying in his books the relationship between industrial psychologists and blue-collar workers (through the fictional approach in *Tempi stretti* (Tight Times, 1957), through an autobiographical account oscillating between a documentarist chronicle and novelistic narrative in *Donnarumma all'assalto* (The Men at the Gate, 1959) and in the form of personal notes on his industrial experience in *La linea gotica* (1962)). At the level of thematics, the introduction of psychology and psychoanalysis into factories resulted in a remarkable emphasis, in industrial literature, on the spreading of working-class neuroses. That is to say, Italian factory writers looked mostly at the devastating effects of industrial society and the tyrannical logic of productivity on workers' psyches. In his article "Astuti come colombe" (Shrewd as Doves, 1962), Franco Fortini used the term "tristezza operaia" (working-class sadness) to label a trend in industrial literature that portrayed factory labor by focusing on the dysphoric reactions it triggered: alienation, depersonalization, melancholia, suicidal thoughts.[27] Ottieri was also the protagonist of this literary trend because he privileged an intimist approach to the factory, describing

---

26 With the expression 'scrittori olivettiani,' I refer to those writers who actively contributed to the Olivetti project while employed by the company in different capacities. Some examples are Leonardo Sinisgalli, Ottiero Ottieri, Giancarlo Buzzi and Paolo Volponi.

27 Fortini, F. 2003. "Astuti come colombe." *Saggi ed epigrammi*. Edited by Luca Lenzini. Milan: Mondadori. 58.

workers' psychological sufferance and employing the perspective of alienated subjects as the vantage point from which to portray industrial realities. However, the "ansia di autointrospezione" (anxiety of self-introspection) and the "rodio psicoanalitico" (psychoanalytic gnawing) that Italo Calvino identified in Ottieri also characterized the work of other writers.[28] The association of blue-collar workers with alienated, neurotic subjects can be found in Paolo Volponi, who in *Memoriale* (My Troubles Began, 1962) stressed the similarities between the alienation provoked by factory labor and clinical madness. As Angelo Guglielmi acknowledged soon after the novel was published, *Memoriale* is in fact "la descrizione di un caso clinico" (the description of a clinical case), representing "la condizione dell'operaio nella fabbrica neocapitalistica. Alla reificazione industriale si sovrappone la paranoia" (the condition of the worker in the neo-capitalist factory. Paranoia is superimposed on industrial reification).[29] Later on, cinema denounced the spreading of a peculiar industrial madness, as made clear by Elio Petri's *La classe operaia va in paradiso* (Lulù the Tool, 1971), where an old worker named Militina, who has been confined to an asylum after a mental collapse resulting from tough working conditions, reveals to his former colleague Lulù that "qui [nell'ospedale psichiatrico] è sempre uguale, come in fabbrica, solo che non ti fanno uscire" (here [in the psychiatric hospital], it's always the same, like in the factory, except they never let you leave). Thus, Petri did not limit himself to stressing the mere similarities between the worker and the psychiatric inmate; he denounced the factory and asylum environments as virtual twins.

Comparisons between industrial organizations and totalitarian institutions of mental health can also be found in literature. In *L'amore mio italiano* (My Italian Love, 1963), Giancarlo Buzzi suggests that the factory presents itself as a reassuring environment, able to provide for the care and health of workers' bodies and minds. At the same time, though, he

---

28 Camerano, V., Crovi, R., and Grasso, G. 2007. *La storia dei gettoni di Elio Vittorini*. Turin: Nino Aragno Editore. 780.
29 Cited in Ferretti, G. C. 1972. *Paolo Volponi*. Florence: La Nuova Italia. 44.

emphasizes how such a seemingly 'good' and efficient system can come to ambiguously embody power and control:

> Era la fabbrica che curava la nostra salute fisica e psichica, che doveva darci la gioia del vivere nell'agio e nella sicurezza, che doveva consentirci di ammogliarci e allevare i figli [...]. Non ci dicevano più: siete cittadini di un mondo in cui esiste anche la fabbrica; bensì: siete operai di una grandiosa fabbrica che è il vostro mondo. [...] La fabbrica intendeva risolvere la nostra vita.
>
> (It was the factory that took care of our physical and psychic health, that was responsible for giving us the *joie de vivre* of ease and safety, for allowing us to find wives and raise children [...]. They no longer told us: you are citizens of a world where there is also the factory; but rather: you are the workers of a great factory that is your world. [...] The factory intended to resolve our lives.)³⁰

Such a view of the factory as a safe, but at once threatening space of salvation also informed *Memoriale*. In Volponi's book, the paranoid protagonist Albino Saluggia believes that he is the victim of a conspiracy through which a group of factory doctors are plotting to remove him from his job. Excluded from work for health reasons, Saluggia dreams of the factory as a place of rebirth and regeneration, seeing in readmission to the industrial world the only path to recovery and happiness:

> Pensavo con piacere [...] di far parte di un'industria così forte e bella e che la sua forza e la sua bellezza fossero in parte mie e pronte ad aiutarmi, così come la fabbrica mi scaldava e mi dava luce. [...] La fabbrica mi appariva sempre più bella e mi sembrava che si rivolgesse a me, come se fossi l'unico o uno dei pochi in grado e ben disposto a capirla.
>
> I thought with pleasure [...] that I was part of a strong and beautiful industry and that part of that strength and beauty belonged to me and was there, ready to help me, the same way that the factory kept me warm and gave me light. [...] The factory seemed to become more beautiful, and I felt as if it spoke to me directly, as if I were the only one or one of the few who could or wanted to understand it.³¹

---

30   Buzzi, G. 2014. *L'amore mio italiano*. Rome: Avagliano. 168–169.
31   Volponi, P. 1962. *Memoriale*. Milan: Garzanti. 63. Volponi, P. 1964. *My Troubles Began*. Translated by Belén Sevareid. New York: Grossman. 44–45.

Consequently, as Tiziano Toracca has argued, Saluggia's final revolt against the 'total factory' is not the exclusive result of his comprehending that industrial labor implies alienation and exploitation.[32] Rather, the protagonist's rejection of the industrial utopia stems from a profound disenchantment: Saluggia feels that he has been betrayed by the factory, a sort of caring mother that has failed to honor its promise of safety, salvation and healing, one that has opted instead to expel the protagonist from its pure body, and because of his malady.

Such an identification of the factory with sanity – understood as both physical and mental health – was also expressed in literature by the recurrent representation of factories as bright and transparent buildings:

> [L']icona della fabbrica di vetro [è un] vero e proprio motivo conduttore che in Ottieri assume i connotati del 'castello orizzontale di vetro' o dell'"immenso parallelepipedo con la parete di vetro' (così in *Donnarumma all'assalto* e nella *Linea gotica*), fino a trasmigrare fra le memorie dell'operaio Volponi nella dimensione di luogo segnato da un particolare stato di *pulchritudo*: 'così è anche bella la fabbrica con i suoi vetri e metalli' [...].
>
> (The icon of the glass factory [is a] real and sustaining theme that in Ottieri takes on connotations of a 'horizontal castle of glass' or an 'immense block with walls of glass' (in *Donnarumma all'assalto* and in *La linea gotica*), even transmigrating among the memories of Volponi the worker in the dimension of a place marked by a particular state of *pulchritude*: 'beauty is also the factory, with its glass windows and metals' [...].)[33]

By idealizing and describing beautiful and luminous structures, writers associated factories with a symbolic and at once concrete idea of Enlightenment, turning them into geometrical incarnations of order and reason. This *topos* aimed at stressing the contrast with the mass of workers, trapped in the darkness of their madness and malady, ready to be cured and controlled within and through the rational and well-organized factory system. The factory was thus portrayed as a twofold organism: on the

---

32 See Toracca, T. 2019. "Paolo Volponi's *Memoriale*: Industry Between Alienation and Utopia." *The Years of Alienation*. Edited by Alessandra Diazzi and Alvise Sforza Tarabochia. Chan: Palgrave Macmillian. 115–132.
33 Lupo, G. 2016. *La letteratura al tempo di Adriano Olivetti*. 61.

one hand, it produced alienation and was the primary cause of workers' psychological deviance; on the other, it was the realm of rationality, order and control. It was, in sum, an institution of care and welfare that provided workers with a cure for the same pains it provoked. Just like the asylum, the factory was organized as a total institution that, while imposing a patronizing conception of care, suppressed the personal freedom, political agency and individuality of workers. In Foucault's terms, industrial literature represented the organization of the factory as a system of at once anonymizing alienation, discipline and recovery. As a result, the factory's fictional imaginary revealed a "disciplinary power" that "has this double property of being 'anonymizing,' that is to say always discarding certain individuals, bringing anomie, the irreducible, to light, and of always being normalizing, that is to say, inventing ever new recovery systems, always re-establishing the rule."[34]

Care or Control? Closing Remarks

This overview of the relationship between the factory and psychology has demonstrated that the employment of psychologists, psychoanalysts and 'psicotecnici' in industry extensively influenced both the development of Italian factories and the fictional imaginary of industrial spaces.

On the one hand, the application of the psychological disciplines to factory labor contributed to the transformation of the factory into what was understood as a 'good space.' On the other hand, industrial psychology became an ambiguous practice which, in its attempt to cure the workers' unconscious, risked moving against the rise of class consciousness. In fact, the medicalization of forms of psychological discomfort triggered by external and unfavorable conditions – rather than by pathological and underlying motives – mitigated and even suppressed the revolutionary potential associated with a collective reflection on, and expression of, unhappiness.

34   Foucault, M. 2008. *Psychiatric Power: Lectures at the Collège de France, 1973–1974*. Edited by Jacques Lagrange. New York: Picador. 54.

Literature, and to a lesser extent cinema, constituted a privileged site for the elaboration of the tension between a new understanding of industrial welfare and the risk of repression resulting from the normalization of discontent. Accordingly, the peculiar 'psicologismo' (psychologizing character) that marked industrial literature did not result, as Calvino and Fortini contended, from an intimist portrayal of the working class that, by focusing on workers as suffering subjects, supposedly failed to show any interest in addressing sociopolitical questions. On the contrary, the emphasis on the psychological consequences of industrialization, as well as the use of psychoanalytic *topoi* to describe the relationship between workers and the 'total factory,' articulated a different and 'softer' form of political commitment, an "engagement with the 'other' (lower case), meaning 'the neighbor,' rather than the 'collective,' or hypostasized, phantasmatic 'Other.'"[35] The psychological perspective characterizing industrial literature constituted a fundamental tool that writers employed in order to denounce the subtle and ambiguous forms of exploitation and repression connected with factory labor. This approach had in fact the paramount importance of reflecting on questions of factory biopolitical control, an aspect of Italian industrialization that remains otherwise mostly overlooked.

35 Antonello, P. and Mussgnug, F. 2009. "Introduction." *Postmodern 'impegno': Ethics and Commitment in Contemporary Italian Culture*. Oxford: Peter Lang. 11.

ANDREA SARTORI

8 Class Struggle and Its Metamorphoses: A Path through Postwar Italian Political Thought

Literary and cinematic production in postwar Italy runs parallel to the development of philosophical categories whose analysis is useful to understand the political and cultural atmosphere in which writers and filmmakers focusing on industry operated. Therefore, this chapter shifts the attention to postwar Italian political thought in order to help answer some questions. For instance: What were the main features of the Marxist debate about class struggle around the years in which Paolo Volponi described Albino Saluggia's intimate discontent in *Memoriale* (My Troubles Began, 1962)? What were the alternatives to Nanni Balestrini's total refusal of both capital and labor in his 1971 novel *Vogliamo tutto* (We Want Everything)? Why did Elio Petri set his film *La classe operaia va in paradiso* (The Working Class Goes to Heaven, 1971) in a factory, while Primo Levi abandoned that scenario when he described the adventures of Faussone in *La chiave a stella* (The Wrench, 1978)? It is not by chance that, through the years and up to our age of precarity, the meanings of labor and struggle have changed.

More specifically, the trajectory of postwar Italian political thought concerning Marxian class struggle illustrates a transition from an emphasis on political party belonging to a more 'heretic' and less ideological perspective. This transition took place against the background of shifting historical conditions and genealogies of thought, both of which caused the notion of struggle to become gradually detached from the notion of class.

In a more or less sequential manner, the trajectory we are about to describe runs from the Partito Comunista Italiano (Italian Communist Party, PCI) leader Palmiro Togliatti's appropriation of Antonio Gramsci's thought (immediately after the Second World War) to Mario Tronti's 1960s 'operaismo' (workerism), and from the philosophy of sexual difference to twenty-first-century biopolitics (Giorgio Agamben, Roberto Esposito and even Antonio Negri). As we will see, Massimo Cacciari's position in the 1970s is peculiar and requires separate description.

Togliatti and Gramsci

After the Second World War, Togliatti wanted to use Gramsci's philosophy of praxis to oppose the long-standing influence of Benedetto Croce's intellectualism and idealism.[1] Togliatti thought that Gramsci's philosophy would, in practical terms, open the possibility of contrasting capitalist exploitation.[2] From his perspective, the Party's 'organic intellectuals' (as Gramsci called the PCI's political pedagogues) needed to spread their cultural hegemony across the country. But as Tronti remarks, Togliatti always nurtured "the myth of capitalist backwardness,"[3] even during the rise of capitalist development in Italy. In other words, Togliatti neglected Gramsci's conclusion that class struggle could originate from within the modern and sophisticated structure of the Fordist factory. For Gramsci, the struggle was an integral part of the process of modernization and the rationalization of modes of production – a process that was always already oriented towards its own completion in communism. In his essay *Americanismo e fordismo* (Americanism and Fordism, 1934), Gramsci argued that the modern relations and modes of production that developed after the First World War (namely Americanism and Fordism) "risulta[ro]no dalla necessità immanente di giungere all'organizzazione

---

1 Gramsci wrote his *Notebooks* in the Fascist prisons from 1929 to 1935, but they were published by Einaudi, under the supervision of Togliatti and editor Felice Platone, between 1948 and 1951. Valentino Gerratana's critical and philologically accurate edition dates only to 1975.
2 Togliatti, P. 1967. "Attualità del pensiero e dell'azione di Gramsci." *Gramsci*. Edited by Ernesto Ragionieri. Rome: Editori Riuniti. 125.
3 Tronti, M. 2012. "Our Workerism." *New Left Review*, vol. 73. 130.

di un'economia programmatica" (derive[d] from an inherent necessity to achieve the organization of a planned economy).[4] Such an achievement had already been reached by Russia, which in the aftermath of the October Revolution (1917) adopted a planned economy, but without first passing through modernity. In other words, Gramsci thought that Americanism and Fordism were not arbitrary conjunctions of events with no lasting significance, since both could be instrumental for abolishing the residues of feudalism in Italy and preparing the 'necessary' transition to communism. According to Gramsci, such residues of feudalism had hindered the economic and social progress of the country, which was essential to developing a modern sense of class-belonging.

Tronti: Workerism

After the Soviet Union's and Nikita Khrushchev's violent 1956 repression of dissent in Hungary, in Italy too the PCI's possible subordination to the Communist Party of the Soviet Union (CPSU) started to raise questions. In 1961, Raniero Panzieri, together with Tronti, Negri, Romano Alquati, Alberto Asor Rosa and Danilo Montaldi, founded the journal *Quaderni rossi*. Tronti split from the group in 1963, opting to publish a different journal, *Classe operaia*, plus the 1966 book *Operai e capitale*.[5] *Classe operaia* closed one year before the fateful protest movements of 1968. During his workerist experience, Tronti distanced himself from the orthodoxy of the PCI and 'togliattismo' (Togliatti-ism) for at least two reasons. First, in the complicated relationships between capital and labor, the latter – as *factory* labor, and by virtue of its qualitative and existential difference from capital – had to take priority over the former, generating

4   Gramsci, A. 1975. *Quaderni dal carcere*. Vol. 3. Turin: Einaudi. 2140. Gramsci, A. 1971. "Americanism and Fordism." *Selections from the Prison Notebooks*. New York: International Publishers. 279.
5   Trotta, G. and Milana, F. (eds). 2008. *L'operaismo degli anni Sessanta. Da "Quaderni rossi" a "classe operaia"*. Rome: DeriveApprodi.

a definite antagonism, and not, as Togliatti believed, a synthesis, a dialectical relationship or even a compromise.⁶ Second, Tronti criticized *de facto* Togliatti's organic intellectual, using a workerist subjectivity that exceeded the PCI's 'logic' and thus challenging the official Party line. More recently, Tronti has written – likely indulging in a melancholic retrospective idealization of his own experience as a workerist – that "*operaismo* [and not the Party] was our university, we graduated in class struggle – entitling us not to teach, but to live."⁷ For the workerists, 'to live' meant to take a stand – to be of a *part* and not a Party – against a common enemy: the factory bosses. From Tronti's perspective, 'struggle' above all linked "a handful of people [...] by a bond of political friendship."⁸ Today, he fully recognizes that the workerist class struggle is a defeated ideal, and that we now live – however evolved we are – in a ferocious state of nature: "l'hobbesiano *homo-lupus* è l'interprete-protagonista dello stato di natura borghese" (the Hobbesian *homo-lupus* is the interpreter-protagonist of the bourgeois state of nature).⁹ For Tronti, Thomas Hobbes' anthropology has defeated Marxist sociology. That is, it has defeated the attempt to *civilize* the struggle (civilizing the struggle entails, in retrospect, the clear and firm rejection of armed insurrection infamously undertaken by the 'Brigate Rosse' (Red Brigades) in 1970). If for Tronti what characterizes today's bourgeois society is the *homo-lupus*, then we might add that Christian Marazzi's and Maurizio Lazzarato's research suggests that it does not matter that work and economy are immaterial. The animal spirits of capitalism, Marazzi and Lazzarato argue, are as ferocious as ever.¹⁰

---

6   As Negri once stated: "il togliattismo era l'ideologia del compromesso" (Togliattism was the ideology of compromise). Negri, A. 2007. *Dall'operaio massa all'operaio sociale. Intervista sull'operaismo*. Edited by Paolo Pozzi and Roberta Tomassini. Verona: ombre corte. 41.
7   Tronti, M. 2012. "Our Workerism." 127.
8   Tronti, M. 2012. "Our Workerism." 119.
9   Tronti, M. 2008. "Noi operaisti". *L'operaismo degli anni Sessanta*. 51.
10 Marazzi, C. 2008. *Capital and Language: From the New Economy to the War Economy*. Cambridge and London: MIT Press. Lazzarato, M. 2012. *The Making of the Indebted Man: An Essay on the Neoliberal Condition*. Cambridge and London: MIT Press.

Sexual Difference and Cacciari's *Krisis*

In the 1970s, the aversion to being of a party as the only way of being of a part – that is, of taking a political stand – and to the idea that between labor and capital there could be some sort of (Hegelian-Marxist) synthesis became acute among feminists too. In 1970, Carla Lonzi published her influential book *Sputiamo su Hegel* (Let's Spit on Hegel) precisely in order to criticize, from a feminist point of view, the dialectical approach in philosophy, and in 1975 a collective of feminists opened the 'Libreria delle donne' (Women's Bookstore) in Milan. But it was only in the 1990s that Adriana Cavarero and Luisa Muraro were able to publish their respective books *Nonostante Platone* (In Spite of Plato, 1990) and *L'ordine simbolico della madre* (The Symbolic Order of the Mother, 1991). With the exception of Leopoldina Fortunati's *L'arcano della riproduzione: Casalinghe, prostitute, operai e capitale* (The Arcane of Reproduction: Housework, Prostitution, Labor and Capital, 1981), no systematic reflection on sexual difference originated from within Marxist thought, hence the antagonistic and anti-dialectical features of the main segment of Italian feminism. However, what these thinkers had in common was the reinterpretation of the notion of struggle in light of sex (gender performance was not yet distinguished from biological identity). Sex, in fact, was for the feminists the key factor determining the subordination of women in patriarchal society. Muraro suggested overcoming such a subordination by opposing the concreteness, the flesh and blood, of the maternal register to the abstractions and intellectualism of the symbolic order of the father. Cavarero, on her end, reworked Hannah Arendt's insights (from *The Human Condition*, 1958) and argued that the individual identity – the answer to the question 'Who am I?' – is rooted in the liminal experience of 'birth,' one exposing the newborn to the world and to the gaze of others. Fortunati focused instead – within the perspective of Marx's *Grundrisse* (1858) – on the changing meaning of reproductive work in the transition from a pre-capitalist to a capitalist society.

The insistence that political struggle could never lead to liberation or redemption – however Marx was interpreted – characterized the philosophy of Massimo Cacciari between the late 1960s and the 1970s. Cacciari upended workerism's perspective and theorized the permanent crisis of capitalism as an inevitable and tragic dimension of political commitment, a dimension that, if it is to be understood, requires some form of *negative* thought. With Cacciari, all faith in Gramsci's "inherent [objective] necessity" of achieving a planned economy was definitely abandoned. Capitalism could not move beyond itself – that is, beyond its own crisis. The pressing and grave issues surrounding the modes and relations of production, social ties and the problem of class struggle itself – in short, the crisis of "the Political"[11] – could not be superseded by any power outside the horizon of internal conflicts proper to bourgeois social structures, whether that power be the working class or another sociopolitical body or identity. As Cacciari wrote in 1969, the three negative thinkers of bourgeois society had been Arthur Schopenhauer, Søren Kierkegaard and, above all, Friedrich Nietzsche,[12] whose notion of 'will to power,' in Cacciari's reading, had nothing to do with irrationality. Will to power, in fact, was the Political itself; it was the way in which the Political rationalized – and found multiple, specific solutions to – its own constantly returning contradictions. From this point of view, as Cacciari wrote in *Krisis* (1976),[13] to struggle *against* the system meant to be totally embedded *in* the system – to share its own (will to) power, which was its true ideology. Empowering 'damaged life' meant integrating it in order to organize and administer (or manage) what was already in existence, not proposing some utopic separatism in search of new foundations. Hence, with *Krisis*, Cacciari shifts our attention from the figures of the worker and organic intellectual to that of the civil servant, whose technical profession Max Weber had analyzed in his 1919 essay *Politics as a Vocation*.

11   Cacciari, M. 1977. *Pensiero negativo e razionalizzazione*. Venice: Marsilio. 12.
12   Cacciari, M. 1969. "Saggio sulla genesi del pensiero negativo". *Contropiano*, vol. 1. 172–173.
13   Cacciari, M. 1976. *Krisis. Saggio sulla crisi del pensiero negativo da Nietzsche a Wittgenstein*. Milan: Feltrinelli.

Negri: Separatism (and Agamben's Sovereign Ban)

Negri, on the contrary, has never abandoned his separatist vocation. But he has also distanced himself from Tronti's 'first' workerism, in response to the decline of Fordism during the 1970s. For Negri, this was a moment for finding a new antagonistic subjectivity. The 'operaio sociale' (which literally means 'social worker') took the place of the 'mass worker', whose environment had been represented (and delimited) by the factory only.[14] The 'operaio sociale' is a worker whose place is society as such – that is, the entire rarefied sphere of circulating money, financial instruments, goods, knowledge, information and images. What is important is that the 'operaio sociale' is incapable of identifying an enemy (the factory boss) against which to be motivated in struggle. As Negri later specified, in a globalized world, capitalist exploitation dominates the social lives of a new typology of worker and goes beyond the borders historically established by the capitalist system. Marx's prophetic and immaterial "general intellect," alongside his notion of "world market," has been made reality in the knowledge economy of global capitalism.[15] In the 'new' world, there is no external opponent against which to struggle, as Tronti thought there was when he limited his view to the factory. Therefore, Negri insists that workers must find the resources of antagonism within themselves: they must 'autovalorizzarsi' (enhance themselves), as he has been writing since the 1970s. Interpretating Baruch Spinoza's ontology at the beginning of the 1980s, Negri attempted to find a new lexicon (and a new conceptuality) that would be able to account for worker autonomy in a post-Fordist age. One new term and concept he found was that of "potere costituente" (constituting power) – in addition to 'multitude' and 'commonwealth' – a kind of power that never changes into "potere costituito" (constituted power)[16] because it maintains its *potentia* open and always

---

14   This is the main topic of: Negri, A. 2007. *Dall'operaio massa all'operaio sociale*.
15   Marx, K. 1993. *Grundrisse: Foundations of the Critique of Political Economy*. London: Penguin Books.
16   Negri, A. 1992. *Il potere costituente. Saggio sulle alternative del moderno*. Rome: manifestolibri.

reproduces its own generativity (its revolutionary drive) without becoming ossified in an institution.[17]

Agamben criticizes Negri's constituting power in *Homo Sacer* (1995) and aims to demonstrate its indissoluble link with constituted power – that is, with sovereignty.[18] According to Agamben, this link is formed by what he calls the "sovereign ban" concerning *homo sacer*. Such a ban was initially issued by exceptional decree, whose origins date back to Roman law. According to this decree (which is 'biopolitical' because it creates the very possibility of political space), "*human life* is included in the juridical order solely in the form of its exclusion (that is, of its capacity to be killed)."[19] From Agamben's point of view, the sovereign ban works as a dispositive of power, that is, as the most important discourse (as Michel Foucault would say) that power put into effect in order to govern life.[20] For Agamben, the sovereign ban about the life of *homo sacer* separates Aristotle's '*zoē*' from '*bíos*.' *Zoē* is bare life, which can be killed, and *bíos* is qualified life, which is worth living. The sovereign ban implemented a decision imposed by decree, and, in Agamben's view, such a ban is no longer an exception at the margins of the political order. He insists that "bare life […] gradually

---

17 More recently, Michael Hardt and Negri have focused on the organization of social movements from below. Hardt, M. and Negri, A. 2017. *Assembly*. Oxford: Oxford University Press.

18 Agamben, G. 1998. *Homo Sacer. Sovereign Power and Bare Life*. Stanford: Stanford University Press. 31.

19 Agamben, G. 1998. *Homo Sacer*. 12. Emphasis mine.

20 The notion of dispositive usually refers to the various institutional, physical and administrative mechanisms and knowledge structures which maintain the exercise of power within society. Foucault used this concept in the 1977 interview "The Confession of the Flesh." Foucault, M. 1980. *Power/Knowledge: Selected Interviews and Other Writings*. New York: Pantheon Books. 194–228. Agamben expanded the notion of dispositive in the essay "What is an Apparatus?" Agamben, G. 2009. *What is an Apparatus? And Other Essays*. Stanford: Stanford University Press. 14. Gilles Deleuze has addressed Foucault's elusive concept of dispositive in another article from 1988 titled "What is a Dispositif?" Armstrong, T. J. (ed.) 1992. *Michel Foucault Philosopher*. Hemel Hempstead: Harvester Wheatsheaf. 159–168. As we will see in the Conclusion of this chapter, the term dispositive is critical for Dario Gentili as well. Gentili traces the genealogy of this concept back to ancient Greek medicine.

begins to coincide with the political realm" so that "inclusion and exclusion, outside and inside, *bíos* and *zoē*, right and fact, enter into a zone of irreducible indistinction."[21] Agamben maintains that this is how biopower functions: bare life is systematically captured, by means of its own exclusion (reclusion, negation or even assassination), by the dispositive of the sovereign ban. No Spinozist *potential* – no life's generativity, no constituting power, much less a class or social identity – exists outside it. Even to be outside the ban means to be included in it as someone who can be isolated, exploited or killed at any moment, *in sum* cursed by the sovereign power.

In the wake of Agamben's criticisms, at the turn of the twenty-first century, Negri seems to have abandoned the notion of constituting power and to have focused more on biopolitics as the sphere of possibility for thinking a way out of capitalism's most coercive aspects. In *Multitude* (2004), Michael Hardt and Negri write that all the conflicts and contradictions characterizing contemporary geopolitics must be understood as an expression of the conflict between the multitude of singularities and the imperial (global) sovereignty – that is, between biopolitics and biopower.[22] The duo tries to rescue antagonism by separating a lively and affirmative biopolitics – "a governing […] *of* life" (as Esposito calls it in *Bíos: Biopolitics and Philosophy*)[23] – from biopower, or the power exerted by capitalism *over* life. Within this perspective:

> *class struggle* in the biopolitical context takes the form of *exodus*. By exodus here we mean, at least initially, a process of *subtraction* from the relationship with capital by means of actualizing the potential autonomy of labor-power. Exodus is thus not a refusal of the productivity of bio-political labor power but rather a refusal of the increasingly restrictive fetters placed on its productive capacities by capital.[24]

---

21 Agamben, G. 1998. *Homo Sacer*. 12.
22 Hardt, M. and Negri, A. 2004. *Multitude: War and Democracy in the Age of Empire*. London: Penguin Books. Unlike Hardt and Negri, Michel Foucault, who coined the terms "biopolitics" and "biopower" in his 1976 book *The History of Sexuality*, never differentiated their meanings.
23 Esposito, R. 2008. *Bíos: Biopolitics and Philosophy*. Minneapolis and London: University of Minnesota Press. 15.
24 Hardt, M. and Negri, A. 2009. *Commonwealth*. Cambridge: Harvard University Press. Emphasis 1 and 2 mine. Emphasis 3 in the original.

Hardt and Negri's new terms for class struggle are "exodus" and "refusal" (of the specific constraints of capitalism), in the absence of a clearly identifiable antagonist and given our post-Fordist mode of globalized production. But having become disillusioned with the possibility of an outside for *Empire* – the title of their 2000 book[25] – Hardt and Negri significantly avoid signaling what the promised land of exodus looks like.

Agamben: Camp, *Lager* and Inoperativity

As we have seen, Agamben's political archeology of the sovereign ban does not share the Marxist premises of thinkers like Tronti, Cacciari and Negri. For Agamben, the sovereign ban still describes our globalized world.[26] He insists that the Nation-State is radically changed: it is no longer based on 'birth' (*nascita*) – that is, birth no longer guarantees that one will be included in the territory where they are born. For Agamben, the crisis of the Nation-State, together with globalization, does not allow for the free and 'happy' circulation of people as promoted in neoliberal propaganda. On the contrary, the dispositive of the sovereign ban, with its inherent ferocity, has been a secretly operating part of the modern world, including the important case of Nazism. The sovereign ban dictates the biopolitical separation of lives worth living from negatable lives: "integrated and sovereign citizens" from "the wretched, the oppressed, and the defeated," who are neither integrated nor sovereign and are instead confined to a "camp" or a "court of miracles."[27] If the camp is the biopolitical paradigm of the modern world,[28] then Agamben is justified in arguing

---

25 Hardt, M. and Negri, A. 2000. *Empire*. Cambridge and London: Harvard University Press.
26 As Dario Gentili writes: "oggi [...] tutti i cittadini sono virtualmente *homines sacri*" (today [...] every citizen virtually is a *homo sacer*). Gentili, D. 2012. *Italian Theory. Dall'operaismo alla biopolitica*. Bologna: Il Mulino. 182.
27 Agamben, G. 1998. *Homo Sacer*. 100.
28 Agamben, G. 1998. *Homo Sacer*. 66–105.

that the Nazi *Lager* made biopower absolute: it made biopolitics coincide with *thanatopolitcs* (the politics of death).[29]

The Auschwitz survivor Primo Levi wrote that in the *Lager*, those inmates capable of struggling for survival did so with very limited, or even non-existent, commitment to solidarity. In his testimonial work *Se questo è un uomo* (If This is a Man, 1947), Levi made extensive recourse to the sociologist Herbert Spencer's terminology of the 'survival of the fittest.'[30] In this light, Agamben might even add that *thanatopolitcs* used the energy of those capable of reacting to absolutize the plain and simple need for survival. This would explain Levi's paradoxical feeling of shame for having survived the *Lager* (especially in *I sommersi e i salvati* (The Drowned and the Saved, 1986)): a shame of de-humanization for having acted as a *homo-lupus* (wolf-man).

What, then, should a "nuova politica" (new politics) look like?[31] In answering this question, Agamben is careful to avoid simply updating the concept of class struggle. He likewise refuses to focus on some identity based in sex or gender, since the act of belonging to similar categories is itself trapped – already included by means of its own exclusion – in the dispositive of sovereignty. Agamben prefers a biopolitical answer, but one that focuses on a minor biopolitics, since the possibility of moving beyond biopolitics is hindered, as Cacciari argued in the 1970s, by the crisis of dialectics. If, as Agamben writes in *Homo Sacer*, "bare life" has now entered into a "zone of irreducible indistinction" from politics,[32] then "bare life" is itself "the one place for both the organization of State power and emancipation from it."[33]

29 Agamben, G. 1999. *Remnants of Auschwitz: The Witness and the Archive*. New York: Zone Books.
30 In the chapter "A Good Day" of *If This is a Man*, Levi implicitly evokes the *Lager*'s social Darwinism when he says: "the group of Greeks, those admirable and terrible Jews of Salonica" are "pitiless opponents in the struggle for life." Levi, P. 1959. *If This is a Man*. New York: The Orion Press. 80. On the "struggle of each one against all," see pages 42 and 106. On the "struggle for life," see pages 100 and 101. On the "struggle for survival," see page 101.
31 Agamben, G. 2003. "Una biopolitica minore." *Intervista a Giorgio Agamben*. Edited by Paolo Perticari. Rome: manifestolibri.
32 Agamben, G. 1998. *Homo Sacer*. 12.
33 Agamben, G. 1998. *Homo Sacer*. 12–13.

But in contrast to Negri, Agamben does not think that the solution is to juxtapose two powers, the biopolitical power (under the form of exodus) and biopower. In his 1990 book *The Coming Community*, Agamben writes that "the novelty of coming politics is that it will no longer be a struggle for the conquest or control of the State, but a *struggle between the State and the non-state (humanity)*."[34] To struggle in the name of "humanity" means to de-activate the dispositive of the sovereign ban by rendering it inoperative, so that life as such (humanity with all its natural and cultural features) is no longer divided into life worth living and life that can be damaged. Once this inoperativity of humanity is reached, struggle will no longer be necessary and contemplation will become possible.[35]

Conclusion: Gentili's Crisis Dispositive (and the Importance of Literature)

This chapter has sought to trace the gradual detachment of the notion of struggle from the notion of class. For 1970s feminists, struggle was something that played out between sexual difference and a patriarchal society that attempted to negate that difference. For Cacciari, empowering the wretched and the defeated meant working (struggling) for them, but from within the system, like the civil servant does. For Negri, class struggle ended up taking on the form of an exodus of biopolitical power. Agamben focused on de-activating the sovereign ban in an attempt to free humanity from all kinds of struggle. What these cases share is that they all differentiate the notion of struggle from Spencer's survival of the fittest – the uncivilized struggle. In Agamben's (and Esposito's) terms, for instance, *thanatopolitics* is the negative side of biopolitics, while for

---

34　Agamben, G. 1993. *The Coming Community*. Minneapolis and London: University of Minnesota Press. 84. Emphasis mine.
35　Agamben's understanding of politics as inoperativity is developed in many texts, but see in particular: Agamben, G. 2011. *The Kingdom and the Glory: For a Theological Genealogy of Economy and Government*. Stanford: Stanford University Press.

Tronti, it is the *homo-lupus* that interprets today's bourgeois state of nature. But as Tronti says, the real uncivilized version of class struggle was the terrorism of the Red Brigades. From this point of view, theorizing different pedigrees of struggle and finding multiple genealogies of thought that are useful in accounting for a critical and effective political commitment have been – and continue to be – the *modus operandi* of postwar Italian political thought that tries to oppose the ferocity of both sides of the political spectrum.

Dario Gentili has recently suggested that the dichotomies used here (many of which he treats in his book *Italian Theory* (2012)) – work and capital, sexual difference and patriarchy, multitude and biopower, *zoē* and sovereignty – have been created by a crisis dispositive (the word 'crisis' comes from the Greek *krinein*, which means to distinguish and judge).[36] Gentili traces the origin of this dispositive back to Hippocrates' medicine (c. 460 BC – c. 370 BC), where life and illness were separated out by a judgment that knew how to distinguish between normative, acceptable life and that which deviated from the norm. For Gentili, this is the real reason why capitalism and, today, neoliberalism have been able to curse (to condemn), one after the other, the working class, women, *zoē* and the multitude. Neoliberalism, in particular, justifies this movement by constantly invoking 'exceptional' crises that necessitate, for instance, periodical austerity measures in economy. But Gentili insists that these crises are not exceptional at all, since the condition of 'crisis' in which we live has been ongoing since the 1970s. Gentili says that crisis has become an art of government, an expression of power that claims to judge who should be saved and who should drown in the age of precarity. For Gentili, the critical answer to the crisis dispositive depends on de-activating it as such, which does not mean that it is possible to supersede crisis, nor that we can move beyond conflict and struggle. On the contrary, it means that it is necessary to detach crisis from political decisions based on the judgment that curses and condemns a person in place of someone else.

---

36   Gentili, D. 2012. *Italian Theory*. 15–16. See also: Gentili, D. 2018. *Crisi come arte di governo*. Macerata: Quodlibet. 21–46.

We might add that, as Levi shows in his non-testimonial work, literature can play an important role in de-activating the crisis dispositive. Levi's case seems to call for an ethics of writing, which should be developed in common, to the advantage of a wide readership. In fact, thirty years after his testimony in *Se questo è un uomo*, Levi wrote *La chiave a stella* (1978), published in the US as *The Monkey's Wrench* (1986). This is Levi's only fictional work, and it is usually considered his most optimistic book. In the novel, Levi's protagonist Faussone is an ironic and comical contractor, a freelance worker constantly travelling around the world. Faussone tells Levi, the narrator, a series of stories about his experiences. With *The Monkey's Wrench*, Levi the author takes the many metaphors issuing from Faussone's job and transforms the meaning of the horrific Auschwitz sign "*Arbeit macht frei*" (Work sets you free) into a reason to live: to be professional in one's work (whether construction, chemistry, writing or some other trade). The novel's rhetorical strategy is at the service of a very complex operation: it attempts to work through the trauma of the *Lager*, and therefore the struggle for survival, according to which someone must be saved and someone must drown.

If we conceive literature (and philosophy) in these terms – that is, as "lived thought"[37] – then we have given one more reason for which it is still worth struggling.

---

[37] Tronti defines the workerist experience as "lived thought." Tronti, M. 2012. "Our Workerism." 119. Esposito also writes "living thought," by which he means the Italian philosophical tradition running from Niccolò Machiavelli, Giordano Bruno and Giambattista Vico to the theorists of conflict and struggle analyzed here. Esposito, R. 2012. *Living Thought. The Origins and Actuality of Italian Philosophy*. Stanford: Stanford University Press.

AMBRA ZORAT

9 Women and/in the Factory

In anthologies of Italian industrial literature before and during the economic boom, the names of women writers are entirely missing. And yet, many women did write, more or less systematically, about factory life. Teresa Noce's novel *Gioventù senza sole* (Dreary Youth) was published in Paris in 1938, then in Italy in 1950, as if to link the earlier period of proto-industrialism to the postwar takeoff. A communist and antifascist from Turin, Noce was among the twenty-one women elected to the Constituent Assembly of the Italian Republic in 1946. From humble origins, she had experienced factory life from a very early age, working first in a pastry factory, then on the lathe at Fiat. *Gioventù senza sole* is the story of Maddalena, whose childhood is defined by a spiral of poverty and eviction. After elementary school, Maddalena abandons her dream of becoming a teacher and begins working, first as a tailor, then at a pastry factory. She is proud and impetuous, always ready to rebel against perceived injustices or abuses of power.

Noce's novel deals with the rise of female industrial labor during the First World War, including the heated debates that such a phenomenon generated throughout society. It also documents the heroic involvement of women in the 1917 Turin strikes, proclaiming: "È l'officina che ha trasformato l'impiegata, la serva, la sartina che nel maggio del '15 scappavano al rumore delle fucilate, nelle superbe eroine del '17!" (It is the factory that turned the female clerk – the servant girl, the little tailoress who ran from the sound of guns in May '15 – into the spirited heroines of '17!)[1] By gathering many women under one roof, the factory creates a sense of class-belonging that is a necessary prerequisite for the development of social movements. In the novel, there are many cases of female solidarity:

1   Noce, T. 1938. *Gioventù senza sole*. Paris: Edizioni Italiane di Coltura. 208–209.

women made provisions to cover for each other in the event of accidents and sickness. For the protagonist of *Gioventù senza sole*, female workers are slaves twice over – in the factory and in the home – and she organizes a protest against the policy of dismissing them to the maternal hearth after four years of factory labor. The novel also treats the question of promiscuity in closed and crowded spaces, denouncing the sexual crimes of the pastry factory's director, who tries to seduce 15-year-old girls by promising them advance pay.

Despite its obvious connections to Noce's life, *Gioventù senza sole* is not a first-person narrative, and the names of the characters are not the names of Noce's family members. On the contrary, it is an exemplary story of labor, self-awareness and revolt. The use of the past tense gives way in the final two pages to present and future verbs, just as the protagonist joins a large group of demonstrators. This stylistic device, together with the accumulation of so many interrogative and exclamative sentences, serves to emphasize the final message of solidarity and hope in socialism conveyed in the closing scene. Though *Gioventù senza sole* indulges the occasional rhetorical flourish, it also anticipates important problems of postwar industry like the relations between workers and bosses and widespread participation in strikes. Moreover, the novel conjugates personal and political perspectives by showing a woman intent on asserting herself through committed activism.

Between the 1950s and 1970s, questions of industry appear in the writings of many women. The factory world is present, for example, in the works of Anna Maria Ortese, Elsa Morante, Dacia Maraini and Nella Nobili.[2] Ortese in particular dedicated her entire oeuvre to representing the oppressed, often with striking realism and at times with fantastic and visionary acumen. Ortese's realism is indissolubly linked to *Il mare non bagna Napoli* (Neapolitan Chronicles, 1953), a critique of the perennially immobile southern city's intellectual class. But it is also manifest in *Silenzio a Milano* (Silence in Milan, 1958), a collection of investigative articles

---

[2] See also Luce d'Eramo, whose 1954 story *La straniera* (The Stranger) tells of a young Italian woman hired in a German factory. The text is largely autobiographical, concentrating on the unfair treatment of Italian workers, who are not allowed to enter the most secure safety bunkers.

commissioned by *L'Europeo* and *L'Unità* that also includes completely invented fiction pieces. Having lived in Milan from 1953 to 1958 and from 1965 to 1970, Ortese used *Silenzio a Milano* to denounce the consequences of industrialization in a "metropoli-matrigna" (wicked metropolis).³

Ortese had intimate knowledge of the city's desolate peripheries and working-class neighborhoods, and she inveighed in her writings on the reification of humanity introduced by the new economic system. Thus the silence of the book's title belongs to those individuals who work the assembly line, transformed by the rhythms of modern production into docile and mute bodies. In the opening article, titled "Una notte nella stazione" (A Night at the Station), Ortese bluntly declares that "si entrava in questa città per essere trasformati in cose, in cifre, o respinti" (one entered this city to be transformed into things, into numbers, or turned down).⁴ Men and women are "senza parola, muti, docili: senza verde, luce, aria; trasformati in cemento, vetro, acciaio; trasformati in lucidatrici frigidaires, essi che magari li desiderarono" (without words, mute, docile: without green, light, air; transformed into cement, glass, steel; transformed into refrigerator polishers – the same people who desired them).⁵

In the last chapter of *Silenzio a Milano*, titled "Lo sgombero" (The Evacuation), Ortese tells the story of two siblings: Alberto Sanipoli, who works in a steel factory, and Masa, who is perennially busy with her sewing machine. In the process of boxing up their modest belongings and moving to a new home, the two protagonists melancholically evoke the lives they have led inside their old apartment. Masa is generally ill-suited for life, weak and sickly from a young age. Both she and her brother Alberto have been scarred by the death of their father, who was "ingoiato come una cosa" (swallowed up like a thing)⁶ in a factory accident.⁷ Alberto and Masa are

3   Baldi, A. 2000. "La metropoli matrigna: *Silenzio a Milano* di A. M. Ortese." *Studi Novecenteschi*, vol. 27, no. 59. 187–209.
4   Ortese, A. M. 1993. *Silenzio a Milano*. Milan: La Tartaruga. 35.
5   Ortese, A. M. 1993. *Silenzio a Milano*. 30.
6   Ortese, A. M. 1993. *Silenzio a Milano*. 121.
7   As Ortese wrote in a letter to Vito Laterza in September 1956, this was inspired by a real accident: "ho sempre in mente i funerali del mastello d'acciaio. Un uomo, a Sesto, un operaio anziano, quest'inveno, cadde, mentre lavorava, nell'acciaio fuso, che lo distrusse completamente" (I'm always thinking about the steel tank funeral. A man, in Sesto, an old worker, this winter, fell, while he was working,

betrayed by a bourgeois intellectual with communist sympathies named Dino Piermattei, who instills in them a sense of hope with his marriage proposal and promises of proletarian liberation, then abandons them both after the 1956 Soviet invasion of Hungary. No longer a virgin, Masa suddenly finds herself "senza marito in una strada che non porta a niente" (without a husband, in the middle of a street that leads nowhere).[8] In the words of Alberto, as soon as a man "oltrepassa la soglia della sua abitazione, ecco è una cosa: e un ingranaggio lo afferra, e lo porta avanti e indietro, su e giù, come una ruota per venti, trent'anni, sotto un cielo plumbeo" (steps out of his home, *voilà* he is a thing: and a mechanism grabs him, and it drags him forward and backward, up and down, like a wheel, for twenty, thirty years, beneath a leaden sky).[9] Brother and sister, worker and woman – already mature yet still unmarried – are both defeated by the new Italian society under construction.

As Andrea Baldi has noted, in Ortese's other texts such an anti-industrial polemic takes on the form of the fantastic.[10] In her novel *L'Iguana* (The Iguana, 1965), the oppressed creature is not the proletarian mass, but rather a half human, half snake servant girl: a monstrous being unable to speak the language of her bosses and therefore condemned to remain misunderstood and exploited. Here the impossibility of the oppressed subject to express herself is reframed with reference to the animal kingdom in a way that is somewhat coherent with *Silenzio a Milano*, where Ortese makes mention of "uomini uccello" (bird men) and "uomini topo" (mouse men),[11] describing Masa as "un grosso cane scuro e dolente" (a big dog, dark and painful)[12] and as a horse "con gli occhi neri colmi di una pura angoscia" (with black eyes filled of pure anguish).[13] Such allusions to the animal

---

      in the molten steel, and it completely destroyed him). Cited in Clerici, L. 2002. *Apparizione e visione. Vita e opera di Anna Maria Ortese*. Milan: Mondadori. 330.

8   Ortese, A. M. 1993. *Silenzio a Milano*. 110.
9   Ortese, A. M. 1993. *Silenzio a Milano*. 121.
10   Baldi, A. 2000. "La metropoli matrigna." 192.
11   Ortese, A. M. 1993. *Silenzio a Milano*. 70–72.
12   Ortese, A. M. 1993. *Silenzio a Milano*. 100.
13   Ortese, A. M. 1993. *Silenzio a Milano*. 139.

kingdom are a frequent feature of industrial literature, most famously in the works of Paolo Volponi. But while for Volponi, the animal represents "un corpo in fuga, irriducibile, nel suo delirio, a ogni ordine compositivo" (a fugitive body, irreducible in its delirium to any constituent order),[14] for Ortese – a writer deeply concerned with animal welfare[15] – the animal shares a plane of existence with humanity, underlining a mutual suffering of impossible communication. Nevertheless, in *L'iguana* and subsequent novels, Ortese's animals are mysterious figures: suspended "fra noto e ignoto" (between the known and the unknown),[16] born of a present challenge yet released from the dimension of history and taking on mythical forms.

The theme of factory life is also addressed, however briefly, in Elsa Morante's novel *La Storia* (History: A Novel, 1974), which takes place during the 1940s. In one of the last chapters, Davide Segre – a young Jewish man with bourgeois origins and anarchist sympathies – begins work at a northern industrial factory. Davide's decision to join the workers is justified by his desire to grow closer to the proletariat, and he crosses the factory threshold "col rispetto dovuto a un recinto sacro" (with the respect due to a holy enclosure).[17] Such an expression harmonizes with associations of factory and church in both Volponi's *Memoriale* (My Troubles Began, 1962) and Leonardo Sinisgalli's short story "L'operaio e la macchina" (The Worker and the Maching, 1949). While for Volponi and Sinisgalli, the religious sensibility is connected to respect for a symbolic space of modernity, for Morante, it evidences Davide's awareness that "quella che per lui era una scelta, per gli altri umani là rinchiusi era una condanna imposta" (what had been for him a free choice was an imposed sentence for the other humans enclosed there).[18] Here, the sacred is a product of the character's sincere compassion for the workers, understood as prisoners of the factory system.

14 Zinato, E. 2010. "Figure animali nella narrativa italiana del secondo Novecento: Sciascia, Primo Levi, Calvino, Volponi, Morante." *Per Romano Luperini*. Edited by Pietro Cataldi. Palermo: Palumbo. 102.
15 See, for example: Ortese, A. M. 2016. *Le piccolo persone*. Milan: Adelphi.
16 Farnetti, M. 1998. *Anna Maria Ortese*. Milan: Mondadori. 37.
17 Morante, E. 2009. *La Storia*. Turin: Einaudi. 412. Morante, E. 1977. *History: A Novel*. Translated by William Weaver. New York: Knopf. 351.
18 Morante, E. 2009. *La Storia*. 412. Morante, E. 1977. *History: A Novel*. 351.

But Morante tinges the affirmation with a note of irony: Davide's longing for insurrection is associated with the hasty enthusiasm of someone about to penetrate "nell'*occhio del ciclone*" (into the *eye of the cyclone*), like "un miliziano d'ultima leva impaziente di provarsi al *battesimo del fuoco*" (a raw recruit eager to prove himself in his *baptism of fire*).[19]

Davide is assigned to work first at a machine press, then at a milling machine. Inside the factory, the light is blinding, the dust and odors are penetrating and the deafening noise prevents Davide from communicating with the other workers. All laboring bodies must keep up with the fast production rhythms, and they soon become indistinguishable from the assortment of ironclad machinery. Even outside the factory, the intellectual becomes incapable of thinking. Davide's working-class experience turns out to be a disaster when his body can no longer resist: he vomits, suffers from migraines and nightmares, and is forced to leave the factory.

As Concetta D'Angeli has argued, Davide Segre's factory experience shares a number of similarities with the biography of Simone Weil (as outlined in *La condition ouvrière* (1934)).[20] But Monica Zanardo has also suggested that the tone of *La Storia*'s prose borders on parody: while the French philosopher worked in a factory from December 1934 to July 1935, Morante's intellectual quits his job after only nineteen days.[21] Morante's intention is to lay bare the contradictions and weaknesses of a character – the only one to have reached political consciousness – whose revolutionary ideals are discredited by his concrete behavior. In fact, the narrating voice even specifies that Davide's story was first reported by a certain Ninnuzzu, who "ne dava un'interpretazione comica (anche se per Davide quella era stata, invero, una tragedia)" (gave it a comic interpretation (even if, for Davide, it had been a real tragedy)).[22] The intellectual's serious self-image

---

19 Morante, E. 2009. *La Storia*. 422–423. Morante, E. 1977. *History: A Novel*. 351.
20 D'Angeli, C. 1993. "La presenza di Simone Weil ne *La Storia*." *Per Elsa*. Edited by Giorgio Agamben et al. Rome: Linea d'ombra. 109–135.
21 Zanardo, M. 2014. "Davide Segre nelle carte manosctritte della *Storia* di Elsa Morante." *I cantieri dell'italianistica. Ricerca didattica e organizzazone agli inizi del XXI secolo*. Edited by Beatrice Alfonzetti et al. Rome: Adi editore. 7.
22 Morante, E. 2009. *La Storia*. 412. Morante, E. 1977. *History: A Novel*. 350.

is thus opposed by a popular and burlesque vision that emphasizes his real ill-suitedness to the proletarian world.

Moreover, Davide's contact with the factory workers is a rare occurrence. Becoming aware of the dearth of topics available for conversation at a working-class dinner, "per un sentimento che a lui pareva di *carità* (ma, assai più invero, per un suo bisogno di simpatia) si buttò lui stesso a raccontare una storiella sconcia" (with a feeling which to him seemed *charity* (but was, really, far more his own need of being liked) he eagerly set out to tell a dirty story) – a story that alarms his listeners, who suspect the presence in his speech of dangerous political allusions.[23] Such an episode reveals the chasm of incommunicability that separates Davide from the workers. The narrating voice's observations – included between parentheses – confirm that Davide's behavior is dictated not so much by a desire to help the workers as by a search for affection and human warmth: an individual need to free one's self from a refined but sterile form of knowledge production.

We should not underestimate the importance of Morante's decision to make the intellectual character a male. While the female in *La Storia* – represented by the exemplary maternal Ida – is tied to an archaic corporeality and an intuitive form of knowledge production excluded from all 'official' History, the male is associated with the *logos*: the reason that orders the real and gives it meaning.[24] Davide Segre therefore becomes the incarnation of a "dramma della conoscenza" (drama of knowledge): his defeat is that of an abstract knowledge form – necessarily violent and inauthentic – inside of a genre founded upon the practice of silencing the female.[25]

Morante thus approaches factory life from the perspective of the complex relationship between the Italian intellectuals and the Italian people. A central focus of Antonio Gramsci's reflections during the 1920s and 1930s, this relationship was intensely elaborated during the 1960s and 1970s. But Morante leaves the contradictions of the relationship unresolved: she refuses

---

23   Morante, E. 2009. *La Storia*. 417. Morante, E. 1977. *History: A Novel*. 355.
24   Bernabò, G. 1991. *Come leggere "La Storia" di Elsa Morante*. Milan: Mursia. 57–67. Benabò, G. 2012. *La fiaba estrema. Elsa Morante tra vita e scrittura*. Rome: Carocci. 207–211.
25   Puggioni, E. 2006. *Davide Segre un eroe al confine della modernità*. Alessandria: Edizioni dell'Orso. 10.

to abandon herself either to a facile populism or to a sturdy faith in the intellectual superiority of writers, remaining ever aware that the dominant culture of her period is managed entirely by men.

Factory life is also confronted in the writings of Dacia Maraini, especially in the short story "Le mani" (These Hands, 1968) and the theatrical piece *Il manifesto* (The Manifesto, 1969). The title of "Le mani" places the concept of manual labor front and center, but it also hints at the protagonist's dream of changing jobs and becoming a manicurist. The story is told by a married woman – her unemployed husband has been sent to prison – who uses a diary and unrefined language to narrate what she does throughout the day: cleaning, shopping and meal preparation, digestion and bowel problems, factory labor, evenings with friends and erotic encounters. The female protagonist is hampered by the drudgery of everyday life, and she remains detached and confused in the face of factory strikes: "In fabbrica sempre con quell'idea dello sciopero mi hanno fatto la testa come un paniere. Ma che vogliono? Lunedì c'è la riunione della Commissione interna. Intanto è da due giorni che non vado di corpo. Per forza a furia di mangiar patate" (At the factory the endless gossip about a strike gives me a splitting headache. What on earth do they want? Monday's the meeting of the Workers' Committee. Meantime I haven't had a crap for two days; no wonder, all I eat is potatoes).[26] Such disinterest is ironically followed by a reference to the pressing demands of everyday life: for a factory worker, digestion and bowel problems are a clear sign of malnourishment, which is a result of insufficient pay. Elsewhere, the protagonist distances herself from factory strikes by entertaining fanciful dreams of a new life: "In fabbrica sono ancora lì che parlano di sciopero. Mi fanno ridere. Io poi alla fine dell'anno me ne vado" (At the factory they make me laugh, still talking strike. Anyway, I'm quitting at the end of this year).[27] Her work makes her sick: "In fabbrica crepo. A respirare sempre quell'acido mi è venuta una tosse da turco. E poi hai voglia di mettere crema e olio. La pelle delle mani se ne va come la buccia

---

26 Maraini, D. 1999. "Le mani." *Mio marito*. Milan: BUR. 119. Maraini, D. 2004. "These Hands." *My Husband*. Translated by Vera F. Golini. Waterloo, Ontario: Wilfrid Laurier University Press. 122.

27 Maraini, D. 1999. "Le mani." *Mio marito*. 120. Maraini, D. 2004. "These Hands." *My Husband*. 123.

della cipolla. Sono gonfie e mangiate dall'acido. I guanti non servono a niente. L'acido passa sotto i guanti, sotto la pelle, sotto tutto" (The factory will be the death of me. Constantly breathing those acid fumes has brought on a devil of a cough. When I put on cream and oil, the skin peels off my hands like an onion. They're swollen and eaten by the acid. Gloves are useless. The acid eats through the gloves, the skin, everything).[28] As a result of these problems, the protagonist is reassigned first to the assembly line, then to the lathe, where she loses a finger in an industrial accident. Her dream of becoming a manicurist evaporates in an instant, and the story ends when she realizes that she no longer even wants to keep a diary: "mi è venuta la stufagna" (I'm fed up).[29] For a woman as lonely and withdrawn as Maraini's protagonist, not even writing remains useful.

As one of Maraini's first theatrical pieces, *Il manifesto* is deeply indebted to Japanese culture, especially to the *Noh* tradition, which frequently casts spirits as protagonists. In *Il manifesto*, a young dead woman tells the story of her tragic but adventurous life, starting with her transfer from Palermo to Monza (Lombardy) to work in a cardboard box factory. In this feminist account, the protagonist provocatively distances herself from all sorts of female-gendered stereotypes like passivity and frailty. On the contrary, she pursues erotic encounters with enthusiasm and encourages the women in the factory to demand the same pay as the men. Once arrested, she leads a revolt from inside a prison, but she is killed by three guards. By providing concrete testimony of working-class and private problems, the short story "Le mani" foregrounds the protagonist's loneliness and distance from organized political action, while Maraini's theatrical piece emphasizes the need for women to join forces and rebel together.[30]

---

28 Maraini, D. 1999. "Le mani." *Mio marito*. 127. Maraini, D. 2004. "These Hands." *My Husband*. 127.
29 Maraini, D. 1999. "Le mani." *Mio marito*. 152. Maraini, D. 2004. "These Hands." *My Husband*. 143.
30 One thinks also of the theatrical pieces by Franca Rame and Dario Fo, especially the monologue *Il risveglio* (The Awakening, 1977) about a working-class mother. Awaking from a nightmare about an industrial accident, the protagonist searches frantically for her house keys so that she can take her child to school and get to work. In order to find the keys, the protagonist must reconstruct the events of the

Excepting parts of Rossana Ombres' collection *Le ciminiere di Casale* (Farmhouse Smokestacks, 1962), the most important Italian poetry to deal with factory life is by Nella Nobili. Born in Bologna to a modest family, Nobili worked from age fourteen as a glassblower in a medicine vial factory (1940–1943). She then joined a glassmaker in Bologna city center (1945–1949). Nobili's poems were published in magazines, and she frequented noted intellectuals like the writers Renata Viganò and Sibilla Aleramo, with whom she shared a concern for women's issues in contemporary society. She also knew painters like Giorgio Morandi, to whom she dedicated the piece "Paesaggio 1926" (Landscape 1926). In 1949, Nobili published *Poesie* (Poems), a critically successful collection with a section of love lyrics dedicated to a woman. She moved to Rome in 1953, then migrated to Paris, where she became an artisan and wrote in French. Nobili's poetry is countercultural by definition: she wrote not only about love for women but also factory labor in *La jeune fille à l'usine* (The Girl at the Factory, 1978). She committed suicide in 1985, and her work was only rediscovered in 2017 by Marie-José Tramuta. In Italy, Maria Grazia Calandrone edited the 2018 volume *Ho camminato nel mondo con l'anima aperta* (I Walked the World with an Open Soul), which includes a selection of poems in Italian and French with translations by Ximena Rodriguez Bradford.

The factory experience recounted in *La jeune fille à l'usine* is not that of an external and detached subjectivity, but rather that of a poetic sensibility that knows the reality of working-class labor from the inside. Moreover, because it employs a plurality of personal pronouns – not only "je" (I), but also "tu" (you), "elle" (she) and "nous" (us) – the tone of *La jeune fille à l'usine* is simultaneously personal and choral. The collection begins with the section "Tendresse" (Tenderness), where the poetic voice confesses the omnipresence of her own childhood ghost and the obsessive thought of her painfully interrupted destiny. Indeed, the happy promises of a childhood cut short by misery and the necessity of labor are nothing but a tender memory. In one part of the section "L'enfance trahie" (Childhood

---

previous evening, at which point she realizes that it is Sunday and that work worries have taken over her free time.

Betrayed), Nobili opposes the sweetness of a pearly city sunset to the electric and eternal lights of the industrial factory.[31]

The harsh world of industrial labor is spotlighted in the section "L'usine" (The Factory), where female workers inhale hot flames as their skin is perforated by shards of glass.[32] During a lunch break, the poetic voice is labeled "la jeanefillequipleure" (the younggirlwhocries) – a one-word name designed to make the act of crying an integral part of her identity – while she consoles herself by eating food brought from home and by secretly reading a book.[33] The infernal atmosphere is reflected in a bottle of compressed air that might explode at any moment,[34] in the factory heat that can be alleviated only by tearing off one's skin[35] and in the quick, repetitive gestures required to maintain the rhythms of labor.[36] At the end of each shift, the factory doors open as if invoked by an incessant prayer for liberation.[37] In the section "Le mur" (The Wall), the factory becomes an inescapable prison where the poetic voice can do nothing but scratch at the cement.[38] In "Les cahiers de l'usine" (Factory Notebooks), the factory shatters the female workers' innards and their souls flow out into the products of their labor.[39] The death of the soul is soon followed by the death of the body. One poem that begins with the pale body of a female worker lying supine on a table ends with the image of a working-class lunch consumed on that same surface.[40] The circular structure of Nobili's poem brings into direct relief the resignation of female workers to the merciless logic of factory production.

It is only by writing that the poetic voice can attempt to resist and survive. As the section "La beauté et la liberté" (Beauty and Freedom) makes

31 Nobili, N. 2018. *Ho camminato nel mondo con l'anima aperta*. Edited by Maria Grazia Calandrone. Milan: Solferino. 160.
32 Nobili, N. 2018. *Ho camminato nel mondo con l'anima aperta*. 173.
33 Nobili, N. 2018. *Ho camminato nel mondo con l'anima aperta*. 175.
34 Nobili, N. 2018. *Ho camminato nel mondo con l'anima aperta*. 177.
35 Nobili, N. 2018. *Ho camminato nel mondo con l'anima aperta*. 181.
36 Nobili, N. 2018. *Ho camminato nel mondo con l'anima aperta*. 188.
37 Nobili, N. 2018. *Ho camminato nel mondo con l'anima aperta*. 184.
38 Nobili, N. 2018. *Ho camminato nel mondo con l'anima aperta*. 193.
39 Nobili, N. 2018. *Ho camminato nel mondo con l'anima aperta*. 215.
40 Nobili, N. 2018. *Ho camminato nel mondo con l'anima aperta*. 218.

clear, what the factory system steals from young female workers is their beauty and freedom, two characteristics that Nobili's poetic voice seeks to restore in verse. Writing becomes a way for the poetic voice to remain worthy of the hopeful girl she used to be: "Jamais mon enfant, je ne t'ai trahie" (Never, my little one, I never betrayed you).[41] Thus Nobili writes about factory life to express a feeling of revolt, but she also does so to keep faith with herself and with her poetic vocation.

This chapter has provided a brief overview of female voices in Italian industrial prose, theater and poetry, with a focus on the economic boom and the 1970s. But it is merely a sketch of the essentials – a starting point for further research and analyses. In order to properly situate the presence of women writers within the historiography of Italian industrial literature, we must remember that the first workers to enter the factory were indeed women. Daily labor during proto-industrialism – between the nineteenth and twentieth centuries, when industrial development was centered on textile production – was predominantly female labor;[42] daily labor from the Second World War through the 1970s was predominantly male labor. Nevertheless, even during this second period, when mechanical production came to dominate, woman continued to work in the textile industry, frequently from home.[43] For women writers like Ada Negri and Jolanda (pseudonym of Maria Majocchi) who worked between the nineteenth and twentieth centuries, industrial labor was generally tied to the quest for identity.[44] But the twentieth century saw women's industrial literature develop quickly and diversify its themes.

41 Nobili, N. 2018. *Ho camminato nel mondo con l'anima aperta*. 251.
42 De Clementi, A. 2015. "Operai e operaie nel primo cinquantennio del capitalismo italiano." *Storia del lavoro in Italia. Il Novecento (1896–1945)*. Edited by Stefano Musso. Rome: Castelvecchi. 24–57. Ortaggi Cammarosano, S. 2009. "Condizione femminile e industrializzazione tra '800 e '900." *Donne, Lavoro, Grande Guerra. Saggi II 1982–1999*. Milan: Unicopli. 63–152. Pescarolo, A. 1996. "Il lavoro e le risorse delle donne in epoca contemporanea." *Il lavoro delle donne*. Edited by Angela Gropi. Bari: Laterza. 299–344.
43 Curtufelli, M. R. 1977. *Operaie senza fabbrica. Inchiesta sul lavoro a domicilio*. Rome: Editore Riuniti.
44 Positano, S. 2014. *Donne e lavoro nella letteratura italiana di fine Ottocento: tra merce di scambio e impresa identitaria*. Bari: Progedit.

The writers treated in this chapter adopt a variety of approaches, but they also exhibit important points of contact and intersection. Noce and Maraini both privilege the question of emancipation: for them, freedom and independence are obtained not through labor, but through a reaction to the injustices of the factory world. Morante and Ortese both explore the complex role of intellectuals: the first by focusing on the figure of Davide Segre, the second by presenting a cast of oppressed characters who are deceived, then abandoned by the communist Dino Piermattei. Noce and Nobili both draw heavily on their own biographical experiences. This is more than evident in final pages of *Gioventù senza sole*, where Noce's expressive *pathos* seems to sacrifice literary quality to the author's political message. At the same time, Nobili's poetry is clearly much more than a personal testimony of extraordinary literary value: it reveals how one can be both a poet and a factory worker without internal contradiction.

Moreover, it is important to note that all these writers connect the theme of factory life to much broader questions: Noce emphasizes political commitment as a potential marker of female identity, Ortese describes the impossibility of the oppressed subject's self-expression and the general reification of humanity in modern society, Morante reflects on the state of an intellectual class separated from both the workers and the female experience, Maraini asserts the urgency of a feminist revolt and Nobili declares the need to resist violence and oppression with literary means. Above all, they demonstrate how questions of industry can be approached from a variety of perspectives: the factory is not, in the end, a hermetic world closed in upon itself.

Translated by Jim Carter

PIERGIORGIO MORI

10 Ecocritical Approaches to Factory Life

What Is Ecocriticism?

Considering the uncertain origin of the term 'ecocriticism' and the wide variety of 'ecocritical' approaches to culture over the past forty years, ecocriticism is both difficult to define and hard to speak of as a fixed practice.[1] Nevertheless, it is useful to begin with Lawrence Buell's affirmation that "è sbagliato credere che l'ecocritica riguardi solo la letteratura che parla di posti rurali e selvaggi" (it is a mistake to believe that ecocriticism concerns only literature about rural and wild places).[2] Such a statement is reminiscent of Elio Vittorini's argument in issue number four (1961) of *Il Menabò di letteratura*[3] that it is not the literature of naturalism – with its focus on factories and companies – that can provide a model for approaching the "cose nuove" (new things)[4] of industrial society, but rather the French *école du regard* of authors like Alain Robbe-Grillet.[5] Vittorini wanted to understand the extent to which the new industrial civilization of the 1950s and 1960s was impacting the general approach to writing literature, thinking and speaking. He knew that millennia before, the

---

1 For an overview of ecocriticism, including its historical development, see Oppermann, S. and Iovino, S. (eds). 2016. *Environmental Humanities: Voices from the Anthropocene*. London: Rowman and Littlefield.
2 This quote comes from a conference held in China. The proceedings were published only in Italian. Buell, L. 2013. "La critica letteraria diventa eco." In *Ecocritica. La letteratura e la crisi del pianeta*. Rome: Donzelli Editore. 4.
3 Issue number four of *Il Menabò* confirmed the birth of a critical reflection on industrial literature in Italian culture.
4 Vittorini, E. 1961. "Industria e letteratura." *Il Menabò di letteratura*, no. 4. 13.
5 Vittorini, E. 1961. "Industria e letteratura." 19.

agricultural revolution had generated a number of literary genres, separated according to historical and geographical context, but with varying links to the practice of farming.

There exists another point of contact between Vittorini's essay and ecocriticism: the rhizomatic effects of the industrial revolution and environmentalism on literature. Vittorini was not interested in discovering the influence of industry on the settings of novels; he wanted to know how the rise of industrial society was modifying literary language in its approach to reality. In a similar way, ecocriticism does not just measure an environmentalism intrinsic to its texts; it explores the importance of the environment and its representation in the literary tradition. Ecocriticism responds to Harold Fromm's warning that "today, man's Faustian posturings take place against a background of arrogant, shocking and suicidal disregard of his roots in the earth."[6]

Did writers of the 1950s and 1960s have a conception of ecology comparable to ours today, as a "insieme dei problemi ambientali e dei provvedimenti da adottare per la salvaguardia dell'equilibrio naturale" (collection of environmental problems and provisions to adopt for safeguarding the natural equilibrium)?[7] If they did, then it was certainly a vague one. With the partial exception of Italo Calvino's short story *La nuvola di smog* (Smog, 1958),[8] Italian industrial literature of the 1950s and 1960s was more concerned with economic development than environmentalism. Nevertheless, as Niccolò Scaffai has indicated,[9] the genre did recognize one properly ecological factor: the transformation of the

---

6   Fromm, H. 1996. "From Transcendence to Obsolescence." *The Ecocriticism Reader: Landmarks in Literary Ecology*. Edited by Cheryll Glotfelty and Harold Fromm. Athens, GA: University of Georgia Press. 39.
7   Scaffai, N. 2017. *Letteratura e ecologia. Forme e temi di una relazione narrata.* Rome: Carocci. 43.
8   The focus of Calvino's short story is not so much ecological as it is ethical and ideological: a Marxist intellectual must live with the torment of his own necessary relation to a capitalist enterprise. Nevertheless, the story's background registers the development of a collective consciousness around questions of ecology in the atomic age.
9   Scaffai, N. 2017. *Letteratura e ecologia.* 183.

landscape, whose representation remained however partially detached from industrial pollution.[10]

We should also consider what Scott Slovic has called "geographic determinism," that is: "the effect of place on language and state of mind."[11] Slovic highlights how different parts of the world – from India to China, Germany to the United States – have developed different ecocritical approaches calibrated to their own cultural and spatial traditions or visions of nature.

Where does Italy fit in? What type of ecocritical approach is suggested by the Italian cultural and literary tradition?

With respect to geographic determinism, and therefore to the development of literature in Italy, one might venture a response by foregrounding the role of nature in the recurring *topos* of the *locus amoenus*. The *locus amoenus* is the domain of the pastoral tradition:[12] that uncontaminated and natural world of the countryside imagined as a space of simplicity, joy and purity that is however a simulacrum and the copy of a non-existent original.

Such a nostalgic tradition of juxtaposing the natural to the artificial (urban) landscape runs through texts like Petrarch's *Canzoniere*, Boccaccio's *Ninfale fiesolano* (The Tale of the Fiesole Nymph) and *Commedia delle Ninfe fiorentine* (Comedy of the Florentine Nymphs) – all 14th C – Jacopo Sannazaro's *Arcadia* (1504), Torquato Tasso's *Aminta* (1573) and Canto VII of the *Gerusalemme liberata* (Jerusalem Delivered, 1581), Angelo Poliziano's *Orfeo* (Orpheus, 1607), Giovan Battista Marino's *Adone* (Adonis, 1623), the work of the Pontifical Academy of Arcadia (17th–20th C), Giovanni Verga and Gabriele d'Annunzio, where the rustic world finally takes on a set of instinctual, almost feral, implications. For more than six centuries, the pastoral tradition provided the background of an uncontaminated nature, as opposed to what was imagined as the corruption of urban life.

---

10   Such was the case in literature (with Carlo Cassola and Paolo Volponi), music (with Adriano Celentano) and television (with Giulio Macchi).
11   Slovic, S. 2015. "Ecocritcism 101: A Basic Introduction to Ecocriticism and Environmental Literature." *Social Sciences & Humanities*, vol. 23. 7.
12   Love, G. 1996. "Revaluing Nature: Toward an Ecological Criticism." *The Ecocriticism Reader*. Edited by Cheryll Glotfelty and Harold Fromm. 231.

From Green to Gray: Ottieri and Cremaschi

With the industrial novels of the twentieth century, something began to change. The transformation of the countryside, the abandonment of farms and the retreat of grazing lands had a profound effect on the imaginations of many writers. The awareness of the Anthropocene began to work its way into their consciousness.[13] Along with Pier Paolo Pasolini's famous fireflies, some of the first elements ushered out by the economic boom were sheep and their designated spaces. Ottiero Ottieri observed the phenomenon in his 1962 journal *Linea gotica* (The Gothic Line):

> Tornando da Sesto, costeggiando la Breda, passo per la Bicocca, invece di fare Viale Monza. Muro lunghissimo, muraglia cinese della Breda, strada d'asfalto, e dall'altro lato di essa, vecchi orti, qualche casetta, prati [...]. Un gregge sparuto di pecore ancora pascola nello zoccolo d'erba rimasto fra l'asfalto e il muro. Da dove departono queste pecore? L'Italia non ha più pascoli?
>
> (Coming back from Sesto, walking alongside the Breda factory, I pass through the Bicocca neighborhood, rather than up Viale Monza. A very long wall, like Breda's own Great Wall of China, an asphalt street, and on the other side of this, old gardens, some little houses, some grasslands [...]. A scant flock of sheep still grazes in the single hoof of grass remaining between the asphalt and the wall. Where are these sheep coming from? Has Italy run out of grazing lands?)[14]

Industrial society (the synecdoche of the factory) snatches up all the pastoral spaces. The world of agriculture declines and dissolves into "spelati campi di football" (barren football fields) and some gardens.[15] Ottieri's question ("L'Italia non ha più pascoli?") reverberates with a sense of lost identity and estrangement.[16] His writings, together with the writings of

---

13   The term 'Anthropocene' was coined by the atmospheric physicist Paul Crutzen and the ecologist Eugen Stoermer to emphasize the strong impact of human activity on the climate and environment.
14   Ottieri, O. 1962. *La linea gotica*. Milan: Bompiani. 60.
15   Cremaschi, I. 1965. *A scopo di lucro*. Milan: Mondadori. 99.
16   This is a curious reversal of the situation denounced by Thomas More in *Utopia* (1516), where it is the practice of enclosure that forces peasants from their lands in

others like Inisero Cremaschi, Paolo Volponi, Calvino, Giovanni Testori, Luciano Bianciardi and Pasolini, charge nature and industry with a chromatic value that invades the space of literature: the traditional green of the *locus amoenus* is displaced by the pervasive tones of a dark gray. In Ottieri's first industrial novel, *Tempi stretti* (Tight Times, 1957), the Sunday air is "nera e gialla" (black and yellow), caught between smog and fog, cold with a blue hue that is "appena intuibile" (barely intuitable).[17] The eclipsed sun contributes to draining any feeling of festivity, foreshadowing the wane of civilization, if not the apocalypse of an era. The colors gray and black return later in *Tempi stretti* as attributes of a factory explicitly connected with the transformation of human moods: "Forse perché le stesse cose, i reparti, i muri, il rumore, la fatica, cambiavano colore secondo lo stato d'animo, il colore dell'animo: La Zanini le appariva grigia e nera" (Maybe because things themselves, the departments, the walls, the noise and the exertion changed color with her mood: To her, the Zanini factory looked gray and black).[18] This is the same impression that Ottieri recounted five years later in his *Linea gotica*, where the writer describes in similar language his own arrival in Milan: "Solo, appoggiato con la testa sul tavolino dello scompartimento, dalla stazione scendo su una Milano nera dentro una malinconia nera" (Alone and with my head leaning on the little table inside the train car, I enter the station and descend on a black Milan in a black melancholy).[19]

Ottieri's Milan is strikingly similar to that of Inisero Cremaschi, a writer whom literary critics have historically marginalized, but who is today ripe for rediscovery. In Cremaschi's 1962 novel *Pagato per tacere* (Paid to Keep Quiet), the protagonist cannot help but remark on "i tetti di Milano, visti nella lente affumicata del pulviscolo nero" (the rooftops of Milan, seen through the smoky lens of a black dust).[20] Such a representation serves to blot out all potential for geo-local specificity, diluting the Milanese

---

      order to make room for grazing. More's analysis has typically been understood as marking the birth of what would become, two centuries later, the proletariat class.
17   Ottieri, O. 1957. *Tempi stretti*. Turin: Einaudi. 99.
18   Ottieri, O. 1957. *Tempi stretti*. 198.
19   Ottieri, O. 1962. *La linea gotica*. 6.
20   Cremaschi, I. 1962. *Pagato per tacere*. Milan: Silva. 21.

peripheries and the city's skyscrapers that reach beyond the steeple of the cathedral with its centuries-old history that slips into an indistinct and social-democratic limbo.[21] Milan becomes just another northern European city, prefiguring Cremaschi's 1965 novel *A scopo di lucro* (Profit-Making).

The protagonist of *A scopo di lucro* is Novello, whose boss charges him with tracking down an attractive woman, Annamaria, glimpsed on the street. A series of vague clues leads Novello to undertake a personal and sociological adventure across two colliding worlds: the advancing Milan of the economic boom and the retreating Milan of the organized crime group "leggera."[22] Cremaschi describes the Milanese air as "fredda e maligna" (cold and malign), with "mele marce" (bad apples) next to "mele sane" (good apples) and little old women with no teeth and withered roses.[23] While this putrefied world awaits redemption, some wonder if the cure might prove worse than the disease: "Costruiscono qui, eh? Fra qualche anno queste topaie non ci saranno più. Case nuove, moderne, piene di luce, basta con queste stamberghe puzzolenti. Senti un po', ma adesso dove andiamo?" (They're building here, huh? In a few years these ratholes won't exist anymore. New houses, modern ones, full of light, enough with these stinky hovels. But what about us? Where will we go?).[24] These are the questions of Sandrino, a boy from the peripheries who offers to help Novello in his quest. The economic boom has little to do with the dissolving Milan of the peripheries, where the landscape teems with sadness and anonymous homogenization, while the Milan of European modernity is not quite the Milan it used to be. Upon returning to his office, Novello remarks that the city is "sempre uguale, le ore non portano variazioni, le due finestre spalancano sul grigio della casa di fronte una proiezione di altre finestre in fila, uffici come il suo, si specchino gli uni negli altri come imitandosi nei desolanti episodi di tutti i giorni, identici in mille altri uffici di Milano, d'Italia, d'Europa, del mondo intero" (always the same, the hours bring no

---

21   Cremaschi, I. 1962. *Pagato per tacere*. 21.
22   'Leggera' (or 'ligera') was an organized crime group active in Milan during the first half of the twentieth century. The group was composed mostly of petty criminals like cheaters, thieves, prostitutes and their protectors.
23   Cremaschi, I. 1965. *A scopo di lucro*. 17.
24   Cremaschi, I. 1965. *A scopo di lucro*. 23.

variety, these two windows project more windows onto the grayness of the house across the way, offices like those are reflected in these; they imitate each other in the desolating episodes of everyday life, just like a thousand other offices in Milan, in Italy, in Europe, in the whole world).[25] Novello sets out for the squalid periphery to explore a world of the senses, where he feels attacked by "folate puzzolenti che dialogano nell'aria" (smelly gusts that whip through the air) and "hanno un punto d'origine, certamente nelle fabbriche che stendono un corpo lungo e seghettato all'orizzonte, dopo ciuffi d'alberi e colline di macerie, rifiuti quasi a pelo di spelati campi di football per ragazzi" (certainly have their origin in the factories that spread their long and serrated bodies across the horizon, beyond tufts of trees and hills of rubble, right next to barren football fields for kids).[26] The intricate folds of Cremaschi's language reveal an aura of uncertainty around a recurrent metaphor of grayness: gray is a mixture of black and white, neither one nor the other, with a hybridity that is both physiognomic – "un uomo semicalvo" (a semi-bald man), the author writes[27] – and ideological, just like the paintings above the couch in a house Novello visits, depicting "Lenin ossuto e cadaverico" (a bony and cadaverous Lenin) or "il faccione sbigottito di papa Giovanni XXIII" (the dismayed face of Pope John XXIII).[28] Its hybridity reverberates in the life choices of Annamaria's friend Mirella, "che ha già ventott'anni, fidanzata da quattro, con un meccanico che guadagna bene ma non si decide a sposarla" (who is already twenty-eight and has been engaged for four years to a mechanic who makes a good living but won't make up his mind to marry her).[29] In this delicately balanced world, human beings have even less imagination than nature, and love is not an irrational passion or choice of devotion, but something to control and homogenize: "Amore, sì l'amore, d'accordo, ma non sposarsi troppo presto, e soprattutto non avere troppi figli" (Love, sure, love, fine, but don't get married too soon, and above all, don't have too many children).[30]

25 Cremaschi, I. 1965. *A scopo di lucro*. 82.
26 Cremaschi, I. 1965. *A scopo di lucro*. 99.
27 Cremaschi, I. 1965. *A scopo di lucro*. 128.
28 Cremaschi, I. 1965. *A scopo di lucro*. 128.
29 Cremaschi, I. 1965. *A scopo di lucro*. 145.
30 Cremaschi, I. 1965. *A scopo di lucro*. 146.

A scopo di lucro is a far cry from the pastoral or bucolic. In Cremaschi's world, what matters most is "i soldi, i capitali, la lotta per arrichirsi" (money, capital, the struggle to get rich).[31] Here "le inique corti" (the sinful courts) of the *Gerusalemme liberata* have been replaced by the corruption of bourgeois and neo-capitalist society.[32] This leads to the disintegration of Aristotle's ideal man – a 'political animal' – and to the creation of a "un uomo sazio di tutto" (fully satiated man) who wants to "impoverire gli altri per arrichire se stesso" (impoverish others in order to enrich himself) but ends up alone because "chi è spietato vive in solitudine" (he who is cruel lives in solitude).[33] Such solitude is the defining feature of a world directed (already in 1965) toward a neutral and dystopic globalization. The events of *A scopo di lucro* have little to do with the specificities of Milan: they could take place, as Cremaschi confirms, "in capo al mondo, nella periferia di Rio de Janeiro, se qui ci fosse il mare, di Tokio, di Alessandria d'Egitto" (at the ends of the earth, in the peripheries of Rio de Janeiro, if [Milan had] a sea, or Tokyo, or Alexandria) – it is the sea, not humanity, that makes the difference.[34]

The chromatic and antipastoral implications of industrial society were already present in Ottieri's 1959 novel *Donnarumma all'assalto* (The Men at the Gate). In an autobiographical passage, the narrator marks a turning point in the chromatic tone of personal experience: "il sole nella fabbrica, il cielo, il verde e il mare, benché li ami, non mi convincono" (it seems strange to me to bring the brightness of sun, sky and sea, and the greenery of lawns and trees, right into a factory, much as I love them).[35] Moreover, he confesses, "l'industria l'ho conosciuta nel nord e la caratteristica di essa rimane sempre quella d'essere grigia, se è un industria vera. Le officine le ho sempre viste nere e senza spazio, come se la loro forza fosse proprio questa" (my experience of industry has been in the north, where, if it is true

---

31 Cremaschi, I. 1965. *A scopo di lucro*. 155.
32 Tasso, T. 1992. *Gerusalemme liberata*. Milan: Mondadori. 152. Tasso, T. 2000. *Jerusalem Delivered*. Translated by Anthony M. Esolen. Baltimore: Johns Hopkins University Press. 136.
33 Cremaschi, I. 1965. *A scopo di lucro*. 165.
34 Cremaschi, I. 1965. *A scopo di lucro*. 7.
35 Ottieri, O. 1959. *Donnarumma all'assalto*. Milan: Bompiani. 24. Ottieri, O. 1962. *The Men at the Gate*. Boston: Houghton Mifflin. 18.

industry, it is always dark in hue. Workshops to me are dim and crowded, as though their very strength lay in these characteristics).³⁶ In the narrator's eyes, the pleasant and the beautiful are simply irreconcilable with the industrial. If it rained, "un raro grigio confondeva il cielo con il mare e rendeva grigio, massiccio anche lo stabilimento nonostante le sue pareti colorate, i suoi tetti leggeri. Lo stabilimento pareva coperto dalla sua aria giusta, industriale" (an unusual gray mist blended sky and sea in one, and made the factory buildings look drab and massive, despite their colored walls and light roofs. They almost took on an appropriately industrial air).³⁷ This is a surprising image of the Olivetti factory in Pozzuoli ('Santa Maria' in the novel), which was supposed to represent a simbiotic relationship between nature and industry. The Olivetti factory in Pozzuoli was designed by Luigi Cosenza as a symbol of the company's progressive attempt to turn the industrial world into a maker of beauty: it was a statement of aesthetic taste in a space unaccustomed to conjugating the artificial with the natural. The factory of *Donnarumma all'assalto* is described as "un castello orizzontale di vetro fluorescente di luci fredde" (a long castle of glass, lit by its fluorescent lights)³⁸ that becomes the background for the president's speech:

> [la fabbrica] si è elevata, nell'idea dell'architetto, in rispetto alla bellezza dei luoghi e affinché fosse di conforto nel lavoro di ogni giorno. [...] Abbiamo voluto che la natura accompagnasse la vita della fabbrica [...] concepita sulla misura dell'uomo [...] strappato alla terra e alla natura dalla civiltà delle macchine.
>
> (the architect's aim has been to build [the factory] in harmony with the beauty of the place, in order that, in your daily work, this beauty should be a comfort to you. [...] We wanted the life of the factory to be in touch with nature [...] conceived in scale with man [...] torn from the land and from contact with nature by the machine age.)³⁹

---

36 Ottieri, O. 1959. *Donnarumma all'assalto*. 24. Ottieri, O. 1962. *The Men at the Gate*. 18.
37 Ottieri, O. 1959. *Donnarumma all'assalto*. 41. Ottieri, O. 1962. *The Men at the Gate*. 34.
38 Ottieri, O. 1959. *Donnarumma all'assalto*. 38. Ottieri, O. 1962. *The Men at the Gate*. 78.
39 Ottieri, O. 1959. *Donnarumma all'assalto*. 117–118. Ottieri, O. 1962. *The Men at the Gate*. 106–107.

With this speech, the president attempts to reconcile the production of beauty with the need to maintain a people-oriented and friendly environment. But does his insistence on people-centered development represent a genuine dedication to human wellbeing or a rhetorical distraction from less charitable goals? In the eyes of the president – a stand-in for Adriano Olivetti, the Enlightened industrialist *par excellence* – nature is a force to be conquered and bent toward the needs of machine civilization: it must be subordinated to the superiority of the human mind. The environmental sensibilities of today remained underdeveloped in the 1950s, while the neo-humanism instilled in Ottieri's novel was not a product of geographies like Pozzuoli: "una civiltà di pescatori senza barca e di contadini senza terra" (a social order consisting of fishermen without boats and peasants without land).[40] *Donnarumma all'assalto* represents these people in Arcadian tones: they are "intontiti nella natura e nel cielo, paghi di una loro felicità da non distruggere" (dazed, suffocated, by their natural surroundings, yet satisfied with a happiness of their own that it would be a pity to destroy), but at the same time "pongono esigenze cittadine e urbane" (their needs [...] are clearly urban).[41] Such disorientation generates a set of novel equilibria between the landscape, the environment and the natural world that, in the most extreme cases, leads some employees to suffer from alienation and neuroses.[42]

Memoriale: The Radical Wilderness of Albino Saluggia

The quintessential victim of this mental crevice opened up by the presence of the factory in nature is Albino Saluggia, the protagonist of Volponi's novel *Memoriale* (My Troubles Began, 1962). The moving confession of

---

40   Ottieri, O. 1959. *Donnarumma all'assalto*. 151. Ottieri, O. 1962. *The Men at the Gate*. 140.

41   Ottieri, O. 1959. *Donnarumma all'assalto*. 165. Ottieri, O. 1962. *The Men at the Gate*. 154–155.

42   Scaffai, N. 2017. *Letteratura e ecologia*. 32–33.

Ecocritical Approaches to Factory Life

a neurotic worker suffering from tuberculosis, Volponi based the story on his own managerial experience at Olivetti, but also on his childhood memories from Urbino (Le Marche): a peaceful and Arcadian geography defined by the soft colors of the central Italian landscape. But Volponi is less chromatic than Ottieri and Cremaschi: he is more concerned with the classical juxtaposition between the country and the city, which in *Memoriale* takes on the guise of an opposition between the natural world and the artificial factory.[43] In Albino's hallucinations, Lake Candia (Piedmont) becomes a synecdoche for all of nature, transforming itself into a living being that can converse with the protagonist. The city is nothing but the strenuous adaptation to the artificial: Albino even distinguishes between a profound respect for the countryside and the illegitimate appropriation it suffers at the hands of peasants. Those who work the land also destroy it, "come certi animali che rovinano il legno" (like those animals that gnaw on trees and ruin the timber),[44] and as Albino retreats to Lake Candia, he exalts the wilderness of the countryside, a virgin and thriving force that he believes is better left to its own devices.[45] Lake Candia is never still: it develops, expands and breathes, articulating the fragile existence of the neurotic Albino, for whom it becomes a sign of redemption and utopian salvation. Albino's infantile faith in a protective mother nature is split apart when he witnesses one fish devour another. The experience breaks the spell of illusion, revealing the true identity of a nature directed by implacable laws and frightening Albino into a vision of identification with the dying fish: "non c'era nulla da fare, anche per me; anch'io muovevo soltanto l'acqua, destinato alla fine" (there was nothing I could do, not even for myself. I could only thrash the water like the dead fish, destined to die).[46] Lake Candia remains forever uncontaminated, but also unresponsive to Albino's cry for help. In the final pages of *Memoriale*, he returns from Turin to observe the lake closely: "respirava

---

43 The relationship between the country and the city is central to at least two of Volponi's novels: Volponi, P. 1965. *La macchina mondiale*. Milan: Garzanti. Volponi, P. 1974. *Corporale*. Turin: Einaudi.
44 Volponi, P. 1962. *Memoriale*. 8–9. Volponi, P. 1964. *My Troubles Began*. 8.
45 Scaffai, N. 2017. *Letteratura e ecologia*. 47–50.
46 Volponi, P. 1962. *Memoriale*. 249. Volponi, P. 1964. *My Troubles Began*. 186.

piano [...] chiuso dentro le sue sponde [...] il suo collore non brillava e non si spandeva all'intorno" (breathing softly between its banks [...] it didn't shine, and its reflection didn't spread along the edges). It is in this moment that Albino understands – as he says – that "nessuno può arrivare in mio aiuto" (no one can help me now).[47]

Conclusion: The Promise of Ecocriticism

The approach to ecocriticism adopted in this chapter is merely indicative of its exegetical and epistemological power. Ecocriticism does not stop at the relationship between human beings and the environment; it goes far beyond this by forcing us to rethink, at the level of industrial civilization, both the pastoral tradition and the *topos* of the *locus amoenus*. In this sense, ecocriticism responds to Vittorini's challenge that writers learn to "vedere a qual punto le 'cose nuove' tra cui oggi viviamo, direttamente o indirettamente, per opera dell'ultima rivoluzione industriale abbiano un riscontro di 'novità' nell'immaginazione umana" (see how the 'new things' among which we live, directly or indirectly, thanks to the last industrial revolution have been reflected in the 'novelties' of the human imagination).[48] On the one hand, the promise of ecocriticism lies in its potential to set in motion a series of responses to similar concerns. On the other hand, the genre of the industrial novel – with all of its questions, ambiguities and confusions – is a favorable frontier for the development in Italian literary studies of an ecocritical awareness.

Translated by Jim Carter

---

47   Volponi, P. 1962. *Memoriale*. 308. Volponi, P. 1964. *My Troubles Began*. 231.
48   Vittorini, E. 1961. "Industria e letteratura." 13.

PAOLO CHIRUMBOLO

11 The City, the Countryside and the 'Great Transformation' in Italian Industrial Literature

The discussion of the importance of space and spatial representations in literary and cultural studies has become, in recent years, quite conspicuous. The so-called 'spatial turn' of the mid-1990s[1] called into question the hegemony of the category of time in literary criticism and paved the way for the development of modern theories that placed emphasis on place and space in literature.[2] However, in order to fully appreciate the impact that space theory has had on the study of literature and the humanities, it is necessary to mention such precursors as Joseph Franck, Gaston Bachelard, Gilbert Durand, Jurij Lotman, Maurice Blanchot and, above all, Mikhail Bakhtin. It is the work of the Russian thinker that established space as a key element to the analysis of literary texts. In "Forms of Time and of the Chronotope in the Novel," Bakhtin defined the chronotope as "the intrinsic connectedness of temporal and spatial relationships that are artistically expressed in literature."[3] The concept

---

[1] The American geographer Edward Soja, one of the most prominent spatial theorists, has defined the 'spatial turn' in the humanities and social sciences as "a response to a longstanding if often unperceived ontological and epistemological bias that privileged time over space in all the human sciences, including spatial disciplines like geography and architecture." Soja, E. 2008. "Taking Space Personally." *The Spatial Turn: Interdisciplinary Perspectives*. Edited by Santa Arias and Barbara Warf. London: Taylor and Francis. 12.

[2] For a good introduction to the study of literature and space in which the author outlines different theoretical approaches, from Bertrand Westphal's 'geocritique' to Franco Moretti's 'literary geography,' see Iacoli, G. 2008. *La percezione narrative dello spazio. Teorie e rappresentazioni contemporanee*. Rome: Carocci.

[3] Bakhtin, M. 1981. "Forms of Time and of the Chronotope in the Novel." *The Dialogic Imagination*. Translated by Caryl Emerson and Michael Holquist. Austin: University of Texas Press. 84.

of the chronotope, and how time and, more importantly, space is represented in literature has been widely used in literary criticism, as it draws attention to the physical locations in which stories take place and characters experience their lives. Among the chronotopes identified by Bakhtin is the "idyllic novel," a particular narrative genre characterized by the unity of space and time and by the organic and wholesome relationship between people and nature.[4] After identifying different kinds of idylls (the love idyll, the family idyll, the idyll with a focus on agricultural labor), Bakthin writes:

> No matter how these types of idylls, and variations within these types, may differ from one another, they all have [...] several features in common, all determined by their general relationship to the immanent unity of folkloric time. This finds expression predominantly in the special relationship that time has to space in the idyll: an organic fastening down, a grafting of life and its events to a place, to a familiar territory with all its nooks and crannies, its familiar mountains, valleys, fields, rivers and forests, and one's own home. Idyllic life and its events are inseparable from this concrete, spatial corner of the world where the fathers and grandfathers lived and where one's children and their children will live.[5]

I will argue that in many respects what several postwar Italian industrial writers describe in their works is the end of that idyll: the end of a world governed by the cycle of nature. A space that was once cohesive and coherent, full of memories and local identities, is in these works disintegrating, disappearing and dying.[6]

Giorgio Bigatti and Giuseppe Lupo, co-editors of the anthology *Fabbrica di carta*, acknowledge the importance of spatial representations in industrial literature and dedicate an entire section of their work to "Panorami dell'Italia industriale" (Landscapes of Industrial Italy), featuring literary samples from authors such as Ottiero Ottieri, Luigi Davì, Lucio Mastronardi, Elio Pagliarani, Carlo Bernari, Giovanni Testori and Paolo Volponi. In the sub-section "Città industriali e periferie" (Industrial Cities and the Suburbs), the two editors explain:

---

4   Bakhtin, M. 1981. "Forms of Time and of the Chronotope in the Novel." 224.
5   Bakhtin, M. 1981. "Forms of Time and of the Chronotope in the Novel." 225.
6   Turri, E. 2004. *Il paesaggio e il silenzio*. Venice: Marsilio. 229.

Il primo dispiegarsi del processo di industrializzazione nel secondo Novecento […] ha sconvolto il tradizionale assetto delle città e la loro imagine. L'inurbamento ha provocato un'incontrollata espansione delle periferie a danno delle campagne circostanti. Gli iconemi della modernità (capannoni, ciminiere, officine, palazzi in cemento armato) hanno preso rapidamente il sopravvento su prati, campi coltivati, rogge, canali, viottoli, orti. Come registrano le pagine di Calvino, Ottieri, Testori, Bianciardi, Sinisgalli e degli altri scrittori di questa sezione, la crescita e le trasformazioni urbane hanno modificato abitudini, stili di vita, bisogni individuali e collettivi. Tutto ciò ha ridefinito nuovi modelli antropologici che sono stati lo specchio delle contraddizioni di un paese, come l'Italia, a lungo diviso tra regioni a vocazione contadina (la dorsale appenninica e le aree interne del Mezzogiorno) e centri di più pronunciato sviluppo industriale (Milano, Torino, Genova, Napoli).

(The industrialization process of the second half of the twentieth century in its full force […] subverted the traditional layout of cities and their appearance. The urban drift provoked an unfettered expansion of suburbs, to the detriment of the countryside. The symbols[7] of modernity (warehouses, chimneys, repair shops, buildings made of concrete) quickly took over the space of grass fields, farmed fields, water channels, alleys, vegetable gardens. As recorded by the pages of Calvino, Ottieri, Testori, Bianciardi, Sinisgalli and other writers, the growth and urban transformations modified habits, lifestyles, individual and collective needs. All this redefined new anthropological models of a country, Italy, for a long time divided between regions with an agricultural vocation (the Apennines and the rural South) and industrial cities (Milan, Turin, Genoa, Naples.)[8]

The impact of industrialism on the Italian territory and countryside can hardly be exaggerated. In *A Short Environmental History of Italy*, Gabriella Corona outlines the various stages of Italian modernization and its impact on the environment. Corona analyzes Italy's industrialization process before and after the unification of the Italian kingdom, discusses the transition of Italy into modernity and addresses the role of environmentalism in contemporary Italy. More importantly, Corona scrutinizes the ecological

---

7   Giorgio Bigatti and Giuseppe Lupo use the term "iconemi," a reference to Turri's semiotic analysis of space and landscapes. For Turri, an "iconema" is an essential element of a given landscape, one that defines its natural or human vocation. See Turri, E. 2004. "La forza degli iconemi." *Il paesaggio e il silenzio*. 127–129.
8   Bigatti, G. and Lupo, G. (eds). 2013. *Fabbrica di carta. I libri che raccontano l'Italia industriale*. Rome: Laterza. 84.

implications of industrialism and economic development during the republican period. As Corona puts it:

> An extraordinary growth began in all sectors of the country's productive and everyday life, including industrial activities, urban areas, transportation, infrastructure, agriculture and families' consumption models. This epochal transition marked the beginning of a period of widespread affluence [...]. This exceptional improvement of life condition, however, came at a cost. The advent of an energivorous society determined very strong pressure by human activities on the environment.[9]

This dramatic and accelerated modernization, described by Eugenio Turri as the "Grande Trasformazione" (Great Transformation) had considerable repercussions on the Italian environment and society.[10] Cities grew, in size and population, at a rate never known before, heavy industries expanded all over the peninsula (from Sesto San Giovanni near Milan to Gela in Sicily) and began employing – and wasting – a vast amount of energy and natural resources, the countryside became extremely industrialized and heavily impacted by the use of chemical products and workers abandoned rural areas to move to more industrialized ones. The works of authors such as Ottieri, Volponi, Bianciardi, Alberto Bevilacqua,[11] Italo Calvino and Franco Fortini, just to mention a few, portray this transition and highlight its social, political, environmental and psychological consequences.

As Ronald Bourneuf and Réal Ouellet note, "space in a novel is not just a decorative element. It is expressed in very specific forms, it carries several meanings, and in some cases it is the main reason for the work."[12] The representative texts analyzed in this chapter use what Giulio Iacoli calls "indici spaziali" (indexical spatial signs)[13] corresponding to rural,

---

9   Corona, G. 2017. *A Short Environmental History of Italy: Variety and Vulnerability*. Winwick, Cambridgeshire: The White Horse Press. 59.
10 Turri, E. 2004. *Il paesaggio e il silenzio*. 10.
11 Alberto Bevilacqua's name is usually not associated with industrial literature. Although I will not argue that Bevilacqua's *La Califfa* should be included in this canon, I will, on the other hand, suggest that some of the elements of the novel lend themselves to an industrial reading.
12 Bourneuf, R. and Ouellet, R. 1976. *L'universo del romanzo*. Turin: Einaudi. 94.
13 Iacoli, G. 2008. *La percezione narrativa dello spazio*. 24.

urban or industrial landscapes that are not just backdrops to their stories and characters but are essential parts of their narration. In fact, space (in all its different facets) can be considered one of the most important characters in these works. In what follows, I will discuss how the poetics (and organization) of space informs at a very deep level the writers' works and their narrative/textual strategies,[14] and I will analyze how they depict the disruption of the once-harmonic and balanced relationship between the city and the countryside.

Ottieri's *La linea gotica* (The Gothic Line, 1962) is a good case in point, as it illustrates well the interplay between spatial/geographical representations and rhetorical strategies. Both the title of the book and its subtitle – *Taccuino (1948–1958)* (Notebook (1948–1958)) – immediately provide the reader with crucial information regarding the nature and content of the text. The Gothic Line was the last line of defense of the German army during the invasion of Italy. It was a fortified line built in 1944 that stretched from Massa and Carrara (in Tuscany) all the way to the Adriatic Sea near Pesaro (in the Marches), dividing the Center-North of Italy from the rest of the country. Since then, the term 'Gothic Line' has become synonymous with division, fragmentation and isolation. It is a spatial metaphor that conjures up images of conflict and separation, including the struggle to overcome a sense of detachment and contradiction. It is exactly in this sense that Ottieri uses this image in *La linea gotica*. The beginning of the book is self-evident:

> Una linea gotica, mentale, per me taglia a mezzo l'Italia. Ci vivo a cavallo. I dilemmi spirituali, dell'anima, si proiettano nella geografia. Una scelta interiore si camuffa da scelta di una città e non è nemmeno del tutto un camuffamento. Roma è il mio essere, Milano il mio dover essere. Sogno una terza città che le unisca, dove avere tutto, conciliare tutto, e stare una buona volta tranquillo.
>
> (For me, a mental gothic line cuts Italy in two. I live on it. Dilemmas of the spirit, of the soul, are projected on the geography. An internal choice is disguised as a choice among cities, and even then, it is not completely disguised. Rome is my being, Milan

---

14   For more on the rhetoric of space, see Moretti, F. 2010. "Spazio e stile, geografie dell'intreccio e storie del Terzo." *Il senso dello spazio. Lo spatial turn nei metodi e nelle teorie letterarie*. Edited by Flavio Sorrentino. Rome: Armando Editore. 69–84.

is my must-be. I dream of a third city that unites these two, where I can have everything, reconcile everything and be at peace for once.)[15]

In this manner, *La linea gotica* establishes a crucial link between geography and psychology, between physical and spiritual landscapes. The "dilemma dell'anima" (dilemma of the soul), as Ottieri calls his neurotic relationship with the world, is mirrored in how the writer experiences and sees the space around him.[16]

Rome and Milan are the two epicenters of Ottieri's spatial biography. Rome, his birthplace, is the place where the writer grows up, where he spends the first twenty-three years of his life, where he has "la letteratura, la casa agiata dei miei, la nevrosi di figlio unico" (literature, the comfortable house of my parents and the neurosis of an only child).[17] Rome is the city where the young Ottiero reads Marx and speculates about working classes and factory workers. As Furio Colombo puts it, Rome is also "la città bianca di sole e colma di vacanza, ma inutile, perché non ci sono né il lavoro né i lavoratori a Roma" (the city white from the sun and filled with vacations, but useless because there is neither work nor workers in Rome).[18] Milan, on the other hand, is the city of business, the capital of Italian economy, the heart of the industrial boom. It is the place where the author can finally see, first-hand, what he is so unwaveringly looking for: factories, workers, union leaders, history in the making. And if Milan turns out to be cold, gray and dark, it is still a city full of life and energy. Milan, he notes, "non è colorata, è monotona. Ma è viva. Ci nascono le situazioni più nuove e tese, complicate dalla civiltà moderna, in mezzo alle quali è bello stare" (is not colored, it is monotonous. But it is alive. The newest and tensest situations are born there, complicated by modern civilization, in the middle of which it is beautiful to be).[19]

La linea gotica is, as its subtitle makes clear, a *taccuino*: a notebook, where Ottieri records personal impressions, metaliterary annotations,

---

15 Ottieri, O. 2001. *La linea gotica. Taccuino (1948–1958)*. Parma: Guanda. 23.
16 Ottieri, O. 2001. *La linea gotica*. 23.
17 Ottieri, O. 2001. *La linea gotica*. 23.
18 Colombo, F. 2001. "L'Italia di Ottieri." In Ottieri, O. *La linea gotica*. 11.
19 Ottieri, O. 2001. *La linea gotica*. 196.

political comments and accurate, detailed descriptions of a disappearing countryside. The years it chronicles are those of the Great Transformation, or what Turri called a "grandioso e stravolgente processo di mutamento" (grandiose and tremendous process of mutation) that changed Italy's territory in a dramatic fashion.[20] Using a realistic and matter-of-fact style – a style that fits the diarist nature of the text – Ottieri records, in real time, the modifications of the Italian territory. The text is rife with descriptions of industrial sites, of changing neighborhoods and of city streets modified by commercial activities. Take, for example, a paragraph in which Ottieri describes Sesto San Giovanni, a little 'borgo' (village) on the outskirts of Milan:[21]

> Anche Sesto S. Giovanni, Stalingrado, cittadella rossa, è Italia. È Lombardia e le tracce dello spirito ottocentesco, manzoniano, continuano negli angoli di verde, nascosti nel piccolo ventre sconosciuto e pittoresco del paese, in una piazza col mercato, in stretti orizzonti ancora aperti verso la larva di campagna invece che verso la Falck. La Sesto vecchia è ancora un borgo lombardo con l'acciottolato di sassi. [...]
>
> Guardando il nord a sinistra, le è cresciuta accanto una Sesto nuova, agglomerato informe dall'Ottocento a oggi, prolungamento violento della città, disarmonico. [...] Sesto nuova è senza quiete e senza misura, né piccola né grande; né città né paese. Non ha anima, né presente, né remota.
>
> (Even Sesto S. Giovanni, Stalingrad, the red citadel, is Italy. It is Lombardy, and the traces of the nineteenth century spirit, Manzonian, continue in the patches of green, hidden in the little, unknown and picturesque stomach of the town, in a *piazza* with a market, in narrow horizons still open toward the larva of the countryside, rather than toward the Falck. Old Sesto is still a Lombard village with cobblestone roads. [...]
>
> Looking north, to the left, a new Sesto has grown up around her: a shapeless agglomeration from the nineteenth century to today, a violent extension of the city, disharmonic. [...] New Sesto is restless and without measure, neither small nor large, neither city nor town. It has no soul, neither present nor remote.)[22]

20   Turri, E. 1979. *Semiologia del paesaggio italiano*. Milan: Longanesi. iii.
21   The urban and industrial outskirts of Milan are also described in Ottieri's first novel, *Tempi stretti* (1957). See, for example, Ottieri, O. 1981. *Tempi stretti*. Bergamo: Minerva Italica. 20–21.
22   Ottieri, O. 2001. *La linea gotica*. 76.

This transition to modernity is, for Ottieri, chaotic and violent. The new industrial space appears amorphous and soulless, and the fragmentation of the old world further enhances Ottieri's own sense of isolation. In many ways, what Ottieri (and other writers of the time – the name of Calvino with his *Marcovaldo* comes to mind) describes here is the subversion of the "human/non-human space" paradigm identified by French anthropologists Francoise Paul-Lévy and Marion Segaud.[23] If in pre-industrial societies the human space is the *locus* of order, security and social life, while the non-human space is the one of chaos, uncertainty and danger, after the industrial revolution this paradigm appears reversed. As Ottieri shows, the human space has lost its protective appeal: it has become a non-place, and it looks like an unintelligible labyrinth. "L'espansione delle metropoli" (The expansion of metropolis), Gianfranco Rubino writes, "è lungi dall'essere rassicurante [...] costituisce essa stessa un fattore di disumanizzazione, di anonimato, di omologazione" (is far from being comforting [...] it is a factor that contributes to dehumanization, anonymity, and homologation).[24]

To overcome this meaninglessness, Ottieri tries to establish a very physical relationship with the landscape. Obsessed by the unwavering desire to experience and understand the space around him – not just intellectually, but also with his body[25] – the narrating subject embarks on several trips (he calls them, rather emphatically, 'pilgrimages') during which he explores industrial sites, visits factories and roams through city outskirts or abandoned country landscapes. To own the landscape, Ottieri must live it directly. As his daughter Maria Pace has observed:

---

23 Paul-Lévy, F. and Segaud, M. 1983. *Anthropologie de l'espace*. Paris: Centre George Pompidou. 37.
24 Rubino, G. 2010. "Spazi naturali, spazi culturali." *Il senso dello spazio*. Edited by Flavio Sorrentino. Rome: Armando Editore. 50.
25 "Giro, giro per Milano, dietro al mio piccolo lavoro tipografico e giornalistico – che mi lascia libertà – ma soprattutto dietro al bisogno accanito di scoperta e di coscienza della città (non più di me)" (I go around Milan, following my little typographic and journalistic job, a job that leaves me a lot of freedom. But especially I go around following my stubborn need to discover the city and be aware of it (and no longer of myself)). Ottieri, O. 2001. *La linea gotica*. 81.

La domenica [Ottieri] esplora le periferie, va in pellegrinaggio a Sesto San Giovanni, sui luoghi delle grandi fabbriche, la Falck, la Pirelli, la Breda. 'Sono un esploratore, cioè un uomo inquieto,' scriverà nel top secret journal 1967–1977; 'trovo la quiete soltanto quando il mondo che voglio esplorare non ha più mistero.'

(On Sundays [Ottieri] explores the peripheries, he goes on pilgrimages to Sesto San Giovanni, to the places of the grand factories, Falck, Pirelli, Breda. 'I am an explorer, that is, a restless man,' he would write in his top-secret journal in 1967–1977; 'I find rest only when the world I want to explore is no longer mysterious.')[26]

Ottieri's is not the leisurely stroll of the bourgeois subject: the *flaneur* looking for aesthetic and spiritual epiphanies. Rather, it is the wandering of "un nomade, un drifter, che finisce per cogliere il rapporto ormai imploso fra comunità territoriale e comunità relazionale" (a nomad, a drifter, who ends up grasping the by-now imploded relation between territorial community and relational community).[27] Ottieri's psychological restlessness and neurotic connection with the world (and with himself) mirrors the futility of a territory that, under the pressure of industrialism, changes quickly to become unrecognizable and incongruous, if not hostile and unfriendly.

A similar manic relationship between character and landscape is found in Volponi's *Memoriale* (My Troubles Began, 1962). In this novel, the disintegration of Bakhtin's spatial idyllic chronotope is on full display, and the whole text is imbued with a melancholic sense of loss and disorientation. As Alfredo Luzi has aptly suggested:

In *Memoriale* Albino Saluggia si colloca al centro della contraddizione tra la tendenza alla reificazione insita nell'esaltazione del lavoro in fabbrica, secondo la teoria del capitalismo avanzato, e la nostalgia per un mondo, idillico e georgico, che sta scomparendo ma che egli ha interiorizzato e alle cui immagini ricorre quando desidera difendersi dagli attacchi della società, tutelando la propria diversità.

(In *Memoriale*, Albino Saluggia is right at the center of the contradiction between the tendency to reification of factory life and work, typical of advanced capitalism, and the nostalgia for an idyllic and pastoral world that is disappearing but that the

---

26   Ottieri, M. P. 2009. "Cronologia." In Ottieri, O. *Opere scelte*. Milan: Mondadori. LXX-LXXI.
27   Nesi, C. 2013. "Due culture, due città. *La linea gotica*." *Le linee gotiche di Ottieri. Percorsi testuali*. Edited by Maria Antonietta Grignani. Novara: Interlinea. 32.

protagonist has internalized so much that he keeps returning to it in order to defend himself from the attacks of society and safeguard his diversity.)[28]

In a telling paragraph, *Memoriale*'s paranoid protagonist and narrating 'I,' Albino Saluggia, talks to a factory workmate Palmarucci, who complains about the city, its emptiness – "stanno tutti dentro la fabbrica" (Everyone is in the factory) – and its lack of life – "È una città questa? Non c'è nemmeno il corso dove la gente vada a passeggio e si possa vederla" (Is this a city? There isn't even a promenade where people go walking to see and be seen).[29] Albino thinks about his hometown, its quiet comfort and how much he dislikes "il disordine della città" (the disorder of the city),[30] then he adds:

> Se avessi fatto il contadino e fossi rimasto a Candia, pensavo, non mi sarei ammalato. Avrei potuto comperare altra terra, prendere un trattore e mettere su una stalla. Avrei potuto vivere per conto mio e decidere ogni giorno il mio lavoro libero per i campi. Le stelle segnano le stagioni e quando seminare, rivoltare la terra, mietere e tagliare i fieni. Le piogge gonfiano i semi e aprono i solchetti al sole che viene dopo. Avrei potuto cambiar strada dietro una lepre o risalire i fossi del confine. Scuotere gli alberi da frutta o sedermi e dare una voce a quelli degli altri campi. [...] Invece ho accettato il lavoro della fabbrica. Mi è stato imposto dai progetti degli altri, che mi hanno scelto come la loro vittima. Lavorare a ore, un minuto dietro l'altro [...] ed essere confuso tra tutti gli altri.

> (If I had become a farmer and stayed in Candia I wouldn't have gotten sick. I would have been able to buy more land, buy a tractor and start a stable. I would have been able to live as I wished and decide what kind of work I would do each day, free in the fields. The stars mark the seasons, and you know when you have to plant, plow, or cut the grain. The rains bloat the seed and open the furrows to the sun. I could have stopped my work to run after a rabbit or follow the furrows to the confines of the land. I could have shaken the fruit trees or sat down and called out to other men working nearby in the fields. [...] Instead I chose to work in the factory. Other people and their plans forced me to do it, and I was their victim, a victim who works by the hour, one minute after another. [...] I was just another faceless worker.)[31]

28 Luzi, A. 2005. "La scrittura di Volponi tra natura e storia. Ideologia ed eros in *Il lanciatore di giavellotto.*" *Cahiers d'études italiennes*, vol. 3. 141.
29 Volponi, P. 1962. *Memoriale*. Milan: Garzanti. 151. Volponi, P. 1964. *My Troubles Began*. Translated by Belén Sevareid. New York: Grossman Publishers. 161.
30 Volponi, P. 1962. *Memoriale*. 152. Volponi, P. 1964. *My Troubles Began*. 162.
31 Volponi, P. 1962. *Memoriale*. 152. Volponi, P. 1964. *My Troubles Began*. 162.

Caught between the familiar space of his hometown (the imaginary Candia), where life still follows the natural cycle of the seasons, and the hostile space of the factory town where he works, a place that only follows the cycle of capitalist production, Albino becomes the perfect symbol of the spatial alienation of modernity. "The modern model," argue Bourneuf and Ouellet, "is rife with examples of this identification between nature and characters, in which the landscape is not only a state of mind, but also clarifies the subconscious life of those who contemplate and imagine it."[32]

As Albino constantly commutes from one place to another, he has to cope not only with the fragmentation of space and time, but also with the loss of his identity. The daily journey that brings him to the factory complex is another example of his bewilderment. As Fabrizio Scrivano has pointed out, Albino repeatedly describes his journey from home to work and back: "Per almeno sedici volte Albino sale su un treno e per altre sei su una corriera; in molte altre occasioni si fa cenno a questo sostamento" (Albino gets on the train at least sixteen times and on the bus another six times; and several other times he refers to this commuting).[33] Moreover, Scrivano notes: "Il viaggio è la porta d'ingresso in un mondo estraneo, quello della città e della fabbrica; è il corridoio attraverso il quale si può raggiungere la salvezza o la perdizione: ma Albino non sa da che parte stia l'una e l'altra. Quello del viaggio è un mondo sospeso [...]. Il viaggio è un non-luogo che possiede una forza estraniante" (The journey is the entrance to a foreign world, that of the city and the factory; it is the passageway through which one can reach salvation or perdition: but Albino does not know which side he is on. That of the journey is a suspended world [...]. It is a non-place with a strong estranging power).[34] Unable to freely experience and live the world of his forefathers, Albino Saluggia remains stuck in between worlds.

---

32 Bourneuf, R. and Ouellet, R. 1976. *L'universo del romanzo*. 109.
33 Scrivano, F. 2000. "Individuo, società e territorio nei romanzi di Paolo Volponi: Le soluzioni narrative di *Memoriale* e *La strada per Roma*." *Esperienze letterarie*, vol. 25, no. 1. 101.
34 Scrivano, F. 2000. "Individuo, società e territorio nei romanzi di Paolo Volponi." 101–102.

The poetics of space are also essential to Alberto Bevilacqua's *La Califfa* (The Calif, 1964). The novel tells the story of Irene Corsini, also known as 'la Califfa,' and her illicit love affair with Annibale Doberdò, the most influential businessman in the community.[35] Set in postwar Italy, *La Califfa* presents an interesting, albeit neglected, depiction of Italian industrialism, where the organization of space plays a crucial role. A masterful writer, Bevilacqua is able to portray the dramatic sociopolitical changes of his time with ease, unobtrusively, using characters and landscapes as paradigms of power and submission. Aware of the striking alterations that the Italian territory underwent during the economic boom, Bevilacqua describes the consequences of this transformation, particularly in the city of Parma, as follows:

> Credo che Parma abbia pagato lo scotto di un altro suo primato, quello di avere fondato il maggiore numero di industrie nel dopoguerra. In una piccola città, questo ha una grande importanza. Sono arrivati molti capitali, anche stranieri. È mutata la mentalità. Da un lato Parma si è imborghesita, dall'altro ha perduto la sua classica sigla popolare. È diventata più internazionale e più caotica.
>
> (I believe Parma has paid the price for one of its many records: that of having founded the largest number of industrial companies in the postwar period. In a small city, this is greatly important. There was a lot of investment, even foreign investment. The mentality changed. On the one hand, Parma was gentrified; on the other hand, it lost its classic popular touch. It became more international and more chaotic.)[36]

The arrival in the city of a large industrial company, and its seizure of the territory, is symbolically staged at the beginning of *La Califfa* when

---

35   In 1970, Bevilacqua adapted and directed a film version of his own novel. The film starred Ugo Tognazzi and Romy Schneider as Annibale Doberdò and Irene Corsi. In many ways, the film is a faithful rendition of the book, especially in its depiction of the melodramatic love affair between the two main characters. But when it comes to historical setting, the filmic adaptation differs strongly from the novel. The film's story does not take place in postwar Parma, but in late 1960s Italy. The difference is substantial: Italian industrialism is not represented during its unstoppable rise, but during a moment of crisis and violent conflict between factory workers and capitalists. See also Carioti, G. 1970. "La Califfa nell'occhio del ciclone: intervista con Alberto Bevilacqua." *Il Dramma*, vol. 46. 117–118.

36   Cited in Marabini, C. 1976. *Le città dei poeti*. Turin: SEI. 60.

Ubaldo Farinacci – a local notable – sets up a food plant that will supposedly employ many of the old city's workers: "c'è bisogno di braccia, non importa quale bandiera abbiano sbandierato" (we need manpower; it doesn't matter which flag they used to wave) he announces.[37] To mark his social prominence, and to bait the workforce, Farinacci organizes a parade – much like a military parade – where the new plant's machines are showcased in the old part of the city. Bevilacqua's heroine is fascinated and excited by this spectacle of efficiency and the promise of a better future:

> 'Ammore [sic], ammore, ammore, ammore mio …' cantò con rabbia gioiosa la Califfa, spalancando con un gran colpo le persiane, quando i macchinari della ditta Farinacci cominciarono la sfilata come tanti carri armati, per quei borghi dove riuscivano appena a passare, sballottati sul selciato sconnesso, con un fragore di ferraglia.
>
> ('Loovve, loovve, loovve, oh myyy love …' sang Califfa with joyous rage, throwing open the shutters with a great bang, when the Farinacci machines began to parade like so many tanks, barely able to pass through those neighborhoods, tossed around by the sloppy cobblestones, with the clamor of metal.)[38]

But despite this carnivalesque display of power, the plant closes soon after, leaving behind it unemployment, desperation and social tension.

The appearance of industrialism in the city of Parma dovetails with another phenomenon typical of the Italian economic boom: property speculation, with its reckless exploitation of the landscape and the countryside. In *La Califfa*, the character responsible for this exploitation is Mastrangelo, a shady entrepreneur who controls all the construction sites in the old part of the city. In one scene, Doberdò attends a ceremony celebrating the construction of a school "in un prato accanto la città" (in a field next to the city).[39] Observing the changing landscape, he laments: "Qui finisce che non ci cresce più nemmeno un cavolfiore! Io sono contrario alle prime pietre, decisamente contrario! Preferisco i cavolfiori!" (Here we will end up unable to grow even one cabbage! I am against the laying of cornerstones, decisively against it! I prefer the cabbages!)[40] If on the one hand Doberdò

37 Bevilacqua, A. 1972. *La Calliffa*. Milan: Rizzoli. 9.
38 Bevilacqua, A. 1972. *La Calliffa*. 9.
39 Bevilacqua, A. 1972. *La Calliffa*. 136.
40 Bevilacqua, A. 1972. *La Calliffa*. 136.

disparages the urban development of the city and the 'distruzione della natura' (destruction of nature),[41] on the other hand, through his presence at the ceremony, he hypocritically endorses it with political and financial support. Profit, in the age of mass industrialism, trumps everything, including the devastation of the environment.

Bevilacqua's novel unfolds across two main spaces: the old 'borgo' (village) Oltretorrente – home of the poor, the wretched, the forgotten, and of Irene and her friends – and the new city – home of the rich, the wealthy bourgeoisie, of culture and power, and where Doberdò and his associates live and thrive. A true tale of two cities, *La Califfa* is rife with depictions of these two irreconcilable worlds separated only by a stream (the Parma River) and a bridge:

> Questa incapacità di allontanare i pregiudizi e di fondersi in un'unica popolazione alterava, dunque, la dimensione delle cose. E quel torrente che lambiva, da una parte, la sponda di un bel viale verde di tigli e, dall'altra, i balconcini di ferro arrugginito, le grate medioevali, le tane dei topi scavate in decrepite facciate, era davvero come un grande oceano che rendesse diversi i cervelli e l'aria di due continenti.
>
> (This incapacity to beat back prejudices and to found life on a single population therefore altered the dimension of things. And that torrent that licked, on the one hand, the shores of a nice boulevard lined with tilia trees and, on the other hand, the little balconies made of rusty metal, the medieval grates, the mouse nests dug in to decrepit façades – it was really like a grand ocean that shaped the brains and the air of two continents in different ways.)[42]

Irene Corsini is the only character in the novel who is able, albeit temporarily, to cross that 'ocean,' to get a glimpse of the high life of the new city. As a result of her illegitimate relationship with Doberdò, Irene is able to move temporarily into a new home and enjoy a life of comfort and leisure: "Proprio così!" (That's right!), she says, "la signora, facevo, e alla faccia di chi sapevo io" (I lived like a lady, and in spite of someone

---

41   I am referring here to Antonio Cederna's seminal book, one of the first studies on construction speculation in Italy. Cederna, A. 1975. *La distruzione della natura in Italia*. Milan: Einaudi. See also Cederna, A. 1956. *I vandali in casa*. Rome: Laterza.
42   Bevilacqua, A. 1972. *La Calliffa*. 55.

I knew).⁴³ The area surrounding her new home is beautiful, unlike anything she has experienced before: "La mattina se ne andava per casa. Io che di letto sono sempre stata pigra, quasi mi alzavo col sole. Guarda un po', mi dicevo, adesso che nessuno ti sta dietro, che potresti dormire comoda fino a mezzogiorno, sembra che devi andare a bottega. Ma bisognava vederlo tutto quel gran bel verde che c'era intorno alla mia camera da letto" (In the mornings, we hung around the house. I, who have always laid lazy in bed, nearly got up with the sun. Will you look at that – I said to myself – now that nobody is prodding you on, when you could comfortably sleep until noon, it seems like you are busy as a bee. You should have seen all that wonderful green around my bedroom).⁴⁴ However, Irene's redemption is only temporary. The blissful relationship between her and Doberdò ends with the latter's sudden death, and she is forced to return to the old city. The countryside, once again, symbolically marks this dramatic change of fortune and the end of illusion: "Anche i campi, quelli che si potevano vedere attraverso la vetrata, se la Califfa girava la testa per appoggiare la guancia nella fredda buca del cuscino, erano gli stessi campi gelati che l'avevano vista partire verso le sue nuove illusioni" (Even the fields that Califfa could see from the windows, turning her head and leaning her cheeks on the cold dip in the cushion, were the same frozen fields that had seen her off toward her new illusions).⁴⁵ Space in *La Califfa* is clearly hierarchical, and its organization reflects the power structure of the city. It is not democratic because rather than cooperation and harmony, it produces antagonism and alienation.

As illustrated by Bourneuf and Ouellet, the analysis of space and its literary representation reveals the presence of places and landscapes indicating relationships of "symmetry or contrast, of attraction, tension, or repulsion."⁴⁶ The works examined in this chapter share a similar outlook on space: they stage a conflictual relationship between characters (real or fictional) and landscapes and question the unity and harmony of the

---

43 Bevilacqua, A. 1972. *La Calliffa*. 130.
44 Bevilacqua, A. 1972. *La Calliffa*. 131.
45 Bevilacqua, A. 1972. *La Calliffa*. 228.
46 Bourneuf, R. and Ouellet, R. 1976. *L'universo del romanzo*. 96.

Bakhtinian idyllic chronotope. As these works make clear, Italian industrial writers demonstrated that in modern Italy such a spatial archetype lost its comforting meaning and that the Great Transformation – with its development of industry and expansion of big cities – changed the Italian landscape forever.

FRANCESCA CANTORE AND ANDREA MINUZ[1]

12   Against Working-Class Idols: Thieves, *Vitelloni*, Hunks and the *Dolce Vita* in 1950s Italian Cinema

This chapter examines 1950s Italian cinema by concentrating on a group of films that called into question the idea of labor as a driving myth for postwar Italian culture, particularly in its Marxist guise. During the first wave of neorealism, despite certain limits imposed by censorship and the cultural climate of the early Cold War, cinematic representations of the working world performed a drama of human, ethical and social (political) dimensions.[2] Films like Vittorio De Sica's *Ladri di biciclette* (Bicycle Theives, 1948) and *Umberto D* (1952), Luchino Visconti's *La terra trema* (1948) and Giuseppe De Santis' *Riso amaro* (Bitter Rice, 1949) used humble characters to tell painful stories of unemployment, intermittent labor and the difficult working conditions of fishermen, shepherds and day laborers. The idea was to provide testimony of the challenges of national reconstruction, the experience of misery, the search for a collective moral redemption and the desire for social justice. But against this set of priorities, popular Italian cinema developed its own comic sub-genres – the *commedia di costume* (comedy of manners), the *bozzetto* (sketch comedy), the *farsa* (farce), the *commedia all'italiana* (comedy Italian style) – that opposed the orthodoxy of the working-class idol with a repertoire of atavistic Italian defects (laziness, laxity, incompetence). Such a contrast generated a set of comic gags poking fun at the 'religion' of labor so important for communist

---

[1]   This chapter is the result of a collaborative discussion. Sections 1 and 4 were written by Andrea Minuz. Sections 2 and 3 were written by Francesca Cantore.
[2]   For an overview of 1950s Italian cinema see: Noto, P. 2011. *Dal Bozzetto ai generi. Il cinema italiano dei primi anni Cinquanta*. Turin: Kaplan. Bernardi, S (ed.). 2004. *Storia del cinema italiano*. Volume IX (1954–1959). Venice: Marsilio.

culture. The films explored in this chapter throw a harsh light on the working world, thus appearing to contrast both the mass-mediated idea of social welfare resulting from economic growth and the spirit of denunciation central to neorealist and Marxist culture.

In his celebrated novel *Il lavoro culturale* (Cultural Labor, 1957), Luciano Bianciardi effectively registered the weight of labor as a topic for discussion in postwar Italian cinema circles. For Bianciardi, film criticism found value only in what was politically expedient, something that placed Italian professionals alongside their Soviet colleagues who tended to exalt socialist realism. From his lonely existence in the province of Grosseto (Tuscany), Bianciardi describes a desperate attempt to give life to a local cinema club. One of the protagonists, Marcello, liaises with the cinema section of the Partito Comunista Italiano (Italian Communist Party, PCI), and a Party delegate arrives from Rome for the screening of De Sica's *Ladri di biciclette*:

> C'era stata grande attesa, in città, per la conferenza del noto critico cinematografico, annunciata persino con i manifesti. La sala era piena; il noto critico era un uomo alto e robusto, con i capelli cortissimi e gli occhiali montati in nero. Parlava a voce bassa, in tono dolce e suadente, ma Marcello rimase un po' male, perché non disse nulla del montaggio, dei carrelli e della sintesi audiovisiva. Poi gliene chiese, timidamente. Gli chiese se a suo avviso c'era un possibile rapporto fra la teoria del cine-occhio di Dziga Vertov e la poetica di *Ladri di biciclette*. Per esempio, la sequenza del furto, con quel procedere a succhiello, bicicletta-bambino-bicicletta-padre-stadio-bicicletta-padre-bambino-bicicletta, non era, a suo avviso, già anticipata? Ma il noto critico lo interruppe e gli disse che quella sua era una posizione ancora precritica, filologica se vogliamo, non ancora storicistica. 'A noi *Ladri di biciclette* interessa solo nella misura in cui riesce a porre in forma popolare un problema d'importanza nazionale. Nel caso specifico il problema della disoccupazione.' Marcello lo stava a sentire. 'Caso mai,' continuò il noto critico, 'possiamo cogliere i limiti assai notevoli di questo film. Per esempio: l'operaio disoccupato non è un lavoratore tipico nell'attuale società italiana. L'operaio Ricci attacca i manifesti, no? Quanti sono, in Italia, gli attacchini? E quanti i braccianti? Quanti i siderurgici? Non ho con me i dati esatti, ma la non tipicità dell'uomo di De Sica mi pare di per sé evidente, no?' Guardava in viso Marcello, duramente, come se la colpa fosse sua, anziché di De Sica.
>
> (There was a lot of hype, in town, about the lecture of this noted cinema critic. There were even flyers. The room was full; the noted critic was a tall and robust man, with very short hair and black rim glasses. He spoke in a low voice, with a sweet and mellow tone, but Marcello was a bit disappointed, because he didn't say anything

about the editing, the tracking shots or the audiovisual synthesis. So he asked him, shyly. He asked him if in his opinion there could be some relation between Dziga Vertov's theory of the Cine-Eye and the poetics of *Ladri di biciclette*. For example, the sequence of the theft, with its punctuated development, bicycle-child-bicycle-father-stadium-bicycle-father-child-bicycle, had it not been, in his opinion, already anticipated? But the noted critic interrupted him and told him that this position was still pre-critical, philological perhaps but not yet historicist. 'We are interested in *Ladri di biciclette* only insofar as it succeeds in posing in popular form a question of national importance. In this case, the question of unemployment.' Marcello heard him out. 'If anything,' the noted critic went on, 'we can understand the very considerable limits of this film. For example: the unemployed worker is not typical of Italian society today. The worker Ricci puts up flyers, right? How many people in Italy put up flyers? And how many are day laborers? How many are ironworkers? I don't have the exact data on me, but it seems self-evident to me that De Sica's man is atypical, right?' He looked Marcello in the eyes, harshly, as if it were his fault and not De Sica's.)[3]

This exemplary passage announces a series of misunderstandings originating in the communist conception of neorealism as an unbiased and objective project of Italian denunciation – one that De Sica and Roberto Rossellini clearly intended as lyrical and existential. With his typically polemic irony, Bianciardi photographs the slow breakdown between various moments of cultural renewal and a communist orthodoxy modelled on Soviet criteria (the book was published in the wake of the 1956 crisis, with the Russian invasion of Hungary, the first public denunciations of Stalin and the opening of a rift between the PCI and Italian intellectuals). By reading *Ladri di biciclette* as a film that deals inadequately with questions of unemployment and class consciousness, the cinema critic actually reveals Marxist analysis' inability to deal adequately with the idea of labor. His approach is directed by a search for 'objective reality' and the criteria of socialist realism (which Visconti's *La terra trema* and De Santis' *Non c'è pace tra gli ulivi* (No Peace Under the Olive Tree, 1950) adopt in their own ways). Moreover, while it is true that the Italian drama of postwar economic and social reconstruction, the political premises of 1960s union struggles and the workerism of magazines like *Quaderni rossi* (1961–1963) and *Classe operaia* (1964–1965) were developed inside the factory,

---

3   Bianciardi, L. 2013. *Il lavoro culturale*. Milan: Feltrinelli. 54–55.

neorealist cinema was much more concerned with peasant labor than industrial labor. Industrial workers remained mostly off-screen through the mid-1950s, when Italian society began an intense process of urbanization. In the meantime, the factory space appeared only rarely, like in Eduardo De Filippo's *Napoletani a Milano* (Neapolitans in Milan, 1953): a decidedly modern film that mixed tragedy and farce in ways unfamiliar to both neorealist canons and the *commedia di costume*. In Camillo Mastrocinque's *Totò, Peppino e la ... malafemmina* (Totò, Peppino and the Hussy, 1956), the image of Totò and Peppino in Piazza del Duomo with fur coats and big hats is a far cry from the idea of Neapolitan migrants wading through the Milanese fog only to be swallowed up by an industrial factory. By the end of the 1950s, in comedies like Dino Risi's *Il vedovo* (The Widower, 1959), the factory world was still a mere background for the staging of impossible dreams like Alberto Nardi (Alberto Sordi)'s transformation into an entrepreneur.

Indolence and Laziness among Postwar Italian Youth

There is no place for labor in the colorless Rimini (Emilia Romagna) of Federico Fellini's *I vitelloni* (1953). The five protagonists, verging on their thirties, lead a sleepy existence, between a game of billiards, a Carnival ball and a winter's stroll down the beach. The group includes Leopoldo (Leopoldo Trieste), who lives with his aunt and dreams of becoming a playwright, Riccardo (Riccardo Fellini), who is a good singer and loves horseraces, and Alberto (Alberto Sordi), who is incapable of supporting his mother and sister but strives nevertheless to impose himself as head of the household. Moraldo (Franco Interlenghi) is the youngest and most reflexive of the group, and his story intersects with that of Fausto (Franco Fabrizi), toward whom Moraldo feels a strange mix of fascination and moral repulsion.

Who exactly are these 'vitelloni' (Italian for 'big calves,' but translatable as 'loafers')? Writing in the popular journal *Cinema* in 1952, the film's screenwriters announced:

Ciascuno di loro ha qualcuno che, bene o male, lo mantiene: un padre, una madre, una sorella, una zia, una famiglia [...]. Nessuno di loro sa bene cosa vorrebbe fare. I piccoli lavori, le piccole occupazioni che la cittadina di provincia potrebbe offrire alla loro scarsa preparazione, li disdegnano. Hanno fatto qualche studio, ma non sono arrivati in fondo. Non hanno attitudini per niente in modo speciale; aspettano sempre una lettera, una offerta, una combinazione che li porti a Roma o a Milano per qualche incarico generico, onorifico e redditizio; e aspettando sono giunti verso i trent'anni; passano la giornata a fare discorsi e scherzetti da ragazzini del ginnasio; e brillano nei tre mesi della stagione balneare, la cui attesa e i cui ricordi occupano tutto il resto dell'anno.

(Each of them has someone who, for better or for worse, supports them: a father, a mother, a sister, an aunt, a family [...]. None of them really knows what he wants to do with his life. They are underprepared and disdain all the odd-jobs and little side projects that provincial life has to offer. They have studied a bit, but not very much. They don't really care about anything; they're always waiting for a letter, an offer, some combination of circumstances that will bring them to Rome or Milan for some generic position, honorary and profitable; but in the meantime, they've hit their thirties; they waste the day chatting and playing schoolboy pranks; and they shine during the three months of beach season, whose anticipation and memories keep them busy for the rest of the year.)[4]

On the one hand, *I vitelloni* is full of autobiographical elements typical in Fellini's films: the province of Rimini and the presence of Riccardo – the director's brother and alter ego. But on the other hand, it takes a deep dive into archetypes of *Italianità* (Italian-ness): that "rilassatezza dello stile di vita italiano" (Italian-style relaxation) that doubles as a symptom of the "diffuso senso di inferiorità rispetto agli altri Paesi ritenuti più moderni e civili" (widespread sense of inferiority with respect to other, supposedly more modern and civil countries).[5]

In sketching the five characters, Fellini, Ennio Flaiano and Tullio Pinelli hesitated the most with Fausto, especially in relation to Moraldo's sister Sandra (Eleonora Ruffo). When Sandra becomes pregnant, Fausto is suddenly forced into maturity: he marries Sandra and begins working in a local shop. Though he seems to be on the right track, Fausto's old vices return with a vengeance: "si sente vittima; e quando pensa ai suoi amici che dormono ancora o che stanno

---

4 Fellini, F. et al. 1952. "Soggetti di film – I vitelloni." *Cinema*, no.s 99–100. 289.
5 Minuz, A. 2012. *Viaggio al termine dell'Italia. Fellini politico.* Soveria Mannelli: Rubbettino Editore. 62–63.

a giocare al biliardo, gli viene un groppo in gola" (he feels like a victim; and when he thinks of his friends still asleep or out playing billiards, it brings a lump to his throat).[6] The entire film is sustained by the *vitelloni*'s casual disregard for serious labor together with its implications (economic independence, responsibility and initiated adulthood). Such an attitude is evidenced by the way Fausto's friends sneer at him through the shop window where he works and by the celebrated scene of Alberto's 'Italian salute' to a group of highway laborers (see Figure 5). It also gives form to a broader generational conflict between fathers and sons, represented by the rift between Fausto's father (a real gentleman who worked his whole life to support his family) and Fausto (who refuses to grow up). It is finally up to Fausto's father Francesco to establish patriarchal order – perhaps once and for all – by beating his son with a belt. But *I vitelloni* also offers an alternative image of youth in Guido, the train station errand boy who runs into Moraldo at three o'clock in the morning. While Moraldo is kicking around, just wasting time, the young Guido is already on his way to work. He thus represents the hope for a new youth with a better future, and he returns to salute Moraldo when the latter finally decides to leave town and find his own way in the world.

Figure 5. Alberto Sordi's 'Italian salute' to a group of highway laborers in Federico Fellini's *I vitelloni* (1953).

6   Fellini, F. et al. 1952. "Soggetti di film – I vitelloni." 290.

Against Working-Class Idols

The gloomy indolence of the provincial *vitelloni* leaves plenty of room for the boisterous activity of city kids like Romolo (Maurizio Arena) and Salvatore (Renato Salvatori), who give themselves to pleasure and the pursuit of every passion in Risi's 1957 film *Poveri ma belli* (Poor but Handsome).[7] The title says it all: who cares about labor (and the prospect of wealth) when one has beauty and the art of love?[8] Indeed, beauty and labor are in open contradiction: "Ma guarda che giornata" (What a day) Romolo tells his friend, "ma ti pare giusto che uno deve andare a lavorare con un sole come questo? [...] Capirei uno che è vecchio, uno che non sta bene, ma un ragazzo come me, sano, robusto, un bel ragazzo è spreccato ad andare a lavorare!" (you think it is right that someone has to go to work under a sun like this? [...] I would understand someone old, someone who isn't well, but a kid like me, healthy, strong, a handsome kid is squandered if he goes to work!) And yet, the two protagonists do have jobs – the big city always has more to offer. Salvatore is a lifeguard at Ciriola, a Tiberside beach under the Ponte Sant'Angelo in Rome, but his swimmers are constantly complaining: "non si trova mai sto bagnino" (this lifeguard's nowhere to be found). Romolo sells records in his uncle's shop, but their professions are merely the background to the sexual escapades that fill their daily lives. Like Fellini's characters, those of Risi exhibit a stubborn resistance to adulthood, but unlike their provincial cinematic cousins, they are also marked by a profound innocence. As Vittorio Spinazzola has written:

> Questi bulli e pupe, questi galletti e pollastrelle trasteverini ostentano continuamente i propositi più bellicosi, ma si guardano bene dal porli in atto: la loro spavalderia è tutta verbale: in realtà sono fior di bravi ragazzi e ragazze, che tranne l'uso del bikini

7 *Poveri ma belli* belongs to the tradition of 'pink neorealism.' The term was first used in: Kezich, T. 1955. "Neorealismo rosa." *Letteratura*, no.s 13–14. According to Enrico Giacovelli, 'pink neorealism' includes all of 1950s Italian comedy up to Mario Monicelli's 1958 film *I soliti ignoti* (Big Deal on Madonna Street). Giacovelli, E. 1990. *La commedia all'italiana. La storia, i luoghi, gli autori, gli attori, i film.* Rome: Gremese. 23.
8 Guido Aristarco's review of *Poveri ma belli* is rightfully famous. With telling disdain, Aristarco announces the "passaggio dal neorealismo al neoerotismo" (transition from neorealism to neoeroticism). Aristarco, G. 1957. "Il mestiere del critico – Poveri ma belli." *Cinema Nuovo*, no.s 101–102. 155.

> e qualche battuta a doppio senso non si sognano nemmeno di dare scandalo sul serio […]. Tutti dimostrano un sano buon senso da fare invidia a qualsiasi morigerato padre di famiglia.
>
> (These guys and dolls, these young bucks and chicks from Trastevere always project the most aggressive intentions, but they are careful not to take any action: their cockiness is entirely verbal: in reality, they are the best of kids who might wear bikinis and crack racy jokes, but would never even dream of causing a serious scandal […]. They all prove to have a healthy common sense that any straight-laced family man would envy.)[9]

They share nothing of Fausto's malicious betrayal of Sandra in *I vitelloni*. If anything, Romolo and Salvatore's antics are victimless crimes: they are innocent kisses under the sun, and if pregnancy is ever broached, then we can be sure that it is just a rumor. Poverty remains a question of very little importance, though in Risi's next two installments – *Belle ma povere* (Pretty but Poor, 1957) and *Poveri milionari* (Poor Millionaires, 1958) – this would quickly change. Deciding to marry each other's sisters, the two friends exchange their obsession with conquest for an obsession with a stable job: they attend night school to learn a trade because they realize that the only way to marry is to work (and therefore to enter into adulthood).

Scams and Cheating in 1950s Italian Cinema

In Mario Monicelli's 1958 film *I soliti ignoti* (Big Deal on Madonna Street),[10] the idea of an honest and dignified 'lavoro' (job) is exchanged for that of an illicit 'lavoretto' (odd job). At the center of the film is a plot to rob the Monte di Pietà charity in Rome. Monicelli introduces a gang of peripheral delinquents: the old but eager Capannelle (Carlo Pisacane), the

9 Spinazzola, V. 1974. *Cinema e pubblico. Lo spettacolo filmico in Italia (1945–1965)*. Milan: Bompiani. 115–116.
10 Film historians generally agree that *I soliti ignoti* was a trailblazer for the *commedia all'italiana* sub-genre. Initially considered a parody of the gangster genre, and especially of Jules Dassin's 1955 film *Du rififi chez les hommes* (Rififi), *I soliti ignoti* previews a series of stylistic and narrative elements that would connote Italian comedy in the years after its release.

Against Working-Class Idols

reluctant thief Mario (Renato Salvatori, fresh from *Poveri ma belli*), the jealous Sicilian Ferribotte (Tiberio Murgia), the photographer Tiberio (Marcello Mastroianni) and the retired boxer Peppe (Vittorio Gassman), alias "Er Pantera" (The Panther), who takes control of the gang by stealing the thunder of the veteran Cosimo (Memmo Carotenuto). They clearly consider themselves professionals in a sort of 'art of the robbery,' turning in preparation to the "maestro dello scasso" (master lock-picker) Dante Cruciani (Totò; see Figure 6). Like workers on an assembly line, each gang member has his own specific competency: "ognuno va adoperato secondo le attitudini sue ... È così che fai un *lavoro scientifico*" (everyone must be employed according to his own aptitude ... That's how you do a *scientific job*), says Peppe, as if to establish a mantra. Even illegal labor is characterized by a hierarchy of professionalism, and when the gang's deposed leader Cosimo dies in a mugging, Dante cannot help but comment: "Un professionista come lui si mette a fare lo scippo?" (A professional like him reduced to mugging?)

Figure 6. Marcello Mastroianni, Renato Salvatori, Carlo Pisacane, Vittorio Gassman and Totò (left to right) in *I soliti ignoti* (Big Deal on Madonna Street, Mario Monicelli, 1958).

Notwithstanding their meticulous attention to detail and the 'scientific' nature of their preparation, the gang's plot is destined to implode. In the words of Enrico Giacomelli, Monicelli's characters share something with the "eroi di borgata degli anni Cinquanta, i poveri-ma-belli" (1950s suburb heroes, the poor-but-handsomes), with the important difference that "a quelli andava tutto bene, a questi non ne va dritta una: sono perdenti nati" (for those [from the 1950s] all went according to plan, for these [of Monicelli's film] nothing does: they are born losers).[11] Common sense and levelheadedness prevail in *I soliti ignoti* too, when the failed robbery unwittingly gives way to the undoing of the gang members themselves (Mario leaves the gang for an honest job, Peppe falls in love with the servant girl he was supposed to deceive and Tiberio returns home as a responsible family man).

While the prospect of honest labor appears self-evidently impractical – "lavorare stanca" (work is tiresome), Peppe confesses with a pointed hint of resignation – robbery is even more difficult because, as Tibero tells his friends over a plate of pasta and chickpeas, "è un mestiere impegnativo, ci vuole gente seria, mica come voi ... Voi al massimo potete andare a lavorare" (it's demanding work, it takes real dedication, not an attitude like yours ... You, if anything, could go get a job).

Such an opposition between honesty and delinquency is crystalized in the *finale* of *I soliti ignoti*. Pockets empty and bellies full after their failed robbery, Capannelle and Peppe hide from the police in a group of construction workers. Labor finally appears to be the only solution. A film that began with prisoners marching in a jail ends when Peppe is literally swallowed by a construction site. He fades into the crowd of workers, among Capannelle's cries: "Peppe, dove vai? Ma ti fanno lavorare sai!" (Peppe, where are you going? You know they'll make you work!).

Another film that explores the dichotomy between honest labor and fraud is Francesco Rosi's *I magliari* (The Magliari, 1959). The film is based on true crime reports from the 1950s, when rival gangs of Italian clothing peddlers called 'magliari' exchanged gunfire in Hamburg and Munich. Set in West Germany, *I magliari* launched a craze – together with Gian Luigi Polidoro's *Le svedesi* (The Swedes, 1960) – for "film sugli italiani all'estero" (films about Italians abroad) by photographing the phenomenon

---

11   Giacovelli, E. 1990. *La commedia all'italiana*. 45.

of migration to northern Europe (and elsewhere) during the 1950s and 1960s.[12] *I magliari* is structured around the opposition between Mario (Renato Salvatori again) – a factory worker from Grosseto who migrates to Hannover in search of a job – and a shady circle of Italian 'magliari', headed by Ferdinando Magliulo, alias Totonno (Alberto Sordi).

Mario is depicted as an honest worker who, in a moment of desperation, gives in to the promise of an easy profit without even posing himself the question of legality. Totonno drags Mario around to show him the ropes of swindling as a business, and when Mario visits his former colleagues in their factory he can hardly contain his excitement: "Ma lo sapete che questi commercianti guadagnano in un giorno quello che noi guardagniamo in un mese? Hanno tutti l'automobile! [...] È gente che ci sa fare, mica come noi che siamo tante pecore" (Did you know that in one day these merchants make as much as we do in a month? They all have an automobile! [...] These people know how to get it done, unlike us: we're a bunch of sheep). Mario's naiveté is set off against Totonno's craftiness – the latter is a professional 'magliaro', and proud of it: "Voi dovete fa la morale perché lavorate in fabbrica e finché c'è la fabbrica tutto va bene. Ma se uno manca, sta fabbrica, da soli ve sapete move? E invece un imbroglione come me riesce a vivere" (You're all goody two-shoes because you work in a factory, and as long as there's a factory everything's good. But what if one day this factory disappears, would you know how to get around on your own? Meanwhile, a con artist like me leads a pretty good life). But not for long: Totonno stumbles and is driven out of the 'magliari', while Mario – who orchestrated Totonno's downfall – returns to Italy and an honest life.

Imagining a Post-Work Society: *La dolce vita*

"E il lavoro come va? Ti rende bene?" (How's work going? Does it pay you well?) So asks Marcello's father, who travels to Rome to visit his son in Federico Fellini's 1960 film *La dolce vita*. Marcello and his father are

---

12   Di Marino, B. 2004. "Transizioni: Tra neorealismo rosa e commedia all'italiana." *Storia del cinema italiano*. Edited by Sandro Bernardi. 118.

seated at an outdoor bar on the Via Veneto with the buzz of Roman high society vibrating up and down the street. "Il mestiere del giornalista, se ci sai fare, rende abbastanza" (If you're good at it, journalism pays enough) Marcello responds. "Io ho avuto fortuna, mi sono introdotto, conosco tutti, e adesso mi sono fatto anche la macchina, ho l'appartamento" (I've been lucky, I made some friends, I know everybody, and now I even have an automobile, I have an apartment). Marcello's father is distracted by the continuous flow of beautiful women and strange people parading among the street-side tables: "Beh, forse hai da fare adesso, avrai un impegno, un appuntamento" (Well, you must be busy now, you must have some commitment, some appointment) he insists, attempting a departure. "Ma no papà, il mio lavoro è anche qui, vedi è qui che capitano i personaggi che ci interessano, una notizia, una fotografia" (No Dad, this too is my work, you see, interesting people turn up here, a news story, a photograph). "Ma insomma …" (And so …) Marcello's father huffs, "ve ne state seduti qui, ecco" (you just plant yourselves here in a seat).

The words of Marcello's father betray a mix of alarm and confusion, but also a poorly concealed jealousy with respect to such a nebulous, abstract and seemingly enjoyable job. "Perbacco che movimento qui di notte" (My goodness there's such movement here at night) he shouts, ogling about, "mentre da noi in provincia tutte le sere un mortorio" (back home in the suburbs every night's like a funeral).

"This too is my work." Marcello's is an emblematic affirmation that marks a significant transition with respect to the question of labor in Italian cinema. Fellini's film casts Marcello Mastroianni as a tabloid journalist who moves in café society circles, between gossip, decadent aristocracy, vein intellectualism and showbusiness. His job has no connection to any idea of manual labor, sacrifice, duty or discipline. In the eyes of his father, Marcello's is an incomprehensible job, but it is also an attractive one: it is a job somehow designed to transform pleasure into work. Not only does *La dolce vita* project the visions of two diverging generations and the conflict between the suburbs and the city; it also marks an epochal shift in the vocational choices of its main protagonist. According to the first version of the script, *La dolce vita* was supposed to tell the next chapter of Moraldo's story from *I vitelloni*, as if to transform all idleness, artistic desire and leisure into its own modish profession. "Lei è un fotoreporter?

Un lavoro interessante, un lavoro *artistico*" (You are a photojournalist? An interesting job, an *artistic* job) Marcello's father tells his son's colleague Paparazzo, grossly overestimating the artistic prospects of the developing mass market for images. Shortly after the release of *La dolce vita*, Luciano Bianciardi published *La vita agra* (It's a Hard Life, 1962), which from its very title offered a critical rereading of the 'dolce vita' (sweet life) myth. But it was Fellini's contribution that furnished a quickly transforming Italian society with a gallery of faces, symbols, situations and jobs like that of the 'paparazzi.' In an effort to emphasize the epochal nature of *La dolce vita*, Spinazzola has compared it to Visconti's *Rocco e i suoi fratelli* (Rocco and His Brothers, 1960), released just months after Fellini's masterpiece:

> Diversissimi per doti e temperamento, Fellini e Visconti fanno entrambi il film giusto al momento giusto: porgono al pubblico un'occasione per uno spettacolare esame di coscienza collettivo, offrono alla nazione uno specchio in cui riconoscersi e giudicarsi. Ciascuno a sua maniera, interpretano stati d'animo di massa, maturati nella nuova realtà del paese. I tempi della ricostruzione e della guerra fredda sono ormai dietro le spalle; l'economia conosce un periodo di espansione, che viene addirittura definito un miracolo. I miti e le parole d'ordine del 'benessere' si diffondono rapidamente.
>
> (Differing greatly in terms of talent and temperament, Fellini and Visconti both make the right film at the right time: they make possible a spectacular analysis of collective consciousness, they give the nation a mirror for recognizing and judging itself. They represent – each in his own way – states of mind that are mass-produced, developed within the country's new reality. The era of the reconstruction and the Cold War have been superseded, the economy is expanding so much that it is even called a miracle. The myths and watchword of 'well-being' are quickly spreading.)[13]

Both watershed moments in the history of Italian cinema and Italian culture, *La dolce vita* and *Rocco e i suoi fratelli* tell stories of social and moral degradation generated by the arrival of modernity. *Rocco e i suoi fratelli* revisits the theme of Italian migration so important to *I magliari*, but from a perspective that is entirely internal, as if to propose an analysis of collective consciousness in the form of an epic melodrama that revolves around the collision of two irreconcilable worlds (the industrially advanced North and the poor, rural South). On the contrary, Fellini's *La*

---

13 Spinazzola, V. 1974. *Cinema e pubblico*. 244.

dolce vita steers clear of any form of social denunciation, but it also evidences the search for a new vision, capable of comprehending, or at least observing, the rapid transformations underway. Thus, the perspective of Marcello as a character who performs some sort of labor takes on a highly symbolic value. Marcello's problem is not that he must flee from duty and responsibility like the *vitelloni*; it is that he must find a place within that society of the spectacle that celebrates and rewards itself and that is reflected in the tabloids, but without feeling empty, disappointed or fatally trapped by new obligations of 'pleasure' and 'permanent amusement' (the price of modernity in Fellini's film). As Alberto Moravia wrote some years after *La dolce vita*'s release:

> Grazie al personaggio di Marcello e al suo mestiere, Fellini sfugge al destino dei crepuscolari consistente per lo più in una specie di derisoria e rassegnata educazione sentimentale; e ferma invece nel suo film il momento storico del passaggio della società italiana dalla realtà della provincia all'irrealtà dei miti, dalla scala dei valori tradizionali a quella dei valori di spettacolo, dall'economia di risparmio all'economia di consumo. Il mestiere di Marcello sta ad indicare che tutto è consumabile, perfino la delusione.
>
> (Thanks to the character of Marcello and his job, Fellini eludes the destiny of the *crepuscolari*, which basically consists in a sort of derisive and resigned sentimental education; on the contrary, he fixes in his film the historical moment of transition from the real Italian society of the suburbs to the unreality of myths, from the hierarchy of traditional values to that of spectacle values, from the savings economy to the consumption economy. Marcello's job demonstrates that everything is consumable, even disappointment.)[14]

The transition evoked by Moravia from a savings economy to a consumption economy neatly sums up the relation of Fellini's film to its historical moment, or its capacity to mark the incompatibility between two models of society: postwar peasant or reconstruction Italy and economic boom Italy. From this point of view, and with special reference to the novel configuration of the worker as interpreted by Marcello Mastroianni, *La dolce vita* is capable of maintaining an intimate relation to that repertoire of film comedies designed to poke fun at Italian labor.

Translated by Jim Carter

14   Moravia, A. 1975. "Roma mille film orsono." *L'Espresso*. October 12.

CARLO BAGHETTI

13 Contemporary Returns to Questions of Industry and Labor

The New Labor Literature

Unlike many other contributions to the present volume, this chapter is a sort of jetty. My intent is to build outward from the solid ground of 'industrial literature,' with its most important authors, into an assortment of texts that is liquid, fluctuating and difficult to dam up with one analysis: the most recent literature on questions of industry and labor. Like a jetty, the chapter serves many purposes: it is a dock, a point of arrival and departure for in-depth explorations; it is a lookout from which to scrutinize the thematic trajectories of industrial literature after the 1970s. In any event, the nature of this chapter is primarily descriptive: it is intended to identify lines of research, isolate broad concepts, reflect on modes of representation that traverse the entire *corpus* and signal texts and authors figuring prominently in the current of contemporary labor literature. It cannot, however, claim to be exhaustive.[1]

We must first consider the chronology of texts to be examined. Between the literary production of the industrial era and that of the contemporary moment, there exists a real caesura. The last two novels covered

---

1   For more complete accounts, see the following books: Chirumbolo, P. 2013 *Letteratura e lavoro. Conversazioni critiche*. Soveria Mannelli: Rubbettino. Bàrberi Squarotti, G. and Ossola, C. (eds). 1997. *Letteratura e industria: Atti del 15° Congresso AISLLI*. Florence: Olschki. Boscolo, C. and Roverselli, F. (eds). 2009. "Scritture precarie attraverso i media: un bilancio provvisorio." *Bollettino '900*, no.s 1–2. Fieni, M. 2010. *Il tema del lavoro nella letteratura italiana contemporanea*. Milan: Principato. Nencioni, B. 2016. *Il posto fisso: rassegnazione, impresa e romanzi. Il caso del Sud d'Italia 1945–2015*. Ariccia: Arcane. Pegorari, D. M. 2018. *Scritture precarie. Editoria e lavoro nella grande crisi 2003–2017*. Bari: Stilo.

in this volume, Primo Levi's *La chiave a stella* (The Wrench) and Tommaso Di Ciaula's *Tuta blu* (Blue Overalls), were both published in 1978, but a recognizable 'filone neoliberale' (neoliberal current)[2] in Italian literature can be dated only to 1994, with the appearance of three novels: Giuseppe Culicchia's *Tutti giù per terra* (We All Fall Down), Antonio Pennacchi's *Mammut* (Mammoth) and Sebastiano Nata's *Il dipendente* (The Employee). The 1980s offered very few – almost zero – literary representations of labor. One might object that Aldo Busi's *Vita standard di un venditore provvisorio di collant* (The Standard Life of a Temporary Pantyhose Salesman) is from 1985, Paolo Volponi's *Le mosche del capitale* (The Flies of Capital) is from 1989 and Pap Khouma's *Io venditore di elefanti* (I Was an Elephant Salesman) is from 1990, the latter having been drafted with the help of journalist Oreste Pivetta during the previous decade. But the existence of these three novels does little to undermine the point: Volponi's book is set in the 1970s and belongs fully to the 'modern' tradition;[3] Busi's is profoundly influenced by postmodern poetics, but it's central theme is the mentality of northern Italian petite bourgeois society, not labor;[4] and Khouma's is primarily interested in questions of migration, cultural encounters and Italian social (im)mobility.

On the contrary, the year 1994 was a real turning point in Italian history.[5] With respect to literature, it charted a new path for Italian prose;[6]

---

2   The term 'neoliberal' is useful for distinguishing the most recent literature from that of the 1950s and 1960s, which is 'liberal' or 'industrial.' Some scholars (see, for example, La Porta, F. 2000. "Albeggia una letteratura postindustriale." *Tirature 2000. Romanzi di ogni genere: dieci modelli a confront*. Edited by Vittorio Spinazzola. Milan: Il Saggiatore. 97–105.) prefer the term 'postindustrial,' though we will see that industry does not disappear from these novels.

3   Fortini, F. 2001. "Volponi moderno." *Volponi*. Edited by Emanuele Zinato. Palermo: Palumbo. 238–241.

4   Tirinanzi De Medici, C. 2018. *Il romanzo italiano contemporanoa. Dalla fine degli anni Settanta a oggi*. Rome: Carocci. 63.

5   Casadei, A. 2002. "1994. I destini incrociati del romanzo italiano." *Italianistica*, vol. 36, no. 1. 253–258. Donnarumma, R. 2014. *Ipermodernità. Dove va la narrativa contemporanea*. Bologna: Il Mulino.

6   The following novels are exemplary: Tabucchi, A. 1994. *Sostiene Pereira*. Milan: Feltrinelli. Ammaniti, N. 1994. *Branchie*. Rome: Ediesse. Siti, W. 1994.

with respect to politics, the year 1994 announced the entrance of Silvio Berlusconi with an unexpected electoral victory that sealed the fate of the old party system and its cultural influence.[7] Such a sea change underwrote the accelerated penetration in Italy of neoliberal economic theories, thanks to the Minister of Economy and Finances Giulio Tremonti and the Minister of Labor and Social Security Tiziano Treu.[8]

Starting in 1994, writers brought their attention back around to the social realities of Italian labor. Their narrative models were inevitably different from those of the industrial era, as the cultural context of their activity had changed. The influences of "giovane" (young),[9] "cannibale" (cannibal) and pulp literatures[10] and the "rinnovata vitalità dei generi letterari" (renewed vitality of literary genres)[11] represented new points of comparison against which labor narratives were constantly measured.

The Factory Lives on: Industrial Novels Today

Notwithstanding the elements of chronological, stylistic and sociocultural discontinuity outlined above, there exist between the old and new

---

Scuola di nudo. Turin: Einaudi. Brizzi, E. 1994. *Jack Frusciante è uscito dal gruppo*. Ancona: Transeuropa.

7   Deaglio, E. 1995. *Besame mucho. Diario di un anno abbastanza crudele*. Milan: Feltrinelli.

8   Especially with law number 196 of June 24, 1997, known as the 'pacchetto Treu' (Treu package).

9   Tirinanzi De Medici, C. 2018. *Il romanzo italiano contemporaneo*. 124–126. For a linguistic analysis of 'giovane' literature, see Arcangeli, M. 2007. *Giovani scrittori, scritture giovani. Ribelli, sognatori, cannibali, bad girls*. Rome: Carocci.

10 Lucamante, S. (ed.). 2001. *Italian Pulp Fiction: The New Narrative of the "Giovani Cannibali" Writers*. London: Associated University Press. Mondello, E. 2007. *In principio fu Tondelli. Letteratura, merci, televisione nella narrativa degli anni novanta*. Milan: Il Saggiatore.

11 Tirinanzi, De Medici. 2018. *Il romanzo italiano contemporaneo*. 147.

currents of industrial literature certain points of contact, especially with regards to theme or setting.

The first point we notice is that the factory has not disappeared from today's industrial literature. Even if it has been joined by other office settings – causing some scholars to propose the term "letteratura aziendale" (company literature)[12] – the factory lives on as the space of production *par excellence* and continues to inspire Italian writers. In 1994, after years of editorial difficulties,[13] Pennacchi finally published *Mammut*, set at the Supercavi factory in Latina (Lazio). Almost ten years later, Ermanno Rea wrote *La dismissione* (The Dismantling, 2002), set in Naples' industrial Bagnoli neighborhood, and Francesco Dezio enjoyed unexpected success with *Nicola Rubino è entrato in fabbrica* (Nicola Rubino Entered the Factory) in 2004, set in an impoverished and ferocious Puglia. The following year, Raffaele Nigro published *Malvarosa*, which tells the story of the Ilva factory in Taranto (Puglia), then two very different novels – both focused on steel production – were published in 2010: Silvia Avallone's *Acciaio* Steel, set in Piombino (Tuscany), and Cosimo Argentina's *Vicolo dell'acciaio* (The Alley of Steel), set like Nigro's novel in Taranto.

Thus the factory endures as a privileged space in the literary discourse on labor. But unlike their predecessors, contemporary writers no longer identify in the casting machines, lathes and presses the instruments for forging a better future at the assembly line.

The factory today appears to be a space dominated by death and destined to oblivion. Some of the works mentioned above evoke this fate in their very titles: *La dismissione*, for example, is the story of painstakingly dismantling – both physically and metaphorically – a steel production plant. The protagonist, a skilled worker named Vincenzo Buonocore, wants to end his brilliant career by dismantling, "a regola d'arte" (with precise

---

12 Contarini, S. (ed.). 2010. "Letteratura e azienda. Rappresentazioni letterarie dell'economia e del lavoro nella letteratura italiana degli anni 2000." Special Issue of *Narrativa*, no.s 31–32. Ceteroni, A. 2018. *Le letteratura aziendale. Gli scrittori che raccontano il precariato, le multinazionali e il nuovo mondo del lavoro*. Novate Milanese: Calibano.

13 Pennacchi, A. 2011. "Introduzione all'edizione Mondadori." *Mammut*. Milan: Mondadori. 5–12.

perfection)[14] and without the destructive force of dynamite, the factory that contributed so much to the construction of his identity. For an entire generation of the Italian South, the factory represented the hopes and dreams of national civic progress: an idea of progress that claimed to resolve the disparities between North and South, rich and poor, while promising the cultivation of class consciousness and a strong work ethic to combat the ever-present threat of mafia corruption. Bolt by bolt, Buonocore dismantles part of the building in what is certainly an extreme act of love for the factory and everything it represented. But at the same time, Buonocore also dismantles his own professional present and future: he knows that the casting machines will be shipped to the Far East, perhaps contributing to the construction of new political identities and leaving Italy with nothing but the pieces, debris and scraps of a consciousness never fully realized.

Mammut too evokes, in its very title, a rather gloomy fate. The novel explores the Supercavi factory in Latina, where the protagonist Benassa was a labor union representative, during an important moment of productive transformation, when power was shifted from the internal commission to the management. Benassa has witnessed the evolution of industry since the struggles of the 1960s and 1970s, and he has no illusions that the working class is destined to oblivion. During his last public speech, in announcing his decision to renounce politics and write a company history (with the blessing of the management, which uses the project as a way to further divide the workers), Benassa compares the working class to animals from past geological epochs: "una specie in via di estinzione" (a species on its way to extinction).[15] The principal cause is "l'automazione, *l'aumento dei computer*. Tra trent'anni, tutte le fabbriche saranno automatiche. Completamente. Gli operai non esisteranno proprio più" (automation, *the increase in computers*. In thirty years, all factories will be automated. Completely. Workers just won't exist anymore).[16] The narrator of *Mammut* does not stop at the moment of value creation; he ruthlessly takes stock of the aspirations and achievements of almost two decades of working-class

---

14   Rea, E. 2014. *Le dismissione*. Milan: Feltrinelli. 38.
15   Pennacchi, A. 2011. *Mammut*. 175.
16   Pennacchi, A. 2011. *Mammut*. 175. Emphasis mine.

struggles: "Culturalmente, poi, non ne parliamo. L'egemonia operaia? Ma per piacere ... Siamo una classe estinta. Ci siamo estinti già da un pezzo. Come il bisonte dell'Europa. Come i mammut ... Non ci stanno più i mammut ... E noi? Ci siamo estinti, amore mio. Culturalmente. Politicamente. Numericamente. Come i mammut" (Culturally, forget about it. Working-class hegemony? Give me a break ... We're an extinct class. We went extinct a while ago. Like the European bison. Like the mammoth ... There aren't any more mammoths ... And what about us? We went extinct, my dear. Culturally. Politically. Numerically. Like the mammoth).[17]

But while both of these novels recount the factory today, they are well aware (perhaps too aware) of the factory before the 1990s. On the contrary, Dezio's *Nicola Rubino è entrato in fabbrica* steers clear of that memory, presenting instead a totally automated factory whose employees maintain short-term or project-based contracts. Such an arrangement requires the employees to pass a never-ending series of tests, examinations and training courses that has eroded job security and rendered the predicament of workers exceedingly fragile. Dezio's merit is to show us how, despite the technologization of the relationship between workers and the assembly line, the damaging psychological effects of industrial labor have not disappeared. The alienation, loneliness and fear that overwhelmed workers in the large factories of Turin and Milan have remained potent and are indeed exacerbated by the mortification and bewilderment of constant subjection to possible termination (the fate of the rebel protagonist). Dezio's novel also foregrounds another theme shared by many contemporary stories that are set away from the neoliberal metropolis:[18] it is in the provinces that the application of capitalist logic seems the most cruel and ferocious. Advanced practices of human relations and marketing are here administered in the most rigid and acritical way, as if the only possibility for existence in the capitalist economy were to adapt to a set of general formulae.

17 Pennacchi, A. 2011. *Mammut*. 175.
18 For example, the Sardegna of Murgia, M. 2006. *Il mondo deve sapere*. Milan: ISBN. or the various provinces of Ferracuti, A. 2006. *Le risorse umane*. Milan: Feltrinelli.

The Tertiary Sector: Office Work and New Spaces of Production

Since the 1990s, Italian literary representations of labor have focused more and more on an aspect already present, though minor, in 'industrial' literature: the tertiary sector.[19] Anticipating the writing style of the anthology *Gioventù cannibale* (Cannibal Youth, 1996), Nata's novel *Il dipendente*[20] introduces the reader to the corridors of a multinational financial services corporation called Siva (probably a metathesis of 'Visa'). The protagonist is a tremendously successful manager who suddenly loses all control over his life. Very quickly, his whole world crumbles: his boss loses all trust in him, and without offering any explanation, hires a new, younger and more energetic manager; the protagonist catches his ex-girlfriend cheating with another woman and leaves her his apartment, going to live instead in a squalid and extremely expensive Roman hotel; he loses touch with his daughter, who already lives with her mother in Brazil; and he maintains affective family relations only with his own mother (his father is nowhere to be found).[21] Isolated, depressed and repeating without conviction the company mantras of labor power and flexibility, the protagonist perishes in an automobile accident that resembles a suicide.

Nata's prose is intimately personal and dominated by the use of parataxis, as if to synthetically render the narrator's fear of articulating thoughts and overcoming the superficial barrier separating him from the depths of his own self. Nata tells the story of a ruthless world: where generating profit

---

19   The most obvious example from the 'industrial' period is Parise, G. 1965. *Il padrone*. Milan: Feltrinelli. See also the novels of Ottiero Ottieri.
20   These two publications grew from of the same editorial grounds. *Il dipendente* was one of the last novels printed by the Roman publishing house Theoria, directed by Severino Cesarei and Paolo Repetti. Cesarei and Repetti then moved to Einaudi, where they published *Gioventù cannibale*, edited by Daniele Brolli.
21   It should be noted that there exists in contemporary labor literature a recurring link between father figures and death, whether from sickness or mere disappearance. Nata elaborates this link in subsequent novels, including in Nata, S. 2010. *Il valore dei giorni*. Milan: Feltrinelli.

is the only imperative, where the ability to generate it orders all human hierarchy and interpersonal relations, where economic value determines human value in a detrimental imbalance whose danger is confirmed by the novel's epilogue.

Unlike Nata, with his concern for the finance world of the economic elite, Andrea Bajani concentrates in *Cordiali saluti* (Kind Regards, 2005) on the 'middle class.' Bajani's narrator never actually introduces himself, but he is nevertheless given the name of 'Killer' by his colleagues, on account of his job: he drafts the company's employee termination letters. All of the attention is concentrated on the internal dynamics of this anonymous Italian office building, including the violence that regulates the relationships between employees and managers and among employees themselves. Bajani's short novel opens with the termination of the sales director Carlo Simoni, the reasons for which are not disciplinary, but rather biological. The middle-aged Simoni has lost all ability to keep up with the advancing production rhythms: he is slow, he lags behind and his long sales experience is no longer considered an asset, but rather a hinderance to the introduction of new working methods on the part of the company's management.

Like Nata, Bajani's goal is to reveal the cruel logic that dominates the Italian tertiary sector: in his novel there exists no sentiment, nor respect, nor loyalty capable of controlling the hegemony of the profit motive and its exaltation of the useful. Yet from a distance, Nata and Bajani offer divergent conclusions: while the protagonist of *Il dipendente* is crushed in the wreckage of a company automobile, the narrator of *Cordiali saluti* rebels against the office environment, laying bare its monstrosity along with that of the human relations director. Though it is true that the latter case still leads to the narrator's termination, Bajani's is at least a message of hope instead of an unconditional surrender.

In *Il mondo deve sapere* (The World Must Know, 2006), Michela Murgia too turns her attention to the impoverished middle class of the working poor. Murgia's characters are telemarketers at a Sardinian call center whose extremely low salaries and short-term contracts are topped off by bonuses awarded for high call volumes. This "romanzo tragicomico" (tragicomic novel), as the book's title page defines it, is the result of a peculiar editorial history: it began as a blog about the misadventures of the telemarketer Camilla de Camillis before being picked up by the publishing company ISBN and printed in physical form. That *Il mondo deve sapere* began as a web-based document is evident in the fragmentary nature of its chapters (for rapid reading), its caricatured individuals (for easy memorization), its continuous experimentation with irony and its absence of a proper ending. Such a model has inspired many imitators, both with respect to the adaptation of web-based to paper-based stories (and vice versa),[22] and with respect to the use of a comic and ironic tone in narrating complex and socially relevant themes like the increasing rate of precarious labor.[23] Notwithstanding certain stylistic limits, *Il mondo deve sapere* is among the first texts to give a large reading public access to the reality of the contemporary call center.[24] It has made of the call center and its difficult working conditions markers of a specific literary category, "un topos del precariato nella letteratura e nel cinema" (a *topos* of precarious labor in literature and cinema).[25] Such a category includes titles like *Viva il call center* (Long Live the Call Center, Paolo Amadio 2005), *Call center* (Angela Ceraso 2005), *Voice center* (Zelda Zeta 2007), *Vita precaria e amore eterno* (Precarious Life and Eternal Love, Mario Desiati 2006), plus short stories from Giorgio Falco's collection *Pausa caffè* (Coffee Break, 2004) like

---

[22] One thinks immediately of the international success (despite widespread critical reservations) of Incorvaia, A. and Rimassa, A. 2006. *Generazione mille euro*. Milan: Rizzoli. This text exists both on the book market and online at <http://www.generazione1000.com>. Accessed July 2, 2019.

[23] As Fulvio Panzeri notes, "L'ironia può essere un antidoto per non prendersi troppo sul serio come 'precari,' per non trasformare un'etichetta sociale in una patologia cronica, che come tutte le patologie indulge al vittimismo e può rappresentare una giustificazione alla mancanza di azione, all'impossibilità di dare una risposta creativa" (Irony can be an antidote to taking ourselves too seriously as 'precarious' workers, to transforming a social label into a chronic pathology that, like all pathologies, induces victim complexes and can represent a justification for renouncing action and dismissing any creative response as impossible). Cited in Chirumbolo, P. 2013. *Letteratura e lavoro*. 65.

[24] Another important 'text' in this regard is Paolo Virzì's 2008 film *Tutta la vita davanti*.

[25] Jansen, M. 2009. "Le vite precarie di Andrea Bajani." *Bollettino '900*, no.s 1–2. 2.

"Cold center," "Position" and "Rep Dance." These examples give an idea of just how prominent the call center has become in the collective literary imaginary: it is the dead end of a generation, the place where dreams and aspirations go to expire.

It would be difficult to close this section on the tertiary sector without saying something more of Falco's debut collection *Pausa caffè*. Falco's text is not a novel in the strict sense, but rather an assemblage of fragments: it is a chorus of voices, with different accents and regional inflections, orchestrated to recount the meanings of labor at the beginning of the twenty-first century. *Pausa caffè* is remarkable for its commitment to formal experimentation, a practice that most of contemporary labor literature gives up in exchange for the development of content and narrative force. Falco's collection seems to echo the lessons of Nanni Balestrini and the 1960s neo-avantgarde experiments, including lapses in narrative, an occasional lack of punctuation, creative figures of speech like zeugmas and syllepses, rhythmic stanzas, internal rhymes and parts that alternate verse with prose. *Pausa caffè* can be read as a medley of different styles, a work that tries to rescue certain of the past century's rhetorical strategies. But at the same time, it tells the ruthless story of an increasingly precarious labor market where jobs are protected no longer by the justice system, but rather by the kindheartedness of entrepreneurs. It explores the neon light of Italian office interiors with a standardized (and vulgar) language that is exceedingly hospitable to foreign influences, especially from English.

Literature and Labor: A Story of Continuity and Discontinuity

This short overview of contemporary Italian labor literature has demonstrated that there exists a thematic continuity between texts of the 1950s–1960s and those of today. The spaces of production have been outfitted with new technologies that have transformed the collective imagination, but in substance those spaces remain mostly the same. The harsh nature of labor and the imperative to struggle for the defense of human rights are likewise elements of representation in both the industrial and the neoliberal period.

And yet, the elements of discontinuity are still more numerous. Among these, we must note the disappearance in neoliberal literature of that yearning for – and belief in – economic and social improvement that characterized the greater part of the industrial period. The assumption of a real link between labor and progress that inspired socialist ideologies has come undone. Across generations, contemporary writers now tell stories of a new Italy, where the priority is to tear down factories and question workers' rights, especially those enshrined in the 1970 Statuto dei lavoratori (Workers' Charter) and those won in labor union struggles.

Balestrini's cry "Vogliamo tutto!" (We Want Everything!) has been replaced by an individualistic and subdued groan: "io non voglio niente" (I don't want anything).[26] The increasing rate of precarious labor and the proliferation of personalized short-term contracts have caused a deep fracture in Italy's social fabric. Barring very rare cases,[27] the worker-characters of contemporary labor literature do not think of themselves as belonging to a social group or class. Quite the contrary: they register both a reciprocal mistrust among individual workers and the declining repute of all forms of organized labor, resulting in the representation of workers as isolated persons who lack the necessary tools to fight a dominating and organized enemy.

Today, contemporary labor literature must be read in conjunction with an understanding of the industrial period, and vice versa. The value of returning to the novels of the 1950s and 1960s is that we can now recognize in them many of the central ideological elements that were destined to disappear, evaporate or fracture. From different historical perspectives, the theme of labor has constituted a gateway to some of Italy's most problematic and painful challenges. Since at least the 1950s, writers have used their language to hold up a mirror – sometimes more distorted, sometimes less – to society. More recently, though in a completely different literary, political and cultural context, we can see how labor literature expresses the

---

26 Trevisan, V. 2016. *Works*. Turin: Einaudi. 528.
27 One such case is Prunetti, A. 2018. *108 metri*. Rome and Bari: Laterza.

"necessità di pronunciarsi sul presente" (necessity of pronouncing on the present),[28] whether by adopting the fictional register of the novel or the directness of non-fiction.[29]

Translated by Jim Carter

---

28 Donnarumma, R. 2014. *Ipermodernità*. 108.
29 For examples of contemporary non-fiction about labor, see the following: Leogrande, A. 2008. *Uomini e caporali. Viaggio tra i nuovi schiavi nelle campagne del Sud*. Milan: Mondadori. Ferracuti, A. 2006. *Le risorse umane*. Rovelli, M. 2009. *Servi. Il paese sommerso dei clandestini al lavoro*. Milan: Feltrinelli.

MALVINA GIORDANA

14 Italian Cinema in the Twenty-First Century: Representing the Precarious Subject

The description of confusion is not the same as a confused description.
— Walter Benjamin, 1939

It's not true that we have lost,
it's just that we have arrived at a more delicate moment.
— Mario Monicelli, *I compagni*, 1963

To reflect on Italian cinema's representation of precarious work under neoliberal post-Fordism, it is first necessary to examine the wider conditions of precarity's expression in contemporary social life and media. In so doing, this chapter aims to better identify what is meant by 'precarious work' and which processes have been key to its depiction in Italian cinema of the last twenty years, particularly as expressed by female protagonists. Furthermore, the analysis here asks whether this recent cinema, which has made a point of representing precarious subjects, has in fact succeeded in accounting for major changes in labor and has created a new popular political imaginary. As will become clear, examining the trends in recent Italian cinema allows us to see a growing prevalence of precarious workers as protagonists and a wider shift in theme to the general conditions of precarious life. Both in the years before and after the 2008 financial crash, several films have employed narrative forms conducive to the critical and mainstream reception of a wide repertoire, a gallery of precarious subjects exceeding the depiction of exploitation in underground and independent film circuits.

From its inception, cinema was used as a tool to animate images of men and women at work. This continues to be true. However, the images have had to change along with the type of labor prevalent today. Typically, the worker characters more recent films represent are highly qualified while also inextricably tied to the unstable and devalued nature of contemporary work, enlivening the discussions on deskilling, and on the nature of precarity itself.[1] This analysis begins from the understanding that the existential conditions of precarity and contemporary forms of "expulsion"[2] – which have worked together to produce current social instability – have become central concerns of much contemporary international film, and that this is particularly true for the Italian context, where this theme is articulated mainly through the conventions of the comedy. I contend that a coherent thematic strand has emerged in many Italian movies of the last two decades, perhaps even a sub-genre, that represents the crisis of self-identification among young, often highly skilled, exploited subjects. These films make use of conventions inherited from the tradition of popular cinema, rather than adhering to the models of artistic commitment or *impegno*, given the former's wider accessibility.[3] Consider, as one example, the specificities of comedy in the Italian context. Ilaria De Pascalis

1   See: Di Nicola, E. 2019. *La dissolvenza del lavoro. Crisi e disoccupazione attraverso il cinema*. Rome: Ediesse.
2   My use of "expulsion" comes from the way sociologist Saskia Sassen describes the logics through which we can understand the vast changes to social life of the last few decades. The term refers to the expulsion of certain subjects from stable work and from social and physical spaces, as well as from certain rights that were defended for some in the Global North during the twentieth century. Sassen writes: "We are confronting a formidable problem in our global political economy: the emergence of new logics of expulsion. The past two decades have seen a sharp growth in the number of people, enterprises, and places expelled from the core social and economic orders of our time." Sassen, S. 2014. *Expulsions: Brutality and Complexity in the Global Economy*. Cambridge, MA and London: The Belknap Press of Harvard University Press. 1. I will borrow her use of this term to describe the predatory logics of contemporary capitalism, and also to underline how 'spaces' of expulsion can be used as political and conceptual spaces from which to agitate and struggle.
3   Consider the historical tradition of British films advancing social critique and of the ability of these films to describe the conditions of British workers and the underclass. Another historical precedent is found in the exploration of the precarious and expulsive spaces portrayed in contemporary French and Belgian social critique cinema. Prominent examples that come to mind: Ken Loach's most recent film *Sorry We Missed You* (2019), which investigates new forms of working-class exploitation,

discusses contemporary Italian comedy as a modality more than a genre: a chain of films with strong intertextual connections. She describes how the comedy – which employs traditional narrative forms and follows a linear resolution to the protagonist's problems – establishes which dynamics are to be considered common and 'normal,' and which 'deviate' from the norm. But she also underlines how rarely the ending is actually 'happy' and completely satisfying.[4]

This coherence between films that I underline is evident in the cultivation of a unifying methodological framework among Italian directors who have attempted to use cinema as a technical device to document precarity, but have instead often rendered it more ambiguous. Precarity must be understood as a historical phenomenon, linked just as much to labor regulations as to the social and individual dynamics of self-identification of working and filmic subjects. Thus, the analysis here appreciates cinema as an expressive form that has represented and continues to correspond to forms of capitalist life in a more direct way than other symbolic forms of visual culture.

Historically, this thematic strand became widely present precisely when the paradigm of flexibility as a credible promise for future stability was contested by workers across the continent: the illusions promised by this flexibility fell apart due to the material conditions of social life. Contemporaneous with the 2008 economic crisis, this moment was characterized by the mass expulsion of 'atypical' workers, those precarious subjects left completely devoid of a functioning socioeconomic safety net or a means of achieving the economic promises of the past.[5] Approximately

---

and the Dardenne Brothers' *Deux jours, une nuit* (2014), which confronts the consequences of being fired, in material as well as existential terms. More broadly, contemporary cinema outside of Europe is full of titles which refer to the conditions of precarious labor as forms of expulsion: *Certain Women* (Kelly Reichardt, 2017) or *The Florida Project* (Sean Baker, 2017). In Italy, titles such as *A Ciambra* (Jonas Carpignano, 2017) and *Fiore* (Flower, Claudio Giovannesi, 2016) quickly come to mind.

4   De Pascalis, I. A. 2012. *La commedia nell'Italia contemporanea*. Milan: Il castoro.
5   We can think of intellectual labor in Italian universities and the drastic consequences of cuts to public spending, which went from 6.7 billion Euro in 2008 to

a decade later, according to Eloisa Betti, we still find a context in which precarious contracts are "the principle modality of entrance into the Italian labor market, and even represent a growing percentage of new employment, due to the difficulties of access to stable positions once accessible with 'atypical contracts.'"[6]

The hypothesis I propose here is that it was possible to use the fragmented nature of precarious work to respond to an urgent need to create a cohesive narrative of precarity in the popular imagination through cinema. The lack of a unified and intelligible subject made it necessary to cinematically represent the spirit of our times, to see these subjects and this subjectivity configured in, where possible, unified and credible terms, and to create an image that corresponds to the specificities of the post-Fordist Italian condition. As we will see, this is most clearly expressed in female protagonists, who have always offered a more radical perspective and continue to demonstrate the tensions between desire and impossibility that characterize the precarious life of those in Italy entering the workforce today. The central questions of this chapter are whether this cinema has fulfilled this goal of forming a unified precarious subject, and whether these films could create this thematic coherence given a generalized impossibility to conceptualize the workforce and the social body with the use of outdated twentieth-century categories.[7] In short, was this cinema able to animate, or more precisely, *invent* an alternative precarious subjectivity amidst the chaos and instability of contemporary life?

4.9 billion in 2015. See: Coin, F. et al. (eds). 2017. *In/disciplinate: soggettività precarie nell'università italiana.* Venice: Edizioni Ca' Foscari.

6   Betti, E. 2015. "Storicizzare la precarietà del lavoro tra fordismo e post-fordismo: una prospettiva di genere." *Di condizione precaria. Sguardi trasversali tra genere, lavoro e non lavoro* Edited by Luca Salmieri and Ariella Verrocchio. Trieste: EUT Edizioni Università di Trieste. 118.

7   See: Bologna, S. 2007. *Ceti medi senza futuro?* Rome: DeriveApprodi. Allegri, G and R Ciccarelli. 2011. *La furia dei cervelli.* Rome: Manifestolibri.

Precarity: From the Political Imaginary to the Cinematic Narrative

Precarious work does not simply refer to strict definitions of labor relations and paradigms. More precisely, this term signifies an all-encompassing general *condition* into which contemporary workers find themselves subsumed. This condition is measurable first in the structural and normative aspects of labor relations, in the instability of wages or the lack of guaranteed contract lengths or continuous work.[8] However, it is also deeply based in social and individual self-representation and self-recognition – or the lack of an ability to recognize oneself – in social life and in media.

In terms of a political imaginary, during the last two decades a symbolic vocabulary was produced from social movements and workers' struggles in Italy. These movements proclaimed themselves 'precarious workers' at the first May Day Parade in Milan in 2001.[9] From the outset, the themes of the political struggle were inscribed into a parable of global exploitation and contingency, often in response to perspectives disseminated by neoliberal

---

8   According to a report by the European Commission, the following are the key characteristics of precarious work: part-time, temporary, freelance or self-employment, under-the-table, on-call contracts, zero-hour contracts, seasonal work, domestic work, care work, and so on. See: European Commission, DG Employment, Social Affairs and Equal Opportunities. 2012. "Study on Precarious work and social rights." <http://ec.europa.eu/social/BlobServlet?docId=7925&langId=en>.

9   I refer here to the 2001 May Day Parade in Milan. Prompted by the Milanese collective Chainworkers and other movements and groups in Italy, participants organized with the intention of networking a generation whose common denominator was not work in the strict sense, but the experiences of precarious social and working conditions that could not be placed any longer on the failures of trade union representation or adequately described in public debate. Among them were temporary workers in call centers or universities, permanent interns or till operators, and so on. See: Foti, A. 2004. "It's a Euro MayDay." *Posse*, no. 8. Fumagalli, A. 2015. "Cognitive, Relational (Creative) Labor and the Precarious Movement for 'Common-fare': 'San Precario' and EuroMayDay." *Creative Capitalism, Multitudinous Creativity*. Edited by Giuseppe Cocco and Barbara Szaniecki. London: Lexington Books.

talk-show political debate. From Milan, the term and the struggle moved through Europe. After this, during the last fifteen years, studies on precarity have become more and more common. They first began between sociology and economics, but have also expanded into fields such as aesthetics and film studies.[10]

At the same time, an interdisciplinary consideration between scholars – many of whom belong to the so-called 'precarious generation' themselves, now in their thirties – has begun to theorize an investigation of work with respect to the category of so-called 'feminized labor' under post-Fordism.[11] Because of a series of historically determined conditions, the female cinematic subject remains the most useful and radically contemporary protagonist for the purposes of depicting exploitation. Given that female subjects have historically been scrutinized much more than males (inspected for their style, fashion, walk, sex appeal and so on), and have always carried greater signs of marginalization, the highly performative female filmic subject provides an entry point to documenting precarious life.[12]

These investigations have been clearly prompted by the complex systems for producing and disseminating images, which have allowed for the creation of an iconographic collection of the precarious condition.

With this in mind, we can assert that mainstream Italian cinema has taken this pluralist and contingent scenario to re-stage widespread disappointment and discomfort toward an atmosphere dominated by the

---

10   See: Chirumbolo, P. 2012. "Il mondo del lavoro nel cinema del nuovo millennio: R. Milani, F. Comencini e A. D'Alatri." *Annali d'Italianistica*, vol. 30. D'Amelio, M. A. 2014. "La commedia del precariato in *Tutta la vita davanti* (P. Virzì, 2008)." *Un nuovo cinema politico italiano? volume 1 Lavoro, migrazione, relazioni di genere*. Edited by William Hope, Luciana d'Arcangeli, and Silvana Serra. Leicester, UK: Troubador Publishing. Agosti, A. 2008. "Lavoro e lavoratori sullo schermo cinematografico: esempi del passato, testimonianze dell'oggi." *RASSEGNA CNOS*, vol. 23, no. 3. 95–113.

11   Regarding the Italian context, see: Fantone, L (ed.). 2011. "Genere e precarietà." *Scriptaweb*. See also a monographic issue devoted to this topic: De Simone, G and S Scarponi (eds). 2010. "Genere, lavori precari, occupazione instabile." *Lavoro e diritto*, vol. XXIV, no. 3.

12   Cardone, L et al. (eds). 2018. "Pelle e pellicola. I corpi delle donne nel cinema italiano." *Arabeschi*, no. 12.

disintegration of social and civil contracts. Rather than representing such collective possibilities, however, these films often propose parables of individualism, seen through the singular protagonist stuck in contemporary isolation. Rather than workers in collective struggle, the characters are often a single man or a woman who suffer from the material consequences of precariousness.

The search for a coherent image became central to cinematographic narratives, just as it was historically key to enact radical self-representation in the performance of social actors during crisis and struggle. The generation of militant subjects referenced above has insisted on the redefinition of prior frameworks in the discourses on labor and has offered a new language to create a political subjectivity from its precariousness.[13] These subjects began to appreciate the individual and social costs of flexibility to describe a new collective and heterogeneous precarious subject.[14]

In the early years of the new millennium, this new imaginary reconfigured the symbolic order of work via a strong investment in the performative dimension. As underlined by Attila Bruni and Giulia Selmi, writing on the Italian May Day movement:

> Attraverso il riferimento a diversi artefatti simbolici (testi, immagini, performance) prodotti dai gruppi e dalle reti che in Italia si mobilitano contro la precarietà, mostreremo come l'aver sostituito al piano della rappresentanza quello della rappresentazione abbia contribuito a far emergere (e, in un secondo momento, a tematizzare esplicitamente) l'ordine simbolico di genere che fa da sfondo tanto alle relazioni lavorative, quanto alla narrazione di nuove identità sociali, problematizzando così le relazioni tra soggettività individuale e collettiva, lavoro e non lavoro, maschile e femminile.

> (Through the reference to diverse symbolic artefacts (texts, images, performances) produced by groups and from networks that in Italy mobilized against precarity [...] they have substituted their political representation for a self-representation, which has contributed to the emergence (and, in a second moment, to explicitly thematize) the symbolic order of gender which creates the background for labor

---

13 See: Standing, G. 2011. *The Precariat: The New Dangerous Class*. London: Bloomsbury Publishing. Allegri, G. and R. Ciccarelli. 2013. *Il Quinto Stato*. Florence: Ponte delle Grazie.
14 Gallino, L. 2001. *Il costo umano della flessibilità*. Bari: Laterza.

relations, as well as for the narratives of new social identities, and thus problematizes the relations between individual subjectivities and the collective, working and non-working, male and female.)[15]

In the first decade of the twenty-first century, while politicians and TV debates remained fixed on the 'flexibility' of labor, social movements such as those described above created a synthesis of images. They re-centered the subject, who thus became material for the first audiovisual expressions of precarity that were disseminated through independent cinema. These were the years of documentary: *Vite flessibili* (The Flexible Lives, Nicola Di Lecce and Rossella Lamina 2003), *Invisibili* (The Invisibles, Tania Pedroni 2003), *L'uomo flessibile* (The Flexible Man, Stefano Consiglio 2003), but also of narrative films such as *Il vangelo secondo Precario – Storie di ordinaria flessibilità* (The Gospel According to the Precarious – Stories of Ordinary Flexibility, Stefano Obino 2005). Just by looking at the titles, we can already see an emphasis on the human cost of this 'flexibility,' and therefore, of the self-reflection of the working subject's experience. The common trait among these films is in the value afforded to testimony, though it is expressed in very different ways. The use of testimony demonstrates the obsolescence of modern class separations, such as those between employed and unemployed, in favor of new relations between work and non-work, between subordination and autonomy. Before all else, what became clear was the impossibility of recounting such diverse subjects through a univocal or undifferentiated subject. These films seem, in fact, to have described the more general tension between desire and impossibility, influenced by the gender and age of the represented subjects, whether atypical, flexible, seasonal or under-the-table workers.

During the 2010s, however, dozens of mainstream Italian films also shifted focus to subjects that demonstrated the impossibility of finding stable work. Many were made by first-time directors, who understood and denounced precarity in films such as *Into Paradiso* (Paola Randi 2010), *Spaghetti Story* (Ciro de Caro 2013), *Smetto quando voglio* (I Can Quit Whenever I Want, Sydney Sibilia 2014, 2017), *Cosa vuoi che sia* (What's

---

15 Bruni, A. and G. Selmi. 2010. "Da san Precario a WonderQueer: Rappresentazioni di genere nell'attivismo precario italiano." *Studi culturali*, vol. 7, no. 3. 365.

the Big Deal, Edoardo Leo 2016) and *In bici senza sella* (On a Bike with No Saddle, 2016). Furthermore, the critique of precariousness also became a central preoccupation in films by established directors like *Giorni e nuvole* (Days and Clouds, Silvio Soldini 2007), *Tutta la vita davanti* (Your Whole Life Ahead of You, Paolo Virzì 2008), *Generazione 1000 euro* (The 1000 Euros Generation, Massimo Venier 2009), *L'intrepido* (Intrepido: A Lonely Hero, Gianni Amelio 2013), *Scusate se esisto* (Do You See Me?, Riccardo Milani 2014) and *Sole cuore amore* (Sun, Heart, Love, Daniele Vicari 2016).

Through these films that had widespread appeal, we begin to see an image of the generation born during and since the legislative provisions of part-time work under the Craxi government (1983–1987), entering the workforce during the last thirty years. These subjects, now in their thirties and forties, began to experience the contemporary forms of legislated exploitation such as 'temporary work' through the Pacchetto Treu (1997), project-based contracts through the Legge Biagi (2003) and labor reform during the 2008 crisis through the Legge Fornero (2012) and the 2014 Jobs Act. In this way, such historic conditions allowed precarity to become a verifiable norm in the popular imagination. Thus, the protagonists of these mainstream and popular films are clearly subjects perpetually in transition: from the precarious subjects of the first documentaries in investigations such as *Vite flessibili*, 'atypical' stories in films such as *Il vangelo secondo Precario*, a long list of brilliant graduates without a future such as Matteo from *Generazione 1000 euro*, researchers who have been 'expelled' from academia such as the protagonists of *Smetto quando voglio* all the way to the skilled female workers who face gender and age discrimination, embodied in characters like Serena Bruno in *Scusate se esisto* or Eli and Vale from *Sole cuore amore*, to cite just some of the most significant examples.

While Italian films had already addressed the uncertainty of life, the struggle of the protagonists was often mediated through family drama, down-and-out youth and the frustration and unhappiness of narcissistic problems.[16] Instead, the directors I mention here abandoned this content,

---

16   The reference here is to titles such as: Gabriele Muccino's *L'ultimo bacio* (The Last Kiss, 2001) and *Baciami ancora* (Kiss Me Again, 2010), Giovanni Veronesi's *Che ne sarà di noi* (What Will Become of Us, 2004) and *Genitori e figli. Agitare bene*

while keeping the form of mainstream films. They made use of the subjective repercussions of the economic crisis, configuring it with expressive codes capable of animating the workers of a chaotic time, the economic logics of exploitation and those of 'expulsion.' For example, the common cinematic trope of depicting a fear of aging was transposed in many films into a fear of an unstable future. Thus, traditional filmic tropes were not so much done away with, as they were strategically employed to describe a new narrative. That being said, while an unstable future should ostensibly speak to a collective subjectivity, these films rather reinforced the individual's place within such crises. Just when the societal faith in work evaporates, we see a deluge of images in mainstream Italian cinema that are articulated with regards to the trajectories of new precarious subjects. During the moment in which work is eclipsed as a singular, monolithic notion, its fragmentation creates a heterogeneous cinematic subject and uses forms like the typical romantic comedy to forge reception and recognition.

Going further, this thematic strand I am teasing out demonstrates a reflection on labor as an incandescent nucleus to be reorganized via a form that takes hints from documentary and narrative film. These are, in fact, the years in which filmmakers moved freely between fiction and documentary, creating hybrids between these poles[17] as in the case of *Mi piace lavorare (Mobbing)* (I Like to Work: (Mobbing), Francesca Comencini 2004), a film that is still underappreciated for how it engaged themes of social exploitation. But most importantly, there were still films that continued to reflect typical and classically constructed representations of labor, such as *Il posto dell'anima* (The Soul's Place, Riccardo Milani 2003) or *Signorinaeffe* (Miss F, Wilma Labate 2007), inspired by the documentary short *Signorina Fiat* (Miss Fiat, Giovanna Boursier 2001). The list continues with titles such as

---

prima dell'uso (Parents and Children: Shake Well Before Using, 2010) and Paolo Genovesi's *Immaturi* (The Immature, 2011).

17   Concerning Italian cinema, see: Montini, F. and Zagarrio, V. 2012. *Istantanee sul cinema italiano. Film, volti, idee del nuovo millennio*. Catanzaro: Rubbettino Editore. Perniola, I. 2014. *L'era postdocumentaria*. Milan and Udine: Mimesis Cinema. Concerning the last two decades of documentary filmmaking in Britain, the US and Europe, see: Bruzzi, S. 2000. *New Documentary: A Critical Introduction*. London and New York: Routledge.

Il mio paese (My Country, Daniele Vicari 2006), *Morire di lavoro* (Dying of Work, Andrea Segre 2008), *Dell'arte della Guerra* (The Art of War, Luca Bellino and Silvia Luzi 2012) about the Innse case in Milan and *7 minuti* (7 Minutes, Michele Placido 2016), inspired by the victory of women workers who struggled against a textile factory in Yssingeaux, France.

Thus, now we can assert that cinema departed from the classic sites of waged labor – the factory, for example – and rather began to elaborate new times and spaces of work and of unemployment. These spaces, and imaginaries, are depicted in contemporary changes to housing policy, the value and eradication of leisure time, in new structures of affective relations and so on. Perhaps we can think these spaces with Mikhail Bakhtin's chronotopes, which he proposed to describe discursive configurations of time and space. As the title of Virzì's film (Your Whole Life Ahead of You) seems to ironically attest, the proposal that a functional future necessitates an intermittent and austerity-ridden economy noticeably collapsed in the perception of young graduates who saw the foreclosure of those promises of stability as they entered these new spatio-temporal realities (see Figure 7).

Marta, Serena and Eli: Female Subjects as Markers of Precarity

In April 2019, the writer Michela Murgia responded to a tweet by former Interior Minister Matteo Salvini in which he referred to her as a "intellettuale radical chic e snob" (chic radical intellectual and a snob). Murgia responded by recounting the entries on her CV as a testament to her work history made up of precarious, short-term, project-base contracts all over Italy, including work in restaurants, small companies, schools and call centers. Her resume made resolutely clear that she was anything but a snob, but rather a typical example of a young precarious worker. Using her experiences from one of the jobs on the list – as a vacuum vendor for the US multinational company Kirby – Murgia created a blog first and then wrote her debut book *Il mondo deve*

Figure 7. Poster for the theatrical release of Paolo Virzì's *Tutta la vita davanti* (Your Whole Life Ahead of You, 2008). The pose of the mass of characters clearly replicates and parodies the famous early-1900s painting *Il quarto stato* (The Fourth Estate) by Giuseppe Pellizza da Volpedo, representing a workers' strike.

sapere. Romanzo tragicomico di una telefonista precaria (The World Must Know: A Tragicomic Novel by a Precarious Telephone Operator). In the book, she describes:

> Quell'anno d'esordio è stato anche quello in cui il precariato divenne per la prima volta un argomento di moda nei talk show televisivi e nei comizi; ce li ricordiamo ancora i politici nei salottini televisivi a pontificare che non bisognava definire 'precarietà' quel deflusso dei diritti legati al lavoro. A sentir loro, allora come oggi, dovevamo chiamarla 'flessibilità.'

> (That debut year was also the one in which precarity became for the first time a fashionable argument in television talk shows and in speeches; we can still remember the politicians in television studios pontificating that the eradication of workers' rights shouldn't be called 'precarity.' In their opinion, just like today, we should call it 'flexibility.')[18]

Among the films from this decade to which we have dated the continual reception of precarious subjects in Italian cinema, it seems that Virzì's *Tutta la vita davanti* – based on the written testimony of Murgia and receiving five David and Donatello nominations while taking in four million euros at the box office – is the most fitting example for the arguments presented here. In the film's portrayal of work as a space of solitary individualism, as claustrophobic and rife with hierarchies that render ambiguous the categories by which workers may recognize themselves, Virzì and the screenwriter Francesco Bruni insert Marta's odyssey into the rhetoric of dreamy comedy. Marta is a young woman who accepts a precarious job as a call-center operator for Multiple India, a company located in the periphery of Rome that sells water filters. She has a degree in philosophy and takes care of her roommate's daughter to make ends meet.

Tutta la vita davanti is a parable of a subject that traverses the jungle of precarity at a historical juncture when the sun has set on union representation, which until recently (in Italy at least) was a dominant

---

18 Murgia, M. 2006. *Il mondo deve sapere. Romanzo tragicomico di una telefonista precaria*. Milan: Einaudi. V.

player in political and theoretical contexts. Giorgio Conforti (played by Valerio Mastandrea) is a trade unionist with the real Nuove identità di lavoro (New Work Identities) and tries in vain to organize the workers and unmask the company's methods of exploitation. Comparing him to a storied example from Italian cinema, he is just a faded version of Professor Sinigaglia (played by Marcello Mastroianni) from *I compagni* (The Organizer, Mario Monicelli 1963). Sinigaglia is a wise and persuasive figure, a catalyst for strikes in a Turin textile factory at the end of the nineteenth century and a reminder of the developing factory-floor unionists who waged class struggles under industrial labor paradigms. Conforti is instead a representative of our times: only the limping posture of Sinigaglia is preserved, condensed into little details such as the typically working-class bike Conforti handles awkwardly. For the phone center operators, who sell their cognitive-relational labor, the flailing unionist lacks a strategy for cultivating solidarity. In fact, his secret talks to extract information only demonstrate to them that he is not a comrade in struggle who can guarantee work but rather a reminder of the threat of being fired.

Returning to Marta, in the context of twenty-first-century pop subcultures, depicted through allegoric and phantasmagoric forms – the dazzling lights of TV sets and the new architectures in the peripheries inspired by the Renaissance ideal for Sunday consumption (see Figure 8) – she confronts a parable that allows her to demonstrate her incompatibility with the social order proposed by the degrading geometries of precarity, described in grotesque ways between surrealism and hyperrealist dramas. A double tension inside the world of the film is sustained in the mise-en-scène that tends to transfigure the real in order to render it more credible.[19]

---

19   See: Zecca, F (ed.). 2011. *Lo spettacolo del reale. Il cinema di Paolo Virzì*. Pisa: Felici.

Italian Cinema in the Twenty-First Century 233

Figure 8. Marta (Isabella Ragonese) works as a telephone operator in the hyper-transparent workspace of precarity in *Tutta la vita davanti* (Your Whole Life Ahead of You, Paolo Virzì, 2008).

Marta is a character who carries a discursive density combined with the so-called contemporary 'globalization of precarity,'[20] as well as the history of precarious work, which upon closer examination, has established roots appearing way before the shift to cognitive post-Fordist labor. Indeed, on the one hand she embodies this generation which boasts the highest levels of education.[21] On the other hand, she also stands to represent the

20 See: Gallino, L. 2004. "Globalizzazione della precarietà." *Precarietà del lavoro e società precaria nell'Europa contemporanea*. Edited by Ignazio Masulli. Rome: Carocci. 9–24.
21 According to the 2018 Alma Laurea Report on the profiles of university graduates from 2017 (where women make up the overall majority, at 59.2%) the percentage of female students who graduate on time is 53.1% (48.2 for men) and the average score for women is 103.5 out of 110 (101.6 for men). This notwithstanding, the same report continues to show persistent gender wage gaps.

image of marginalized labor,[22] jobs historically held by the so-called peripheral workforce, namely women, children and migrants.[23] She is one of the female subjects whose experience demonstrates the relations between subjective identity and the collective horizon, through mechanisms of imitation, adjustment, refusal and subversion. Performative entities are capable of condensing a well-defined social landscape in their character and, moreover, passing through discursive spheres like fashion, aesthetic canons and lifestyle models.

Apart from Marta, this type of female character is also exemplified by Serena Bruno: the architect in *Scusate se esisto*. She is an independent woman finishing an excellent international training course. She pretends to be a man to get a job she has already secured through a public announcement, after finding out that the organization expects her to be a man. Yet another example is Eli, a barista and mother of four children in *Sole cuore amore* who belongs to a less-educated working class. She embodies the history of marginalized work more explicitly, as well as the phenomenon of the so-called 'feminization of atypical work.'[24] Furthermore there are the two women in the love triangle in *Generazione 1000 euro*. In this film, even though the protagonist is Matteo, a brilliant mathematician who ends up working in marketing, his story is told through the experiences of two women with completely different backgrounds. Metaphorically, they express the two horizons of stable or precarious work, symbolically embodied in different models which the two women express in their lifestyles, aesthetic choices and ethical considerations. In this film – the aspect that makes it particularly pertinent for the arguments presented here – the dispositive of precarity becomes the narrative motor which allows it to continue along the lines of the classic love triangle comedy. This means that the form is preserved but also reflects an entirely different socioeconomic condition.

---

22   See: Paci, M. 1973. *Mercato del lavoro e classi sociali in Italia*. Bologna: Il Mulino. Meldolesi, L. 1972. *Disoccupazione ed esercito industriale di riserva in Italia*. Rome and Bari: Laterza.
23   Betti, E. 2019. *Precari e precarie: una storia dell'Italia repubblicana*. Rome: Carocci.
24   See, for example: CENSIS. 2000. *L'impatto della flessibilità sui percorsi di carriera delle donne*. Milan: Franco Angeli.

Therefore, in the filmic representation of work and workers, some bodies become privileged over others, inscribed into diverse contexts, valorized via stereotypically masculine and feminine characteristics. The construction of a symbolic universe for the codification of the precariat exploits gender features in a rather simplistic way in order to help make visible issues such as "salari rubati" (wage theft), the reduction of welfare and the social safety net and the weakening of modes of collective organization.[25]

Inside such a framework, the contribution of contemporary Italian cinema does not seem to lie in posing the political problem of the production of subjectivity under an advanced capitalist world in an effective way. Rather, Italian cinema helps shine a light on the ways in which the *force* of capital conditions the *forms* of life, allowing new subjects to take center stage in their complex and political identity, instead of reducing them to the mere individuality of their experiences, bordering on a complete self-focus.

These films produce therefore a description, more or less accurate, of a generational condition in a precarious present now normalized. On the one hand, such a mapping is effective in showing the narrative potential of stories about precarity; on the other hand, it proves only able to draw the image of a summation of individuals, rather than organizing a collective of subjects.[26]

That being said, the task of cinema is not to solve issues, but rather to offer momentary montages to activate in the spectator the autonomy in which they might find their reflection. If this is true, then perhaps contemporary Italian cinema can contribute to our understanding of the effects of precarity in public discourse, and to the creation of new subjectivities away from the exploitation of contemporary modes of labor.

---

25   See: Coin, F (ed.). 2017. *Salari rubati. Economia politica e conflitto ai tempi del lavoro gratuito*. Verona: ombre corte. For a key text on the relations between feminized labor and wage theft, see: Federici, S. 2014. *Revolution at Point Zero: Housework, Reproduction, and Feminist Struggle*. New York: Autonomedia.
26   An important reference in this context is the reflection proposed by Japanese philosopher Hirose about the so-called "cine-capitalistic mode of production." See Hirose, J. F. 2018. *Le ciné-capital: d'Hitchcock à Ozu. Une lecture marxiste de Cinéma de Gilles Deleuze*. Paris: Hermann.

PART II

Italian Industrial Literature

UGO FRACASSA

15 Luigi Davì: The Caliber of a Working-Class Writer

Together with the ambitious factory story "Il capolavoro" (The Masterpiece, 1961), the forty-five chapters of *Gymkhana-Cross* (1957) – a debut collection of short stories – make up the industrial nucleus of Luigi Davì's narrative production. Davì's subsequent works – two more short story collections titled *L'aria che tira* (What's in the Air, 1964) and *Il vello d'oro* (The Golden Fleece, 1965) – testify to the variety of interests, subjects and environments available to the writer from the Valle d'Aosta. Starting with his debut for Elio Vittorini's Einaudi book series *I Gettoni*, Davì mixed representations of industrial reality from inside the 'boite' (dialect for 'factory,' but also 'prison') with episodes from the everyday life of a country in demobilization – in the *Gymkhana-Cross* chapter "Smobilitati" (Demobilized) – where the memory of Nazis and partisans was alive and present. Davì also described non-factory spaces, from pauses in industrial production – in "Intervallo due ore" (Two-hour Pause) – to sketches of military life – in "La marcia notturna" (The Night March) – sports – in "La prova del nove" (Casting Out Nines) – and lighter themes – in "Accompagnare una bambola" (Accompanying a Doll). After a rather brief literary career, during the early 1960s, Davì transitioned into television and theater, where he created a short-lived narrative project dedicated to mountaineering.

Born and raised in the Alpine village of La Salle, before relocating to the working-class suburbs of Turin, the author of *Gymkhana-Cross* and "Il capolavoro" was at the center of Italian industrial literature during the 1950s and 1960s. He worked in the Fiat factory, then in the Olivetti company sales organization and finally in pharmaceutical communications. Italo Calvino, who 'discovered' and mentored Davì, called him the "unica autentica voce di scrittore uscita dal mondo della fabbrica" (only authentic writer's voice to come out of the world of the factory).¹ Calvino met Davì in 1948 in the editorial office of the Partito Comunista Italiano (Italian Communist Party, PCI) newspaper *L'Unità*. The aspiring writer was not even twenty years old, but he had already published two short stories. From that moment on, Davì's literary career was hitched to the figure of Calvino: Calvino joined the Einaudi editorial team and recommended Davì to Vittorini, who published the young author in the book series *I Gettoni* and in issue number four (1961) of the journal *Il Menabò di letteratura*, dedicated to "Industry and Literature." Calling Vittorini's attention to the case of the "giovane operaio di Grugliasco" (young worker from the Grugliasco neighborhood), Calvino wrote in June 1955: "Visto che il romanzo cui aveva molto lavorato non andava, gli ho detto di radunarmi tutti i suoi racconti, per vedere se, ora che sono un certo numero, fanno libro" (Seeing as the novel that he had worked hard on wasn't going anywhere, I told him to gather me all his short stories, to see if, now that there is a good number of them, they'll make a book).² Calvino had also counseled Valerio Bertini, draftsman of the Galileo company factory in Florence and author in 1957 of the industrial novel *Il bardotto* (The Hinny), to conceive his book in a freely oriented manner, as a succession of "quadri di vita operaia" (slices of working-class life) rather than trust himself to the structure of the novel, which Calvino considered a "grossa catena al piede" (heavy shackle on the feet) of contemporary "letteratura progressista" (progressive literature).³

During the late 1950s, the book series *I Gettoni* was certainly the best place to experiment with new narrative forms and contemporary themes, especially because it printed small, unadorned volumes at relatively low production costs. Davì's *Gymkhana-Cross* opens with the story "Le mie mani" (My Hands), a very brief fragment that the author considered little more than an impressionistic note on industrial life: "vicino al polso, la

1   Calvino, I. 1961. "Notizia su Luigi Davì." *Il Menabò di letteratura*, no. 4. 184.
2   Cited in Camerano, V., Crovi, R. and Grasso, G. (eds). 2007. *La storia dei Gettoni di Elio Vittorini*, vol. 3. Letter from Italo Calvino to Elio Vittorini. June 7, 1955. Turin: Aragno. 1506.
3   Calvino, I. 1991. Letter from Italo Calvino to Valerio Bertini. March 7, 1956. *I libri degli altri: lettere, 1947–1981*. Turin: Einaudi. 178.

pelle della palma è diventata cuoio, il suo disegno spicca, per la polvere di ghisa nei tessuti" (near the wrist, the skin of the palm has become leather, its design stands out against the iron dust of the fabric).⁴ Notwithstanding its brevity, this first bit of prose introduces some fundamental elements of the collection: the theme of factory labor, but also the constant use of dialog (reminiscent of Ernest Hemingway) triggered by the words of a co-worker: "Fredo mi batteva sulla spalle. Diceva – Mani di meccanico: più sono rovinate più valgono" (Fredo tapped me on the shoulder. He said – Hands of a mechanic: the more they're ruined, the more they're worth).⁵ Starting with the very first line, Davì also uses similes to evoke the presence of a female figure: "Erano come quelle di una femmina. Mani fatte per reggere una penna o per sfogliare un libro" (They were like a woman's. Hands made to hold a pen or to leaf through a book).⁶

The internal variety of *Gymkhana-Cross* – progressively overshadowed by its reception as an intervention into the debate on literature and industry – is confirmed not only by the book's title ('gymkhana,' in both English and Italian, means an assortment of games or sports), but also by the drafts of the table of contents that Davì, Vittorini and Calvino circulated right up to the moment of publication. Davì and Vittorini agreed on a version organized into "racconti d'epoca 1943-'45" (historic stories, 1943-'45), "della provincia" ([stories] from the provinces), "dei ragazzini" (of boys) and "delle ragazze" (of girls), followed by a "racconto sportivo" (sporting story) and, only at the end, stories "di fabbrica" (of factories) and "dei disoccupati" (of the unemployed).⁷ But it was Calvino who insisted on reorganizing the book to really catch the attention of literary critics. He wrote: "Non sono però d'accordo sull'ordine [...] cominciare con racconti del tempo di guerra, vuol dire dare al lettore per primi dei racconti come già ne conosce tanti [...]. Io comincerei con quelli che sono la novità del libro, cioè coi racconti di fabbrica" (But I do not agree on the order [...]

---

4   Davì, L. 1957. *Gymkhana-Cross*. Turin: Einaudi. 13.
5   Davì, L. 1957. *Gymkhana-Cross*. 13.
6   Davì, L. 1957. *Gymkhana-Cross*. 13.
7   Cited in Camerano, V., Crovi, R. and Grasso, G. (eds). 2007. *La storia dei Gettoni di Elio Vittorini*, vol. 3. Letter from Luigi Davì to Italo Calvino. May 30, 1956. 1536–1537.

beginning with wartime stories would mean giving the reader stories they already know [...]. I would begin with the book's novelty, that is, the factory stories).[8] Between March and July 1956, the three also decided on the book's title, after many hypotheses that proved, for one reason or another, unsatisfactory. On Daví's suggestion, they adopted "Gymkhana-Cross," the original title of the sporting story, dedicated to a motocross race (the story's new title became "La prova del nove" (Casting Out Nines)). Such an intuition demonstrated the self-awareness of a young and supposedly inexperienced author who was frequently considered both simple and naïve. Daví wrote: "Per il titolo suggerirei ancora [...] *Gymkhana-Cross* che è uno dei racconti più lunghi; l'insieme dei racconti dà peraltro l'idea di una corsa ad ostacoli" (For the title, I would still suggest [...] *Gymkhana-Cross*, which is one of the longest stories; for that matter, the whole set of stories gives the idea of an obstacle course).[9]

One signature of Daví's factory writings is the unscrupulous use of jargon, not only when it comes to the technical specificities of industrial labor, but also – as the book's title suggests – to life in general. Jargon is the distinct sign of a particular expertise; it works best when inaccessible or foreign to the literary ear (in the penultimate story, "L'argine del Reno" (The Banks of the Rhine), Daví employs the jargon of navigation to narrate a flood in the province of Rovigo (Veneto)). Jargon's reactionary quality can be glimpsed in one of the "racconti di montagna" (mountain stories), where the young protagonist, fed up with the haughty ways of his city friends who during a vacation "vengono pei sentieri" (saunter down the walking trails), devises a linguistic 'vendetta.' The protagonist aspires to a factory job in the valley. He makes friends with "uno della piana" (a kid from the plains), who shares a "libretto pieno zeppo di porcherie, roba di fabbrica del suo mestiere" (booklet jampacked with filth, factory stuff from his trade). Thanks to this booklet, the protagonist can respond to all the "gente beneducata che usa parlare tricolore" (educated folks with their

---

8   Cited in Camerano, V., Crovi, R. and Grasso, G. (eds). 2007. *La storia dei Gettoni di Elio Vittorini*, vol. 3. Letter from Italo Calvino to Elio Vittorini. June 8, 1956. 1540.
9   Cited in Camerano, V., Crovi, R. and Grasso, G. (eds). 2007. *La storia dei Gettoni di Elio Vittorini*, vol. 3. Letter from Luigi Daví to Italo Calvino. May 30, 1956. 1536.

patriotic talk).[10] As he declares: "se mi fanno ancora le parole grosse come case ci rispondo con quelle del libretto lì, che al confronto sono palazzi" (if they tell me those words again, big like houses, I'll respond with those from that booklet there that in comparison are palaces).[11] We can imagine the effect such language had on the average reader of *Gymkhana-Cross*, unaccustomed as they were to industrial terminology. Davì's lexical bravura is on full display in "Il calibro" (The Caliber), where he tells the story of an apprentice determined to learn the tools of the trade: "A tornire gli stampi, un calibro che tirasse almeno 250 mm e fosse preciso, ci voleva.' [...] S'era riempita la testa di 'cinquantesimale,' 'originale,' 'micrometrico,' 'inossidabile.' [...] Glielo portarono a casa avvolto nella carta velina [...] guardò che la prima e l'ultima delle tacche del corsoio corrispondessero con quelle del nonio" (To lathe the plate, we needed a caliber that cast at least 250 mm and was precise. [...] We filled our heads with 'fiftieth,' 'original,' 'micrometric,' 'non-oxidizable.' [...] I brought it home for him wrapped in tissue paper [...] he made sure that the first and last sliding notches corresponded to those of the vernier).[12]

The reactionary character of Davì's writing was a result of inevitable feelings of marginality: the author had left school at the age of fourteen and now he was publishing in Vittorini's prestigious book series. The last story in *Gymkhana-Cross*, titled "Un operaio Biondo" (A Blond Worker), gives voice to his inferiority complex. The protagonist – a stand-in for Davì himself – requests time off from the factory so that he can attend a nearby conference on the works of Ernest Hemingway and Mark Twain. But when he arrives at the conference center, he discovers that the event has been postponed: "Dalla mancata conferenza, Marcello aveva ricavato la sensazione d'essere stato preso a gabbo, schernito. Forse un sesto senso li aveva avvertiti che sarebbe intervenuto un intruso. [...] Un operaio vero tra studenti veri [...] che barzelletta scema" (From the cancelled conference, Marcello had experienced a sensation of being fooled, taunted. Maybe a

---

10 Davì, L. 1957. *Gymkhana-Cross*. 149.
11 Davì, L. 1957. *Gymkhana-Cross*. 149.
12 Davì, L. 1957. *Gymkhana-Cross*. 18.

sixth sense had warned them that an intruder was going to participate. [...] A real worker among real students [...] what a stupid joke).[13]

It would be impossible not to mention the echo effect produced by *Gymkhana-Cross*, when in 1979 Davì described his last visit to the book's editor: "Per il terzo incontro partii da Torino sotto un diluviare tremendo. [...] Elio Vittorini era morto e noi si andava a vederlo quest'ultima volta" (For the third meeting, I left from Turin during a tremendous downpour. [...] Elio Vittorini had died, and we were going to see him for the last time). Together with his wife, Davì reached Vittorini, and this was his immediate reaction: "a porgere l'estremo saluto c'erano tutti i grossi nomi, com'era giusto: pittori, scrittori, musicisti [...] e in breve ci sentimmo soli e sperduti; tornammo in strada e poi via, verso Torino" (all the big names were there to say goodbye, as was right: painters, writers, musicians [...] and, in brief, we felt alone and lost; we went back out into the street and then away, back towards Turin).[14]

Another important feature of these stories is the creative use of the ending, something that distinguished Davì's work from his literary debut to his later involvement in television. Davì's narrative mode is often adventurous, playful or picaresque, but his ending always introduces a note that is, if not quite bitter, certainly inspired by the reality principle: a sudden move grounding both author and reader. This is most evident in stories like "Cani senza padrone" (Dogs without Owners), "Il plotone degli osservanti" (The Platoon of Observers) and "L'argine del Reno," where a series of ideal and sentimental narrative hypotheses are transformed, in the ending, to reveal the causes of each story's action: a dog's hunger, a soldier's instincts and the laws of hydrology, respectively. Such a strategy of narrative build-up is exemplified in the factory story "Tutto a posto" (Everything's in Order), whose length is literally regulated by the mental calculation of one of the characters: "Alla fresatrice Vanni borbottava di vigliaccheria alla matematica, non riuscendogli il conto dei giri dei fori pel divisore. Aveva da tagliare un ingranaggio di 35 denti e da sbollire i postumi d'una festicciola" (At the

---

13   Davì, L. 1957. *Gymkhana-Cross*. 249.
14   Cited in Camerano, V., Crovi, R. and Grasso, G. (eds). 2007. *La storia dei Gettoni di Elio Vittorini*, vol. 3. 1599.

milling machine, Vanni grumbled cowardly about math, since he couldn't figure out the answer to the number of drill holes times the divisor. He had to cut a 35-tooth gear and cool the after-effects of a little party).[15] The story ends on a happy note once the character finishes his calculation, but it also confirms the force of the reality principle and the laws regulating production (emblematically contrasted with the "after-effects of a little party"): in Marxian terms, the prevalence of the structure over the superstructure.

The 1961 publication of "Il capolavoro" marked the consecration of Davì as Italy's industrial writer *par excellence* of working-class extraction. The short story was printed in number four of Vittorini's journal *Il Menabò*, and it represents the highest development of Davì's writing on the complexities of factory life in the years before the economic boom. *Gymkhana-Cross'* industrial reality was still that of the 'boite,' the small plants awkwardly inserted into the urban fabric: "quell'officina come lama di coltello infissa a forza tra le case dell'isolato" (those factories like knife blades forcefully fixed between apartment blocks).[16] In such a setting, where worker camaraderie was still palpable, it was not uncommon for the boss himself to take to a machine: "Il padrone si piazzò al tornio [...] e prese a centrarsi il pezzo col comparatore" (The boss positioned himself at the lathe [...] and began to center the piece with the indicator).[17] If there was a conflict, Davì evoked it only playfully: "Tu! Che fai in giro? –Missione speciale. Stiamo preparando l'insurrezione. –Fila al tuo posto!" (You! What are you doing out and about? –Special mission. We're preparing an insurrection. –Get back to your post!)[18]

Such an environment, where the relationship among workers was more reminiscent of conscripted soldiers than of unionized factory committees, was at risk of remaining invisible to intellectuals like Calvino and Vittorini. Calvino also misunderstood Davì's novel *Uno mandato da un tale* (He Who Was Sent By a Guy, 1959), provoking an early break between the working-class writer and the Einaudi team. Calvino thought the characters were too schematic, and he urged the aspiring Davì to work instead on pinpointing

15   Davì, L. 1957. *Gymkhana-Cross*. 29.
16   Davì, L. 1957. *Gymkhana-Cross*. 24.
17   Davì, L. 1957. *Gymkhana-Cross*. 14.
18   Davì, L. 1957. *Gymkhana-Cross*. 16.

"drammi" (dramas), concrete situations and "calde di vita" (pungent slices of life).[19] Davì retorted in accordance with his own direct knowledge of working-class conditions: "La fabbrica è più complessa di quanto possa sembrare al prendere atto di ordini del giorno o che so io: la fabbrica è tante persone, ed ognuna cammina a modo proprio, ed ogni modo ha la sua motivazione celata o palese, qualunque essa sia" (The factory is more complex than what you see in official reports or, I don't know: the factory is many people, and everyone walks their own way, and every way has its own hidden or clear motivation, whatever that may be).[20] Davì rejected Vittorini's request for 'racconti di agitazione' (agitation stories) with equal firmness. Vittorini wrote: "Mancano nel suo libro racconti di scioperi, di agitazioni, ecc. che completerebbero la visione dell'ambiente" (Your book is missing stories about strikes, agitations, etc. that would complete the vision of the environment).[21] In his response, Davì limited himself to re-asserting his own working methods, based on the narration of "cose viste o partecipate" (things seen or experienced), before conceding Vittorini the lack of "agitazioni" (agitations).[22]

Moreover, the industrial reality of open conflict was already dwindling during the late 1950s, when Davì was hired by Fiat. It was here that he was acquainted with the new production model represented in "Il capolavoro", a complex industrial reality that was nonetheless already prefigured in *Gymkhana-Cross* (for example, in the story "Reparto che vai" (You Can Tell a Department), where an unusual air of suspicion spreads across the production floor during interdepartmental transfers, even within the same factory). As Davì wrote to Vittorini, "Il capolavoro" is "una storia un po'

19   Cited in Camerano, V., Crovi, R. and Grasso, G. (eds). 2007. *La storia dei Gettoni di Elio Vittorini*, vol. 3. Letter from Italo Calvino to Luigi Davì. December 13, 1954. 1498.
20   Cited in Camerano, V., Crovi, R. and Grasso, G. (eds). 2007. *La storia dei Gettoni di Elio Vittorini*, vol. 3. Letter from Luigi Davì to Italo Calvino. December 11, 1954. 1502.
21   Cited in Camerano, V., Crovi, R. and Grasso, G. (eds). 2007. *La storia dei Gettoni di Elio Vittorini*, vol. 3. Letter from Elio Vittorini to Luigi Davì. October 29, 1955. 1515.
22   Cited in Camerano, V., Crovi, R. and Grasso, G. (eds). 2007. *La storia dei Gettoni di Elio Vittorini*, vol. 3. Letter from Luigi Davì to Elio Vittorini. November 5, 1955. 1516.

complessa, anche se in fondo non si tratta che d'uno che cambia fabbrica" (a somewhat complex story, even if, after all, it is just about someone who moves to a different factory).²³

The protagonist's future depends on his ability to make some sort of product – the 'capolavoro' (masterpiece) – and he labors away at a press. His colleagues are friendly, but also strangely reticent, and his first lesson is to memorize the numbers on his time card: "Lei guardi il numero, invece: la rintraccia prima [...] i numeri sono tutto e i nomi niente, voleva fargli capire il segretario" (Just look at the number: you'll find it quicker [...] numbers are everything and names are nothing, the secretary wanted to make him understand).²⁴ Tossed between fears of snitching and sneaking suspicions, the story barrels towards a vote for labor union representation, but the protagonist cannot fully grasp the importance of the situation. It is only in the closing lines that he finally achieves awareness and understanding. In accordance with Davì's penchant for jargon, the bitter moral of "Il capolavoro" is disclosed in an aural and lexical context displeasing to the ear of the average reader: "Da in cima al reparto l'utensile, un Widia, continuava a straziare i timpani" (From the top of the department, the utensil – a Widia – continued to tear apart the eardrums).²⁵ Davì's intention is to show the reader the rigid and secret logic of capitalism that poisons the working class with the potion of suspicion while progressing toward a totalizing and cohesive organization of social life. From the perspective of the individual worker, "ogni cosa si esauriva in sé, sempre episodica, singola, marginale, mai più che frammento" (everything referred only to itself, always episodic, singular, marginal, never more than a fragment).²⁶ The precision of the system succeeds in involving the workers as a whole. In the final words of "Il capolavoro," the protagonist comes face-to-face with the truth of his condition: "Molto meglio di lui, s'avvicinò all'intuire, il capolavoro l'avevano fatto degli altri. Molto meglio di lui e di qualsiasi

---

23 Cited in Camerano, V., Crovi, R. and Grasso, G. (eds). 2007. *La storia dei Gettoni di Elio Vittorini*, vol. 3. Letter from Luigi Davì to Elio Vittorini. October 23, 1957. 1566.
24 Davì, Luigi. 1961. "Il capolavoro." *Il Menabò di letteratura*, no. 4. 158.
25 Davì, Luigi. 1961. "Il capolavoro." 183.
26 Davì, Luigi. 1961. "Il capolavoro." 183.

di loro. 'Che stai ad almanaccare? Lascia perdere.' D'una precisione che li toccava tutti. Tutti" (He drew near to listen: the others had made their masterpiece much better than him. Much better than him, and than any of them. 'What are you racking your brains for? Let it go.' With a precision that they all needed to have. All of them).[27]

The intervention of the editors was decisive for "Il capolavoro" too. Calvino declared himself satisfied with the story – he wrote: "sei riuscito a rappresentare rapporti umani e stati d'animo complessi e difficili" (you succeeded in representing complex and difficult human relationships and moods)[28] – but together with Vittorini, he convinced Davì to perform a quick revision eliminating all the scenes of recreation, where young workers dressed as bourgeois gentlemen to court women in coffee bars. Once "Il capolavoro" was "ridotto quasi solo agli episodi di fabbrica" (reduced almost to only the factory episodes),[29] it could be packaged in a way that would make Davì what his editors called "il trionfatore di questo attesissimo 'menabò'" (the star of this highly anticipated number of 'menabò').[30]

In 1994, Davì participated in a conference on "Literature and industry" at the historic headquarters of the Fiat company. The author of *Gymkhana-Cross* and "Il capolavoro" looked retrospectively on his own narrative activity:

> Mentre sul versante operaio si scrivevano piccoli episodi, *tranche de vie*, racconti, impressioni, 'noterelle' e appunti, Volponi ci ha dato con il *Memoriale* il romanzo industriale nella sua pienezza. [...] Naturalmente gli scrittori operai non erano certo in parità di chance: vedevano la fabbrica da relegati nel proprio angolo, dal repartino angusto [...] mentre Volponi aveva in favore lo stare nei piani alti col vantaggio di una cultura organica più che adeguata e di una visione panoramica [...] del problema fabbrica.

---

27 Davì, Luigi. 1961. "Il capolavoro." 183.
28 Cited in Camerano, V., Crovi, R. and Grasso, G. (eds). 2007. *La storia dei Gettoni di Elio Vittorini*, vol. 3. Letter from Italo Calvino to Luigi Davì. December 5, 1957. 1568.
29 Cited in Camerano, V., Crovi, R. and Grasso, G. (eds). 2007. *La storia dei Gettoni di Elio Vittorini*, vol. 3. Letter from Italo Calvino to Elio Vittorini. April 3, 1958. 1575.
30 Cited in Camerano, V., Crovi, R. and Grasso, G. (eds). 2007. *La storia dei Gettoni di Elio Vittorini*, vol. 3. Letter from Italo Calvino to Elio Vittorini. May 15, 1961. 1581.

>(Some workers were concerned with writing brief episodes, slices of life, stories, impressions, 'little notes' and annotations, but Volponi gave us with *Memoriale* the industrial novel in its full development. [...] There was naturally no way that working-class writers could do this: they saw the factory from their own relegated corners, from their little narrow departments [...] while Volponi was favored by his position on the top floors and by the vantage of a more than adequate organic culture: a panoramic vision of the factory question.)[31]

Such words are a testament to the self-awareness and the intellectual stature of an author who was always deemed too "grezzo" (rough) to "subire crescite letterarie senza snaturarsi" (suffer literary growth without betraying his nature).[32] In his Fiat intervention, Davì recognized the superiority of the most celebrated industrial novel – Paolo Volponi's *Memoriale* (1962), influenced by the context of Adriano Olivetti's Ivrea – but he also decentered it in comparison with the compulsory fragmentation of his own narrative universe as a working-class writer.

Translated by Jim Carter

---

31   Davì, L. 1997. "Narrativa di fabbrica." *Letteratura e industria: Atti del 15° Congresso AISLLI*. Edited by Giorgio Bàrberi Squarotti and Carlo Ossola. Florence: Olschki. 1234–1235.

32   Cited in Camerano, V., Crovi, R. and Grasso, G. (eds). 2007. *La storia dei Gettoni di Elio Vittorini*, vol. 3. Letter from Italo Calvino to Elio Vittorini. June 7, 1955. 1505.

FABRIZIO DI MAIO

16 Mechanization and Exploitation in Ottiero Ottieri: *Tempi stretti* (1957) and *Donnarumma all'assalto* (1959)

This chapter sets out to examine how Ottiero Ottieri represented the dark side of the Italian industrial world in two novels: *Tempi stretti* (Tight Times, 1957) and *Donnarumma all'assalto* (The Men at the Gate, 1959).[1] Thanks to his personal experiences as human resources manager at Olivetti, Ottieri was able to convert industrial themes into literary texts from a privileged point of view, being at the same time writer and employee in a factory.

First, I will concentrate on the readings (of texts by Karl Marx and Simone Weil) and experiences that pushed Ottieri to look for a direct connection with the industrial world. In so doing, my analysis will be mostly based on some significant events of Ottieri's life, namely his employment in the Olivetti factories. Second, I will analyze how Ottieri shed light on two recurrent elements in the changing relationship between workers and the product of their labor in the capitalist mode of production: mechanization and exploitation. With the term mechanization, I refer to the process of using machines in order to produce something previously made by hand. Exploitation, from Marx's definition, is any underpaid or unpaid labor, which became routine practice across Italian factories during the

---

1   Apart from these works, it is worth mentioning that Ottieri wrote a comedy, *I venditori di Milano* (1960) and a diary, *La linea gotica* (1962) around industrial themes. For many critics, Ottieri was considered the front runner of Italian industrial literature. See the following references: Bulgheroni, M. 1957. "Tempi Stretti, un romanzo della fabbrica." *La Gazzetta del Libro*. October. Placido, B. 2004. "Ottiero Ottieri tra i operai meridionali." *La Repubblica*. April 4. Ferrata, G. 1962. "Ottieri e le esperienze di fabbrica." *Rinascita*. December 22.

economic boom. Finally, I will focus on the main consequence that arises from the interaction of mechanization and exploitation: industrial alienation. According to Marx, in brief, workers become alienated because, in industrial production under capitalism, they inevitably lose control of their work and thus, ultimately, of their lives and selves.

Ottieri's interest in the industrial world began developing in the 1940s, when he read the works of Karl Marx and Simone Weil. Ottieri carefully studied Marx's materialistic conception of alienation, by which workers become disconnected from what they produce.[2] This theme subsequently emerged strongly in Ottieri's factory novels.

Apart from Marx's theories, Weil's *La condition ouvrière* was a fundamental text for Ottieri's understanding of the conditions of the working class.[3] In her book, Weil gave first-hand testimony of the brutality and inhumanity of working conditions, describing the physical harshness of factory work and the moral impact of inhumane working cycles. She also compared the unjust balance of power between managers and workers to slavery. Ottieri was intensely impressed by Weil's descriptions of labor conditions from the inside. Influenced both by Weil's experience and her book, Ottieri wanted to "vedere con i miei occhi il problema del rapporto tra l'operaio e la macchina così come l'avevo letto in Marx. Sono stato una specie di piccola Simone Weil" (to see with my own eyes the problem of the relationship between workers and machines, just as I had read about it in Marx. I was a sort of little Simone Weil).[4]

Having studied the workers' conditions, Ottieri felt the need to plunge himself directly into the industrial world, knowing that it was only through personal experience that he would be able to appreciate the concreteness of the situation. For this reason, Ottieri decided to find a job in a

---

2   Marx, K. 1994. *Selected Writings*. Edited by Lawrence H. Simon. Indianapolis: Hackett Publishing Company.
3   Weil, S. 1951. *La Condition ouvrière*. Paris: Gallimard. Simone Weil, who was a teacher, took a one-year leave of absence (from December 1934 to November 1935) from her teaching position to work as a laborer in an Alsthom factory in Paris. She believed that only this form of experience, from inside, would allow her to connect with the working class.
4   Cited in Vergine, L. 1990. *Gli ultimi eccentrici*. Milan: Rizzoli. 233.

factory – somewhere where he could be close to the workers in their daily struggle.⁵ In 1953, he was hired as human resources manager at Olivetti, working in the factory in Ivrea (Piedmont) before moving to the factory in Pozzuoli (Campania) in 1955. Although his managerial position clearly distanced Ottieri from Weil's experience as a manual laborer, the position did allow him to have some direct observation of the workers' conditions during the economic miracle. The next step was the transposition of this direct experience into a literary narrative.

Elio Vittorini and Italo Calvino wrote about the relationship between Italian industry and literature in journals like *Nuovi argomenti* (issue numbers thirty-one from March-April 1958 and thirty-two from May-June 1958) and *Il Menabò* (issue numbers four from 1961 and five from 1962).⁶ As industry became an essential factor during the postwar economic reconstruction, Vittorini and Calvino wanted Italian literature to produce narratives directly from the industrial environment. But according to Vittorini, and despite some thought-provoking debates about the necessity of creating an 'industrial novel,' still by the mid-1950s, an industrially themed novel set inside a factory had not yet been published. The main issue was that laborers, clerks, employers and managers who worked for Italian companies did not have the suitable competencies (those of intellectuals, writers or poets) to describe such a complex reality. Regarding this crucial point, Ottieri was convinced that only a writer working in a factory would have the ability to make a contribution:

5   In an unpublished note from March 1947 housed at the Università di Pavia's Centro Manoscritti (Fondo Manoscritti), Ottieri wrote: "Sono convinto che solo attraverso [gli operai] possiamo raggiungere l'altra classe, il proletariato e vivere finalmente questa esperienza che è nel cuore del nostro secolo e della nostra situazione interiore. Perciò il mio ideale adesso sarebbe entrare in una fabbrica, in una Società, in un'industria, dove avvicinare padroni e servi nella loro lotta quotidiana." (I am convinced that it is only through [the workers] that we can reach that other class, the proletariat, and finally live out the experience that is at the heart of our century and of our interior condition. For this reason, my ideal now would be to join a factory, a company, an industry – somewhere where I can get close to the masters and servants in their daily struggle).

6   For more on *Il Menabò*, see Fiaccarini Marchi, D. 1973. *Il Menabò 1959–1967*. Rome: Edizioni dell'Ateneo.

> Il mondo delle fabbriche è un mondo chiuso. Non si entra – e non si esce – facilmente. Chi può descriverlo? Quelli che ci stanno dentro possono darci dei documenti, ma non la loro elaborazione: a meno che non nascano degli operai o impiegati artisti, il che sembra piuttosto raro. Gli artisti che vivono fuori, come possono penetrare in un'industria?
>
> (The world of factories is a closed world. One does not enter or exit it easily. Who can describe it? Those on the inside can give us documents, but not their elaboration – as long as no worker-artists or employee-artists are born, something that seems rather rare. Those artists living on the outside, how can they penetrate into an industry?)[7]

Because Ottieri was at once a writer and employee at Olivetti, he was able to bring to the surface the hidden world of the factories. With *Tempi stretti* (1957) and *Donnarumma all'assalto* (1959), Ottieri shed light on some significant features of industrial life that otherwise would have remained in the dark.

Tempi stretti is set in the mid-1950s in Milan and in Sesto San Giovanni (Lombardy), one of the most industrialized towns of the period, where "l'idea del lavoro e del mutamento sono per forza di casa, non essendoci da rispettare né alberi, né pietre antiche, né ponti sui fiumi. L'unica anima del luogo era la speranza operaia" (the idea of labor and of change are necessarily at home, seeing as there is no need to respect trees, nor ancient rocks, nor bridges over rivers. Working-class hope was the place's only soul).[8]

The main characters of *Tempi stretti* are Giovanni Marini, a manager at the Alessandri company, and Aldo Comolli, a worker at the Zanini company who, at the end of the novel, is fired because of his participation in trade union activism. Ottieri uses these two protagonists to give the reader the opportunity to grasp some important aspects of working life from two opposite perspectives. From a vertical perspective – from on high – the manager Giovanni observes the characteristics of the working cycles. From a horizontal perspective – from below – Aldo gains first-hand experience of the workers' conditions, which grow worse day after day. *Tempi stretti* highlights the main issues facing workers in their daily struggles: low wages, workplace humiliation, fear of being fired and nervous breakdowns.

---

7   Ottieri, O. 2004. *La linea gotica*. Parma: Guanda. 183.
8   Ottieri, O. 1957. *Tempi stretti*. Turin: Einaudi. 130.

Thanks to his managerial position, Giovanni (Ottieri's *alter-ego*) succeeds in acknowledging that the workers – the driving force of the economic miracle – are ruthlessly exploited by their superiors.

Ottieri drew particular attention to the mechanization that was changing the relationship between the workers and the products of their labor in the capitalist mode of production. The 'tight times' – the *tempi stretti* of the title – were a big issue in every factory: the machine converted work into time, while working times diminished in parallel with the machine's improvement. Ottieri describes the working process in the novel:

> I capisquadra giravano per le macchine, le preparavano. Un cronometrista rilevava il tempo. [...] A non sbagliare sono sei tempi. [...] Sei tempi, sei tempi, sei tempi e il sesto e il primo si rincorrevano. [...] Il tempo va vinto, non farsi vincere dal tempo. [...] La macchina riduce il lavoro a tempo puro, sebbene anche le macchine siano più veloci. Il progresso è questo. [...] Con il progresso, i tempi tendono a zero.
>
> (The foremen wandered around the machines, they prepared them. A timekeeper indicated the pace. [...] If done right, it takes six steps. [...] Six steps, six steps, six steps and steps six and one follow each other closely. [...] You need to beat the pace, do not let the pace beat you. [...] The machine reduces labor to pure time, even if machines are faster themselves. This is progress. [...] With progress, time tends toward zero.)[9]

Ottieri also highlights the slow but steady evolution of working conditions, from the predominance of physical labor to the prevalence of nervous struggles. On the one hand, thanks to the technological development of the machine, the workers' physical burden is lightened; on the other hand, the workers progressively lose their humanity and become automatons synchronized with the machine: "Qui la sincronia uomo-macchina era perfetta e ambedue correvano di volata, la pressa a divorare, l'uomo a rifornirla, pedalando sulla leva come uno scatenato ciclista con una gamba sola. Egli compiva movimenti fulminei, la fronte appena inclinata in avanti, fissando e consumando la strada invisibile dei pezzi e del tempo" (Here, the synchrony between man and machine was perfect, and both sprinted ahead, the machine press devouring, the man feeding it, pedaling the lever like a wild one-legged cyclist. He performed lightening-fast movements,

---

9 Ottieri, O. 1957. *Tempi stretti*. 51, 52, 64.

his forehead tilted slightly forward, fixing and consuming the invisible street of pieces and time).[10]

The critical reception of *Tempi stretti* was divided. Vittorini, Calvino and Pier Paolo Pasolini criticized the narration for being too 'bourgeois': in their eyes, it served to distance the reader from industrial reality. At the same time, however, they greeted it as the first attempt to write an 'industrial novel' in Italian literature. The same was expressed by Walter Mauro, who suggested that

> Questo libro ci porta proprio all'interno di questa Milano operaia, delle grandi industrie italiane, mostrandocene la vita in un momento di trasformazioni, di sviluppi e di difficili lotte sociali. [...] È proprio nelle testimonianze della vita di fabbrica, mi sembra più che negli scorci patetici e sentimentali, che l'autore rivela notevole forza narrativa.
>
> (This book brings us right into working-class Milan, with its grand Italian companies, showing us its life in a moment of transformations, of developments and of difficult social struggles. [...] It seems to me that it is precisely in the testimony of factory life, more than in the pathetic and sentimental moments, that the author demonstrates a notable capacity for narration.)[11]

After the publication of *Tempi stretti*, Ottieri continued to narrate the industrial world from new perspectives. Based on his experience at the Olivetti factory in Pozzuoli (which in literature he renamed "Santa Maria"), in *Donnarumma all'assalto* (1959) Ottieri narrated the dark side of industrialization in southern Italy in relation to the Southern Question. The Southern Question refers to a set of issues arising from the extreme economic, social and cultural differences that characterized the historical development of southern Italy with respect to the North. These issues were identified shortly after Italy's unification, at the end of the nineteenth century.

In Pozzuoli, Ottieri noticed three main problems: the forced industrialization of the South, its economic imbalance compared to the wealthier North and the farmers' industrial dream of being employed in a factory. As human resources manager, Ottieri's job was to select from among

---

10 Ottieri, O. 1957. *Tempi stretti*. 154.
11 Mauro, W.1957. "Un documento di vita italiana, Tempi stretti." *Il Paese*. October 24.

thousands of candidates the most suitable people for factory labor. Using a psychotechnics aptitude test, he was in charge of assessing each candidate's intellectual and physical abilities to perform specific tasks inside a factory. As his protagonist recounts in *Donnarumma all'assalto*:

> Qui giudichiamo un popolo intero. […] Non si seleziona, si screma. […] È più facile che un cammello passi attraverso la cruna di un ago che uno di Santa Maria attraverso l'esame psicotecnico. […] C'è una abitudine fissa, antica, di cercare lavoro più che di lavorare, […] una abitudine alla disoccupazione così profonda che ha generato i suoi vizi e le sue difese naturali.
>
> (Here we are judging a whole people. […] One does not select, one skims. […] It would be easier for a camel to pass through the eye of a needle than for an inhabitant of Santa Maria to get through this psychological examination. […] They are spurred on by a blind, restless desire for work combined with a fixed, inveterate habit of seeking work rather than working, […] they are inured to a state of unemployment, which is so deeply rooted that it has generated its own vices and its own natural defenses.)[12]

Illiteracy and unemployment are key features of the historical, sociological and economic background of the South. However, instead of showing improvement during the reconstruction period, Ottieri underlines that the situation has actually worsened. In his 1959 analysis of the novel, Ferdinando Virdia correctly emphasized this crucial point:

> Ma è possibile tollerare in una nazione uno squilibrio così angoscioso come quello che si presenta nell'Italia di oggi? L'esperienza del sociologo si inserisce profondamente, è vero, non solo nella scoperta di un mondo e di una società e di contrasti che sono tra i più angosciosi del nostro tempo, ma direi che essa è la leva che sorregge e solleva la fantasia dello scrittore.
>
> (Is it possible for a nation to tolerate such an anguished imbalance as the one present in Italy today? It is true: the experience of the sociologist is profoundly embedded not only in the discovery of a world and of a society of contrasts that are among the most anguished of our time, but I would say that this experience is also a lever that supports and raises the imagination of the writer.)[13]

---

12   Ottieri, O. 2004. *Donnarumma all'assalto*. Milan: Garzanti. 173. Ottieri, O. 1962. *The Men at the Gate*. Boston: Houghton Mifflin. 12, 29.
13   Virdia, Ferdinando. 1959. "Donnarumma all'assalto." *La Fiera Letteraria*. July 26.

The most important element of the novel is the farmers' alienation. Once they are employed in a factory, they lose their nature, and they experience two types of alienation. First, farmers are driven from their original environment and forced to adapt to a new industrial one. Second, in the factories, they lose connection with the objects they produce. As in *Tempi stretti*, so too in *Donnarumma all'assalto*, Ottieri relates what he has seen with his own eyes: the materialistic conception of alienation, in which workers lose control of their lives because they have no command over the product of their work.

> Il tema cupo e catastrofico dell'alienazione marxista risuona nel fondo di tutte queste interpretazioni. Causata dal non possesso degli strumenti produttivi o dalla sola organizzazione scientifica e dalla suddivisione del lavoro, insomma dovuta al capitalismo o problema anche di una società socialista, l'alienazione è il cancello di ferro che trattiene chi lavora, lo isola in una responsabilità così frazionata e lontana dagli ultimi scopi, da violare l'istinto, la volontà, l'intelligenza.

> (The somber Marxist theme of the alienation of the workers from society is to be discerned at the root of all these interpretations. Owing to the fact that they do not own the means of production, or because of scientific organization and the subdivision of labor – in other words, owing to the capitalist system, and a problem also in a socialist society – the worker is kept apart and isolated in a responsibility so fragmented and remote from any ultimate aims as to violate his instincts, his will and his intelligence.)[14]

Beniamino Placido has called *Donnarumma all'assalto* "un classico della letteratura italiana del dopoguerra" (a classic of postwar Italian literature), underlining Ottieri's successful attempt to narrate a 'war' fought inside a (theoretically) peaceful Italy. It is about the social conflicts related to the growth of industry during the reconstruction period, especially the protracted struggle between industry and agriculture on the one hand and the impoverishment of the South as a direct consequence of industrial development on the other: "Fra le tante guerre che hanno attraversato e straziato il nostro Paese ce ne sono state due che meritano di essere raccontate insieme: la guerra provocata dal conflitto fra industria

---

14 Ottieri, O. 2004. *Donnarumma all'assalto*. 173. Ottieri, O. 1962. *The Men at the Gate*. 164.

e agricoltura, fra lavoro industriale e lavoro di fabbrica e il suo rovescio" (Among the many wars that have played out and torn apart our country, there are two of them that deserve to be recounted together: the war provoked by the conflict between industry and agriculture, between industrial work and factory work and its opposite).[15]

In conclusion, with *Tempi stretti* and *Donnarumma all'assalto*, Ottieri criticized the Italian industrial dream with a painful depiction of daily factory life during the postwar reconstruction. Thanks to his first-hand experience as human resources manager at Olivetti, his writing was inspired by what he actually saw from the inside. Ottieri described how workers and laborers, although protagonists of the reconstruction, were constantly alienated from the products of their labor, and thus could not enjoy the fruits of the economic miracle. No matter what the geographical setting (Milan for *Tempi stretti*, Pozzuoli for *Donnarumma all'assalto*), mechanization and exploitation were the two key factors that characterized the workers' poor conditions.

---

15   Placido, B. 2004. "Ottiero Ottieri tra i operai meridionali."

TIZIANO TORACCA

17 Giovanni Arpino's Industrial Novels: *Gli anni del giudizio* (1958) and *Una nuvola d'ira* (1962)

Giovanni Arpino considered *Gli anni del giudizio* (The Years of Judgement, 1958) his real literary debut: "Arpino si convince, intorno alla metà degli anni Cinquanta, di dover scrivere un romanzo d'ambientazione operaia, che rappresenti il suo vero esordio impegnativo dopo quello invece 'spensierato'" (around the mid-1950s, Arpino became convinced that he needed to write a novel set in the industrial world that would represent his real and committed literary debut after the 'frivolous' book) *Sei stato felice, Giovanni* (You Were a Happy One, Giovanni).[1] This last book had caught the attention of Elio Vittorini, who printed it in the Einaudi publishing house's *I Gettoni* series in 1952.

In order to dedicate himself to *Gli anni del giudizio*, Arpino abandoned two ongoing projects: *Incanto e verità* (Enchantment and Truth, a collection of four short stories written in 1956) and *Regina di cuoi* (Queen of Leather – but almost *Regina di cuori*, Queen of Hearts – more short stories written between 1948 and 1953). But despite the efforts and expectations of *Gli anni del giudizio*, Arpino's literary success would have to wait for the publication of *La suora giovane* (The Novice) in 1959. In the opinion of Eugenio Montale, *La suora giovane* was a more idyllic and introverted work,[2] one toward which Arpino would remain forever ambiguous.

Gli anni del giudizio is set in Bra (Piedmont), between the territory of the Langhe and the city of Turin: two places close to Arpino's heart and present in many of his writings. As a child, Arpino took many trips to Bra, and he lived there between 1942 and 1952 while studying at the Liceo

1 Damiani, R. 2005. "Arpino e la sua ombra." in Arpino, G. *Opere scelte*. Milan: Mondadori. XIV.
2 Montale, E. 1960. "Arpino. *La suora giovane*." *Corriere della Sera*. March 25.

Classico Virgilio (Virgil Classical Lyceum). He returned as a commuter to work at the Law Department, then moved to the Literature Department at the University of Turin, where he wrote a thesis on the Russian poet Sergei Yesenin. Turin can certainly be considered Arpino's "città patria" (hometown).[3] Together with Caterina Brero, Arpino made his home in a working-class neighborhood that had developed around the Leumann textile factory. He remained there all his life, working as a writer and journalist for newspapers like Turin's *La Stampa* and Milan's *Il Giornale*.[4]

The story of *Gli anni del giudizio* unfolds during the two intense weeks of political campaigning that led up to the Italian elections of June 7, 1953. These elections, which Italo Calvino also wrote about in *La giornata d'uno scrutatore* (The Watcher, 1963), were of great historical importance: in March 1953, despite strong opposition and with an approval process that was hotly contested, the Democrazia Cristiana (Christian Democrats, DC) promulgated what became known as the 'legge truffa' (swindle law). Departing from the model of proportional representation inaugurated in 1946, the law (which was repealed by 1954) introduced a majority bonus for the coalition that received more than half of all votes. This meant that the winner automatically controlled 65% of the Italian Chamber of Deputies.[5] The protagonist of *Gli anni del giudizio* is a worker named Ugo Braida – Arpino's original title was *Braida e la sua parte* (Braida and His Part) – who agitates against the swindle law and in favor of the Communist Party. Braida is a 30-year-old ex-partisan who works "alle officine delle ferrovie a Torino" (at the Turin railway factory)[6] and lives in Bra together with his wife Ester

---

[3] Quaranta, B. 1989. *Stile Arpino. Una vita torinese*. Turin: Società editrice internazionale. 89.

[4] Dughera, A. 2006. *Per una biografia di Giovanni Arpino*. Bra: Istituto Storico di Bra e dei braidesi. Quaranta, B. 2018. "Il Piemonte di Arpino." *'La vita o è stile o è errore.' L'opera di Giovanni Arpino*. Edited by Maria Cala Papini, Federico Fastelli and Teresa Spignoli. Pisa: ETS. 103–112.

[5] The centrist coalition led by the Christian Democrats was short lived, and it failed to obtain half of all votes.

[6] Arpino, G. 1965. *Gli anni difficili*. Turin: Einaudi. 17.

and her mother.⁷ Ester is seven months pregnant when she is fired from the local textile factory, so she begins working from home as a seamstress. Ugo is an honest laborer who sacrifices his own private life (the cinema, walks around town, personal hobbies) in the name of political commitment: he studies, reads the newspapers, attends meetings, agrees to deliver an electoral speech for the party and spends his nights hanging campaign posters with his comrades. But even though Ugo is the protagonist of *Gli anni del giudizio*, the narrating voice is that of Ester. If we exclude Ugo's monologues and some short scenes reported by an extradiegetic narrator, Ester is "il filtro del dramma umano e degli interrogativi esistenziali dell'operaio" (the filter of the human drama and of the worker's existential questions).⁸ She is the author of Ugo's biography and thus of the novel's fundamental theme, which is not – as it may seem – the political commitment of a 'typical' worker during a crucial historic moment, but rather the values of activism and sacrifice implied by politics: the formation of a critical consciousness.⁹ Ugo's every gesture is characterized by an uncertain sense of anxiety that complicates the story's apparently realist development.¹⁰

From the beginning, Ugo is both a reasoning and problematic character. His reflections and the words he uses to address others are fused with hope and impotence, will and frustration. Ester fully recognizes these complexities, and her point of view serves to bring them into sharp focus. In her eyes, Ugo is an exemplary man and communist: a worker respected in the factory and in the party, able to think, to get the job done,¹¹ to

---

7   Berardo, L. 1990. "'*Gli anni del giudizio*': il romanzo 'elettorale' come moderna epopea." *Giovanni Arpino. L'uomo, lo scrittore*. Edited by Cetta Berardo. Bra: Cassa di risparmio di Bra. 51–58.
8   Romano, M. 1974. *Invito alla lettura di Arpino*. Milan: Mursia. 42.
9   Barberi Squarotti, G. 1978. *Poesia e narrativa del secondo Novecento*. Milan: Mursia. 356.
10 Tortora, M. 2018. "Il primo Arpino: 1952–1962." *Filologia e critica*, vol. 43, no. 4.
11 In contrast to Ester's father, "senza misericordia davanti al lavoro" (who, when it comes to work, has no mercy), Ugo is a good worker. In one of his many dialogues with Ester, Ugo expresses an extremely interesting idea: "Chissà perché – mi aveva detto un giorno – chissà perché la vita non è tutta così, come il lavoro per un uomo che lavora. Se smetti di lavorare la vita è diversa, non basta l'esperienza, ci vogliono subito i soldi" (Who knows why – he told me one day – who knows why life is not all like this, like work for a man who works. If you stop working, then life is different, experience is not enough, you need money right away). In the opinion of

appreciate labor and even love it. In a word, Ugo is responsible, especially when compared with the local party secretary Pagliaro, who cowardly abandons the pregnant Antonietta, departs before the end of the leader Palmiro Togliatti's speech in Cuneo and somehow seems to be a different type of communist.[12] Ester depicts her husband as a tragic hero driven by a "desiderio di verità e di onestà" (desire for truth an honesty),[13] able to "vedere le cose, di capirle" (see things, to understand them), but with the awareness "di non poterle modificare mai, non potere mai mettere le mani nel mondo" (that he cannot ever change them, that he cannot lay hands on the world).[14]

Ugo's anxiety, sharpened by Ester's depiction, has a precise root that is partially revealed by a question he asks her in chapter three: "Non è venuto nessuno a cercarmi?" (Nobody came looking for me?)[15] It is, in fact, an ideological anxiety: time and again, Ugo discovers that his own ideals are out of line with the party's bureaucratic logic and dogmatism,[16] and he becomes aware of the distance that separates his own flexible vision of the world from that of his comrades. The maturation of a personal *Weltanschaung* (worldview)[17] culminates in Ugo's decision to speak out publicly – first against a party functionary from Rome, then at a speech in San Matteo – and results in his estrangement from the party. Ugo's resentment toward both Pagliero (who scolds him for acting out) and a certain professor (who follows Togliatti's speech with pessimistic discussion of the Hungarian

---

Gian Mario Veneziano, Arpino uses this idea to make labor the "paradigma di quel che dovrebbe essere la politica" (paradigm of an ideal politics). Arpino, G. 1965. *Gli anni difficili*. 173. Veneziano, G. M. 1994. *Giovanni Arpino*. Milan: Mursia. 30.

12 That Pagliaro is somehow a different type of communist enters Ugo's mind during a drive to Cuneo, where Togliatti is scheduled to speak. Arpino, G. 1965 *Gli anni difficili*. 148–149.

13 Scrivano, R. 1979. *Arpino*. Florence: La nuova Italia. 42.

14 Arpino, G. 1965. *Gli anni difficili*. 217.

15 Arpino, G. 1965. *Gli anni difficili*. 19.

16 Fioretti, D. 2013. *Carte di fabbrica. La narrativa industrial in Italia (1934–1989)*. Pescara: Tracce. 89–90. Merola, N. 2018. "Temi forti e uomini deboli nei romanzi di Arpino." *'La vita o è stile o è errore.' L'opera di Giovanni Arpino*. Edited by Maria Carla Papini et al. Pisa: Edizioni ETS. 11.

17 Baldini, A. 2008. "La trilogia della disillusione di Arpino." *Il comunista. Una storia letteraria dalla Resistenza agli anni Settanta*. Turin: UTET. 87.

Revolution, the Polish protests and popular movements in Germany) betray a developing distrust that will lead the protagonist into sudden isolation. Nevertheless, Ugo's crisis is never absolute; it is always accompanied by the awareness of being a worker and therefore of needing others – of not being able to "fare il comunista da solo" (be a communist by one's self).[18] Ugo never loses his ability to judge, nor his pride in being a good worker who gets the job done.[19] In chapter thirty-two, he rides his bike to the neighborhoods of Falchetto and Pollenzo to hang campaign posters with his comrades. After, and despite being extremely tired, he joins the group at a late-night bar full of patrons. But when Ugo decides to return home, he realizes that he no longer recognizes the city. Even Turin seems far away, and this sudden bewilderment forces him to reflect upon his own solitude, class membership and the need to accept the party line: "Sono in colpa. Un operaio non è un uomo che possa alzare la cresta. Un operaio deve sapere capire e dar retta. Poche storie. Ma che credevo di essere, di fare? Di cambiare il cervello agli altri con la mia bella facia?" (It's all my fault. A worker can't get too cocky. A worker must be able to understand and heed the word. Don't put up a fuss. Who did I think I was? Did I think I could change people's minds with my pretty little face?)[20]

Deep down, Ugo Braida remains a problematic character. He is aware of not being able to live without his comrades, their political struggle and the priorities of the party – "Ha ragione Pagliero" (Pagliero's right), he admits[21] – but this does nothing to temper his ideals and doubts. At the end of the novel, a group of Christian Democrat activists come for Ugo's elderly and unconscious mother-in-law, whom they want to help cast a vote against the Communists. Ugo and Ester take away her voter's license and pretend that nobody is home. Their opposition to the DC's "assedio" (siege)[22] is firm and legitimate,[23] but it is also tormented. It is the resistance

18 Arpino, G. 1965. *Gli anni difficili*. 142.
19 Arpino, G. 1965. *Gli anni difficili*. 17.
20 Arpino, G. 1965. *Gli anni difficili*. 207.
21 Arpino, G. 1965. *Gli anni difficili*. 207.
22 Baldini, A. 2008. "La trilogia della disillusione di Arpino." 85.
23 As Giorgio Barberi Squarotti pointed out, Ugo could easily have his mother-in-law vote for the communists, but he decides not to. Barberi Squarotti, G. 1992.

of those who understand the impossibility of thinking "da solo e per noi soli" (alone and for ourselves),[24] of those who believe in socialism, but will not renounce the practice of meditating on their own actions and choices.[25]

Una nuvola d'ira (A Cloud of Rage, 1962) was Arpino's fifth novel. In the afterword to the first Rizzoli edition (1982), significantly titled "Confessione" (Confession), the author revealed that the story upset the leaders of the Partito Comunista Italiano (Italian Communist Party, PCI). Arpino wrote that "lo stesso Palmiro Togliatti, segretario del partito comunista, ne discusse con Mario Alicata, suo 'ministro' alla cultura, perché il romanzo incontrasse ostacoli" (the secretary of the Communist Party, Palmiro Togliatti himself, discussed it with his 'minister' of culture Mario Alicata, intending to impede the novel).[26] Carlo Salinari, one of the literary critics closest to the Party, excoriated *Una nuvola d'ira* and argued fiercely with Arpino.[27] As Arpino wrote to Bruno Quaranta, these Communist politicians and critics took issue with the novel's three protagonists, who did not transparently reflect the condition of the working class and were therefore dismissed as "surreali, bugiardi, 'incredibili'" (surreal, deceitful, 'unbelievable').[28] In hindsight, it is precisely this fact that gave *Una nuvola d'ira* its power: the novel represented the transformation of the working class during the economic boom, its gradual integration into capitalist society and the beginnings of what Pasolini denounced, in the 1970s, as an apocalyptic process of homogenization.[29]

Una nuvola d'ira is the story of a *mènage a trois* that suddenly breaks down. The narrating voice is Sperata. She is married to Matteo, but has

---

"Introduzione." *Giovanni Arpino. Opere. Storie de nostro tempo*, vol. 4. Edited by Giorgio Barberi Squarotti. Milan: Rusconi. 11.

24 Arpino, G. 1965. *Gli anni difficili*. 216.
25 Fioretti, D. 2013. *Carte di fabbrica. La narrativa industrial in Italia (1934–1989)*. 90.
26 Arpino, G. 1982. "Confessione." *Una nuvola d'ira*. Milan: Rizzoli. 164.
27 Salinari, C. 1962. "Un amore a tre nella Torino '61." *Vie Nuove*. March 8. Salinari, C. 1962. "Salinari risponde a Arpino." *Vie Nuove*. March 22. Arpino, G. 1962. "Lettera a Salinari." *Vie Nuove*. March 15.
28 Quaranta, B. 1989. *Stile Arpino. Una vita torinese*. 80.
29 Pasolini, P. P. 1999. "Scritti corsari." *Scritti sulla politica e sulla società*. Edited by Walter Siti and Silvia De Laude. Milan: Mondadori.

an affair with Angelo, and the three begin living together under the same roof. They are all convinced that their acceptance of such an unconventional arrangement is a sign of their individuality and ability to challenge the culture imposed by "le confusioni che fanno i cattolici" (Catholic confusion)[30] and bourgeois morality.[31] But the arrangement suddenly breaks down, revealing the conformism and hypocrisy of all three characters. More generally, it reveals that "presumersi diversi non basta per esserlo davvero" (presuming ourselves different is not the same thing as really being different),[32] and that separating ourselves from others and believing ourselves the free "depositari d'una verità e d'una armonia che ancora non esiste" (guardians of a truth and harmony that does not yet exist) results only in alienation.[33]

The real protagonist of *Una nuvola d'ira* is the "labirinto di parole" (labyrinth of words)[34] in which Angelo and Sperata – the self-styled "eroi di un'umanità nuova" (heroes of a new humanity)[35] – turn about. They scramble frantically in an effort to justify their own "specialità" (specialty) and status as "rinnovati" (renewed),[36] individual human beings.[37] Nevertheless, some distinctions should be made: while Angelo is the one always preaching formulas, theorizing and inveighing against everything and everyone, Sperata is the one who is more uncertain and confused. "Forse sbagliavo" (Maybe I was wrong), she wonders, "ma mi parve che anche [Angelo] come me, in quel momento s'affidasse a una forza che si sperava soltanto di possedere" (but it seemed to me in that moment that [Angelo] was, like me, trusting himself to a strength that he only hoped to

30   Arpino, G. 2009. *Una nuvola d'ira*. Milan: BUR. 54.
31   Arpino, G. 2009. *Una nuvola d'ira*. 44.
32   Raffaeli, M. 2009. "Una sfida operaia." in Arpino, G. *Una nuvola d'ira*. VII.
33   Calvino, I. 1962. "A Giovanni Arpino – Milano." *Lettere 1940–1985*. Edited by Luca Baranelli. Milan: Mondadori. 703.
34   Arpino, G. 2009. *Una nuvola d'ira*. 55.
35   Romano, M. 1974. *Invito alla lettura di Arpino*. 58.
36   Arpino, G. 2009. *Una nuvola d'ira*. 54.
37   It is not a coincidence that the novel's epigraph cites Antonio Gramsci and Nâzim Hikmet. Gramsci: "Il vecchio uomo rinnovato negativamente …" (The old man negatively renewed …). Hikmet: "Siamo al punto a cui è il nostro mondo" (We are at the same point, this world and ourselves).

possess).[38] Matteo is completely excluded from this whirlwind of thoughts and words. The only time he enters Sperata's room, he refuses to speak his mind: "A cosa vuoi che servano tutti questi brodi di parole ... Si parla anche troppo qui dentro ... A chi ha mai cambiato la vita il parlare ..." (What's the point of all these jumbly words ... You speak too much in here ... Whose life was ever changed by speaking ...).[39] Matteo is a lonely and reserved former peasant and ex partisan. He works in a small factory as a leather tanner and, despite his forty years, seems immediately aged and sorrowful. Matteo is sick with an ulcer, and his habits associate him with the past: alcohol, cards, bocce and motorcycles. As a relic of the early twentieth century, he is completely estranged from Sperata and Angelo's dimension of modernity. He loves fishing and hunting, and eventually searches for refuge in the countryside whence he came. In the *mènage a trois*, Matteo finds nothing but suffering, and his degeneration is due in part to his not accepting the arrangement from the beginning. Angelo, on the contrary, is fifteen years younger. Though he is a skilled mechanic, his political activism has confined him to a small role in a factory warehouse. Angelo is energetic and loquacious, always looking for an argument and fond of criticism: "Questo è il buon esempio che deve dare un marxista: interpretare storicamente le cose, la sua parte, non mollare mai" (This is the good example that every Marxist must give: use history to interpret things and his part in them, don't ever give up).[40]

The novel begins at a hospital. Matteo is recovering from an operation, and Sperata and Angelo come to visit him: "la grigia, smagrita, trasandata figura di Matteo s'allinea al grigiore tetro dell'ospedale" (Matteo's gray, thinned, run-down figure lines up with the gloomy grayness of the hospital).[41] After the visit, Angelo and Sperata decide to see the Fiera della Tecnica (Technology Fair), a historical reference that grounds the plot in Turin during the hundred-year anniversary of Italian Unification (1861–1961) and also an extraordinary symbol of the economic boom. Some pages

---

38   Arpino, G. 2009. *Una nuvola d'ira*. 47.
39   Arpino, G. 2009. *Una nuvola d'ira*. 50.
40   Arpino, G. 2009. *Una nuvola d'ira*. 33.
41   Scrivano, R. 1979. *Arpino*. 93.

later, this culminates in a veritable catalog of industrial goods and modern pastimes, from Sperata's hairdryer – "persino il ronzio era consolante" (even the buzz of it was comforting)[42] – to car rides, film outings, museums and cafés that announce the arrival of a consumer society and the integration of the working class.[43] In chapter two, Sperata initiates a series of flashbacks evoking episodes from her past: political discussions with Angelo and Matteo, her own detachment from her husband and an engagement party where Angelo, supported by Matteo, reprimands the feted couple for their opinions on fidelity and cheating.[44] Such ambivalent memories reveal the hidden neuroses and contradictions of a piddling antibourgeois society that Angelo and Sperata struggle to legitimate.

In the following chapter, Sperata and Angelo arrive by car at the Fiera della Tecnica. They are both mesmerized: Sperata by a Cinerama movie screen; Angelo by a diesel engine. The night drags on, and their tiresome wanderings among piazzas, pizzerias and cafés function as "una premonizione angosciosa" (an anguished premonition)[45] of the future that awaits them. This is confirmed by the verses Sperata recites, taken from Yevgeny Yevtushenko's poem "Se porti il bene o il male, davvero non so" (Whether You're Good or Evil, I Truly Don't Know)[46] and transcribed with Italics in Arpino's novel: "*Ma appena sto con te, io divento peggiore ... Che cosa far con te? Che fare con me stesso?*" (But as soon as I am with you, I am worsened ... What shall I do with you? What shall I do with myself?)[47] The first half of *Una nuvola d'ira* culminates in a dramatic scene announced by the novel's title (partly inspired by Vladimir Mayakovsky's epic poem *Vladimir Ilyich Lenin*, 1924). Sperata and Angelo return home to find out

42   Arpino, G. 2009. *Una nuvola d'ira*. 29.
43   Raffaeli, M. 2009. "Una sfida operaia." IX.
44   In this scene, Angelo anticipates the novel's central drama: "Saremo bravi, saremo cambiati, ma novanta volta su cento siamo ancora gente che fa sogni borghesi. I sogni sono ancora tutti borghesi" (We may be good, we may be transformed, but ninety times out of a hundred, we are still folks with bourgeois dreams. Our dreams are all still bourgeois). Arpino, G. 2009. *Una nuvola d'ira*. 60.
45   Scrivano, R. 1979. *Arpino*. 97.
46   Arpino must have read the poem in Ripellino, A. M. 1961. *Nuovi poeti sovietici*. Turin: Einaudi. The original Russian title is "К добру ты или к худу."
47   Arpino, G. 2009. *Una nuvola d'ira*. 77.

that Matteo has escaped from the hospital and committed a "massacro di elettrodomestici" (massacre of household appliances).[48] Matteo symbolically directs his rage at the physical objects of consumer society that penetrate the intimacy of the working-class home and express an existential condition from which he feels excluded. Matteo's 'nuvola' (cloud) is set off against another cloud evoked in the novel: the "nuvola d'argento" (silver cloud) that scientists say will disseminate "una luce d'argento" (a silver light) over Moscow for the (fictional) 1967 Universal Exposition Inspired by Reason and Labor.[49] Behind such symbols of progress and their claim to provide a foundation for new social relations, Matteo glimpses nothing but selfishness and hypocrisy. Nevertheless, his is a "violenza autodistruttiva" (self-destructive violence).[50] In the second half of *Una nuvola d'ira*, Angelo and Sperata desperately search for Matteo. They visit the hospital, the local party section, a cultural club, the countryside, the hills around Alba and finally the house of Matteo's stepbrother, Antonio. Tired and anguished, they bicker at length, but they also reach a critical awareness of their own delusions. The closer they get to the truth (Matteo is dead), the more they perceive it as their own failure. For Sperata, this is immediately evident: " 'Basta' replico. 'Non siamo migliori. Siamo come tutti gli altri, e magari peggio. Inutile che ci si dia tante arie di migliori. Siamo come tutti' " ('Enough' I responded. 'We're no better. We're just like everyone else, and maybe worse. There's no sense in putting on airs. We're just like everyone').[51] Moreover, as Matteo's wife, Sperata's search is much more personal than Angelo's: it is punctuated by intimate memories, omens and epiphanies.[52] Angelo recognizes the failure of his "utopia privata" (private utopia)[53] only shortly before finding Matteo: "Abbiamo fatto un gran pasticcio. Così finisce. Uno si crede meglio, scavalca tutto, pesta i piedi, e così finisce. Ho messo sotto gli amici del Partito, e Matteo, e anche te. Chiamala

---

48   Raffaeli, M. 2009. "Una sfida operaia." V.
49   Arpino, G. 2009. *Una nuvola d'ira*. 35.
50   Fioretti, D. 2013. *Carte di fabbrica. La narrativa industrial in Italia (1934–1989)*. 91.
51   Arpino, G. 2009. *Una nuvola d'ira*. 108–109.
52   Arpino, G. 2009. *Una nuvola d'ira*. 127.
53   Baldini, A. 2008. "La trilogia della disillusione di Arpino." 90.

superbia, chiamala come vuoi […] È colpa mia" (We've got ourselves into a real mess. Here's how it all ends. You think you're better than everyone else, you rise above it all, you stomp your feet, and here's how it all ends. I brought down my friends in the Party, and Matteo, and you too. Call it arrogance, call it what you will […] It's all my fault).[54] Not by chance, Sperata's conclusion recalls Ugo Braida's exhortation to reconcile the self with the other: "cercare di fare meglio, da soli, è impossibile" (striving to do better, by ourselves, is impossible).[55]

Translated by Jim Carter

---

54 Arpino, G. 2009. *Una nuvola d'ira*. 149.
55 Arpino, G. 2009. *Una nuvola d'ira*. 151.

SILVIA CAVALLI

18 Industrial Absurdities and Utopia in Giancarlo Buzzi's *Il senatore* (1958) and *L'amore mio italiano* (1963)

An Allegory of the Modern

Giancarlo Buzzi was born in Como (Lombardy) in 1929 and died in Milan in 2015. He completed his humanistic studies in Pavia and began a career in the industrial world. A writer and a manager, he contributed to the definition of the corporate identity of some of the most important Italian companies, including Pirelli, Olivetti and the publishing house Mondadori, where he worked as marketing director in the 1960s.

He made his literary debut with *Il senatore* (The Senator), a novel published by Feltrinelli in 1958 and set inside an unnamed industrial factory, which is however identifiable with Pirelli, where Buzzi worked as a copywriter from 1953 to 1955. Some clues at the beginning of the novel corroborate this identification: "il pavimento in linoleum verde brillante" (the bright green linoleum flooring)[1] of the main character's office and the ergonomic armchairs with "il sedile in gommapiuma, elastico ma non molle" (the elastic yet not soft foam rubber seat).[2]

These objects were located at the Milanese company, whose plants are in the Bicocca district. The well-known flooring material was produced by the Società Italiana del Linoleum (Italian Linoleum Company) – part of the Pirelli group – whereas foam rubber, invented at the end of the 1920s, played

---

1   Buzzi, G. 1958. *Il senatore*. Milan: Feltrinelli. 11.
2   Buzzi, G. 1958. *Il senatore*. 12.

a leading role, alongside tires, in the company's imagination, thanks to a series of billboards devised and promoted by the poet Leonardo Sinisgalli.

But the narration of *Il senatore* does not center on the items produced in the industrial complex. Where Buzzi relates his own experience at the company, he focuses on a feature peculiar to the working world of the 1950s: the changing complex of relationships between workers, middle management and upper management, all of which were administered by a set of rules imported from the United States and known as human relations. In his novel, Buzzi concentrates most of his attention on the relationship between middle management and upper management.

Il senatore is a parody of human relations, highlighting the paradox of a company owner who, although essential to the factory, is at the same time absent and invisible. "In questo grande macchinario tutti gli ingranaggi funzionano obbedendo a leggi ferree" (In this great machine world, all the gears work abiding by iron laws), remarks the main character of *Il senatore*, the middle manager Tullio Masi, "ma colui che muove gli ingranaggi, colui che aziona le leve non si vede" (but he who moves the gears, he who operates the levers is unseen).[3] Interpersonal relations, deprived of their human component, are illusory and subtle to the extent that they become phantasmal.

Searching for the upper management, the protagonist loses himself in a bureaucratic labyrinth, and Buzzi narrates the situation in a Kafkian key. Italo Calvino – author of *La nuvola di smog* (Smog, 1958) and a book editor for the publishing house Einaudi – also noted this point, providing one of the first critical interpretations of *Il senatore*. In a letter addressed to Buzzi in December 1957, Calvino was the first to suggest Kafka as a template not only for Buzzi's book, but also for industrial literature as a whole, identifying in "kafkismo aziendale" (corporate Kafkianism) one possible approach "per rappresentare certi aspetti della realtà contemporanea" (to represent certain aspects of contemporary reality).[4]

According to Giuseppe Lupo, *Il senatore* "rappresenta il primo tentativo di narrare il capitalismo (non la fabbrica) in forma di meccanismo

---

[3] Buzzi, G. 1958. *Il senatore*. 76.
[4] Calvino, I. 1991. *I libri degli altri: Lettere 1947–1981*. Edited by Giovanni Tesio. Turin: Einaudi. 243.

complicato e asfissiante" (represents the first attempt to narrate capitalism (and not the factory) as a complicated and suffocating mechanism), operating with the rules of "un gioco alienante e inverosimile, che si basa sul paradigma/paradosso dell'assenza" (an alienating and absurd game that is based on the paradigm/paradox of absence).[5] This fully accounts for the resemblance of Buzzi's novel with the work of the Prague writer.

In order to better understand the Kafkianism of *Il senatore*, we must refer to another author who engaged in an imaginary, indirect dialogue with Kafka. In 1960, Roland Barthes wrote "La réponse de Kafka (Kafka's Answer)" for the *France-Observateur*, a review – later included in *Essais critiques* (Critical Essays, 1964) – of a monograph by Marthe Robert published by Gallimard. Inspired by Robert's work *Kafka*, Barthes argued that the question answered by short stories such as *Die Verwandlung* (The Metamorphosis, 1915) is not the obvious "pourquoi écrire?" (why write?), but rather "comment écrire?" (how should one write?), implying therefore that "l'être de la littérature n'est rien d'autre que sa technique" (the being of literature is nothing but its technique).[6]

Kafka's answer is that narrative should be conducted through allusions rather than symbols. In Barthe's words, Kafka "fonde son œuvre en en supprimant systématiquement les *comme si*: mais c'est l'événement intérieur qui devient le terme obscur de l'allusion" (creates his work by systematically suppressing the *as ifs*: but it is the internal event which becomes the obscure term of the allusion).[7] *Die Verwandlung* is an excellent example: a man feels that his life is dull, like that of an insect. One morning, when he wakes up, he finds himself turned into the cockroach to which he fears comparison. The term of comparison is placed at the center of the story: "La technique de Kafka implique donc d'abord un accord au monde, une soumission au langage courant" (Kafka's technique implies first of all an agreement with

---

5 Lupo, G. 2016. *La letteratura al tempo di Adriano Olivetti*. Rome and Ivrea: Edizioni di Comunità. 141.
6 Barthes, R. 1993. *Œuvres completes: Tome I (1942-1965)*. Edited by Éric Marty. Paris: Éditions du Seuil. 1271. Barthes, R. 1972. *Critical Essays*. Translated by Richard Howard. Evanston, IL: Northwestern University Press. 135.
7 Barthes, R. 1993. *Œuvres completes: Tome I (1942-1965)*. 1272. Barthes, R. 1972. *Critical Essays*. 136.

the world, a submission to ordinary language), says Barthes, "mais aussitôt après, une réserve, un doute, un effroi devant la lettre des signes proposés par le monde" (but immediately afterwards, a reservation, a doubt, a fear before the letter of the signs the world proposes).[8]

Such reasoning can also be extended to *Il senatore*, on the basis of the clues provided by Robert and Barthes. The factory owner pursued by Tullio Masi is so evanescent that he does not exist as a recognizable figure: he can be thought of *as if* a ghost, something that effectively turns him into a ghost.

Thus, while searching for the upper management, the protagonist comes into contact with the ghost of the founder: a former senator in the Italian parliament, and the father of the current company owner. This helps to explain the title of the book: the senator's ghost, through the suppression of the *as ifs* glimpsed in Barthes, becomes the narrative representation both of the degeneration of the old ruling class and of the lack of a human component at the helm of industry.

It appears as a classic case of alienation: the manager suffers from hallucinations and sees the senator's picture, hanging on the wall of his office, come to life. But if this were the case, then we would expect Buzzi's novel to adopt the traditional expedients of fantastic literature in recounting an unprecedented situation in the work world. Instead, the apparition of the ghost challenges us to shift the present discussion from Kafka to Pirandello: that is, from the condition of the absurd, typical of Kafkianism, to a Pirandellian theater of the absurd, made of masks (and indeed ghosts).

The figure of the senator is therefore not the outcome of a hallucination, but a 'character' in the Pirandellian sense of the term. According to the interpretation provided by Angelo R. Pupino, the characters in Pirandello's work – above all, in short stories like *Personaggi* (Characters, 1906), *La tragedia d'un personaggio* (The Tragedy of a Character, 1911), *Colloquii coi personaggi* (Conversations with Characters, 1915) and the play *Sei personaggi in cerca d'autore* (Six Characters in Search of an Author, 1921) – owe a debt to the theosophical and spiritistic culture of the early twentieth century.[9] George Pitoëf's historic Paris staging of *Sei personaggi*

---

8   Barthes, R. 1993. *Œuvres completes: Tome I (1942-1965)*. 1272. Barthes, R. 1972. *Critical Essays*. 136.
9   Pupino, A. R. 2000. *Pirandello: Maschere e fantasmi*. Rome: Salerno. 15.

in cerca d'autore in 1923 corroborates the interpretation of characters as ghosts looking forward to seeing their own events played before an audience, and in the *novellas*, the writer is depicted in the dim light of his own study receiving characters who ask to be included in his works.

The circumstances of these last apparitions are very similar to the first encounter between the senator and Tullio Masi, which takes place in a deserted and poorly lit office: "Col modesto mezzo della lampada da tavolo mi compiacevo di creare un'atmosfera raccolta" (With the modest means of a table lamp, I was pleased with the cozy atmosphere I was able to create), recalls the narrator.[10] In both cases, a request must be granted: the Pirandellian characters ask to live through literature and theater; the senator asks that his son be found. But in both cases, such wishes are bound to be frustrated.

The senator's apparitions are however surrounded by a veil of ambiguity, thus providing the reader with a text that seems to hesitate at the borders of the fantastic genre as codified by Tzvetan Todorov. In *Introduction à la littérature fantastique* (The Fantastic, 1970) Todorov defines the fantastic as a genre that lasts the time of a hesitation shared between the reader and the character.[11] Both the reader and the character must decide whether what they read or see is a real, even though strange, phenomenon, or if it belongs instead to the dimension of wonder. This is also the case for *Il senatore*, where the protagonist briefly considers, then rejects, the reality of a séance: "mi venne da ridere" (it made me laugh), he remarks immediately after having examined its possibility.[12]

More precisely, *Il senatore* straddles the border between the fantastic and the allegorical, following a pattern of short stories exemplified in Edgar Allan Poe's *William Wilson* (1839). According to this interpretation, the ghost that appears in the book acquires an emblematic meaning. His presence is not a simple *topos*, typical of the fantastic genre, but one of the many "immagini della modernità" (images of modernity) or "allegorie del moderno" (allegories of the modern) that Stefano Lazzarin (with Romano

---

10   Buzzi, G. 1958. *Il senatore*. 24.
11   Todorov, T. 1970. *Introduction à la littérature fantastique*. Paris: Éditions du Seuil. 29.
12   Buzzi, G. 1958. *Il senatore*. 50.

Luperini) insists haunt the narratives of the nineteenth and twentieth centuries.[13]

In this sense, *Il senatore* can be read as an allegory of the transformations of industrial society. The power at the top of the hierarchy is no longer in the hands of a single individual or a family, but rather diluted in the fragmentary and anonymous ownership of corporate acquisitions, thus leading to the disappearance of the role of the company owner, who is divested of his functions and shares with all the employees the anguish of not knowing who is actually in charge in the factory.

The Community of Welfare

In 1963, Buzzi published his second novel, *L'amore mio italiano* (My Italian Love), printed by Mondadori and inspired by the author's experience at the Olivetti company in Ivrea from 1955 to 1959. In these years, Buzzi was the cultural manager of the community centers for the Movimento Comunità (Community Movement), a political-cultural organization founded in 1947 by Adriano Olivetti and broadly advocating liberal-democratic and federalist reforms.

The city and the factory where the story takes place are again unnamed, but Ivrea and Olivetti are easily recognizable through the veil of fiction. Just like in *Il senatore*, in *L'amore mio italiano* the plot is a pretext to describe the distinguishing features of midcentury Italian industry. While the first book is an allegory of human relations in a corporation, *L'amore mio italiano* is the story of two relationships – the marriage between Paolo and Dina, and the affair between Paolo and Daniela – that provokes a reflection on economic and social welfare during the economic boom – the 'economic miracle' at which the book's title hints.

In *L'amore mio italiano*, material wealth and welfare are compared to the flood of a river that cannot be contained by the embankments built with

---

13 Lazzarin, S. 2008. *Fantasmi antichi e moderni: Tecnologia e perturbante in Buzzati e nella letteratura fantastica otto-novecentesca*. Pisa and Rome: Fabrizio Serra. 50.

the debris of a world that has now disappeared. The "piena di benessere" (flood of welfare) sweeps away the small city: it erases poverty, evens out anything it submerges, blunts the contours and hides the differences.[14] Those who escape the flood share the destiny of the "vinti" (defeated) described by Giovanni Verga in the preface to *I Malavoglia* (The House by the Medlar Tree, 1881): overwhelmed by "la fiumana del progresso" (the stream of progress).[15] Similarly, Buzzi writes that "i superstiti della società in sfacelo" (the survivors of the deteriorating society) suffer "la sorte di tutto il vecchiume già inghiottito dall'onda" (the fate of all the junk that has already been swallowed by the wave).[16]

At the sight of this spectacle, Paolo, the protagonist of *L'amore mio italiano* (a company executive, like Tullio Masi), is perplexed: he expresses his doubts through the biblical metaphor of the advent of the "regno" (kingdom), refusing at the same time to believe in a "paradiso" (paradise) on Earth.[17] The image is ambiguous: it is not clear in which paradise the protagonist does not believe; nor is it clear which God his fellow citizens are expecting. Whether the kingdom represents God or money, the question remains deliberately open.

When Paolo asks Daniela "Qui l'uomo può esser felice?" (Can man be happy here?), she responds "Come Adamo" (Like Adam).[18] But the completion of the sentence (… in Eden) is implicit, and partly conceals the aporia: placing the possibility of happiness in a mythical age implies a cyclical view of time, as opposed to that of a prophecy, which is linear and cast into the future. It is tantamount to saying, with Jean-Jacques Rousseau, that men can be happy only in a pre-industrial society where they are ignorant of welfare. The hypothesis is supported by the addition of a gloss in the revised edition published in 2014: "Come Adamo? Non proprio. Il peccato anche qui è già stato commesso, da tempo immemorabile" (Like

---

14   Buzzi, G. 1963. *L'amore mio italiano*. Milan: Mondadori. 37.
15   Verga, G. 2014. *I Malavoglia*. Catania and Novara: Fondazione Verga/Interlinea. 11-13.
16   Buzzi, G. 1963. *L'amore mio italiano*. 37.
17   Buzzi, G. 1963. *L'amore mio italiano*. 73.
18   Buzzi, G. 1963. *L'amore mio italiano*. 162.

Adam? Not quite. Here too sin has already been committed, from time immemorial).[19]

The story of Paolo is poised between Old Testament quotes and Gospel parables and can be placed between the extremities of the concepts suggested by the biblical verses constituting the epigraphs of each part of the novel. These quotes have an obvious undertone of wisdom and clearly mark the transition from, in the first part, the feeling of discomfort in welfare society – "C'è chi fa il ricco e non possiede nulla, un altro fa il povero tra molte ricchezze" (There is that maketh himself rich, yet hath nothing: there is that maketh himself poor, yet hath great riches)[20] – to, in the second part, the acceptance of a model of active participation in the Olivetti project – "Il pigro vuole e disvuole ma l'animo degli operosi sarà soddisfatto" (The soul of the sluggard desireth, and hath nothing: but the soul of the diligent shall be made fat).[21] Despite some reluctance, Buzzi recognizes the need to contribute to the construction of a utopia like Adriano Olivetti's in Ivrea, one that embodies the redemptive dreams of an economically and culturally backward country.

While he was writing *L'amore mio italiano*, Buzzi was also seeking an effective solution to these questions with an essay on the sociocultural and political aspects of advertising, titled *La tigre domestica* (The Domestic Tiger, 1964). Buzzi was aware of the contradiction between the dissent against consumerism and the adoption of a lifestyle that cannot ignore it, and he ultimately choose to compromise with economic, industrial or politic power rather than to refuse participation.

This reasoning recalls the arguments made by Julien Benda in his 1927 pamphlet *La Trahison des clercs* (The Betrayal of the Intellectuals). *L'amore mio italiano* does not explicitly mention the French philosopher, nevertheless the concept of betrayal is treated from the same angle: the intellectual rejects the capitalistic economic model and corporate structure in words, but he adheres to it in deed. Buzzi thus dodges the objections expressed by intellectuals such as Franco Fortini in the pages of *Il menabò* (issue number

---

19 Buzzi, G. 2014. *L'amore mio italiano*. Edited by S. Cavalli. Rome: Avagliano. 198.
20 Proverbs 13:7.
21 Proverbs 13:4.

5, 1962), and he leans neither towards Marxism nor capitalism, adopting the Third Way solution advocated by Olivetti on the basis of philosophers like Jacques Maritain, Emmanuel Mounier and Simone Weil.

Given this context, we are lead to understand that the meaning of the tangled relations between Paolo, his wife Dina and his mistress Daniela goes far beyond the simple extramarital love story. The protagonist lacks the courage to bring about a revolt against the system in which he lives and the factory that employs him, attaching instead a connotation of rebellion to his personal betrayal of Daniela. It will take him the entire novel to realize that this is just a ploy (and an ineffective one), to shun the responsibility of deciding if and how to *betray*, to use the language of Benda.

In the final pages of *L'amore mio italiano*, Paolo decides to contribute to the creation of a territorial plan, putting into practice his willingness to participate in the fields of architecture and urban planning. Designing houses, neighborhoods and villages is an opportunity to address the demands for the revival and refoundation of humanity. Buzzi calls this a "conversione" (conversion), a term that gives full weight to the series of religious metaphors in the first part of the novel.[22] But the 'kingdom' now takes on the reassuring features of a project aimed at developing a new residential district with the characteristics of Le Corbusier's unrealized garden city, the *Ville Radieuse* (Radiant City). What Buzzi describes is not yet an actual city; it is a utopia.[23]

This is the real "città dell'uomo" (city of man)[24] imagined by Adriano Olivetti and built with the contributions of architects, urban planners and sociologists who appeared, starting in 1954, in the catalog of the Edizioni di Comunità – Olivetti's own publishing house. None of this would have been possible without the work and the contribution of, among others, Giancarlo De Carlo, Luigi Figini, Marcello Nizzoli, Gino Pollini, Ludovico Quaroni and Renato Zveteremich. They made the Olivetti utopia a concrete utopia, erecting in Ivrea a large complex of factories, buildings and

---

22   Buzzi, G. 1963. *L'amore mio italiano*. 164.
23   Buzzi, G. 1963. *L'amore mio italiano*. 159-160.
24   Olivetti, A. 1960. *Città dell'uomo*. Milan: Edizioni di Comunità.

neighborhoods that are today part of an open-air museum and a UNESCO World Heritage Site.

L'amore mio italiano draws its inspiration from their works too, and the landscape of Ivrea has to be considered – like Paolo, Dina and Daniela – one of the protagonists of the novel, with its delicate balance between industrialization and the protection of farming land, between respect for tradition and the advent of welfare society, between aspirations of material wealth and criticism of consumerism.

GIOVANNI CAPECCHI

19 Failure and Solitude in the Boom Years: The Vigevano Stories of Lucio Mastronardi

The city of Vigevano, in the province of Pavia (Lombardy), is inextricably linked to the personal history and writing experience of Lucio Mastronardi. Mastronardi was born in Vigevano in 1930 (his father was a school inspector from Abruzzo; his mother was a school teacher from Vigevano), and he spent his entire life in the small town. He was particularly fond of two public spaces. First, the *piazza*, where the routine of everyday life flowed forth, characterized by what Mastronardi calls daily "fatterelli" (happenings), where one could observe the world as it changed humanity. And second, the Ticino river, which represents an escape from collective life, and from Mastronardi's detested job as a school teacher: a space for solitary walks that he pursued until the very end, April 24, 1979. On that day, the writer left his house without telling anybody, and making an effort to cover his tracks. On April 27, 1979, his body was found by a fisherman, five kilometers downstream from the bridge that connects Vigevano to Milan.[1] It was an epilogue to a tormented existence, characterized by depression and angry outbursts broken up by periods of recovery in psychiatric clinics and a brief stint in prison. Such a *finale* to a life "scorciato vivo" (cut short), in the words of Mastronardi's friend Italo Calvino,[2] had been foretold by a first, unsuccessful, suicide attempt in 1974, an attempt that was recounted in striking detail (though by a fictional character) in Mastronardi's last

1   De Gennaro, R. 2012. *La rivolta impossibile. Vita di Lucio Mastronardi*. Rome: Ediesse. 202–206.
2   Calvino, I. 1983. "Ricordo di Lucio Mastronardi." *Per Mastronardi. Atti del Convegno di studi su Lucio Mastronardi*. Edited by Maria Antonietta Grignani. Florence: La Nuova Italia. 13–14.

book, 7 minut (At Your Home They are Laughing, 1971). The protagonist Pietro is a rich and solitary industrialist who, despite his economic success, is unfit for modern life (his name reminds us of Federigo Tozzi's *Con gli occhi chiusi*). He jumps into the Ticino river, and his body sinks to the bottom, but it gets stuck in a tangle of algae: "Il vestito era diventato pesante come lo scafandro. Il corpo andava sotto. Pietro si sentiva scendere. Planava. Nell'acqua colorata dai riflessi azzurri il corpo seguitava planare. Sopra il tappeto di sabbia. Trascinato. Pietro si sentiva impigliare nelle alghe. Essere come allacciato alle alghe" (His clothes became heavy like a diver's suit. His body was going under. Pietro felt himself sinking. He was gliding. His body kept gliding through the shiny blue water. On a carpet of sand. Dragged along. Pietro felt himself wrapped up in algae. Like he was tied to a bunch of algae).[3]

For Mastronardi, Vigevano is a microcosm for recounting Italy and the general experience of life. It is a source of inspiration and a place of action for his fictional characters, who become protagonists on the written page. It is a "musa teatrale" (theatrical muse) and a "palcoscenico" (stage), in the words of Maria Corti, a space where everyone is invited to recite their own tragicomedy.[4] Starting with the 'Vigevano cycle,' all of Mastronardi's work is connected to this marginal space: *Il calzolaio di Vigevano* (The Shoemaker from Vigevano, published in the first issue of Elio Vittorini and Italo Calvino's journal *Il Menabò*, then as a book by Einaudi in 1962), *Il maestro di Vigevano* (The Teacher from Vigevano, also published by Einaudi in 1962) and *Il meridionale di Vigevano* (The Southerner from Vigevano, Einaudi, 1964). Mastronardi enjoyed a good deal of success: *Il maestro* sold eighty thousand copies, thanks in part to Elio Petri's 1963 film adaptation staring Alberto Sordi. Even after the 'Vigevano cycle,' and the writer's editorial migration from Einaudi to Rizzoli, Mastronardi's work continued to revolve around the microcosm of Vigevano. Following the publication of the novel *A casa tua ridono* and the short story collection

---

[3] Mastronardi, L. 2002. *A casa tua ridono e altri racconti*. Turin: Einaudi. 218.
[4] Corti, M. 1983. "Prefazione." *Per Mastronardi. Atti del Convegno di studi su Lucio Mastronardi*. Edited by Maria Antonietta Grignani. Florence: La Nuova Italia. 8.

L'assicuratore (The Insurance Man, 1975), the Rizzoli editor Sergio Pautasso pushed to have the original trilogy reprinted in a single volume titled *Gente di Vigevano* (People from Vigevano, 1977).

Mastronardi's Vigevano was the capital of the Italian shoemaking industry from the 1930s through the 1960s. Day and night, it seemed that everyone in Vigevano had but one dream: to set up a shoemaking factory and accumulate a fortune. The hustle and bustle, the rhythms of domestic and warehouse labor, the pride of great success and the shame of great failure are all central to Mastronardi's novels between 1959 and 1964. The protagonist of *Il calzolaio*, Mario Sala, leaves Vigevano for Italian-occupied Albania, and as the train car withdraws from the little world of daily labor and 'danè' (money), he watches intently from the window: "Il treno si mosse e Mario vedeva operare ferme al passaggio a livello con borsoni di tomere, operari in saia, garzoni con ceste; fabbriche fabbrichine che lentamente si girano mostrandosi in tutte le parti, tricicli carichi di scatole bianche, ciminiere fumare ..." (The train began to move, and Mario saw some female workers waiting at the railroad crossing with big handbags, male workers in smocks, shop boys holding baskets; little bity factories turning slowly around, revealing all their sides, tricycles full of white boxes, smoking chimneys ...).[5] *Il calzolaio* describes this world between the 1930s and the end of the Second World War (but with the hindsight of the economic boom): a world where wealth and success are at arm's reach, but so are errors, mishaps and failure. It is not a coincidence that Mastronardi's introduction echoes Giovanni Verga's *I Malavoglia*: "A Vigevano l'hanno sempre conosciuto come Micca" (In Vigevano, he had always been known as Micca) recalls the Sicilian writer's "Li avevano sempre conosciuti per Malavoglia" (They had always been known as the Malavoglias).[6] Mastronardi's protagonist rushes up the ladder of success, falls violently to the ground and, in the end, decides to get up and try again. He has become aware of the fact that

---

5   Mastronardi, L. 1994. *Il maestro di Vigevano, Il calzolaio di Vigevano, Il meridionale di Vigevano*. Turin: Einaudi. 269.
6   Mastronardi, L. 1994. *Il maestro di Vigevano, Il calzolaio di Vigevano, Il meridionale di Vigevano*. 209. Verga, G. 2006. *I grandi romanzi. I Malavoglia. Mastro don Gesualdo*. Milan: Mondadori. 9.

"il commercio è un giro, come la vita" (commerce is, like life, a cyclical adventure).[7]

At the moment of its publication, *Il calzolaio* presented itself as a book capable of recounting Italian society during the boom years. Starting in the late 1950s, the market for literature had seen Ottiero Ottieri, Luigi Davì and Paolo Volponi's industrial novels, Italo Calvino's short stories about real estate speculation and urban pollution, Giovanni Testori's accounts of factory life and what seemed like a collective medical record of a new, healthy Italy (where, as Luciano Bianciardi showed, sickness still lurked beneath the surface). From the perspective of Vigevano, *Il calzolaio* recounts a society where the rhythm of production grows faster every day, with the transformation of manufacturing methods and the passage from craftsmanship to heavy industry with the introduction of the assembly line: "Si lavorava all'americana, i misté, grandi e piccoli che sia, li fanno tutti i macchinari, gli operari fanno sempre lo stesso verso" (We worked like Americans, every stage, whether big or small, was done by machines, the workers always aped their part).[8] Readers and critics were attracted to Mastronardi's novel for its unconventional linguistic choices. *Il calzolaio* constructs a hybrid language that draws on dialect words, expressions and grammatical structures. As Maria Antonietta Grignani has written, dialect "è proprio una sorta di morbillo, che investe racconto e dialogato" (is truly a sort of disease that infects both narrative and dialogue).[9] *Il calzolaio* also incorporates much technical jargon tied to the world of shoemaking, linguistically calling the narrative back to the microcosm of Vigevano with both mimetic and expressive force. When for lack of culture and confidence some standard Italian sayings are botched beyond recognition – "è bello perché è avariato" (it's beautiful because it's rotten *instead of* it's beautiful

---

7   Mastronardi, L. 1994. *Il maestro di Vigevano, Il calzolaio di Vigevano, Il meridionale di Vigevano*. 339.
8   Mastronardi, L. 1994. *Il maestro di Vigevano, Il calzolaio di Vigevano, Il meridionale di Vigevano*. 332.
9   Grignani, M. A. 1983. "Lingua e dialetto ne *Il calzolaio di Vigevano*." *Per Mastronardi. Atti del Convegno di studi su Lucio Mastronardi*. Edited by Maria Antonietta Grignani. Florence: La Nuova Italia. 50.

because its varied)¹⁰ – these become emblematic expressions of the folly and cruelty integral to this world.

Just after the publication of *Il calzolaio*, Einaudi also released *Il maestro di Vigevano*. Calvino, one of Mastronardi's most attentive readers, and his constant interlocutor, immediately noticed a fundamental difference between the two novels: "*Il calzolaio* è un libro più bello perché la stessa visione dell'umanità è espressa in modo più o meno oggettivo e più o meno unitario; ma *Il maestro* è un libro più infernale e ricco e impressionante" (*Il calzolaio* is a more pleasing book, because its vision of humanity is expressed in a more or less objective and uniform way; but *Il maestro* is more infernal and rich and striking).¹¹ *Il maestro* recounts Vigevano's boom years by focusing closely on the figure of maestro Mombelli, a teacher through whom Mastronardi presents both the scholastic world (grotesquely described, between irony and rage) and the shoemaking industry. It centers on the everyday struggles of a man who is unable to come to terms with reality, suffocated by the "catrame" (tar) that prevents all free and comfortable movement. The frenetic compulsion to 'fare danè' (make money) and open a modest factory are here incarnated in Mombelli's wife, a factory worker who scorns her husband's socially and economically useless job: "Prima di sposarti le amiche mi dicevano: la Ada sposa un maestro!, con aria invidiosa. Ora dicono: povera Ada. Ha sposato un maestro!" (Before I married you, my friends would say to me: Ada is going to marry a school teacher!, as if they were jealous. Now they say: poor Ada. She married a school teacher!)¹² Ada forces Mombelli to leave the school and use his severance pay to buy a shoemaking factory. Mastronardi concentrates his attention on the dark side of the boom, which in the words of Luciano Bianciardi reveals the "balordaggine del miracolo" (foolishness of the miracle).¹³ This is an economic miracle accompanied by feelings of solitude and egoism, where the funeral of an active and lifelong school employee goes

10 Mastronardi, L. 1994. *Il maestro di Vigevano, Il calzolaio di Vigevano, Il meridionale di Vigevano*, 250.
11 De Gennaro, R. 2012. *La rivolta impossibile. Vita di Lucio Mastronardi*. 49.
12 Mastronardi, L. 1994. *Il maestro di Vigevano, Il calzolaio di Vigevano, Il meridionale di Vigevano*. 8.
13 Bianciardi, L. 1999. *La vita agra*. Milan: Bompiani. 157.

practically unattended, a miracle mixed with a profound and irremediable sense of marginality and uselessness for all those who fail to insert themselves like cogs in a machine. Mombelli thinks: "Solitudine dolorosa [...]. Ma forse non è proprio solitudine. È la consapevolezza di essere inutili" (Painful solitude [...]. But maybe it's not exactly solitude. It's the awareness of being useless).[14] Such meditations characterize both the school and the factory, where due to his total incompetence Mombelli is at risk of crippling production. The distinguishing feature of Mastronardi's protagonists remains their propensity to failure: first Mario Sala, then maestro Mombelli, with his useless days – "Mi accorgo cha la mia vita è tutto un seguito di ore bruciate, di tempo perduto" (I realize that my whole life is a succession of wasted hours, of lost time)[15] – and his obsessive, neurotic fears, emblematically represented by the recurring image of toes, which Mombelli examines and thinks about constantly. Mombelli is a disoriented and incompetent character whose supposed greatness is entirely latent. In sleeping and waking dreams, he reworks reality, imagining himself as a champion cyclist who can easily beat Fausto Coppi or Gino Bartali.

In a review published in *La Stampa* on June 6, 1962, Franco Antonicelli underlined the "agitarsi buffonesco" (clownish excitement) typical of Mastronardi's "umanità comico-dolente" (comic and painful humanity).[16] Antonicelli's review inaugurated two images of the writer's work that would recur through its reception history: the clownish or farcical character of many situations and the tragic nature of the human condition in all its infernal aspects. With respect to the former, Mastronardi tends to adopt forcefully grotesque forms of representation, whether in descriptions of the scholastic world or of the shoemaking industry. With respect to the latter, he is concerned with revealing an empty abyss below and within humanity. The *piazza*s of Vigevano stage the process of economic and

---

14   Mastronardi, L. 1994. *Il maestro di Vigevano, Il calzolaio di Vigevano, Il meridionale di Vigevano*. 112.
15   Mastronardi, L. 1994. *Il maestro di Vigevano, Il calzolaio di Vigevano, Il meridionale di Vigevano*. 39.
16   Cited in Tesio, G. 2002. "L'ultimo Mastronardi: la sfida di un moralista insocievole tra demoni e clown." in Mastronardi, L. *A casa tua ridono e altri racconti*. Turin: Einaudi. IX.

social transformation, with industrialists who flaunt their money from the windows of brand-new cars. But they also become a metaphor for life's repetitiveness, its rhythms "tra crisi e lisi" (between crises and lesions), in the words of Italo Svevo,[17] its wasted hours, lost time, neuroses and bouts of depression. Mastronardi's is "una provincia apocalittica, sottratta a ogni ipoteca di riforma e di salvezza" (an apocalyptic and provincial existence, immune to all reform or salvation).[18]

Survival is a challenge wherever the ability to make money is considered the only criteria for dividing capable from incapable, useful from useless human beings. In *Il meridionale di Vigevano*, the industrialist Girini despises the employees he sees sitting at a coffee shop: "Al dí d'inco, disoma la verità, chi gh'ha no un miliún, l'è propi una bestia, a l'è" (To which I say, let's be serious, whoever doesn't have a million bucks is a beast, that's right).[19] Such contempt is meant to represent a new and popular way of thinking, a dominant mindset in Italian society during the boom years and in a Vigevano full of riches but lacking in culture. The journalist Giorgio Bocca described this attitude in a justly famous note: "Fare soldi, per fare soldi, per fare soldi: se esistono altre prospettive, chiedo scusa, non le ho viste. Di abitanti cinquantasettemila, di operai venticinquemila, di milionari a battaglioni affiancati, di librerie neanche una" (Make money, to make money, to make money: if there are other points of view, sorry, but I didn't see them. Population: 57,000; workers: 25,000; millionaires: many battalions all lined up; bookshops: not even one).[20] *Il meridionale* was published in 1964, and it belongs to the same narrative project as the previous two novels. The language is less forceful with respect to *Il maestro*, but with evocative descriptions of Vigevano and the ubiquitous noise of shoe-making machines. It deals with the evolving economic situation, capital investments in real estate and the growing interest among industrialists in construction development. It announces the end of a civilization based

17 Svevo, I. 2006. *Romanzi e "continuazioni"*. Milan: Mondadori. 1083.
18 Jacomuzzi, A. 1983. "Il maestro di Vigevano." *Per Mastronardi. Atti del Convegno di studi su Lucio Mastronardi*. 68.
19 Mastronardi, L. 1994. *Il maestro di Vigevano, Il calzolaio di Vigevano, Il meridionale di Vigevano*. 368.
20 Cited in De Gennaro, R. 2012. *La rivolta impossibile. Vita di Lucio Mastronardi*. 38.

on farming, transforming agricultural workers into factory laborers – in the words of a female glue mixer: "Prima fiva il pastón per i besti; adesso fo il pastón per le scarpe!" (Before, I made the paste for the beasts; now, I make the paste for the shoes!)[21] – and it lingers on the lives of southern migrants who have come to Vigevano. One of these migrants is the protagonist, who is respected by tax evaders only because he works in a tax office, and he is surrounded by a large community of migrants whose lives are connected to a set of narrative spaces: the payphone room at the local telephone company (to call home on Sundays), the waiting room at the train station (to celebrate holidays and welcome new arrivals, in search of work and hope) and the countryside (to sell their manpower, cheaper and less unionized than northern labor).

After *Il meridionale*, Mastronardi's literary adventures began to come to a close. In letters to friends and publishers, he wrote of his struggle to find new narrative possibilities and his desire to experiment with new forms, especially with an eye toward the neo-avantgarde and their reworking of narrative time and space. But the results were disappointing, and his readers (for example, Calvino) were quick to criticize Mastronardi during this period of increasingly frequent personal crises. Nevertheless, this writer still produced some interesting material, like *La ballata del vecchio calzolaio* (The Dance of the Old Shoemaker, published in *L'approdo letterario* (The Literary Landing) in 1969, then reprinted in the collection *L'assicuratore*). Giovanni Tesio sums up *L'assicuratore* with the following words: "Tutti i dodici racconti mettono in scena creature fuggiasche, braccate dalle proprie ossessioni, personaggi votati all'imbarazzo, all'impaccio, alla timidezza, alla storditaggine, all'indecisione, alla frustrazione, all'umiliazione, alla pesantezza, alla sconfitta" (All twelve short stories present fugitive creatures, hunted by their own obsessions, characters prone to embarrassment, to blunders, to shyness, to bewilderment, to indecision, to frustration, to humiliation, to heaviness, to defeat).[22] Although Mastronardi had discussed this composite collection very early with Einaudi, it was only printed in

---

21 Mastronardi, L. 1994. *Il maestro di Vigevano, Il calzolaio di Vigevano, Il meridionale di Vigevano.* 426.
22 Tesio, G. 2002. "L'ultimo Mastronardi." XVII.

1975 by Rizzoli, as if to backfill a creative gap that had produced so much anguish and depression. Most of the short stories of *L'assicuratore* belong to the intellectual climate and narrative forms of the Vigevano trilogy, while some like *La ballata del vecchio calzolaio* mark a clear moment of transition. A number of Mastronardi's noted contexts and themes resurface: the protagonist of *La ballata del vecchio calzolaio* is a successful shoemaker from Vigevano, who despite his riches remains somehow hindered, disconnected and lonely. But the forms of expression change: Mastronardi narrates the protagonist's life across one single day, using flashbacks to make past moments reemerge and juxtaposing with the present slices of life from previous periods. In the words of Gian Carlo Ferretti, the story is

> una mera successione di gesti nevrotici, di tic esteriori, di idee fisse, accentuata dall'uso ossessivo del verbo infinito, dalla giustapposizione di brevi frasi staccate, tronche, iterate. Il microcosmo vigevanese ne risulta come frantumato e fissato in tanti vitrei frammenti, allineati l'uno accanto all'altro, che lasciano tuttavia intravedere un'angoscia segreta incapace di esprimersi, un senso oscuro di degradazione avanzata e di morte incombente, un freddo ghigno che è ormai la proiezione dell'estremo limite di una scrittura e di una vita.
>
> (a mere succession of neurotic gestures, of outward tics, of fixations, accentuated by the obsessive use of verbs in the infinitive, by the juxtaposition of short, staccato sentences, truncated and iterated. The microcosm of Vigevano ends up shattered into so many glass fragments, lined up one beside the other but nevertheless leaving exposed a secret anguish that is unable to express itself, a dark sense of advancing degradation and of impending death, a cold sneer that has become the projected far limit of a way of writing and living.)[23]

The story concludes fittingly and emblematically with a sneer. The protagonist imagines what he will see when he enters his bedroom, where his wife is sleeping: "Nell'andare in letto la guarderà dormire. La testa spettinata. La fronte corrugata. Le guance spiritate. La bocca scarnita. Il respirare contratto. Il mento appuntito. Le narici dilatate. Gli occhi gli andranno allora sul comodino. Il bicchiere: la dentiera: il ghigno" (Going

---

23 Ferretti, G. C. 1983. "Il mondo in piccolo (ritratto di Lucio Mastronardi)." *Per Mastronardi. Atti del Convegno di studi su Lucio Mastronardi.* Edited by Maria Antonietta Grignani. Florence: La Nuova Italia. 33.

to bed, he will see her sleeping. Her head all messy. Her brow all furrowed. Her cheeks quivering. Her mouth all fleshy. Her breathing contracted. Her chin pointed. Her nostrils dilated. Then, his eyes will wander across the nightstand. A glass, some dentures, a sneer).[24]

For Mastronardi, the only way forward was to formulate new variations on the old themes of anguish and death. After a long process of writing and rewriting, he finished the novel *A casa tua ridono*. In a letter to Giorgio Bocca, Mastronardi describes the ambition behind this last book: while the previous works "si accontentavano di osservare i padroncini del miracolo, questo, direi, piange sulla condizione umana" (were happy to observe the petty bosses of the economic miracle, this one, I would say, mourns the human condition).[25] The Rizzoli editor Pautasso wrote to encourage Mastronardi, saying that the novel could be a sign of the author's "rinascimento" (rebirth).[26] But the writing process had cost Mastronardi an enormous effort. He responded to Pautasso: "Caro Sergio quando leggerai questa lettera io sarò chiuso nella clinica psichiatrica. Il medico mi ha trovato arrangiato come uno straccio; la mente logorata" (Dear Sergio, by the time you read this letter, I will be locked up in the psychiatric clinic. The doctor found me to be tangled up in knots, my mind worn out),[27] and the publication of his novel resounded like a death knell. *A casa tua ridono* is truly the epilogue to a tormented career. The novel returns to Vigevano, where the rhythm of the shoemaking industry has become fixed in the everyday routine of the assembly line: "I dipendenti si sentono intercambiabili come se fossero dei pezzi d'ingranaggio. Ciascuno può fare il lavoro dell'altro" (The employees feel themselves interchangeable, as if they were gears. Anyone can do the job of anyone else).[28] The values of success and money in contemporary society are paired with the expressive choices pioneered in the short stories of the late 1960s. The maelstrom of life grows unstoppable, cutting off all escape. In a private latter, Mastronardi wrote

24 Mastronardi, L. 2002. *A casa tua ridono e altri racconti.* 81.
25 Cited in De Gennaro, R. 2012. *La rivolta impossibile. Vita di Lucio Mastronardi.* 177.
26 Cited in De Gennaro, R. 2012. *La rivolta impossibile. Vita di Lucio Mastronardi.* 176.
27 Cited in De Gennaro, R. 2012. *La rivolta impossibile. Vita di Lucio Mastronardi.* 175.
28 Mastronardi, L. 2002. *A casa tua ridono e altri racconti.* 219.

that *A casa tua ridono* "è la sintesi del dolore" (is the synthesis of pain).[29] The delirious thoughts of Pietro, who has just attempted suicide in the nearby river, are interrupted by the rhythm of an obsessive refrain: "A casa tua ridono" (At your home they're laughing). Everyone is laughing at him. And it is an evil, injurious laugh, that stigmatizes and signals scorn, that raises an insurmountable barrier between him and all others.

Translated by Jim Carter

---

29 Cited in Tesio, G. 2002. "L'ultimo Mastronardi." XX.

MARK PIETRALUNGA

20   Luciano Bianciardi and the New Frenetic Era of Labor

In 1954 Luciano Bianciardi left his hometown of Grosseto and moved to Milan, determined to participate in the culture industry that was in its nascent stages. He joined the newly formed Feltrinelli publishing house as a member of its editorial staff. Seven months after his arrival in Milan, Bianciardi published in February of 1955 the article "Lettera da Milano" (Letter from Milan) in the journal *Contemporaneo*.[1] Bianciardi acknowledged having been warned that he would find the city too harsh, closed and confined. He was especially struck by the difficulty of establishing steadfast and sincere human relationships. Even visually, the city appeared to be a type of "labirinto di griglie scure, fra le quali scorrono lunghe, eguali, monotone le strade" (labyrinth of dark grids, between which there flowed streets that were long, indistinguishable and monotonous).[2] Moreover, Bianciardi saw the northern metropolis as a place where the intellectual would become just another piece of the bureaucratic and commercial apparatus. He asked his readers to consider how many writers, journalists, artists and photographers worked in advertising. It was that same advertising that taught you that success in life, and in business, was based on the type of shoe polish and electric razor you used and how you marketed yourself. Consequently, he asserted, "questa non è la Milano che produce, ma quella che vende e baratta, e in questa società si vende e si baratta proprio presentandosi col volto ben rasato, le scarpe lucide ecc" (this is not the Milan that

---

1   Bianciardi, L. 2008. *L'antimeridiano. Tutte le opere*, vol. 2. Milan: ExCogita. 700–705.
2   Bianciardi, L. 2008. *L'antimeridiano*, vol. 2. 701.

produces, but rather the one that sells and barters, and in this society one sells and barters just showing up with a cleanly shaved face, shoes shined etc).³ What emerges from this article is an outspoken sense of disorientation on the part of the affected intellectual, who clearly distinguishes the new environment of the Lombard capital from the provincial world he has just left. The "Lettera da Milano" is a fundamental text above all because it anticipates questions and problems, such as the role of the intellectuals, central to Bianciardi's 'Milanese' novels.

In 1960 Bianciardi published the novel *L'Integrazione* (The Integration), a social satire of the myth of the culture industry during the economic boom that traced his own discouraging experiences in the publishing industry. In the 1961 issue of the journal *Il Menabò di letteratura*, dedicated to the topic "Industry and Literature," Marco Forti's essay on industrial themes in Italian literature included Bianciardi's *L'integrazione* in its analysis.⁴ Forti highlighted Bianciardi's "umorismo tetramente rivelatore" (gloomily revealing humor) as he encountered the new protagonist of the metropolis, the "anonimo robot eter-diretto che ha nome di uomo-massa" (anonymous, hetero-directed robot known as mass-man).⁵ Forti noted how the novel's opening pages captured the frenetic, mechanical and conditioned movements and behaviors that defined Milan in its daily activities, as the anonymous crowd piled into buses at rush hour, walked swiftly along the streets in a military marching motion, ate quickly at a *tavola calda* (self-service restaurant) while listening to a portable radio, at night went to a movie or watched television, or rapidly made love in the car. Equally affected by a climate coldly conditioned by the all-consuming economic life and by its obsession with organization was the publishing world: "Guardali in faccia: stirati, con gli occhi delle febbre, dimentichi di tutto tranne che dei soldi che ci vogliono ogni giorno, e che servono soltanto quanto basta per stare in piedi, per lavorare, trottare ancora, e fare altri soldi" (Look in their faces: strained, with feverish eyes, unmindful of everything except

---

3   Bianciardi, L. 2008. *L'antimeridiano*, vol. 2. 703.
4   Forti, M. 1961. "Temi industriali della narrativa italiana." *Il Menabò di letteratura*, no. 4. 213–239.
5   Forti, M. 1961. "Temi industriali della narrativa italiana." 235.

for the money that is necessary each day, that is sufficient enough to stay on one's feet, in order to work, to still scamper, and make more money).[6] In a letter dated May 23, 1960 to his friend Mario Terrosi, shortly after the completion of *L'integrazione*, Bianciardi summarized the environment of the publishing industry that had fallen victim to the law of production:

> La verità è che le case editrici son piene di fannulloni frenetici: gente che non combina una madonna dalla mattina alla sera, e riesce, non so come, a stancarsi lo stesso, e a dare l'impressione, fallace, di star lavorando. Si prendono persino l'esaurimento nervoso. La cosa migliore [...] è prendersela calma e possibilmente sfotterli. Come ho fatto ne *L'integrazione*.
>
> (The truth is that the publishing houses are full of frenetic loafers: people who do not accomplish a damn thing from morning to evening, and manage, I don't know how, to exhaust themselves, and to give the impression, deceptive as it may be, of working. They even end up having a nervous breakdown. The best thing [...] is to take it slow and possibly mock them, as I did in *L'integrazione*.)[7]

In another letter to Terrosi dated February 4, 1961, Bianciardi provided insight into the motivation behind his new novel about Milan that reflected the chaos, alienation and indifference prevailing in a country in the process of modernization:

> In preparazione avrei un altro libro più grosso, più cattivo, su Milano. Nonostante il passare degli anni, la rabbia contro questa città cresce di continuo. Hai ragione tu a dire che Grosseto è la piu bella città d'Italia. Qui c'è un vantaggio: che ti danno lavoro e ti pagano. Per il resto, non è una città, non è un paese, non è niente. È solo una gran macchina caotica, senza cielo sopra, e senza anima dentro. Andrebbe minata. Eppure tanti si ostinano a dire che è il cuore d'Italia.
>
> (I am preparing another book, even bigger and nastier, about Milan. Even with the passing of years, my anger against this city only grows. You're right when you say that Grosseto is the most beautiful city in Italy. Here there is one advantage: you find work and they pay you. For the rest, it's not a city, it's not a country, it's nothing. It's only a big, chaotic machine, with no sky above and no spirit inside. It needs to be blown up. And yet so many insist on saying that it is the heart of Italy.)[8]

6   Forti, M. 1961. "Temi industriali della narrativa italiana." 235.
7   Gessani, A. and Terrosi, M. 1985. *L'intellettuale disintegrato: Luciano Bianciardi*. Rome: Ianus. 103–104.
8   Gessani, A. and Terrosi, M. 1985. *L'intellettuale disintegrato*. 90.

The announced book is *La vita agra* (It's a Hard Life, 1962). In it Bianciardi recounts his own personal experiences in a stifling society that attempts to conceal a moral squalor and a lack of human interaction by an overabundance of superficial stimuli. The author gives his reasons for writing a story about an ordinary man who, like many others, is caught in a rat race:

> Questa è a dire parecchio una storia mediana e mediocre, che tutto sommato io non me la passo peggio di tanti altri che gonfiano e stanno zitti. Eppure proprio perché mediocre a me sembra che valeva la pena di raccontarla. Proprio perché questa storia è intessuta di sentimenti e di fatti già inquadrati dagli studiosi, dagli storici sociologi economisti, erano un fenomeno individuato, preciso ed etichettato. Cioè il miracolo italiano.
>
> (It is paying this story a compliment to call it ordinary and commonplace, and that, is to say a lot, and that, all things considered, I'm no worse off than a lot of others who put up with things without making such a fuss. But the story seemed to me to be worth the trouble of telling just because it is so ordinary. Just because it is made up of facts and feelings already classified by scholars, historians, sociologists and economists, I wanted to describe a single, definite, carefully documented case. A case history, that is to say, of the Italian miracle.)[9]

The reference to himself as "ordinary" is a motif that appears in Bianciardi's early writings. It suggests a desire of the intellectual to lose himself in anonymity, to become one with the masses. This identification with the working class and the proletarian values of his native region of Grosseto was expressed in an autobiographical piece for the journal *Belfagor* in 1952 entitled "Nascita di uomini democratici" (The Birth of Democratic Men):

> Io sono con loro, i badilanti e i minatori della mia terra, e ne sono orgoglioso; se in qualche modo la mia poca cultura può giovare al loro lavoro, alla loro esistenza, stimerò buona questa cultura, perché mi permette di restituire, almeno in parte, lavoro che è stato speso anche per me [...]. Non mi pare di aver detto grandi cose e non le potevo dire, perché so bene d'essere, senza modestia, un uomo mediocre, eguale, né migliore né peggiore di centomila altri come me. Ma appunto per questo io credo che

---

9 Bianciardi, L. 1962. *La vita agra*. Milan: Rizzoli. 174. Bianciardi, L. 1965. *It's a Hard Life*. Translated by Eric Mosbacher. New York: The Viking Press. 151.

> la mia testimonianza abbia qualche interesse, perché è la tipica della mia generazione. Della quale generazione, la 'generazione bruciata,' si son dette e si dicono tante cose amare. E per la verità, se guardo a questi trent'anni, non vedo molte ore liete.
>
> (I'm with them, the diggers and the miners of my land, and I'm proud of it. If in some way the little culture I have acquired can be of any use to their labors and to their existence, I'll consider it worthwhile, because it allows me to repay, at least in part, the labor that has been spent also for me [...]. I don't claim to have said great things, nor could I say them, because I am, without modesty, fully aware of being an ordinary man, equal to, not better nor worse, one hundred thousand others like me. But precisely for this reason I think my testimony can be of interest, because it is typical of my generation. Many bitter things have been said and continue to be said about this generation, the 'wasted generation.' And in all truthfulness, if I look at these past thirty years, I do not see many happy hours.)[10]

In his 1961 essay "Il lavoro del traduttore" (The Job of the Translator), Bianciardi's identification with the working class was reflected in the parallels he drew between his activity as translator and the labors of the miners:

> Già, perché si è detto finora di lavoro artigianale, e va invece ricordato che tradurre è oltre tutto una fatica fisica e psicologica da sterratore [...]. I 'movimenti di terra' il traduttore li fa con la vanga e la barella, come i terrazzieri delle mie parti quando lavorano al fossone [...]. Come un terrazziere delle parti mie, cartella dopo cartella, libro dopo libro, e a volte, la domenica, col fiasco del vino davanti, mi diverto a cantare una vecchia storia, a inventare un 'dispetto.'
>
> (We have spoken up to this point about manual labor, but instead what should be remembered is that the act of translating is above all the psychological and physical fatigue of a digger [...]. The translator does his 'earthworks' with a shovel and a handbarrow, like the diggers of my hometown when they work at an excavation [...]. Like a digger back home I continue to excavate, page after page, book after book, and sometimes on Sunday, with a bottle of wine in front of me, I enjoy singing an old story and creating a little 'mischief.')[11]

La vita agra tells the story of a passionate intellectual from the provinces who comes to Milan to blow up the headquarters of a chemical giant. The chemical company's relentless quest for profits over human welfare

---

10 Bianciardi, L. 2008. *L'antimeridiano*, vol. 2. 295–296.
11 Ibid., 875–876.

has resulted in the death of forty-three miners in an explosion near the protagonist's hometown in 1954. However, before he can accomplish his mission, the protagonist must earn a living. He finds work in the publishing industry and learns immediately the reality of life in a white-collar world: his creativity and humanitarianism must succumb to the reality of bureaucratic planning and the demands of specialization. When he tells his future employer that he would like to write a story about the mine explosion, the reply is that it is old news; besides, it falls outside his specialized sector:

> "Ma bada bene, Qui si tratta di prendersi un incarico preciso, da svolgere puntualmente, mese per mese." "Ma sullo scoppio non ti serve niente? Io sarei informato …" "Te l'ho detto" fece, impaziente. "È una notizia invecchiata, e poi andrebbe in pagina sindacale. Vuoi farlo o no, questo spoglio della stampa periodica, per il settore sociologico?"
>
> ("But you realise, don't you, that it means undertaking a definite commitment and turning in the material punctually every month?" "But don't you want anything about the explosion? I know all about …" "I've told you, it's stale, and in any case it would go on the trade union page. Are you willing to try your hand at a review of the sociological press, or are you not?")[12]

In Milan where time is money and where everyone is busy working and consuming, no one has time for revolutions. Not even the working class, with whom the protagonist felt a strong affinity in his hometown, is interested:

> Nemmeno ci rassegnavamo all'impossibilità di serbare i contatti con la classe operaia, che aveva orari sfasati rispetto ai nostri, giungeva alle sei del mattino coi treni del sonno e ripartiva alle sei del pomeriggio, oppure, terminato il lavoro, rincasava in fretta per travestirsi da ceto medio e andarsene al cinema o al bar.
>
> (We did not even resign ourselves to the impossibility of making contact with the working class, whose time-table was out of gear with ours, as they arrived by train at six o'clock in the morning and left again at six in the evening, or hurried home as soon as their day's work was over to disguise themselves as members of the middle class and go to the cinema or the café.)[13]

---

12   Bianciardi, L. 1962. *La vita agra*. 49. Bianciardi, L. 1965. *It's a Hard Life*. 43.
13   Bianciardi, L. 1962. *La vita agra*. 80–81. Bianciardi, L. 1965. *It's a Hard Life*. 71.

The protagonist's struggles against a mechanized and bureaucratized world are captured in his eventual job of translator who, like the novel's author, spends his days frantically producing translations in order to meet the culture industry's demands. It is a trade that fits the needs of a world obsessed with the accomplishment of purely technical tasks:

> In una città come questa, cioè piena di gente terziaria e quartaria, col mercato comune in vista e il miracolo in prospettiva, c'era molto da tradurre in materia aziendale, specialmente testi chiamati operativi, e siccome c'era molta fretta, si contentavano anche di me, senza badare troppo agli apostrofi e alle rime ato ato, ente ente e zione zione.
>
> (In a city like this, full of tertiary and quaternary people, that is to say, with the common market round the corner and the economic miracle in sight, there was a great deal of commercial and industrial material to translate, particularly books on so-called business efficiency, and, as these were always wanted in a great hurry, they even put up with me, without worrying too much about apostrophes and having words that rhymed in the same sentence.)[14]

During the economic boom there was a tendency in the new societal force of the middle class to consider the acquisition of books as an occasion to display its new social condition. Consequently, translators found themselves inundated by the new consumer's demand. The protagonist of *La vita agra* is depicted as being bombarded by the words on the page. The books he translates have lost their sense of humanity and have become a means for survival in the city: "Riuscivamo a fare anche quindici, anche venti cartelle al giorno. Due a Mara, una al padrone di casa, una per luce-gas-telefono-pane e latte, un'altra per le rate dei mobili e dei vestiti, due per il companatico e le sigarette" (We managed to do as much as fifteen or twenty pages a day. Two for Mara, one for rent, one for light, gas, telephone, bread and milk, another for the instalments on furniture and my clothes, and two for extras and cigarettes.)[15] The novel's innovative style and language reflect the disoriented state of its protagonist, as Bianciardi chooses to mix a variety of styles, genres and languages from his numerous translations in order to illustrate the chaotic condition of contemporary society:

---

14   Bianciardi, L. 1962. *La vita agra*. 142. Bianciardi, L. 1965. *It's a Hard Life*. 124.
15   Bianciardi, L. 1962. *La vita agra*. 144. Bianciardi, L. 1965. *It's a Hard Life*. 126.

Proverò l'impasto linguistico, contaminando da par mio la alata di Ollesalvetti diobò, e 'u dialettu d'Ucurdunnu, evocando in un sol periodo il Burchiello e Rabelais, il Molinari Enrico di New York e il lamento di Travale – guata guata male no mangiai me mezo pane – Amarilli Etrusca e zio Lorenzo di Viareggio. Ma anche vi darò il romanzo tradizionale, con tre morti per forza, due gemelli identici e monocoriali e un'agnizione. Il romanzo neocapitalista, neoromantico o neocattolico, a scelta. Ci metterò dentro la monaca di Monza, la novizia del convento di ***, il curato di campagna e il prete bello. Datemi il tempo, datemi i mezzi, e io toccherò tutta la tastiera – bianche e neri – della sensibilità contemporanea. Vi canterò l'indifferenza, la disubbidienza, l'amore coniugale, il conformismo, la sonnolenza, lo spleen, la noia e il rompimento di palle.

(Or I shall compose a linguistic medley of my own, combining a variety of regional dialects, recalling in a single paragraph Burchiello and Rabelais, Enrico Molinari of New York and the lament of men of Travale (the earliest recorded phrase in colloquial Italian, complaining about how little they eat), Amarilli Etrusca and Uncle Lorenzo of Viareggio. And I shall also give you the traditional, with at least three deaths, two pairs of identical twins and a legal acknowledgement. The neo-capitalist, neo-Romantic or neo-Catholic novel, as you will. And I'll include in it the nun of Monza, the novice in the convent of ***, the country priest and the handsome priest. Give me the time and give me the means and I'll touch all the keys, both black and white, of contemporary sensibility. I'll give you indifference, disobedience, married love, conformism, sleepiness, spleen, boredom and indignation.)[16]

Bianciardi's novel is an attempt to revive the individual's declining consciousness, as humans become absorbed by mass communication and mass consumption, with knowledge administered and confined. In order to recapture some sense of his own individuality, the protagonist of *La vita agra* is driven to hallucinate a world that lives exclusively for the sexual act. However, to achieve what he calls a "neocristianesimo a sfondo disattivistico e copulatorio" (anti-agitative and copulatory neo-Christianity),[17] he recognizes that "non basta sganasciare la dirigenza politico-economico-social-divertentistica italiana" (it is not enough to get rid of the political, economic, social and entertainment management in Italy).[18] Instead, "la rivoluzione deve cominciare da ben più lontano,

---

16   Bianciardi, L. 1962. *La vita agra*. 30. Bianciardi, L. 1965. *It's a Hard Life*. 27.
17   Bianciardi, L. 1962. *La vita agra*, 162. Bianciardi, L. 1965. *It's a Hard Life*. 157.
18   Bianciardi, L. 1962. *La vita agra*. 178. Bianciardi, L. 1965. *It's a Hard Life*. 155.

deve cominciare in interiore homine" (the revolution needs to begin elsewhere, in the interior of man).[19] He thus imagines a utopian world in which every kind of mechanical device has been abandoned and industrial production has ceased: "Tutto ciò che ruota, articola, scivola, incastra, ingrana e sollecita sarà abbandonato" (Everything that revolves, slides, engages, or accelerates will be given up).[20] In this fantasy world all those jobs that feed off and exploit the materialistic and consumerist mania that has invaded the city will vanish: "Saranno scomparse le attività quartarie, e anzitutto i grafici, i PRM, e i demodossologi" (All the quaternary occupations will disappear, and first of all typographers, public relations officers and demodoxologists).[21]

Once work is reduced almost to nothing, leisure, another obsessive byproduct of the economic boom, will no longer be coveted and capitalized on: "Il problema del tempo libero non si porrà più essendo la vita intera una continua distesa di tempo libero" (The problem of leisure will no longer arise, for the whole of life will consist of nothing else).[22] By viewing leisure as a problem and a product of the new frenetic era of labor, Bianciardi appears to subscribe to the Gramscian notion that leisure is not free. Karl Spracklen has observed: "Although some people […] may have some agency and freedom to choose their leisure, the working classes and other marginalized and disempowered social groups are denied that freedom." Moreover, as Spracklen continues, "that leisure, in its commodified state, is a way in which the ruling classes keep the working classes ignorant of their oppression."[23] In a 1959 essay entitled "L'alibi del progresso" (The Alibi of Progress), Bianciardi even posed the question of whether it were right to organize conferences on the useful employment of leisure time when two million Italians did not have jobs and when many more were employed just six months per year.[24] However, at a time of tremendous growth in wealth

19   Bianciardi, L. 1962. *La vita agra*. 178. Bianciardi, L. 1965. *It's a Hard Life*. 155.
20   Bianciardi, L. 1962. *La vita agra*. 179. Bianciardi, L. 1965. *It's a Hard Life*. 155.
21   Bianciardi, L. 1962. *La vita agra*. 179. Bianciardi, L. 1965. *It's a Hard Life*. 155.
22   Bianciardi, L. 1962. *La vita agra*. 180. Bianciardi, L. 1965. *It's a Hard Life*. 156.
23   Spracklen, K. 2009. *The Meaning and Purpose of Leisure: Habermas and Leisure at the End of Modernity*. London: Palgrave Macmillan. 19.
24   Bianciardi, L. 2000. *L'alibi del progresso. Scritti giornalistici ed elzeviri*. Milan: ExCogita. 293.

and technological invention for many and when the market for products to satisfy wants rather than needs was drastically increasing, leisure time became a major topic of the critical discourse on the contemporary culture industry. In fact, the thirteenth Triennale di Milano (the Milan Triennial, an international exhibition of art and design) in 1964, curated by Umberto Eco and Vittorio Gregotti, examined the theme of leisure time in connection with the modes of production and consumption of design. It did so from a similar demystifying and critical perspective to that of Bianciardi's treatment of the metropolis not only in his novels *L'integrazione* and *La vita agra*, but also in his many journalistic writings and short stories.[25] Like Bianciardi, the organizers of the thirteenth Triennale embraced the political commitment of protest against mass civilization and the alienation of the contemporary age. In an exhibition space called the "Corridor of Captions," one such caption, warned of the danger posed by industrial civilization and delivered the central thesis of this section: "Uno dei pericoli della CIVILTÀ INDUSTRIALE è che il *Tempo Libero* sia organizzato dagli stessi centri di potere che controllano IL TEMPO DEL LAVORO. In questo caso il *Tempo Libero* è consumato secondo lo stesso ritmo DEL TEMPO LAVORATIVO. Diverstirsi significa FARSI INTEGRARE." (One of the dangers of the INDUSTRIAL CIVILIZATION is that *Free Time* could be organized by the same centers of power that controlled work time. For this reason, *Free Time* is consumed according to the same pace OF WORK TIME. Having fun means BEING INTEGRATED).[26] It is that same danger of being swallowed up by the furious industrious and frantic activity of the impersonal metropolis and the fear of being absorbed in the cult of material progress that leads the protagonist of the *La vita agra* to withdraw, if only for a short while, to a world of fantasy. In doing so, he refuses to sacrifice individual instincts in the name of progress and repudiates the whole working world and its recreation.

La vita agra is one of the few novels of protest that emerged during the Italian economic boom, and it is an angry statement of a man's failure

---

25 For more on the Milan Triennale, see Ciliberto, G. 2012. *La Triennale di Milano fra costruzione e critica del design in Italia*. Venice: Università Iuav di Venezia. Thesis.
26 Ciliberto, G. 2012. *La Triennale di Milano fra costruzione e critica del design in Italia*. 179.

to defeat that phenomenon. Both the protest and failure are depicted by the protagonist's attempt to undermine the capitalistic system that ultimately consumes him. His reluctant but eventual integration into a culture obsessed with material pursuits is accompanied by a complete disintegration of the self. Bianciardi's tenacious opposition to the conformism that was rampant during the boom years is clearly evident in the choice of an unconventional narrative expression.

DANIELE FIORETTI

21 Writing the Factory: Paolo Volponi's Industrial Novels

It is impossible to understand Paolo Volponi's industrial novels without making reference to the Olivetti factory and, in particular, to Adriano Olivetti, an entrepreneur who developed an idealistic conception of what industry is and what its role in society should be. For this reason, the present chapter is focused specifically on two important novels written by Volponi, *Memoriale* (My Troubles Began, 1962) and *Corporale* (Corporal, 1974), in order to show how Volponi's experience as a manager of the Olivetti factory shaped his views on industry and allowed him to depict with great effectiveness several problematic issues related to industrial work. Adriano Olivetti never considered the factory only as a profit-making device. On the contrary, he believed that a successful industrial company should redistribute its profits to enhance the wellbeing of its workers and of the surrounding community. The Olivetti company provided its workers with affordable housing near the factory and social services, like daycare for children, free health services, cultural centers and libraries, including a comprehensive library inside the main factory, open to all the workers.[1] Adriano Olivetti was not only an entrepreneur; he was also a reformer. One of his most revolutionary moves was to attract intellectuals, offering them jobs at Olivetti: not only technicians, engineers and psychologists, but also writers and poets like Leonardo Sinisgalli, Franco Fortini, Ottiero Ottieri and Paolo Volponi.

---

1 Gallino, L. 2001. *L'impresa responsabile. Un'intervista su Adriano Olivetti*. Turin: Edizioni di Comunità. 57.

Olivetti hired Volponi in 1956 as director of the Social Services for the factory in Ivrea (Piedmont), and since the beginning, Volponi truly believed in Adriano Olivetti's cultural project. Unfortunately, the sudden death of Adriano Olivetti in 1960 represented a setback for Volponi; from his position inside the company, the writer was able to witness the slow waning of Adriano's social vision. Volponi's growing disappointment over the industrial environment is clearly expressed in his first novel, *Memoriale*. *Memoriale* is centered on a protagonist who is exactly the opposite of the working-class hero that populated the novels celebrated by the critics close to the Partito Comunista Italiano (Italian Communist Party). In fact, Albino Saluggia is a paranoid, tuberculotic young man, a former prisoner during the Second World War – in short, a marginalized individual. Since the novel is narrated in the first person, the reader's only source of information is Albino's clearly hallucinatory and psychotic perspective, a choice that forces the reader to approach a well-known reality – the factory, in this case – in a completely uncanny, estranged way.

Albino is physically ill, and therefore an outcast. He suffers from tuberculosis, a marginalizing illness that was considered for many years the result of a reckless lifestyle and a waste of vitality, characterized by "spells of euphoria, increased appetite, exacerbated sexual desire."[2] Furthermore, the protagonist is also mentally ill, another form of 'disease' that creates marginalization. The mental patient, in fact, has always been considered a challenge to a modern industrial society based on discipline, good health and work.[3] Unable to perform the basic functions of production and consumption, individuals with mental health issues provide a model of existence that is unassimilable to capitalism. It is important, then, that the factory where Albino is sent to work is centered on discipline. The protagonist's hopes that his new job will represent a fresh start in his life, after all the sufferings of war, are quickly vanquished at the first job interview. The examiner wears a military shirt and a black tie (a combination that recalls Italy's Fascist past); he addresses the protagonist by underlining Albino's military background and praises the value of discipline: "Tu hai fatto il soldato per molti anni e conosci il valore della disciplina e dell'ubbidienza. Queste due

---

2   Sontag, S. 1978. *Illness as Metaphor*. Toronto: McGraw-Hill Ryerson Ltd. 13.
3   Basaglia, F. 1981. *Scritti*. Turin: Einaudi. 365–366.

virtù sono basilari anche nella fabbrica" (You've been a soldier for many years, so you must know the value of discipline and obedience. These are also two basic principles of the factory).[4] What Albino finds in the factory is essentially the same kind of oppression he thought he could escape.

Volponi uses Albino's physical and mental sufferings in order to underline the reification and the helplessness that workers experience in the industrial environment. Little by little, the narrator-protagonist becomes convinced that the doctors in the factory are plotting to fire him because of his tuberculosis. At first glance, it seems clear that this belief is a symptom of Albino's paranoia, while the company seems to be taking care of him scrupulously, paying for his medical expenses and for his recovery in a sanatorium. A more in-depth analysis, though, makes clear that the company leaves him no freedom of choice, something that should be the foundation of the patient-doctor relationship (if the patient is not a factory worker, an already objectified individual). Social aid, devoid of any empathy, becomes formal and constraining. When examined from this standpoint, Albino's attempts to find other doctors outside of the factory for a second opinion on his illness can be interpreted as an effort to reclaim his agency and to withdraw himself from the oppression of industrial power. However, when Albino approaches physicians outside of the factory, they refuse to visit him. The official reason, according to them, is that Albino is already receiving the best medical care available through his employer. But it is also possible that these doctors are afraid to challenge the power of big industry. It is true that the company seems to take good care of Albino, and it even excuses his outbursts of rage and his whimsical behavior. However, it soon becomes clear that the factory managers want to use Albino's vulnerability to turn him into a spy. One manager promises to deal with the doctors, Albino's 'enemies,' provided that the protagonist reports to him whatever the workers say when they are among themselves, especially if they bad-mouth the managers or plan to strike. The health tracking provided by the company becomes here a way to put pressure on the employee, instead of working for his own good and protection. Here we see the importance of Volponi's choice to center the narration on a paranoid character. It is

---

4   Volponi, P. 1962. *Memoriale*. Milan: Garzanti. 22. Volponi, P. 1964. *My Troubles Began*. Translated by Belén Sevareid. New York: Grossman. 23.

precisely by virtue of his alienated condition, and his confused subjectivity, that Albino succeeds in perceiving the repressive nature of the factory system. The subversive nature of the deviant individual is a central element for Volponi who uses it to force the reader to look at everyday reality from an estranged point of view. As Romano Luperini has written, the "razionalità irrazionale" (irrational rationality) of the system is highlighted by the "irrazionalità razionale" (rational irrationality) of the fool.[5]

The end of the novel is rather pessimistic: Albino loses his job as a result of organizing a strike. Alone and unemployed at his mother's house, he realizes that no one will come to his help. But Volponi's negative judgement of the factory does not come from a rejection of Adriano Olivetti's project. Rather, it comes from the acknowledgement that Olivetti as a factory represented only a partial, imperfect realization of its own original plan. Volponi worked for Olivetti until 1971, doing his best to develop the utopian potentialities of the industrial company. According to him, industry should not be seen as an instrument of alienation, but as a liberating force that can free people from need, toil, illnesses and the countless slaveries that still influence human life.[6] This is why, in other parts of *Memoriale*, industry is depicted – at least potentially – as a place of solidarity, especially when Albino describes an episode of mutual help between two excavators. This scene in the novel, apparently unrelated to the main plot, has a strong allegorical significance: that within industry, one can find not only selfishness, but also solidarity.

Nonetheless, according to Volponi, *Memoriale* is not a fully industrial novel, because in the 1950s and early 1960s Italy was not a truly industrialized country – it was transitioning from a rural to an industrial economy. *Corporale*, on the contrary, is the first novel that really comprises industry, because it is industrial not only in its theme, but also in its language and style. *Corporale* brings to the extreme some experimental traits that were already present in *Memoriale* and in Volponi's second novel, *La macchina mondiale* (The Worldwide Machine, 1965), especially the idea of narrating

[5] Luperini, R. 1980. "Sperimentazione e neoavanguardia nell'ultimo ventennio." *Letteratura italiana. Storia e testi*, vol. 10, tome 1. Edited by Carlo Muscetta. Rome and Bari: Laterza. 359.
[6] Ferretti, G. C. 1972. *Paolo Volponi*. Florence: La Nuova Italia. 49.

the story from the estranged point of view of a 'fool.' The first draft, written between 1965 and 1966 and similar in style to the first two books, was later completely transformed, and *Corporale* became a complex, experimental novel, both structurally and linguistically. One of the most notable features is the way in which the narrator's point of view shifts between the first and third person. When the protagonist is the middle-aged intellectual Gerolamo Aspri, the narration is in the first person; when the story focuses on the bandit/gangster Joaquìn Murieta there is a linguistic shift to the third person. Only later in the novel does the reader realize that Murieta is a pseudonym of Gerolamo. Such a shift therefore underlines the inherently schizophrenic nature of the main character, as well as Volponi's intention to maintain a critical distance from Murieta's illegal plans.

One of the most important themes of *Corporale* is the threat of a nuclear catastrophe which, according to Volponi, is nothing but the logical consequence of neo-capitalist imperialism. Not by chance, the epigraph of *Corporale* is a quotation from Elsa Morante's essay *Pro o contro la bomba atomica* (For or Against the Atomic Bomb, 1965), where Morante defined the atomic bomb as the natural expression of the imperialist, neo-capitalist society.[7] But the apocalypse can also be interpreted as a metaphor for the neurosis of the protagonist Gerolamo. It was Sigmund Freud, in his essay on the Schreber case, who stated that fantasies about the end of the world in paranoid subjects can be interpreted as an unintentional metaphor of the complete withdrawal of libidinal investment from the people around the patient and from the world outside as a whole.[8] Such an analysis can be applied to *Corporale* as well: in this sense, it is justified to say that Volponi used the theme of nuclear catastrophe as a metaphor for the crisis of Gerolamo himself as a leftist intellectual marginalized by industry. There is a clear connection between Gerolamo and Volponi himself as an intellectual who progressively detached himself from the entrepreneurial world. When the president of Olivetti, Bruno Visentini, offered Volponi the chance to become the CEO of the company in 1971, the latter saw this proposal as an opportunity to transform the factory into a tool for spreading culture and

---

7 Morante, E. 1987. *Pro o contro la bomba atomica*. Milan: Adelphi. 99.
8 Freud, S. 2003. *The Schreber Case*. London and New York: Penguin. 59.

social justice by implementing the teachings of Adriano Olivetti. However, the company had changed since Adriano Olivetti's death. The 1960s saw a dramatic slowdown in the Italian economy, and Olivetti, which had made a large investment in the American market, became very indebted. In order to save the company, the Olivetti family sold 70% of its shares to investors like Fiat and Pirelli – two companies whose managers never believed in Adriano Olivetti's philosophy. If it is true, as *Fortune Magazine* insisted in 1967, that no company could fail with the help of Fiat and Pirelli, it is also true that it could not go on unchanged.[9] Instead of appointing Volponi the new CEO, the board of directors opted for a former navy admiral, the much more conservative figure Ottorino Beltrami. Volponi saw this move as a betrayal of Visentini's promises, and resigned.

All these events are reflected in *Corporale*: Gerolamo/Murieta is a partially autobiographical projection of Volponi, and the engineer Salsamiti is a representation of Visentini. In one scene, the protagonist and Salsamiti have a discussion about the importance of the human factor in industrial production:

> – Ma le imprese le fanno gli uomini al 90%, – disse Salsamiti, e ostentò molto cinismo per buttare là questa conclusione, imbattibile come la diagnosi fatale di un cancro. – Quali uomini? – disse Murieta, – i consiglieri? i direttori? No! Le imprese le fanno gli uomini al 100%, ma tutti gli uomini che vi lavorano: tutti, con tutto il lavoro.
>
> (But companies are made 90% by people – Salsamiti said, showing a very cynical attitude in drawing this conclusion, unbeatable like the diagnosis of a cancer. – Which people? – said Murieta, – members of the board? Counselors? Managers? No! Companies are made 100% by people, but all the people, all the workers: every one of them, with their work).[10]

As Volponi revealed years later, this conversation is an almost literal transcription of a real conversation that the author himself had with Visentini before leaving Olivetti.[11]

---

9 Soria, L. 1979. *Informatica: un'occasione perduta. La divisione elettronica dell'Olivetti nei primi anni del centrosinistra*. Turin: Einaudi. 46.
10 Volponi, P. 2002. *Romanzi e prose*, vol. I. Turin, Einaudi. 724–725.
11 Bettini, F. (ed.). 1995. "Paolo Volponi. Per una letteratura di liberazione e di conflitto. Incontro con gli studenti di Frascati." *Critica marxista*, no. 2. 86.

Notwithstanding his personal defeat, Volponi continued to believe in the cultural potentiality of the factory, but he also had to acknowledge that this progressive potential could not be fully developed within an industrial framework supported by elites who preferred a model at odds with Adriano Olivetti's project. Volponi believed that only a radical, catastrophic event could make change possible, and in *Corporale* the nuclear catastrophe also represents the possibility to start over with a clean slate, to rethink society as we know it: a paradoxical utopia that will be born from the ashes of a dystopia.

After the failure of Murieta's criminal plan, Gerolamo decides to move to the countryside of the Marche region (Volponi's native land) to build a fallout shelter that will allow him to survive a supposedly imminent nuclear catastrophe. Gerolamo tries to imagine a new human subject, one who will be mutated by so much radiation and – at least in the mind of the protagonist – will resemble more an animal than a human. The new being could look like a lizard or a bird, a virus or even a species of seaweed: the only important thing would be its vitality. The author repeats the terms "vivo" (alive) and "diverso" (different) three times in order to characterize a subject radically other than the creature that humans have become in neocapitalist industrial society: pitiful beings in constant search of services to give and masters to serve.[12] Nonetheless, in *Corporale*, this catastrophic regeneration never occurs. After being hospitalized in an accident, Gerolamo gives up on the project, implicitly acknowledging the fact that isolation is not an effective strategy for changing society. At the end of the novel, the protagonist disappears, leaving behind only a text: a diary written under the name Joaquìn Murieta, a metaphor for the novel itself. It is literature, therefore, more than fallout shelters, that must serve as a hopeful witness of the future and its insuppressible utopian impulses.

It may seem strange that Volponi defined *Corporale* as his only real industrial novel – after all, there are no representations of factories or workers in the book. Nonetheless, the novel is written from the point of view of an atypical industrial manager, just like Volponi. In parts of the text, the protagonist interrogates himself on the degree of freedom that factory workers enjoy on the job, a freedom that is deeply connected to

---

12   Volponi, P. 2002. *Romanzi e prose*, vol. I. 884.

the possibility of varying the rhythm of their work.[13] Following Adriano Olivetti's ideas, Gerolamo thinks that assembly line production denies the workers any kind of freedom and control on their work. This is why the "industrie liberanti" (freeing industries) that Gerolamo/Murieta has in mind are not aimed only to improve production, but also to create a model of industrial development that is human in a deeper sense.[14] This new industrial model, according to Volponi, should not be focused only on the subdivision of work: production and fragmentation should be integrated in a socialist-oriented organization of labor, so that the union of the two systems can eliminate the drawbacks of both. On the one hand, this model will maintain the productivity of capitalism; on the other hand, the socialist vision allows every worker a more artisanal approach to their job.[15] This reflection evidences Volponi's deep connection to the thought of Adriano Olivetti, since it was one of Adriano Olivetti's main concerns to transform industrial work from a necessary evil into a chance for factory workers to express their spirit and creativity.[16]

It is only in *Le mosche del capitale* (The Flies of Capital, 1989) that Volponi's view of industry became more negative and desolate. Two characters, the progressive manager Bruto Saraccini – another partly autobiographical representation of Volponi himself – and the factory worker Antonino Tecraso, are both marginalized and defeated by the factory. The novel witnesses a historic defeat of the Italian working class: the 1980 failure of a thirty-five-day strike at Fiat that marked the decline of the labor unions. But Volponi did not see this defeat as a repudiation of Adriano Olivetti's ideas. Rather, he dedicated *Le mosche del capitale* to Adriano Olivetti, "maestro dell'industria mondiale" (*maestro* of world industry), a man endowed with a quality that, according to the author, even Italian politicians lacked: "una fervida fantasia istituzionale" (a lively institutional imagination).[17]

---

13 Volponi, P. 2002. *Romanzi e prose*, vol. I. 553.
14 Volponi, P. 2002. *Romanzi e prose*, vol. I. 692.
15 Volponi, P. 2002. *Romanzi e prose*, vol. I. 693.
16 Cadeddu, D. 2012. *Reimagining Democracy. On the Political Project of Adriano Olivetti*. New York: Springer. 8.
17 Camon, F. 1973. *Il mestiere di scrittore*. Milan: Garzanti. 137.

RICCIARDA RICORDA

22 Reversing the Coming-of-Age Story in Industrial Society: *Il padrone* (1965) by Goffredo Parise

Goffredo Parise began writing *Il padrone* (The Boss) in 1964, five years after the publication of his previous novel, *Amore e fervore* (Love and Excitement, 1959). He worked intensely for a few months, finishing the book in October of the same year. Parise offered the manuscript to the Garzanti publishing house, which had already printed his successful novel *Il prete bello* (Don Gastone and the Ladies) in 1954, but Garzanti refused it, and *Il padrone* came out with Feltrinelli in 1965 (a second edition was printed by Einaudi in 1971).

From the Countryside to the Metropolis

A young man from the Venetian countryside, about twenty years old, moves to a big city to work for an important company. His story is told in the first person, though he is never named, and it is unclear what sort of products or services the company offers. Such lack of detail was not uncommon in Italian industrial novels, but in Parise's case it has a precise motivation: to abstract from the dimension of history and, as the author himself declared, turn the company represented into a metaphor for "la vita" (life).[1] Parise is thus able to offer an interpretation of 1960s alienation from a very broad political perspective. What counts here are the processes of failure and defeat integral to small 'ecosystems' like the

---

1 Grillandi, M. 1965. "*Il padrone* dice Parise non è un romanzo di fabbrica." *Il Gazzettino*. July 20.

family, the company or the city. Parise identifies the ultimate causes of such processes in the order of biology: the 'survival of the fittest' from Darwin's study *On the Origin of Species* (1859), which was recommended to him by Carlo Emilio Gadda.

The first chapter of *Il padrone* tells the story of the young protagonist's first day in the city. He is excited to report to work immediately, where the space has a strong impact on him: the entrance hall is silent and dark, but beyond a glass door he can see "macchie di un verde luminoso e mobile" (spots of a luminous green, mobile).[2] The protagonist's first encounter is with a bald and somewhat apish doorman whose gloomy gaze is reminiscent of an orangutan. The doorman promptly points the protagonist up the stairs, where another disquieting usher introduces him to the man who got him the job: Diabete. Diabete knows the protagonist's father, and he immediately starts talking about Dottor Max, the son of the owner who now runs the company while his elderly father is out whaling.

The names of the characters amplify the allegorical dimension of *Il padrone*. If, on the one hand, the protagonist remains unnamed, on the other hand, the names of the other characters are iconic, and they point to a variety of semantic traditions. These include the world of Disney comics for the boss' girlfriend Minnie and the company employees Pippo, Pluto and Orazio, or the world of classical mythology for the boss Max (Jupiter Maximus) and his parents Saturno and Uraza (possibly an allusion to Uranus). Moreover, some character names have strongly parodic connotations, like Diabete and Bombolo: grotesque figures whose physical traits are brought to life via comparison to the animal or vegetable kingdoms, as if to signify an intensifying process of depersonalization and reification.

The protagonist goes to Diabete's house: a small, comfortable and rational but also sterile apartment where Diabete lives with his loveless wife and daughter. The bus ride to Diabete's apartment and the length of the visit give the protagonist time to think about his far-away parents. He is proud of his job, which should guarantee his parents a serene retirement,

---

2 Parise, G. 1987. "Il padrone." *Opere*, vol. 1. Edited by Bruno Callegher and Mauro Portello. Milan: Mondadori. 836. Parise, G. 1966. *The Boss*. Translated by William Weaver. New York: Knopf. 5.

but he is also proud to belong to a real community: a "collettività lavorativa" (working aggregate).³ The beginning of *Il padrone* announces itself as a classic coming-of-age story, with the promise of character development for a protagonist who leaves adolescence behind and enters a new social context.

At first, Dottor Max reminds the protagonist of "uno studente romantico, un giovane idealista che rincorra alti ideali di ordine e di classicità" (a romantic student, a young idealist who is pursuing lofty ideals of order and classicism), but he soon exhibits animalesque features like a "secrezione biancastra alla bocca" (whitish secretion at his mouth) and the voice of an "insetto ferito" (wounded insect).⁴ Already in his first words, which exalt life in the countryside at the expense of "la mania di correre nella grande città" (mania for coming to the big city),⁵ the protagonist senses the power relationship that will develop between the boss (on high) and him (down below). But he also senses something positive for the immediate future: the "dolcezza di vivere in funzione della ditta commerciale" (sweetness of living for the firm) and of taking part in the "grande involucro protettivo della specie umana" (great protective shell of the human species) – that is, labor.⁶

After meeting the painter and advertiser Orazio and Dottor Bombolo – an unsettling character with complex relations to Dottor Max – the protagonist ends his first working day with a walk around the city, stopping to purchase (by installments) an elegant brown overcoat. He also stops in a bar to order a costly drink called "Sexy Gin."⁷ This gives him a light buzz, then after a bit of wandering, he returns to the rented room that Diabete has found him. He falls asleep, his head filled with nostalgic thoughts of home, his girlfriend and parents. Parise clarifies in this way the juxtaposition between two types of spaces: the metropolis, which revolves around labor and production, with its social rites and designated consumption sites – the luxury shop, the fashionable cocktail lounge – and the countryside, with its comforting dimensions.

3   Parise, G. 1987. "Il padrone." *Opere*, vol. 1. 849. Parise, G. 1966. *The Boss*. 18.
4   Parise, G. 1987. "Il padrone." *Opere*, vol. 1. 855. Parise, G. 1966. *The Boss*. 23–24.
5   Parise, G. 1987. "Il padrone." *Opere*, vol. 1. 858. Parise, G. 1966. *The Boss*. 26.
6   Parise, G. 1987. "Il padrone." *Opere*, vol. 1. 859. Parise, G. 1966. *The Boss*. 27.
7   Parise, G. 1987. "Il padrone." *Opere*, vol. 1. 883. Parise, G. 1966. *The Boss*. 51.

It is not difficult to recognize in Parise's descriptions the city of Milan, never mentioned by name, but metaphorically alluded to in discussions of the "magma dinamico della grande città" (dynamic magma of the big city) that "travolge e distrugge tutto ciò che non è utile" (overwhelms and destroys everything that is not useful).[8] The plot unfolds in a setting dominated by the company. The entire city gravitates around spaces of labor and the shadows of industrial buildings are spread even across the parks.

In chapters two and three, the narrative of workplace integration continues: the protagonist is assigned a tiny office (part of Dottor Max's personal bathroom), he meets more employees, including the secretary Selene, and he falls into the company's routine. The protagonist describes himself as feeling "abbastanza felice" (fairly happy), despite the usual ups and downs caused by everyday interactions with his colleagues.[9] The most difficult to deal with is Dottor Max, whose unstable behavior results from a fundamental contradiction: "se sia morale o no essere il padrone e comportarsi come tale" (whether or not it is moral to be the boss and to behave like one).[10] The question emerges frequently in discussions with the protagonist, even though the boss is beginning to take a liking to him. Aside from such moral qualms, Dottor Max wants to have control over everybody who works for the company. The protagonist must learn to adapt himself, becoming an object in the hands of his employer, who in return offers an almost religious sense of depersonalization that separates the protagonist from his previous life and family affections.

The protagonist also meets Dottor Max's parents: his mother Uraza, whose face is dominated by an "enorme massa di capelli soffici e fiammeggianti" (enormous mass of soft, flaming hair)[11] reminiscent of a lion's mane, and his father Saturno, who is described as "vecchio, molto vecchio, vecchissimo, ma dall'aria ancora robusta" (old, very old, extremely old, but he seemed still robust).[12] As the founder of the company, Saturno is constantly humiliating his son in an effort to show everybody who is really

---

8   Parise, G. 1987. "Il padrone." *Opere*, vol. 1. 1037. Parise, G. 1966. *The Boss*. 209.
9   Parise, G. 1987. "Il padrone." *Opere*, vol. 1. 899. Parise, G. 1966. *The Boss*. 68.
10   Parise, G. 1987. "Il padrone." *Opere*, vol. 1. 909. Parise, G. 1966. *The Boss*. 78.
11   Parise, G. 1987. "Il padrone." *Opere*, vol. 1. 934. Parise, G. 1966. *The Boss*. 103.
12   Parise, G. 1987. "Il padrone." *Opere*, vol. 1. 937. Parise, G. 1966. *The Boss*. 106.

in charge. The protagonist also meets Dottor Max's girlfriend Minnie, who expresses herself with the words and gestures of a comic book character: *szip, smak, ron ron, splak*. Such childish language is intended to illustrate the reduced possibilities of communication in contemporary society, a theme to which Parise will return at the end of the novel.

As the power relationship between Dottor Max and the protagonist develops, the former is quick to assure the latter of his ultimate freedom: "è [il dipendente] che liberamente diventa proprietà della ditta e dunque del padrone, non il padrone che lo acquista in proprietà" (he [the employee] is the one who freely becomes the property of the firm and therefore of the boss; it isn't the boss who buys him).[13] Nevertheless, things get strange: every morning, the doorman Lotar – embodiment of a perfect employee, "oggetto meccanico, e allo steso tempo vivente e umano, della proprietà assoluta, totalitaria e demiurgica" (the mechanical and, at the same time, living and human object of absolute, totalitarian, and demiurgic property)[14] – gives the protagonist painful and useless vitamin injections that testify to Dottor Max's total control.

A brief trip home to the countryside sanctions the unbridgeable gap separating the protagonist from his previous life, and it turns out to be the last contact he has with the old world. Even when his father visits the city, in an attempt to rescue his son from the reification of modernity, all efforts prove useless.

The protagonist's colleagues are archetypical characters. Pluto and Pippo exemplify two antithetical models of company employee: the first is completely attached to his job, the second is a hangover from a defunct social class who is out of step with the times and destined to commit suicide after an argument with Dottor Max (the argument revolves around whether human labor is a law of nature).

Pippo's drama and the arrival of the new general manager Rebo exacerbate the psychology of the protagonist, who becomes obsessed with Dottor Max and even thinks about killing him. The idea is to plan the perfect (and

---

13   Parise, G. 1987. "Il padrone." *Opere*, vol. 1. 949. Parise, G. 1966. *The Boss*. 118.
14   Parise, G. 1987. "Il padrone." *Opere*, vol. 1. 959. Parise, G. 1966. *The Boss*. 128.

impossible) crime, using cyanide poison or perhaps a knife – these thoughts are interrupted on occasion by telephone calls from Dottor Max himself.

The final four chapters of *Il padrone* revolve around the last and most disconcerting imposition that Dottor Max and his family bring to the protagonist. Uraza introduces him to Zilietta, a young girl with Down syndrome, and proposes that he marry her. The protagonist reacts with disbelief, knowing that such a marriage would mean "catalogare e immobilizare" (establishing and freezing) forever his role at the company.[15] But then, he begins to reason through the possibilities: marry Zilietta, bide his time, find a new company. The protagonist rejects this last approach and attempts to postpone his decision, but punishment follows promptly: his salary is cut, his office is moved twice and he must complete a series of absurd premarital medical exams. He also gets to see Zilietta up close: her condition is evident in her face, while he says her body is beautiful. In his words, she is not "completamente idiota" (a complete idiot).[16] She recognizes objects and knows how to identify them, but cannot remark on their quality.

In the end, he accepts the marriage, together with a new house, an automobile and "tutto quello che occorre per vivere nella società" (everything necessary to live in society).[17] Dottor Max is happy, seeing in his family the prototype of the ideal social unit: "il capolavoro della proprietà assoluta" (the masterpiece of absolute property).[18]

Contrary to the protagonist's expectations, life with Zilietta shows all the signs of a "vita normale" (normal life). Theirs is a relationship devoid of verbal communication, but since language has become a mere instrument of attack and defense, this actually sanctions their happiness. The couple is expecting a son, whom the protagonist hopes will lack his own sense of reason so that he can instead be happy like his mother "nella beatitudine pura dell'esistenza" (in her pure bliss of existence).[19] Only by becoming an object – the protagonist imagines – can one avoid all pain and suffering.

---

15   Parise, G. 1987. "Il padrone." *Opere*, vol. 1. 1040. Parise, G. 1966. *The Boss*. 212.
16   Parise, G. 1987. "Il padrone." *Opere*, vol. 1. 1041. Parise, G. 1966. *The Boss*. 213.
17   Parise, G. 1987. "Il padrone." *Opere*, vol. 1. 1072. Parise, G. 1966. *The Boss*. 245.
18   Parise, G. 1987. "Il padrone." *Opere*, vol. 1. 1073. Parise, G. 1966. *The Boss*. 246.
19   Parise, G. 1987. "Il padrone." *Opere*, vol. 1. 1073. Parise, G. 1966. *The Boss*. 246.

Thus, the conclusion of *Il padrone* proposes a reversal of the coming-of-age story. The protagonist's development brings him to accept the destiny of alienation in a society dominated by reification, consumerism and violent interpersonal relations.[20] Distancing oneself from this sort of society is impossible: one needs to accept things as they are – this is the paradoxical lesson of the novel.

The complex content of *Il padrone* is easily accommodated by Parise's tense and blunt writing style. In the words of Guido Piovene, the novel was even "divertente come pochi altri libri d'oggi, con il suo umorismo feroce, le sue trovate impreviste e bizzare, i personaggi a fondo funebre, ma vivi sulla pagina, sui quali lo scrittore infierisce da cima a fondo" (amusing like very few books today, with its ferocious humor, unexpected and bizarre wit, characters straight out of a funeral but also alive on the page, whom the author storms over from top to bottom).[21]

A Divided Reception

Il padrone won the prestigious Viareggio Prize in the summer of 1965. As part of the jury's official motivation, the renowned author Giacomo Debenedetti applauded Parise for navigating "tra vita individuale e massificazione neocapitalistica" (between individualism and neo-capitalist massification) in a novel that lent itself to various interpretations, from the representation of a profound antagonism between literature and industry to a religious parable of Kafkian inspiration.[22]

---

20 It should be noted that Parise's is a paradoxical conclusion. From a presentist perspective, such a representation of Zilietta as a bearer of Down syndrome who enjoys a privileged condition deriving from her lack of reason and her status as a mere object appears, to say the least, problematic.
21 Piovene, G. 2016. "Il nuovo romanzo di Parise (1965)." *Riga*, vol. 36. Special issue on Goffredo Parise. Edited by Marco Belpoliti and Andrea Cortellessa. Milan: Marcos y Marcos. 272.
22 Debenedetti, G. 2016. "Parise? L'unico erede di Kafka (1965)." *Riga*, vol. 36. Special issue on Goffredo Parise. 278–279.

The book was immediately translated into many languages, including French, English, German, Spanish, Russian and others, and it gave rise to a number of controversies that were both literary and ideological. Critics like Carlo Bo and Paolo Milano maintained that it was the expression of an unhappy phase of Parise's life: they accused the author of excessive nihilism and the renunciation of responsibility because they could not accept the total desperation and alienation of *Il padrone*'s protagonist.[23] Others like Carlo Salinari and Pietro Citati rejected the exaggerated attributes of the characters, the grotesque forms of personality that alternated between the abstract and the surreal.[24] Whether the novel belonged to the tradition of industrial literature was brought into question by Parise himself, who in a 1965 interview with Massimo Grillandi declared: "*Il padrone* non c'entra niente con la letteratura di fabbrica" (*Il padrone* has nothing to do with factory literature).[25] The book also provoked a series of paradoxical misunderstandings, like that of the Éditions du Seuil editorial director François Wahl who, in a letter to the author, proclaimed that he was shocked by the lack of references to labor unions.[26]

Other readers were more attentive, and many were convinced admirers. In a review for the *Corriere della Sera*, Eugenio Montale wrote that *Il padrone* "ribocchi da capo a fondo" (overflows from top to bottom) with a type of poetry that combined "la crudeltà espressiva" (expressive cruelty) with "la precisione del taglio chirurgico" (the precision of a surgeon's cut).[27] Guido Piovene underlined Parise's move away from history and toward biology, remarking that *Il padrone*'s treatment of "comando e servitù" (master-slave) relations was of a religious stamp.

---

23 Bo, C. 1965. "Siamo tutti un barattolo al servizio del Padrone". *L'Europeo*. May 9. Milano, P. 1965, "Il ludibrio gioioso del servo perfetto". *L'Espresso*. April 25.
24 Salinari, C. 1965. "Gli uomini-barattolo della società capitalistica". *L'Unità*. May 25. Citati P. 1965. "Un mare di psicologia nell'azienda moderna". *Il Giorno*. May 5.
25 Grillandi, M. 1965. "*Il padrone* dice Parise non è un romanzo di fabbrica."
26 Portello, M. 1987. "Note e notizie sui testi. *Il padrone*." in Parise, G. *Opere*, vol. 1. 1594. For a good review of critical responses to the novel's publication, see Altarocca, C. 1972. *Parise*. Florence: La Nuova Italia. 119–125.
27 Montale, E. 1965. "Una precisione d'alta chirurgia". *Corriere della Sera*. April 18.

The Adelphi publishing house released a new edition of *Il padrone* in 2011, to the enthusiasm of many critics like Alfonso Berardinelli and Ferdinando Camon, who have written of a story ripe for rediscovery, somehow still relevant and 'real' today.[28] The most recent scholarly accounts, like that by Niccolò Scaffai, have tended to underline the importance of the novel within the context of Parise's lifetime literary production.[29]

Il padrone and Parise's Other Novels

After the release of his novel *Amore e fervore* in 1959, Parise did not publish anything for five years. In 1960, he moved from Milan to Rome, where he frequented writers like Gadda, Elsa Morante and Alberto Moravia. He flirted briefly with the world of cinema, collaborating on a few screenplays and travelling to the United States on the commission of producer Dino De Laurentiis to develop a story for a new film, an experience that Parise later defined as a "trauma conoscitivo" (cognitive trauma).[30]

Parise was already the author of a rich literary *œuvre* that included the novel *I movimenti remoti* (Remote Movements), written in 1948 but unpublished until 2007, and *Il ragazzo morto e le comete* (The Dead Boy and the Comets), his official debut in 1951. The latter was the remarkably original story of an adolescent boy set in the days after the Second World War, and distinguished by a disjointed style that juxtaposed its chapters as if in a collage. Even while describing the reality of wartime horrors, *Il ragazzo morto e le comete* touched on the dimensions of fantasy and lyricism by employing a plurality of voices and a variety of stylistic approaches. The novel mixed many different languages, including the language of cinema.

---

28 Berardinelli, A. 2011. "Il fumetto (kafkiano) del potere." *Corriere della Sera*. June 19. Camon, F. 2011. "*Il padrone* e il suo barattolo." *Ttl Supplemento de la Stampa*. June 18.
29 Scaffai, N. 2018. "Goffredo Parise." *Il romanzo in Italia. Il secondo Novecento*. Edited by Giancarlo Alfano and Francesco de Cristofaro. Rome: Carocci. 218.
30 Barbato, A. 1965. "Il Colosseo di plastica". *L'Espresso*, April 11.

Parise's next book, *La grande vacanza* (1953), preserved the adolescent point of view from *Il ragazzo morto e le comete*, introducing many autobiographical details into a non-linear story. This novel used cinema-like flashbacks to restore a degraded present to the radical 'otherness' of childhood. If on the one hand, it announced a stronger commitment to realism, on the other hand, it was also traversed by a continuous process of alteration.

Parise moved to Milan to work for the Garzanti publishing house, but his third printed novel was set, like the first two, in the Venetian countryside. *Il prete bello* was one of the first bestsellers of the postwar period, published in 1954 and telling the story of Sergio, a young boy during the Fascist years. This novel was firmly grounded in the tradition of realism, juxtaposing to the children of proletarian families the milieu of the dashing Don Gastone and his bigoted female admirers.

In his next two books, *Il fidanzamento* (The Engagement, 1956) and *Amore e fervore* (1959), Parise abandoned the world of childhood and turned to the themes of marriage and desire, framing them in a utilitarian context of petite bourgeois provincialism.

Writing for the *Corriere della Sera* in July 1958, Parise remarked on the uselessness of the novel as a literary form. In his opinion, the life and ideological force of the novel had always been tied to "epoche drammatiche della storia" (dramatic historical eras), while the present representation of reality in novel form was rendered entirely pointless by the "mutamento o degradazione dell'animo umano in stadio ogni giorno più simile al materialismo di tipo animale" (intensifying mutation and degradation of the human soul toward an animalesque materialism) and the "polverizzazione delle ideologie in un grande numero di desideri immediati e possibili" (pulverization of ideologies into a large number of immediate and satisfiable desires).[31] Parise also wrote of an impending transition from Western-based humanism to a civilization of robots. It was from these reflections, and from the stress of his voyage to the United States, that *Il padrone* was born. If on the one hand, the book acknowledged the uselessness of the novel as a literary form in the era of "animalesque materialism," on the other

---

31   Parise, G. 1987. "Inutilità del romanzo (1958)." *Opere*, vol. 1. 1541. See also Scaffai, N. 2018. "Goffredo Parise." *Il romanzo in Italia*. 226–228.

hand, it used the novel precisely for the purpose of representing that same era. While there were certainly elements of continuity with Parise's previous literary production, *Il padrone* marked a turning point in the writer's career: his stories moved from the countryside to the metropolis, from an environment dominated by the church to the company, from a fluid style to a logical and argumentative prose.

The result was a novel that abstracted from the dimension of history, casting a shadow over events that in reality belonged to Parise's own biography: his employment at Livio Garzanti's publishing company and the difficult relationship with Garzanti himself. *Il padrone* documents a moment in the Milanese industrial world, sustained by families with a long tradition and strong values, but beset by deep generational conflicts, where sons were searching for an identity. In its powerful specificity and originality, the book evoked the new and complex working world of the early 1960s. In this regard, as Nico Naldini has written, Parise succeeded in applying "le sonde più sensibili per definire in immagini la società alienata del suo tempo, in un'epoca in cui questo fenomeno storico era ancora tutto da scoprire e descrivere" (the most sensitive probes to define with images the alienated society of his time, during an era in which such an historical phenomenon was ripe for discovery and description).[32]

Similar themes and situations resurfaced in the short stories of *Crematorio di Vienna* (Vienna Crematory, 1969), where Parise elaborated arguments like alienation, consumerism, reification, human aggression and animality.

After the period of dramatic representation that produced *Il padrone* and *Crematorio di Vienna*, the writer rediscovered the natural world, the ideal of the primitive and the simplicity of reality. This culminated in an attempt to found a new alphabet of human feelings with two *Sillabari* (Syllabary n. 1 and Syllabary n. 2, 1972 and 1982).

Translated by Jim Carter

---

32 Naldini, N. 1997. "Il nuovo padrone di Milano." *Goffredo Parise*. Edited by Ilaria Crotti. Florence: Olschki. 165–172.

PASQUALE VERDICCHIO

23 When Nothing Meets the Needs of Everything: Nanni Balestrini's *Vogliamo tutto* (1971)

Nanni Balestrini's novel *Vogliamo tutto* (We Want Everything) was published in 1971 by Feltrinelli and, given the timeliness of the issues treated within it, quickly became a bestseller. Its content ignited an immediate series of debates in Italy and beyond, but while it was quickly translated into other languages, it did not appear in English until recently.[1]

The anonymous narrating voice is that of a young worker from Campania. He is hired by Ideal Standard for a plant that will open in Salerno, but he is first sent to the northern city of Brescia (Lombardy) to train in an already operating factory. It is here that our anonymous worker, whom we shall refer to as the *voice*, first meets unionized workers, but he initially disregards their attempts to recruit him. But as the *voice* gains a better understanding of his role as a worker and of the relationship of those who own and manage the plant to those who produce and maintain it, he becomes more antagonistic and is fired. He moves to Milan, then to Turin, where his sister lives, and finds work on the Fiat production line. The rhythm of the production line and the piecework requirements are excessive, so the *voice* fakes an accident in order to have time off with pay. After initiating a protest on the production floor, coming to blows with an engineer during a union meeting and also with the guards at the plant's main gate, the *voice* is fired from this position too. He decides to dedicate himself whole-heartedly to the workers' struggles. Here, the novel parallels the actual history of the workers' movement in Italy, which led to the

---

1   Balestrini, N. 2014. *Vogliamo Tutto*. Translated by Matt Holden. Melbourne: Telephone Publishing. Balestrini, N. 2016. *We Want Everything: The Novel of Italy's Hot Autumn*. Translated by Matt Holden. New York: Verso.

'autunno caldo' (hot autumn) of 1969 and the founding of the protest group Potere Operaio (Workers' Power). The aim of this group was to achieve political and economic power on its own terms, without the mediation of unions that were seen as compromised by their relationship with a corrupt system. The long-term objective was not only an improvement in working conditions, but also the abolition of work as such. The increasingly successful workers' struggles eventually joined up with the actions and efforts of university students, and they culminated in the great demonstration of July 3, 1969, which degenerated into a series of violent encounters between protesters and police. Balestrini's novel reconstructs these events, in which his character, the *voice*, avoids being arrested during similar clashes, and flees the scene along the rooftops.

Vogliamo tutto marks a transition in the changing social, economic and cultural environment of postwar Italy. Coming in the years that followed the much celebrated economic boom, the novel could be said to represent the cumulative effects of the culture clash made apparent by that shift from a mostly pre-industrial to a postindustrial society. By the same set of circumstances, *Vogliamo tutto* calls attention to the exciting period of cultural activism and innovation that gave the novel its life and that announced a season – perhaps a movement – of more politically engaged literary expression.

The organizing institution behind such a movement was the literary journal *Il Verri*. Founded in 1956 by Luciano Anceschi, *Il Verri* counted among its young collaborators Giulia Niccolai, Antonio Porta and Balestrini himself. Anceschi's editorial from the first number, titled "Discorso generale" (General Introduction), outlined the practices of what became regarded as a neo-avantgarde movement: the Italian 'neoavanguardia.'[2] The journal's goal was to use experimental research into the functions and structures of language in order to explore the relationship between society, technology and the period's great developments in a variety of disciplines. In fact, *Il Verri*'s field of exploration and dissemination included innovations

2   Anceschi, L. 1956. "Discorso generale." *Il Verri*, no.1. 1–6. See also: Vetri, Lucio (ed.). 1988. *Interventi per "il verri" (1956–1987)*. Ravenna: Longo. Barilli, R. 1995. *La neoavanguardia italiana. Dalla nascita del "Verri" alla fine di "Quindici"*. Bologna: Il Mulino.

in psychoanalysis, philosophy, structuralism and various scientific fields. Today, *Il Verri* is mostly remembered for its introduction and support of what became the 'neoavanguardia,' a term meant to distinguish the movement from other avantgardes of the early twentieth century. Among those who helped Anceschi to promote literary experimentalism through creative and critical texts were Edoardo Sanguineti, Elio Pagliarani, Alfredo Giuliani, Porta and Balestrini, all of whom appeared in the anthology *I Novissimi* (The Very New Ones, 1961). The publication, which gave the group its name, became the occasion to announce a new, emerging poetics.[3] The editor Alfredo Giuliani's introduction to the first edition – which reads as a sort of manifesto – emphasized the group's intolerance toward an old and worn-out linguistic register that was in his view out of step with Italy's postwar transformations. For the Novissimi, language represented more than an instrument with which to describe reality; it was a primary site of engagement, experimentation and activism.

In 1963, the Novissimi joined up with other writers, artists, philosophers and intellectuals for an epochal conference in Palermo: a gathering self-baptized the 'Gruppo 63' (Gruppo of 63). Balestrini and Giuliani's introductory essay to the conference's proceedings – published the following year by Feltrinelli as *Gruppo 63* and collecting experimental materials, theoretical essays, position pieces and creative work – begins with the following observation:

> Che cosa ci si aspetta dagli scrittori? Che nelle loro finzioni introducano dosi più o meno cospicue di verità, lampi di conoscenza sui mondi reali o immaginabili. La

---

[3] In a recent video interview, Giuliani stated that Anceschi had "un piede nell'accademia e uno nella rivoluzione culturale permanente" (one foot in the academy and another in the permanent cultural revolution). Di Oscar Alicicco, A. C. et al. (eds). 2010. *I novissimi: ricostruzione del fenomeno editoriale*. Rome: Oblique Studio. 5. Before the 'Novissimi,' Ancheschi had already published a collection of experimental hermetic poetry titled *I lirici nuovi* (1943), and inaugurated a publishing series on contemporary poetry titled *Linea lombarda* (1952). But Anceschi was not satisfied with these, and he declared some years later: "se ci sono nuovi poeti, non ci sono invece poeti nuovi" (though there are poets who are new, there are however no new poets). Di Oscar Alicicco, A. C. et al. (eds). 2010. *I novissimi*. 5.

lingua della scrittura letteraria non è mai innocente e 'naturale.' È invece storicamente determinata e sempre in lotta con se stessa per non ripetere il già fatto. In una certa epoca si può, con qualche profitto, variare e arricchire; in altre epoche, quando si avverte l'esaurimento irrimediabile dei correnti modelli linguistici e formali, si è spinti, se vogliamo dallo spirito dei tempi, a ricercare il nuovo, a escogitare inediti modi di raccontare, di fare poesia o teatro.

(What do we expect of writers? That they introduce more or less conspicuous doses of truth in their fiction, flashes of understanding into worlds real or imagined. The language of literary writing is never innocent or 'natural.' It is, rather, historically determined and always struggles with itself so as not to repeat what has been done. In a certain epoch one might, with some success, vary and enrich it; at other times, when one becomes aware of the irremediable exhaustion of current linguistic and formal models, one is required, possibly by the spirit of the times, to look for something new, to come up with unusual ways to tell stories, to write poetry or do theater.)[4]

My brief overview of this period is not meant to suggest that *Vogliamo tutto* represented the activities of the Gruppo 63, but that it was an expression of the challenges brought forth by that group. Far from a conventional work, *Vogliamo tutto* performs its artistry by generating a form and a language that reflects the social, historical and political situation that it narrates. It is an innovative and experimental novel that, as such, achieves a three-fold status: *Vogliamo tutto* is an expressive work of art, a document of an era and a political witness to the activism and inside operations of the factory floor.

As stated above, the narrative *voice* that carries forward these three statuses is that of a southern worker. Rachel Kushner is of the opinion that the *voice* was fashioned after Alfonso Natella, a Fiat worker to whom the book is dedicated, and who seems to have provided Balestrini with insights into working conditions in the factory.[5] Despite this identification, the *voice's* identity as an individual matters little for the trajectory of the novel. It is because Balestrini's novel gives voice to, and details factory work conditions in the 1970s, and because for factory owners, workers were faceless,

4   Balestrini, N and Giuliani, A. 1964. "Introduzione." *Gruppo 63. La nuova letteratura. Palermo 1963*. Edited by Nanni Balestrini and Alfredo Giuliani. Milan: Feltrinelli. 19.
5   Kushner, R. 2016. "Introduction." in Balestrini, N. *We Want Everything*. xi.

nameless and easily replaceable components, that I have chosen to refer to the narrator as the *voice*. Any factory worker could be easily replaced by numerous other individuals in search of opportunity and a better life for themselves and their families. The *voice* is blunt, aggressive and sometimes intimate; other times it is reluctant, insolent and demanding. But what is most evident, in the progression of the novel, is that the *voice* progresses from a self-interested individual, through its acquisition of a political and class consciousness, through the exploitative practices of the factory, to a voice willing to speak out on the general condition of all workers who find themselves in a similar position. Historically, the *voice* is that of countless workers who migrated to northern Italy to train and work in factories, and *Vogliamo tutto* dives deep into the dysfunctionality of labor relations and the cultural contrasts resulting from these mass migrations. Moreover, it is recounted in a language that illustrates and represents the contradictions of contemporary Italian society, some of which have continued into the present. The linguistic hybrid of the *voice*'s southern syntax/language, layered with standard Italian and the technical terminology required by its work, together with the political vocabulary acquired, is one of the traits that mark this novel as contemporary. In other words, it is written not in a literary register, but in a language that reflects the reality of working bodies of the period.

The first part of *Vogliamo tutto* is a self-reflective document compiled by the *voice*, who witnesses the conditions and conflicts that came to define that historical period. Most importantly, the *voice* addresses itself to those who were not present at the events narrated, filling in the gaps in a history that still today remains largely untold from the point of view of workers. The problems associated with the migration of workers from southern to northern Italy quickly become evident upon the workers' arrival in the North. In an exemplary illustration of how industry exploited migrant workers and public institutions, the *voice* recounts the 1970s situation at the Turin train station:

> c'erano dei disgraziati che hanno dormito per tre o quattro giorni e molti anche per un mese nella stazione nella sala d'aspetto di seconda classe a Porta Nuova. E erano anche controllati dalla polizia che non lasciava nessun giornalista li avvicinasse. Per entrare la notte nella sala d'aspetto di seconda classe a Porta Nuova uno doveva

> mostrare il tesserino Fiat se già lavorava alla Fiat oppure la carta della visita cioè la lettera della Fiat che ti dice di presentarti a passare la visita. Se no la polizia non fa entrare nessuno in questo dormitorio che c'ha la Fiat gratis alla stazione a Torino.
>
> (There were some unlucky ones who spent a few days in the station, and lots even a month, in the second-class waiting room at Porta Nuova. It was patrolled by police who made sure that journalists didn't get near it. To get into the second-class waiting room at Porta Nuova at night you had to show your Fiat ID card if you were already working there, or the letter from Fiat that said you should come for an interview. Without it the police wouldn't let anyone into this dormitory that Fiat had, for free, at Torino station.)[6]

While the *voice* is lucky enough to sleep at a sister's apartment, others are relegated to the makeshift dormitory of the station. Integration into the Fiat workforce is fiercely competitive, the work schedules are demanding and the *voice* is one among twenty thousand job candidates. Many cannot sustain the pace of the assembly line, and they leave after one or a few days. But the *voice* is one of those "mostri, [...] gli orribili lavoratori" (monsters, [...] the horrible workers) who fiercely take on the work required of them, and it just as fiercely challenges its own working conditions.[7]

The whole process, from interview to hiring and work, is rather farcical. Instead of making a selection based on actual skills, the interview process is designed to instill in all future employees a productive sense of competition. The medical exam that follows is as ridiculously performative as the interview, and in the end, everyone is hired. The farce is fueled by both the factories and the workers willing to dispense with regulations, given, on the one hand, the constant need for manpower and, on the other, the need for employment.

While *Vogliamo tutto* offers a truly revealing scrutiny of the world inside Italian factories, it also makes obvious Balestrini's admiration for those faceless and apparently identity-less workers with a sophisticated understanding of national politics. The *voice* is aware that the Cassa per il Mezzogiorno (Fund for the South) – a postwar financial aid program meant

---

6   Balestrini, N. 2004. *Vogliamo tutto*. Rome: Derive Approdi. 62. Balestrini, N. 2016. *We Want Everything*. Translated by Matt Holden. 58.
7   Balestrini, N. 2004. *Vogliamo tutto*. 69. Balestrini, N. 2016. *We Want Everything*. Translated by Matt Holden. 65.

for the development of southern Italy – was merely a pretext to ensure the availability of a labor force for the North.⁸ In a succinct description, northern development required "il nostro [meridionale] sottosviluppo" (our [southern] underdevelopment).⁹

As a founding member of the extra-parliamentary left-wing group Potere Operaio in 1968, Balestrini was well practiced in communicating with and recounting the stories of workers.¹⁰ It was this direct experience that enabled him to reproduce the very effective voice and overall working experience represented in *Vogliamo tutto*. Alfonso Natella was also a member of Potere Operaio, and had likely shared his experiences with Balestrini in the context of that group. Such direct practices of reporting have their roots in Marxism and, in Italy, in the workers' movement known as Operaismo (Workerism), and they have been labelled 'inchiesta' (enquiry). In the postwar period, the 'inchiesta' as a genre took on different forms in the work of Danilo Dolci, Nuto Revelli, Rocco Scotellaro and Carlo Levi.

These writers also shared an approach to work and activism that found correspondence beyond their political activism and social theories. Balestrini successfully blended the practices of 'inchiesta' into his art, revolutionizing forms of expression and injecting a new level of consciousness into their production and consumption. *Vogliamo tutto* is only one example, and Balestrini maintained such an approach in later novels, including *La violenza illustrata* (Violence Illustrated, 1976), *Gli invisibili* (The Unseen, 1987), *La Grande Rivolta* (The Great Revolution, 1999) and *Sandokan* (2004). Most of these works are narrated in the first-person by protagonists whose stories are rooted in direct experience, which makes of them historical accounts, whether they are about the militancy of the 1977 Autonomist movement, or the violence and destructive influence of the Camorra in

8   The Cassa per il Mezzogiorno was established in 1950 to provide funds for an industrially undeveloped South. While this effort had some effect in very localized situations, the overall results and effects were less than hoped for. In fact, in the early years of the fund, about ten million southerners migrated to the North.
9   Balestrini, N. 2004. *Vogliamo tutto*. 15. Balestrini, N. 2016. *We Want Everything*. Translated by Matt Holden. 5–6.
10 For a good account of Potere Operaio, see Wright, S. 2002. *Storming Heaven: Class Composition and Struggle in Italian Autonomist Marxism*. London and Sterling, VA: Pluto Press. 131–151.

southern Italy. Like *Vogliamo tutto*'s narrating voice, these voices too are anonymous and represent a multitude. They are different from the classical subjectivity of nineteenth-century novels and closer to more vernacular forms of expression, oral traditions, epic tales and mythological explications.

The arduous nature of factory work, where wages were tied to productivity, and the repetitive motions that took their toll on the workers, caused great physical and psychological strife among the labor force. These conditions were further aggravated by the alienation that workers experienced in foreign social and cultural environments, the distance from their families and the lack of after-work activities. It was this situation that drove workers like the *voice* of *Vogliamo tutto* to explore other radical directions meant to strengthen activism:

> Una sera uscivo dalla Fiat e vedo uno studente che mi fa Vuoi venire a una riunione li al bar? Io decido che mi va e gli dico va bene che ci vado. Che cazzo non c'ho niente da fare mi vado a vedere questi stronzi che vogliono che dicono. Li vedevo tutti i giorni questi studenti e li giudicavo stronzi. Non sapevo neanche quello che dicevano non leggevo nessuno dei loro volantini.

> (One evening I was coming out of Fiat and I see a student who goes: Do you want to come to a meeting at the bar? It sounded OK to me and I told him OK, I'll go. What the fuck, I didn't have anything to do, it was OK to see what these assholes want, what they say. I saw these students every day, and I figured they were assholes. I didn't know what they were talking about, I never read their leaflets.)[11]

In response to workplace passivity, management-organized strikes, alienation and the knowledge that all work benefits the factory owners, the *voice* presents everything from the point of view of direct lived experience. Apparently contradicting the very title of the book, Balestrini's own workers are ready to risk everything. This is well documented in the second half of the book, as the collective nature of the workforce is actually defined by the *voice*'s own organizational meetings, coordinated strikes, workplace actions and direct challenges to the factory bosses. The developing consciousness of the factory hierarchy, with its manipulation from above, soon becomes clear in the workers:

---

11   Balestrini, N. 2004. *Vogliamo tutto*. 80. Balestrini, N. 2016. *We Want Everything*. Translated by Matt Holden. 79.

Ora l'abbiamo capito l'organizzazione che ci siamo dati ci ha consentito di condurre la lotta nell'officina ma non ci ha permesso di superare l'isolamento in cui commissione interna e sindacato ci hanno tenuti. Rifiutandosi di portare avanti le nostre richieste. Separando la lotta delle Fonderie Nord da quelle delle Fonderie Sud. Non informando gli operai delle altre sezioni Fiat. Ma i motivi per cui ci siamo mossi rimangono in piedi. Come siamo riusciti a organizzarci nell'officina così bisogna sapersi organizzare in tutta Mirafiori. Come? Solo organizzandoci con gli operai di altre officine potremo organizzare lotte con il minimo di danno per noi e con il massimo di danno per il padrone. Solo facendo sentire tutta la nostra forza organizzata costringeremo il padrone a mollare.

(Now we get it: the organisation we have created has allowed us to carry out the struggle in the factory, but it hasn't allowed us to overcome the isolation forced on us by the internal commission and the union. Refusing to carry our claims forward. Dividing the struggle of North Foundry from South Foundry. Not informing workers in Fiat's other sections. But the reasons we acted still hold. Just as we were able to organise ourselves in the workshop, we need to be able to organise all of Mirafiori. How? Only by cooperating with the workers of the other workshops will we be able to organise struggles that cause the least harm to us and the most harm to the boss. Only by making our full organised force felt will we force the boss to surrender.)[12]

Here is part of the greater meaning of the insistent request 'vogliamo tutto,' which during this period became the workers' call to arms. What is 'everything?' According to the testimony given in Balestrini's novel – the 'inchiesta' into the lives and working conditions of the workers – 'everything' does not seem to be anything too extraordinary. What the workers 'want' is a workplace that honors their work and that does not require them to work long and difficult hours, while struggling to make ends meet. They 'want' time to spend with their families, time to enjoy themselves after work, and to receive adequate compensation for maintaining a respectable life.

Vogliamo tutto is a novel, a testimony and an anti-capitalist essay that has not exhausted its narrative. Whether in Italy or elsewhere, the struggles of workers seem always centered around the same issues: the resolution of exploitative practices, and the achievement of respect for laboring bodies.

---

12   Balestrini, N. 2004. *Vogliamo tutto*. 131. Balestrini, N. 2016. *We Want Everything*. Translated by Matt Holden. 141.

PIERPAOLO ANTONELLO

24 *La chiave a stella* (1978): Labor *sub specie* Faussone

Primo Levi's *La chiave a stella* (The Wrench), published in 1978 by Einaudi, is something of an anomaly in the constellation of novels clustered under the heading 'industrial literature.' It comes late, by comparison with the main corpus of this sub-genre of contemporary Italian literature, and coincides with the peak in 1970s Italy in ideological and political tensions, characterized by pivotal historical events, such as the kidnapping and assassination of former Prime Minister Aldo Moro. By contrast with other writers in the sub-genre, whose direct experience of industry and corporate entities was more brief or sporadic, Levi had worked in chemicals companies for thirty years, both on the technical side and in management, becoming Technical Director of the paint manufacturer SIVA in 1950, and then CEO in 1966.

Though labeled a novel, *La chiave a stella* is structured as a collection of linked short stories, defined as a "romanzo in quattordici racconti" (novel in fourteen stories) or an "antologia di avventure di lavoro" (anthology of labor adventures).[1] It is the confessional autobiography of Libertino Faussone, a 35-year-old rigger, or mechanical worker, who recounts a series of adventures relating to the resolution of engineering problems encountered during the construction of major mechanical projects such as oil-rigs, bridges, and cranes in different parts of the world, including the Middle East, India, the former Soviet Union and Alaska. Faussone is a fictional character, whom Levi nonetheless considers real, in the sense of authentic, for Faussone is a "conglomerato di persone reali, che ho conosciuto" (a mixture of real people whom I've met), "un condensato di

---

1 Levi, P. 2018. *Opere complete*, vol. 3. Turin: Einaudi. 125.

trent'anni di incontri in fabbrica" (a condensation of thirty years of meetings in the factory).² Specifically, Levi met various engineers and specialist workers from Fiat, who worked on the production of the Lada car brand, manufactured by AvtoVAZ Žiguli, during his trips to Togliattigrad in Russia between 1972 and 1973. The setting of these stories outside Italy's national borders, thereby maintaining a view from afar in geographical terms,³ further differentiates this book from other industrial novels, which are invariably set in Italy.

In his protagonist, Levi plots an archetype that had been underrepresented or indeed completely overlooked by contemporary Italian writers. Faussone is a solitary hero, a man of industry, but not of the factory floor. He is not the emblematic worker who stands for the blue-collar masses featuring in many industrial novels or films, but rather an exceptional character who had the privilege to make autonomous decisions about his engineering projects, representing a marginal element of the workforce that emerged in twentieth-century industrial Italy. Faussone is part of a "aristocrazia operaia di origine settentrionale che dopo il miracolo economico è diventata una componente minoritaria dell'intera classe lavoratrice" (northern workers aristocracy that, after the economic miracle, became a marginal component of the whole working class).⁴ Levi is not interested in the average worker, or the average case, but in those outlier examples that can provide narrative salience by describing a type of work that is personally and cognitively enhancing, bringing both psychological and epistemological grace and fulfillment to the worker.

By comparison with standard themes in industrial literature, Levi's book is remarkable for its reaction against the general ideological and

---

2 Levi, P. 2018. *Opere complete*, vol. 3. 130.
3 Precisely because of this view from afar, *La chiave a stella* was labelled by Claude Levi-Strauss an "ethnographic" book. Cited in Belpoliti, M. 2015. *Primo Levi di fronte e di profilo*. Milan: Guanda. 297.
4 Fioretti, D. 2013. *Carte di fabbrica. La narrativa industriale in Italia (1934–1989)*. Pescara: Edizioni Tracce. 189.

intellectual climate in Italy at that time,⁵ with the dominant radical Marxist criticism of the capitalist organization of society that embraced the belief "that all work, particularly factory work, was oppressive and alienating," and enacted a "consequent refusal to consider it as one of the bases of human identity."⁶

Levi's book is in fact a eulogy of *homo faber*, man as maker, articulating a close interconnection between work, morality and ethical imperatives, both as necessary precondition but also contribution to the needs of the community in a complex society like an industrialized one. Faussone is "uno di quelli che il suo mestiere gli piace" (one of those guys who like their profession), one who defends and proudly extols his taste for work, one who treats the day of a crane inspection "sempre un po' come una festa" (always [with] a festive atmosphere).⁷ The book explicitly stands in contrast to those ideological theses in which work is the great enemy of the people and must be rejected in favor of the "macchine desideranti" (desiring machines) and the pleasure principle that circulated through the reception of Nietzsche and in the youth movements of the 1970s.⁸ As Levi explained in an interview, "Ero io stesso infastidito, come molti, da una certa posizione insulsa: il lavoro si rifiuta! Se il lavoro si rifiuta e tutti lo rifiutano, si muore di fame in sostanza" (Like many others, I was annoyed by this dull political position: we must refuse to work! If one refuses to work and everybody refuses to work, then we would basically starve).⁹

---

5   The working title of *La chiave a stella* was *Vile meccanico* (Vile Mechanic), showing the clear polemical dimension of Levi's book in relation to the intellectual and political climate of the period. The reference is to chapter 4 of Alessandro Manzoni's *I promessi sposi* (The Betrothed, 1827).
6   Cicioni, M. 1995. *Primo Levi: Bridges of Knowledge*. Oxford: Berg. 84.
7   Levi, P. 1997. "La chiave a stella." *Opere*, vol. 1. Turin: Einaudi. 1071. Levi, P. 2015. "The Wrench." *The Complete Works of Primo Levi*, vol. 2. Translated by Nathaniel Rich. New York and London: Liveright Publishing Corporation. 1078–1079.
8   Zinato, E. 2015. *Letteratura come storiografia? Mappe e figure della mutazione italiana*. Macerata: Quodlibet. 68–69.
9   Cited in Grassano, G. 1979. "Conversazione con Primo Levi." in Levi, P. *Opere complete*, vol. 3. 172.

Ideological moderation, a trait uncommon in Italian political and intellectual discourse, is at the center of Levi's approach to any ethical and political discussion. It is typical of Levi to reject ideological polarizations and political maximalism: "siamo estremisti: ignoriamo le vie intermedie [...]; dovremmo respingere questa nostra innata tendenza alla radicalità, perché essa è fonte del male. Sia lo zero, sia l'uno, ci spingono all'inazione" (we are extremists: we overlook the middle ground [...] we ought to reject this inborn tendency of ours toward the radical, because it's the root of evil. Both the zero and the one push us toward inaction).[10]

Levi's position is characterized by 'common sense,' and it aims to reestablish "un clima di ragionevolezza dopo l'esasperazione del conflitto sociale, aperto nel 1968 ed esploso con nuovo vigore nel 1977" (a climate of reason, after the exacerbation of social conflict, which started in 1968 and exploded with new force in 1977).[11] He explicitly rejects the rhetoric of those who least know this "sconfinata regione del rusco, del boulot, del job, insomma del lavoro quotidiano" (vast region – the region of the *trade*, of the *boulot*, of the *job*, in short, of daily work), indeed "ne parlano di più, e con più clamore, proprio coloro che meno l'hanno percorsa" (the people who speak about it the most, who make the greatest racket, are the ones who know the least about it).[12] From a political standpoint, Levi positions himself at the midpoint of the ideological spectrum: he is polemical both against those who exalt work "nelle cerimonie officiali [dove] viene mobilitata una retorica insidiosa, cinicamente fondata sulla considerazione che un elogio o una medaglia costano molto meno di un aumento di paga e rendono di più" (in official ceremonies [where] an insidious rhetoric comes into play, based on the cynical belief that a medal and a few words of praise cost less, and are more valuable, than a pay increase), but he equally opposes

---

10 Levi, P. 1997. *Opere*, vol. 2. Turin: Einaudi. 855. Levi, P. 2015. "Other People's Trade." *The Complete Works of Primo Levi*, vol. 3. Translated by Antony Shugaar. New York and London: Liveright Publishing Corporation. 2250.

11 Fioretti, D. 2013. *Carte di fabbrica. La narrativa industriale in Italia (1934–1989)*. 189.

12 Levi, P. 1997. *Opere*, vol. 1. 1015. Levi, P. 2015. "The Wrench." *The Complete Works of Primo Levi*, vol. 2. Translated by Nathaniel Rich. 1023.

La chiave a stella (1978): Labor sub specie Faussone

> una retorica di segno opposto, non cinica ma profondamente stupida, che tende a denigrarlo, a dipingerlo vile, come se del lavoro, proprio od altrui, si potesse fare a meno, non solo in Utopia ma oggi e qui: come se chi sa lavorare fosse per definizione un servo, e come se, per converso, chi lavorare non sa, o sa male, o non vuole, fosse per ciò stesso un uomo libero. È malinconicamente vero che molti lavori non sono amabili, ma è nocivo scendere in campo carichi di odio preconcetto: chi lo fa, si condanna per la vita a odiare non solo il lavoro, ma sé stesso e il mondo.
>
> (a rhetoric on the other side, not so much cynical as profoundly stupid, that tends to denigrate work, to portray it as vile, as if we could do without work, our own or that of others, not just in some future utopia but here, today: as if anybody who works were by definition a servant, and as if, conversely, anyone who doesn't work, or doesn't know how to, or doesn't want to, were therefore a free man. It's the depressing truth that many jobs are undesirable, but it's a mistake to rage against them if you're prejudiced from the start: anyone who does so condemns himself to a lifetime of hatred – not only of his work but of himself and the world.)[13]

Levi's position also reflects phenomenological observations: among the various different Faussones he himself encountered in Italy and abroad, he found no overriding ideological positions – unsurprisingly, they were "per metà comunisti e per metà anticomunisti" (half communists and half anti-communists).[14] Levi explicitly claims to want to outline a "lay" character, starting from a distinctive anthropological makeup, "il misurarsi con le cose non è né di destra né di sinistra. Fa parte del meccanismo dell'animale uomo e deve essere riconosciuto come tale" (weighing the facts of reality is not an activity of the right, nor of the left. It is part of the mechanism of the human-as-animal, and must be acknowledged as such).[15] Moreover, we should consider that "l'amore del lavoro non è poi così tanto raro come si crede: e chi ama il lavoro non è necessariamente un reazionario" (loving one's job is not as rare as we tend to think, and a person who loves their job is not necessarily a reactionary).[16]

---

13 Levi, P. 2018. *Opere complete*, vol. 3. 130. Levi, P. 2015. "The Wrench." *The Complete Works of Primo Levi*, vol. 2. Translated by Nathaniel Rich. 1023–1024.
14 Levi, P. 2018. *Opere complete*, vol. 3. 130.
15 Levi, P. 2018. *Opere complete*, vol. 3. 144.
16 Levi, P. 2018. *Opere complete*, vol. 3. 124. Levi is aware that his book could be understood as ideologically reactionary. See Levi, P. 2018 *Opere complete*, vol. 3. 144.

Consequently, Levi engages with the general discourse on the alienation of work in contemporary industrial society, focusing his attention on the individual over the collective. Love or hatred of work reflect an inner, personal existential trajectory, "che dipende molto dalla storia dell'individuo, e meno di quanto si creda dalle strutture produttive entro cui il lavoro si svolge" (which depends greatly on the story of the individual and less than is believed on the productive structures within which the work is done).[17] He always insists on individual responsibility as a cornerstone of morality: "La malattia più grave, fra le molte che ci affliggono è il rifiuto della responsabilità" (The most serious disease, among the many that afflict us, is the rejection of responsibility),[18] "di colpa e errori si deve rispondere in proprio, altrimenti ogni traccia di civiltà sparisce dalla faccia della terra" (a person has to answer for his sins and errors, otherwise every trace of civilization would disappear from the face of the Earth).[19]

Unsurprisingly, after the publication of *La chiave a stella*, various radical leftist commentators heavily criticized Levi's book for presenting an unexacting eulogy to manual and industrial work. In an interview, Levi recalled certain harsh articles published by the radical paper *Lotta continua*, in which he was denounced for daring to write about the condition of the working class, being himself an outsider to that demographic.[20] While it may be partially true that in Levi's writing there is very little explicit political or ideological discussion in relation to the development of a capitalistic society[21] – or, more precisely, discussion that does not conform to the

17 Levi, P. 1997. *Opere*, vol. 1. 1016. Levi, P. 1987. *The Monkey's Wrench*. Translated by William Weaver. New York: Penguin. 80.
18 Levi, P. 1997. *Opere*, vol. 1. 1220. P. Levi. 2015. "Letter to Lattanzio: 'Resign.'" *The Complete Works of Primo Levi*, vol. 2. Translated by Alessandra Bastagli and Francesco Bastagli. 1231–1232.
19 Levi, P. 1997. *Opere*, vol. 2. 1133. Levi, P. 2015. "The Drowned and the Saved." *The Complete Works of Primo Levi*, vol. 3. Translated by Michael F. Moore. 2545.
20 Levi, P. 2001. *The Voice of Memory*. Cambridge: Polity. 129. See also Di Ciaula, Tommaso. 1979. "L'operaio Faussone è per caso analfabeta?" *Lotta continua*. January 14.
21 See also Mario Spinella's criticism of Levi in the review of *Vizio di forma*, in *Rinascita*, 4 June 1971, cited in Ferrero, F (ed.). 1996. *Primo Levi: un'antologia della critica*. Turin: Einaudi. 333.

La chiave a stella (1978): Labor sub specie Faussone

common ideological parameters of the period – he did nonetheless have extensive personal experience of "*le boulot*, the job, *il rusco* – daily work." Levi in fact had worked at every level of industry: from his enslavement of the *animal laborans* of the *Lager* right up to his leadership role as CEO at SIVA.

From a Marxist standpoint, it is evident that Levi skirts the issue of manufacturing conditions and labor relations and essentially justifies the capitalistic organization of modern society, while his discourse seems to be tainted by a sort of resigned fatalism in the acknowledgement that there are too many, in his euphemistic phrase, "lavori non amabili" (undesirable jobs).[22] As Daniele Fioretti has written

> Levi non affronta direttamente i presupposti politico-ideologici da cui partono i movimenti, magari per criticare l'utopia su cui sono fondati. Al contrario, *La chiave a stella* propone un'utopia più simmetrica ma al contempo regressiva, che guarda esplicitamente al passato, cioè al modo di produzione semi-artigianale tipico degli anni Cinquanta.
>
> (Levi does not directly confront the political and ideological presuppositions at the root of protest movements, something that would have allowed him to criticize the vision of utopia on which they are founded. On the contrary, *La chiave a stella* proposes an even more symmetrical, but at the same time regressive utopia: one that looks explicitly to the past – that is, to the semi-artisanal mode of production typical of the 1950s.)[23]

In the chapter "Batter la lastra" (Metalwork), Levi demonstrates nostalgia for the kind of manual labor and craft that separates the moral and aesthetic value of a given achievement from its economic and commercial value. This is specifically and emblematically embodied by Faussone's father, who was a tinsmith, or worker in light metals. After he had finished his handmade copper stoves,

> stava lì a guardare i suoi lambicchi dopo che li aveva finiti e lucidati. Quando venivano i clienti a portarseli via, lui gli faceva una carezzina e si vedeva che gli dispiaceva; se

---

22   Levi, P. 1997. *Opere*, vol. 1. 1098.
23   Fioretti, D. 2013. *Carte di fabbrica. La narrativa industriale in Italia (1934–1989)*. 190.

> non erano troppo lontani, ogni tanto prendeva la bicicletta e andava a riguardarli, con la scusa di vedere se tutto andava bene.
>
> (you could see it in the way he looked at his stills after he had finished and polished them. When his clients came to take them away, he gave them a little caress and you could tell that he was sorry; if they didn't end up too far away, he'd sometimes take his bike and go look at them, with the excuse of making sure that everything was working all right.)[24]

In this respect, the novel bears witness to a particular moment in labor history, when workers who had developed methods, techniques and manual skills in the context of craftsmanship were coopted by corporate industry. Levi's meditation on work is moved not by the perspective of a blue-collar worker, but by what Enrico Mattioda identifies as a long tradition of Piedmontese thought, characterized by human self-actualization through work: a sort of secular religion of commitment and labor.[25] Faussone embodies a particular regional culture, underlined by his partial use of dialect and by his technical Piedmontese jargon,[26] systematically adopted by Levi in an attempt to fill an ecological niche: that is, seeking to give "diritto di cittadinanza al nuovo italo-piemontese che si parla oggi nella Torino operaia, con le sue nuove metafore e il nuovo lessico tratto dal mondo tecnologico" (citizenship rights to the new Piedmontese Italian that is spoken today in working-class Turin, with its new metaphors and vocabulary taken from the world of technology).[27]

At the basis of the Levian disposition and understanding of technical-industrial work is not the logic of production, but rather the creative force behind it: both objectively (in terms of the actual manufacture of material and technical objects), and subjectively (in terms of the construction of the self, channeled through a dedication to well-made work, itself linked with intrinsic pleasure, and ultimately thereby with freedom). The idea of

---

24 Levi, P. 1997. *Opere*, vol. 1. 1018. Levi, P. 2015. "The Wrench." *The Complete Works of Primo Levi*, vol. 2. Translated by Nathaniel Rich. 1026.
25 Mattioda, E. 2011. *Levi*. Rome: Salerno. 117–124.
26 On Levi's use of language, see Mengaldo, V. 1996. "Lingua e scrittura in Levi." *Primo Levi: un'antologia della critica*. 169–242. See also Villata, B. 2018. *Primo Levi e il piemontese. La lingua de "La chiave a stella"*. Turin: Fondazione Enrico Landri.
27 Levi, P. 2018. *Opere complete*, vol. 3. 131.

La chiave a stella (1978): Labor sub specie Faussone 345

freedom had not previously been associated with the theme of labor, which had tended instead to be discussed as an instrument of alienation, both in economic and Marxist terms, and in psychiatric and Foucauldian terms: "Il termine libertà ha notoriamente molti sensi, ma forse il tipo di libertà più accessibile, più goduto soggettivamente, e più utile al consorzio umano, coincide con l'essere competenti nel proprio lavoro, e quindi nel provare piacere a svolgerlo" (The term 'freedom' has many meanings, but perhaps the most accessible form of freedom, the most subjectively enjoyed and most beneficial to the social order, derives from being competent in one's own work, and thus taking pleasure in doing it).[28] *La chiave a stella*, with its eulogy for work well done as a fundamental value for social organization and for individual subjectivity, could be summarized in the well-known phrase: "Se si escludono istanti prodigiosi e singoli che il destino ci può donare, l'amare il proprio lavoro (che purtroppo è privilegio di pochi) costituisce la migliore approssimazione concreta alla felicità sulla terra: ma questa è una verità che non molti conoscono" (If you put aside those prodigious, singular moments that destiny gives us, love of one's work – a privilege enjoyed, unfortunately, only by a few – is the best, most concrete approximation of happiness on earth – but most people don't realize this).[29] And, to paraphrase Bertrand Russell from *The Conquest of Happiness*, "non c'è felicità senza sforzo" (there's no happiness without effort).[30]

However, Faussone rejects factory work in the Fordist sense of the assembly line and the obligation to work for a boss: "fare tutta la vita gli stessi gesti attaccato al convogliatore fino che uno non è più buono a fare altro e gli danno la liquidazione e la pensione e si siede sulle panchine" (making the same movements all your life, stuck on the assembly line until you're no good for anything else and they give you your severance pay and your

---

28 Levi, P. 1997. *Opere*, vol. 1. 1074. Levi, P. 2015. "The Wrench." *The Complete Works of Primo Levi*, vol. 2. Translated by Nathaniel Rich. 1081.
29 Levi, P. 1997. *Opere*, vol. 1. 1015. Levi, P. 2015. "The Wrench." *The Complete Works of Primo Levi*, vol. 2. Translated by Nathaniel Rich. 1023.
30 Levi, P. 2018. *Opere complete*, vol. 3. 174. The actual quote by Russell is: "the mere absence of effort from his life removes an essential ingredient of happiness." Russel, B. 1958. *The Conquest of Happiness*. New York: Liveright. 34.

pension and you sit on a park bench).³¹ Consequently, Faussone's labor is not rife with the experience of alienation, but is powered by an autonomous creative drive which fully corresponds to his own existential tension and interest. His work is free in the sense that Faussone independently imagines, invents and executes the solutions to the technical problems he encounters. To reinforce this point, Levi names his protagonist Libertino – literally, 'free man' – surely a subversive response to the grotesque inscription on the gate of Auschwitz, 'Arbeit Macht Frei' (work sets you free). As Philip Roth remarked in his interview with Levi, "Faussone is Man the Worker made *truly* free through his labor."³²

Because of its picaresque dimension and its epos of a solitary hero, *La chiave a stella* has been deemed less dated than other factory novels which relate more closely to the economic, political and industrial reality of their time, and it has continued to find new readers. In this sense, the reception of *La chiave a stella*, including judgments about the figure of Faussone, acts as a kind of cultural probe in the context of late twentieth century Italy. It is compelling to compare the ideological polemics of its reception at the time of its publication with a contemporary moment like the late 2010s, characterized by systemic crisis in the Italian economic and political landscape, de-industrialization and the progressive disappearance of jobs. What we observe is that the horizon of understanding has been reversed with respect to the rhetoric of the 1970s. In reporting the spread of what he terms the "funzione-Levi" (Levi-code) in contemporary criticism and journalism, Andrea Rondini signals the

> penetrazione, nell'immaginario sociale contemporaneo, della rappresentazione del lavoro *sub specie* Faussone: un incrocio di passione, competenza, orgoglio del lavoro ben fatto, onestà, che evidentemente costituiscono un paradigma di riferimento, sia per mettere in luce esperienze positive sia per segnalare situazioni di crisi.
>
> (penetration in the contemporary collective consciousness of the representation of labor *sub specie* Faussone: a mix of passion, competence, pride in a job well-done and

---

31 Levi, P. 1997. *Opere*, vol. 1. 1017. Levi, P. 1987. *The Monkey's Wrench*. Translated by William Weaver. 81.
32 Cited in Levi, P. 2018. *Opere complete*, vol. 3. 638.

honesty that evidently constitutes a paradigmatic model, both to highlight positive experiences and to signal crisis situations.)[33]

Rondini highlights the general nostalgia for that most dynamic of economic moments in the history of Italy as a nation state, and calls for a return to valuing labor expertise and know-how in a tenor compatible with the new economic, social and technological order. "Il recupero di una memoria industriale e dell'orgoglio per questa tradizione" (The recovery of an industrial memory and a pride in that tradition), Rondini concludes, "trova un codice e una radice proprio nelle pagine de *La chiave a stella*" (finds a language and a root right here in the pages of *La chiave a stella*).[34] This resonates with the shift over time in the reception of Levi's *oeuvre*, which has progressively moved from the margins of the Italian canon to its center. This has happened not only because Levi produced one of the most lucid and compelling accounts of the Lager experience at the international level, but also because of his eccentricity in respect to modern Italian literature and intellectual life, and his ability to interpret key aspects of contemporary culture.

---

[33] Rondini, A. 2012. *Anche il cielo brucia. Primo Levi e il giornalismo*. Macerata: Quodlibet. 158–159. See also Ranieri, A. 2010. "Lavoro e conoscenza." *Bruno Trentin. Lavoro, libertà, conoscenza*. Edited by Alessio Gramolati, Giovanni Mari. Florence: Firenze University Press. 127.

[34] Rondini, A. 2012. *Anche il cielo brucia. Primo Levi e il giornalismo*. 160.

ERICA BELLIA

25 Tommaso Di Ciaula's *Tuta blu* (1978): The Voice and Body of the Working Class

Tommaso Di Ciaula's *Tuta blu. Ire, ricordi e sogni di un operaio del Sud* (Blue Overalls: Rages, Memories and Dreams of a Worker from the South) is a first-person consideration of its author's experience as a metalworker in a factory in Puglia in the 1970s.¹ Born in 1941 to an Apulian peasant family, Di Ciaula was employed from a young age in the Pignone Sud factory. This was a large plant located in the area of Bari and owned by ENI, the Italian public oil and gas company. Di Ciaula made his debut as a writer in 1970 with a self-published poetry collection titled *Chiodi e rose* (Nails and Roses).² *Tuta blu* was his first prose work, published by Feltrinelli in 1978 in the series 'Franchi Narratori' (free narrators – a play on the term 'franchi tiratori,' sharpshooters). The

---

1   Di Ciaula, T. 1978. *Tuta blu. Ire, ricordi e sogni di un operaio del Sud*. Milan: Feltrinelli. From now on, I will refer to and quote from the most recent edition: Di Ciaula, T. 2003. *Tuta blu. Ire, ricordi e sogni di un operaio del Sud*. Jesolo: Zambon. Translations are available in French, Spanish, German and Russian, but not yet English. The translations provided in this chapter are mine. Apart from the reviews published immediately after the publication (a list of which is available in the Zambon edition), the book is often mentioned in reflections on industrial literature, but it is not the subject of any monographic study. The following are major contributions on *Tuta blu*: Giacomazzi, G. 1997. "Tematiche e strategie testuali della letteratura 'selvaggia.'" *Letteratura e industria: Atti del 15° Congresso AISLLI*. Edited by Giorgio Bàrberi Squarotti and Carlo Ossola. Florence: Olschki. 1009–1024. Panella, C. 2016. "Scritture di rabbia e scritture di desiderio. La letteratura italiana di fabbrica degli anni Settanta." *Lavoro! Storia, organizzazione e narrazione del lavoro nel XX secolo*. Edited by Novella di Nunzio and Matteo Troilo. Rome: Aracne. 53–66.
2   The collection was republished in 2006 as Di Ciaula, T. 2006. *Chiodi e rose. Poesie operaie*. Foggia: Rainoneditore.

series was launched by the neo-avantgarde writer Nanni Balestrini and the critic Aldo Tagliaferri, and included autobiographical texts by non-professional writers. In comparison to the dominant tradition of earlier industrial literature, the main element of novelty in *Tuta blu* is that its author is a working-class writer who decided to recount his story first-hand, without the mediation of professional writers.[3] The voice that says 'I' from within the factory is therefore simultaneously the author, the narrator and the protagonist. This chapter will consider the book's title and its implications, its genre and its main features in terms of both style and content, including discussion of fragmentation, obscene language, irony and reflections on labor, the body and the factory.

Tuta blu's title refers to the blue overalls of the metalworkers, and it alludes metonymically to the narrator's identity as a blue-collar factory worker. Labor and the factory are evoked from the beginning: "La fabbrica dove lavoro è a 6 chilometri da Bari" (The factory where I work is six kilometers from Bari).[4] They seem to constitute the book's thematic core: many of the events recounted in it concern Di Ciaula's experience in the factory. The counterpoint to this is his rural background, an aspect that aligns *Tuta blu* with earlier industrial novels such as Paolo Volponi's *Memoriale* (My Troubles Began, 1962),[5] where the factory is described as a new and troubling object in opposition to the countryside.

A starting point for understanding how *Tuta blu* relates to the tradition of industrial literature in Italy is the question of genre. In his 1978 foreword to *Tuta blu*, Volponi found it difficult to define the book's genre. He fell back on vague definitions such as 'book,' 'text' or 'story.' Volponi pointed out that the most recognizable likeness was with poetry, due to both the inclusion of fragments of lyric within the novel and the lyrical

---

3   There are other examples of industrial literature written by working-class writers, such as Luigi Davì and Vincenzo Guerrazzi. However, Davì's writing was not in conflict with bourgeois literature to the extent that Di Ciaula's was. See Lupo, G. 2011. "Postfazione." In Davì, L. *Gymkhana Cross*. Matelica: Hacca edizioni. 303–313. Guerrazzi will be discussed further below.
4   Di Ciaula, T. 2003. *Tuta blu*. 11.
5   Volponi, P. 1962. *Memoriale*. Milan: Garzanti.

tone that informs many of the prose passages.⁶ In the words of its author, *Tuta blu* can be read as a diary,⁷ whereas critics have classified it as an example of 'letteratura selvaggia' (savage literature). This label was created in the early 1970s to account for a certain type of new literary object which is the closest antecedent to *Tuta blu*: a cluster of texts written by working-class or non-professional writers, often autobiographical. Perhaps the best example of 'letteratura selvaggia' is Vincenzo Guerrazzi's *Nord e Sud uniti nella lotta* (North and South United in Struggle, 1974).⁸ The adjective 'selvaggia' echoes Claude Lévi-Strauss's category 'pensée sauvage' (savage thinking), but it also evokes an idea of instinctive, uncultivated and consciously disheveled writing. With such a constellation of meanings, 'letteratura selvaggia' works as a critical category to describe the attitude of those writers to linguistic experimentalism: an angry vitalism and a refusal to comply with the rules of more institutional and bourgeois literature. Literary critics looked to 'savage' texts with both curiosity and hope, interested in the innovations these texts could bring to exhausted literary standards and traditions.⁹

The framing and grouping of such texts demonstrated a general disorientation and the need to define and circumscribe a literary phenomenon that institutional writers were unsure how to handle properly. Such efforts were seen by Di Ciaula as acts of disempowerment, perpetrated in order to patronize working-class writers, appropriate their voices, domesticate and neutralize their subversive power:

> era una maniera per ghettizzarci ... selvaggi, franchi narratori ... quante ce ne hanno dette!... scrittori naïf, ruspanti ... Avevano paura di noi, i grandi scrittori! Perché noi del popolo le cose le sappiamo scrivere, e anche bene! Con i nostri libri nessuno si è mai annoiato! Scriviamo fra lacrime, polvere, sperma, sangue, sofferenze, gioie timide.

---

6   Besides *Chiodi e rose*, Di Ciaula's most important poetry collection is Di Ciaula, T. 1980. *L'odore della pioggia*. Bari: Laterza.
7   Telephone interview with the author. December 13, 2018.
8   Guerrazzi, V. 1974. *Nord e Sud uniti nella lotta*. Venice: Marsilio.
9   For early discussions of 'letteratura selvaggia,' see the following sources: Giuliani, A. 1975. "Scriversi addosso." *Il Messaggero*. January 31. 3. Golino, E. 1976. *Letteratura e classi sociali*. Bari: Laterza. 179–185.

(it was a way to ghettoize us ... savage, free narrators ... the stuff they said about us!... naive, rustic writers ... Great writers were afraid us! Because we belong to the people, we know how to write and how to write well! No one has ever gotten bored from our books! We write among tears, dust, sperm, blood, sufferings, timid joys.)[10]

According to Di Ciaula, his major revolution was the narrating voice's authenticity as well as its intrinsic legitimacy, set off in opposition to the canonized factory novel of the 1960s. 'Savage' writers were factory workers and thus the only ones entitled to tell their own stories. Their voices deserved to be heard and listened to more than those of professional industrial writers who wrote only about second-hand experience. Di Ciaula's harsh criticism of Primo Levi's *La chiave a stella* (The Wrench, 1978) is revealing: "Il romanzo mi pare sinceramente conservatore e stakonovista [sic]. Tanto valeva che invece di Levi glielo scriveva Gianni Agnelli! [...] Per caso l'operaio 'aristocratico specializzato' Faussone è analfabeta? Non se la sapeva scrivere da solo la sua storia come fa Guerrazzi o il sottoscritto modestamente?" (The novel seems to me truly conservative and Stakhanovite. Levi may as well have let Gianni Agnelli write it! [...] Does the 'aristocratic specialized' worker Faussone happen to be illiterate? Wasn't he perfectly able to write his story by himself, as Guerrazzi and as I do, if you don't mind my saying?)[11]

The bourgeois narration of factory workers' lives was perceived as imposturous as well as a falsification of the real conditions of workers: "Per noi hanno sempre parlato gli intellettuali, e questo non è giusto" (Intellectuals have always spoken on our behalf, and this is not fair).[12] It was exactly

10   Cited in Giacomazzi, G. 1997. "Tematiche e strategie testuali della letteratura 'selvaggia.'" 1010–1011.
11   Di Ciaula, T. 1979. "L'operaio Faussone per caso è analfabeta?" *Lotta continua*. January 15. 5. In *La chiave a stella* (1978), Levi created the character of a travelling mechanical worker who was happy in his own job and praised labor. This sounded inauthentic to working-class writers. But on a different level, Di Ciaula's and Levi's writing – especially Levi's *Se questo è un uomo* (1947) – seem to have something in common: they both write as witnesses, they both involve the reader in ethical reflections and they both reflect on total institutions.
12   Di Ciaula, T. 1978. "Vita da operai. Dibattito tra i lavoratori dell'Alfa." *Corriere della Sera*. June 24. 4. In the same article, the factory worker Alfonso Rossi raises the question of *Tuta blu*'s reception, suggesting that the cost of the book prevented its circulation among factory workers. An annotated edition for schools was

through their rejection of bourgeois literary conventions that the 'savage' writers pursued their revolution in writing.

How did this claim for literary independence, immediacy and dignity translate into form and content in *Tuta blu*? Di Ciaula dismissed the traditional structure of the bourgeois unitary novel and opted for fragmentation. *Tuta blu* results from the juxtaposition of short, typographically separated paragraphs whose montage creates an effect of estrangement. The tone of the fragments is heterogeneous: it ranges from reportage to invective, from satire to document, to lyrical prose. One of the most frequent figures of speech in the text is accumulation, evident in this spontaneous and chaotic accretion of different materials.

The language is spontaneous. In *Tuta blu*, Di Ciaula does not simply mimic the workers' language – he does not 'regress' to the language of the subaltern in order to gain an effect of realism. On the contrary, he uses his own language and charges it with literary dignity. One significant metalinguistic passage addresses this question about halfway through the book:

> Studiosi del movimento operaio, partiti di sinistra, fiumi di libri sul movimento operaio che poi risultano ostrogoti incomprensibili proprio agli operai. Conferenze, dibattiti, tavole rotonde ecc … E i risultati? I risultati sono che gli operai stanno più nella merda di prima. […] È ora quindi di parlare chiaro, tutti debbono parlare chiaro, basta con i linguaggi a doppio senso, chi parla difficile vada a fare in culo chiunque egli sia: deputato, presidente, dottore, avvocato, studioso, comunista, socialista, sindacalista … quindi diffidare dei linguaggi ermetici e borghesi, a morte le chiacchiere, vogliamo i fatti.

> (Researchers of the working-class movement, left-wing parties, loads of books on the working-class movement that are incomprehensible precisely to factory workers. Conferences, debates, roundtables etc … And the result? The result is that factory workers are up shit creek even more than before. […] It's time to speak plainly, everybody should speak plainly, enough with ambiguous languages, those who speak abstrusely should fuck off, whoever they are: deputies, presidents, doctors, lawyers, scholars, communists, socialists, unionists … So let us distrust inscrutable and bourgeois languages, enough with the gossip, we want facts.)[13]

---

    released in 1983: Di Ciaula, T. 1983. *Tuta blu. Ire, ricordi e sogni di un operaio del Sud*. Turin: Loescher.

13   Di Ciaula, T. 2003. *Tuta blu*. 67.

To gain clarity and ultimately truth, language should adhere to facts and real people: it should be open. The editorial spirit of the 'Franchi Narratori' series had already started in such a direction, in an attempt to expand the spectrum of what could be considered literature. For its part, *Tuta blu* includes dialect expressions without glosses or annotations, plus frequent obscene language in an attempt to de-sublimate literature. The same applies to the use of irony – ironic debunking is directed at every expression of authority: "Abbiamo avuto un medico in fabbrica eccezionale [...]. Veramente un brav'uomo. Un gran pezzo di carogna" (We had an exceptional doctor in the factory [...]. Really a good man. A swine).[14] The aim is to create something disturbing and to wrong-foot even allegedly progressive intellectuals.

When it comes to themes and images, Di Ciaula's revolution against the tradition of factory novels is less evident. In *Tuta blu*, a few especially prominent themes emerge: the body and its phenomenology, the dialectic between nature and history and that between the countryside and the factory.

Industrial labor involves first and foremost the body, and it is from the body that the alienation process begins. Healthy bodies are exploited in the factory. They are wounded by hellish machines; they are worn out through repetitive work. They are entirely devoted to production and, by this, exhausted: "Con il mio Schaublin debbo fare il contorsionista, il tornio è piccolino e mia madre mi ha fatto lungo. Per stare un po' comodo debbo infilare le gambe nel cavo del tornio, con una gamba ne inverto il movimento, con il piede aziono la frizione, sembro proprio un suonatore di jazz. Però debbo suonare quando vogliono loro e mai quando ne ho voglia io" (With my Schaublin I have to be a contortionist; the lathe is pretty small, and my mother made me tall. To be even a little comfortable, I have to place my legs in the cavity of the lathe; with one leg I invert the movement, with my foot I press the clutch; I really look like a jazz player. But I have to play when they want me to play, and never when I want to).[15]

14 Di Ciaula, T. 2003. *Tuta blu*. 29.
15 Di Ciaula, T. 2003. *Tuta blu*. 16.

Di Ciaula's reference to jazz seems to open labor in the factory up to the possibility of a playful, creative, even enjoyable side. However, this dimension is immediately rejected and reversed: if the nature of jazz lies in improvisation and freedom, Tommaso's movements at the lathe are instead hetero-directed. The worker's body is not free, even in dreams or love. Sexuality is affected by industrial labor and procreation becomes a nightmare, as it means more people to support:[16]

> Sempre sogni angosciati facciamo noi poveri disgraziati. Sempre l'ossessione del lavoro o del sesso. Per esempio, un altro sogno ricorrente che mi angoscia è questo: sto a fare all'amore con una ragazza, le lecco la fica, le orecchie, il collo, poi mentre sto per ficcarglielo dentro mi prende una paura folle di metterla incinta e subito mi sveglio atterrito.

> (We poor wretches always have anguished dreams. Always the obsession with work and sex. For example, another recurring dream which scares me is this: I am about to make love with a girl, I lick her pussy, her ears, her neck, then, when I am about to shove it in her, I get crazily scared of making her pregnant, and I immediately wake up, terrified.)[17]

The workers' individual and collective unconscious, as much as their body, is colonized by labor. Relationships and sex are mediated and determined by the economic structure of society. In Italy, 1978 was the year of a major referendum that ratified the possibility of legal abortion. Thus, *Tuta blu*, although recounting events occurring in the years before, is imbued with these discourses and was conveniently released at the beginning of 1978, in the conflictual climate of gender awareness and feminist struggles.[18] Di Ciaula sees his body, conversely, as a means of resistance: "Non bastano i partiti e i sindacati per difendere gli operai! Abbiamo questo meraviglioso corpo che potrebbe difendersi da solo. Un corpo sano vale

---

16 For his survey *L'altra cultura*, Vincenzo Guerrazzi asked a sample of factory workers about various aspects of their life. Their answers concerning sexual life are particularly interesting, as they give voice, however indirectly, to women and to the complex gender dimension which characterizes all discourse on labor. Guerrazzi, V (ed.). 1975. *L'altra cultura: inchiesta operaia*. Venice: Marsilio.
17 Di Ciaula, T. 2003. *Tuta blu*. 23.
18 See also Di Ciaula, T. 2003. *Tuta blu*. 96–97.

più di un colpo di cannone" (Parties and unions are not enough to defend the factory workers! We have this amazing body which could defend itself all on its own. A healthy body is worth more than a cannon shot).[19]

Unlike the inauthentic realm of words, the body can become an invaluable instrument of struggle. Factory workers do not need the patronizing and ambiguous words of trade unionists, if only they use their bodies as political weapons. Di Ciaula's political proposal passes through a repossession of voice and body, ultimately of agency:

> Stamattina, io, operaio metalmeccanico, figlio di cgil cisl uil, nipote della flm, come ho messo le mani sulle maniglie del tornio mi sono sentito uno stronzo mi sono messo a gridare come un pazzo che volevo morire, che volevo tornare a zappare la terra, tornare ad incantare serpenti, a mescere erbe velenose, a ballare la pizzica pizzica e la tarantella, che volevo tornare ad inculare le capre.

> (This morning I, a metalworker, a son of the cgil, cisl, uil, a nephew of the flm, when I put my hands on the lathe's handles, I felt like an asshole, I started shouting like a madman that I wanted to die, that I wanted to go back to hoeing the earth, back to charming snakes, pouring out poisonous herbs, dancing the pizzica pizzica and the tarantella, that I wanted to go back to buggering goats.)[20]

Through this desperate cry, the factory worker reclaims what has been taken from him by a double alienation: the alienation of industrial labor and of his voice, seized by intellectuals and unionists.

The anaphoric 'I wanted to go back to' introduces an important dialectic between nature and history, between the rural and industrial worlds. *Tuta blu* is set in southern Italy, where the transition from rural to industrial labor that had largely occurred in the North was still incomplete at the end of the 1970s. Many men and women migrated to the North to work. Di Ciaula, on the contrary, remained in his native Puglia and described its socioeconomic as well as environmental transformation.

Industry here was still in the process of becoming a 'second nature,' as Marx would put it, and this is reflected in Di Ciaula's analogies, similes and metaphors. In the space of two pages, we find two utterly different examples. In the first example, something pertaining to history (broadly intended as the realm of human actions) is compared to a metahistorical detail: "Lungo

---

19   Di Ciaula, T. 2003. *Tuta blu*. 25.
20   Di Ciaula, *Tuta blu*, p. 112.

il percorso le solite gocce di sangue luccicano per terra, sembrano foglioline del melograno" (Along the path, the usual drops of blood sparkle on the ground; they resemble the tiny leaves of a pomegranate tree).[21] Di Ciaula is commenting on a work-related injury. As often happens with descriptions of the body, we are offered here a close-up detail: the drops of blood, which are likened to an image from Di Ciaula's peasant background. The text achieves an effect of estrangement by associating something violent with the tender and innocuous leaves of a pomegranate tree. Two pages later, the process is reversed: "Mi sono avvicinato ad una rosa e mi sono punto ad una spina più tagliente di un truciolo di acciaio di quelli che faccio a quintali nell'officina" (I got close to a rose, and I pricked myself with a thorn that was sharper than one of the steel shavings I produce by the ton in the workshop).[22] A natural element, a rose thorn, is compared to a metal shaving, which appears to be more familiar to Di Ciaula. He is not at ease with nature anymore. He deals better with metal shavings than with a natural object. These two similes reflect well Di Ciaula's dialectic condition, on the threshold between nature and history.

In conclusion, we should put some pressure on *Tuta blu*'s subtitle: "Ire, ricordi e sogni di un operaio del Sud." The book is undoubtedly driven by rage and anger. A reference to wrath also allows for an epic reading in the spirit of the 'Franchi Narratori' series, which in Balestrini's words was precisely to "costruire un 'controromanzo epico,' che desse voce al sotterraneo" (build an 'epic counter-novel' that could give voice to the underground).[23] Nonetheless, *Tuta blu* is also about memories and dreams: daydreams and nightmares, aspirations as well as troubling manifestations of the unconscious. Between epic, lyric and tragic, the book is readable in the name of Di Ciaula's multi-level conflicts, with the all-pervasive economic system, with intellectuals and unionists reproducing that economic system, with machines and objects, with the narrator's own inner world, dialectically suspended between a rural past and an industrial present. But more than anything else, *Tuta blu* is a claim to voice, a claim to agency.

21 Di Ciaula, T. 2003. *Tuta blu*. 47–48.
22 Di Ciaula, T. 2003. *Tuta blu*. 49.
23 Cited in Vadrucci, F. 2010. *Quando la penna esplode di vita. La collana Franchi Narratori Feltrinelli 1970–1983*. Rome: Oblique studio. 23.

PART III

Italian Industrial Film

PAOLA D'AMORA

26 "Casa e lavoro": Southern Labor and the Housing Problem in Eduardo De Filippo's *Napoletani a Milano* (1953)

Towards the end of Eduardo De Filippo's 1953 film *Napoletani a Milano* (Neapolitans in Milan), Don Salvatore Aianiello (played by Eduardo De Filippo himself) succinctly sums up his feelings about the Italian postwar reconstruction effort: "Progress has never set foot here. When it comes, we will leave." The scene takes place in Naples, a city still devastated by the hunger and bombs of the war that has found a way of getting by in the midst of ruins and misery. The protagonists are the occupants of what the voiceover calls "le borgate," a conglomerate of barracks erected with makeshift materials layered atop abandoned buildings.[1] Semiliterate and self-taught, the respected Don Salvatore is regarded as the mayor of his *borgata* (see Figure 9); he provides legal and medical advice to community members in need. Inspired by real events, *Napoletani a Milano* narrates the vicissitudes of the barracks'

---

1   As a term for popular housing in postwar Italy, 'borgata' indicates a type of makeshift and self-made accommodation built on the remains of Fascist-era government projects for residential areas, also called 'borgate,' on the outskirts of big cities. These projects were known as 'sventramenti' (disembowelments), and they led to the construction of 'borgate rapidissime': neighborhoods built quickly with low-cost materials. In the context of *Napoletani a Milano*, 'borgata' indicates the rural, provisional dwellings of the otherwise homeless Neapolitans, opposed both to the Fascist-era projects and the State-funded postwar housing construction (which Pier Paolo Pasolini considered a continuation of Fascist policy. See Pasolini, P. P. 2003. "The Concentration Camps." *Stories from the City of God: Sketches and Chronicles of Rome 1950–1966*. Translated by Marina Harss. New York: Handsel. 174.

occupants, who are forced to evacuate their homes in order to make room for a new industrial plant which, in the film, is owned by the fictional Industrie Lombarde Acciaierie Riunite (United Steel Industries of Lombardy, ILAR). Shot in the northern Dalmine industrial plant, *Napoletani a Milano* subverts the idea of industrialization as an unhampered upward trajectory of progress and development. In what follows, I will contextualize this claim with a comparative analysis of sponsored films from the same period.

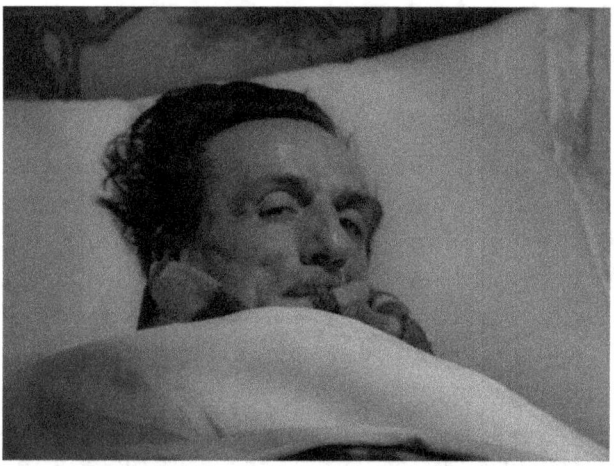

Figure 9. Eduardo De Filippo as Don Salvatore, the unofficial mayor of the *borgata* in *Napoletani a Milano* (Neapolitans in Milan, Eduardo De Filippo, 1953).

The screenplay for *Napoletani a Milano* was written by Eduardo De Filippo himself, the first he conceived of and specifically created for the cinema. Widely known to a national and international audience simply as 'Eduardo,' he was and is considered one of the greatest Italian playwrights. A native of Naples, De Filippo imbued his work with the spirit and language of his city by depicting the day-to-day struggle of the lower classes against deprivation, poverty and oppression. De Filippo was the creative genius behind some of Vittorio De Sica's most well-known films, like the Neapolitan episode of "Adelina" from *Ieri oggi e domani* (Yesterday, Today and Tomorrow, 1963), and *Matrimonio all'italiana* (Marriage Italian Style, 1964), both featuring Sofia Loren and Marcello Mastroianni.² An extraordinarily prolific and versatile actor and writer, De Filippo authored over forty-five plays, dozens of films, poems and short stories in a career spanning more than fifty years, from 1933 to 1984. In addition to *Napoletani a Milano*, De Filippo's postwar cinematic production includes the critically acclaimed *Napoli milionaria!* (Side Street Story, 1950), *Filumena Marturano* (1951), *Marito e moglie* (Husband and Wife, 1952), and *Ragazze da marito* (Girls to be Married, 1952).

Stylistically indebted to the theater, *Napoletani a Milano*'s narrative progression relies on a series of dialogical exchanges that gradually displace the action from the southern Neapolitan setting to the northern industrial city of Milan.³ At first, Don Salvatore and the *borgata* community refuse to make way for the ILAR factory, but then they surrender, leaving only five last-stand occupants to be crushed in the collapse of a decrepit building. The tragedy prompts Don Salvatore to go to Milan in order to request compensation from ILAR for the victims' families. Because there are no legitimate relatives, he instructs dozens of *borgata* residents to pretend. But the ILAR management team refuses to pay, and instead offers Don Salvatore and the group industrial employment. In the lighthearted tones of comedy, the film openly sets out to challenge the widespread stereotype of southern aversion for work – the Neapolitans accept the job to make a good impression (*fare bella figura*) with the Milanese management team and even exceed expectations by saving the factory from bankruptcy.

Relocating from their native *borgata*, the Neapolitans find new housing in Milan and gradually adjust, but do not fully blend in, to their new sociocultural milieu (with the noticeable exception of the factory). From their cheap hotel, the southerners recreate their gregarious lifestyle and preserve

---

2   "Adelina" is based on De Filippo's homonymous play, while *Matrimonio all'italiana* is based on a 1946 play which originally saw De Filippo's own sister Titina in the titular role of Filumena Marturano.
3   On the anti-cinematic nature of De Filippo's theatrical production and its adaptation to film, see Frezza, G. 2007. "Il cinema 'idea' di Eduardo." *Quaderns d'Italià*, no. 12. 37–52.

their language, habits, preferences and, ultimately, values. Translated into a repertoire of nationally intelligible gags, the film capitalizes on cultural and linguistic differences between Naples and Milan, but without ever resolving them. While preserving their individual identities, the Neapolitan and the Milanese workers find common ground in factory occupations and resistance against the closing of the plant. Cultural differences are displaced in a class struggle between the blue-collar workers and the ILAR's management team, which votes unanimously for layoffs. Among the fiercest proponents of closing the plant is Nocera, a Neapolitan lawyer – now part of ILAR's executive board – who has slowly and painfully adjusted to the lifestyle of Milan. Nocera accuses the Neapolitans of speculating on a tragedy, and Don Salvatore attacks him with insults. But by showing contempt for his own people, Nocera exacerbates the class divide by invalidating the equation of geographical provenance with empathetic disposition. The Milanese and Neapolitan workers join forces, take over the factory, reinvigorate production and save jobs.

Fancy housing and the opportunity of labor are instrumental to the Neapolitans' transition from unemployed barrack dwellers to diligent and productive contributors to the national wealth. Released during the postwar reconstruction, *Napoletani a Milano* engages directly with the discourses of modernization and progress from which, at least in the beginning, the Neapolitan characters are excluded. The *borgata* residents consider Don Salvatore an unofficial mayor – their physician and lawyer. He represents the state, its jurisdiction and the institutions even when they are apparently absent. He is the semiliterate authority tasked with translating the eviction notice: "Siamo fregati" (We're screwed), he announces to a concerned crowd anxiously awaiting their sentence. To borrow from Antonio Gramsci, Don Salvatore is an 'organic intellectual' – or a parody thereof, for his literacy is only partial. He can read and he has memorized the laws, but he does not know how to write. Yet on the matters he truly wishes to settle, Don Salvatore's real competence speaks volumes of a Neapolitan resourcefulness that compensates for the lack of proper support and institutions while parodying and undermining all non-sustainable solutions. By acting on behalf of his people, Don Salvatore mediates between the sub-proletarian mass and the ILAR management team, whose language seems to obscure communication (see Figure 10).

"Casa e lavoro": Southern Labor and the Housing Problem 365

Figure 10. Don Salvatore (Eduardo De Filippo) mediates between the sub-proletarian mass and the ILAR management team in *Napoletani a Milano* (Neapolitans in Milan, Eduardo De Filippo, 1953).

Napoletani a Milano portrays labor migration while touching upon stereotypes about the southern ineptitude for real work, a structural assumption of the Southern Question present in foreign and domestic reports about the cultural and economic disparity between the pre-modern South and the modernized North.[4] When the Neapolitans relocate from their barracks to a northern industrial city, they accomplish a radical re-articulation of the perceived and actual Italian territory. One of the film's *leitmotifs* involves Don Salvatore's dream of a train that would connect Piazza Fontana in Milan to the Neapolitan neighborhood of Posillipo. Trains, he claims, overwhelm people's spirit with the very idea of traveling, making them dread distance – he envisions the abolition of city names, replaced only by signs for squares and streets. *Napoletani a Milano* uproots the Southern Question; it is not to *migrate* that the Neapolitans board a train – the working-class mode of transportation *par excellence* – but rather to go to work.

4 See, for example: Banfield, E. 1958. *The Moral Basis of a Backward Society*. Glencoe: The Free Press.

The change in social status from unemployed sub-proletarians to working-class immigrants is intrinsically connected to the southerners' housing problem. They leave their *borgata*, which is not rehabilitated but rather configured as a peripheral, rural area to be forsaken in the pursuit of personal, social and financial betterment. The very term 'borgata' evokes the idea of state funded Fascist-era housing projects which were in many ways continued by the Christian Democrat government during reconstruction. After the Second World War, a parliamentary inquiry into Roman poverty found 95,054 people living in shacks and lacking basic amenities (Paul Ginsborg also reports that between 1948 and 1952, 29,000 housing applications were submitted to the Italian Institute for Popular Housing, which could accommodate a maximum 1,511 people).[5] By 1952, it was clear that employment and unemployment were the cause and solution of the housing crisis. The 'anni duri' (hard years)[6] of working-class life – the first half of the 1950s – saw massive layoffs and explicit repression of the powerful trade unions that had rose to prominence during the liberation and resistance. Afflicted by poverty and threatened by unemployment, blue-collar workers responded to factory lockouts with lengthy occupations and coordinated work-ins that would ensure production.[7] The struggles of these years culminated in defeat due to employer confidence and violent clashes between workers and the police, a situation that produced thousands of court cases, hundreds of wounded individuals and two deaths in major Italian cities.[8]

On the contrary, the optimistic *finale* of De Filippo's film brings about a seemingly positive resolution of class conflict achieved through the sympathetic cooperation of workers, and eventually the police. Summoned to intervene, the *celere* (Italian police's rapid intervention unit for the enforcement of public order) is instructed to shield the factory gate in

5 Ginsborg, P. 1990. *A History of Contemporary Italy: Society and Politics, 1943–1988*. New York: Palgrave Macmillian. 188.
6 Ginsborg, P. 1990. *A History of Contemporary Italy*. 186.
7 Ginsborg, P. 1990. *A History of Contemporary Italy*. 190.
8 In Bologna, legal action against left-wing organizations, in Ginsborg's words, reached "heights which were never to be surpassed in the postwar period." Moreover, between April 1948 and May 1954, "733 people were hurt and two killed" while there were "13,935 trials for offences against public order, and 7,531 verdicts of guilty." Ginsborg, P. 1990. *A History of Contemporary Italy*. 187.

"Casa e lavoro": Southern Labor and the Housing Problem   367

order to prevent women from introducing food provisions into the plant. A casual exchange of insults between a police officer and a worker reveals a linguistic community that becomes a vehicle for class solidarity and disobedience – the *celere* squad is in fact made of working-class youth from southern villages. Worker solidarity thus provides a positive resolution to all conflict, along with comic relief while the Neapolitans' anxiety about relocating to a 'foreign' land are consumed in a demonstration of traditional values like cooperation and mutual help.

In its depiction of internal and external industrial spaces, *Napoletani a Milano* is one of the few fictional, non-sponsored films to move beyond the factory gates.[9] Close-ups of machines complement the film narrative, transitioning to panning shots of a quiet, deserted floor – a space that best represents the lockout of workers and the suspension of activities. After the Neapolitans' plant-rescuing intervention, the machines are triumphantly presented in their full operating potential, lifting and pushing incandescent metal cylinders of considerable proportions. De Filippo shot the sequences inside the Dalmine steel factory located in the homonymous town in the province of Bergamo (Lombardy).

The Dalmine factory is featured in over 500 audiovisual productions preserved by the Dalmine Foundation's historical archive, and present – in part – in the collections of the Istituto Luce (L'Unione Cinematografica Educativa (Educational Film Union), founded in 1924 by Benito Mussolini). Released between the early 1940s and late 1970s, these short films were either part of the Settimana Incom newsreel or produced by the Istituto Luce to showcase Dalmine's activities and its contribution to the progress of national production, as demonstrated in, for example, the eighteen-minute documentary *Arterie d'acciaio* (Steel Arteries, 1953).[10] In fact, Dalmine steel was used to create a 160 kilometer 'artery': a pipeline to bring methane gas to remote rural locations in the Northwest of the country. *Arterie d'acciaio* places emphasis on the primeval, the infernal and the mythological, the prelude to an incredible human enterprise: the domination of nature and

---

9   Giannarelli, A. 1995. "Introduction." *La sortie des usines: Il lavoro industriale nei cento anni del cinema*. Edited by AAMOD. Rome: Ediesse. 9.
10 *Arterie d'acciaio* is accessible at: <https://patrimonio.archivioluce.com/luce-web/search/result.html?query=dalmine&jsonVal=> Last accessed December 10, 2018.

the manipulation of its elements for the creation of something new and pure. The extraction of methane gas from "le viscere della Terra" (the bowels of the Earth) is illustrated with natural landscapes of fields and waters, made to dance with shots from inside the factory, where metal is melted and shaped into its final form. Unusable raw material is transformed into something whole and functional, thanks to the intervention of machines: those structures that are capable of alleviating man's toil and labor, praised and dignified by a quasi-human benevolence.

Dalmine's accomplishment consists in delivering methane pipelines to seemingly impenetrable geographies: an arduous challenge of the natural configuration of the Italian territory. Aerial shots make the viewer aware of the land where excavations take place, explaining in great detail how "lunghe fatiche" (lasting labors) are wisely complemented by "geniali soluzioni" (ingenious solutions). Man's demanding expenditure is presented as an honorable task, for it is directed to a greater good and, ultimately, to the progress of the country. A recurring parallel between the Dalmine factory's work and the natural world amplifies the magnitude of the industrial enterprise – the pipelines run like arteries (as the title suggests) through a living organism, bringing methane, blood and life to the body of the nation. The workers' fatigue is thus removed and sublimated in an act of godly creation.

Arterie d'acciaio is not the only example of an industry- and state-sponsored educational documentary. There are many others, which are contextualized and examined in Paola Bonifazio's recent publication *Schooling in Modernity* (2014). Bonifazio considers the ways in which industrial films responded to a precise political agenda by informing and educating viewers on public and private practices conducive to modernization and industrialization. Bonifazio demonstrates how one Fascist-era documentary – Michele Gandin's *Un villaggio modello* (A Model Town, 1941) – about the town of Dalmine (where the factory was located) evidences continuities between the prewar and postwar period because it attempts to govern the population by blurring the boundary between family and work life.[11] Here, Dalmine is the ideal town for starting a family while working at

---

11   Bonifazio, P. 2014. *Schooling in Modernity: The Politics of Sponsored Films in Postwar Italy*. Toronto: Toronto University Press. 85–86.

the factory and enjoying entertainment through its after-work initiatives. "Industrial films," Bonifazio explains, "focused on the welfare of workers and their families and aimed to demonstrate the company's involvement in the economic recovery of the nation."[12]

While *Napoletani a Milano* touches on family issues only marginally, it speaks directly to postwar labor culture and especially the role of industry in reconstructing the nation. Like many contemporary sponsored films, De Filippo's interprets the relocation of a southern workforce and its prospects for integration in northern industrial cities, all while raising issues of language, class and culture. On the heels of landmark neorealist productions, De Filippo's film effectively espouses narrative devices reminiscent of comedy from previous decades (especially from his collaboration with his brother Peppino) and includes stylistic elements openly evocative of auteur cinema. The *vicoli*, or narrow city streets, and the background of Piazza Mercato become the stage for the Neapolitan sub-proletariat's response to hunger, devastation and unemployment. A stylistically complex work, *Napoletani a Milano* reaches a positive resolution for class conflict when Don Salvatore delivers a timely monolog to ILAR's reception party in celebration of the plant's rescue. A trademark of De Filippo's theatrical production, the conclusive speech that serves to settle all of the play's actors is, in many cases, an address to the audience and their conscience. It is a lesson in humanity, sometimes oneiric in nature but always optimistic for the future. De Filippo's work for the stage and for the screen represents a valuable and dear portrait of the Italian past, engraved and preserved in our collective memory.

---

12   Bonifazio, P. 2014. *Schooling in Modernity*. 5.

ANNA MASECCHIA

27　*Giovanna* (1955) and the Others: Factory Women in Reconstruction Italy

Recounting Female Labor: A Political and Collective Undertaking

The dawn of cinema coincided with an important short film about workers leaving a factory. In the year 1895, the Lumière Brothers opened their *cinématographe* onto the reality that they knew best, bestowing on history bodies and faces as they appeared at the end of the working day. One is still struck by the prevalence here of women: they have a certain pride in their step, some even a wry smile. In any case, these women are not *femmes fatales* or damsels in distress; they are workers in the act of completing the daily toil required by their employment. Although their work brings them daily into a closed space, it also affords them a role outside the domestic sphere: a role that is neither mother nor hearth angel.

Sixty years and two world wars later, the Women's International Democratic Federation (WIDF) promoted an international project that sought to tell the story of working women in five different countries. As the WIDF secretary Marie Claude Vaillant-Courturier wrote on several occasions, the purpose was to offer a tapestry of the daily lives of women in France, Brazil, China, the Soviet Union and Italy, following the model of Joris Ivens' 1954 film *Das Lied der Ströme* (The Song of the Rivers). The WIDF asked Ivens to coordinate the project, titled *Die Windrose* (The Wind Rose), which took the double form of an episodic film for exportation to all capitalist countries and a more militant short film. The long version, preserved by the Bundesarchiv in Berlin, includes an explanatory prologue by Melene Weigel – wife of Bertolt Brecht. Silvia Pagni has summarized the episodes thus:

> L'episodio brasiliano ripercorre l'itinerario di poveri braccianti verso San Paolo; la giovane protagonista Ana induce i suoi compagni a ribellarsi al caporale e alla schiavitù del loro lavoro.
>
> L'episodio sovietico, che in parte fu modificato accogliendo alcuni suggerimenti della Vaillant-Couturier, è basato sul contrasto amoroso fra Nadesha e Geisha: la giovane donna vuole imbarcarsi e abbandonare il suo kolchoz, il suo innamorato alla fine decide di seguirla.
>
> L'episodio francese segue l'insegnante progressista Jeanine nella sua lotta per evitare che le povere famiglie dei suoi alunni vengano sfrattate dalle loro case.
>
> Dopo l'episodio italiano, segue quello cinese a chiudere il racconto. Chen Hsiu Hua è una giovane donna alla guida di una fattoria collettiva nella Cina socialista, gli uomini contestano questo suo ruolo dirigenziale, ma alla fine la donna ottiene un bel raccolto dimostrando le sue capacità.
>
> (The Brazilian episode follows the path toward São Paulo of poor day-laborers; the young protagonist, Ana, incites her companions to rebel against the foreman and against the servitude of their work.
>
> The Soviet episode, which was partially modified according to the suggestions of Vaillant-Couturier, is based on the romantic conflict between Nadesha and Geisha: the young woman wants to depart and abandon her kolkhoz, and her partner decides, in the end, to follow her.
>
> The French episode follows the progressive teacher Jeanine in her struggle to prevent the eviction of her students' families.
>
> After the Italian episode, the Chinese episode concludes the film. Chen Hsiu Hua is a young woman directing a collective farm in socialist China. The men object to her managerial role, but in the end, she obtains a good harvest, demonstrating her ability.)[1]

As is often the case for projects of this sort, the WIDF film was poorly financed and required the collaboration of many militant directors and crew members. Giuseppe De Santis was first recruited for the Italian episode, then Giuliano De Negri, who, in turn, involved Gillo Pontecorvo. Franco

---

[1] Pagni, S. 2014. "*Giovanna* di Gillo Pontecorvo: Un film sulla problematica del lavoro femminile nei documenti d'archivio." *Il Mondo degli Archivi – Studi*. 4.

Solinas collaborated as screenwriter, Mario Caino and Franco Giraldi (former film critic for the Partito Comunista Italiano (Italian Communist Party, PCI) daily *L'Unità*) as assistants, Erico Menczer as cinematographer, Mario Zafred as composer and Giuliano Montaldo as the episode's administrator.[2] Guided by Pontecorvo and Solinas, the Italian group followed a Rossellinian trajectory, adopting many of the aspirations and stylistic devices of neorealism. The rest was a direct result of their surrounding reality: the people of Prato – a city chosen for its factories, but also for its leftist government – strongly supported the film. The Communist-dominated Confederazione generale italiana di lavoro (Italian General Confederation of Labor) union facilitated the film's production.

Directed by Pontecorvo and titled *Giovanna* (1955), it focused on the development of female class consciousness and the women's struggle against layoffs.[3] Factory occupations and 'strikes in reverse' (working without pay) were hot button topics in an Italy still gripped by the crisis of the early 1950s. The Christian Democrat government was pursuing its own pro-American, anticommunist campaign with intimidating and repressive tactics, while the PCI was drifting toward a more centrist position. In 1953, Italian neorealism was 'dyed pink,' so to speak: critics dubbed the dilution of social concerns with elements of comedy 'neorealismo rosa.' Yet even those neorealist films that attempted to remain 'pure' – like *Il sole negli occhi* (Empty Eyes, 1953) by the Soviet realist disciple Antonio Pietrangeli – were dyed 'pink,' for another reason: they presented female protagonists. Pietrangeli's film tells the story of Celestina, a girl from the countryside who goes to Rome to work as a servant. In an Italy moving toward the economic boom, *Il sole negli occhi* weaves the nineteenth-century model of the moralistic novel with modernist innovations to recount the story of young servant women who are unprepared to live outside their familiar environment and thus get lost as soon as they come into contact with a social system devoid of values and devoted to outward appearances and consumption. Before the big screen

2   For a detailed account of the film's planning and production, see: Medici, A. 2002. "Il collettivo cinematografico internazionale de *La rosa dei venti*." *Giovanna: Storia di un film e del suo restauro*. Edited by Antonio Medici. Rome: Ediesse. 17–23.
3   Montaldo, G. 2002. [No title]. *Giovanna*. Edited by Antonio Medici. 140. Pagni, S. 2014. "Giovanna *di Gillo Pontecorvo*."

debut of the busty 'maggiorata' (big sweater girl) in her shameless conquest of a place in the sun (and here we must remember Alessandro Blasetti's 1954 film *Peccato che sia una canaglia* (Too Bad She's Bad)), Pietrangeli's Celestina embodies – in a similar way to the protagonists of Luciano Emmer's 1952 film *Le ragazze di Piazza di Spagna* (Three Girls from Rome) – an Italy in transition, giving shape to a still hopeful female lead.[4] During the Fascist years, the female protagonists of popular cinema were frequently secretaries (private and not so private). But even in the 1930s, the working woman was almost always a 'Cinderella' in disguise; her entry into the workplace was intended as a step towards assuming the role of wife and mother, with so many *risotto* dishes to prepare and no time to waste away from home.[5]

After the Second World War, the role of women in Italian society was completely transformed. Following years of great ferment, the Christian Democrat platform failed to meet women's desire for work, while in 1951 a newspaper like *L'Unità* could dedicate articles to women's work in the rice fields (on the heels of a successful film like Giuseppe De Santis' *Riso amaro* (Bitter Rice, 1949)).[6] Reflections on women's labor began to take on a political meaning. Christian Democrats often emphasized that conceding women the right to work would enable them to purchase ephemeral goods and risked accelerating the race of consumerism, which would lead to what became known as the economic boom.

In this climate, Pontecorvo and Solinas' choice to film inside a factory, representing women by focusing only on the daily activities of labor at an industrial machine, showing female life devoid of both makeup and domestic

---

4   For a discussion of the female body as a marker of national identity see: Grignaffini, G. 2006. *La scena madre. Scritti sul cinema*. Bologna: Bologna University Press. Gundle, S. 2007 *Bellissima: Feminine Beauty and the Idea of Italy*. New Haven and London: Yale University Press.

5   In particular, the reference is to films like *La segretaria privata* (The Private Secretary), directed by Goffredo Alessandrini in 1931, and *Gli uomini, che mascalzoni …* (What Scoundrels Men Are!) directed by Mario Camerini in 1932. For more on working women in Italian cinema, see: Villa, F. 2014. "Fatica." *Lessico del cinema italiano. Forme di rappresentazione e forme di vita*, vol. I. Edited by Roberto De Gaetano. Milan and Udine: Mimesis. 373–432.

6   One such article was published on April 12, 1951. Cited in Sarasina, B. 1997. "Meglio il fascino o l'impegno?" *L'Unità*. August 28.

concerns and conceding nothing to mainstream images of the female body had clear political and ideological power that renders the film – made by men – an important case in the history of women in 1950s Italian cinema.

Truth in Fiction: Speaking Faces, Full of Light

Pontecorvo's career had already hit a turning point a few years before making *Giovanna*, when his passions for politics and photography came together in the making of several documentary films. As a veteran of the anti-fascist resistance, in 1946 Pontecorvo had collaborated with the Associazione nazionale partigiani d'Italia (National Association of Italian Partisans) on the making of Aldo Vergano's film *Il sole sorge ancora* (Outcry), in which he also acted. But it was through still images that Pontecorvo developed his mechanical, filtered and re-elaborated approach to reality. Like some of his contemporaries, he turned to cinema only subsequently, and like those same contemporaries, the moment of revelation was his encounter with Rossellini. Especially *Paisà* (Paisan, 1946), whose sixth episode, set in the valleys of Comacchio, Pontecorvo recalled in a 1953 documentary titled *Missione Timirazev* (Mission Timirazev), which was made with photographs and 16mm film clips. In these years, Pontecorvo completed many projects tied to neorealism: *Porta Portese* (1954), *Cani dietro le sbarre* (Dogs Behind Bars, 1954), *Festa a Castelluccio* (Celebration at Castelluccio, 1955), *Uomini del marmo* (Men of Marble, 1955) and *Pane e zolfo* (Bread and Sulfur, 1956).

A militant intellectual, Pontecorvo sought to capture a dynamic truth in filmic images. His encounter with the activist Franco Solinas – younger, and with firm leftist politico-ideological convictions – gave life to a collaboration that immediately moved in this direction and would find full expression in the 1966 film *La battaglia di Algeri* (The Battle of Algiers).

Those directors, assistant directors and collaborators who, in the aftermath of the Second World War, travelled across Italy in search of particular faces capable of giving reality and truth to everyday lives in a moment of sorrow and hope struck Pontecorvo as entirely epic. Even the producer Franco Giraldi recalled passing through markets looking for the faces of striking women who could illustrate Pontecorvo's veneration for "l'autenticità del volto umano" (the authenticity of the human face). According to Pontecorvo, "più che un attore interessava una faccia che esprimesse una luce, un segreto" (more than an actor, we were after a face that might express a light, a secret).[7] In this way, *Giovanna* fully inscribes itself within the context of neorealism's preference for non-professional actors. As Jacqueline Nacache has shown, the non-professional has the virtue of offering a rather fertile hybridization of reality and art to a cinema that wants to be both narrative and political.[8] With "un piede nella realtà e uno nella finzione" (one foot in reality and another in fiction),[9] the women and female laborers of Pontecorvo's film render the gravity of that historical moment and the shared daily struggle, which for the first time on screen is oriented toward women themselves. If Anna Magnani had already opened the way for female civil protests in Luigi Zampa's 1947 film *L'onorevole Angelina* (Angelina) – other films from an urban and petit bourgeois setting, like Giuseppe De Santis' *Roma ore 11* (Rome 11:00, 1952), followed suit[10] – Pontecorvo's female laborers shift the discursive focus from daily life to class struggle, thus amplifying the dimension of politics. *Giovanna*'s opening epigraph is not to be overlooked: "Questo film è interpretato da un gruppo di operaie tessili" (This film features a group of female textile workers). The collective inspiration animating neorealism is here explicated, and placed, moreover, at the very beginning of the filmic text. The actresses are not credited with their names and surnames, but rather with a collective denomination meant to represent an entire class. The face of the non-professional Giovanna, the 'actress' Armida Gianassi, was selected in the dance hall of a small leftist club and effectively stands in for all Italian

7   Rivenni, G. (ed.). 2002. Giovanna *di Gillo Pontecorvo e gli anni '50 a Prato. Testimonianze e ricordi*. Prato: Mediateca della memoria. 11.
8   On non-professional actors, see: Pitassio, F. and Noto, P. 2010. *Il cinema neorealista*. Bologna: Archetipolibri. 31. Pitassio and Noto take the idea of the non-professional actor as someone just 'passing through' from Nacache, J. 2003. *L'acteur de cinéma*. Paris: Armand Colin.
9   Pitassio, F and Noto, P. 2010. *Il cinema neorealista*. 140.
10 Villa, F. 2014. "Fatica." 384–388.

female workers: a symbol, as Gianassi herself recalled, of so many women "dal doppio lavoro, di giorno in fabbrica e la sera in casa, in famiglia" (with two jobs, in the factory by day and at home with the family by night).[11]

The Factory as a Social Space

Cinema creates spaces that are simultaneously concrete and symbolic. Choosing a location is thus always difficult, especially when the space in question wishes to be, and must be, real. For his location, Pontecorvo chose the real Romita factory in Prato, a Tuscan city about fifteen kilometers northwest of Florence. As Alessandro Bernardi has remarked, the city was chosen not only because

> era uno dei grandi distretti industriali italiani, ma anche perché aveva ancora fabbriche vecchie, di tipo ottocentesco, come quella, che aveva accanto un canale per la raccolta degli scarichi, e che venne utilizzato anche nel film, per drammatizzare la messa in scena delle visite serali dei mariti alle mogli chiuse dentro la fabbrica, che sembra quasi una prigione.
>
> (it was one of the great Italian industrial districts, but also because there were still the old, nineteenth-century factories, like the one with a canal alongside for draining waste, which was used in the film to dramatize the spectacle of the evening visits the husbands paid to the wives closed inside the factory, which seems almost like a prison.)[12]

The representation of factory labor is, of course, one of the film's driving features: the realism of spaces, faces and daily movements both inside and outside the factory contribute to the configuration of a workplace that is there for the action but also to convey a sense of imprisonment. If this is the nature of all factories for all workers, *Giovanna*'s emphasis on women amplifies these dimensions. From this point of view, the film's first

---

11 Cited in Bernardi, A. 2011. *Da "città del silenzio" a città delle macchine. Prato nel cinema degli anni '50*. Florence: Firenze University Press. 14.
12 Bernardi, A. 2011. *Da "città del silenzio" a città delle macchine*. 13.

sequence is vitally important because it takes place *outside* the factory, in the domestic sphere of the protagonist. Early in the morning, before going to work, Giovanna and her husband discuss the layoffs of some female workers, including what they ought to do about it. While glossing this as a political problem, she continues to care for her child, prepare breakfast and prepare her husband for his own day's work. Giovanna's husband is dedicated to politics and the labor union struggles, and he maintains that his wife should not bother with such matters, since they are no business of a woman. But Giovanna is unsatisfied; her gaze embraces the collective, not content to dwell on the conventional spaces of kitchen and bedroom. Indeed, the film's first frame shows exactly this: Giovanna looks outside, facing the camera from behind a glass door where we spy a domestic interior. We can only guess that other workers are already walking toward the factory.

This sequence also ends with Giovanna, who follows her husband outside to wish him a good day, all while holding the baby in her arms. A cut carries us to the next sequence, where a shot from above shows a small stream of female workers hurrying toward the factory. The camera's eye picks out a few women whose discussion revolves around the imminent layoff of some twenty workers. The voice of Giovanna quickly clarifies the rules and limits of the film's regime of representation: what we are seeing is an after-the-fact chronicle of the events presented as though they really happened (and indeed the 'sciopero al rovescio' was a common practice in these years).[13] Giovanna's voice, which seals the narrative truth within a dimension of witness testimony, offers to take us on this journey. This is a defense of the awareness

---

13   Giovanna's voice narrates: "A quell'epoca, una delle forme di lotta tipiche in Italia, dove il problema del lavoro era fondamentale, era lo sciopero a rovescio: contro la chiusura di una fabbrica, cioè, si reagiva occupando la fabbrica e lavorando" (At the time, one of the typical forms of political struggle in Italy, where the problem of labor was crucial, was the strike in reverse: that is, the workers would protest against the closing of a factory by occupying it and working). Pontecorvo describes the inspiration for the script in: Pontecorvo, G. *Giovanna*. 133. Danilo Dolci, who helped clarify the dynamics of the 'sciopero a roverscio' by farmers and factory workers, chronicles his experiences in: Dolci, D. 2011. *Processo all'articolo 4*. Palermo: Sellerio. See also: Cantarano, G. 1989. *Alla riversa: per una storia degli scioperi a rovescio, 1951–1952*. Bari: Dedalo.

and empowerment of a housewife and devoted mother who, closing the factory gate behind her, disobeys her husband to affirm her place in the world as woman, laborer and active human being. As the film unfolds, the space of the occupied factory becomes more and more confining: when the authorities close the street to access the factory, it becomes difficult for the women's relatives to bypass the restrictions and communicate from the outside. As Bernardi pointed out, the canal divides the factory even further from the town, intensifying the dimension of segregation. There are more signs of this progressively carceral isolation, which seems to cast over the women a deplorable sense of guilt, perceived as they are to shirk their duties as angels of the hearth: the machines turn off because there is no electricity; and even worse, the call of their relatives' voices, sounding metallic because they emanate from loudspeakers, arrives from afar as in the long nights of the imprisoned. For the female workers, this is the most difficult moment: as mothers, they are accustomed to a life of labor, but also of physical care for the body of an 'other' – a body they can no longer see, rendered all the more phantasmatic by the sole presence of its voice.

Sounds and noises are an essential part of *Giovanna*. The narrating voice authorizes the film's truthfulness like the voiceover of a documentary while also attesting to the presence of a subject who recounts, in definite neorealist style, an experience both singular and collective. Then there is the sound of the machines, which becomes a symbol of freedom, especially in the open ending. Once again, it is outside the factory that a fully feminist discourse imposes itself: at night, Giovanna slips out to ask the men for help in returning electricity to the machines, and it is here that she expresses all of her acquired awareness. Regarded with admiration, Giovanna is welcomed by her respectful husband and rewarded for her strength. Consequently, she returns to the factory, stronger than before. The electricity kicks in, the looms resume their work and resistance becomes possible once again: the laborers continue their struggle together. All the remaining female workers rush the factory – now framed in a long shot – and even the boss' spokesperson Teresa reaches the inside. It is an open and hopeful ending, accompanied by the sound of the looms and Giovanna's own words: "Trentaquattresimo giorno. Resistevamo ancora e nessuna avrebbe più abbandonato la lotta ormai, nessuna, sino alla fine"

(Thirty-fourth day. We still resisted and no one would abandon the struggle at this point, no one, until the end).

Before the Italian comedy appropriated and deformed the image of the Italian at work, Pontecorvo undertook to tell the story not so much of the toil of labor[14] as of the right to work, which for women has always meant a different centrality in the social sphere and an access, in a political and human sense, to independence from the patriarchy. Women are born fighters, engaged on several fronts, including worker's rights, civil rights and rebellion against the patriarchy, as Cecilia Mangini recounts in *Essere donne* (1965), this time in a documentary that restores the complexity of another profound moment of change and tremendous hope for Italy, namely when the feminist revolt was getting under way. *Giovanna* takes shape out of the will to an organized feminist politics, and even if the film was not realized by women, it is the fruit of the labor of a group of cineastes politically engaged and coordinated by Gillo Pontecorvo: for these reasons, while one cannot define it as a properly feminist film, because in Italy the times were not ripe to assume this kind of perspective yet, *Giovanna* may be said to be the expression of a "pink" neorealism, albeit a very different one, of course, from the comedic sub-genre that is usually characterized with this tag and that was among the most successful trends of Italian cinema at the beginning of the 1950s. Pontecorvo's film is hence a film realized "for" women, but an Italian cinema made "by" women was still to come, and it is (still) to be realized.

Translated by Patrick Waldron

---

14 Fondazione Gramsci PM. PM.1553. For a reflection on the concept of "fatica" (labor, strain, effort) in Italian culture and film, see F. Villa, *Fatica*, cit., who, in relation to comedy Italian style also refers to the study by Edoardo Zaccagnini, *I "mostri" al lavoro! Contadini, operai, commendatori ed impiegati*, Sovera, Roma 2009, that goes, however, in a different direction than the one we are following here. About female labor in the acceptation that interests us here see, at least, F. Loreto, *"Ma j'òm a i capissu nèn!" Le donne nei settori del tessile e dell'abbigliamento*, in *Mondi femminili in cento anni di sindacato*, ed. by G. Chianese, vol. I, Ediesse, Roma 2008, pp. 143–208; M. L. Righi, *Il lavoro delle donne e le politiche del sindacato dal boom economico alla crisi degli anni Settanta*, in *Mondi femminili in cento anni di sindacato*, ed. by G. Chianese, vol. II, Ediesse, Roma 2008, pp. 123–139.

FEDERICO VITELLA

28 Love Is Not a Many Splendored Thing: Pietro Germi's *L'uomo di paglia* (1958)

> Non coglierò questa occasione per spiegare ai lettori e al pubblico che cosa significhi il titolo del mio nuovo film: *L'uomo di paglia*. Molti me l'hanno già chiesto, e sono certo che la stessa domanda finiranno col farsi quanti lo vedranno. Nel film, infatti, non c'è nulla che spieghi in modo palese questo titolo. […] C'è, sì, un uomo la cui storia è strana ed eccezionale solo in quanto è inventata; ma il suo comportamento è comune e semplice, non diverso da quello di tanti italiani comuni e semplici come lui, che hanno una moglie e un'amante.
>
> (I will not take this occasion to explain to the readers and the public what the title of my new film means: *A Man of Straw*. Many have already asked me, and I am sure it will be asked by all those who see it. Indeed, in the film there is nothing to explain this title in an obvious way. […] There is, yes, a man whose story is strange and exceptional only insofar as it is made up; but his conduct is common and simple, not different from that of many common and simple Italians like him, who have a wife and a lover.)
>
> Pietro Germi, 1958[1]

Enter Vides

L'uomo di paglia (A Man of Straw, 1958) began when producer Franco Cristaldi was struck by the aesthetics of Pietro Germi's film *Il ferroviere* (The Railroad Man, 1956) and its resounding success in the cinemas of

---

1   Germi, P. 1989. *Pietro Germi. Ritratto di un regista all'antica*. Edited by Adriano Aprà and Patrizia Pistagnesi. Parma: Pratiche. 35.

small-town Italy, after a poor showing on the first-run urban circuit.[2] Germi and his screenwriter Alfredo Giannetti, who were galvanized by their unexpected success, were already thinking about a new story with a proletarian setting. They wanted their next protagonist to be similar to Andrea Marcocci, the unlucky Roman train conductor in *Il ferroviere* who is swept up in the winds of the economic boom. Germi and Giannetti took the opportunity to team up with the new production company Vides, whose approach to film was less industrial and more artisanal, attentive to creative value and known for respecting the freedom of authorship. The partnership quickly generated a treatment and, within six months, a shooting script, and production began in July 1957 at Cinecittà studios. Together with Germi were trusted collaborators like Leonida Barboni (cinematography), Carlo Egidi (art direction), Dolores Tamburini (editing) and Carlo Rustichelli (music), but also actors from previous films like Saro Urzì, Edoardo Nevola and Luisa Della Noce. These three had played the best friend, young son and wife of the "ferroviere," respectively. Together with Cristaldi was the most reliable of all Italian production companies, Renato Gualino's Lux, which functioned both as a majority production partner (at 47%) and the film's main Italian distributor. Documents preserved at the Archivio Centrale dello Stato (Central State Archive) report fourteen weeks of shooting and a relatively meagre (and partially unused) budget that amounted to about 250 million lira, only thirty million of which was allotted for "artistic personnel" – that is, actors.[3] The film had no famous faces, completely overlooking the dynamics of stardom, and Germi opted for a traditional black-and-white format (1.33:1) in a moment when Technicolor was establishing its international dominance. Such a choice was certainly intended to economize production, but also to advance an anti-spectacular

---

2   On its initial release, *L'uomo di paglia* garnered only 56 million lira, but its overall box office earnings reached 811 million lira subsequently. Levi, O. (ed.). 1977. *Catalogo Bolaffi del cinema italiano (1945–1956)*. Turin: Bolaffi.
3   All financial details are from production documents preserved in the "Cinema" section of the archive: Ministero del Turismo e dello Spettacolo dell'Archivio Centrale dello Stato di Roma (fascicolo CF 2692).

alternative to mainstream cinema, inheriting the noblest principles of neorealism and subordinating form to content.

A Big Love Story

As Germi perhaps imprudently told Fausto Montesanti (curator of a book of materials still indispensable for locating the film in its historical and cultural context), *L'uomo di paglia* was intended as a sort of *Brief Encounter* (David Lean, 1945) in the world of Vittorio De Sica's film *Ladri di biciclette* (Bicycle Thieves, 1948): "una grossa storia d'amore, una vicenda di famiglia anzi, e precisamente un adulterio, ambientato però anziché nella borghesia in un mondo popolare, e da svolgersi in chiave intimista, ma in un clima non romantico, bensì realistico" (a big love story, or rather a family affair, and more precisely, the story of adultery set in a popular environment, rather than among the middle class, and to be developed in an intimate key, in a realistic rather than a romantic mood).[4] More precisely, the film shows how a factory worker named Andrea Zaccardo (Pietro Germi), happily employed in the Roman periphery, engages in a problematic amorous relationship with a young typist named Rita (Franca Bettoia), all while his wife Luisa (Luisa Della Noce) takes their young son Giulio (Edoardo Nevola) far away so that he might recover from a severe pulmonary ailment. Andrea's affair puts the entire family to the test: his abandoned lover commits suicide by dramatically throwing herself from a balcony, while the protagonist is tortured by guilt. In an attempt to heal, but also in a gesture of extreme cowardice, Andrea finds no other solution than to tell his incredulous spouse everything (the consequences of which action I will return to later). The film's title – evocative, picturesque and trenchant – was borrowed from

---

4   Montesanti, F (ed.). 1958. *L'uomo di paglia di Pietro Germi*. Bologna: Cappelli. 20. This small volume contains a plethora of material, including the film treatment and part of the shooting schedule.

T. S. Eliot's poem *The Hollow Men* (1925),[5] and it was chosen over the more commercial proposal *L'amore non è una cosa meravigliosa* (Love is Not a Many Splendored Thing). *L'uomo di paglia* thus alludes to the protagonist's reprehensible behavior: he is easily 'inflamed' by the prospect of spending time with an attractive woman who makes him feel young at forty, but also 'extinguished' just as soon as his wife returns with their son and his clandestine encounters become impractical. Andrea loses himself in an affair that seems completely fortuitous, with the same passivity with which he later dismisses the sorrowful Rita and sheepishly returns to his family.

A Relatable Character

Nonetheless, it would be a mistake to paint Andrea as a 'negative' character. The narration works systematically to 'align' the audience with Andrea, always ensuring full access to his actions, states of mind and feelings, and granting him a presence on the screen that is unrivalled by any other character. The film also works to construct what analytic-cognitive scholars of the 'philosophy of film' call the "moral allegiance" between spectator and character: the spectator's favorable disposition with respect to a fictional character, accomplished on the basis of that character's presumed morality.[6] In other words, the moral evaluation of a character's behavior is strongly influenced by the axiological position assumed by other characters, and Andrea is clearly loved by his wife, idolized by his son, esteemed by his colleagues, with whom he passes a good part of his free time, and supported like a brother by his friend Beppe

---

5   "We are the hollow men / We are the stuffed men / Leaning together / Headpiece filled with straw." Eliot, T. S. 1936. "The Hollow Men." *Collected Poems, 1909–1935*. London: Faber & Faber Ltd. 87.
6   For more on this analytic-cognitive approach, see: Smith, M. 1994. "Altered States: Character and Emotional Response in the Cinema." *Cinema Journal*, no. 4. 34–56. For a more general account by the same author, see: Smith, M. 1995. *Engaging Characters: Fiction, Emotion and the Cinema*. Oxford: Clarendon Press.

(Saro Urzì). Moreover, the film continually calls on the protagonist's own extradiegetic commentary; Andrea looks back upon his actions after the fact and explicitly expresses his malaise, remorse and repentance for the extramarital relationship and for the consequences it brings to the lives of his loved ones. Such narration conditions in real time our own perception of the event and circumstances. Finally, the representation of Andrea as a specialized worker is significantly influenced by the positive characterization of *Il ferroviere*'s protagonist Andrea Marcocci. Both Andreas share an attitude and social position; both are played by the director-actor Pietro Germi himself, with the same tones, accents and style. Yet such moral allegiance between the film character and the audience – an indispensable condition for sharing in Andrea's emotions – does not imply the total approval of his behavior: in the interest of maintaining a moral allegiance with the character, what matters is not that he always act as the audience wishes, but rather that he appear fundamentally 'good,' so to speak.

'The Visible' and the Working Class

Sympathy for a character in a film is not the same thing as moral allegiance, but the audience's growing affection for Andrea Zaccardo is facilitated, if not by shared character traits, certainly by a familiarity with his environment: suburban buses, cheap restaurants, peripheral dance halls, billiard rooms and similar spaces. *L'uomo di paglia* continues strategically in the direction, already outlined in *Il ferroviere*, of an expansion of what is 'visible' in relation to the working class. In comparison to the earlier film, however, *L'uomo di paglia* distinguishes itself, in this respect, for the specific attention it gives to industrial labor.[7] Besides the markedly ideological disapproval of the Communist press (especially the

---

7   With the concept of 'the visible,' the film historian Pierre Sorlin synthesizes what can be represented and perceived within a given historical society. For more, see the following two books: Sorlin, P. 1977. *Sociologie du cinéma*, Paris: Aubier Montaigne. Sorlin, P. 2015. *Introduction à une sociologie du cinéma*, Paris: Klincksieck.

journal *Cinema Nuovo* (New Cinema)), late 1950s Italian film criticism praised Germi's engagement with the 'questione operaia' (working-class question), and today such an insistance must be considered a recognition of the territory that the director mapped out and that had not quite been adequately explored in postwar Italian cinema, neorealism included.[8] In particular, I am referring to three sequences showing the protagonist's workshop, which serve to punctuate the story. Each of these sequences is narrated in a new way: first, Andrea works at the lathe after showing his colleagues his son's hopeful x-ray results; second, he and Beppe examine the new apprentices and Andrea tries to help Rita's brother Gino (Luciano Marin) distinguish himself and obtain employment as a day-laborer; and third, Andrea interrupts the production of a machine part to speak with his wife on the phone – she has just returned to the city, and she asks Andrea to run some errands on his way home. Beyond their specific narrative functions, in all three sequences the width of the camera's shots, the depth of field, the slow pace of editing and the character's spatial movements confer on these segments a descriptive quality, capable of presenting an environment typical enough to seem real, yet generic enough to allow for identification. Clearly the film's ideal spectator is a provincial public that, living in suburban neighborhoods, enjoys shared entertainment and factory employment and understands the Zaccardo family's daily struggles.

The Melodramatic Mode

Nevertheless, the pseudo-neorealism of *L'uomo di paglia* does nothing to hinder the powerful dramatization of its narration. This quality of Germi and Giannetti's cinema was little appreciated by contemporary critics,

[8] For a discussion of the ideological reservations of communist film criticism in the face of the scarce class consciousness of Germi's worker-character, see: Donghi, L. 2016. "Né allineati, né alienati. Gli operai di Pietro Germi ne *Il ferroviere* e *L'uomo di paglia*." *Il cinema di Pietro Germi*. Edited by Luca Malavasi and Emiliano Morreale. Rome: Edizioni di Bianco e Nero. 117–124.

who were annoyed by the story's supposedly low-brow tone and by the apparent abuse of "sentimentalismo" (sentimentalism) and "effettacci" (cheap effects), that is, the strategic recourse to cliché.[9] The film consciously mobilizes the instruments of the melodramatic tradition to optimize the emotive potential of the narrative material and to maximize the participation of a lower-class public. For example, Andrea and Rita's romance responds to the rules of the 'sudden reversal plot' so diffuse in Hollywood genre films and linked to eighteenth-century English sentimental literature (especially Samuel Richardson and his imitators). Moreover, an important role is played by chance, action is deliberately reduced to a minimum and events appear immediately functional as triggers of character (and audience) emotion. The story's pace repeatedly inflects the classic 'tearjerker' theme of the familiar separation and reunion, varying its meaning as the case requires. Andrea and Luisa suffer at first because their detachment is forced, but then it becomes the necessary condition of Andrea's affair with Rita. Finally, detachment is the punishment Andrea must suffer for betrayal, not to mention the pretext of his family's reunion. The greatest plot reversal, Rita's suicide, which follows an initial but provisory 'return to normalcy' in the Zaccardo household, assumes the dramaturgic configuration of a typical 'death notice' scene, when it is Andrea and Luisa's son who must inform the parents, provoking his father's histrionic reaction. While Luisa carries little Giulio home, Andrea wanders around the neighborhood like a ghost, shaken by the news, the hasty explanations and expressions of compassion from the curious bystanders gathered at the site of the tragedy. On Andrea's pallid face, dominating the screen, one can read for the first time his dismay, anguish and humiliation.[10]

---

9 Leftist criticism is still particularly sensitive to this issue. For an historical example, see: Vice. 1958. "L'uomo di paglia." *L'Avanti*. March 12.

10 For more on melodrama from a reception perspective, see: Tan, S. H. and N. H. Frijda. 1999. "Sentiment in Film Viewing." *Passionate Views: Film, Cognition, and Emotion*. Edited by Carl Plantinga and Gregg Smith. Baltimore: John Hopkins University Press. 48–64.

The Issue of the Ending

We could continue at length on the melodramatic structure of *L'uomo di paglia*, but it is the film's much criticized *finale* that still merits some remarks.[11] First, I want to briefly recapitulate the main elements. Andrea recognizes his wrongdoing, and, seeking relief, confesses everything to his wife. This he does while they are at church, and just as his wife is about to offer thanks for having overcome some danger: having intuited something from her husband's strange behavior, she has already tacitly forgiven him. But the new burden is too heavy for her to bear, and it divides the couple again for several months, until New Year's Eve, when Andrea, having hit rock bottom and plunged into crisis, returns home at night to find his wife and son unexpectedly welcome him. In fact, Giannetti wanted to end the film on the day of Rita's funeral, with a stunned Andrea watching the procession from his window, but without his wife so much as suspecting the role her husband played in the girl's suicide. But Germi insisted on an emotional coda, partly with encouragement from a test screening in Parma.[12] What was important was not the relatively light conclusion – tarnished, in any case, by Luisa's voiceover, which reminds the viewer of the gravity of Andrea's actions – but rather the completion and clarification of the protagonist's transformational arc, furnishing Andrea with a microplot of sorrow and affliction to serve a partly rehabilitative function. This meant representing the solitude of Andrea's apartment, his isolation at work, his anxious anticipation of a letter from his family, his calls home in vain hope of an answer and, above all, the drunkenness of New Year's Eve, with his affliction juxtaposed to the extravagant partiers around him, first in a restaurant, then in the streets of Rome, illuminated by fireworks as though it were the middle of the day. Germi was interested in highlighting the sincerity of Andrea's repentance and the depth of his suffering, so that the audience, in agreement with the

---

11 Most reviewers criticized the script for its ending, even when they appreciated the film as a whole. See, for example: P, V. 1958. "L'uomo di paglia." *Il Popolo*. March 12.
12 Pal. 1958. "Il tempo dei telefoni neri", in *Lo Specchio*, March 23.

"criterial pre-focusing" typical of melodrama, might finally be nudged into 'negative' fictional emotions like sadness and compassion, despite the frivolousness of Andrea's behavior.[13] For in Germi's eyes, Andrea is fundamentally a man among many: a normal man fallen into disgrace by some trick of destiny.

An Antimodernist Male Weepy

L'uomo di paglia is a good example of the male weepy: a family melodrama with a male protagonist, designed to provoke an emotional response from an audience that is not exclusively female. By adopting the category of the 'male weepy' – an interpretive label used in the United States to discuss a certain tendency in Hollywood melodrama from the 1950s – I intend to juxtapose Germi's film with some of its contemporaries like Nicholas Ray's *Bigger Than Life* (1956) and Vincente Minnelli's *The Cobweb* (1955), both of which renegotiated models of traditional masculinity in light of the rapid sociocultural changes of their time.[14] Andrea Zaccardo is, however, an antimodernist hero. What is at stake in all the tears spilt for Germi's protagonist is the adhesion to a traditional gender model as it is being put on trial during the sociocultural reorganization of a country. Germi clearly stigmatized such a reorganization in a December 1956 interview for *Oggi* (Today), unambiguously titled "Ho girato 'Il ferroviere' per gente all'antica" (I Made 'Il ferroviere' for the Old-timers). If *Il ferroviere*'s protagonist Andrea Marcocci struggled "contro il Jazz [...] contro il sex-appeal [...] contro il neon [...] contro la pubblicità [...] contro i figli che

---

13   For a discussion of criterial pre-focusing in melodrama, see: Carrol, N. 1999. "Film, Emotion, and Genre." *Passionate Views*. 21–47.

14   Lutz, T. 2000. "Men's Tears and the Roles of Melodrama." *Boys Don't Cry: Rethinking Narratives of Masculinity and Emotion in the U.S.* Edited by Milette Shamir and Jennifer Travis. New York: Columbia University Press. 182–2004. Stella Bruzzi is particularly attentive to this context in her book: Bruzzi, S. 2005. *Bringing Up Daddy: Fatherhood and Masculinity in Postwar Hollywood*. London: BFI.

vorrebbero i pantaloni all'americana" (against Jazz [...] against sex appeal [...] against neon [...] against advertisements [...] against the children who want to wear American-style pants), *L'uomo di paglia*'s protagonist Andrea Zaccardo is a victim of that general relaxation of social mores in the years of Americanization that refused to spare even the least prosperous classes.[15] This is also the reason why Germi himself plays Andrea, why Andrea is characterized in such a sympathetic way, why his context is a popular one and why he demands, first and foremost, pity. At its most profound, *L'uomo di paglia* relates a classic theme typical of the melodramatic tradition: morality under seduction. Moreover, melodrama functions here – by the book – by encouraging the audience to moral reasoning, putting viewers on the spot by making them clearly capable of discriminating right from wrong and conveniently charged with handing out morality permits for the characters' behaviors, beliefs and values. Andrea's (melo)drama is the tragedy of an old-timer, a man with cuffs on his pants who, despite himself, has lost his way. His poor example has the value of a warning aimed at elevating the morality of observers called to put themselves in the uncomfortable shoes of a man of straw.

Translated by Lorenzo Marmo

---

15   Germi, P. 1956. "Ho girato 'Il ferroviere' per gente all'antica" *Oggi*, no. 51. December 20. 31.

VALERIO COLADONATO AND DALILA MISSERO

29 Rocco e i suoi fratelli (1960): Patterns of Labor, Space and Integration

Following the death of their father, the Parondi family migrates from the southern region of Lucania (Basilicata) to the prosperous northern city of Milan, where the eldest son Vincenzo already lives. Luchino Visconti's film *Rocco e i suoi fratelli* (Rocco and His Brothers, 1960) is articulated in five parts – each named after one of the family's brothers – tracing the struggles of adaptation to a new context, where there are opportunities for economic gain and social integration, but also temptations and threats in a modern city that drives the group's members apart. The film is inspired by some tales and characters from Giovanni Testori's collection of short stories *Il ponte della Ghisolfa* (Ghisolfa Bridge), published in 1958.

Rocco e i suoi fratelli was the major hit at the Italian box office in 1960–1961. Around 75% of its earnings came from peripheral and provincial theaters, attended mainly by working-class audiences.[1] A group of factory workers interviewed after a screening affirmed that their favorite character was the hardworking and pragmatic middle brother, Ciro.[2] This is not surprising: Ciro is a factory worker himself, and he is the Parondi family member who best exemplifies a trajectory of successful integration to the city of Milan.[3] Such an experience was very close to the aspirations of many southern migrants, and therefore the character delineates a wide,

---

1   Spinazzola, V. 1985. *Cinema e pubblico: Lo spettacolo filmico in Italia 1945–1965.* Rome: Bulzoni. 255.
2   Pravadelli, V. 2006. "Visconti's 'Rocco and His Brothers': Identity, Melodrama, and the National-Popular." *Annali d'Italianistica*, vol. 24. 241.
3   For a recent critical study of the scholarship on 'integration,' with a specific focus on Milan, see: Foot, J. 2001. *Milan Since the Miracle: City, Culture, and Identity.* Oxford: Berg.

collective process of identity formation. Nevertheless, Visconti paints Ciro with mixed and contrasting tones that only partially overlap with the two prevailing hegemonic contemporary discourses about progress: modernity and integration. On the one hand, there was an emphasis on the conflicts generated by internal migration, focusing on aspects like housing, unemployment and the cultural clash between 'locals' and migrants and with special attention to the supposed 'backwardness' of the South.[4] Such concerns – all present in Visconti's film – were related to concrete social issues, which were perceived as the by-products of modern capitalism.[5] On the other hand, there was the triumphalist image of progress disseminated by the Italian government and entrepreneurs through newsreels, documentaries and illustrated magazines.[6]

Visconti's choice of Milan as a shooting location and the film's treatment of urban space are intertwined with such images, and they strongly influence the ways in which labor is represented. As John Foot has noted, *Rocco e i suoi fratelli* is exceptional in its choice to portray Milan, the capital of Italy's economic boom, almost exclusively through the peripheries and margins.[7] In the film's opening, several episodes foreshadow the process of integration and highlight the movement of transition – from the outside to the inside – that the Parondi family will face. For instance, either through an editing cut or a camera movement, emphasis is put on a physical barrier that separates the interior and the exterior of a space that the characters will

---

[4] It is interesting to note that in 1960 – the year of *Rocco e i suoi fratelli*'s release – two influential texts about the social and cultural issues of integration also appeared: Luciano Bianciardi's essay-novel *L'integrazione* (The Integration) and the sociologist Francesco Alberoni's *Contributo allo studio dell'integrazione sociale dell'immigrato* (Contribution to the study of the migrant's social integration).

[5] That the boom years represent a missed opportunity for fixing some of Italy's structural problems is emblematically expressed in: Crainz, G. 2003. *Il paese mancato. Dal miracolo economico agli anni Ottanta*. Rome: Donzelli.

[6] There are very good examples of this iconography in many Settimana Incom government newsreels, such as "Italia in cammino" (Italy On The March, 1958) and "L'industrializzazione italiana nelle parole di illustri industriali ed imprenditori" (Italian Industrialization in the Words of Illustrious Entrepreneurs, 1961), both available online at: <https://www.archivioluce.com>

[7] Foot, J. 1999. "Cinema and the City: Milan and Luchino Visconti's Rocco and His Brothers (1960)." *Journal of Modern Italian Studies*, vol. 4, no. 2. 209–235.

traverse. The first two shots of the film, after the titles end, show the tracks of Milan's central station: in these two shots the perspectives are similar, but the first one is blocked by the vertical bars of a gate, while the second one is taken from the other side of that same gate. Shortly after, when Vincenzo asks for shelter at the Vecchi brothers' construction company, the camera positions itself outside, then climbs over the fence with an elaborate (and narratively 'superfluous') dolly shot. The Parondi family's arrival to their first apartment is shot in a similar way: the movement of the gate, which opens from the inside, is highlighted by the camera, which follows the family's slow walk through their courtyard, carrying their belongings on a cart under the othering gaze of various tenants, who exchange racist comments and laugh with scorn.

This peculiar treatment of urban space works via a multilayered use of the existing city imagery by privileging transitions and passages, but also by strategically avoiding Milan's most renown symbols of capitalism. Indeed, there are very few clear references to the iconography of the economic boom. The first can be found in the tram journey that takes the family from the station to Vincenzo's apartment: here the lights of the shop windows symbolize the irresistible lure of commodities: "lo spettacolo delle merci che inebria, stordisce e acceca" (the inebriating, dizzying and blinding spectacle)[8] that will contribute to the 'corruption' of traditional family values.[9] Another is the brief sequence set in front of the Standa department store, where Vincenzo is waiting to meet Ginetta. As the first department store chain in Italy, Standa was an icon of mass consumerism, but in Visconti's film it merely functions as a site for a quick and 'forbidden' meeting between two lovers. A third moment linked to the iconography of the boom – and also the most important one for our purposes, as it is the only one explicitly tied to the representation of industrial labor – portrays Ciro in the Alfa Romeo car factory where he is employed.

8   Canova, G. 2000. "*Rocco e i suoi fratelli*: Visconti e le aporie anestetiche della modernità." *Il cinema di Luchino Visconti*. Edited by Veronica Pravadelli. Rome: Fondazione Scuola Nazionale di Cinema. 182.
9   As Mauro Giori notes, in order to achieve this effect, the geography of the city was altered: whereas the tram is supposed to connect the central station to Lambrate, the scene was actually shot in the very central via Manzoni. Giori, M. 2011. *Luchino Visconti. Rocco e i suoi fratelli*. Turin: Lindau.

This is the only time we see Ciro in his professional context, in a tracking shot that lasts no more than five seconds: the camera approaches him as he stands at the assembly line, between two other workers, fastening a bolt to an engine all while engaged in conversation (we cannot hear his words; see Figure 11). It is important to underline that the shot in question constitutes an anomaly with respect to the film's visual style and narrative: these images are evoked through the mother Rosaria's voiceover, as Rocco reads her letter, sent to update him on various family matters.[10] The factory shot is exceptional for several other reasons: it is the only part of the letter that is visually 'translated,' the only instance of nonchronological editing and the only shot without synchronous sound. Moreover, in contrast to the general underplay of locations and symbols typically associated with 'progress' and 'modernity,' this shot is also the only part of the film perfectly compliant with the established iconography of the economic boom, and especially with the epic of labor celebrated by corporate and governmental media outlets.

Figure 11. Ciro (Max Cartier) in his professional context, at the Alfa Romeo assembly line in *Rocco e i suoi fratelli* (Rocco and His Brothers, Luchino Visconti, 1960).

---

10   Rosaria's narration also emphasizes the link between education and Ciro's role as a skilled worker: "He has been hired at Alfa Romeo now that he got his diploma from night school."

In fact, at the time of the film's release, even a fleeting image of factory work would have been sufficient to recall the larger repertoire of visual culture associated with industrial labor. In particular, the assembly line, where the worker employs sophisticated robots to build new models of Italian-designed cars, became a symbol of the advent of modern capitalism. As such, Ciro, the integrated factory worker, embodies aspects of both economic boom narratives: one that warned against negative social effects, and one that celebrated promises of wealth.

The eccentricity of this shot confirms the film's complex and conflicting position with respect to modernization and integration. As Veronica Pravadelli has rightly noted, "Visconti seems to favor the transformation of the southern peasantry into the proletarian class of the northern industrial society,"[11] but at the same time, many crucial aspects of *Rocco e i suoi fratelli* reveal a feeling of 'cultural apocalypse' similar to that found in the writings of Pier Paolo Pasolini and the anthropologist Ernesto De Martino.[12] As a specialized factory worker engaged to the daughter of a local entrepreneur, Ciro is destined to join the middle class and take part in the most profound experience of social mobility in postwar Italy. Nevertheless, this particular experience is only secondary to the film's plot, which uses the melodramatic mode to prioritize the sense of loss and displacement felt by Rocco and Simone.[13] Conversely, Ciro's steps towards integration are placed in the realm of normalcy and everydayness, as when he is shown bowed over his desk, where he studies to obtain his diploma, or when his brothers comment sharply on his graduation.

If Ciro's hard work, determination and sacrifice do not fit the melodramatic frame of Visconti's film, his real centrality emerges when he reveals, in a farewell dialogue with the younger brother Luca, his strong feelings for the Lucania region. This conversation takes place after Ciro has already left the family house and interrupted any viable relationship with

---

11 Pravadelli, V. 2006. "Visconti's 'Rocco and His Brothers.'" 239.
12 Giuliani, G. 2018. *Nation and Gender in Modern Italy: Intersectional Representations in Visual Culture*. Basingstoke: Palgrave Macmillan. 124.
13 On the application of theories of melodrama to Visconti's film, see: Pravadelli, V. 2006. "Visconti's 'Rocco and His Brothers.'" Bayman, L. 2014. *The Operatic and the Everyday in Postwar Italian Film Melodrama*. Edinburgh: Edinburgh University Press.

the group. Ciro represents the eradicated subaltern subject – his choice of integration ends up costing him the affective ties of family life and the chance to return to the South. But despite all this, Ciro still believes in the righteousness of his decision and in the positive effects of progress on his people.[14] He envisions that someday southerners too will understand the necessity of progress and modernity, and at that point he believes that his younger brother Luca will have a chance to return 'home.'[15]

Therefore, in order to fully grasp the implications of Ciro's trajectory, it is necessary to juxtapose it – as the film itself demands – with the full "spectrum of available ways of dealing with integration" embodied by the other brothers.[16] Along these lines, we could also argue that, in order to deconstruct the film's portrayal of industrial labor through the character of Ciro, we should juxtapose it with the other kinds of labor and the respective characters that embody them. In particular, the film articulates different kinds of labor through the eroticized bodies of Nadia, Rocco and Simone, as well as through the multiple gazes that they attract. These three characters are involved in an ill-fated love triangle that fuels the plot's tragic component. But Rocco and Simone also make up (together with the manager Morini) another tragic triangle, propelled by the illusion of easy social mobility and professional success through the sport of boxing.[17] These two triangles are sometimes marked in the film by episodes of 'excess'

---

14   Taking a cue from Visconti's own statements, many scholars have established parallels between this speech and Antonio Gramsci's call for an alliance between northern workers and southern peasants in the struggle to overcome the Southern Question (the North-South divide). For an overview of these interventions, see: Rohdie, S. 1992. *Rocco and His Brothers*. London: British Film Institute.
15   Though this might be seen as pointing to a circular understanding of time and history, Veronica Pravadelli argues that "the absence of the prologue [...] undo[es] the relationships with the ending," thus undermining the circular trajectory and the melodramatic structure. Therefore, "the narrative structure of the film supports integration." Pravadelli, V. 2006. "Visconti's 'Rocco and His Brothers.'" 238–239.
16   Pravadelli, V. 2006. "Visconti's 'Rocco and His Brothers.'" 236.
17   The film highlights the parallels between these two tragic triangles by crosscutting, especially in the famous climatic sequence that juxtaposes Simone's murder of Nadia with Rocco's boxing match. For a recent analysis of this key scene, see: Bayman, L. 2014. *The Operatic and the Everyday in Postwar Italian Film Melodrama 168–171*.

in the mise-en-scène (in typical melodramatic fashion): a combination of close-ups or extreme close-ups, showing an insisted gaze that eroticizes the bodies of the protagonists. This form of stylistic punctuation occurs when erotic desire overlaps with the impulse to confine a given body to its 'professional' identity.

Figure 12. Nadia (Annie Girardot) at the Parondi family home in *Rocco e i suoi fratelli* (Rocco and His Brothers, Luchino Visconti, 1960).

Let us briefly illustrate three such moments. The first occurs in the sequence that foreshadows the tragic love triangle, when Nadia is introduced to the Parondi family through a chance encounter (see Figure 12). She purposely exhibits her eroticized body for the eyes of the brothers, while the editing anticipates this visuality with a double close-up of Rocco and Simone. It is here that, observing the photograph of Vincenzo as a boxer, Nadia instils in the brothers the idea of easy money through a fighting career. A second sequence takes place in the shower, following Simone and Rocco's first training session. Morini emerges out of the dark to stare at the boys' naked bodies with a gaze that replicates the spectator's own (in a prolonged shot that highlights the spectacle of the brothers' nude torsos). Morini nods with satisfaction: a gesture that refers ambiguously to his anticipation of 'professional' success (he realizes that Simone has what it takes to become a professional boxer), but also to the beginning of his erotic seduction.[18] In a third sequence, that of Nadia's rape, Simone invokes Rocco's gaze toward the victim and forces him to see her as a prostitute: "He must see who you are" Simone yells, as he brutally assaults Nadia under Rocco's and the audience's eyes.

The 'ideological work' on labor in *Rocco e i suoi fratelli* can thus be found in the formal and narrative slippage between, on the one hand, male homosexual desire or the love for a prostitute and, on the other hand, the exploitation of physical labor. This is achieved through the "constant parallels the film draws between prostitution and boxing" as different but ultimately akin forms of "exploitation of the body of poorer classes by the richer as a form of social sacrifice."[19] Both forms of labor involve the spectacle of the body eroticized through class difference, and they also carry with them representational generic codes.[20] The conversion of a 'desired' subject into an 'exploited' one also highlights the interchangeability of the commodified body: in the Rocco-Simone-Nadia triangle, the woman is exchanged by the two men, whereas in the Morini-Rocco-Simone triangle, one boxer is replaced by another.

Nadia provides the most explicit commentary on this slippage, she being arguably the only character capable of demonstrating a higher awareness of the conditions of her exploitation. Nadia tells Simone: "If

18 For a close reading of this sequence, see: Bolongaro, E. 2010. "Representing the Un(re)presentable: Homosexuality in Luchino Visconti's Rocco and His Brothers." *Studies in European Cinema*, vol. 7, no. 3. 221–234.

19 Hipkins, D. 2006. "I Don't Want to Die": Prostitution and Narrative Disruption in Visconti's *Rocco e i suoi fratelli*." *Women in Italy, 1945–1960: An Interdisciplinary Study*. New York and Basingstoke: Palgrave. 200.

20 On *Rocco e i suoi fratelli*'s engagement with – but also challenge to – the trope of the female prostitute in postwar Italian cinema, see: Hipkins, D. 2006. "I Don't Want to Die." For a contextualization of the film within the boxing genre, which suggests situating its representation of exploited physical labor and 'othered' bodies (in terms of class and ethnicity) within an international canon, see: Hennessey, B. 2016. "Patterns of Pugilism: *Rocco e i suoi fratelli* (1960) and the Boxing Film. *The Italianist*, vol. 36, no. 2. 214–242.

I understood correctly, you do boxing like I do life." Conversely, Simone seems completely oblivious to the ways in which he has fallen prey to a system designed "to exploit misery in the form of a spectacle."[21]

Unlike Ciro's factory labor, which produces a successful integration, the work of these marginalized bodies does not allow them to transcend their condition of subalternity: Nadia remains trapped in the patriarchal dichotomy of wife and prostitute, Simone's aspirations of social mobility are tragically thwarted and even if Rocco's trajectory seems more successful (he joins the national boxing team), he remains alien to the forms of consumption and lifestyle that distinguish 'modern' Italian masculinity during the economic boom.[22] Several critics have identified this as a potential weakness of the film's declared political intent: Brendan Hennessey, for example, writes that the "brothers and their love interest pressed representations of factory work and workers to the film's margins."[23] Nevertheless, the film's reception at the time of its release, as well as the legacy of *Rocco e i suoi fratelli* as an epitome of life during the economic boom, seem to contradict such concerns. As we argued, Visconti's emphasis on the visual and narrative melodrama is not detrimental to the role of Ciro; on the contrary, it is only against the backdrop of these failed integrational trajectories that the symbolic value of Ciro's industrial labor comes into full relief. Moreover, the film's specificity lies in its ability to fully evoke and intercept, even in the apparent 'marginality' with which it represents factory work, the real centrality of labor as a social experience and the conflicting discourses and images of progress and modernity circulating in Italy at the time.

21 Giori, M. 2011. *Luchino Visconti*. 204.
22 Bellassai, S. 2003. "Mascolinità, mutamento, merce. Crisi dell'identità maschile nell'Italia del boom." *Genere, generazione e consume. L'Italia degli anni Sessanta*. Edited by Paolo Capuzzo. Rome: Carocci. 105–137.
23 Hennessey, B. 2016. "Patterns of Pugilism." 221. Ruth Ben-Ghiat makes a similar argument, remarking that Visconti's film "draw[s] in viewers with an emphasis on sexuality and spectacle that undercuts and threatens to overwhelm didactic messages about the virtues of honest labor and class solidarity." Ben-Ghiat, R. 2001. "The Italian Cinema and the Italian Working Class." *International Labor and Working-Class History*, no. 59. 37.

VERONICA PRAVADELLI

30 *Il posto* (1961) and the Gender of Italian Modernity

Ermanno Olmi's *Il posto* (1961) is a key film in the context of 1960s Italian auteur cinema even though its status in critical and scholarly debates is, and has been, far less relevant than other major films by Michelangelo Antonioni, Federico Fellini, Luchino Visconti and Pier Paolo Pasolini. However, *Il posto* deserves consideration because it contributes in original ways to the (canon) formation of modern cinema as well as to the mise-en-scène of Italian modernity.

Work and working conditions are a major theme in Olmi's career at least up to *L'albero degli zoccoli* (The Tree of Wooden Clogs, 1978). Olmi usually focuses on industrial labor as in many of his early documentaries and *I fidanzati* (1963). *Il posto* is peculiar in this regard as the story of young Domenico Cantoni develops in the context of urban white-collar work. The representation of white-collar labor and upward mobility in early 1960s Milan drive Olmi's peculiar take on modernity as a filmic mode and as a sociocultural scenario.

In "The Modern Cinema and Narrativity" (1966) Christian Metz lists Olmi as one of the authors who, along with Jean-Luc Godard, François Truffaut and Antonioni, subscribe to a fundamental realism, "a certain type of truth [...] that is extremely difficult to define [...] It is the exactness of an attitude, of the inflection of a voice, of a gesture, of a tone [...] [It is] the most precious conquest of modern cinema."[1] Metz's essay pioneered the study of auteur cinema as modern cinema by capturing the peculiarity of this 'new form' vis-à-vis classical cinema in terms of filmic language, style and narration. Along with Metz's essay, David Bordwell's "The Art

---

1   Metz, C. 1991. "The Modern Cinema and Narrativity." *Film Language: A Semiotics of the Cinema*. Chicago: University of Chicago Press. 197–198.

Cinema as a Mode of Film Practice" (1979) and *Narration in the Fiction Film* (1985) have contributed enormously to a definition of art cinema as a peculiar filmic mode. Focusing chiefly on French New Wave and 1960s Italian *cinema d'autore*, Bordwell states that art cinema is a specific mode of film practice "possessing a definite historical existence, a set of formal conventions, and implicit viewing procedures."[2] In contrast to classical narration, art cinema privileges character over plot. As is the case with literary modernist novels, the art film's purpose is to pass judgment on modern life and the human condition. The art cinema protagonist must admit to themselves that they are facing "a crisis of existential significance."[3] Olmi's *Il posto* could well be analyzed along these lines, that is, as a modern film in terms of character, style and narrative. Here, however, I would like to consider these issues from a different perspective, namely, by looking at the way the film tackles the relation between subjectivity, gender and modernity in the age of the economic miracle.

In "Modernity: The Troubled Trope" (2011) Thomas Elsaesser argues that the concept of modernity is "a divided semantic field of force" that has undergone shifts and changes.[4] While 1960s auteur cinema is not one of Elsaesser's main objects of study, I believe that it is possible to reorient

---

2   Bordwell, D. 1999. "The Art Cinema as a Mode of Film Practice." *Film Theory and Criticism*. Edited by Leo Braudy and Marshall Cohen. New York: Oxford University Press. 716.

3   Bordwell, D. 1985. *Narration in the Fiction Film*. Madison: The University of Wisconsin Press. 207. It is important to stress that for Bordwell modern cinema is to some extent the 'filmic version' of the modernist novel as it shares important features such as the crisis of the subject and the critique of modernization and modern life. However, the issue of modernity in cinema only partially overlaps with the critical debate about literary modernism. Besides the authors cited, for an extensive treatment of modern cinema see: Kovács, A B. 2007. *Screening Modernism: European Art Cinema, 1950–1980*. Chicago: University of Chicago Press. For an in-depth analysis of Italian auteur/modern cinema see also: Pravadelli, V. 2017. "Italian 1960s Auteur Cinema (and beyond): Classic, Modern, Postmodern." *A Companion to Italian Cinema*. Edited by Frank Burke. West Sussex, UK: Wiley Blackwell. 228–248.

4   Elsaesser, T. 2011. "Modernity: The Troubled Trope." *The Visual Culture of Modernism*. Special Issue of *SPELL: Swiss Papers in English Language and Literature*, vol. 26. Edited by Deborah L. Madsen and Mario Klarer. Tübingen: Natt. 22.

his thesis in relation to 1960s art cinema, and specifically to *Il posto*, in productive ways. The 'modern' is a troubled concept because it has developed three different terms and fields of inquiry: Modernism, Modernization and Modernity. In the 1950s and 1960s modernism and modernization were seen as antagonistic. Modernism defined avantgarde literary and artistic movements between the end of nineteenth century and early twentieth century and "designated the high-culture critique and ultimate rejection of what modernization stood for: the technologically driven, capitalist modes of consumption and leisure, responsible for creating a mass-culture whose outwardly most striking sign was the cinema, with its immense and near-universal popularity, at least since the end of WWI."[5] The concept of modern cinema developed by Metz, Bordwell and others is part of this line of inquiry since it subtends an opposition between art cinema as high art and Hollywood cinema as mass-culture.[6] Elsaesser further comments that modernity as a separate term is a creation of the 1970s and 1980s due to the rediscovery and reinterpretation of the writings of Walter Benjamin. It is "a compromise formation" that "offered a solution in the antagonism between modernism and 'modernization,' because it bridged the ideological gap between" high modernism, "generally technophobe and elitist," and modernization which supported "technology and popular culture."[7] Modernity has thus a dual nature: on the one hand, "it identifies mobility" as a key phenomenon "of everyday life, and it recognizes that mass production has led to the commodity status of all activities and services." On the other hand, it criticizes some of these tendencies and highlights "the fragmentation, alienation and anomie of the individual in the crowd, and above all, the shock to the senses and trauma to the body that resulted from perceptual overload." Both Benjamin and Siegried Kracauer valued modernity's dual nature and had an interest in popular culture. This version of modernity "had another consequence: it tied modernity to the

---

5   Elsaesser, T. 2011. "Modernity: The Troubled Trope." 22.
6   See also: Deleuze, G. 1989. *Cinema 2: The Time-Image*. Minneapolis: University of Minnesota Press. Kovács, A B. *Screening Modernism*.
7   Elsaesser, T. 2011. "Modernity: The Troubled Trope." 23.

metropolis" and such a conjunction "came to signal epoch-defining changes in consciousness and mental life."[8]

As is well known, the episteme cinema/modernity/metropolis has redefined scholarly work in cinema studies since film historians have been able to redesign the contours of early and silent cinema in original ways. Italian 1960s auteur cinema is a terrific candidate for a reorientation of 'cinema and modernity studies' as the conjunction modernity/metropolis defines in different ways the films of all major Italian authors, including Olmi. To do this, we must think of modernity in light of Fernand Braudel's notion of 'longue durée.' Modernity is a social, cultural and economic phenomenon whose "structure" persists for a long time: "By structure observers of social questions mean an organization, a coherent and fairly fixed series of relationships between realities and social masses. For us historians, a structure is of course a construct, an architecture, but over and above that it is a reality which time uses and abuses over long periods. Some structures, because of their long life, become stable elements for an infinite number of generations."[9]

Il posto can be interpreted in relation to the paradigm of modernity as it foregrounds the dual nature of the subject's experience in the modern metropolis. As early as 1903 in *The Metropolis and Mental Life* Georg Simmel, "the first sociologist of modernity,"[10] sketched a dialectical theory of modernity which is still quite suitable to describe Italy's urban context in the early 1960s. For Simmel modernity is a particular mode of lived experience in which the outer world is incorporated into the individual's inner world. To understand modernity requires "the investigation of the adaptations made by the personality in its adjustment to the forces that lie outside of it."[11] Moreover, modernity "assures the individual of a type and degree of

8   Elsaesser, T. 2011. "Modernity: The Troubled Trope." 24.
9   Braudel, F. 1980. "History and the Social Sciences. The *Longue Durée*." *On History*. Chicago: University of Chicago Press. 31.
10 The definition is David Frisby's. See: Frisby, D. 1986. *Fragments of Modernity. Theories of Modernity in the Work of Simmel, Kracauer and Benjamin*. Cambridge: The MIT Press. 39.
11 Simmel, G. "The Metropolis and Mental Life." *The Blackwell City Reader*. Edited by Gary Bridge and Sophie Watson. Chichester, West Sussex, UK and Malden, MA: Wiley-Blackwell. 11.

personal freedom to which there is no analogy in other circumstances."[12] But it is "the obverse of this freedom that, under certain circumstances, one never feels as lonely and as deserted as in this metropolitan crush of persons. For here, as elsewhere, it is by no means necessary that the freedom of man reflect itself in his emotional life only as a pleasant experience."[13] The 'trope' of modernity can thus be understood only if we accept the co-presence of opposite aspects. Simmel's paradigm is a helpful starting point for discussing the representation of modern subjectivities in 1960s Milan.

For *Il posto*'s protagonist, young Domenico Cantoni, coming from the small rural town of Meda, urban Milan is the place where he can lead a modern lifestyle in which working and having fun mingle according to the structures and schedules of capitalist industrialization and mass entertainment. But there is a negative side to all this as the metropolis can also be the site of alienation and loneliness. The film's position vis-à-vis modernity can thus be assessed by looking at the way Olmi negotiates the two sides of modernity. Though gender is not a conscious theme of the film, in *Il posto*, men and women face modernity in strikingly different ways.

Presented at the Venice Film Festival, *Il posto* is the second film of Olmi's 'trilogia del lavoro' (labor trilogy), along with *Il tempo si è fermato* (Time Stood Still, 1959) and *I fidanzati*. While overall the film did well with both critics and audiences, its reception was actually quite diverse. Catholic film magazines were among the most supportive, while a Marxist journal like *Cinema Nuovo* and the new left journals *Filmcritica* and *Cinemasessanta* were quite critical. The film's neorealist elements – such as Cesare Zavattini's technique of 'pedinamento' (tailing), the choice of non-professional actors and on-location shooting – were highly appreciated but the film's intimate tone was deemed inadequate to give voice to class struggle.[14] Lino Miccichè, for example, official film critic for the Socialist newspaper *Avanti!*, argued that Olmi's analysis of reality only touches "costumi" (lifestyles) and "sentimenti" (feelings) and that it "sembra rinunciare […] all'ideologia

---

12   Simmel, G. "The Metropolis and Mental Life." 15.
13   Simmel, G. "The Metropolis and Mental Life." 16.
14   On the film's reception, see: Buffoni, L. 2003. "La fortuna critica." *Ermanno Olmi. Il cinema, i film, la televisione, la scuola*. Edited by Adriano Aprà. Venice: Marsilio Editori. 95–116.

tout court" (seems to give up ideology completely). According to him, Olmi neither celebrated nor condemned the world of the 'economic miracle,' and it is this "sorta di agnosticità a caratterizzare i limiti, soprattutto ideologici" (kind of agnosticism that defines the limits, especially the ideological limits) of the film. While Miccichè praises other aspects such as "la spontaneità dell'interpretazione" (the spontaneity of actors' interpretation) and "l'autenticità di una lingua non 'sceneggiata'" (the authenticity of 'non-scripted' language), which make Olmi "una personalità tra le più originali degli iniziali anni '60" (one of the most original personalities of the early 1960s), the issue of ideology is the key element of his critique.[15] If we look more closely, in fact, we realize that Olmi is only apparently neutral vis-à-vis industrial neo-capitalism. The film is structured around the dichotomy between the "immagine grottescamente orrorifica" (grotesquely horrific depiction) of white-collar workers and the "teneramente idillica" (tenderly idyllic) world of Domenico and his girlfriend, between "il mondo 'disumanizzato' del lavoro seriale e dell'anonimato impiegatizio" (the 'dehumanized' world of serial work and white-collar anonymity) and "il mondo 'autentico' dei cuori semplici" (the 'authentic' world of simple hearts). The film's narrative and style show that there is "un'alternativa tra i valori individuali e i disvalori industriali" (an alternative between individual values and industrial disvalues). Miccichè concludes that in the age of mature capitalism such an alternative is no longer in place since individual autonomy and authenticity have been offset by alienation and heteronomy.[16]

Miccichè's comment is useful because it reveals how helpful the concept of modernity is. The Italian critic singles out the main features of the film, but his critique subtends a non-dialectical notion of modernity. On the one hand, he believes that outer and inner worlds are separate entities and that the former has neutralized the latter. On the other hand, he reproaches Olmi for believing that inner worlds and individual feelings can be autonomous from outer reality.[17] If we re-inscribe these conceptual tools

---

15 Miccichè, L. 1995. "I cuori semplici di Ermanno Olmi." *Cinema italiano: gli anni '60 e oltre*. Venice: Marsilio. 227.
16 Miccichè, L. 1995. "I cuori semplici di Ermanno Olmi." 227–228.
17 More recently Antonio Daniele has similarly argued that in *Il posto* Ermanno Olmi has "preferito raffigurare la resistenza dei sentimenti alla forza dei mutamenti

within a dialectical mode we can better address the issues at stake. How does *Il posto* address modernity and how does office work shape young men's and women's lived experience in 1960s Milan?

Olmi's biography helps us to broach the issue and provides significant context for understanding the author's worldview. Domenico Cantoni's meanderings from rural Meda to urban Milan in the (successful) attempt to raise his social status through a white-collar job is very close to the director's own biography. Olmi's father was a railroad worker from Bergamo (Lombardy) and later an *operaio* (laborer) for the gas company Edison in Milan; his mother was a peasant from Treviglio (Lombardy) who moved to the city after marrying. Olmi spent his childhood in Bovisa, at the time Milan's largest industrial and working-class neighborhood, and frequently visited his much beloved grandmother, a peasant. After losing his parents, he decided to join the company his father had worked for as an *impiegato* (employee) and to live in the suburb of San Siro with his grandmother. Olmi has admitted that his grandmother was a constant source of affection, support and advice.[18] From the start, his life seemed to be torn between the present and the past, industrialization/urbanization and the rural setting, the city and the countryside. This dichotomy fuels all his cinema and Italian culture at large.[19] Olmi started his career in the early 1950s by making

---

sociali. Che il film dovesse chiamarsi *Due fermate a piedi* ne è la più evidente delle conferme: al regista premeva la prospettiva del breve intrico sentimentale, premeva – ancor di più – che esso avesse la forza di sopraggiungere e di restare a galla proprio mentre i due ragazzi tentavano il concorso" (preferred to show the resistance of feelings instead of social changes. The film's title was supposed to be *Due fermate a piedi* (Two Stops on Foot): the director was more interested in the short sentimental plot and moreover he wanted it to happen precisely while the two protagonists were competing for a position). Daniele, A. 2014. "Italiani e lavoro: il cinema di Ermanno Olmi negli anni del *Boom*." *Annali d'italianistica*, vol. 32. 359.

18   On Olmi's biography, see: Mazzei, L. 2003. "Amori di confine. Olmi fra società industriale e mondo contadino." *Ermanno Olmi*. 20–37.

19   Michele Guerra has stated: "Soprattutto però, [Olmi] è un autore tra la città e la campagna, che in quei primi anni Sessanta voleva dire tra il futuro e il passato, tra la modernità e la tradizione, tra due diverse *necessità*" (But above all, Olmi is an author moving between the city and the country, which in the early 1960s meant between the future and the past, between modernity and tradition, between two different

industrial films produced by Edisonvolta, the company he worked for. From 1952 to 1959 he made about forty short industrial films (according to his own estimate) on the theme of work, working conditions and workers' lives, often placed in natural settings and far away from the metropolis. Olmi was intrigued by the mechanics and rhythms of workers' everyday routine and fatigue. His documentary apprenticeship is evident in *Il posto* – and even more in *I fidanzati* – but the story of Domenico Cantoni recalls first of all Olmi's own biography and family history.

The film maps out a clear geography of human movements, locations and social statuses that depict a phase of transition in Italian economic and cultural life. Such a transition also accounts for the generational gap between parents and children: in the film, a real change from one generation to the other is tangible. Domenico's father lives a harsh life: he works hard to support his family and to pay for his kids' education. At the outset, we learn that Domenico is going to have a job interview in a big Milanese company and that he has just quit studying to give the same opportunity to his younger brother. Both Domenico and his brother can get a white-collar job, a 'better' job than their father. Olmi seems to disagree, since he represents office work as the most alienating activity one can do.

Let us start from the ending. After working as an errand boy for some time, Domenico is promoted to the position of clerk. A fellow worker has died and as a consequence his position, that is, his desk, is free. Being the youngest, Domenico will sit in the last row of the office – a relatively small space with several desks in two vertical rows, a bonsai version of the huge office in King Vidor's *The Crowd* (1928). As Domenico finally takes his *posto* (place), he is framed in close-up: the young man looks mesmerized at the camera while we hear, from off-screen, the incessant and monotonous sound of a mimeograph machine. The alienating sound of the mimeograph machine welcomes Domenico and prepares him for a boring life as getting the "secure job so vaunted by his parents is simply a way of marking time – the interval between the bells for lunch and for dismissal, or in Domenico's case, the interval between adolescence

---

necessities). Guerra, M. 2010. *Gli ultimi fuochi. Cinema italiano e mondo contadino dal fascismo agli anni Settanta*. Rome: Bulzoni. 211. Emphasis in the original.

and retirement."[20] The ending suggests that Domenico's future is sealed from the start. Indeed, his fate is somewhat anticipated in earlier episodes when we are shown his colleagues doing nothing or being bored at work, or at home, in lonely rented rooms. The *impiegato* is for Olmi a loser, a solitary and lonely man living an empty life with no pleasure or affective relations.

And yet, despite the ending and despite the film's author, *Il posto* entails other moments, episodes and situations which complicate greatly the configuration of modernity. The first aspect concerns the representation of the rural setting and lifestyle, which Olmi so enthusiastically embraced in his life – he will spend a large part of his adult life in the small town of Asiago (Veneto). The fact that Meda and Domenico's family life are not presented positively clearly undermines the critique of modern life in the metropolis. Domenico's father is a severe patriarch: he works hard, but shows no affection or warmth for his kids and wife. At home during meals he sits silent at the table and reads the paper hiding his face behind it. The paper works as a screen separating the *paterfamilias* from the rest of the family: such a separation is furthered by a precise mise-en-scène of the gaze. While the father only looks at the paper, he is unaware that the mother and sons exchange complicit looks around him: simply by looking at each other the three take decisions the father is unaware of. We gather he tends to deny permission to his sons to do what they like, like going out after dinner. For Domenico family life is coercive and claustrophobic. And so is Meda. The town is presented with a few shots in the early morning when it is still dark and people, like Domenico and his brother, get out to catch a train. There is nothing interesting or fun in Meda. In the countryside it is impossible to get a good job and to indulge in leisure and consumption, true cornerstones of modernity and modern lifestyles.

In *The Salaried Masses* (1930), a study of 1920s Berlin office workers, Siegfried Kracauer argued that "the decisive difference between the office

---

20   Marcus, M. 1986. *Italian Film in the Light of Neorealism*. Princeton: Princeton University Press. 215.

Figure 13–14. Domenico and Antonietta (Sandro Panseri and Loredana Detto) look through the window shop, look at the city and look at themselves, and the look becomes the active agent fueling desire in *Il posto* (Ermanno Olmi, 1961).

workers and wage laborers, is the different hierarchy in terms of the sphere of consumption. While wage laborers spend more money on food, lodging, heating and clothing – that is, on basic needs – the office workers spend a disproportionate amount of money on culture."[21] The cultural needs include means of transport, but also tobacco wares, pubs, intellectual and

---

21   Koch, G. 2000. *Siegfried Kracauer. An Introduction*. Princeton: Princeton University Press. 42. Kracauer, S. 1998. *The Salaried Masses. Duty and Distraction in Weimar Germany*. London: Verso.

social events, entertainment such as movies, dancing halls and amusement parks, shopping in department stores, etc. Modernity's *long durée* is evident since Kracauer's picture of 1920s Berlin office workers is not very different from that of Olmi: the relations between classes and generations as well as the dichotomy city/countryside in a belated modern country like Italy recall the sociocultural dynamics of early twentieth century in Germany or the United States.

For Domenico, Milan is not only the place to find a good job: the metropolis is the site of leisure and consumption, of strong sensations and thrills, of energy, incessant change and chance. The city also favors romantic encounters: the trope of couples falling in love in the metropolis – *L'amore in città* (love in the city), as the 1953 Italian omnibus film aptly suggested – has been part of (global) film history at least since the 1920s. Referring to Mario Camerini's *Gli uomini che mascalzoni ...* (What Scoundrels Men Are!, 1932), Laura Mulvey has argued that "while *trasporto* is linked to the speed of the city, the constantly shifting patterns of people and transport also convey the contingent nature of the romantic encounter. The city is the site of chance and the casual pick-up is typical of its modernity."[22] After taking the exam, Domenico wanders in the city and crosses by chance Antonietta whom he had met at the firm. The girl is one of three females also applying for the job. Domenico and Antonietta need to kill some time before returning to the firm to continue their examination. While conversing and getting to know each other they stroll in the city, look at window shops and drink a coffee in a bar. Domenico and Antonietta enjoy each other's company as well as the city's energized atmosphere: several shots frame the two within the urban space full of traffic, smoke, construction sites, shops, cafés, etc. The episode is a startling example of how inner and outer worlds blend; the mise-en-scène of the gaze is also telling. Domenico and Antonietta look at the city and at themselves, and the look becomes the active agent fueling desire (see Figures 13–14). The film's modern ethos

---

22   Mulvey, L. 2007. "The Young Modern Woman of the 1920s: A Convergence of Feminist Film Theory and Gender Studies." *La valle dell'Eden*, no.s. 10 and 19. 2007. 22.

is rendered through an emphasis on pleasure and distraction.[23] The camera follows the two with tracking movements as they walk in the city streets. Olmi is close to his characters and registers the emergence of a mutual feeling; at the same time the camera frames the city as a spectacle, for characters and viewers of the film alike. This section is an ode to the city and to modern life and, quite tellingly, one of the few moments of happiness for Domenico. Both characters will get a job, but their schedules will not match and the two won't see each other again for quite some time. They will meet once more only to lose sight of each other again. One can speculate that the film's overall ideology owes a lot to the main character: Olmi has chosen a weak and naïve protagonist who is clearly at odds with city life. But besides Olmi's conscious choices, *Il posto* is riddled with 'unconscious' materials which contradict its main take on modernity. The film is troubled by gender, as women seem much better equipped than men to face modernity.

Let us start from Antonietta. The young girl has grown up in the city and captures immediately Domenico's difference, his retro upbringing. When the young man tells her his name she comments that "è un po' antico come nome" (it is an old-fashioned name), and that, after all, "you are a bit old-fashioned yourself." His old-fashioned manners are clearly a sign of his non-urban upbringing. By contrast, Antonietta is a modern young girl eager to find a job and have some fun. At the same time, she must cope with her controlling mother and knows that her freedom is limited. She tells Domenico that she wanted to study foreign languages but then did not, "tanto poi una donna si sposa" (at any rate, a woman eventually marries) implying that after marriage women are expected to quit working. This is rather ironic, since Antonietta, played by Loredana Detto, will indeed stop acting after this film as a result of her engagement to (and later marriage with) the director. While Domenico is quite out of place in the big city, Antonietta is a smart girl who is accustomed to urban habits and better understands social and gender relations. She also does better

---

23 On this and other aspects of modernity, see Rita Felski's wonderful book, from which I draw the title of my chapter: Felski, R. 1995. *The Gender of Modernity*. Cambridge, MA: Harvard University Press.

Il posto (1961) and the Gender of Italian Modernity   413

than Domenico since she gets an office job right away. Her feelings for the young man might not be as strong as Domenico's for her, but she likes him and is happy to entertain herself with him. When they meet the second time, one can infer she would have expected Domenico to look for her. It is Christmas time and Antonietta suggests she might go to the firm's New Year's Eve celebration if her mother will let her go. Domenico goes to the event full of hope, but the girl does not show up.

Overall, in Antonietta one can seize "the blasé outlook" that Simmel considered the "psychic phenomenon [...] so unconditionally reserved to the city." Being blasé is a defense mechanism allowing modern individuals to protect themselves from the excessive stimulations of the metropolis. "The blasé attitude is an indifference toward the distinction between things;" blasé people never get too close to experience and "every child of a large city evinces [the blasé attitude] when compared with the products of the more peaceful and stable milieu."[24] Domenico falls in love at first sight and gets too involved with Antonietta. But since he doesn't really understand the rhythms and schedules of the metropolis he is unable to devise a way to see the girl again and develop a relationship with her. Antonietta's emotional involvement with Domenico is less strong because in the metropolis young people entertain multiple social relations. Urban dwellers are accustomed to frequent chance meetings and casual encounters and thus cannot react with "the required amount of energy" to each stimulation they experience.[25]

Not only is Antonietta better equipped than Domenico to face modernity and urban life, but female office workers inhabit the workplace in more appropriate ways than men. Though the film devotes large sections and episodes to Domenico's current and future male colleagues, one can capture important gender implications in Olmi's depiction of white-collar work. Male clerks, all middle-aged or closer to retirement, are passive individuals waiting for the end of the workday (and of their lives). On the contrary, women, mostly young girls like Antonietta, seem to enjoy their jobs. They are efficient, polite, active, soberly but nicely dressed. They have

24 Simmel, G. "The Metropolis and Mental Life." 14.
25 Simmel, G. "The Metropolis and Mental Life." 14.

an elegant demeanor and are at ease in the firm's locales: overall they have the right skills to cope with modernity. In *I fidanzati* a colleague of the protagonist, Giovanni, comments that Sicilians "non hanno una mentalità industriale: all'inizio quando pioveva rimanevano a casa e non venivano a lavoro" (do not have an industrial mentality: at first when it rained they stayed at home and didn't go to work), as in the countryside. But this behavior concerns a specific generation: Giovanni's co-worker concludes that young people are probably different. In *Il posto* we face a similar generational gap.[26] Office work is alienating for an older generation. Perhaps, Domenico's fate is not sealed. After all, he might learn to be like the girls of his age and be modern.

---

26 Such a generational gap is confirmed by the one older female office clerk Olmi devotes some attention to: this character's performance on the job is hindered by familial problems and she is consequently often reprimanded by the boss. Trapped in traditional patriarchal structures, she has been clearly denied access to the same chances for emancipation available to younger women.

LUCIA CARDONE

31 Earth and Water: The Market of Bodies in *La ragazza in vetrina* (1961)

At the beginning of the 1960s, the Italian screen was dramatizing the contradictions, the desires and the novel social identities generated by the economic boom, among which emerged unemployment and the migratory movements northward, the central role played by youth and their distance from previous generations and the affirmation of styles of life and transgressive sexual behaviors. *La ragazza in vetrina* (Girl in the Window, 1961) weaves together these themes in the characteristically episodic and intimate progression of Luciano Emmer's films,[1] holding together, not without unevenness,[2] two apparently opposed stories: the terrifying work of Italian migrants in the mines of Belgium and the tender love story between one among their ranks, Vincenzo (Bernard Fresson), and the beautiful Else (Marina Vlady), a girl in the window in the red light district of Amsterdam. In this way, the feature film, which passed the censors with great difficulty,[3] explores two

1   Moneti, G. 1992. *Luciano Emmer*. Milan: Il castoro. Villa, F. 1999. *Il narratore essenziale della commedia cinematografica italiana degli anni Cinquanta*. Pisa: Edizioni ETS. 97–122.
2   Contemporary criticism emphasized, beside the elegance with which the narration is conducted, the fragility of such an openly bipartite and patchy structure. See, for example: Castello, G. C. 1961. "La ragazza in vetrina." *Il Ponte*. February 11. Guglielmino, G. M. 1961. "La ragazza in vetrina." *Gazzetta del Popolo*. April 15. Moravia, A. 1961. "La ragazza in vetrina." *L'Espresso*. May 7. Pellizzari, L. 1961. "La ragazza in vetrina." *Cinema Nuovo*, vol. 10. Visentini, G. 1961. "La ragazza in vetrina." *Il giornale d'Italia*. April 26. Rondi, G. L. 1961. "L'imprevisto. La ragazza in vetrina." *Giornale dello spettacolo*, vol. 17.
3   For more on the censors' treatment, see the relations and repeated requests for revision presented to the Direzione generale dello spettacolo at: <http://cinecensura.com/sesso/la-ragazza-in-vetrina/> (last consultation March 30, 2019). After *La ragazza in vetrina*, because of the bitterness over censorship, Emmer avoided

distinct 'productive landscapes,' and offers itself as an exemplary case study for examining the representation of women and men who work in the nascent 'cinema of modernity.' Consequently, I will reflect here on the way in which the film stages the lives of Italian migrants abroad, especially in relation to the dichotomy between violence in the mine and the violence, fleeting but equally cruel, of sexual exploitation. In both situations, the body and corporality fulfill, naturally, a crucial role: *La ragazza in vetrina* takes the body into account in purely cinematic terms. I would like, indeed, to demonstrate by analyzing in particular the choices enacted by the camera and the strategies employed in the editing how the handling of the gaze and the processes of identification connected to it are able to intimately represent with ineffable carnality the coercive pressure exercised on the characters' bodies and, passing through the film to the flesh, on the bodies of the spectators themselves.

Underground

The film begins with the arrival of the migrants' train: the locomotive approaches along the tracks to the left of the frame, and the Italians descend from the clanking convoy. The camera, placed on the platform, welcomes them into the Belgian night. Dimly illuminated by the lights of the mining town, which we can glimpse in the background, the scene is resolved into a single, lasting shot,[4] articulated at the center by a horizontal pan to keep the new arrivals in the frame. There are four of them, and they come from different regions: all generically southerners, except for Vincenzo, immediately marked out as the protagonist, who is from Veneto. The attitude

---

full-length films for almost twenty years, working in television instead. For more on this, see the following: Moneti, G. 1992. *Luciano Emmer*. Emmer, L. 1997. *Quel magico lenzuolo blu. Divagazioni non troppo serie sul cinema*. Mantova: Circolo del cinema.

4   The duration of this scene is about one minute, fifty seconds.

of the camera from the beginning announces an orientation of the gaze, which will be constant throughout the narration, where the choice of the long take and the fluidity of the camera movements register the actions of the characters, privileging the lasting dimension of time and conceding very little to the conventions of classical editing.[5]

Within the span of three shots, the young Italians reach a tavern, in which they are offered a room and accommodated in the dormitory; a cut swallows up the first sleep of the miners and carries us to the entrance of the mineshaft,[6] where the new arrivals present themselves to the shift manager and are swiftly given shovels, lamps and helmets. Disoriented, Vincenzo and the others gird themselves with a somewhat forced gaiety, and the camera follows them, rendering the operations preparatory to their descent through rather prolonged takes. Such an insistence on the long take accentuates the feverish development of their activities, and it is accompanied by a sound close-up of ambient noises: we hear primarily the squeaking, the clicks, hissing and whistles of the siren, which emphasize the mechanical nature of the industrial space.

At the shift change, however, the meeting by the elevator with the team that has just finished its shift assumes a different rhythm: as the grate opens, the dark, sooty faces of the miners coming out are shot in close-up, while the editing fractures into four shorter but dynamic shots, which juxtapose the still clean skin of those who are about to descend into the mine with the bronzed, shiny skin of the others. The greeting of the veterans is jovial, and the entrance of the novices into the cage is rapid. With the click of the bars that close, the camera finds itself, together with the miners, inside the elevator and gives way to the unnerving experience of plunging into the mine, which constitutes the dramatic heart of the entire story. Beyond

---

5   The result is a film whose style is modern, thanks also, as the screenwriter Rodolfo Sonego recalls, to the freedom of action and improvisation that Emmer cultivated during production. In the spectacular underground sequence, such a freedom was possible thanks also to the studio reconstruction of the mine environment. For more on this, see: Sanguineti, T. 2015. *Il cervello di Alberto Sordi. Rodolfo Sonego e il suo cinema*. Milan: Adelphi Edizioni.
6   This is the fifth shot of the film, over which appears the title, written in white characters.

its duration in absolute terms,[7] this macrosequence constructs a fleeting temporality, which seems to extend indefinitely, disorienting both the characters and the spectators. The immersion into the darkness is rendered all the more distressing by the shrieking of the ropes, which encumber the soundtrack, and moreover, by the tilting upward of the camera, which dives down into the well, showing only a mouth of light, which becomes smaller and smaller at the center of the otherwise black frame. One has the sensation of a vertiginous freefall, obtained by the combination of the movement of the elevator with the use of zoom. The descent is marked both by the voice of the foreman who calls out the different depths as they are reached, and, on a visual level, by the increasingly thick darkness. The tension is increased by the editing, which alternates among the mute faces of the miners and that of the assertive team leader. Having arrived at the bottom, at 1035 meters underground, the camera seems to acclimate itself and begins to move in a fluid manner, with more expansive frames. The environment is dark and hostile, pervaded by cables, looming beams and by tracks over which heavy carts full of coal suddenly dart, threatening to crush the miners. The constant deafening noise, together with the flashes of the helmet lights that show, all of a sudden, the darkened faces of the workers distorted by their strain, and most of all the slightness of the ever-narrower trenches, casts the characters into an infernal dimension. The spectator is plunged into such a dimension too, thanks to the handling of the gaze and the processes of identification that derive from it.[8] Here, the psycho-physical involvement of the audience is obtained through both the

7   This sequence lasts eighteen minutes and is composed of 101 shots. It opens and closes with two pairs of specular shots, which signal the plunge into the mineshaft and the unhoped-for re-ascent, using the motif of the black frame pierced by the opening of the elevator, preceded (in the descent) and followed (in the escape) by a brief glance outward from the cage.
8   Metz defined the mechanism of the viewers' identification by distinguishing two typologies: primary and secondary. In virtue of the first, the spectator identifies herself with the apparatus, with the gaze of the film (and consequently with the camera) which allows her to look at the world represented on the screen; only later, with the secondary identification, the spectator sees herself in the characters who inhabit that world. Metz, C. 1982. *The Imaginary Signifier: Psychoanalysis and the Cinema*. Translated by Celia Britton. London: McMillan. 45–52.

mobility of the camera and an employment of the editing that enhances the pathos. Consider, for example, the path that Vincenzo undertakes to reach his post: the narrow gallery is reduced to a tunnel in which the young man is forced to crawl; his slow progress, impeded by innumerable obstacles, is captured without breaks in an uninterrupted tracking shot. The result is a markedly long sequence, capable of capturing, in the foreground, what emerges from the darkness, obstructs the field of view and prevents one from seeing with ease, thus translating the rugged advance of the protagonist in visual terms (see Figure 15).

Figure 15. Vincenzo (Bernard Fresson) is plunged in the dark, narrow, infernal dimension of the mine in *La ragazza in vetrina* (Girl in the Window, Luciano Emmer, 1961).

A few hours into Vincenzo's first day of work, the mine suddenly caves in. The editing assumes the task of transmitting the drama and the fear of impending danger. Indeed, if the stylistic regime prevalent in the film is, as I have said, that of the long take and of a tenacious continuity, this section takes an entirely different approach. The sequence articulates itself in a rapid juxtaposition of shots.[9] These shots are for the most part close-ups

9   The sequence of the cave-in lasts around thirty seconds and is composed of twelve shots.

and very dark, and consequently, they are quite difficult to decipher. Yet they prove to be effective in their swift succession. The clarity of the exposition of events is sacrificed in favor of a skillful emotional construction, obtained, we might say, rhythmically; in this way, the frames, indistinctly filled with details of bodies and objects, arrange themselves through editing into a discordant and syncopated score, voiced by the screams of the men and the crashes of falling rocks.

A fade to black signals the end of the collapse and the beginning of a period of waiting: the darkness and the silence which follow are broken only by the helmet lights and by the coughing of one of the miners buried alive. Here begins a sequence of episodes composed of five scenes, each broken up by a fade to black. These are the only underlined transitions present in the film,[10] and they are not used to punctuate a precise chronology, but, on the contrary, serve to emphasize the mysterious passing of a fleeting, terrifying temporality. In the darkness of the frame, one can scarcely make out the shapes of faces, the whites of eyes, and the glow of the lips of the three remaining workers trapped underground. Federico (Lino Ventura), the most skilled, displays an unhinged optimism and encourages Vincenzo and Mustafà; he even sings and assures them he will be able to keep track of the hours as they go by. This is not the case, though: the minutes and days run together, but the rescuing excavation team does not arrive. The darkness becomes increasingly thicker, the perception of space tightens, and the buried men start to lack air as well as lose hope of salvation. The struggle wreaks havoc on their bodies, as they lay exhausted, caked in sweat, mouths agape trying to draw any leftover oxygen. Thanks to the insistence and proximity of the camera, which seems to hunt and almost loom over the characters, even the spectator feels a very strong, disturbing sense of claustrophobia and shortness of breath.

The final fade to black is riven by the beam of light from the elevator shaft, marking the ascent of the survivors and overturning the theme of descent which had opened the sequence. The rescue operation is utterly erased

10   There is, in fact, another fade to black, which closes the romantic digression shared by the two lovers in Else's seaside house. This fade, however, obeys the conventions of filmic syntax, as it canonically signals the fact that the characters have spent the night together.

with an ellipsis. This choice signals once and for all the representation in infernal terms of the industrial extraction of coal. A horrifying kingdom, despite the mechanization, the mine is an untamable space, a place in which the rationality of technology, the expertise of specialized work and human compassion have no business. For this reason, we are not witnessing the liberation of the survivors, and indeed we learn nothing of the slain miner left behind, nor have we any idea of the seriousness of Mustafà's wound, as he cries strongly while he is carried away in an ambulance. For Vincenzo, who has understood all this and has decided to return to Italy, all that remains is to follow Federico for a weekend of excitement: Amsterdam, with its exotic and erotic promises, will perhaps allow him to forget the horror of the mine.

On the Water

The extraordinary multimedia impact of Alessandro Blasetti's documentary film *Europa di notte* (European Nights, 1959)[11] resounds in the sequence dedicated to Amsterdam, tinged with a bizarre Nordic exoticism, in particular in some passages dedicated to dancing. Consider, for example, the corpulent women who dance in the various bars, or the grotesque scene in the gay bar, into which an unwitting Federico,

---

11   On the success and resonance of the films of Blasetti, and more generally of the 'mondo movie' genre, see the following: Spinazzola, V. 1985. *Cinema e pubblico. Lo spettacolo filmico in Italia 1945–1965*. Rome: Bulzoni. 318–336. Goodhall, M. 2006. *Sweet & Savage: The World Through the Shockumentary Film Lens*. London: Headpress. Dalla Gassa, M. 2014. "'Tutto il mondo è paese.' I mondo movies tra esotismi e socializzazione del piacere." *Cinergie*, vol. 5. 83–95. De Berti, R. 2016. "*Europa di notte*. Lo spettacolo di rivista nell'Italia del boom economico." *L'avventura*, vol. 2. 337–356. Previtali, G. 2016. "'Siamo fatti così: aiuto!' La rappresentazione dell'identità di genere nei mondo movies." *Bianco e Nero*, vol. LXXVIII, no. 585. 74–82. On the representation of sexuality in Italian cinema, see, in general: Maina, G. and Zecca, F. (eds). 2014. *Sessualità nel cinema italiano degli anni Sessanta: forme, figure e temi*. Special issue of *Cinergie*, vol. 5.

already drunk, enters. The bodies marked by excess and the exhibitions of nonheteronormative sexualities punctuate the film like real attractions, in both a cinematic and touristic sense. In any case, the city is introduced by a kind of postcard image: from an elevated position, the gaze of the camera caresses the evening traffic of a canal-side street in a morbid panoramic shot, while in the background jut the towers of a church and the Dutch flag waves through the air.

The night is clear and still, and the two miners, having escaped from the collapse, begin their exploration, walking through the neighborhood where what is for sale is sex. The camera captures in a long take the protagonists' aimless steps, until they stop in front of a window inside which a young woman is sitting. "Quella è in vendita" (She's for sale) explains Federico, "ti metti d'accordo sul prezzo e la comperi [...] come un chilo di parmigiano!" (you come to an agreement on the price [...] and you buy her like a kilo of parmesan cheese!) They keep walking, and he continues his coarse banter, commenting on the girls in display one after another. The camera frames these girls without interruption, illuminating their movements, glances and postures: one smiles, another knits, another, somewhat older, beckons their attention by lifting up her arms, while another lowers a basket from a window, as if by routine, on an improvised pulley. Federico's commentary is vulgar, comradely, and attests to a certain familiarity with prostitution that seems to bring the two men closer:[12] "Questa è roba di lusso!" (This is some fancy stuff!) And again: "Quella lì fa almeno venti chili a coscia, scommetti?" (That one there weighs at least twenty kilos a thigh, wanna bet?) Vincenzo is quiet until Else appears. The camera shoots her with a fluid movement, running up from her ankle to her face, taking in her delicate features. "Bell'*occio*, bella coscia, bella bestia" (Pretty eyes, pretty thighs, a pretty beast) observes the young man from Veneto, spoiling the elegance of the image and consigning it to the realm of flesh for sale, somewhere between brothel and butcher.

---

12 This custom should not surprise, given that the closing of brothels had occurred in Italy only a few years earlier, in 1958, in the wake of the troubled Merlin law. For more on this, see: Bellassai, S. 2006. *La legge del desiderio. Il progetto Merlin e l'Italia degli anni Cinquanta*. Rome: Carocci.

The film offers an anachronistic representation of the Amsterdam sex industry, and Emmer himself later emphasized this residual quality of the film, revealing how, in those years, the windows were "ormai destinate alla soddisfazione dei desideri sado-masochistici" (by that point dedicated to the satisfaction of the sadomasochistic desires) of foreign tourists.[13] Showing little interest for this new landscape, with *La ragazza in vetrina* the director chose to depict prostitutes that still resembled the ancient consolers of sailors far from home. Moreover, they appear rather different from the figures we find circulating in contemporary Italian cinema:[14] they have a rather cold appearance, they wear elegant and almost proper clothes, from which emerge their long legs and white skin, similar to porcelain. Some are slender and slim, while others have big hips, full breasts and matronly features. Together they make up a sort of catalogue of conjugality, albeit temporary and venal. Their windows mimic certain coy dollhouses, and if we look closely, these Nordic women embody, more than transgression, the dream of 'normal,' comfortable, and petit bourgeois happiness. In the tidiness of their exhibition parlors, the women appear as domestic sirens, who promise wayfarers the joys of the homeward journey, offering "l'illusione di un focolare e di una compagna subito pronta a fare l'amore" (the illusion of a hearth and of a companion ready to make love immediately).[15] Perhaps, in Else's window, Vincenzo is searching for (and finds) just this: a safe place, like a home, where he might overcome the trauma of the mine. Indeed, what occurs between the miner and the prostitute has more to do with love than with carnal exchange. Emmer tells the story of their love in an elliptical fashion, focusing on their linguistic misunderstandings and leaving the principal developments of their relation unspoken. Such a choice translates into a specific kind of gaze: the film uses camera movements and editing to present the fragility of normative exchanges and

---

13 Emmer, L. 1997. *Quel magico lenzuolo blu*. 81.
14 See the following two sources: Hipkins, D. 2014. "The Fantasy Harem: Prostitution and the Battle of the Sexes in Italian Film Comedy of the Early to Mid-1960s." *Cinergie*, vol. 5. 45–57. Hipkins, D. 2016. *Italy's Other Women: Gender and Prostitution in Italian Cinema, 1940–1965*, Oxford: Peter Lang.
15 Emmer, L. 1997. *Quel magico lenzuolo blu*. 81.

valorize the mysterious encounter, the "amore puro" (pure love)[16] taking place between them. One need only think of the failure of the first dialogue between Vincenzo and Else, mediated by the bossy words and gestures of Federico: the protagonists are unable to understand each other and cannot make plans for the weekend. The scene is put together in a classical way, with a series of frames that adhere perfectly to the common practice of shot/countershot, only to underline the communicative inexpediency of canonical editing conventions. The rules of cinematic syntax are ineffectual: their rigidity is unable to account for what is really happening, that is to say, the nascent emotional tension destined to shatter current relational models. On the contrary, the characters grow closer precisely in a common swerving from language, their communion occurring in that uncertain space which both exposes them to the risk of misunderstanding but also allows, in the end, the authenticity of understanding. This is clear during the resplendent sequence on the beach, with a strong wind blowing, and the camera holding the two young characters stubbornly together, no matter the words that are spoken (see Figure 16). Here, on the one hand, an irritable joust begins between them, caused by their exchange and the trivial responses of Vincenzo, who does not know how to respond to Else's coded requests. On the other hand, the proxemic insistence of the camera and the joint point of view shot, which unites the gazes of the two characters onto the sea, that vital element and link to "a fantasy of female eroticism,"[17] are all signs of a hidden and irreversible process that has been triggered between them. The dynamic of such a process is relegated to an off-camera intimacy that spills back into the story in an allusive manner, but influences the ending in a profound way.

16   Some reviewers discuss this pure love. See, for example: Pellizzari, L. 1961. "La ragazza in vetrina." 365.
17   Bruno, G. 1993. *Streetwalking on a Ruined Map: Cultural Theory and the City Films of Elvira Notari*. Princeton: Princeton University Press. 99.

Figure 16. Vincenzo (Bernard Fresson) and Else (Marina Vlady) on the beach in *La ragazza in vetrina* (Girl in the Window, Luciano Emmer, 1961).

Indeed, in order to remain with Else, Vincenzo ultimately decides against returning to Italy. Federico's coarse and closing quip – "Sai come la chiamano al mio paese? La prugna!" (You know what they call that in my parts? The plum!) – ought not deceive: it is not the pulsating shadow of sex but a luminous act of love that pushes Vincenzo to descend back into the darkness of the mine, to submerge himself in the pernicious maze of tunnels together with his silent companions and the rats, emblematic figures of a looming destiny, which the camera laconically records.

Translated by Patrick Waldron

ANDREA MARIANI

32 The Working Class in Post-Neorealist Italian Cinema: Times and Politics of Mario Monicelli's *I compagni* (1963)

On the evening of October 25, 1963, Mario Monicelli's new film *I compagni* (The Organizer, 1963) premiered at Rome's Palazzo dei Congressi convention hall. The occasion was the inaugural meeting of the thirty-fifth National Conference of the Partito Socialista Italiano (Italian Socialist Party, PSI). Monicelli, a Socialist himself, was seated next to Party secretary Pietro Nenni. Lino Miccichè reported for the Socialist newspaper *Avanti!*:

> I temi e i personaggi de *I compagni* costituiscono infatti un'assoluta novità rispetto all'intera storia del cinema italiano che, spesso fervidamente presente rispetto alla realtà attuale, finora non ha mai saputo, né potuto, guardare indietro agli anni in cui l'Italia unita si andava formando e nei quali la lotta tra progresso e reazione aveva ancora aspetti primordiali. È in quegli anni che nacque il Partito Socialista Italiano ed ebbero inizio le prime grandi lotte operaie.
>
> (The themes and characters of *I compagni* indeed constitute an absolute novelty with respect to the entire history of Italian cinema that, often enthusiastically present with respect to today's world, has not yet figured out how – nor has it tried – to look back on the years when Italy was being formed, when the struggle between progress and reaction was still of a primordial nature. It is in those years that the Italian Socialist Party was born and the great working-class struggles began.)[1]

The next day, the same newspaper *Avanti!* printed the following:

> La prima giornata congressuale si è chiusa con la proiezione dello stupendo film *I compagni* di Mario Monicelli, sottolineato, nelle sequenze più significative, da grandi

---

1 Miccichè, L. 1963. "Cominciò così la lotta dei 'compagni.'" *Avanti!*. October 25. 5.

applausi e salutato, alla fine, da un'interminabile ovazione. Anche questa proiezione ha un suo significato di profondo rinnovamento: la più giovane delle arti è venuta al nostro Congresso come a documentare con le immagini delle prime lotte del Socialismo, l'ampiezza di un arco storico insostituibile se si vuol comprendere un secolo di vita italiana.

(The first day of the conference concluded with the projection of Mario Monicelli's stupendous film *I compagni*, accompanied in its most meaningful scenes by fervent applause and greeted at the end by an interminable ovation. Film projection has its own profoundly transformational significance: the youngest of the arts entered our Conference as if to document, with images of Socialism's early struggles, the scope of an historical development critical to the understanding of a century of Italian life.)[2]

But such an emphatic account conflicts with Monicelli's own memory of the evening: "Ero seduto vicino a Nenni quando scoppiarono i tafferugli. Dovettero interrompere la proiezione. Lui si scusò molto. Si respirava un clima di grandi conflitti. Era in corso una spaccatura all'interno del partito" (I was sitting near Nenni when the scuffle broke out. They had to stop the projection. He apologized profusely. There was great conflict in the air. The party was splitting from the inside).[3] Disregarding the questions of credibility raised by two such diverging memories, the thirty-fifth National Conference of the PSI is a topic rife with political and ideological tensions that express one of the most delicate periods in the anguished history of the Party's identity.

On the national political stage, the year 1963 announced a restless dynamism for Catholic, Communist and Socialist fronts. The elections of April 28 were marked by a difficult alliance between Aldo Moro's Democrazia Cristiana (Christian Democrats, DC) and Nenni's PSI: the DC opened to the (first) center-left government with the objective of creating a reformist version of capitalism, founded on the progressive liberation of the PSI from the Partito Comunista Italiano (Italian Communist Party, PCI). But as elections approached, alliances were all but certain: "La DC restava divisa tra riformatori e conservatori. […] Il PSI assunse posizioni sempre più polemiche, di fronte alla scelta democristiana di rallentare il processo

2   Buttitta, P. A. 1963. "Perché tanta gente." *Avanti!* October 26. 10.
3   Monicelli, M. 2016. *La commedia umana. Conversazioni con Sebastiano Mondadori.* Milan: Il Saggiatore. 116.

riformatore" (The DC was still divided between reformists and conservatives. [...] The PSI assumed evermore polemical positions in the face of the DC's choice to slow down the reform process).[4] The elections of 1963 were traumatic and the governing alliance did not help either party: the DC lost some votes and the PSI barely broke even, while the PCI scored big.

Tensions continued to mount in the PSI, and the following year the Party's left wing broke off to form the Partito Socialista di Unità Proletaria (Italian Socialist Party of Proletarian Unity, PSIUP). This new party was home to those militants who had opposed direct collaboration with the DC during the first center-left government, preferring instead a left-wing alliance in opposition together with the PCI.

Given such historical premises, it is not surprising that a film like *I compagni* aroused wide-ranging reactions, nor that a portion of the audience strongly disapproved. Using cinema to represent the birth of working-class and socialist movements in Italy meant rubbing salt in the traumatic and decisive wounds that defined the historical identity of the Party.

I compagni tells the story of a group of textile factory workers in late nineteenth-century Turin. These are the years of Prime Minister Francesco Crispi's reactionary politics,[5] "un periodo in cui la neonata classe operaia italiana lavora in condizioni di intollerabile sfruttamento e povertà, mentre il movimento socialista e sindacale, combattuto in tutti i modi dal potere economico e politico, sta muovendo i primi passi ed è ancora debole e isolato" (a period when the fledgling Italian working class labored under conditions of intolerable exploitation and poverty while the socialist labor union movement, attacked on all sides by economic and political powers, was taking its first steps, weak and isolated as it was).[6] Following the latest industrial accident, a product of exhausting labor conditions (a worker

---

4 Formigoni, G. 2016. *Storia d'Italia nella Guerra fredda (1943–1978)*. Bologna: Il Mulino. 309.
5 Crispi was Prime Minister from 1887 to 1892, then again from 1893 to 1896. His politics were remarkably authoritarian, characterized by conflicts with socialist movements and labor unions and by a number of rebellions. Crispi's reactionary politics lead to the dissolution in 1894 of Filippo Turati's budding PSI.
6 Consoli, G. P. 2011. *Mario Monicelli: La storia siete voi. Commedia, Guerra, lotta di classe*. Rome: Carocci. 33.

dozes off at the end of a fourteen-hour shift and loses his hand), the bosses begin to hear requests for shorter days and better compensation, like breaks and salaries (see Figure 17). Nevertheless, these voices go unheeded until an intellectual (a professor) arrives and organizes them in the direction of a long-term strike. After thirty days and a violent clash with strikebreakers from the adjacent neighborhoods, the workers are at the end of their tether. But the professor incites them to one last act of revolt and they move in with the intention of occupying the factory. The revolt is suppressed by the army: the professor is arrested and the workers are shot at, killing one. At the end of the film, the defeated workers return to the factory, but the seeds of future revolts have been planted.

Figure 17. Prodromes of the strike in the factory in *I compagni* (The organizers, Mario Monicelli, 1963).

While *I compagni* presents itself as an historical film, its close relation to the politics and culture of the 1960s reflects a clear stylistic and poetic choice on the part of the director. Monicelli stages an attentive balance of philological research and contemporary sociopolitical currency that underscores a crucial period of Italian cinema after neorealism. In what follows, we wish to linger on these very aspects.

(Post-Neorealist) Italian Cinema between History and Style

During the late 1950s and early 1960s, the Italian film industry underwent a process of reorganization. A 1949 law promulgated by Undersecretary for the Ministry of Arts Giulio Andreotti, which was designed to protect the Italian industry from American competition, expired in 1954 and was quickly followed by an administrative void, a decline in production and the first significant drop in ticket sales since the end of the war. Law number 897 of July 31, 1956 allowed for a swift recovery, characterized by a significant change of strategy on the part of the surviving production companies, now intent on moving beyond the overabundance of low-cost productions and toward high-quality films. "A partire dal 1962 si assiste non solo al definitivo sorpasso del cinema italiano su quello americano [...] ma anche allo sfruttamento sempre più intensivo delle prime visioni" (Not only did Italian cinema finally outpace the Americans, but starting in 1962 it also began to exploit the practice of film premieres with growing intensity), something that ultimately rewarded "le realtà minori che decidono di investire in produzioni prestigiose e quindi remunerative anche sulla lunga distanza, come fanno la Vides di Franco Cristaldi" (minor players who decide to invest in productions that were prestigious and therefore profitable, if only in the long run, like Franco Cristaldi's company Vides).[7] The Turinese Cristaldi was the producer of *I compagni* and one of the most interesting figures in the panoply of new Italian cinema, especially for his role in *auteur* films that addressed the heritage of neorealism. Starting in the mid-1950s, Cristaldi produced films by Luchino Visconti, Francesco Rosi, Monicelli, Pietro Germi, Gillo Pontecorvo, Antonio Pietrangeli and Luigi Comencini. As András Bálint Kovács has noted, Italian cinema was undergoing a process of stylistic and aesthetic transition:

> The year 1950 was an end and a beginning. It was the end of political neorealism (although De Sica's *Umberto D.* appeared only in 1952), and the beginning of a slow

---

[7] Di Chiara, F. 2013. *Generi e industria cinematografica in Italia. Il caso Titanus (1949–1964)*. Turin: Lindau. 30.

process where stylistic and narrative principles of neorealism were gradually emptied of their social contents to become mere surface effects ready to absorb and express different intellectual contexts other than the political. Neorealism did not disappear; it went through a substantial metamorphosis.[8]

I compagni thus belongs to a period of change in Italian cinema, and yet it is an original, autonomous and even ambiguous film.

When it was released in 1963, *I compagni* had a rather poor commercial showing. But years later, at the end of the 1960s, it found a new mass audience in the young militants of protest movements who were in a better position to appreciate Monicelli's political aspirations.[9] Such historical dyscrasia speaks volumes of the originality and innovation of using genre cinema to energize the politics of everyday life. In 1963, *I compagni* seemed to upset both politicized audiences – who were in the midst of their own minor crisis – and the general public, which was still celebrating the economic boom and conforming its tastes to that complex transformation of neorealism that Kovács summarizes in a stylistic model emptied of any social, ideological or moral considerations. Neorealism was altered through folkloristic aestheticization – like in Comencini's *Pane, amore e fantasia* (Bread, Love and Dreams, 1953) – psychological overdetermination – like in Federico Fellini's *8 ½* (1963) – and the radical evacuation of character attributes and the enhancement of the dramatic visual power of landscapes – like in Michelangelo Antonioni's films.[10]

Monicelli's film does not fit into any of these categories. Thanks to its meticulous construction of space, the realism of *I compagni* is charged with a political and sociological function that is inscribed in the characters themselves. It creatively reworks Roberto Rossellini's lesson that "the environment does not exist outside of the character, and vice versa, the character is always depicted in relation to his environment [...]. Morality, so to speak, was encoded in the environment."[11] Monicelli's set designer Mario

---

8   Kovács, A. B. 2007. *Screening Modernism: European Art Cinema, 1950–1980*. Chicago and London: The University of Chicago Press. 255.
9   Consoli, G. P. 2011. *Mario Monicelli*. 70.
10 Kovács, A. B. 2007. *Screening Modernism*. 256.
11 Kovács, A. B. 2007. *Screening Modernism*. 263–264.

Garbuglia said as much: "Basti pensare alle case degli operai, ognuna con le sue caratteristiche, che denotano chi aveva radici contadine, chi veniva da un'altra cultura, chi era operaio già da due generazioni" (Just think about the workers' houses, each with its own characteristics, which indicate who was of peasant origins, who came from another culture, who had already been a worker for two generations).[12]

Another decisive contribution came from the cinematographer Giuseppe Rotunno. On the one hand, Rotunno's camera wants to document the iconography of the period by correlating archival images with photographic reproductions in a way that seems to evoke the social documentaries of Jacob Riis (Monicelli searched high and low for an authentic location, finally settling on a nineteenth-century factory in Zagreb, Croatia). But on the other hand – and on Monicelli's explicit request – Rotunno systematically avoided the temptation to shoot a period piece of purely historical reconstruction. As the costume designer Piero Tosi recalled: "Monicelli era terrorizato di fronte ai pericoli di un film in costume: voleva che lo spettatore si scordasse che il film era in costume [...]. Si trattava di immergersi fino in fondo nell'ambiente in modo da conferirgli la naturalezza di cose che avvengono oggi" (Monicelli was terrified by the prospect and dangers of a costume drama: he wanted the audience to forget that the characters were in costume [...]. He wanted the audience to be completely immersed in the world of the film, so that it took on the natural feeling of things that happen today).[13]

It was this relation to contemporary Italian society that confirmed *I compagni*'s place in the new Italian cinema. A recent study by Luca Barattoni has made it possible to clarify at least two central elements from the development and production of *I compagni*, both of which are of an historical and sociological order. "One of the most traumatic events in the process of cultural change taking place between the mid-1950s and the end of the economic boom, circa 1962," Barattoni writes, "was the desacralization of

---

12   Cited in Pintus, P. (ed.). 1958. *Commedia all'italiana, parlano i protagonisti*. Rome: Gangemi. 88.
13   Cited in Baldelli, P. (ed.). 1963. *I compagni di Mario Monicelli*. Bologna: Cappelli. 47–48.

the family and, extensively, of the bourgeoisie as a class and as a provider of stable values for the nation."[14] Moreover, he continues:

> the new cinema of the 1960s was less interested in processes of nation-building. Rather, many of the seminal works were prescriptive and nation-constructing, elaborating mirror images of an Italian society that was celebrating its disengagement from and inadequacy for a violent modernization (Antonioni) or even venturing into a nightmarish, post-human territory ([Marco] Ferreri). Neorealism was also about forging a nation: post-neorealist film is already about individuals and micro-communities after the failure of such an enterprise.[15]

In essence, neorealism functioned by excavating Italian identity via processes of subtraction, while the new Italian cinema functioned – under the influence of the ideological and stylistic necessities of various national cinemas and the European or international new 'waves' – by piling up fragments (individual or communal) of a society negotiating its identity and its position in the modern world. In Barattoni's words, this was "a constant struggle to define Italian identity and 'mission' in the modern, industrialized, westernized world."[16] Family and the negotiation of an industrialized modernity in relation to national identity are also broached by Marcia Landy, who has foregrounded Italian cinema's function in the formation or problematic negotiation of a national identity.[17]

As Alan O'Leary and Catherine O'Rawe have polemically suggested, genre cinema and 'national-popular' culture were part and parcel of this process.[18]

14 Barattoni, L. 2012. *Italian Post-Neorealist Cinema*. Edinburgh: Edinburgh University Press. 194.
15 Barattoni, L. 2012. *Italian Post-Neorealist Cinema*. 193.
16 Barattoni, L. 2012. *Italian Post-Neorealist Cinema*. 50.
17 Barattoni, L. 2012. *Italian Post-Neorealist Cinema*. 53. Barratni refers here to: Landy, M. 2000. *Italian Film*. Cambridge: Cambridge University Press.
18 O'Leary, A. and O'Rawe, C. 2011. "Against Realism: Italian Film Criticism." *Journal of Modern Italian Studies*, vol. 16, no. 1. 107–128. Monicelli himself insisted on the idea of 'national-popular' culture: "La commedia è sempre stata nazional-popolare [...]. In Italia c'è questa vena popolare che è sanguigna, violenta, grassa, sbracata e quindi anche volgare" (Comedy has always been national-popular [...]. In Italy there's this popular streak that is sanguine, violent, carnal, slovenly and hence also vulgar). Cited in Borghini, F. 1985. *Mario Monicelli. Cinquant'anni di cinema*. Pisa: Master. 9.

Family, Modernization and Comedy

In the words of Mariapia Comand, "se il neorealismo invoca un personaggio in stretto rapporto con il tempo e con l'ambiente, oltre che con altri elementi narrativi (personaggi e oggetti), gli scrittori della commedia all'italiana onorano questa lezione poiché immergono il personaggio in una fitta rete di relazioni, all'interno del film e tra il film e il mondo a cui esso appartiene" (if neorealism invokes a character in close relation to a time and place, not to mention to other narrative elements (characters and objects), the writers of the *commedia all'italiana* [comedy Italian style] honor this lesson insofar as they immerse their characters in a thick web of relations, both inside a single film and between each film and the world to which it belongs).[19] In *I compagni*, such a tangle of identity-based and sociohistorical ties is incorporated in the language of comedy, but without losing anything of its effect and indeed gaining in both concentration and incisiveness. As an account of a small community of workers that is also a small family community, Monicelli charges his film with the symbolic value of both a class (the proletariat) and a social institution (the family). From the start, the organization of life in the factory and the transformations of the social life of the individual in response to industrial modernization have a detrimental effect on the family dimensions of the proletariat. The film tellingly opens with a family portrait that is already compromised: the absence of a household head means that all responsibility falls on the oldest son, Omero. Through tragic and hopeless irony, Omero is an emblematic character and a fallen symbol of the struggle for the recognition of basic rights. The world of industry piles victim upon victim, which in turn blocks all social mobility. Omero is forced to renounce his studies in order to support his mother, sister and younger brother, just as his younger brother will himself be forced to leave school to take the place of the dead Omero. The chaos of the family as a social institution accompanies the entire film: the dehumanizing rhythms of factory labor force a father to see his son only during lunch breaks – "quando esco di casa dorme, quando rientro a casa

---

19   Comand, M. 2010. *Commedia all'italiana*. Milan: Il castoro. 9.

la sera tardi dorme" (when I leave home, he's asleep; when I come home late at night, he's asleep). Family members are picked off by community tragedies (the absence or disappearance of Omero's father prematurely forces the boy to take up a position of authority) while social roles are frequently inverted by the conventions of comedy, which skillfully animates the historical narrative (the son asking the professor about his old father's behavior in school, in a perfect reversal of Edmondo De Amicis' 'socialismo dei professori' (socialism for professors)).[20]

The construction of gender in *I compagni* deserves further attention, even if it is largely beyond the scope of this chapter. Monicelli's female characters are the harbingers of an emancipation: the proud prostitute Niobe (Annie Girardot), Omero's sister (Raffaella Carrà), the demagogue and proto-unionist Cesarina (Elvira Tonelli) and the circumspect little migrant Gesummina (Anna di Silvio). The prostitute Niobe is particularly relevant in this regard: on the one hand, she reclaims a social practice denounced even in popular working-class songs (daughters forced to 'sell themselves' rather than earn a respectable paycheck, an extreme solution adopted only for survival that in *I compagni* severs the ties of the traditional family). On the other hand, she links up to the bourgeois world of the factory bosses, whose family relations are already strained by their usual practice of extramarital affairs. If it is true, as Marcia Landy has argued, that "the national community is forged through the assumed common bonds of unitary language, the nation as a family [and] conceptions of gender and ethnicity that rely on an identity of origins, culture and interests," then the comic approach of *I compagni* must burst the radical base asunder.[21] The Italian horizon of identity is dominated by the uncertainty produced by fractures in the body of the 'family-nation' and by a proliferation of regional cultures and languages that are still in need of interaction and translation (quite literally). Moreover, if the social institution of the family begins to take on water, then even the Kingdom of Italy and the fact of belonging to it start to capsize. In this regard, the representation of political affiliation in

---

20   See: Levy, C. 2001. "The people and the professors: socialism and the educated middle classes in Italy, 1870–1915". *Journal of Modern Italian Studies*, Vol. 6, No. 2. 195–208.
21   Landy, M. 2000. *Italian Film*. 1.

I compagni is provocatively incongruous: the workers write "a morte il re" (death to the king) on the chalkboard, then arrive at a factory occupation carrying the flag of the monarchy.

In the long run, for Monicelli, comedy always steals the show. As Mariapia Comand has noted, "alla base della commedia all'italiana ci sarebbe il nucleo problematico dell'identità sociale, il conflitto tra il singolo e il suo ingresso nell'arena pubblica" (the *commedia all'italiana* is founded on the central problem of social identity, the conflict between the individual and their entrance to the public arena).[22] In this regard, *I compagni* confirms the rule as a collective film: Monicelli's star (Marcello Mastroianni) steps back to make room for a plural, even communitarian, protagonist (see Figure 18).

It is the fate of such a collective protagonist to end in tragic defeat, a loser battered by history in the best traditions of popular comedy.

Translated by Jim Carter

Figure 18. Professor Sinigaglia (Marcello Mastroianni, far right), leader and inspirer of the strike's organization, makes room for a plural protagonist in *I compagni* (The organizers, Mario Monicelli, 1963).

22 Comand, M. 2010. *Commedia all'italiana.* 9.

ELEONORA LIMA

33 The Factory as a Work of Art and an Alienating Force in Michelangelo Antonioni's *Deserto rosso* (1964)

Watching Michelangelo Antonioni's *Deserto rosso* (Red Desert, 1964), it is almost with reluctance that we allow ourselves to appreciate the majestic shapes of the industrial complex, the intricate net of the electric trellis, the stark contrast of colors that the polluting fumes, the steaming pipes and the cargo ships create. For all the beauty displayed on the screen, the viewer knows that the industrial society and its technological ethos are responsible for the protagonist Giuliana's sense of displacement and alienation as well as for the destruction of the natural landscape on the outskirts of Ravenna (Emilia-Romagna).[1]

However, aesthetic appreciation and a sense of unsettlement are not mutually exclusive: *Deserto rosso* indeed depicts the industrial environment as a source of alienation, since the new way of life it establishes amplifies Giuliana's neurosis and makes her effort of regaining mental health and balance more arduous, but the film also celebrates it for its iconic beauty. The closing scene is possibly the most powerful in visually summarizing this tension: Giuliana, having just reassured her son that no birds will fly through the poisonous smoke of the factory chimneys, walks with the

---

1   Giuliana and the landscape or Ravenna are indeed the two main characters of *Deserto rosso*. The protagonist, married to the owner of a petrochemical plant on the outskirts of Ravenna, has just been released from a mental health clinic when she meets Corrado, an old friend and collaborator of her husband. Giuliana finds in Corrado someone who understands her struggle to adapt to modern life, hypostatized in the image of the polluting factory. But as the man leaves for Patagonia to oversee a mining site, Giuliana realizes that she can only count on herself to conquer her fears and regain her balance.

Figure 19. Giuliana (Monica Vitti) and her son walk by the factory's chimneys, and in the background a row of steaming smokestacks paint yellow stripes against the gray sky in *Deserto rosso* (Red Desert, Michelangelo Antonioni, 1964).

boy towards the camera and exits the frame, revealing in the background a landfill full of yellow, green and blue jugs of nitric acid and a row of steaming smokestacks that paint yellow stripes against the gray sky (see Figure 19). The attractiveness of the visual elements – the pictorial quality of the shot, the contrast between the acid colors of the factory and the earthy ones of the protagonists' clothes – contradicts the sense of a looming threat arising from the scene.[2] It is precisely this incongruity, along with the disquieting experience of watching Giuliana's mental struggle unfold

---

2   As with his other films, Antonioni's aesthetic research behind the pictorial composition of scenes for *Deserto rosso* took inspiration from the work of a multiplicity of modern painters: Jean Fautrier, Mark Rothko, Alberto Burri, Giorgio Morandi and others. See the following sources: Dalle Vacche, A. 1996. *Cinema and Painting: How Art Is Used in Film*. Austin: Continuum International Publishing Group. Gandy, M. 2003. "Landscapes of Deliquescence in Michelangelo Antonioni's 'Red Desert.'" *Transactions of the Institute of British Geographers*, vol. 28, no. 2. 227–229. Liehm, M. 1986. *Passion and Defiance: Italian Film from 1942 to the Present*. London: University of California Press. 228–230. Tyson, J. "Industrial Arts: Michelangelo Antonioni's *Red Desert* and Minimalism and Land Art." *New*

against the background of an eerily fascinating petrochemical complex, that upset many critics when the film was first released. Not surprisingly, this prompted them to write negative reviews of *Deserto rosso*, castigating its incoherent message about industrial alienation which, in their opinion, made it hard for viewers to sympathize with Giuliana's situation and invalidated the credibility of any possible political outcry.[3]

However, Antonioni's choice to treat the wasteland of the industrial district of Ravenna like an artistic object, worthy of being contemplated in its sheer beauty, is not incongruous nor is it unprecedented: as this chapter aims to establish, this dissonant depiction, first, serves to convey the director's view on technological progress and, second, pays homage to the well-established cinematic aesthetics of industrial documentaries, with which Antonioni had experimented at the beginning of his career.

The apparent incoherence between formal and narrative aspects creates an essential tension on which the entire film relies and that allows the director to adopt a diplopic vision. The medical term 'diplopia,' borrowed by Clément Chéroux to talk about the visual aesthetics of photo coverage during and after the 9/11 attacks, indicates a dysfunction that causes people to see two images where there is only one.[4] It is thus a particularly apt concept to explain how *Deserto rosso* approaches the industrial environment: in the film, Antonioni's vision and that of his protagonist Giuliana coexist alongside each other, but without merging, as the director tried to explain to a perplexed Charles Samuels in a 1969 interview. Starting from the assumption that all of Antonioni's works "suggest a revulsion against

---

Waves: Transatlantic Bonds between Film and Art in the 1960s. Washington: National Gallery of Art. Blog. <https://www.nga.gov/features/new-waves/industrial-arts.html>. Accessed May 15, 2019.

3   See, for example: Sarris, A. 1965. "Red Desert." *Village Voice*. February 11. Taylor, S. 1965. "The Red Desert: Neurosis à La Mode." *The Hudson Review*, vol. 18, no. 2. 258–259. Grazzini, G. 1977. *Gli anni Sessanta in cento film*. Bari: Laterza. Chatman, S. 1985. *Antonioni: Or, the Surface of the World*. Berkeley: University of California Press. 165. Rohdie, S. 1990. *Antonioni*. London: British Film Institute. 165–166. Arrowsmith, W. 1995. *Antonioni: The Poet of Images*. Oxford University Press. 85–86.

4   Chéroux, C. 2009. *Diplopie. L'image photographique à l'ère des médias globalisés: essai sur le 11 septembre 2001*. Cherbourg and Octeville: Le Point du Jour.

technology," the journalist became puzzled by the aesthetic sophistication displayed in shooting the Ravenna petrochemical complex: "You paint the factory pipes so that they become rather attractive. On the one hand, you show that technological modern life is bad; on the other, you're saying it's good."[5] What escaped Samuels, though, was that Antonioni had no intention of condemning technology: he was not a Luddite, as Karen Pinkus points out,[6] but rather a supporter of industrial development and, more generally, of any technological advancement, which he saw as a sign of progress. Samuels is right that the film is centered on the anxious struggle of Giuliana who, after having attempted suicide and been released from a mental clinic, is desperately trying to find her place in a mechanized, unnatural environment. And yet, *Deserto rosso* bears no ethical judgment over the industrialization of society: technology is not inherently alienating but rather has this effect on people only because they fail to keep up with the changes, as Antonioni elucidated for Samuels:

> I'm not saying that technology is bad, something we can do without. I'm saying that present day people can't adapt to it. These are merely terms of a conflict: 'technology' and 'old fashioned characters.' I'm not passing judgment, not at all. [...] In *Red Desert*, I [...] confronted this technology and these machines with human beings who are morally and psychologically retarded and thus utterly unable to cope with modern life.[7]

The idea that human beings and not machines are faulty and out of pace and that therefore Giuliana is not a heroine, resisting the process of mechanization of the human race, but rather the victim of her

---

5   Samuels, C. 2008. "Michelangelo Antonioni (July 29, 1969)." *Michelangelo Antonioni Interviews*. Edited by Bert Cardullo. Jackson: University Press of Mississippi. 85.
6   Pinkus, K. 2011. "Antonioni's Cinematic Poetics of Climate Change." *Antonioni: Centenary Essays*. Edited by Laura Rascaroli and John David Rhodes. London: Palgrave. 263.
7   Samuels, C. 2008. "Michelangelo Antonioni (July 29, 1969)." 85. Antonioni made the same argument in an article published in the French magazine *Humanité dimanche* soon after *Deserto rosso* was released. See: Antonioni, M. 1996. *The Architecture of Vision: Writings and Interviews on Cinema*. Edited by Carlo di Carlo and Giorgio Tinazzi. Chicago: University of Chicago Press. 288.

inability to adapt, emerges also from a previous interview, conducted in 1964 by Jean-Luc Godard, in which Antonioni delved even deeper into the issue.[8] Commenting on the scene of Giuliana's son's toy robot (see Figure 20), Antonioni explained to Godard that the robot is not a menacing presence, but rather a benevolent one: just like any other game, it serves to prepare the child for adulthood, so he can acquaint himself with technology and not suffer from it like his mother. Rejecting the idea of a mechanized society as a tragic prospect does not mean that Antonioni refused to consider the alienating impact of industry. Indeed, he was no stranger to the uneasiness that Giuliana experiences – he told Godard that he envied the character of the young boy, perfectly attuned to the new industrial world – and it is precisely this clash between individual perception and collective progress that makes the struggle inevitable, in life as in the film.[9]

Figure 20. Giuliana's son (Valerio Bartoleschi) sleeps as his toy robot watches over him in *Deserto rosso* (Red Desert, Michelangelo Antonioni, 1964).

8   Godard, J.-L. 1966. "The Night, The Eclipse, The Dawn (November 1964)." *Cahiers Du Cinema in English*, no. 1. 19–29.
9   Godard, J.-L. 1966. "The Night, The Eclipse, The Dawn (November 1964)." 25.

It is perhaps because of this consonance between Antonioni and his protagonist that Pier Paolo Pasolini chose to read *Deserto rosso* as the result of the perfect superimposition of their two views, in order to make sense of the otherwise unresolved tension structuring the film. In his famous essay "The 'Cinema of Poetry,'" Pasolini interpreted the film as a stylistic exercise in what he called cinematic free indirect discourse. He maintained that Antonioni and Giuliana's visions converge rather than clash, as the director's desire to mimetically reproduce the protagonist's neurotic gaze is precisely what enabled Antonioni to adopt his own cinematic aesthetics. In Pasolini's words, Antonioni "has finally been able to represent the world seen through his *eyes, because he has substituted in toto for the worldview of a neurotic his own delirious view of aesthetics*, a wholesale substitution which is justified by the possible analogy of the two views."[10]

The poetic quality of the film that Pasolini observed is thus instrumental in expressing Giuliana's neurotic condition. The unrealistic use of color – Antonioni had walls, street carts and even grass, trees and toxic waste artificially painted before shooting[11] – the eerie musical commentary, which is not mimetic and descriptive, but rather has a distancing effect,[12] the use of unfocussed shots and telephoto lens so as to eliminate depth of field[13] – these elements all serve, in Pasolini's interpretation, to express Giuliana's distorted perception of reality. According to this analysis, Antonioni's point of view is entirely replaced by Giuliana's, as the two coincide. Even more, the woman's neurotic gaze is fundamental for

---

10 Pasolini, P. P. 1988. *Heretical Empiricism*. Translated by Ben Lawton and Louise K. Barnett. Bloomington: Indiana University Press. 179–180. Emphasis in the original.

11 On Antonioni's use of color on set, see: Aristarco, G. 1985. "Il cinema. Dalla chimica ai processi elettronici." *Il nuovo mondo dell'immagine elettronica*. Edited by Guido Aristarco and Teresa Aristarco. Bari: Edizioni Dedalo. 16–17. Arrowsmith, W. 1995. *Antonioni*. 96–99. Rohdie, S. 1990. *Antonioni*. 156–164. Chatman, S and Duncan, P. 2004. *Michelangelo Antonioni: The Investigation*. Köln and London: Taschen. 91. Pierotti, F. 2016. *Un'archeologia del colore nel cinema italiano. Dal technicolor ad Antonioni*. Pisa: Edizioni ETS. 200–206.

12 Chatman, S. 1985. *Antonioni*. 133–135.

13 Chatman, S and Duncan, P. 2004. *Michelangelo Antonioni*. 92. Tinazzi, G. "The Gaze and the Story." *The Architecture of Vision: Writings and Interviews on Cinema*. XXI.

the film's aspirations of retaining some sort of coherence between the level of style and that of narration.

However, as Antonioni and many critics have made clear,[14] the director does not disappear behind his character: it is not a matter of substitution, but rather of juxtaposition and it is precisely this diplopic vision that allows *Deserto rosso* to show the factory as an alienating force and, at the same time, as an object worthy of aesthetic contemplation. Furthermore, to explain the film's style through a mimetic principle as Pasolini does, is not only to deny its diplopic vision, but also to affirm a realistic approach that Antonioni wanted instead to escape. In Antonioni's interview with Godard, when the French director asked if the film's expressionistic use of color replicates Giuliana's distorted perception, Antonioni replied that to mimetically reproduce the world through sensual experience would have been an artificial "trick."[15] What Antonioni wanted to express, instead, were the repercussions of the industrial turn on his own aesthetics, and he was by no means alone in this artistic quest.

Indeed, to fully understand the reasons behind the exquisite formalism with which Antonioni depicts Ravenna's industrial landscape, we must link *Deserto rosso* to the vast production of industrial films, the so-called 'cinema d'impresa' of the late 1940s to the 1960s, whose intention was not simply to promote the social utility of the companies that financed them, nor to engage in self-congratulations of managers and governments by showing citizens economic and technical innovations.[16] If these were surely the main factors prompting the creation of such films, they also played a crucial role in allowing many directors the space to experiment in order to develop a cinematic language able not only to narrate stories set in the factory, but

14   Chatman, S. 1985. *Antonioni*. 97–98. Rhodes, J. D. "Antonioni and the Development of Style." *Antonioni: Centenary Essays*. 293–294.
15   Godard, J.-L. 1966. "The Night, The Eclipse, The Dawn (November 1964)." 29.
16   Bertozzi, M. 2008. "L'arte, l'industria e la cultura." *Storia del documentario italiano. Immagini e culture dell'altro cinema*. Venice: Marsilio. 129–158. Bonifazio, P. 2014. *Schooling in Modernity: The Politics of Sponsored Films in Postwar Italy*. Toronto: University of Toronto Press. Frescani, E. 2014. *Il cane a sei zampe sullo schermo. La produzione cinematografica dell'Eni di Enrico Mattei*. Naples: Liguori. Latini, G. 2011. *L'energia e lo sguardo: il cinema dell'Eni e i documentari di Gilbert Bovay*. Rome: Donzelli.

to express the spirit of the industrial turn and the paradigmatic change it announced on all levels of human perception. This was indeed the case for Ermanno Olmi, whose career in filmmaking began at Edisonvolta, then Italy's largest energy company: Olmi shot almost forty sponsored films between 1947 and 1961.[17] This was also the case for Bernardo Bertolucci, who in 1967 shot the three-part television documentary *La via del petrolio* (The Oil Route), commissioned by the oil and gas company ENI, as a way of finding new inspiration and overcoming his creative block through experimentation with a new genre.[18] Finally, it was the case for the French director Alain Resnais, who first experimented with color in the industrial documentary *Le chant du styrène* (The Song of the Styrene, 1958), commissioned by the French company Pechiney and dedicated to the production process of Styrofoam.[19] For these directors and many others, experimenting with industrial cinema was not simply a way of getting by, especially in the early days of their careers; it was a creative and formative experience.

Antonioni also passed through a similar apprenticeship, which later informed his style in *Deserto rosso*: in 1949, he authored the ten-minute documentary *Sette canne, un vestito* (Seven Reeds, One Suit), which follows the manufacturing process of rayon in the SNIA Viscosa factory near Trieste, starting with the creation of yarn and ending with the tailoring of dresses. The documentary, rediscovered in the factory archives in 1995, aims to tell "la favola del rayon, una favola moderna scritta con le formule magiche dei libri di chimica" (the fairy tale of rayon, a modern fairy tale written with the magic formulas of the chemistry books), as the voice-over announces, inspired by a 1938 poem by the Futurist writer Filippo Tommaso Marinetti and dedicated to the same rayon factory as a successful

---

17   Mazzei, L. 2004. "I documentari industriali di Ermanno Olmi." *Storia del cinema italiano, vol. 9*. Edited by Sandro Bernardi. Venice: Marsilio. 282–288.
18   Banita, G. 2014. "From Isfahan to Ingolstadt: Bertolucci's *La via del petrolio* and the Global Culture of Neorealism." *Oil Culture*. Edited by Ross Barrett and Daniel Worden. Minneapolis: University of Minnesota Press. 145–168.
19   Dimendberg, E. 2005. "'These Are Not Exercises in Style': Le Chant Du Styrène." *October*, vol. 112. April 1. 63–88. Pierotti, F. 2016. *Un'archeologia del colore nel cinema italiano*. 113–118.

example of Italian autarchy.[20] Far from any intended political implications, *Sette canne, un vestito* is nevertheless a testament to the positive aspects of industrial development, tracing a metaphorical journey from the muddy reeds of the marshes, needed to make wood pulp, to the modern environment of the factory.[21] But the manufacturer is not only a beacon of technological progress; it is also regarded by Antonioni as an aesthetic object, to be explored with the means of cinema. The shots composed to reveal the symmetries of the volumes, the high angles and slow panning to display the clean geometric shapes of the chimneys, the intricate grid of the pipes, the power of the steam that surrounds and swallows the factory workers, the fascination for the materiality of the industrial products: all this will return sixteen years later in *Deserto rosso*, only in color and charged with an existential meaning.

Comparing the two cinematic works is, of course, far from suggesting that Antonioni aimed at promoting the two companies whose factories are portrayed in *Deserto rosso*: the refinery SAROM and the public petrochemical firm ANIC. Instead, I intend to recognize Antonioni's prior adherence to a codified style, aligning with the fascination of many other directors for the beauty of the factory and of its products. For a 1964 spectator to see the interior of a petrochemical plant, with its bright colors and pumping machines, was not an unprecedented experience. Quite the opposite: what Antonioni does in *Deserto rosso* is a transcoding experiment, that brings the aesthetics of sponsored industrial films into the realm of artistic cinema.

20   Marinetti, F. T. 1938. *Gli aeropoeti futuristi dedicano al Duce il poema di Torre Viscosa: parole in libertà futuriste*. Torviscosa: SNIA Viscosa Ufficio propaganda. For further references, see: Blanc, P. 2016. *Fake Silk: The Lethal History of Viscose Rayon*. New Haven: Yale University Press. 129–164.
21   The documentary tellingly ends with the images of a fashion show accompanied by the following words: "genio di scienziati, potenza di macchine, valore di tecnici, lavoro intelligente e instancabile di operai hanno trasformato la canna fangosa della palude in variopinto, elegantissimo tessuto" (the genius of scientists, the power of machines, the valuable input of technicians and the intelligent and restless labor of the workers have transformed the muddy reed into a colorful, extremely elegant dress).

When framed within Antonioni's personal aesthetics, as well as within the search for a new cinematic language common among many directors, it is not at all surprising that *Deserto rosso* refused to depict the factory as a malign force that condemns humans to alienation. The conflict was deeper than that, and it was an unsolvable one: it was the fact of seeing the utility and beauty of the factory yet being incapable of uniting with it.

LUCA PERETTI

34 *Italiani nel mondo* (1965): The Glorification of Italian Labor Abroad

Nontheatrical, ephemeral and sponsored films have received renewed attention in recent years. Some of these films can be classified as industrial, as many companies, especially between the end of the 1950s and the beginning of the 1970s, produced and sponsored films that were then screened in a variety of settings, from trade fairs and expositions to regular film theaters. *Italiani nel mondo* (Italians the World Over, 1965) is one of the many non-fiction films produced in this golden era of Italian industrial cinema. It is a unique case because it is a publicly funded film that promoted private and state funded companies alike, providing a sort a catalogue of places and works that Italians perform around the world. The film is directed by Ugo Fasano, a veteran of ephemeral cinema, with a voiceover commentary written by Ettore Della Giovanna, a journalist who worked in different settings around the world,[1] and it is sponsored by the Presidenza del Consiglio dei Ministri (Presidency of the Council of Ministers, PCM). In this chapter, I will first present some archival issues linked to this film. Then I will present the general topic of the film and finally, I will demonstrate how *Italiani nel mondo* is a fruitful example of the discourse on Italians abroad at the time.

---

1 See the following: Della Giovanna, E. 1961. *Le lettere non spedite*. Rome: Rotosei. Della Giovanna, E. 1997. *Scherzi della memoria*. Casale Monferrato: Piemme.

Archival Issues

Before speaking more in detail about the film and the discourse it promoted, a few words on its preservation are needed: as often happens when one is researching ephemeral cinema, in fact, copies are not easy to find, and it is not entirely clear how to attribute credits. In the case of ephemeral films, then, preservation and archival location also partially determine what they are.

There are at least three copies of *Italiani nel mondo* available in Italian archives: two of the complete film and one of about two thirds. Two copies, one in Italian and one in English, can be found in the film archive of the Istituto del Commercio Estero (Institute for Foreign Business, ICE), a government agency that deals with several aspects of Italian trades and business abroad, from construction projects to fairs and expositions. An additional copy – only 39' long, and not the full 59' – is in a more unusual place: the large archive of the United States Informational Service in Trieste, which holds the films produced by the European Recovery Program (ERP), more commonly known as the Marshall Plan.[2] *Italiani nel mondo* is the most recent film in the archival unit, and it is unclear how a film from 1965, unrelated to the reconstruction of Italy or to US subjects, ended up there.[3]

---

2   Carucci, P. 2007. "Prefazione." *United States Information Service di Trieste. Catalogo del fondo cinematografico (1941–1966)*. Edited by Giulia Barrera and Giovanna Tosatti. Rome: Ministero per i Beni e le Attività Culturali, Direzione Generale per gli Archivi. ix-xii.

3   The archival unit, composed of 674 reels and 506 films, was recovered in the northeastern border city of Trieste, and given to the Archivio Centrale dello Stato (Central Archives of the State, ACS) in February 1987. In 1991, ACS collaborated with the Archivio Audiovisivo del Movimento Operaio e Democratico (Audiovisual Archive of the Democratic and Labor Movement, AAMOD) to archive, identify and transfer the copies of the films. See: Cova, U. 2007. "I filmati USIS di Trieste: vicende storico-istituzionali di un archivio cinematografico." *United State Information Service di Trieste*. 53–62. Tosatti, G. 2007. "Propaganda e informazione nell'Italia del secondo dopoguerra: il fondo audiovisivo dell'USIS di Trieste." *United State Information Service di Trieste*. 63–85.

ICE gave its film and photograph archives to the Archivio Nazionale Cinema d'Impresa (The National Archive for Industrial Film), founded in Ivrea (Piedmont) in 2006 as a branch of the Fondazione Centro Sperimentale di Cinematografia (Experimental Film Center Foundation). There the films were digitized and some of them uploaded to YouTube and other online platforms.[4] Nowhere does *Italiani nel mondo* indicate who sponsored the film, but it does name the production company that made it (Opus Film, by producer Gastone Ferranti). Even though the film is preserved in the ICE archive, however, the likelihood is that it was not sponsored by this institution, but rather given to it as promotional material: research into the ICE archive has not yielded any result. Conversely, in three different places, the film is attributed to the PCM: a small label on the film reel at ICE reads "Presidenza del Consiglio,"[5] while the catalogue of the United States Information Service in Trieste lists *Italiani nel mondo* as a PCM production[6] and finally – and most importantly – the film is listed in the little-known catalogue *Per immagini* (Through Images), compiled by the PCM in 2009.[7] That a copy of a film that represents Italian

---

4   They can be found at the following links: <https://www.youtube.com/watch?v=AZ2fNcWcLsQ (full Italian version)>; <https://www.youtube.com/watch?v=FmvjQ93-GWc (full English version)>; <https://www.youtube.com/watch?v=mNqO4NnaUAs (shorter Italian version)> [last accessed June 25, 2019].
5   As Maria Luisa Battaglia, whom I thank dearly for the kind help and assistance, at ICE showed me, several archival documents do not make any mention of the film. For example, in a detailed "Progetto di iniziative per lo sviluppo delle esportazioni – Esercizio finanziario 1962/1963," fairs and expositions are listed and explained, for several worldwide locations, but there is no trace of *Italiani nel mondo*. See: Istituto nazionale per il commercio estero, Comitato Esecutivo, Verbale della riunione del giorno 18 maggio 1962. Furthermore, the reports of the institution's presidency meetings include a section for new publications, but films are never mentioned there.
6   The film is listed as one of the documentaries produced by the PCM. Barrera, G and Tosatti, G (eds). 2007. *United States Information Service di Trieste. Catalogo del fondo cinematografico (1941–1966)*. Rome: Ministero per i Beni e le Attività Culturali, Direzione Generale per gli Archivi. 323.
7   Presidenza del Consiglio dei Ministri, Dipartimento per l'Informazione e l'Editoria. 2009. *Per immagini. Gli audiovisivi prodotti dalla Presidenza del Consiglio dei Ministri*. Rome: Istituto Poligrafico e Zecca dello Stato S.p.A. 178.

labor abroad would end up at an agency like ICE, which deals with Italian trade and business abroad, seems absolutely normal: so it is that the film was produced in several different languages, including English.⁸

Italiani nel mondo: Art and Industry

Several films, fiction and non-fiction alike, were made about Italians working abroad during the economic miracle. Usually sponsored by big companies, such as the firm Innocenti with *Italiani nel Venezuela* (Italians in Venezuela, directed by Armando Tamburelli in 1963–1965) and *Attacco alla Savana* (Attack on the Savannah, by Mario Damicelli in 1964) or ENI with *Gli uomini del petrolio* (The Oil Men, by Gilbert Bovay in 1965) and *La via del petrolio* (The Oil Route, by Bernardo Bertolucci in 1967),⁹ such films depicted and fueled a change of perspective regarding what Italians were doing abroad: as the language of *Italiani nel mondo* puts it, "in the second half of the twentieth century there has been a radical change in their [Italians'] foreign relationships." The film in fact participates in this shift, and its clear thesis is well expressed in the very first lines:

> Some time back Italy used to export labor, especially unskilled labor, along the sorrowful path of indiscriminate emigration; nowadays it's exporting talents in the shape of keenly-sought technicians, skilled laborers and products which the world markets are crying out for. Once upon a time the Italian who left home to make his fortune abroad was looked upon as gone forever. Today the pattern has changed. Whether he is a professional or a worker, after making his useful contribution to the life of other nations, he comes back to the vital center of all his initiatives. In the past hundred years millions of Italians throughout the world have played an important part

---

8   All citations in this chapter are taken from this version. When the English version differs significantly from the Italian, I cite both.
9   On ENI and the cinema, see the following: Frescani, E. 2014. *Il cane a sei zampe sullo schermo. La produzione cinematografica dell'Eni di Enrico Mattei*. Naples: Liguori. Bonifazio, P. 2014. "United We Drill: ENI, Films, and the Culture of Work." *Annali d'Italianistica*, vol. 32. 329–350.

The Glorification of Italian Labor Abroad 453

> in the progress of mankind, in North and South America, in Africa, Asia, Australia. But up to recently, at what a price? The emigrant ways across the world were filled with hardship, tears and sacrifices. In a genuine pioneers' spirit the old emigrants set up many new societies. That's all gone and it's hope forever. Italians today remain Italians collaborating with whomever comes to them for assistance in the arts and sciences, in a relationship based on mutual respect and an idealism which formerly was nonexistent in peace time work.

This long, overtly rhetorical quotation sets the tone for the rest of the film, and it is particularly poignant because it resembles the rhetoric embodied by many Italian companies that worked abroad at the time. It emphasizes change in the type of emigration, from "unskilled labor" to "keenly sought technicians," even though this is largely not accurate based on figures of the time. However, pointing to a lack of adherence to reality is less interesting than discussing the type of discourse that government agencies, public companies and even private firms were trying to build. The emigrant is not "gone forever," he (almost never she) comes back after having helped others, thanks to his Italian-ness. Italians do not merge with the new society, but remain Italians even when they go abroad. The last sentence highlights how a new world, in peace time, can be built thanks to labor, and it implies that Italy could play a fundamental role, thanks to its peculiar position: the country was in fact simultaneously part of NATO, therefore allied with the US, and also able to do business and communicate with countries in the Eastern bloc and recently decolonized or decolonizing countries.

The film mostly wants to convey two aspects of Italian labor abroad. On the one hand, it illustrates Italians working for firms like ENI, the tire manufacture Pirelli and the chemical company Montecatini. On the other hand, it shows artists who perform in places as different as Amsterdam and Buenos Aires, painters like Amedeo Modigliani in Paris and Italian art books (like those made by the publishing house Fabbri) exported worldwide. These two components, which we could identify as art and industry, are often shown together – in the Argentinian section, for example, we see how Olivetti builds a city within a city, just as the company did in Ivrea, and at the same time we see Italian opera performers touring in the local theaters.

The constant link between Italy and abroad is also shown in how the film returns periodically to show how Italian companies create, in Italy, things and projects that will be exported abroad. We see laboratories in Milan with a very emphatic voiceover: "When we say that Italy is no longer exporting brawn but brains, or rather the talent of its people, we are describing a fundamental revolution that is taking place in its relations with the other countries in the world." We see images from project locations: "Not just Africa, Asia, South America, but even the United States and the USSR," where "they [foreigners] do not ask us [Italians] for unskilled laborers, but genius solutions and practices for the great problems of our era."[10] In another laboratory in Rome, we are told how refineries are planned and how "teams of highly qualified Italian specialists leave for the site of the new refinery and supervise its installation. When the job is done, they return to Rome and begin work on the next project." During the economic boom the discourse in Italy shifted: Italy now exported the 'Italian genius' – its creativity, not manpower (or at least, not only manpower). The idea of the 'genius' is obviously ambiguous and even fallacious, but it became an extremely powerful tool to promote and even justify the presence of Italian workers abroad: to answer, first and foremost for Italians themselves, the question 'why are our countrymen still emigrating if there is an economic boom right here at home?' Talking about 'Italian genius' also became a way to link the present to the glorious past of the great 'geniuses' like Leonardo, Dante, Michelangelo and others.

A Tour of the World

Italiani nel mondo illustrates how wherever they go Italians help the locals build their infrastructure, learn about great art and culture and forge mutual respect and acceptance. It focuses on Italians and Italian

10   This second sentence is only present in the Italian version: "non si chiedono manovali, bensì soluzioni geniali e pratiche per i grandi problemi di questa nostra epoca."

labor, without distinguishing between different countries and contexts, whether building the Parisian 'borgate,'[11] working in the mines in Belgium or in the African pipelines. In other words, the film does not emphasize the specificity of the foreign places but rather the character of Italians.

The first part of *Italiani nel mondo* focuses on industrialized countries, then after the first return to Italy, a plane brings us to Iran – depicted in strong Orientalist tones – and to the Zambezi river in Africa. The film betrays a formulaic structure that is typical of many contemporary industrial films set abroad: starting with the past glory of the given country, it illustrates how Italians – with the collaboration of the local population – overcome huge difficulties to bring progress and freedom. The second part of *Italiani nel mondo* is dedicated to countries that are especially important for Italian business and culture, like former colony Ethiopia:

> The work done by Italians in recent years has led to a restoration of well-balanced relations between the two countries after the stormy years from 1935 to 1943. Italians are still sentimentally attached to Ethiopia with feelings of genuine affection in spite of the thorns of colonization and war. What was carried out by Italians in Ethiopia deserves an honest word of praise. Ethiopians regard Italians with friendly esteem. Right now, there are countless Italians that work in the country on behalf of 215 Italian firms and Italian is still the *lingua franca*.

In Italian, rather than 'stormy years' the voice over says "tragiche traversie" (tragic plights), a euphemism for some hundreds of killings. Italy is loved "laggiù" (over/down there, another word used in the Italian version) and the Italian language is still used. The discourse on colonization is in place only to minimize its impact, as was and still is largely common.[12]

In Nigeria, the film focuses on ENI's work. Here, the use of footage from a film sponsored by the oil company (Gilbert Bovay's *Gli uomini del petrolio*) attests to the intense circulation and reuse of images in non-fiction cinema. At the time, ENI was the most important and successful

---

11 The word 'borgate,' used in the Italian version of the film, is largely associated with Pier Paolo Pasolini, and in Anglophone literature has become a synonym for periphery. However, it is a rather charged term, close to shantytowns, and usually refers to the peripheries of Rome.
12 Del Boca, A. 2008. *Italiani, brava gente? Un mito duro a morire*. Vicenza: Neri Pozza.

company working abroad. It comes as no surprise that the film dedicates a few sequences to the company, explaining how ENI can cover all aspects of oil exploration and distribution, including training its specialists and technicians in its own schools.[13] Somehow paradoxically for our contemporary understanding of how fuel structures geopolitical relationships, oil is seen as a tool for peace and collaboration among peoples: "While our hope for peace still lasts [in Italian: mentre si alimentano le speranze di pace], there is international cooperation toward the solution of one of the worst problems in this trade: transport. The volume of oil being shipped from one part of the world to another has reached unmanageable proportions by current standards." Italy and ENI excel in building international pipelines that cross nations and, by virtue of its peculiar geopolitical position, the country perceives itself and is perceived as an agent of peace – one that manages to cooperate with different nations and peoples, from major US oil companies to the Soviet oil industry.

The three Latin American countries addressed in *Italiani nel mondo* are those that have seen an historical presence of Italians: Argentina (where Olivetti operates), Brazil and Venezuela, where the machinery company Innocenti works. Finally, after South America, the film ends in North America, in Canada and the USA. In these countries, where Italians have had a solid presence since the second half of the nineteenth century, the narrative that presents them as new and skilled workers is even more fraudulent. The voiceover narration needs to find strange ways to justify this move: for example, by claiming that Montreal lacks manpower because it prefers commerce to construction. Yet Italian migration to Canada in the postwar era was still largely that of former peasants.[14] In his book on the Italians in Toronto, historian Stefano Agnoletto notes how "the greater part of [the immigrants] came from a rural background and experienced

---

13   This is the subject of one of the company's most well-known films, *Oduroh* (Gilbert Bovay, 1964). A DVD of the film was released with the following book: Latini, G. 2011. *L'energia e lo sguardo. Il cinema dell'Eni e i documentari di Gilbert Bovay*. Rome: Donzelli.
14   Boissevain, J. 1970. *The Italians of Montreal: Social Adjustment in a Plural Society*. Ottawa: Studies of the Royal Commission on Bilingualism and Biculturalism.

The Glorification of Italian Labor Abroad 457

in Toronto their first contact with urban capitalist society."[15] Even more complicated is justifying how these Italians are temporary workers in the US. The film does mention important moments for Italian Americans, like the Columbus Day parade or the feast of San Gennaro (when "they reveal their numerical strength"), and it notes how Italians in the US have fully adopted the American way of life. But then with a twist, we also hear how "there has been considerable emigration to America since the war but not permanent settlement. Those who have gone and returned are businessmen, research workers, contractors and technicians." In other words, those unskilled workers who came before the war were Americanized, while the skilled workers come and go. Once again, this is a narrative functional to the economic boom and the idea that Italians do not need to emigrate anymore, and those who have emigrated are now lost.

New York is where the penetration of the new Italian products can be best illustrated: the Olivetti typewriters can be seen in the famous Olivetti shop on Fifth Avenue,[16] and the Vespa is supposedly used throughout the city. But New York City also speaks to more specific cinematic references: the way the city is filmed is similar to how contemporary fictional films (like Alberto Lattuada's *Mafioso* from 1962) depict it, with jazzy music and low angle shots of skyscrapers. Moreover, cinema – like other forms of art and culture – is also a vehicle for the penetration of Italian culture in the US, and *Italiani nel mondo* shows how on certain weeks, as many as ten out of twenty-two film theaters in Time Square screen Italian movies. It is precisely here that Roberto Rosselini's *Roma città aperta* (Rome, Open City, 1945) became a worldwide hit. Perhaps more importantly, the camera lingers on a gigantic poster in Times Square: *The Bible* (directed by John Huston in 1966[17]), which was produced Dino De Laurentiis (whose name

15   Agnoletto, S. 2014. *The Italians Who Built Toronto: Italians Workers and Contractors in the City's Housebuilding Industry, 1950–1980*. Bern: Peter Lang. 1.
16   See: Carter, J. 2018. "Italy on Fifth Ave: From the Museum of Modern Art to the Olivetti Showroom." *Modern Italy*, vol. 23, no. 1.
17   This poster poses some chronological issues because *Italiani nel mondo* was made in 1965: either this poster is an announcement of *The Bible*, a film that will come out the following year (it is impossible to confirm this from the images), or all the catalogues that list *Italiani nel mondo* are wrong.

on the poster is second only to that of the American director), one of those successful Italians who could work both at home and abroad.

The ending of *Italiani nel mondo* connects ancient and modern times:

> Our tour of the worldwide achievements of Italians need never end. There is no end to the story. More than 2000 years ago the Romans sent their first technicians abroad to rebuild Saguntum in Spain and to restore the devasted country around Carthage. At the time, and in later periods of history, the benefits of civilization were often preceded by the sore. But times have changed. In her export of goods and talents today, Italy is making an outstanding contribution to peace and progress in the world.[18]

Like several industrial films of the time, *Italiani nel mondo* glorifies Italians abroad, their work and (supposed) ability to create connections and cooperate with the locals. It is an official position expressed by governments and managers of public and private companies, for a country that had a peculiar position in the new geopolitical spectrum merely twenty years after the end of the Second World War. In this way, *Italiani nel mondo* illustrates the dynamic and anxieties of a country in transformation.

---

18   The second part of this sentence in the Italian version is significantly different: "Ma mentre allora e poi per due millenni le mirabile opere della civiltà italiana dovevano quasi sempre seguire l'azione energica dei condottieri, oggi gli italiani ricercano ed acquistano nuovo prestigio con il loro talento e la loro laboriosità, contribuendo alla concordia tra i popoli." (But if then and for the next two millennia the marvelous work of Italian civilization had to follow almost always the energetic operation of a *condottiero*, now Italians work and acquire new prestige with their talent and their industriousness, contributing to the harmony between peoples).

LOUIS BAYMAN

35 A Spanner in the Works: Elio Petri from *Il maestro di Vigevano* (1963) to *La classe operaia va in paradiso* (1971)

One of the most commercially successful directors of what has been called Italy's *cinema politico* (engaged, or civic cinema), Elio Petri offers a social panorama of the conflicts besetting Italy of the 1960s and 1970s, from breakneck consumerism – in his sci-fi pop-art satire *La decima vittima* (The 10th Victim, 1965) – to the Sicilian Mafia – in his adaptation of Leonardo Sciascia's *A ciascuno il suo* (We Still Kill the Old Way, 1967). His dramatic strategy is to bring to the surface the contradictions inherent to a particular mindset, showing in the process how that mindset is conditioned by the social position of its holder. This can be seen in the proto-fascist mentality of the police chief in the crime thriller *Indagine su un cittadino al di sopra di ogni sospetto* (Investigation of a Citizen Above Suspicion, 1970), the petit bourgeois greed of the family butcher in *La proprietà non è piu un furto* (Property Is No Longer a Theft, 1973) or the cult-like inner workings of Christian Democracy in *Todo Modo* (1976). More specifically, his films revolve around a crisis that ensues when the protagonist's motivating logic can no longer make sense of the environment that has produced it. They thus expose the varied class and institutionally based identities of contemporary Italy, as well as the limitations through which that society might reach its own destruction. The development of this strategy can be seen in his two films about industrial production in Italy, the comedy about the economic boom *Il maestro di Vigevano* (The Teacher from Vigevano, 1963) and the more artistically ambitious *La classe operaia va in paradiso* (The Working Class Goes to Heaven, 1971). The eight years that separate them saw not only the passage from early to mature Petri, but a major historical shift in Italian society, from the economic boom to the bitter civil strife of the 1970s.

Beginning as a screenwriter for the most politically committed of neo-realist directors Giuseppe De Santis, Elio Petri's directorial career belongs however to a later period in Italian film history. For all the humanism of films such as Roberto Rosselini's *Paisà* (Paisan, 1946) or Vittorio De Sica's *Ladri di biciclette* (Bicycle Thieves, 1948), neorealism had not tended to take much interest in the unique character, or the inner lives, of its protagonists, who are more often general types defined by the struggle for physical survival, such as in confrontation with German occupation or poverty and unemployment. But neorealism was over by the late 1950s, and Italy was going through the industrial and consumerist boom of the economic boom whose cinematic counterpart was the caustic, cynical satire of the *commedia all'italiana* (comedy Italian style). In some ways a response to the apparent failure of neorealism's more radical hopes, the *commedia all'italiana* tended to blame the inability to achieve a deeper social revolution in modern Italy on the stubborn insistence of certain characteristics or vices of national character.[1] In *Il maestro di Vigevano*, an adaptation of the book by Lucio Mastronardi (1962) and a vehicle for the popular comedian Alberto Sordi, the drama revolves around what was thus a relatively new element in critical commentary: the idiosyncratic way that a particular character *feels* about the situation.

The setting is the northern industrial town of Vigevano (Lombardy), and the story that of the declining social importance of the educated professional, embodied in the figure of Antonio Mombelli. Mombelli introduces himself in his opening monologue as an elementary school teacher in his nineteenth year of service on the first day of "an important year for me: in six months and one day I'll have the right to a minimum pension." His life is defined by petty precision, in a school that stands in for institutional structures in general, seeming variously part prison, part seminary, part army

---

[1] See Gundle, S. 2017. "The Question of Italian National Character and the Limitations of Commedia all'italiana: Alberto Sordi, Federico Fellini and Carlo Lizzani." *Wiley-Blackwell Companion to Italian Cinema*. Edited by Frank Burke. Oxford: Wiley-Blackwell. 198–214.

barracks, part factory (see Figure 21). Its sternly authoritarian headmaster calls the school "a big family," but he exercises his power through arbitrary acts of public cruelty. If it is a family then, it is because of the infantilizing nature of institutional authority, with hints at the psychology of fascist self-abnegation through the headmaster's overblown insistence on mass obedience. Although Mombelli is a conformist, his rebellious imagination fantasizes of semi-aristocratic consumerist luxury, of seizing the headmaster by the lapels and eventually, in the delirium of an extended fever dream, of returning as Adam with Eve in the Garden of Eden, blissfully living "rustically, primitively." His son, who has already dropped out of school to make a living working in a factory, brings him to his senses with an admonition not to dream, for "life is made of other things."

Figure 21. Antonio Mombelli (Alberto Sordi) in his classroom in *Il maestro di Vigevano* (The Teacher from Vigevano, Elio Petri, 1963).

Mombelli's loss of status is measured as much in offenses to his dignity as in financial cost. He claims to be "humiliated" by his son dropping out of school to work, and is ashamed by the daring public comportment of his wife. Where school replaces the traditional family, industrial production disrupts it: his wife gets a job in a footwear factory, before the couple sets up a small-scale production line at home, which Mombelli then bankrupts by carelessly admitting to tax evasion. He returns to teaching because it is where he finds his "inner balance." It is a mark of its pre-feminist era that the film equates his wife's financial independence with prostitution, as in an unexpectedly tragic ending where Mombelli discovers that her newfound wealth comes from infidelity with the rich industrialist Bugatti, whose son's grades Mombelli had previously refused to fraudulently improve.

At one point before losing their cottage industry, Mombelli has an accident that leads him to wrap his index finger in an overlarge bandage, in one of the film's suggestions of castration. The psychosocial import of such an injury returns in *La classe operaia va in paradiso*, Petri's epic satire of industrial strife in the wake of the 1969 protest season. The film treats a work stoppage against piecework and a speedup of production. At its center is Lulù Massa, and his journey from Stakhanovite worker, then, after an industrial accident, to an unlikely strike leader, unemployment, and then finally to being a member of the production line like any other. Lulù begins the film as the archetypal worker who lacks consciousness – the credits open on him literally asleep. He insults his southern Italian workmates, traditionally a source of cheap labor but also victims of prejudice, and he ignores the pleas of his fellow workmates to stop helping the company set an unreasonably fast rate for the new piecework requirements. But in his concentrated zeal for productivity, he loses a finger in an accident, eventually pits himself against management and urges the workers to take all-out strike action.

The fragile industrial peace holding together Italy's breakneck postwar boom ended in 1969 with a wave of strikes, lockouts and occupations that was named the 'hot autumn.' The breadth and depth of Italy's industrial militancy during this autumn marked a period of working class combativity that remains unparalleled in postwar Europe. *La classe operaia va in paradiso* ranks as the most developed dramatic treatment of its immediate aftermath, as factories remained strike-bound amidst a bitter political impasse. But the film transcends this context to also be one of the great – and indeed rare – cinematic treatments of the social, psychic and political effects of the Fordist production line.

It was a commonplace in the nineteenth century for visitors to the new-style factories to lament how such work reduced human beings into objects, which Karl Marx described as the distinguishing feature of capitalism in his theory of alienated labor.[2] Yet Italian communist Antonio Gramsci noted that the monotony specific to the Fordist production line would forge not only a new type of production, but a new kind of man, whose personal life as much as his working life would be altered by the changed forms of labor, invested in gender difference through the sexual division of labor, catered to by forms of mass consumerism that alleviated the exhaustion of work and that provided a market for him to spend his wages.[3] In Petri's film, titled *Lulu the Tool* for its US release, Lulù embodies the physical and spiritual ruination wrought by factory life; he is developing an ulcer, is too exhausted to contemplate sex and responds to a colleague who tells him "you won't die in bed, you'll die here at the machine" with the nihilistic "and what difference would that make?" The problem is not that he is materially deprived, but the way that mass production determines his psychic energies. Lulù sits in the kitchen at home each evening with his girlfriend and her son incommunicatively facing the television in a line, their silent faces lit by its cold blue mechanical light. Lulù motivates his superfast piecework by alternating thoughts of production with sex, repeating "a piece, an arse" with each thrust into the machinery, as the white cleansing liquid from the mechanism forms ejaculatory droplets on his face (see Figure 22), and he falls asleep at night repeating "a piece, an arse." When Lulù has sex in his car with the female worker he was thinking of, the jouissance is once again that of union with the machine, as the cramped vehicle places gear shift and driver's wheel in the way of the lovers' congress in possibly the most deliberately awkward sex scene in cinema.

2   Marx, K. 1959. *Economic and Philosophic Manuscripts of 1844*. Translated by Martin Mulligan. Moscow: Progress Publishers.
3   Gramsci, A. 1971. "Americanism and Fordism." *Selections from the Prison Notebooks*. Translated by Geoffrey Nowell Smith. New York: International Publishers. 558–622.

Figure 22. Lulù Massa (Gian Maria Volonté) in the factory, as the white cleansing liquid from the mechanism forms ejaculatory droplets on his face in *La classe operaia va in paradiso* (The Working Class Goes to Heaven, Elio Petri, 1971).

At the start of each day the workers enter the factory to loudspeaker announcements telling them to treat their machine with love and let their body become one with the machine. The film reveals the violence latent in this relationship. Ennio Morricone's score, a stern, steady march, incorporates insistent bursts of machinery that sound like machine gun fire, timed after the opening credits to coincide with Lulù's morning alarm clock, whose loud ticking sounds like a time bomb. The dispute over piecework eventually turns the factory into a theater of war, as squads of police drive into the pickets and petrol bombs are thrown. But this violence is merely a more open form of the violence the factory has already wrought upon the worker. Mark Seltzer has elsewhere described how Fordism requires "*assemblages* of body and machine,"[4] making the human operative an appendage of flesh. Lulù's loss of his finger is both a gruesome disruption of the industrial mechanism and a physical literalization of the bodily investment the factory requires, a merging of boundaries of human and machine as his blood flows into the liquid of the works.

---

[4] Seltzer, M. 1998. *Serial Killers: Death and Life in America's Wound Culture.* New York: Routledge. 74. Emphasis in original.

Italy's rich tradition of politicized fiction filmmakers has historically found it difficult to dramatize the situation of industrial labor: in *Il maestro di Vigevano* the factory setting, rather like Mombelli's wife herself, is marginal to Mombelli's experience as a teacher, briefly shown merely to establish its relevance to the plot. Even when a committed communist such as Luchino Visconti made his epic of migrant labor into Milan *Rocco e i suoi fratelli* (Rocco and His Brothers, 1960), he was only able to bring the spectator to the factory gates, where the film ends as the workers enter an apparently new, but future and unseen, dawn of social progress. It would seem that the monotony, de-individualization and manual effort that characterize the production line are hard to elaborate into an interesting dramatic situation. Political comedies contemporary to *La classe operaia va in paradiso*, namely Lina Wertmüller's *Mimì metallurgico ferito nell'onore* (The Seduction of Mimì, 1972) and Ettore Scola's *Trevico-Torino: Viaggio nel Fiat-Nam* (Trevico-Turin: Voyage in Fiatnam, 1973), feature laboring protagonists chiefly engaged in their private or public, but not working, lives. This means admittedly that, away from the male-dominated worksite, these films are able to put more emphasis on a female perspective – compare the role of Mariangela Melato in Lina Wertmüller's communist-feminist film *Mimì metallurgico ferito nell'onore*, and her relative underuse here in *La classe operaia va in paradiso* becomes even more pronounced. Although it is fun to see her in a different wig in each scene, her role as Lulù's hairdresser girlfriend is to be little more than a mouthpiece for the benefits of an aspiring petit bourgeois consumerism.

The brilliance of Petri's cinematic vision lies however in how it employs the nature of factory work at its dramatic and aesthetic basis. The dramatic conflicts are those of the workers in relation to their work. Montages incorporate the dynamic energies of the rhythms of production, cutting in series of close-ups from the workings of industry to the concentration of Lulù in his operations upon it. This editing continually alternates with panoramic camera movements that sweep further upwards, giving a grandeur to the setting and presenting the workplace in its totality. But while the 1920s Soviet montage practitioners who inspire Petri's artistic vision were fired up by a revolutionary positivity about the prospects of the industrial proletariat, the epic perspective provided in *La classe operaia va in paradiso* is not one that the workers can attain, serving instead a detachment that belongs to Petri's skepticism regarding social change.

The factory is an impassive and frozen setting, surrounded by iron railings and a layer of thick snow. Outside the gates each morning, trade union representatives call for an orderly approach to management, limiting their demands to contractual negotiation. They are continually interrupted by student revolutionaries who shout common slogans from the student struggle of the era, calling for the total abolition of the system and for "everything now! More money and less work!" As alternative responses to the drudgery of factory life, the antagonism between trade union representatives and Maoist students presents an irreconcilable conflict between a politics of official procedure and responsibility and one of total refusal. Lulù initially seems to break this impasse, in an outlet of pent-up pressure aided by a suitably intense performance by a constantly red-faced, physically overwrought Gian Maria Volonté. After losing his finger, he takes the microphone during a union assembly to urge his workers into all-out strike. His impassioned plea leads to an explosion of combustible anger as police try to bus in management and strikebreakers. But Lulù loses his job, his workmates return to the factory and the student revolutionaries move on to agitate elsewhere. We never see the process through which the union finally wins Lulù back his job, and rather than a new proletarian order it signifies only a return to the basic situation at the start.

While the students' search for a vanguard indicates their Maoist affiliations, *La classe operaia va in paradiso* can be seen as the major feature film reflection on the radical political current of autonomism. Born in the 1960s out of frustration with the institutional cooptation of official Communist and Socialist politics, Italian autonomism was one of the main ideological beneficiaries of the militant tide of the period. For autonomists the focus of politics is not parliament but the factory, which is where value is created and where workers find their autonomous, collective strength. In Mario Tronti's idea of the "social factory," the concept of the factory is extended to mean the modern organizational expression of bourgeois society.[5] In the social factory, all spheres – university, consumption, civic life – are modelled according to principles of standardization, efficiency,

---

5   Tronti, M. 2013. "Factory and Society." Translated by Guio Jacinto. <https://operaismoinenglish.wordpress.com/2013/06/13/factory-and-society/>.

compartmentalization and systematization. Indeed when Lulù picks his son up at the school gates, he remarks that the schoolchildren look like little workers. Against the docile obedience of mass uniformity produced by such social organization, autonomism sought to instill the values of spontaneity, antagonism, militancy and struggle.

As with *Il maestro di Vigevano*, the conflicts are not solely economic, but about the organization of life, and the inadequacy of existing systems of thought to make sense of the worker's experience. The action begins with a white-coated time and motion inspector, clutching his clipboard as he prowls the factory looking for ways to increase efficiency. He embodies scientific detachment, denying the operatives their basic human attributes, complaining about a worker who needs the toilet and chastising two others who have long hair. After Lulù's injury an onsite psychologist inspects his mental and sexual attitudes for the clear purpose of ensuring the continued smooth running of the factory through psychic conformity to conventions of normality. All forms of thought, even the oppositional ones, are subordinated to the machine. Correspondingly, the workers' official representatives and the student revolutionaries – whose doctrinaire faith in objective historical forces are no less impersonal than any other system of thought in the film – offer little answer either, seeking to impose their own ideological strictures upon the workers. Elio Petri was a director of more working-class background than the bourgeois-bohemianism of most of his contemporaries, and his rejection of facile political solutions to the problems facing the working class had a particular intimacy.[6] The workers in *La classe operaia va in paradiso* are surrounded by people offering solutions that are equally disconnected from the actual personal involvement unique to the workers themselves.

A different rationality is presented however by Lulù's two visits to his friend Militina, a former workmate who now resides in a mental asylum. Militina's somewhat cryptic function in the film is to unbalance the delicate separation of madness from rationality, and so to indicate the absurdity of a system which after all is geared towards the irrationality of meaningless

---

6   Michalczyk, J. 1986. *The Italian Political Filmmakers*. London: Farleigh Dickinson University Press. 210.

repetition. It is after his first visit that Lulù gets fired up to take action. Militina compares the asylum with the factory, saying that the only difference being that you do not get to leave the asylum in the evening – to which Lulù asks where he would go anyway. After his second visit, Lulù stays and Militina goes to leave, before the two realize they have mistakenly swapped positions. Militina defines madness as the brain going on strike and beats his hands against the wall in the asylum, an action which ultimately explains the film's title. In the final scene, Lulù is back at work, where he recounts a dream he had of a wall. The machines are now running louder than ever, causing Lulù to speak in an insistent, repetitive way that assumes a poetic-allegorical manner. In his dream he was dead, facing a wall, but Militina appeared, to tell him that on the other side is paradise. They break the wall but beyond it is only a thick fog, through which Lulù can see the other workers. In an image of the archetypal futility of continual physical labor, Polish revolutionary Rosa Luxembourg compared the constant setbacks inherent to trade union struggle to the mythical labor of Sisyphus, who was condemned for eternity to roll a boulder up a hill only always to see it roll back down the other side again.[7] Here however, labor means endless brick walls, while the passage to the workers' paradise reveals only fog and more walls. Reality cannot be adequately glimpsed, let alone transformed. The noise of the machines drowns out the end of the conversation, before the camera itself is loaded onto the conveyor belt. Our final perspective is that of a component entering the mechanism: our identification with the mass-produced commodity becomes complete and we finally enter the darkness of imprisonment within the production line.

---

7   Luxemburg, R. 2006. *Reform or Revolution and Other Writings*. Translated by Integer. Mineola, NY: Dover Publications. 50.

ILARIA A. DE PASCALIS

36 The Seduction of a Worker in Lina Wertmüller's *Mimì metallurgico ferito nell'onore* (1972)

As broadly described in this volume, industrial labor was one of the issues addressed by Italian cinema after the Second World War. Still, some critics have repeatedly stated that feature films did not represent the factories and the most practical aspects of industrial labor.[1] According to them, the camera stopped at the plants' limits: the vision of the gates, along with the sirens and with workers entering or picketing, was considered the synecdoche for the whole industrial working experience, its cultural world and meanings.[2]

A famous instance of this rhetorical configuration of industrial work as something left out of the frame, while still molding every aspect of characters' lives, is addressed in this volume by Mattia Lento: Ettore Scola's *Trevico-Torino: Viaggio nel Fiat-Nam* (Trevico-Turin: Voyage in Fiatnam, 1973). This is a documentary film following a young man on his journey from Campania to Turin and his new job in the Fiat factory. The Fiat company refused Scola permission to film beyond the gates of its main factory, the Mirafiori plant, and Scola transformed this problem into a formal strategy to address the disciplinary role of economics and institutions in the lives of young men.[3]

1   See, for example: Cineclub Arsenale (ed.). 1989. *Il cinema e il lavoro*. Pisa: Arsenale. Associazione Stranamente (ed.). 1994. *Bulloni & tute: cinema e lavoro*. Associazione Stranamente.
2   Pierre Sorlin underlines how Italian cinema from the 1950s and 1960s narrates the arrival of young men from the rural South to the industrial North, but how it also stays away from the actual representation of the economic and social transformation. Sorlin, P. 1979. *Sociologia del cinema*. Milan: Garzanti. 288, 294–296.
3   See: Miccichè, L. 1980. *Cinema italiano degli anni '70. Cronache 1969–1979*. Venice: Marsilio. 163.

The same Mirafiori neighborhood,[4] however, was one of the locations of another film about a young man who migrates from southern Italy to Turin: Lina Wertmüller's *Mimì metallurgico ferito nell'onore* (The Seduction of Mimì, 1972). The film can be considered the rhetorical opposite of Scola's because it is a feature film with heavily grotesque tones[5] that represents the main character's everyday life as a whirlwind sequence of (mis)adventures. As with other films by Wertmüller, *Mimì metallurgico ferito nell'onore* represents the intersection between private and public life through an exasperation of the stylistic traits of *commedia all'italiana* (comedy Italian style), making fun in particular of the idea that 'the personal is political' at the core of second wave feminism.[6]

The constant imbrication of romantic and working experiences is explicated in the film's Italian title: on the one hand, it defines the young Carmelo 'Mimì' Mardocheo by his being a metalworker ('metallurgico'); on the other hand, it characterizes him for being wounded in his 'honor' ('ferito nell'onore'). The idea of 'honor' is deeply embedded in the patriarchal structures of southern Italian culture and society, as it implies that women's sexual behavior is considered only in terms of its consequences for men's (fathers', brothers', and husbands') reputation. In this way, the film strongly locates itself as close to the male perspective, presenting honor,

---

4   See the entry "Quartiere Mirafiori" in the *Enciclopedia del cinema in Piemonte*, online at <http://www.torinocittadelcinema.it/schedaluogo.php?luogo_id=371&stile=large>. Last accessed March 23, 2019.
5   For a discussion of grotesque tones in Italian comedy, see: De Pascalis, I. A. 2012. *La commedia nell'Italia contemporanea*. Milan: Il castoro. 68–69.
6   For the conflicted relationship between Wertmüller and feminism, see: Diaconescu-Blumenfeld, R. 1999. "Regista di Clausura: Lina Wertmüller and Her Feminism of Despair." *Italica*, vol. 76, no. 3. 389–403. I have already discussed the fascinated but controlling gaze Wertmüller projects on Mariangela Melato's body and face in: De Pascalis, I. A. 2017. "Sfidare i confini dell'inquadratura: il corpo e i costumi di Mariangela Melato." *Arabeschi*, vol. 10. 372–376. For the problematic representation of women's bodies in Wertmüller's cinema, see: Rigoletto, S. 2013. "Laughter and the Popular in Lina Wertmüller's *The Seduction of Mimì*." *Popular Italian Cinema*. Edited by Louis Bayman and Sergio Rigoletto. Basingstoke: Palgrave Macmillan. 117–132.

jealousy and homicide as 'crimes of passion' and the basis of a set of cinematic jokes.

This was a recurring theme in *commedia all'italiana* films: a couple of famous examples are Pietro Germi's *Divorzio all'italiana* (Divorce, Italian style, 1961), and Mario Monicelli's *La ragazza con la pistola* (The Girl with the Pistol, 1968). However, the comedies of the 1960s were still part of Italian auteur cinema, and one of their roles was to examine national culture from a distant and problematic perspective, discussing in particular the conflict between tradition and modernity.[7] The unusual location of Wertmüller at the crossroads between authorship and popular cinema was instead the trigger for many dismissive reviews of *Mimì metallurgico ferito nell'onore* by Italian film critics who considered the film 'cheap' and 'vulgar.'[8] The fact that 'male honor' is such a notorious idea in the Italian imagination is likely to be one of the reasons that the international title focuses only on the erotic and sentimental implications for the main characters as it addresses Mimì's 'seductions.'

The film's plot follows the same complex causal order proposed by its Italian title, as it continuously oscillates between Mimì's public and private life. In the beginning, Mimì (Giancarlo Giannini) works in a Sicilian sulfur mine and is affiliated with the Communist Party.[9] When he refuses to vote for the mafia candidate in the local elections, the mobsters target him, taking away every possibility for him to work. Mimì decides

---

7   See: Pravadelli, V. 2017. "Italian 1960s Auteur Cinema (and beyond): Classic, Modern, Postmodern." *Wiley-Blackwell Companion to Italian Cinema*. Edited by Frank Burke. Oxford: Wiley-Blackwell. 228–248.

8   On the misfortunes of Wertmüller in Italian film culture, see: Rigoletto, S. 2014. *Masculinity and Italian Cinema: Sexual Politics, Social Conflicts and Male Crisis in the 1970s*. Edinburgh: Edinburgh University Press. 77–78. Rigoletto, S. 2013. "Laughter and the Popular in Lina Wertmüller's *The Seduction of Mimì*." 118–119.

9   The film is set at the end of the 1960s, when the Partito Comunista Italiano (Italian Communist Party) was the main political reference for Italian workers. For reference, see the entry in the Treccani Encyclopedia: <http://www.treccani.it/enciclopedia/partito-comunista-italiano_%28Dizionario-di-Storia%29/>. Last access April 3, 2019. For a broader view of Italian politics in this period, see Parker, S. 1996. "Political Identities." *Italian Cultural Studies: An Introduction*. Edited by David Forgacs and Robert Lumley. Oxford: Oxford University Press. 107–121.

to leave for northern Italy, convinced that there he can live legally, join the union as a worker and prosper. He leaves his wife Rosalia behind and arrives in Turin only to discover that the mafia controls the workers everywhere as well as the unions. The mafia is wherever power expresses itself. After witnessing a work-related accident on a construction site, and worried for his life, he declares himself to be a member, through his wife, of a mafia family. Mimì thus is able to ask for and obtain qualified work in a factory, and he writes to Rosalia about his newly gained pride in being a metalworker.

In the meantime, Mimì enrolls in the Communist Party and becomes involved with the Trotskyist and feminist Fiore (Mariangela Melato), who becomes pregnant with his child. Again, Mimì involuntarily witnesses a mafia murder; and because he refuses to cooperate with the authorities, the hitman decides to protect him. Assuming that he wants to return home, the mob finds Mimì a better job at a refinery in Catania. Here, his private life becomes even more complicated. Fiore accompanies Mimì to Catania together with their newborn child, and Rosalia, now a qualified worker who drives, smokes and is tired of being set apart, becomes the lover of the officer Amilcare. When Mimì discovers that Rosalia is pregnant by her lover, he gets his revenge by seducing Amilcare's wife, Amalia. Finally, a mafia hit man kills Rosalia's lover but lays the blame on Mimì to repair the wound to his honor. Mimì is briefly incarcerated according to the Italian law punishing 'crimes of passion,' and upon release, he finds himself with three women (Fiore, Rosalia and Amalia) and numerous children, all demanding his care and attention. He is hence forced to accept a position among the mobsters, in order to support all of his families, provoking the departure of Fiore, the only woman he actually loves. In the film's *finale*, Fiore leaves with their child and Mimì's communist friend.

As can be inferred from this synopsis, work in this film is ancillary, changing as a consequence of Mimì's personal life and of his adventurous ability to face the unknown. Its visual representation is however of great interest, predominantly because of its different declination in relation to gender. Many scenes show Mimì at work: at the beginning of the film in the mine, in the factory of Turin and back in Catania where Mimì is repeatedly shown as a team leader in the refinery. These moments are interestingly offset with sequences representing female work: underprivileged women at home working for the men, Rosalia at a dry cleaner, Amalia working in the sweatshop and Fiore selling handmade sweaters along with the 'workerist' magazine *Potere operaio* (Workers' Power).[10]

In showing its characters at work, the film engages with a broader conversation about class representation and politics in Italian and transnational leftist cinema. *Mimì metallurgico ferito nell'onore* proposes a layered structure that creates a development in the relation between the male character and his working environment, in contrast with the more fortuitous and static representation of women at work. The visual configuration of the very first sequence locates Mimì in an all-male working environment, visually characterized according to a perspective that flirts with literary *Verismo* and with the remnants of neorealism: sweaty and dirty male bodies, covered with rugged clothes and sulfur powder, arranged in a pyramid that mirrors the power relations in the mine.[11] The landscape is a white canvas, but it also entraps the men. The underprivileged workers cannot but submit to the hierarchical power of the mafia that possesses the mine because it provides the only source for survival and regulates every aspect of social and personal life. In the southern environment, work is hence just one of the elements that contribute to establishing the absolute power of mafia families.[12]

10   The 'movimento operaista' (workerist movement) was of great importance to Italian politics during the 1960s and 1970s, and was the cultural basis for the 'autunno caldo' (hot autumn) of 1969: a series of strikes and demonstrations mainly involving the industrial workers in Turin and other cities in the North.

11   See: Schoonover, K. 2012. *Brutal Vision: The Neorealist Body in Postwar Italian Cinema*. Minneapolis: University of Minnesota Press. Minneapolis. See especially Schoonover's Chapter 5: *"Neorealism Undone: The Resistant Physicalities of the Second Generation."*

12   The description of Sicilian society proposed by *Mimì metallurgico ferito nell'onore* reminds one of the problematic analysis in: Banfield, E. 1958. *The Moral Basis of a Backward Society*. Glencoe: The Free Press. Notwithstanding the wide criticism rightfully directed at Banfield's thesis, the idea of 'amoral familism' still circulated in Italian public discourse during the 1960s, sometimes infecting the cultural and visual representation of southern society. See, for instance, the following article, originally published in 1967: Pizzorno, A. 2001. "Familismo amorale e marginalità storica ovvero perché non c'è niente da fare a Montegrano." *Quaderni di Sociologia*, vol. 26, no. 27. 349–362.

The visual representation of mining work is aligned with the description of the behavior of southern peasants according to Antonio Gramsci: the need to survive in a brutal society, the impossibility of relying upon social relations outside of the family and the same individualism even in fighting the absolute power of those who detain the means of production.[13] Moreover, Gramsci's early proposal to change these relations and give power to the peasants is the same as that embraced by Mimì: to become a part of the industrialized North, and to participate in the communist fight for the modernization of society. Gramsci wrote about working class solidarity as something already within reach for northerners, while Mimì proposes something similar in leaving Sicily and its mafia rule to seek hope in Turin.

But soon, he realizes that the same power that rules Sicily has also colonized Turin, and that to continue the working-class struggle for a socialist revolution, individuals must compromise themselves. In the sulfur mine, however, Mimì is prevented from relating with his fellow workers by their criminal supervisor. In Turin, he can immediately become part of a social community of men, even if they are all subjected to mafia infiltrations. Mimì's social skills and his ability to adapt to the rules of the male group are the elements that keep him alive. But the film creates an underlying fracture between the main character and the other men. Because Mimì's position is never a consequence of working merit, it cannot be an active part of his social class as a point of resistance. He cannot indeed participate in the celebration of male effort and physical fatigue that is represented as an essential part of manual labor.[14] The film portrays an insurmountable gap between Mimì and any 'truth': he is aware of it but cannot act on his awareness.

Mimì can perform the gestures of the working position that the mafia assigns him, but he cannot bring his role to its extreme consequences: he acts like a metalworker, and the film visually celebrates the epic integration of human bodies with machines. But Mimì cannot participate in the fight for the communist revolution, as he becomes progressively more and

---

13   Gramsci, A. 1966. "Operai e contadini." *La questione meridionale*. Rome: Editori Riuniti.
14   See: Villa, F. 2014. "Fatica." *Lessico del cinema italiano. Forme di rappresentazione e forme di vita*, vol. I. Edited by Roberto De Gaetano. Milan and Udine: Mimesis. 373–432.

The Seduction of a Worker 475

more involved with the hegemonic power. Mimì's curse is not the alienation of being an effective tool in the assembly line – like Lulù in Elio Petri's *La classe operaia va in Paradiso* (The Working Class Goes to Heaven, 1971) – but rather, the impossibility of escaping the claws of traditional and hegemonic power. Such a difficulty is particularly clear when Mimì is sent to work in the refinery in Catania. The Turin factory is represented as epic, an environment where the human body dominates machines, the two visual elements combining in an organic composition made of metal, skin, light, muscles and fire. But the Catania refinery is shot as if it were a metal Moloch: a dark entanglement of tubes and knobs towering against the pale sky (see Figure 23). The frame is entirely void of humanity. The impossible celebratory dream of the mechanic symphony becomes the symbolization of the human submission to the system, where the individual is subjugated to the apparatus.[15] In the Catania plant, Mimì is often shown in close proximity to metal barriers or fences; his conversations with

Figure 23. In *Mimì metallurgico ferito nell'onore* (*The Seduction of Mimì*, Lina Wertmüller, 1972), the refinery is a metal Moloch, a dark entanglement of tubes and knobs towering against the pale sky.

15 For the dialectic between the celebration of machines and the subjugation of humanity in cinema, see Bertetto, P. 2001. *Fritz Lang Metropolis*. Turin: Lindau. 105–107.

other people become more and more fragmented and his work consists of surveilling and reprimanding other workers.

Still, Mimì is part of various male groups: at work, at the union, at the Communist Party meetings and when speaking with the mobsters. It is only in the film's final shot that he is forced to surrender to absolute loneliness, as Fiore and his former friend leave together and Mimì becomes a tiny spot in the broad wasteland of the sulfur mine. With this shot, the film attests to the failure of Mimì's adaptive behavior along with the impossibility of compromising with power and avoiding irreversible conditioning.

The brief representations of Rosalia, Fiore and Amalia as workers typically involve their isolation by the camera. They are associated with their lines of work, traditionally considered female tasks. Moreover, all three women are employed in the textile and apparel industry: Rosalia works in mechanized laundry, Amalia is a seamstress and Fiore is a knitter.[16]

Again, *Mimì metallurgico ferito nell'onore* adopts a contradictory position with respect to female working conditions and agency in a male-dominated world. The film's second sequence casts an awkward gaze on the female world: wives and daughters wash the feet of men while discussing the upcoming political elections. The elders of the Maddocheo family are entirely aligned with traditional expressions of power as they are part of the 'amorphous, disintegrated mass' that Gramsci discussed in the 1920s. The Maddocheo women obey a strict hierarchical order and rigid economy of labor, their job being to take care of the men's bodies – washing them or submitting to their sexual desires.[17] In the following sequence, politics and gender explicitly interlace: Mimì wants to have sexual intercourse with Rosalia, who passively resists him. Frustrated by his physical desire, Mimì verbally abuses the woman and imposes his political views by forbidding her to vote for the mafia candidate.

---

16   For women in the textile and apparel industries, see: Pescarolo, A. 2001. "Il lavoro e le risorse delle donne." *Storia sociale delle donne nell'Italia contemporanea*. Edited by Anna Bravo. Rome and Bari: Laterza. 127–178, 158.

17   For the patriarchal family as part of the discourse inventing southern Italy, see: Gribaudi, G. 1996. "Images of the South." *Italian Cultural Studies: An Introduction*. Edited by David Forgacs and Robert Lumley. Oxford: Oxford University Press. 72–87. See especially Page 84.

Once disconnected from her husband, however, Rosalia expresses her abilities and empowerment: she dismisses the reproductive system and becomes part of the productive one. To be free from the Maddocheos' economic restraints, she finds employment in a dry cleaner and expresses in a letter to her husband her pride in being an industrial worker herself. The film shows Rosalia fully mastering a series of machines: the huge press, but also her new Vespa scooter. While in the aforementioned second sequence she was detached from the other women of the family, isolated and silent in a two-shot with her husband, Rosalia now interacts with other women, including one who teaches her how to drive the scooter and others who smoke with her during the factory lunch break. These other women are at the margins of the frame: silenced, out of focus, discarded as visually unimportant. Still, they exist. Beneath the surface of the film – and importantly through her work – Rosalia briefly creates a counter narrative, enabled by the genealogic transmission of knowledge among women of the same age and social background.[18] The segregation of the female workplace, instrumental to the protection of male 'honor,' becomes the crucible where new lifestyles can begin through the sharing of experiences and potentially subversive practices.

We can interpret this passage according to feminist theories: the women create a network to help each other in dealing both with the technology of machines (Rosalia and her Vespa) and the technology of gender. Here, my primary reference is Teresa de Lauretis, who emphasizes the need "to think of gender as the product and the process of a number of social technologies, of techno-social or bio-medical apparati," going beyond even Michel Foucault in considering a feminist perspective of gender and power.[19] In *Mimì metallurgico ferito nell'onore*, being in the public sphere of a work environment contributes to shaping the dialectic between men and women through the differing representation of the spaces and the relationships between coworkers. Men can speak to each other and create a

---

18   See: Ferguson, K. E. 1991. "Interpretation and Genealogy in Feminism." *Signs*, vol. 16, no. 2. 322–339.

19   de Lauretis, T. 1987. *Technologies of Gender: Essays on Theory, Film and Fiction.* Bloomington: Indiana University Press. 3. De Lauretis herself quotes from: Foucault, M. 1980. *The History of Sexuality, Vol. I: An Introduction.* New York: Vintage Books.

visible community at the workplace, discussing how power shapes the work as 'dispositif.' Women can be in the same visual frame, but their discourses are made silent by the power of representation (paradoxically articulated through another woman's gaze, that of Lina Wertmüller). The film visually confirms the women's ability to gather and transmit knowledge, but tames the revolutionary potential of such a practice by literally silencing the multiplicity of female voices.

The representation of the gendered division of labor environments hence contributes to a broader discourse about sexism in Italy in the late 1960s and early 1970s, even in Communist culture. At the same time, *Mimì metallurgico ferito nell'onore* underlines the impossibility of pursuing an actual revolution when every aspect of social life is tainted by power as asymmetric energy that induces men into a dialectic between enforcement or submission that cannot be escaped. In other words, work is one of the apparati of the representation and (re)production of power, and as such is organized according to the same rules as all other aspects of social life. The mafia and communism are ideologically opposed, but they coexist as forces: the former a parasitical growth within the too rigid heart of the latter.

MATTIA LENTO

37 Migration, Industry and Class Struggle in *Trevico-Torino: Viaggio nel Fiat-Nam* (1973)

Italian cinema between the 1960s and 1970s is populated with laborers. Figures of industrial workers can already be found in previous eras, but it is during this period that they acquire a specific visibility, across genres. It is in particular the laborer of southern origins, eradicated and lost in the industrial North, who emerges as the emblematic figure of the years of the so-called economic boom and, later, of the 1968 protests.[1] Italy's postwar development was of course the source of enormous richness for the country, but also of deep imbalances and social tensions, caused in part by the inability of the Italian state to handle the huge changes it provoked.[2]

Several authors of the period answered the call of industrial laborers to political and cinematic action. Among them were also some directors who were not accustomed to the representation of the proletariat, at least not in an explicitly political and militant way. Ettore Scola, for example, had mostly been active, up to that moment, as a comedic screenwriter and director. Yet at the beginning of the 1970s he made three films focused on characters connected to the world of industrial labor: *Dramma della gelosia* (The Pizza Triangle, 1970), *Permettete? Rocco Papaleo* (My Name is

1 Zaccagnini, E. 2009. *I mostri al lavoro. Contadini, commendatori ed impiegati all'italiana*. Rome: Sovera. 78–90. On the Italian economic miracle, starting at the end of the 1950s and continuing throughout the 1960s, see: Castronovo, V. 2012. *Il miracolo economico*. Rome: Laterza. On the workers' protest movement at the end of the 1960s, with specific reference to the southern presence in Turin, see: Gallo, S. 2012. *Senza attraversare le frontiere. Le migrazioni interne dall'Unità a oggi*. Rome: Laterza. 183–204.
2 This is the thesis advanced by historian Paul Ginsborg. See: Ginsborg, P. 1989. *Storia d'Italia dal dopoguerra a oggi*. Rome: Einaudi.

Rocco Papaleo, 1971) and *Trevico-Torino: Viaggio nel Fiat-Nam* (Trevico-Turin: Voyage in Fiatnam, 1973).[3]

The first two films share a protagonist of the caliber of Marcello Mastroianni, and they are hence ambitious productions from an economic standpoint. The third film, on the contrary, has played a less important role in Scola's career. It was basically self-produced with a scant budget, and it had a rather complex life (to say the least) in terms of distribution. *Trevico-Torino* is perhaps not an entirely successful film; it might not be on par with Scola's later films such as *Brutti, sporchi e cattivi* (Down and Dirty, 1974), *Una giornata particolare* (A Special Day, 1976) and *La famiglia* (The Family, 1987). Yet it is able to render with great efficacy the many contradictions that characterized Italy at the time, and in particular the city that was the symbol of Italian industrial development: Turin, historic headquarters of Fiat, one of twentieth-century Italy's most successful companies.[4]

The aim of this chapter is to synthetically enucleate the themes, discourses and historical facts presented in *Trevico-Torino*, while at the same time analyzing some formal features of the film, often sidelined by a critical tradition that has come to pay outsized attention to its political and ideological aspects.

The Film

Trevico-Torino was shot with 16 mm film in 1971 and 1972, and produced by Unitelefilm, the production company of the strongest communist party in western Europe: the Partito Comunista Italiano (Italian

[3] This period also marks Scola's passage from socialist to communist militancy and the beginning of his commitment to political documentary. See: Santi, P. M. and Vittori, R. 1987. *I film di Ettore Scola*. Rome: Gremese. 11–114.

[4] In 1952, the company created a new department called 'Cinefiat' that began producing films about its own industrial activities. 'Cinefiat' remained in operation until the end of the 1970s. For more on this, see: Bonifazio, P. 2014. *Schooling in Modernity: The Politics of Sponsored Films in Postwar Italy*. Toronto: Toronto University Press. 51–86.

Communist Party, PCI).[5] Despite already being a successful director, Scola could not find a producer for his story, which was considered too political and unattractive for the market. He thus decided to produce the film himself, then turned to the small production company of the PCI, which sustained the project by lending resources and equipment.[6] The fundamental Communist support came, however, from Diego Novelli: a journalist who – at the time[7] – wrote for the Party newspaper *L'Unità*[8] and a great connoisseur of Turin. Novelli introduced Scola to the social reality of the city and even contributed to making the film.[9]

Trevico-Torino tells the story of Fortunato Santospirito, a young man from Trevico, the same small town of the southern province of Avellino (Campania) where Scola himself was born. Fortunato arrives in Turin to start work at Fiat. The film's title is thus a reference to the migratory path of the protagonist and the subtitle "Viaggio nel Fiat-Nam" refers both to the narrative structure of the film, a sort of visual itinerary of knowledge and to the definition of Turin, taken from "uno slogan d'uso comune" (a common slogan)[10] that points to the analogy of the "città-fabbrica" (factory city)[11] with Vietnam during its war with the United States.

The film opens at Turin's central train station: Fortunato has just arrived, and he is faced with a typical northern Italian winter cityscape of frenzy, fog and grayness. He soon realizes that the Fiat hiring process will not be a speedy affair. Virtually penniless, he is forced to look for a makeshift

---

5 See: Carbone, L. R. 2015. *Il cinema documentario di militanza. L'ordinamento delle carte della sezione filmica del fondo Unitelefilm*. Università della Tuscia: M. A. Thesis.
6 See: Scola, E and Bertini, A. 1996. *Il cinema e io. Ettore Scola*. Rome: Officine. 114–115.
7 Novelli would become mayor of Turin in 1975.
8 *L'Unità* was founded in 1924 by the philosopher and communist Antonio Gramsci.
9 See: Novelli, D. 2002. "Il caso Trevico-Torino." *Trevico-Cinecittà. L'avventuroso viaggio di Ettore Scola*. Edited by Vito Zagarrio. Venice: Marsilio. 116–119.
10 Ellero, R. 1988. *Ettore Scola*, Venice: La Nuova Italia. 47.
11 On the cinematic representation of Turin as a factory city, see: Prono, F. 2002. "Cinegrafia di una città-fabbrica." *Ombre metropolitane. Città e spettacolo nel Novecento*. Edited by Giaime Alonge and Federica Mazzocchi. Turin: DAMS. 259–271.

accommodation. The housing situation in Turin is dramatic and Fortunato is forced back to the train station for shelter, a space populated at night by the city's outcasts. The next day, he turns to a Catholic institution that assists southern migrants and meets Don Luciano Mais, a progressive priest who plays himself in the film. Don Mais advises Fortunato on the next steps, suggesting that, once he is admitted to the factory, he partake in workers' struggles to gain a stronger class and political consciousness. In spite of himself, the priest cannot offer any material help, and Fortunato is forced to wander for several days between soup kitchens and public dormitories, where he meets several people who have fallen through society's cracks.

Upon entering the factory, Fortunato also finds an accommodation, however poor, and he falls in with the Communist Party first, then with the extra-parliamentary left. In particular, he meets Vicky, a young student of bourgeois extraction, who is an activist with Lotta Continua (Continuous Struggle), an extreme left-wing organization. Fortunato takes a fancy to Vicky, who is a *volontaria politico* (political volunteer)[12] in the working-class neighborhoods, and through her he comes into contact with the problems of laboring families, of the proletarian tenements and of the city as a whole. In the meantime, Fortunato attends a night school to earn a diploma and better his condition, but he finds no support in Vicky, who expects him to rebel more completely against the system. The socio-cultural gap between them grows wider and Fortunato, not reciprocated sentimentally, distances himself from her. The film ends when Fortunato, after a quarrel with his team leader, is moved from the assembly line to the ironworks, where he struggles more and more to combine school with work.

After shooting his film, Scola had quite some trouble finding distributors and was only able to show it in a few theaters: the film was thus a financial failure. In some interviews, the director points to a boycott by the Fiat owner Gianni Agnelli.[13] In the second half of the 1970s, however, the film became "un piccolo hit nelle Feste dell'Unità, nelle università, nelle scuole occupate, nei circoli sindacali, nelle sezioni del PCI e in decine di

---

12   In Italy, where the idea of volunteer work has been historically tied up with the Catholic world, the *volontariato politico* is explicitly connected to a left-wing social engagement.
13   Scola, E. 1980. *Parla il cinema italiano, Volume 2*. Edited by Aldo Tassone. Foligno: Il Formichiere. 311.

Migration, Industry and Class Struggle

altre occasioni pubbliche legate al composito palcoscenico della sinistra" (a minor hit at the *Feste dell'Unità*, in the universities, in occupied schools, in the union circles, in the PCI sections and in many other public contexts connected to the composite landscape of the left).[14] In 1978, *Trevico-Torino* was finally broadcasted on national television (RAI), and exactly forty years later a restored version was presented at the Turin Film Festival.[15]

Themes

It is not easy to sum up the themes, the historical issues and the discourses concerning *Trevico-Torino*: their density and complexity is extraordinary. We could start by saying that the plot of Scola's film revolves around an automobile factory that the spectator is only allowed to see from the outside. The director was indeed denied authorization for filming the assembly line and he had to work around this prohibition by inserting still, black and white images of the factory, overlaid with titles describing Fortunato's supposed activity inside.[16] Paradoxically, this solution reveals itself in the film as a strength: what emerges is not the reality of the factory so much as the life of the quintessential Italian factory city – Turin between the 1960s and 1970s – brimming with historical events. The term 'factory city' is warranted by the fact that Turin and its inhabitants have been strongly affected by the presence of Fiat ever since the first decades of the twentieth century. In the second postwar era, with the economic boom and the start of the great exodus from the South to the North, the factory and the

14 Masi, S. 2006. *Ettore Scola*. Rome: Gremese. 40.
15 My analysis is based on the unrestored copy of the film, preserved at the Archivio Audiovisivo del Movimento Operaio e Democratico (Audiovisual Archive of the Democratic and Labor Movement, AAMOD). The film is available online here: <http://patrimonio.aamod.it/aamod-web/film/detail/IL8600002014/22/trevico-torino.html>. Last accessed September 4, 2020.
16 Masi, S. 2006. *Ettore Scola*. 38–40. Fiat only allowed filmmakers employed by its own cinema department to enter company premises. This policy ended in the early 1990s, when Mimmo Calopresti filmed *La seconda volta* (The Second Time, 1995) in what was already a postindustrial factory.

city truly seemed to coincide, at least in common perception. The industrial production process is thus excluded from Scola's representation, but its social consequences emerge for this exact reason with even more force.

The housing problem is among the most important associated with Fiat's presence in the city. At the beginning of the film, it seems that Fortunato's story is only a pretext for showing the deplorable housing conditions of the factory city. It was Diego Novelli, Scola's 'Virgil,'[17] who introduced the director to the hell of run-down lodgings, to the shabby attics and anonymous barracks where the Turin proletariat lived. Connected to the theme of housing is the problem of strong social exclusion: all those who do not contribute to the local production cycle, dominated by Fiat and its satellite activities, become outcasts. Fortunato experiences the so-called 'margins'[18] of the city and risks getting caught there: he meets hopeless people at the train station, in the dormitories and in the charity kitchens, and the only road of escape seems to be Fiat. When he first sees the factory, it appears to Fortunato almost as a mirage (see Figure 24).

Figure 24. The Fiat factory appears almost as a mirage in *Trevico-Torino: Viaggio nel Fiat-Nam* (Trevico-Turin: Voyage in Fiatnam, Ettore Scola, 1973).

17 Scola, E and Bertini, A. 1996. *Il cinema e io*. 118.
18 On the theme of social exclusion in Italy, see: Forgacs, D. 2014. *Italy's Margins: Social Exclusion and Nation Formation since 1861*. Cambridge: Cambridge University Press.

Migration, Industry and Class Struggle

Fortunato's engagement with the Communist Party forces him to confront a political and unionist left that, in that historical post-1968 moment, seems out of touch with the needs and aspirations of the working class as a whole. But Fortunato also has to deal with a maximalist and extra-parliamentary left, which is pushing for an uncompromising rebellion against the dominant classes and enjoying a consensus among younger workers. Nevertheless, the film foregrounds the weaknesses of this new left's political propositions, exceedingly idealistic and too tied up in the aspirations of enlightened students from the bourgeoisie.[19] Though it was produced by the PCI, Scola's film is not merely a work of political propaganda. Its *raison d'être* is the representation of twentieth century Italy's last great internal exodus through the exemplary story of Fortunato, a young southern migrant uprooted by his contact with the industrial North.

Style and Critical Reception

The style of *Trevico-Torino* is strongly influenced by the scant economic resources Scola had at his disposal. First of all, the choice of 16 mm for the film format, much cheaper than the classic 35 mm, endows the film with a strong documentary or even amateurish quality.[20] The actors, almost all of whom are non-professionals and often play themselves,[21] reinforce the film's underlying ambiguity, which at times even seems to inhibit the ability of the spectator to buy into the fiction, pushing them towards a

---

19   Masi, S. 2006. *Ettore Scola*. 40. On the relationship between southern migration and social conflict in Turin, see: Gallo, S. 2012. *Senza attraversare le frontiere*. 183–188.
20   The 16 mm format was introduced in the 1920s and it later became, thanks its reduced costs, the preferred format of documentarians and independent filmmakers.
21   The lead, Paolo Turco, had already been acting for a few years: in 1969 he had even co-starred, together with diva Gina Lollobrigida, in Mauro Bolognini's *Un bellissimo novembre* (That Splendid November).

documentary reading of the text.[22] Scola's initial project was indeed a documentary, only later developing into as a full-fledged fictional film.[23] Moreover, the shooting took place without a proper screenplay, especially for the first half of the film.[24]

From a narrative standpoint, the first half is thinner, but it is also stronger aesthetically. The camera follows Fortunato during the first moments of his migration, and it seems almost to achieve the sort of character *pedinamanto* (tailing) theorized by one of neorealism's most influential intellectuals: Cesare Zavattini.[25] What emerges from this itinerary, which initially resembles a descent into hell, is the reality of southern migration to Turin. The film's migrants become a sort of collective and suffering character.

More than a full-fledged character, Fortunato seems to function here as a medium, a filter necessary to recount the reality that surrounds him. In one of the first scenes, Fortunato meets a group of workers who, at his urge, disclose the serious problem of lodging southerners in Turin. As many critics have noted, Scola's style is close here to social documentary or *cinéma vérité*, thanks to the synchronous sound of voices, uncontrolled camera movements and the proximity of the camera to the subjects represented (see Figure 25).

Such a direct style returns several times during the first half of the film, albeit with different outcomes. In one scene, Fortunato, still without a place

---

22   According to Roger Odin, film texts are endowed with 'modes of production' – that is, suggestions for reading that the spectator may or may not receive through 'modes of reading.' These are influenced, among other things, by the film's shooting context. See: Odin, R. 2000. *De la fiction*. Bruxelles: De Boeck Université.
23   On this process, see: Iaccio, P (ed.). 2004. *La storia sullo schermo. Il Novecento*. Cosenza: Pellegrini. 79–80.
24   Scola, E and Bertini, A. 1996. *Il cinema e io*. 118–119.
25   On this theme, see: Haaland, T. 2012. *Italian Neorealist Cinema*. Edinburgh: Edinburgh University Press. 50–57. The link between Scola's film, on the one hand, and neorealist and documentary aesthetics, on the other hand, was also noted by contemporary critics. See, for example: Argentieri, M. 1973. "'Trevico-Torino.' Semplicità ed efficacia." *Cinemasessanta*, n. 93. 58–60. Zavattini's writings are collected in: Zavattini, C. 1979. *Opere*. Milan: Bompiani.

Figure 25. In some scenes of *Trevico-Torino: Viaggio nel Fiat-Nam* (Trevico-Turin: Voyage in Fiatnam, Ettore Scola, 1973), Ettore Scola's style is close to social documentary or *cinéma vérité*, thanks to the synchronous sound of voices, uncontrolled camera movements and the proximity of the camera to the subjects represented.

to stay, is forced to seek shelter at the train station at night, where he meets the urban sub-proletariat. The darkness, together with the shouting and the type of subjects represented, transform this scene into a veritable nightmare tinged with strongly expressionistic tones. In general, the film's style is characterized by discontinuity and fast changes in rhythm. It seems at times to be witnessing a modification in the intentions of the director himself.

In the second half of the film, the drama gains the upper hand, together with Scola's ideology, though without achieving thoroughly convincing results. This was also the opinion of contemporary critics: they generally appreciated the film, even awarding it some prizes, but they also recognized its narrative weaknesses, criticizing the dramaturgic structure "con le sue scarse svolte e la sua schematica linearità" (with its scarcity of turning points and its schematic linearity), and a certain superficiality on Scola's part in relation to "certe regole strutturali e di linguaggio" (some structural and stylistic rules).[26] The writer Alberto Moravia, who often

---

26 Guglielmino, G. M. 1982. *Cinema sì. I film segnalati dal Sindacato nazionale critici cinematografici italiani. Volume I*. Rome: Bulzoni. 141–142.

doubled as a film critic throughout his career, appreciated *Trevico-Torino*'s "piglio documentario [...] quella sobrietà e verità che [...] diventano automaticamente indignazione e denunzia" (documentary attitude (...) that sobriety and truth (...) that automatically become indignation and condemnation); he appeared less convinced of the "sentimentalismo" (sentimentalism) of the second half.[27] One review by the celebrated critic Goffredo Fofi went so far as to associate the second half with the *commedia all'italiana* (comedy Italian style), a genre in which Ettore Scola had already made a name for himself as a screenwriter and director. Fofi wrote:

> Qui si torna a criteri di cinema-verità, però impuri in quanto a essi si giustappongono furbizie spettacolari tipiche della commedia di costume all'italiota [...]. Così *Trevico-Torino* non è poi nella sostanza così diverso dai precedenti film di Scola. Lo è soltanto in una pregevole e importante superficie: il fatto cioè di spostarsi dalla visione romana della realtà italiana verso la periferia; nello scoprire quantomeno una dimensione documentaria e di denuncia a partire da facce vere e strade vere; nel dire cosa è Torino oggi.
>
> (Here, we must return to *cinéma vérité* criteria, but to impure criteria insofar as they are juxtaposed with the spectacular shrewdness typical of the dimwitted Italian *commedia di costume* (comedy of manners) [...]. *Trevico-Torino* is not substantially different from Scola's previous films. It is different only on one commendable and important surface level: it moves us from the Roman vision of Italian reality toward the peripheries; at the very least, it discovers a documentary and denunciatory dimension, starting with real faces and real street; it tells us what Turin is today.)[28]

Fofi's review is rather harsh on the film's style, but it also recognizes in Scola the merit of having highlighted a reality that had remained, until that moment, cinematically peripheral, a reality that Fofi himself, in 1964, had already documented in a pioneering ethnographical report (still considered a precious reference for the study of Italy's internal migration today).[29] Just

---

27   Moravia, A. 1975. *Al cinema*. Milan: Bompiani.
28   Fofi, G. 1973. "Qualche film." *Quaderni piacentini*, no. 50.
29   Fofi, G. 1964. *L'immigrazione meridionale a Torino*. Milan: Feltrinelli. On the editorial vicissitudes of the report and its republication in 2009, see: Battaglia, F. M. 2009. "Una Torino proibita 35 anni dopo." *Cronache di Liberal*. October 2. 20.

like that report, *Trevico-Torino* – albeit a as minor title in the filmography of a canonical director – still remains a precious text for comprehending many aspects of a fundamental moment in Italian industrial, economic and political history.

Translated by Lorenzo Marmo

APPENDIX
Italian Industrial Literature and Film – A Tentative Canon

Literature

Giovanni Arpino (Pola, 1927-Turin, 1987)
   Gli anni del giudizio (Einaudi, 1958)
   Una nuvola d'ira (Mondadori, 1962)

Nanni Balestrini (Milan, 1935-Rome, 2019)
   Vogliamo tutto (Feltrinelli, 1971)

Alberto Bevilacqua (Parma, 1934-Rome, 2013)
   La Califfa (Rizzoli, 1964)

Luciano Bianciardi (Grosetto, 1922-Milan 1971)
   Il lavoro culturale (Feltrinelli, 1956)
   L'integrazione (Bompiani, 1960)
   La vita agra (Rizzoli, 1962)

Romano Bilenchi (Colle Val d'Elsa, 1909-Florence, 1989)
   Il capofabbrica (Circoli, 1935)

Giancarlo Buzzi (Como, 1929-Milan, 2015)
   Il senatore (Feltrinelli, 1958)
   L'amore mio italiano (Mondadori, 1963)

Italo Calvino (Santiago de Las Vegas de La Habana 1923-Siena 1985)
    La nuvola di smog (Einaudi, 1958)
    La speculazione edilizia (Einaudi, 1963)

Inisero Cremaschi (Fontanellato, 1928-Palazzolo sull'Oglio, 2014)
    A scopo di lucro (Mondadori, 1965)

Luigi Davì (Valdigna d'Aosta, 1929)
    Gymkhana-Cross (Einaudi, 1957)
    Uno mandato da un tale (Parenti, 1959)
    Il capolavoro (Einaudi, 1964)

Tommaso Di Ciaula (Adelfia, 1941)
    Tuta blu (Feltrinelli, 1978)

Vincenzo Guerrazzi (Mammola, 1940-Genoa, 2012)
    Nord e Sud uniti nella lotta (Marsilio, 1974)

Primo Levi (Turin, 1919-Turin 1987)
    La chiave a stella (Einaudi, 1978)

Dacia Maraini (Fiesole, 1936)
    "Le mani" in *Mio marito* (Bompiani, 1968)

Lucio Mastronardi (Vigevano, 1930-Vigevano, 1979)
    Il maestro di Vigevano (Einaudi, 1962)
    Il calzolaio di Vigevano (Einaudi, 1962)

Elsa Morante (Rome, 1912-Rome, 1985)
    La Storia (Einaudi, 1974)

Anna Maria Ortese (Rome, 1914-Rapallo, 1998)
    Silenzio a Milano (Laterza, 1958)

Appendix: Italian Industrial Literature and Film 493

Ottiero Ottieri (Rome, 1924-Milan, 2002)
    Tempi stretti (Einaudi, 1957)
    Donnarumma all'assalto (Bompiani, 1959)
    La linea gotica: Taccuino industriale 1948-1958 (Bompiani, 1962)

Goffredo Parise (Vicenza, 1929-Treviso, 1986)
    Il padrone (Feltrinelli, 1965)

Giovanni Testori (Novate Milanese, 1923-Milan, 1993)
    Il ponte della Ghisolfa (Feltrinelli, 1958)
    La gilda di MacMahon (Feltrinelli, 1959)

Paolo Volponi (Urbino, 1924-Ancona, 1994)
    Memoriale (Garzanti, 1962)
    La macchina mondiale (Garzanti, 1965)

Fiction Film

Michelangelo Antonioni (Ferrara, 1912-Rome, 2007)
    Il grido (1957)
    Deserto rosso (1964)

Alberto Bevilacqua (Parma, 1934-Rome, 2013)
    La califfa (1970)

Mauro Bolognini (Pistoia, 1922-Rome, 2001)
    Metello (1970)

Eduardo De Filippo (Naples, 1900-Rome, 1984)
    Napoletani a Milano (1953)

Vittorio De Sica (Sora, 1901-Neuilly-sur-Seine, 1974)
   Lo chiameremo Andrea (1972)
   Una breve vacanza (1973)

Luciano Emmer (Milan, 1918-Rome, 2009)
   La ragazza in vetrina (1961)

Giuseppe Fina (Lesa, 1924-Villasimius, 1998)
   Pelle viva (1962)

Pietro Germi (Genoa, 1914-Rome, 1974)
   L'uomo di paglia (1958)

Ugo Gregoretti (Rome, 1930-Rome, 2019)
   Omicron (1963)

Alberto Lattuada (Vaprio d'Adda, 1914-Orvieto, 2005)
   Mafioso (1962)

Carlo Lizzani (Rome, 1922-Rome, 2013)
   Achtung! Banditi! (1951)
   La vita agra (1964)

Raffaello Matarazzo (Rome, 1909-Rome, 1966)
   I figli di nessuno (1951)

Mario Monicelli (Rome, 1915-Rome, 2010)
   I compagni (1963)
   Romanzo popolare (1974)

Ermanno Olmi (Bergamo, 1931-Asiago, 2018)
   Il tempo si e fermato (1959)
   Il posto (1961)
   I fidanzati (1963)

Appendix: Italian Industrial Literature and Film

Elio Petri (Rome, 1929-Rome, 1982)
  Il maestro di Vigevano (1963)
  La classe operaia va in paradiso (1972)

Gillo Pontecorvo (Pisa, 1919-Rome, 2006)
  Giovanna (1955)

Francesco Rosi (Naples, 1922-Rome, 2015)
  Le mani sulla citta (1963)
  Il caso Mattei (1972)

Roberto Rossellini (Rome, 1906-Rome, 1977)
  Europa '51 (1952)

Luciano Salce (Rome, 1922-Rome, 1989)
  Il sindacalista (1972)

Ettore Scola (Trevico, 1931-Rome, 2016)
  Trevico-Torino: Viaggio nel Fiat-Nam (1973)

Steno (Rome, 1917-Rome, 1988)
  Il padrone e l'operaio (1975)
  La patata bollente (1979)

Luchino Visconti (Milan, 1906-Rome, 1976)
  Rocco e i suoi fratelli (1960)

Lina Wertmüller (Rome, 1928)
  Mimì metallurgico ferito nell'onore (1972)

Literature in Translation

Balestrini, N. 2016. *We Want Everything: The Novel of Italy's Hot Autumn*. Translated by Matt Holden. London and New York: Verso.

Bianciardi, L. 1965. *La vita agra: It's a Hard Life, a Novel*. Translated by Eric Mosbacher. New York: Viking Press.

Calvino, I. 2018. "A Plunge into Real Estate." *Difficult Loves: Smog, A Plunge into Real Estate*. Translated by D. S. Carne-Ross. London: Vintage.

——. 2018. "Smog." *Difficult Loves: Smog, A Plunge into Real Estate*. Translated by William Weaver. London: Vintage.

Levi, P. 2017. *The Monkey's Wrench*. Translated by William Weaver. New York: Simon & Schuster.

Maraini, D. 2004. "These Hands." *My Husband*. Translated by Vera F. Golini. Waterloo, Ontario: Wilfrid Laurier University Press.

Morante, E. 1977. *History: A Novel*. Translated by William Weaver. New York: Knopf.

Ottieri, O. 1962. *The Men at the Gate*. Translated by I. M. Rawson. Boston: Houghton Mifflin.

Parise, G. 1966. *The Boss*. Translated by William Weaver. New York: Knopf.

Volponi, P. 1964. *My Troubles Began*. Translated by Belén Sevareid. New York: Grossman.

——. 1967. *The Worldwide Machine: A Novel*. Translated by Belén Sevareid. New York: Grossman.

Bibliography

The following is a cumulative bibliography of all published sources cited in this book.

Acland, C R and Massoon, H (eds). 2011. *Useful Cinema*. Durham: Duke University Press.
Agamben, G. 1998. *Homo Sacer. Sovereign Power and Bare Life*. Stanford: Stanford University Press.
——. 1999. *Remnants of Auschwitz: The Witness and the Archive*. New York: Zone Books.
——. 1993. *The Coming Community*. Minneapolis and London: University of Minnesota Press.
——. 2011. *The Kingdom and the Glory: For a Theological Genealogy of Economy and Government*. Stanford: Stanford University Press.
——. 2003. "Una biopolitica minore." *Intervista a Giorgio Agamben*. Edited by Paolo Perticari. Rome: manifestolibri.
——. 2009. *What is an Apparatus? And Other Essays*. Stanford: Stanford University Press.
Agnoletto, S. 2014. *The Italians Who Built Toronto: Italians Workers and Contractors in the City's Housebuilding Industry, 1950–1980*. Bern: Peter Lang.
Agosti, A. 2008. "Lavoro e lavoratori sullo schermo cinematografico: esempi del passato, testimonianze dell'oggi." *RASSEGNA CNOS*, vol. 23, no. 3.
Alicata, M. 1946. "La corrente *Politecnico*." *Rinascita*, vol. 3, no.s 5–6.
Alighieri, D. 1996. *The Divine Comedy of Dante Alighieri*. Translated by Robert M. Durling. New York and Oxford: Oxford University Press.
Allason, B. *Unrra-Casas: contributo alla ricostruzione*. 1950. Rome: Istituto Grafico Tiberino.
Allegri, G and Ciccarelli, R. 2013. *Il Quinto Stato*. Florence: Ponte delle Grazie.
——. 2011. *La furia dei cervelli*. Rome: Manifestolibri.
Alovisio, S and Carluccio, G (eds). 2014. *Introduzione al cinema muto italiano*. Turin: UTET.
Alovisio, S. 2020. "'In verità le sue didascalie furono una palla di piombo'. La collaborazione tra d'Annunzio e Pastrone alla luce di una nuova fonte d'archivio." *Fotogrammi a parole*. Avellino: Edizioni Sinestesie.
Altarocca, C. 1972. *Parise*. Florence: La Nuova Italia.
Ammaniti, N. 1994. *Branchie*. Rome: Ediesse.
Anceschi, L. 1956. "Discorso generale." *Il Verri*, no.1.

Anon. 2011. "C'erano una volta nelle scuole i documentari della Cineteca," *Corriere della Sera*. 14 December.
Antonello, P and Mussgnug, F. 2009. "Introduction." *Postmodern 'impegno': Ethics and Commitment in Contemporary Italian Culture*. Oxford: Peter Lang.
Antonioni, M. 1996. *The Architecture of Vision: Writings and Interviews on Cinema*. Edited by Carlo di Carlo and Giorgio Tinazzi. Chicago: University of Chicago Press.
Aquarone, A. 1995. *L'organizzazione dello Stato totalitario*. Turin: Einaudi.
Arcangeli, M. 2007. *Giovani scrittori, scritture giovani. Ribelli, sognatori, cannibali, bad girls*. Rome: Carocci.
Argentieri, M. 1973. "'Trevico-Torino.' Semplicità ed efficacia." *Cinemasessanta*, n. 93.
Aristarco, G. 1985. "Il cinema. Dalla chimica ai processi elettronici." *Il nuovo mondo dell'immagine elettronica*. Edited by Guido Aristarco and Teresa Aristarco. Bari: Edizioni Dedalo.
——. 1957. "Il mestiere del critico – Poveri ma belli." *Cinema Nuovo*, no.s 101–102.
Armstrong, T J (ed). 1992. *Michel Foucault Philosopher*. Hemel Hempstead: Harvester Wheatsheaf.
Arpino, G. 1982. "Confessione." *Una nuvola d'ira*. Milan: Rizzoli.
——. 1965. *Gli anni difficili*. Turin: Einaudi.
——. 1962. "Lettera a Salinari." *Vie Nuove*. 15 March.
——. 2009. *Una nuvola d'ira*. Milan: BUR.
Arrowsmith, W. 1995. *Antonioni: The Poet of Images*. Oxford University Press.
Associazione Stranamente (ed). 1994. *Bulloni & tute: cinema e lavoro*. Associazione Stranamente.
Bakhtin, M. 1981. "Forms of Time and of the Chronotope in the Novel." *The Dialogic Imagination*. Translated by Caryl Emerson and Michael Holquist. Austin: University of Texas Press.
Baldelli, P (ed). 1963. *I compagni di Mario Monicelli*. Bologna: Cappelli.
Baldi, A. 2000. "La metropoli matrigna: *Silenzio a Milano* di A. M. Ortese." *Studi Novecenteschi*, vol. 27, no. 59. 187–209.
Baldini, A. 2008. "La trilogia della disillusione di Arpino." *Il comunista. Una storia letteraria dalla Resistenza agli anni Settanta*. Turin: UTET.
Balestrini, N. 1988. *Vogliamo tutto*. Milan: Mondadori.
——. 2004. *Vogliamo tutto*. Rome: Derive Approdi.
——. 2014. *Vogliamo Tutto*. Translated by Matt Holden. Melbourne: Telephone Publishing.
——. 2016. *We Want Everything*. Translation by Matt Holden. London: Verso.
Balestrini, N and Giuliani, A. 1964. "Introduzione." *Gruppo 63. La nuova letteratura. Palermo 1963*. Edited by Nanni Balestrini and Alfredo Giuliani. Milan: Feltrinelli.

Banfield, E. 1958. *The Moral Basis of a Backward Society*. Glencoe: Free Press.
Banita, G. 2014. "From Isfahan to Ingolstadt: Bertolucci's *La via del petrolio* and the Global Culture of Neorealism." *Oil Culture*. Edited by Ross Barrett and Daniel Worden. Minneapolis: University of Minnesota Press.
Barattoni, L. 2012. *Italian Post-Neorealist Cinema*. Edinburgh: Edinburgh University Press.
Barbato, A. 1965. "Il Colosseo di plastica". *L'Espresso*, 11 April.
Barbera, G and Tosatti, G (eds). 2007. *United States Information Service di Trieste. Catalogo del fondo cinematografico 1941–1966*. Rome: Pubblicazione degli Archivi di Stato.
Bàrberi Squarotti, G and Ossola, C (eds). 1997. *Letteratura e industria: Atti del 15° Congresso AISLLI*. Florence: Olschki.
Barberi Squarotti, G. 1992. "Introduzione." *Giovanni Arpino. Opere. Storie de nostro tempo*, vol. 4. Edited by Giorgio Barberi Squarotti. Milan: Rusconi.
——. 1978. *Poesia e narrativa del secondo Novecento*. Milan: Mursia.
Barilli, R. 1995. *La neoavanguardia italiana. Dalla nascita del "Verri" alla fine di "Quindici"*. Bologna: Il Mulino.
——. 1964. *La barriera del naturalismo. Studi sulla narrativa italiana contemporanea*. Milan: Il Saggiatore.
Barnett, V. 1955. "Competitive Coexistence and the Communist Challenge in Italy." *Political Science Quarterly*, vol. 70, no. 2.
Barrera, G and Tosatti, G (eds). 2007. *United States Information Service di Trieste. Catalogo del fondo cinematografico (1941–1966)*. Rome: Ministero per i Beni e le Attività Culturali, Direzione Generale per gli Archivi.
Barthes, R. 1972. *Critical Essays*. Translated by Richard Howard. Evanston, IL: Northwestern University Press.
——. 1993. *Œuvres completes: Tome I (1942-1965)*. Edited by Éric Marty. Paris: Éditions du Seuil.
Basaglia, F. 1981. *Scritti*. Turin: Einaudi.
Battaglia, F M. 2009. "Una Torino proibita 35 anni dopo." *Cronache di Liberal*. 2 October.
Bayman, L. 2014. *The Operatic and the Everyday in Postwar Italian Film Melodrama*. Edinburgh: Edinburgh University Press.
——. 2017. "The Popularity of Italian Film Comedy." *Wiley-Blackwell Companion to Italian Cinema*. Edited by Frank Burke. Oxford: Wiley-Blackwell. 180–197.
Bayman, L and Rigoletto, S (eds). 2013. *Popular Italian Cinema*. Basingstoke: Palgrave Macmillan.
Bellassai, S. 2006. *La legge del desiderio. Il progetto Merlin e l'Italia degli anni Cinquanta*. Rome: Carocci.

———. 2003. "Mascolinità, mutamento, merce. Crisi dell'identità maschile nell'Italia del boom." *Genere, generazione e consume. L'Italia degli anni Sessanta*. Edited by Paolo Capuzzo. Rome: Carocci.

Bellotto, A. 1994. *La memoria del futuro: film d'arte, film e video industriali Olivetti: 1949–1992*. Ivrea: Fondazione Adriano Olivetti and Archivio Storico del Gruppo Olivetti.

Belpoliti, M. 2015. *Primo Levi di fronte e di profilo*. Milan: Guanda.

Ben-Ghiat, R. 1999. "Liberation: Italian Cinema and the Fascist Past, 1945–50." *Italian Fascism: History, Memory, and Representation*. Edited by Patrizia Dogliani and Richard J. B. Bosworth. New York: Palgrave.

———. 2001. "The Italian Cinema and the Italian Working Class." *International Labor and Working-Class History*, no. 59.

Benjamin, W. 1968. "The Work of Art in the Age of Mechanical Reproduction." *Illuminations*. New York: Schocken Books.

Berardinelli, A. 2011. "Il fumetto (kafkiano) del potere." *Corriere della Sera*. 19 June.

Berardo, L. 1990. "'*Gli anni del giudizio*': il romanzo 'elettorale' come moderna epopea." *Giovanni Arpino. L'uomo, lo scrittore*. Edited by Cetta Berardo. Bra: Cassa di risparmio di Bra.

Bernabò, G. 1991. *Come leggere "La Storia" di Elsa Morante*. Milan: Mursia.

———. 2012. *La fiaba estrema. Elsa Morante tra vita e scrittura*. Rome: Carocci.

Bernardi, A. 2011. *Da "città del silenzio" a città delle macchine. Prato nel cinema degli anni '50*. Florence: Firenze University Press.

———. 2002. *Il paesaggio nel cinema italiano*. Venice: Marsilio.

Bernardi, S (ed). 2004. *Storia del cinema italiano*. Volume IX (1954–1959). Venice: Marsilio.

Bertetto, P. 2001. *Fritz Lang Metropolis*. Turin: Lindau.

Bertozzi, M. 2008. "L'arte, l'industria e la cultura." *Storia del documentario italiano. Immagini e culture dell'altro cinema*. Venice: Marsilio.

Betti, E. 2019. *Precari e precarie: una storia dell'Italia repubblicana*. Rome: Carocci.

———. 2015. "Storicizzare la precarietà del lavoro tra fordismo e post-fordismo: una prospettiva di genere." *Di condizione precaria. Sguardi trasversali tra genere, lavoro e non lavoro* Edited by Luca Salmieri and Ariella Verrocchio. Trieste: EUT Edizioni Università di Trieste.

Bettini, F (ed). 1995. "Paolo Volponi. Per una letteratura di liberazione e di conflitto. Incontro con gli studenti di Frascati." *Critica marxista*, no. 2.

Bevilacqua, A. 1972. *La Calliffa*. Milan: Rizzoli.

Bianciard, L. 2013. *Il lavoro culturale*. Milan: Feltrinelli.

———. 1965. *It's a Hard Life*. Translated by Eric Mosbacher. New York: The Viking Press.

———. 2000. *L'alibi del progresso. Scritti giornalistici ed elzeviri*. Milan: ExCogita.

———. 2008. *L'antimeridiano. Tutte le opere*, vol. 2. Milan: ExCogita.

——. 1962. *La vita agra*. Milan: Rizzoli.
——. 1999. *La vita agra*. Milan: Bompiani.
Blanc, P. 2016. *Fake Silk: The Lethal History of Viscose Rayon*. New Haven: Yale University Press.
Bo, C. 1965. "Siamo tutti un barattolo al servizio del Padrone". *L'Europeo*. 9 May.
Boissevain, J. 1970. *The Italians of Montreal: Social Adjustment in a Plural Society*. Ottawa: Studies of the Royal Commission on Bilingualism and Biculturalism.
Bologna, S. 2007. *Ceti medi senza futuro?* Rome: DeriveApprodi.
Bolongaro, E. 2010. "Representing the Un(re)presentable: Homosexuality in Luchino Visconti's Rocco and His Brothers." *Studies in European Cinema*, vol. 7, no. 3.
Bonifazio, P. 2014. *Schooling in Modernity: The Politics of Sponsored Films in Postwar Italy*. Toronto: University of Toronto Press.
——. 2014. "United We Drill: ENI, Films, and the Culture of Work." *Annali d'Italianistica*, vol. 32.
Bordwell, D. 1985. *Narration in the Fiction Film*. Madison: The University of Wisconsin Press.
——. 1999. "The Art Cinema as a Mode of Film Practice." *Film Theory and Criticism*. Edited by Leo Braudy and Marshall Cohen. New York: Oxford University Press.
Borghini, F. 1985. *Mario Monicelli. Cinquant'anni di cinema*. Pisa: Master.
Boscolo, C and Roverselli, F (eds). 2009. "Scritture precarie attraverso i media: un bilancio provvisorio." *Bollettino '900*, no.s 1–2.
Bourdieu, Pierre. *The Rules of Art: Genesis and Structure of the Literary Field*. Translated by Susan Emanuel. Cambridge: Polity Press, 1996.
Bourneuf, R and Ouellet, R. 1976. *L'universo del romanzo*. Turin: Einaudi.
Branca, R. 1952. *Curva di fatica del bambino nella visione del film a colori e in bianconero*. Rome: Ministero della Pubblica Istruzione.
——. 1952. *Funzioni e limiti cineteca scolastica italiana*. Rome: Edizioni Ministero Della Pubblica Istruzione.
——. 1956. *Società e scuola negli Stati Uniti*. Rome: Edizioni Ministero Della Pubblica Istruzione.
Braudel, F. 1980. "History and the Social Sciences. The *Longue Durée*." *On History*. Chicago: University of Chicago Press.
Brizzi, E. 1994. *Jack Frusciante è uscito dal gruppo*. Ancona: Transeuropa.
Brunetta, G P. 2009. *The History of Italian Cinema: A Guide to Italian Film from Its Origins to the Twenty-first Century*. Translated by Jeremy Parzen. Princeton: Princeton University Press.
Bruni, A and Selmi, G. 2010. "Da san Precario a WonderQueer: Rappresentazioni di genere nell'attivismo precario italiano." *Studi culturali*, vol. 7, no. 3.
Bruno, G. 2002. *Atlas of Emotions: Journeys in Art, Architecture, and Film*, London and New York: Verso.

——. 1993. *Streetwalking on a Ruined Map: Cultural Theory and the City Films of Elvira Notari*. Princeton: Princeton University Press.
Bruzzi, S. 2005. *Bringing Up Daddy: Fatherhood and Masculinity in Postwar Hollywood*. London: BFI.
——. 2000. *New Documentary: A Critical Introduction*. London and New York: Routledge.
Buccheri, V. 2010. *Lo stile cinematografico*. Rome: Carocci.
Buell, L. 2013. "La critica letteraria diventa eco." In *Ecocritica. La letteratura e la crisi del pianeta*. Rome: Donzelli Editore.
Buffoni, L. 2003. "La fortuna critica." *Ermanno Olmi. Il cinema, i film, la televisione, la scuola*. Edited by Adriano Aprà. Venice: Marsilio Editori.
Bigatti, G and Lupo, G (eds). 2013. *Fabbrica di carta. I libri che raccontano l'Italia industriale*. Rome: Laterza.
Bulgheroni, M. 1957. "Tempi Stretti, un romanzo della fabbrica." *La Gazzetta del Libro*. October.
Buttitta, P A. 1963. "Perché tanta gente." *Avanti!* 26 October.
Buzzi, G. 1958. *Il senatore*. Milan: Feltrinelli.
——. 1963. *L'amore mio italiano*. Milan: Mondadori.
——. 2014. *L'amore mio italiano*. Rome: Avagliano.
Cacciari, M. 1976. *Krisis. Saggio sulla crisi del pensiero negativo da Nietzsche a Wittgenstein*. Milan: Feltrinelli.
——. 1977. *Pensiero negativo e razionalizzazione*. Venice: Marsilio.
——. 1969. "Saggio sulla genesi del pensiero negativo". *Contropiano*, vol. 1.
Cadeddu, D. 2012. *Reimagining Democracy. On the Political Project of Adriano Olivetti*. New York: Springer.
Caesar, M. 1996. "Industrial Novels." *The Cambridge History of Italian Literature*. Edited by Peter Brand and Lino Pertile. Cambridge: Cambridge University Press.
Calvino, I. 1991. "A Gerda Niedieck, Frankfurt am Main." December 19, 1963. *I libri degli altri: lettere, 1947–1981*. Turin: Einaudi.
——. 1962. "A Giovanni Arpino – Milano." *Lettere 1940–1985*. Edited by Luca Baranelli. Milan: Mondadori.
——. 1991. *I libri degli altri: Lettere 1947–1981*. Edited by Giovanni Tesio. Turin: Einaudi.
——. 1967. *Il menabò di letteratura*, vol. 10.
——. 1974. *Invisible Cities*. Translated by William Weaver. San Diego, New York and London: Harcourt Brace Jovanovich.
——. 2002. *Le città invisibili*. Milan: Mondadori
——. 1991. Letter from Italo Calvino to Valerio Bertini. March 7, 1956. *I libri degli altri: lettere, 1947–1981*.
——. 1961. "Notizia su Luigi Davì." *Il Menabò di letteratura*, no. 4.

---. 1983. "Ricordo di Lucio Mastronardi." *Per Mastronardi. Atti del Convegno di studi su Lucio Mastronardi*. Edited by Maria Antonietta Grignani. Florence: La Nuova Italia.

Camerano, V, Crovi, R, and Grasso, G. 2007. *La storia dei gettoni di Elio Vittorini*. Turin: Nino Aragno Editore.

Camerini, C. 1990. *Acciaio. Un film degli anni Trenta*. Turin: Nuova Eri.

Caminati, L. 2012. "The Role of Documentary Film in the Formation of Neorealist Cinema." *Global Neorealism: The Transational History of a Film Style*. Edited by Saverio Giovacchini and Robert Sklar. Jackson: University Press of Mississippi.

Camon, F. 1965. *Il mestiere del poeta*. Milan: Lerici.

---. 1973. *Il mestiere di scrittore*. Milan: Garzanti.

---. 2011. "*Il padrone* e il suo barattolo." *Ttl Supplemento de la Stampa*. 18 June.

Cantarano, G. 1989. *Alla riversa: per una storia degli scioperi a rovescio, 1951–1952*. Bari: Dedalo.

Canova, G. 2000. "*Rocco e i suoi fratelli*: Visconti e le aporie anestetiche della modernità." *Il cinema di Luchino Visconti*. Edited by Veronica Pravadelli. Rome: Fondazione Scuola Nazionale di Cinema.

Caracciolo Aricò, A. 1997. "L'industria dei pastori d'Arcadia da Virgilio a Jacopo Sannazaro." *Letteratura e industria: Atti del 15° Congresso AISLLI*. Edited by Giorgio Bàrberi Squarotti and Carlo Ossola. Florence: Olschki.

Carbone, L R. 2015. *Il cinema documentario di militanza. L'ordinamento delle carte della sezione filmica del fondo Unitelefilm*. Università della Tuscia: M. A. Thesis.

Cardone, L et al (eds). 2018. "Pelle e pellicola. I corpi delle donne nel cinema italiano." *Arabeschi*, no. 12.

Carioti, G. 1970. "La Califfa nell'occhio del ciclone: intervista con Alberto Bevilacqua." *Il Dramma*, vol. 46.

Carter, J. 2018. "Italy on Fifth Ave: From the Museum of Modern Art to the Olivetti Showroom." *Modern Italy*, vol. 23, no. 1.

Carucci, P. 2007. "Prefazione." *United States Information Service di Trieste. Catalogo del fondo cinematografico (1941–1966)*. Edited by Giulia Barrera and Giovanna Tosatti. Rome: Ministero per i Beni e le Attività Culturali, Direzione Generale per gli Archivi.

Casadei, A. 2002. "1994. I destini incrociati del romanzo italiano." *Italianistica*, vol. 36, no. 1.

Casalini, M. 2016. "Tra Hollywood e Cinecittà: modelli di genere nell'Italia fascista." *Donne e cinema*. Edited by Maria Casalini. Rome: Viella.

Casetti, F. 2008. *Eye of the Century: Film, Experience, Modernity*. New York: Columbia University Press.

Castello, G C. 1961. "La ragazza in vetrina." *Il Ponte*. 11 February.

Castronovo, V. 2012. *Il miracolo economico*. Rome: Laterza.
Cavalli, S. 2017. *Progetto «Menabò» (1959–1967)*. Venice: Marsilio.
Cederna, A. 1956. *I vandali in casa*. Rome: Laterza.
——. 1975. *La distruzione della natura in Italia*. Milan: Einaudi.
CENSIS. 2000. *L'impatto della flessibilità sui percorsi di carriera delle donne*. Milan: Franco Angeli.
Cerchi, P. 2014. "Lavoro e letteratura dall'antichità al Rinascimento." *Annali d'Italianistica*, vol. 32.
Cesarani, R, Domenichelli, M and Fasano, P. 2007. *Dizionario dei temi letterari*. Milan: Garzanti.
Ceteroni, A. 2018. *Le letteratura aziendale. Gli scrittori che raccontano il precariato, le multinazionali e il nuovo mondo del lavoro*. Novate Milanese: Calibano.
Chatman, S. 1985. *Antonioni: Or, the Surface of the World*. Berkeley: University of California Press.
Chatman, S and Duncan, P. 2004. *Michelangelo Antonioni: The Investigation*. Köln and London: Taschen.
Chemello, A. 1991. *La biblioteca del buon operaio*. Milan: Unicopli.
Chéroux, C. 2009. *Diplopie. L'image photographique à l'ère des médias globalisés: essai sur le 11 septembre 2001*. Cherbourg and Octeville: Le Point du Jour.
Chirumbolo, P. 2012. "Il mondo del lavoro nel cinema del nuovo millennio: R. Milani, F. Comencini e A. D'Alatri." *Annali d'Italianistica*, vol. 30.
——. 2013 *Letteratura e lavoro. Conversazioni critiche*. Soveria Mannelli: Rubbettino.
Cicioni, M. 1995. *Primo Levi: Bridges of Knowledge*. Oxford: Berg.
Ciliberto, G. 2012. *La Triennale di Milano fra costruzione e critica del design in Italia*. Venice: Università Iuav di Venezia. Thesis.
Cineclub Arsenale (ed). 1989. *Il cinema e il lavoro*. Pisa: Arsenale.
Citati P. 1965. "Un mare di psicologia nell'azienda moderna". *Il Giorno*. 5 May.
Clerici, L. 2002. *Apparizione e visione. Vita e opera di Anna Maria Ortese*. Milan: Mondadori.
Coin, F et al (eds.). 2017. *In/disciplinate: soggettività precarie nell'università italiana*. Venice: Edizioni Ca' Foscari.
Coin, F (ed.). 2017. *Salari rubati. Economia politica e conflitto ai tempi del lavoro gratuito*. Verona: ombre corte.
Colombo, F. 2001. "L'Italia di Ottieri." In Ottieri, O. *La linea gotica*.
Comand, M. 2010. *Commedia all'italiana*. Milan: Il castoro.
Consoli, G P. 2011. *Mario Monicelli: La storia siete voi. Commedia, Guerra, lotta di classe*. Rome: Carocci.
Contarini, S (ed). 2010. "Letteratura e azienda. Rappresentazioni letterarie dell'economia e del lavoro nella letteratura italiana degli anni 2000." Special Issue of *Narrativa*, no.s 31–32.

Corona, G. 2017. *A Short Environmental History of Italy: Variety and Vulnerability.* Winwick, Cambridgeshire: The White Horse Press.
Carrol, N. 1999. "Film, Emotion, and Genre." *Passionate Views: Film, Cognition, and Emotion.* Edited by Carl Plantinga and Gregg Smith. Baltimore: John Hopkins University Press.
Corti, M. 1983. "Prefazione." *Per Mastronardi. Atti del Convegno di studi su Lucio Mastronardi.* Edited by Maria Antonietta Grignani. Florence: La Nuova Italia.
Cova, U. 2007. "I filmati USIS di Trieste: vicende storico-istituzionali di un archivio cinematografico." *United State Information Service di Trieste.* Edited by Giulia Barrera and Giovanna Tosatti. Rome: Ministero per i Beni e le Attività Culturali, Direzione Generale per gli Archivi.
Crainz, G. 2003. *Il paese mancato. Dal miracolo economico agli anni Ottanta.* Rome: Donzelli.
Cremaschi, I. 1965. *A scopo di lucro.* Milan: Mondadori.
———. 1962. *Pagato per tacere.* Milan: Silva.
Curtufelli, M R. 1977. *Operaie senza fabbrica. Inchiesta sul lavoro a domicilio.* Rome: Editore Riuniti.
Dalla Gassa, M. 2014. "'Tutto il mondo è paese.' I mondo movies tra esotismi e socializzazione del piacere." *Cinergie,* vol. 5.
Dalle Vacche, A. 1996. *Cinema and Painting: How Art Is Used in Film.* Austin: Continuum International Publishing Group.
D'Amelio, M A. 2014. "La commedia del precariato in *Tutta la vita davanti* (P.Virzì, 2008)." *Un nuovo cinema politico italiano? volume 1 Lavoro, migrazione, relazioni di genere.* Edited by William Hope, Luciana d'Arcangeli, and Silvana Serra. Leicester, UK: Troubador Publishing.
Damiani, R. 2005. "Arpino e la sua ombra." in Arpino, G. *Opere scelte.* Milan: Mondadori.
D'Angeli, C. 1993. "La presenza di Simone Weil ne *La Storia.*" *Per Elsa.* Edited by Giorgio Agamben et al. Rome: Linea d'ombra. 109–135.
Daniele, A. 2014. "Italiani e lavoro: il cinema di Ermanno Olmi negli anni del *Boom.*" *Annali d'italianistica,* vol. 32.
D'Annunzio, G. 1995. *Il piacere.* Milan: Mondadori.
———. 1991. *The Child of Pleasure.* Translated by Georgina Harding. Sawtry, Cambs: Dedalus.
Davì, L. 1957. *Gymkhana-Cross.* Turin: Einaudi.
———. 1961. "Il capolavoro." *Il Menabò di letteratura,* no. 4.
———. 1997. "Narrativa di fabbrica." *Letteratura e industria: Atti del 15° Congresso AISLLI.* Edited by Giorgio Bàrberi Squarotti and Carlo Ossola. Florence: Olschki.
Deaglio, E. 1995. *Besame mucho. Diario di un anno abbastanza crudele.* Milan: Feltrinelli.

De Berti, R. 2016. "*Europa di notte*. Lo spettacolo di rivista nell'Italia del boom economico." *L'avventura*, vol. 2.
De Clementi, A. 2015. "Operai e operaie nel primo cinquantennio del capitalismo italiano." *Storia del lavoro in Italia. Il Novecento (1896–1945)*. Edited by Stefano Musso. Rome: Castelvecchi. 24–57.
Debenedetti, G. 2016. "Parise? L'unico erede di Kafka (1965)." *Riga*, vol. 36. Special issue on Goffredo Parise. Edited by Marco Belpoliti and Andrea Cortellessa. Milan: Marcos y Marcos.
De Gennaro, R. 2012. *La rivolta impossibile. Vita di Lucio Mastronardi*. Rome: Ediesse.
——. 2012. "Tra fabbrica e clinica, in preda al plusdolore." *Il manifesto*. 3 August.
Del Boca, A. 2008. *Italiani, brava gente? Un mito duro a morire*. Vicenza: Neri Pozza.
Della Giovanna, E. 1961. *Le lettere non spedite*. Rome: Rotosei.
——. 1997. *Scherzi della memoria*. Casale Monferrato: Piemme.
de Lauretis, T. 1987. *Technologies of Gender: Essays on Theory, Film and Fiction*. Bloomington: Indiana University Press.
Deleuze, G. 1989. *Cinema 2: The Time-Image*. Minneapolis: University of Minnesota Press.
De Pascalis, I A. 2012. *La commedia nell'Italia contemporanea*. Milan: Il castoro.
——. 2017. "Sfidare i confini dell'inquadratura: il corpo e i costumi di Mariangela Melato." *Arabeschi*, vol. 10.
De Simone, G and S Scarponi (eds). 2010. "Genere, lavori precari, occupazione instabile." *Lavoro e diritto*, vol. XXIV, no. 3.
Diaconescu-Blumenfeld, R. 1999. "Regista di Clausura: Lina Wertmüller and Her Feminism of Despair." *Italica*, vol. 76, no. 3.
Di Chiara, F. 2013. *Generi e industria cinematografica in Italia. Il caso Titanus (1949–1964)*. Turin: Lindau.
Di Ciaula, T. 2006. *Chiodi e rose. Poesie operaie*. Foggia: Rainoneditore.
——. 1980. *L'odore della pioggia*. Bari: Laterza.
——. 1979. "L'operaio Faussone è per caso analfabeta?" *Lotta continua*. 14 January.
——. 1978. *Tuta blu. Ire, ricordi e sogni di un operaio del Sud*. Milan: Feltrinelli.
——. 1983. *Tuta blu. Ire, ricordi e sogni di un operaio del Sud*. Turin: Loescher.
——. 2003. *Tuta blu. Ire, ricordi e sogni di un operaio del Sud*. Jesolo: Zambon.
——. 1978. "Vita da operai. Dibattito tra i lavoratori dell'Alfa." *Corriere della Sera*. 24 June.
Di Marino, B. 2004. "Transizioni: Tra neorealismo rosa e commedia all'italiana." *Storia del cinema italiano*. Volume IX (1954–1959). Edited by Sandro Bernardi. Venice: Marsilio.
Dimendberg, E. 2005. "'These Are Not Exercises in Style': Le Chant Du Styrène." *October*, vol. 112. April 1.

Di Nicola, E. 2019. *La dissolvenza del lavoro. Crisi e disoccupazione attraverso il cinema*. Rome: Ediesse.
Di Oscar Alicicco, A C et al (eds). 2010. *I novissimi: ricostruzione del fenomeno editoriale*. Rome: Oblique Studio.
Dolci, D. 2011. *Processo all'articolo 4*. Palermo: Sellerio.
Donghi, L. 2016. "Né allineati, né alienati. Gli operai di Pietro Germi ne *Il ferroviere* e *L'uomo di paglia*." *Il cinema di Pietro Germi*. Edited by Luca Malavasi and Emiliano Morreale. Rome: Edizioni di Bianco e Nero.
Donnarumma, R. 2014. *Ipermodernità. Dove va la narrativa contemporanea*. Bologna: Il Mulino.
Duggan, C. 2014. *A Concise History of Italy*. Cambridge: Cambridge University Press.
———. 1995. "Italy in The Cold War Years and The Legacy of Fascism." *Italy in the Cold War: Politics, Culture and Society 1948–1958*. Edited by Christopher Duggan and Christopher Wagstaff. Oxford: Berg.
Dughera, A. 2006. *Per una biografia di Giovanni Arpino*. Bra: Istituto Storico di Bra e dei braidesi.
Eliot, T S. 1936. "The Hollow Men." *Collected Poems, 1909–1935*. London: Faber & Faber Ltd.
Ellero, R. 1988. *Ettore Scola*, Venice: La Nuova Italia.
Elsaesser, T. 2011. "Modernity: The Troubled Trope." *The Visual Culture of Modernism*. Special Issue of *SPELL: Swiss Papers in English Language and Literature*, vol. 26. Edited by Deborah L. Madsen and Mario Klarer. Tübingen: Natt.
Emmer, L. 1997. *Quel magico lenzuolo blu. Divagazioni non troppo serie sul cinema*. Mantova: Circolo del cinema.
Esposito, R. 2008. *Bíos: Biopolitics and Philosophy*. Minneapolis and London: University of Minnesota Press.
Esposito, R. 2012. *Living Thought. The Origins and Actuality of Italian Philosophy*. Stanford: Stanford University Press.
European Commission, DG Employment, Social Affairs and Equal Opportunities. 2012. "Study on Precarious work and social rights." <http://ec.europa.eu/social/BlobServlet?docId=7925&langId=en>
Fantone, L (ed). 2011. "Genere e precarietà." *Scriptaweb*.
Farnetti, M. 1998. *Anna Maria Ortese*. Milan: Mondadori.
Federici, S. 2014. *Revolution at Point Zero: Housework, Reproduction, and Feminist Struggle*. New York: Autonomedia.
Fellini, F et al. 1952. "Soggetti di film – I vitelloni." *Cinema*, no.s 99–100.
Felski, R. 1995. *The Gender of Modernity*. Cambridge, MA: Harvard University Press.
Ferguson, K E. 1991. "Interpretation and Genealogy in Feminism." *Signs*, vol. 16, no. 2.
Ferracuti, A. 2006. *Le risorse umane*. Milan: Feltrinelli.
Ferrata, G. 1962. "Ottieri e le esperienze di fabbrica." *Rinascita*. 22 December.

Ferrero, F (ed). 1996. *Primo Levi: un'antologia della critica*. Turin: Einaudi.
Ferretti, G C. 1983. "Il mondo in piccolo (ritratto di Lucio Mastronardi)." *Per Mastronardi. Atti del Convegno di studi su Lucio Mastronardi*. Edited by Maria Antonietta Grignani. Florence: La Nuova Italia.
——. 1972. *Paolo Volponi*. Florence: La Nuova Italia.
Feuerbach, L. 2008. *The Essence of Christianity*. Mineola, New York: Dover Philosophical Classics.
Fiaccarini Marchi, D. 1973. *Il Menabò 1959–1967*. Rome: Edizioni dell'Ateneo.
Fieni, M. 2010. *Il tema del lavoro nella letteratura italiana contemporanea*. Milan: Principato.
Fioretti, D. 2013. *Carte di fabbrica. La narrativa industrial in Italia (1934–1989)*. Pescara: Edizioni Tracce.
Fofi, G. 1964. *L'immigrazione meridionale a Torino*. Milan: Feltrinelli.
——. "Qualche film." *Quaderni piacentini*, no. 50.
Foot, J. 1999. "Cinema and the City: Milan and Luchino Visconti's Rocco and His Brothers (1960)." *Journal of Modern Italian Studies*, vol. 4, no. 2.
——. 2001. *Milan Since the Miracle: City, Culture, and Identity*. Oxford: Berg.
Forgacs, D. 2014. *Italy's Margins: Social Exclusion and Nation Formation since 1861*. Cambridge: Cambridge University Press.
——. 2008. "Neorealismo, identità nazionale, modernità." *Incontro al neorealismo. Luoghi e visioni di un cinema pensato al presente*. Edited by Luca Venzi. Rome: Fondazione Ente dello Spettacolo. 41–47.
Formigoni, G. 2016. *Storia d'Italia nella Guerra fredda (1943–1978)*. Bologna: Il Mulino.
Forti, M. 1961. "Temi industriali della narrativa italiana." *Il Menabò di letteratura*, no. 4.
Fortini, F. 2003. "Astuti come colombe." *Saggi ed epigrammi*. Edited by Luca Lenzini. Milan: Mondadori.
——. 1969. "Verifica dei poteri." *Verifica dei poteri. Scritti di critica e di istituzioni letterarie*. Milan: Il Saggiatore.
——. 2001. "Volponi moderno." *Volponi*. Edited by Emanuele Zinato. Palermo: Palumbo.
Foti, A. 2004. "It's a Euro MayDay." *Posse*, no. 8.
Foucault, M. 1986. "Of Other Spaces." *Diacritics*, no. 16.
——. 1980. *Power/Knowledge: Selected Interviews and Other Writings*. New York: Pantheon Books.
——. 2008. *Psychiatric Power: Lectures at the Collège de France, 1973–1974*. Edited by Jacques Lagrange. New York: Picador.
——. 1980. *The History of Sexuality, Vol. I: An Introduction*. New York: Vintage Books.
Frabotta, M A. 2002. *Il governo filma l'Italia*. Rome: Bulzoni.
Franchini, A. 2011. "Prefazione." in Bernari C. *Tre operai*. Venice: Marsilio.

Frankforter, A and Spellman, W. 2009. *The West: A Narrative History, Vol. 2 -- 1400 to the Present*. Upper Saddle River: Pearson Education.
Frescani, E. 2014. *Il cane a sei zampe sullo schermo. La produzione cinematografica dell'Eni di Enrico Mattei*. Naples: Liguori.
Freud, S. 2003. *The Schreber Case*. London and New York: Penguin.
Frezza, G. 2007. "Il cinema 'idea' di Eduardo." *Quaderns d'Italià*, no. 12.
Frisby, D. 1986. *Fragments of Modernity. Theories of Modernity in the Work of Simmel, Kracauer and Benjamin*. Cambridge: The MIT Press.
Fromm, H. 1996. "From Transcendence to Obsolescence." *The Ecocriticism Reader: Landmarks in Literary Ecology*. Edited by Cheryll Glotfelty and Harold Fromm. Athens, GA: University of Georgia Press.
Fumagalli, A. 2015. "Cognitive, Relational (Creative) Labor and the Precarious Movement for 'Common-fare': 'San Precario' and EuroMayDay." *Creative Capitalism, Multitudinous Creativity*. Edited by Giuseppe Cocco and Barbara Szaniecki. London: Lexington Books.
Gallino, L. 2004. "Globalizzazione della precarietà." *Precarietà del lavoro e società precaria nell'Europa contemporanea*. Edited by Ignazio Masulli. Rome: Carocci.
———. 2001. *Il costo umano della flessibilità*. Bari: Laterza.
———. 2001. *L'impresa responsabile. Un'intervista su Adriano Olivetti*. Turin: Edizioni di Comunità.
Gallo, S. 2012. *Senza attraversare le frontiere. Le migrazioni interne dall'Unità a oggi*. Rome: Laterza.
Gandy, M. 2003. "Landscapes of Deliquescence in Michelangelo Antonioni's 'Red Desert.'" *Transactions of the Institute of British Geographers*, vol. 28, no. 2.
Gentile, E. 2008. *La via italiana al totalitarismo*. Rome: Carocci.
Gentili, D. 2018. *Crisi come arte di governo*. Macerata: Quodlibet.
———. 2012. *Italian Theory. Dall'operaismo alla biopolitica*. Bologna: Il Mulino.
Germi, P. 1956. "Ho girato 'Il ferroviere' per gente all'antica" *Oggi*, no. 51. 20 December.
———. 1989. *Pietro Germi. Ritratto di un regista all'antica*. Edited by Adriano Aprà and Patrizia Pistagnesi. Parma: Pratiche.
Gessani, A and Terrosi, M. 1985. *L'intellettuale disintegrato: Luciano Bianciardi*. Rome: Ianus.
Giacomazzi, G. 1997. "Tematiche e strategie testuali della letteratura 'selvaggia.'" *Letteratura e industria: Atti del 15° Congresso AISLLI*. Edited by Giorgio Bàrberi Squarotti and Carlo Ossola. Florence: Olschki.
Giacovelli, E. 1990. *La commedia all'italiana. La storia, i luoghi, gli autori, gli attori, i film*. Rome: Gremese.
Giannarelli, A. 1995. "Introduction." *La sortie des usines: Il lavoro industriale nei cento anni del cinema*. Edited by AAMOD. Rome: Ediesse.

Ginsborg, P. 1990. *A History of Contemporary Italy: Society and Politics, 1943–1988*. London: Penguin Books.

———. 2003. *A History of Contemporary Italy: Society and Politics 1943–1988*. New York: Palgrave Macmillan.

———. 1989. *Storia d'Italia dal dopoguerra a oggi*. Rome: Einaudi.

Giori, M. 2011. *Luchino Visconti. Rocco e i suoi fratelli*. Turin: Lindau.

Giuliani, A. 1975. "Scriversi addosso." *Il Messaggero*. 31 January.

Giuliani, G. 2018. *Nation and Gender in Modern Italy: Intersectional Representations in Visual Culture*. Basingstoke: Palgrave Macmillan.

Godard, J-L. 1966. "The Night, The Eclipse, The Dawn (November 1964)." *Cahiers Du Cinema in English*, no. 1.

Golino, Enzo. 1976. *Letteratura e classi sociali*. Rome and Bari: Laterza.

Goodhall, M. 2006. *Sweet & Savage: The World Through the Shockumentary Film Lens*. London: Headpress.

Gramsci, A. 1971. "Americanism and Fordism." *Selections from the Prison Notebooks*. New York: International Publishers.

———. 1966. "Operai e contadini." *La questione meridionale*. Rome: Editori Riuniti.

———. 1975. *Quaderni dal carcere*. Turin: Einaudi.

Grassano, G. 1979. "Conversazione con Primo Levi." in Levi, P. *Opere complete*, vol. 3.

Grazzini, G. 1977. *Gli anni Sessanta in cento film*. Bari: Laterza.

Gribaudi, G. 1996. "Images of the South." *Italian Cultural Studies: An Introduction*. Edited by David Forgacs and Robert Lumley. Oxford: Oxford University Press.

Grignaffini, G. 2006. *La scena madre. Scritti sul cinema*. Bologna: Bologna University Press.

Grignani, M A. 1983. "Lingua e dialetto ne *Il calzolaio di Vigevano*." *Per Mastronardi. Atti del Convegno di studi su Lucio Mastronardi*. Edited by Maria Antonietta Grignani. Florence: La Nuova Italia.

Grillandi, M. 1965. "*Il padrone* dice Parise non è un romanzo di fabbrica." *Il Gazzettino*. 20 July.

Guerra, M. 2010. *Gli ultimi fuochi. Cinema italiano e mondo contadino dal fascismo agli anni Settanta*. Rome: Bulzoni.

Guerrazzi, V. 1974. *Nord e Sud uniti nella lotta*. Venice: Marsilio.

Guerrazzi, V (ed). 1975. *L'altra cultura: inchiesta operaia*. Venice: Marsilio.

Guglielmino, G M. 1982. *Cinema sì. I film segnalati dal Sindacato nazionale critici cinematografici italiani. Volume I*. Rome: Bulzoni.

———. 1961. "La ragazza in vetrina." *Gazzetta del Popolo*. 15 April.

Gundle, S. 2007 *Bellissima: Feminine Beauty and the Idea of Italy*. New Haven and London: Yale University Press.

———. 2017. "The Question of Italian National Character and the Limitations of Commedia all'italiana: Alberto Sordi, Federico Fellini and Carlo Lizzani."

Wiley-Blackwell Companion to Italian Cinema. Edited by Frank Burke. Oxford: Wiley-Blackwell.

Haaland, T. 2012. *Italian Neorealist Cinema.* Edinburgh: Edinburgh University Press.

Hardt, M and Negri, A. 2017. *Assembly.* Oxford: Oxford University Press.

——. 2009. *Commonwealth.* Cambridge: Harvard University Press.

——. 2000. *Empire.* Cambridge and London: Harvard University Press.

——. 2004. *Multitude: War and Democracy in the Age of Empire.* London: Penguin Books.

Hediger, V and Vonderau, P (eds.). 2009. "Introduction." *Films that Work: Industrial Film and the Productivity of Media.* Amsterdam: Amsterdam University Press.

Hennessey, B. 2016. "Patterns of Pugilism: *Rocco e i suoi fratelli* (1960) and the Boxing Film." *The Italianist*, vol. 36, no. 2.

Hipkins, D. 2006. "'I Don't Want to Die'": Prostitution and Narrative Disruption in Visconti's *Rocco e i suoi fratelli*." *Women in Italy, 1945–1960: An Interdisciplinary Study.* New York and Basingstoke: Palgrave.

——. 2016. *Italy's Other Women: Gender and Prostitution in Italian Cinema, 1940–1965,* Oxford: Peter Lang.

——. 2014. "The Fantasy Harem: Prostitution and the Battle of the Sexes in Italian Film Comedy of the Early to Mid-1960s." *Cinergie*, vol. 5.

Hirose, J F. 2018. *Le ciné-capital: d'Hitchcock à Ozu. Une lecture marxiste de* Cinéma *de Gilles Deleuze.* Paris: Hermann.

Iaccio, P (ed). 2004. *La storia sullo schermo. Il Novecento.* Cosenza: Pellegrini.

Iacoli, G. 2008. *La percezione narrative dello spazio. Teorie e rappresentazioni contemporanee.* Rome: Carocci.

Incorvaia, A and Rimassa, A. 2006. *Generazione mille euro.* Milan: Rizzoli.

Jacomuzzi, A. 1983. "*Il maestro di Vigevano.*" *Per Mastronardi. Atti del Convegno di studi su Lucio Mastonardi.* Edited by Maria Antonietta Grignani. Florence: La Nuova Italia.

Jansen, M. 2009. "Le vite precarie di Andrea Bajani." *Bollettino '900*, no.s 1–2.

Kezich, T. 1955. "Neorealismo rosa." *Letteratura*, no.s 13–14.

Koch, G. 2000. *Siegfried Kracauer. An Introduction.* Princeton: Princeton University Press.

Kovács, A B. 2007. *Screening Modernism: European Art Cinema, 1950–1980.* Chicago and London: The University of Chicago Press.

Kracauer, S. 1998. *The Salaried Masses. Duty and Distraction in Weimar Germany.* London: Verso.

Kushner, R. 2016. "Introduction." in Balestrini, N. *We Want Everything.* Translated by Matt Holden. London: Verso.

Landy, M. 2000. *Italian Film.* Cambridge: Cambridge University Press.

La Porta, F. 2000. "Albeggia una letteratura postindustriale." *Tirature 2000. Romanzi di ogni genere: dieci modelli a confront*. Edited by Vittorio Spinazzola. Milan: Il Saggiatore.
Latini, G. 2011. *L'energia e lo sguardo. Il cinema dell'Eni e i documentari di Gilbert Bovay*. Rome: Donzelli.
Laura, E. 2004. *Le stagioni dell'aquila: Storia dell'Istituto Luce*. Rome: Istituto Luce.
Lazzarato, M. 2012. *The Making of the Indebted Man: An Essay on the Neoliberal Condition*. Cambridge and London: MIT Press.
Lazzarin, S. 2008. *Fantasmi antichi e moderni: Tecnologia e perturbante in Buzzati e nella letteratura fantastica otto-novecentesca*. Pisa and Rome: Fabrizio Serra.
Leogrande, A. 2008. *Uomini e caporali. Viaggio tra i nuovi schiavi nelle campagne del Sud*. Milan: Mondadori.
Levi, C. 1947. *Christ Stopped at Eboli*. Translated by France Frenaye. New York: Farrar, Strauss and Co.
———. 1945. *Cristo si è fermato a Eboli*. Turin: Einaudi.
Levi, O (ed). 1977. *Catalogo Bolaffi del cinema italiano (1945–1956)*. Turin: Bolaffi.
Levi, P. 1959. *If This is a Man*. New York: The Orion Press.
———. 1997. "La chiave a stella." *Opere*, vol. 1. Turin: Einaudi.
———. 2015. "Letter to Lattanzio: 'Resign.'" *The Complete Works of Primo Levi*, vol. 2. Translated by Alessandra Bastagli and Francesco Bastagli. New York and London: Liveright Publishing Corporation.
———. *Opere*, vol. 2. Turin: Einaudi.
———. 2018. *Opere complete*, vol. 3. Turin: Einaudi.
———. 2015. "Other People's Trade." *The Complete Works of Primo Levi*, vol. 3. Translated by Antony Shugaar. New York and London: Liveright Publishing Corporation.
———. 2015. "The Drowned and the Saved." *The Complete Works of Primo Levi*, vol. 3. Translated by Michael F. Moore. New York and London: Liveright Publishing Corporation.
———. 1987. *The Monkey's Wrench*. Translated by William Weaver. New York: Penguin.
———. 2001. *The Voice of Memory*. Cambridge: Polity.
———. 2015. "The Wrench." *The Complete Works of Primo Levi*, vol. 2. Translated by Nathaniel Rich. New York and London: Liveright Publishing Corporation.
Levy, C. 2001. "The people and the professors: socialism and the educated middle classes in Italy, 1870–1915". *Journal of Modern Italian Studies*, Vol. 6, No. 2.
Liehm, M. 1986. *Passion and Defiance: Italian Film from 1942 to the Present*. London: University of California Press.
Love, G 1996. "Revaluing Nature: Toward an Ecological Criticism." *The Ecocriticism Reader*. Edited by Cheryll Glotfelty and Harold Fromm.

Lucamante, S (ed). 2001. *Italian Pulp Fiction: The New Narrative of the "Giovani Cannibali" Writers*. London: Associated University Press.
Lukács, G. 1968. *History and Class Consciousness*. Cambridge, Massachusetts: The MIT Press.
Luperini, R. 1980. "Sperimentazione e neoavanguardia nell'ultimo ventennio." *Letteratura italiana. Storia e testi*, vol. 10, tome 1. Edited by Carlo Muscetta. Rome and Bari: Laterza.
Luperini, R and Tortora, M (eds). 2012. *Sul modernismo italiano*. Naples: Liguori.
Lupetti, F et al. 1974. *La polemica Vittorini-Togliatti e la linea culturale del PCI nel 1945–47*. Milan: Lavoro Liberato.
Lupo, G. 2016. *La letteratura al tempo di Adriano Olivetti*. Rome and Ivrea: Edizioni di Comunità.
———. 2013. "Orfeo tra le macchine." *Fabbrica di carta. I libri che raccontano l'Italia industriale*. Edited by Giorgio Bigatti and Giuseppe Lupo. Rome and Bari: Laterza.
———. 2011. "Postfazione." In Davì, L. *Gymkhana Cross*. Matelica: Hacca edizioni.
Lussana, F. 2019. Cinema Educatore: *L'Istituto Luce dal fascismo alla Liberazione (1924–1945)*. Rome: Carocci.
Lutz, T. 2000. "Men's Tears and the Roles of Melodrama." *Boys Don't Cry: Rethinking Narratives of Masculinity and Emotion in the U.S*. Edited by Milette Shamir and Jennifer Travis. New York: Columbia University Press.
Luxemburg, R. 2006. *Reform or Revolution and Other Writings*. Translated by Integer. Mineola, NY: Dover Publications.
Luzi, A. 2005. "La scrittura di Volponi tra natura e storia. Ideologia ed eros in *Il lanciatore di giavellotto*." *Cahiers d'études italiennes*, vol 3. 141.
Maina, G and Zecca, F (eds). 2014. *Sessualità nel cinema italiano degli anni Sessanta: forme, figure e temi*. Special issue of *Cinergie*, vol. 5.
Manzoli, G. 2012. *Da Ercole a Fantozzi. Cinema popolare e società italiana dal boom economico alla neotelevisione (1958–1976)*. Rome: Carocci.
Marabini, C. 1976. *Le città dei poeti*. Turin: SEI.
Maraini, D. 1999. "Le mani." *Mio marito*. Milan: BUR.
———. 2004. "These Hands." *My Husband*. Translated by Vera F. Golini. Waterloo, Ontario: Wilfrid Laurier University Press.
Marazzi, C. 2008. *Capital and Language: From the New Economy to the War Economy*. Cambridge and London: MIT Press.
Marcus, M. 1986. *Italian Film in the Light of Neorealism*. Princeton: Princeton University Press.
Marcuse, H. 1955. *Eros and Civilization: A Philosophical Inquiry into Freud*. Boston: Beacon Press.

Marinetti, F T. 1938. *Gli aeropoeti futuristi dedicano al Duce il poema di Torre Viscosa: parole in libertà futuriste.* Torviscosa: SNIA Viscosa Ufficio propaganda.

———. 2008. "Fondazione e manifesto del futurismo." *Manifesti del futurismo.* Edited by Viviana Birolli. Milan: Abscondita.

———. 1973. "The Founding and Manifesto of Futurism." *Futurist Manifestos.* Edited by Umbro Apollonio. New York: Viking Press.

Marx, K. 1990. *Capital, volume 1.* London and New York: Penguin Books.

———. 1959. *Economic and Philosophic Manuscripts of 1844.* Translated by Martin Mulligan. Moscow: Progress Publishers.

———. 1975. "Estranged Labor." *Economic and Philosophic Manuscripts of 1844. Collected works of Karl Marx and Frederick Engels,* vol. 3. New York: International Publishers.

———. 1993. *Grundrisse: Foundations of the Critique of Political Economy.* London: Penguin Books.

———. 1994. *Selected Writings.* Edited by Lawrence H. Simon. Indianapolis: Hackett Publishing Company.

———. 1976. *The Poverty of Philosophy: Collected Works of Karl Marx and Frederick Engels,* vol. 6. New York: International Publishers.

Masi, S. 2006. *Ettore Scola.* Rome: Gremese.

Mastronardi, L. 2002. *A casa tua ridono e altri racconti.* Turin: Einaudi.

Mastronardi, L. 1994. *Il maestro di Vigevano, Il calzolaio di Vigevano, Il meridionale di Vigevano.* Turin: Einaudi.

Mattioda, E. 2011. *Levi.* Rome: Salerno.

Mauro, W. 1957. "Un documento di vita italiana, Tempi stretti." *Il Paese.* 24 October.

Mazzei, L. 2003. "Amori di confine. Olmi fra società industriale e mondo contadino." *Ermanno Olmi. Il cinema, i film, la televisione, la scuola.* Edited by Adriano Aprà. Venice: Marsilio Editori.

———. 2004. "I documentari industriali di Ermanno Olmi." *Storia del cinema italiano, vol. 9.* Edited by Sandro Bernardi. Venice: Marsilio.

Medici, A. 2002. "Il collettivo cinematografico internazionale de *La rosa dei venti*." *Giovanna: Storia di un film e del suo restauro.* Edited by Antonio Medici. Rome: Ediesse.

Meldolesi, L. 1972. *Disoccupazione ed esercito industriale di riserva in Italia.* Rome and Bari: Laterza.

Meneghelli, D. 2010. "Gli operai hanno ancora pochi anni di tempo? Morte e vitalità della fabbrica." *Letteratura e azienda. Rappresentazioni letterarie dell'economia e del lavoro nell'Italia degli anni 2000.* Edited by Silvia Contarini. Special issues of *Narrativa,* no.s 31–32.

Mengaldo, V. 1996. "Lingua e scrittura in Levi." in Ferrero, F. *Primo Levi: un'antologia della critica.* Turin: Einaudi.

Merola, N. 2018. "Temi forti e uomini deboli nei romanzi di Arpino." *'La vita o è stile o è errore.' L'opera di Giovanni Arpino*. Edited by Maria Carla Papini et al. Pisa: Edizioni ETS.

Metz, C. 1982. *The Imaginary Signifier: Psychoanalysis and the Cinema*. Translated by Celia Britton. London: McMillan.

———. 1991. "The Modern Cinema and Narrativity." *Film Language: A Semiotics of the Cinema*. Chicago: University of Chicago Press.

Miccichè, L. 1980. *Cinema italiano degli anni '70. Cronache 1969–1979*. Venice: Marsilio.

———. 1963. "Cominciò così la lotta dei 'compagni.'" *Avanti!*. 25 October.

———. 1995. "I cuori semplici di Ermanno Olmi." *Cinema italiano: gli anni '60 e oltre*. Venice: Marsilio.

Michalczyk, J. 1986. *The Italian Political Filmmakers*. London: Farleigh Dickinson University Press.

Milano, P. 1965, "Il ludibrio gioioso del servo perfetto". *L'Espresso*. 25 April.

Minardi, M. 1966. "Cinema e industria." *Notizie Olivetti*, vol. 14, no. 88.

Minuz, A. 2012. *Viaggio al termine dell'Italia. Fellini politico*. Soveria Mannelli: Rubbettino Editore.

Mondello, E. 2007. *In principio fu Tondelli. Letteratura, merci, televisione nella narrativa degli anni novanta*. Milan: Il Saggiatore.

Moneti, G. 1992. *Luciano Emmer*. Milan: Il castoro.

Monicelli, M. 2016. *La commedia umana. Conversazioni con Sebastiano Mondadori*. Milan: Il Saggiatore.

Montale, E. 1960. "Arpino. La suora giovane." *Corriere della Sera*. 25 March.

———. 1965. "Una precisione d'alta chirurgia". *Corriere della Sera*. 18 April.

Montaldo, G. 2002. [No Title.] *Giovanna: Storia di un film e del suo restauro*. Edited by Antonio Medici. Rome: Ediesse.

Montesanti, F (ed.). 1958. *L'uomo di paglia di Pietro Germi*. Bologna: Cappelli.

Montini, F and Zagarrio, V. 2012. *Istantanee sul cinema italiano. Film, volti, idee del nuovo millennio*. Catanzaro: Rubbettino Editore.

Morante, E. 1977. *History: A Novel*. Translated by William Weaver. New York: Knopf.

———. 1987. *Pro o contro la bomba atomica*. Milan: Adelphi.

———. 2009. *La Storia*. Turin: Einaudi.

Moravia, A. 1975. *Al cinema*. Milan: Bompiani.

———. 1961. "La ragazza in vetrina." *L'Espresso*. 7 May.

———. 1975. "Roma mille film orsono." *L'Espresso*. 12 October.

Moretti, F. 2010. "Spazio e stile, geografie dell'intreccio e storie del Terzo." *Il senso dello spazio. Lo spatial turn nei metodi e nelle teorie letterarie*. Edited by Flavio Sorrentino. Rome: Armando Editore.

Mulvey, L. 2007. "The Young Modern Woman of the 1920s: A Convergence of Feminist Film Theory and Gender Studies." *La valle dell'Eden*, no.s. 10 and 19. 2007.
Murgia, M. 2006. *Il mondo deve sapere*. Milan: ISBN.
———. 2006. *Il mondo deve sapere. Romanzo tragicomico di una telefonista precaria*. Milan: Einaudi.
Musatti, C et al. 1980. *Psicologi in fabbrica. La psicologia del lavoro negli stabilimenti Olivetti*. Turin: Einaudi.
———. 1976. *Riflessioni sul pensiero psicoanalitico*. Turin: Boringhieri.
Musso, S. 2011. *Storia del lavoro in Italia. Dall'Unità a oggi*. Venice: Marsilio.
Muzzarelli, A. 2014. *Il guaritore ferito*. Rome: Armando.
Nacache, J. 2003. *L'acteur de cinéma*. Paris: Armand Colin.
Naldini, N. 1997. "Il nuovo padrone di Milano." *Goffredo Parise*. Edited by Ilaria Crotti. Florence: Olschki.
Nata, S. 2010. *Il valore dei giorni*. Milan: Feltrinelli.
Negri, A. 2007. *Dall'operaio massa all'operaio sociale. Intervista sull'operaismo*. Edited by Paolo Pozzi and Roberta Tomassini. Verona: ombre corte.
———. 1992. *Il potere costituente. Saggio sulle alternative del moderno*. Rome: manifestolibri.
Nencioni, B. 2016. *Il posto fisso: rassegnazione, impresa e romanzi. Il caso del Sud d'Italia 1945–2015*. Ariccia: Arcane.
Nesi, C. 2013. "Due culture, due città. *La linea gotica*." *Le linee gotiche di Ottieri. Percorsi testuali*. Edited by Maria Antonietta Grignani. Novara: Interlinea.
Nobili, N. 2018. *Ho camminato nel mondo con l'anima aperta*. Edited by Maria Grazia Calandrone. Milan: Solferino.
Noce, T. 1938. *Gioventù senza sole*. Paris: Edizioni Italiani di Coltura.
Noto, P. 2011. *Dal Bozzetto ai generi. Il cinema italiano dei primi anni Cinquanta*. Turin: Kaplan.
Novara, F. 1980. "Organizzazione del lavoro: gli equivoci della ragione scientifica." in Musatti et al. *Psicologi in fabbrica*.
———. 1997. "Psicologia del lavoro: vita, opere, e morte di un'esperienza." *Per una storiografia italiana della prevenzione occupazionale ed ambientale*. Edited by Antonio Grieco and Pier Alberto Albertazzi. Milan: Franco Angeli.
Novelli, D. 2002. "Il caso Trevico-Torino." *Trevico-Cinecittà. L'avventuroso viaggio di Ettore Scola*. Edited by Vito Zagarrio. Venice: Marsilio.
Odin, R. 2000. *De la fiction*. Bruxelles: De Boeck Université.
O'Leary, A and O'Rawe, C. 2011. "Against Realism: Italian Film Criticism." *Journal of Modern Italian Studies*, vol. 16, no. 1. 107–128.
Olivetti, A. 1960. *Città dell'uomo*. Milan: Edizioni di Comunità.
Oppermann, S and Iovino, S (eds). 2016. *Environmental Humanities: Voices from the Anthropocene*. London: Rowman and Littlefield.

Orabona, A and Bellumori, C. 1978. *25 Anni di documentari della Presidenza del Consiglio dei Ministri*. Rome: Tipografia Artistica.
O'Rawe, C. 2017. "Back for Good: Melodrama and the Returning Soldier in Postwar Italian cinema." *Modern Italy*, vol. 22. 123–142.
Ortaggi Cammarosano, S. 2009. "Condizione femminile e industrializzazione tra '800 e '900." *Donne, Lavoro, Grande Guerra. Saggi II 1982–1999*. Milan: Unicopli. 63–152.
Ortese, A M. 2016. *Le piccole persone*. Milan: Adelphi.
———. 1993. *Silenzio a Milano*. Milan: La Tartaruga.
Ossola, C. 1984. "Introduzione." In Cantù, C. *Portafoglio di un'operaio*. Milan: Bompiani.
Ottieri, M P. 2009. "Cronologia." In Ottieri, O. *Opere scelte*. Milan: Mondadori.
Ottieri, O. 1963 *Donnarumma all'assalto*. Milan: Bompiani.
———. 2004. *Donnarumma all'assalto*. Milan: Garzanti.
———. 1962. *La linea gotica*. Milan: Bompiani.
———. 2001. *La linea gotica. Taccuino (1948–1958)*. Parma: Guanda.
———. 2004. *La linea gotica*. Parma: Guanda.
———. 1961. "Taccuino industriale." *Il Menabò di letteratura*, no. 4.
———. 1957. *Tempi stretti*. Turin: Einaudi.
———. 1964. *Tempi stretti*. Turin: Einuadi.
———. 1981. *Tempi stretti*. Bergamo: Minerva Italica.
———. 2012. *Tempi stretti*. Matelica: Hacca.
———. 1962. *The Men at the Gate*. Boston: Houghton Mifflin.
P V. 1958. "L'uomo di paglia." *Il Popolo*. March 12.
Pace, A. 1958. *Benjamin Franklin and Italy*. Philadelphia: The American Philosophical Society.
Paci, M. 1973. *Mercato del lavoro e classi sociali in Italia*. Bologna: Il Mulino.
Pagni, S. 2014. "*Giovanna* di Gillo Pontecorvo: Un film sulla problematica del lavoro femminile nei documenti d'archivio." *Il Mondo degli Archivi – Studi*.
Pal. 1958 "Il tempo dei telefoni neri", in *Lo Specchio*, March 23.
Panella, C. 2016. "Scritture di rabbia e scritture di desiderio. La letteratura italiana di fabbrica degli anni Settanta." *Lavoro! Storia, organizzazione e narrazione del lavoro nel XX secolo*. Edited by Novella di Nunzio and Matteo Troilo. Rome: Aracne.
Parise, G. 1987. "Il padrone." *Opere*, vol. 1. Edited by Bruno Callegher and Mauro Portello. Milan: Mondadori.
———. 1965. *Il padrone*. Milan: Feltrinelli
———. 1999. *Il padrone*. Milan: Rizzoli.
———. 1987. "Inutilità del romanzo (1958)." *Opere*, vol. 1. Edited by Bruno Callegher and Mauro Portello. Milan: Mondadori.

———. 1966. *The Boss*. Translated by William Weaver. New York: Alfred A. Knopf.
Parker, I. 2007. *Revolution in Psychology: Alienation to Emancipation*. London and Ann Arbor: Pluto Press.
Parker, S. 1996. "Political Identities." *Italian Cultural Studies: An Introduction*. Edited by David Forgacs and Robert Lumley. Oxford: Oxford University Press.
Pasolini, P P. 1988. *Heretical Empiricism*. Translated by Ben Lawton and Louise K. Barnett. Bloomington: Indiana University Press.
———. 1999. "Scritti corsari." *Scritti sulla politica e sulla società*. Edited by Walter Siti and Silvia De Laude. Milan: Mondadori.
———. 2003. "The Concentration Camps." *Stories from the City of God: Sketches and Chronicles of Rome 1950–1966*. Translated by Marina Harss. New York: Handsel.
Paul-Lévy, F and Segaud, M. 1983. *Anthropologie de l'espace*. Paris: Centre George Pompidou.
Pegorari, D M. 2018. *Scritture precarie. Editoria e lavoro nella grande crisi 2003–2017*. Bari: Stilo.
Pellizzari, L. 1961. "La ragazza in vetrina." *Cinema Nuovo*, vol. 10.
Pennacchi, A. 2011. "Introduzione all'edizione Mondadori." *Mammut*. Milan: Mondadori.
Peretti, L. 2019. "Between Auteurism and Sponsored Cinema: Joris Ivens, Bernardo Bertolucci, and ENI." *Journal of Italian Cinema and Media Studies*. vol. 7, no. 2.
Perniola, I. 2014. *L'era postdocumentaria*. Milan and Udine: Mimesis Cinema.
Pescarolo, A. 1996. "Il lavoro e le risorse delle donne in epoca contemporanea." *Il lavoro delle donne*. Edited by Angela Gropi. Bari: Laterza.
———. 2001. "Il lavoro e le risorse delle donne." *Storia sociale delle donne nell'Italia contemporanea*. Edited by Anna Bravo. Rome and Bari: Laterza.
Pierotti, F. 2016. *Un'archeologia del colore nel cinema italiano. Dal technicolor ad Antonioni*. Pisa: Edizioni ETS.
Pinkus, K. 2011. "Antonioni's Cinematic Poetics of Climate Change." *Antonioni: Centenary Essays*. Edited by Laura Rascaroli and John David Rhodes. London: Palgrave.
Pintus, P (ed). 1958. *Commedia all'italiana, parlano i protagonisti*. Rome: Gangemi.
Piovene, G. 2016. "Il nuovo romanzo di Parise (1965)." *Riga*, vol. 36. Special issue on Goffredo Parise. Edited by Marco Belpoliti and Andrea Cortellessa. Milan: Marcos y Marcos.
Pitassio, F and Noto, P. 2010. *Il cinema neorealista*. Bologna: Archetipolibri.
Pizzorno, A. 2001. "Familismo amorale e marginalità storica ovvero perché non c'è niente da fare a Montegrano." *Quaderni di Sociologia*, vol. 26, no. 27.
Placido, B. 2004. "Ottiero Ottieri tra i operai meridionali." *La Repubblica*. 4 April.

Portello, M. 1987. "Note e notizie sui testi. *Il padrone*." in Parise, G. *Opere*, vol. 1. Edited by Bruno Callegher and Mauro Portello. Milan: Mondadori.

Positano, S. 2014. *Donne e lavoro nella letteratura italiana di fine Ottocento: tra merce di scambio e impresa identitaria*. Bari: Progedit.

Pravadelli, V. 2017. "Italian 1960s Auteur Cinema (and beyond): Classic, Modern, Postmodern." *Wiley-Blackwell Companion to Italian Cinema*. Edited by Frank Burke. Oxford: Wiley-Blackwell.

——. 2006. "Visconti's 'Rocco and His Brothers': Identity, Melodrama, and the National- Popular." *Annali d'Italianistica*, vol. 24.

Prelinger, R. 2007. *The Field Guide to Sponsored Films*. National Film Preservation Foundation.

Presidenza del Consiglio dei ministri and Dipartimento per l'informazione e l'editoria, 1995. *Per immagini: gli audiovisivi prodotti dalla Presidenza del Consiglio dei Ministri: 1952–1995*. Rome: Ufficio per l'informazione e la documentazione istituzionale.

Previtali, G. 2016. "'Siamo fatti così: aiuto!' La rappresentazione dell'identità di genere nei mondo movies." *Bianco e Nero*, vol. LXXVIII, no. 585.

Prono, F. 2002. "Cinegrafia di una città-fabbrica." *Ombre metropolitane. Città e spettacolo nel Novecento*. Edited by Giaime Alonge and Federica Mazzocchi. Turin: DAMS.

Prunetti, A. 2018. *108 metri*. Rome and Bari: Laterza.

Pupino, A R. 2000. *Pirandello: Maschere e fantasmi*. Rome: Salerno.

Puggioni, E. 2006. *Davide Segre un eroe al confine della modernità*. Alessandria: Edizioni dell'Orso.

Quaranta, B. 2018. "Il Piemonte di Arpino." *'La vita o è stile o è errore.' L'opera di Giovanni Arpino*. Edited by Maria Cala Papini, Federico Fastelli and Teresa Spignoli. Pisa: ETS.

——. 1989. *Stile Arpino. Una vita torinese*. Turin: Società editrice internazionale.

Raffaeli, M. 2009. "Una sfida operaia." in Arpino, G. *Una nuvola d'ira*.

Ranieri, A. 2010. "Lavoro e conoscenza." *Bruno Trentin. Lavoro, libertà, conoscenza*. Edited by Alessio Gramolati, Giovanni Mari. Florence: Firenze University Press.

Rea, E. 2014. *Le dismissione*. Milan: Feltrinelli.

Rhodes, J D. "Antonioni and the Development of Style." *Antonioni: Centenary Essays*. Edited by Laura Rascaroli and John David Rhodes. London: Palgrave.

Rigoletto, S. 2013. "Laughter and the Popular in Lina Wertmüller's *The Seduction of Mimì*." *Popular Italian Cinema*. Edited by Louis Bayman and Sergio Rigoletto. Basingstoke: Palgrave Macmillan.

——. 2014. *Masculinity and Italian Cinema: Sexual Politics, Social Conflicts and Male Crisis in the 1970s*. Edinburgh: Edinburgh University Press.

Rinaldi, R. 1985. *Il romanzo come deformazione. Autonomia ed eredità gaddiana in Mastronardi, Bianciardi, Testori, Arbasino*. Milan: Mursia.
Ripellino, A M. 1961. *Nuovi poeti sovietici*. Turin: Einaudi.
Rivenni, G (ed). 2002. *Giovanna di Gillo Pontecorvo e gli anni '50 a Prato. Testimonianze e ricordi*. Prato: Mediateca della memoria.
Rohdie, S. 1990. *Antonioni*. London: British Film Institute.
———. 1992. *Rocco and His Brothers*. London: British Film Institute.
Romano, M. 1974. *Invito alla lettura di Arpino*. Milan: Mursia.
Rondi, G L. 1961. "L'imprevisto. La ragazza in vetrina." *Giornale dello spettacolo*, vol. 17.
Rondini, A. 2012. *Anche il cielo brucia. Primo Levi e il giornalismo*. Macerata: Quodlibet.
Rousseau. J-J. 2008. *The Social Contract*. New York: Cosimo Books.
Rovelli, M. 2009. *Servi. Il paese sommerso dei clandestini al lavoro*. Milan: Feltrinelli.
Rozzi, R. 1977. *Psicologi e operai: Soggettività e lavoro nell'industria italiana*. Milan: Feltrinelli.
Rubino, G. 2010. "Spazi naturali, spazi culturali." *Il senso dello spazio*.Edited by Flavio Sorrentino. Rome: Armando Editore.
Russel, B. 1958. *The Conquest of Happiness*. New York: Liveright.
Salinari, C. 1965. "Gli uomini-barattolo della società capitalistica". *L'Unità*. 25 May.
———. 1962. "Salinari risponde a Arpino." *Vie Nuove*. 22 March.
———. 1962. "Un amore a tre nella Torino '61." *Vie Nuove*. 8 March.
Samuels, C. 2008. "Michelangelo Antonioni (July 29, 1969)." *Michelangelo Antonioni Interviews*. Edited by Bert Cardullo. Jackson: University Press of Mississippi.
Sangiovanni, A. 2006. *Tute blu: La parabola operaia nell'Italia repubblicana*. Turin: Donzelli.
Sanguineti, T. 2015. *Il cervello di Alberto Sordi. Rodolfo Sonego e il suo cinema*. Milan: Adelphi Edizioni.
Santato, G. 1988. "Follia e utopia nella narrativa di Volponi." *Studi Novecenteschi*, vol. 25, no. 55.
Santi, P M and Vittori, R. 1987. *I film di Ettore Scola*. Rome: Gremese.
Sarasina, B. 1997. "Meglio il fascino o l'impegno?" *L'Unità*. 28 August.
Sarris, A. 1965. "Red Desert." *Village Voice*. February 11.
Sassen, S. 2014. *Expulsions: Brutality and Complexity in the Global Economy*. Cambridge, MA and London: The Belknap Press of Harvard University Press.
Sassi, E. 2009. "Il duce di spalle e altre scene proibite," *Corriere della Sera*. 7 December. 39.
Scaffai, N. 2018. "Goffredo Parise." *Il romanzo in Italia. Il secondo Novecento*. Edited by Giancarlo Alfano and Francesco de Cristofaro. Rome: Carocci.

———. 2017. *Letteratura e ecologia. Forme e temi di una relazione narrata*. Rome: Carocci.
Scalia, G. 1961. "Dalla natura all'industria." *Il Menabò di letteratura*, no. 4.
Schoonover, K. 2012. *Brutal Vision: The Neorealist Body in Postwar Italian Cinema*. Minneapolis: University of Minnesota Press. Minneapolis.
Scola, E. 1980. *Parla il cinema italiano, Volume 2*. Edited by Aldo Tassone. Foligno: Il Formichiere.
Scola, E and Bertini, A. 1996. *Il cinema e io. Ettore Scola*. Rome: Officine.
Scrivano, F. 2000. "Individuo, società e territorio nei romanzi di Paolo Volponi: Le soluzioni narrative di *Memoriale* e *La strada per Roma*." *Esperienze letterarie*, vol. 25, no. 1.
Scrivano, R. 1979. *Arpino*. Florence: La nuova Italia.
Seltzer, M. 1998. *Serial Killers: Death and Life in America's Wound Culture*. New York: Routledge.
Sereni, V. 1961. "Una visita in fabbrica." *Il Menabò di letteratura*, no. 4.
Simmel, G. "The Metropolis and Mental Life." *The Blackwell City Reader*. Edited by Gary Bridge and Sophie Watson. Chichester, West Sussex, U.K. and Malden, MA: Wiley- Blackwell.Siti, W. 1994. *Scuola di nudo*. Turin: Einaudi.
Sitney, P. 2005. "The Autobiography of a Metonymy." *Shoot! The Notebooks of Serafino Gubbio, Cinematograph Operator*. Chicago: The University of Chicago Press.
———. 1995. *Vital Crises in Italian Cinema: Iconography, Stylistics, Politics*. Austin: University of Texas Press.
Slovic, S. 2015. "Ecocritcism 101: A Basic Introduction to Ecocriticism and Environmental Literature." *Social Sciences & Humanities*, vol. 23.
Smith, K. 1999. *Mental Hygiene: Better Living Through Classroom Films 1945–1970*. New York: Blast Books.
Smith, M. 1994. "Altered States: Character and Emotional Response in the Cinema." *Cinema Journal*, no. 4.
———. 1995. *Engaging Characters: Fiction, Emotion and the Cinema*. Oxford: Clarendon Press.
Soja, E. 2008. "Taking Space Personally." *The Spatial Turn: Interdisciplinary Perspectives*. Edited by Santa Arias and Barbara Warf. London: Taylor and Francis.
Soldati, M. 1964. *Le due città*. Milan: Garzanti.
Sontag, S. 1978. *Illness as Metaphor*. Toronto: McGraw-Hill Ryerson Ltd.
Soria, L. 1979. *Informatica: un'occasione perduta. La divisione elettronica dell'Olivetti nei primi anni del centrosinistra*. Turin: Einaudi.
Sorlin, P. 2015. *Introduction à une sociologie du cinéma*, Paris: Klincksieck.
———. 1979. *Sociologia del cinema*. Milan: Garzanti.
———. 1977. *Sociologie du cinéma*, Paris: Aubier Montaigne.

Spracklen, K. 2009. *The Meaning and Purpose of Leisure: Habermas and Leisure at the End of Modernity*. London: Palgrave Macmillan.

Spinazzola, V. 1974. *Cinema e pubblico. Lo spettacolo filmico in Italia (1945–1965)*. Milan: Bompiani.

——. 1985. *Cinema e pubblico: Lo spettacolo filmico in Italia 1945–1965*. Rome: Bulzoni.

Standing, G. 2011. *The Precariat: The New Dangerous Class*. London: Bloomsbury Publishing.

Steimatsky, N. 2008. *Italian Locations. Reinhabiting the Past in Postwar Cinema*. Minneapolis: University of Minnesota Press.

Svevo, I. 2006. *Romanzi e "continuazioni"*. Milan: Mondadori.

Tabucchi, A. 1994. *Sostiene Pereira*. Milan: Feltrinelli.

Tan, S H and Frijda, N H 1999. "Sentiment in Film Viewing." *Passionate Views: Film, Cognition, and Emotion*. Edited by Carl Plantinga and Gregg Smith. Baltimore: John Hopkins University Press.

Tasso, T. 1992. *Gerusalemme liberata*. Milan: Mondadori.

——. 2000. *Jerusalem Delivered*. Translated by Anthony M. Esolen. Baltimore: Johns Hopkins University Press.

Taylor, S. 1965. "The Red Desert: Neurosis à La Mode." *The Hudson Review*, vol. 18, no. 2.

Tesio, G. 2002. "L'ultimo Mastronardi: la sfida di un moralista insocievole tra demoni e clown." in Mastronardi, L. *A casa tua ridono e altri racconti*. Turin: Einaudi.

Tessari, R. 1973. *Il mito della macchina: Letteratura e industria nel primo novecento italiano*. Milan: Mursia.

Tinazzi, G. "The Gaze and the Story." *The Architecture of Vision: Writings and Interviews on Cinema*. Edited by Carlo di Carlo and Giorgio Tinazzi. Chicago: University of Chicago Press.

Tirinanzi De Medici, C. 2018. *Il romanzo italiano contemporanoa. Dalla fine degli anni Settanta a oggi*. Rome: Carocci.

Todorov, T. 1970. *Introduction à la littérature fantastique*. Paris: Éditions du Seuil.

Togliatti, P. 1967. "Attualità del pensiero e dell'azione di Gramsci." *Gramsci*. Edited by Ernesto Ragionieri. Rome: Editori Riuniti.

Toracca, T. 2019. "Paolo Volponi's *Memoriale*: Industry Between Alienation and Utopia." *The Years of Alienation*. Edited by Alessandra Diazzi and Alvise Sforza Tarabochia. Chan: Palgrave Macmillian.

Torchio, M. 2003. "Cinefiat e l'egemonia possibile." *Cinemambiente 2003: Enviromental Film Festival*. Turin: Associazione Cinambiente.

Tortora, M. 2018. "Il primo Arpino: 1952–1962." *Filologia e critica*, vol. 43, no. 4.

Tosatti, G. 2007. "Propaganda e informazione nell'Italia del secondo dopoguerra: il fondo audiovisivo dell'USIS di Trieste." *United State Information Service di Trieste*. Edited by Giulia Barrera and Giovanna Tosatti. Rome: Ministero per i Beni e le Attività Culturali, Direzione Generale per gli Archivi.

Trevisan, V. 2016. *Works*. Turin: Einaudi.
Tronti, M. 2013. "Factory and Society." Translated by Guio Jacinto. <https://operaismoinenglish.wordpress.com/2013/06/13/factory-and-society/>.
——. 2008. "Noi operaisti". *L'operaismo degli anni Sessanta. Da "Quaderni rossi" a "classe operaia"*. Rome: DeriveApprodi.
——. 2012. "Our Workerism." *New Left Review*, vol. 73.
Trotta, G and Milana, F. (eds). 2008. *L'operaismo degli anni Sessanta. Da "Quaderni rossi" a "classe operaia"*. Rome: DeriveApprodi.
Turri, E. 2004. *Il paesaggio e il silenzio*. Venice: Marsilio.
——. 2004. "La forza degli iconemi." *Il paesaggio e il silenzio*.
——. 1979. *Semiologia del paesaggio italiano*. Milan: Longanesi.
Tyson, J. "Industrial Arts: Michelangelo Antonioni's *Red Desert* and Minimalism and Land Art." *New Waves: Transatlantic Bonds between Film and Art in the 1960s*. Washington: National Gallery of Art. Blog. <https://www.nga.gov/features/new-waves/industrial-arts.html>
Vadrucci, F. 2010. *Quando la penna esplode di vita. La collana Franchi Narratori Feltrinelli 1970–1983*. Rome: Oblique studio.
Vené, G. 1963. *Letteratura e capitalismo in Italia dal '700 ad oggi*. Milan: Sugar.
Veneziano, GM. 1994. *Giovanni Arpino*. Milan: Mursia.
Verga, G. 2006. *I grandi romanzi. I Malavoglia. Mastro don Gesualdo*. Milan: Mondadori.
——. 2014. *I Malavoglia*. Catania and Novara: Fondazione Verga/Interlinea.
Vergine, L. 1990. *Gli ultimi eccentrici*. Milan: Rizzoli.
Vetri, Lucio (ed). 1988. *Interventi per "il verri" (1956–1987)*. Ravenna: Longo.
Vice. 1958. "L'uomo di paglia." *L'Avanti*. March 12.
Villa, F. 2014. "Fatica." *Lessico del cinema italiano. Forme di rappresentazione e forme di vita*, vol. I. Edited by Roberto De Gaetano. Milan and Udine: Mimesis.
——. 1999. *Il narratore essenziale della commedia cinematografica italiana degli anni Cinquanta*. Pisa: Edizioni ETS.
Villata, B. 2018. *Primo Levi e il piemontese. La lingua de "La chiave a stella"*. Turin: Fondazione Enrico Landri.
Virdia, Ferdinando. 1959. "Donnarumma all'assalto." *La Fiera Letteraria*. 26 July.
Visentini, G. 1961. "La ragazza in vetrina." *Il giornale d'Italia*. 26 April.
Vittorini, E. 1961. "Industria e letteratura." *Il Menabò di letteratura*, no. 4.
——. 2008. "Industria e letteratura." *Letteratura arte società. Articoli e interventi 1938–1965*. Edited by Raffaella Redondi.
——. 2008. "Premessa al Menabò 6." *Letteratura arte società. Articoli e interventi 1938-1965*. Edited by Raffaella Redondi. Turin: Einaudi.
——. 1960. "Una nuova cultura." *Il Politecnico. Antologia critica*. Edited by Marco Forti and Sergio Pautasso. Milan: Lerici.
Volponi, P. 1974. *Corporale*. Turin: Einaudi.

———. 1965. *La macchina mondiale*. Milan: Garzanti.
———. 1962. *Memoriale*. Milan: Garzanti.
———. 1964. *My Troubles Began*. Translated by Belén Sevareid. New York: Grossman.
———. 2002. *Romanzi e prose*, vol. I. Turin, Einaudi.
———. 2012. *Romanzi e prose*, vol. 1. Turin: Einaudi.
Weil, S. 1951. *La Condition ouvrière*. Paris: Gallimard.
Wright, S. 2002. *Storming Heaven: Class Composition and Struggle in Italian Autonomist Marxism*. London and Sterling, VA: Pluto Press.
Zaccagnini, E. 2009. *I mostri al lavoro. Contadini, commendatori ed impiegati all'italiana*. Rome: Sovera.
Zagarrio, V. 2004. *Cinema e fascismo*. Venice: Marsilio.
Zamagni, V. 1993. *The Economic History of Italy, 1860–1990*. Oxford: Oxford University Press.
Zanardo, M. 2014. "Davide Segre nelle carte manosctritte della *Storia* di Elsa Morante." *I cantieri dell'italianistica. Ricerca didattica e organizzazone agli inizi del XXI secolo*. Edited by Beatrice Alfonzetti et al. Rome: Adi editore.
Zapperi, R. 2013. *Freud e Mussolini: La psicoanalisi in Italia durante il periodo fascista*. Milan: Franco Angeli.
Zavattini, C. 1979. *Opere*. Milan: Bompiani.
Zecca, F (ed.). 2011. *Lo spettacolo del reale. Il cinema di Paolo Virzì*. Pisa: Felici.
Zinato, E. 2018. "Ciclostilati in proprio. La critica dei '*Quaderni piacentini*.'" *Sistema periodico. Il secolo interminabile delle riviste*. Edited by Francesco Bortolotto et al. Bologna: Pendragon.
———. 2010. "Figure animali nella narrativa italiana del secondo Novecento: Sciascia, Primo Levi, Calvino, Volponi, Morante." *Per Romano Luperini*. Edited by Pietro Cataldi. Palermo: Palumbo.
———. 1990. "'Il Menabò di letteratura': La ricerca letteraria come riflessione razionale." *Studi Novecenteschi*, vol. 17, no 39.
———. 2009. "L'esperienza del *Menabò*." *Il demone dell'anticipazione. Cultura, letteratura, editoria in Elio Vittorini*. Edited by Edoardo Esposito. Milan: Il Saggiatore.
———. 2015. *Letteratura come storiografia? Mappe e figure della mutazione italiana*. Macerata: Quodlibet.

Author Affiliations

Pierpaolo Antonello, University of Cambridge

Carlo Baghetti, École des hautes études hispaniques et ibériques

Louis Bayman, University of Southampton

Erica Bellia, University of Cambridge

Paola Bonifazio, University of Texas Austin

Francesca Cantore, Università degli Studi "La Sapienza" di Roma

Giovanni Capecchi, Università per Stranieri di Perugia

Lucia Cardone, Università degli Studi di Sassari

Jim Carter, Boston University

Silvia Cavalli, Università Cattolica del Sacro Cuore

Paolo Chirumbolo, Louisiana State University

Valerio Coladonato, American University of Paris

Paola D'Amora, Independent Scholar

Ilaria A. De Pascalis, Università degli Studi Roma Tre

Alessandra Diazzi, Università del Piemonte Orientale Amedeo Avogadro

Fabrizio di Maio, University of California Irvine

Sergio Ferrarese, College of William and Mary

Daniele Fioretti, Miami University

Ugo Fracassa, Università degli Studi Roma Tre

Malvina Giordana, Università degli Studi Roma Tre

Mattia Lento, Swiss National Science Foundation

Eleonora Lima, Trinity College Dublin

Andrea Mariani, Università degli Studi di Udine

Lorenzo Marmo, Università degli Studi di Napoli "L'Orientale"

Anna Masecchia, Università degli Studi di Napoli "Federico II"

Andrea Minuz, Università degli Studi "La Sapienza" di Roma

Dalila Missero, Università degli Studi di Milano

Piergiorgio Mori, Independent Scholar

Claudio Panella, Università degli Studi di Torino

Luca Peretti, University of Warwick

Mark Pietralunga, Florida State University

Veronica Pravadelli, Università degli Studi Roma Tre

Ricciarda Ricorda, Università Ca' Foscari Venezia

Andrea Sartori, Brown University

Author Affiliations

Tiziano Toracca, Ghent, Università degli Studi di Torino

Pasquale Verdicchio, University of California San Diego

Federico Vitella, Università degli Studi di Messina

Emanuele Zinato, Università degli Studi di Padova

Ambra Zorat, Université de Bourgogne

Index

900 36
1844 Manuscripts (1844) 105–6
3000 Metri sotto il suolo (Three Thousand Meters Below the Surface, 1949) 72
7 minuti (7 Minutes, 2016) 229
8½ (1963) 432
A casa tua ridono (At Your Home They are Laughing, 1971) 284, 288, 292–3
A ciascuno il suo (We Still Kill the Old Way, 1967) 459
A me la libertà (Freedom for Me, 1931) 39
A scopo di lucro (Profit-Making, 1965) 168, 170–2, 492
Acciaio (Steel, 1933) 11, 32–5
Acciaio (Steel, 2010) 210
accidents 29, 52, 152–3, 159, 213, 313, 327, 429, 462, 472
Achtung! Banditi! (Attention! Bandits!, 1951) 42, 46, 494
Acland, Charles 59
Adone (Adonis, 1623) 167
Agamben, Giorgio 138, 143–8
Agnelli, Gianni 73, 352, 482
Agnoletto, Stefano 456
albero degli zoccoli, L' (The Tree of Wooden Clogs, 1978) 401
Aleramo, Sibilla 160
"L'alibi del progresso" (The Alibi of Progress, 1959) 303
Alicata, Mario 266
alienation *see also* exploitation 13, 16, 17, 19, 31–2, 45, 46–52, 83, 102, 105–18, 120–2, 124–5, 129–31, 133–4, 174, 187, 191, 212, 252, 258–9, 267, 275–6, 297, 304, 310, 315, 321–2, 325, 334, 339, 342, 345–6, 354, 356, 403, 405, 406, 408, 414, 439–48, 463, 474
Alighieri, Dante 8–9
Alquati, Romano 139
Amadio, Paolo 215
Amelio, Gianni 227
Americanismo e fordismo (Americanism and Fordism, 1934) 112, 138
Aminta (1573) 167
Amore e fervore (Love and Excitement, 1959) 315, 323, 324
amore in città, L' (Love in the City, 1953) 411
amore mio italiano, L' (My Italian Love, 1963) 16, 131, 273–82, 491
Anceschi, Luciano 92, 328–9
Andreotti, Giulio 431
anni del giudizio, Gli (The Years of Judgement, 1958) 16, 261–71, 491
Antonicelli, Franco 288
Antonioni, Michelangelo 3, 11, 19–20, 45–6, 48, 75, 401, 432, 434, 439–48
Arbasino, Alberto 97
Arcadia (1504) 9, 167
arcano della riproduzione: Casalinghe, prostitute, operai e capitale, L' (The Arcane of Reproduction: Housework, Prostitution, Labor and Capital, 1981) 141

Argan, Giulio Carlo 91
Argentina, Cosimo 210
aria che tira, L' (What's in the Air, 1964) 239
Arias, Adelardo Fernández 29
Armonie Pucciniane (Puccini's Harmonies, 1938) 67
Arpino, Giovanni 16, 37, 80, 97, 261–71
Arterie d'acciaio (Steel Arteries, 1953) 367–8
Asor Rosa, Alberto 139
assicuratore, L' (The Insurance Man, 1975) 285, 290–1
Attacco alla Savana (Attack on the Savannah, 1964) 452
autonomism *see also* operaismo 17, 114–5, 143, 333, 466–7
Avallone, Silvia 210
Avanti! 405, 427

Bachelard, Gaston 177
Bajani, Andrea 214
Bakhtin, Michail 14, 177–8, 185, 192, 229
Baldi, Andrea 154
Balestrini, Nanni 17, 97, 111, 115, 117, 137, 216–7, 327–35, 350, 357
Balla, Giacomo 30
ballata del vecchio calzolaio, La (The Dance of the Old Shoemaker, 1969) 291–1
Barattoni, Luca 433–4
Barbaro, Umberto 38
Barboni, Leonida 382
bardotto, Il (The Hinny) 240
Barilli, Renato 99
Bartali, Gino 288
Barthes, Roland 275–6
Bartoleschi, Valerio 443
Bassani, Giorgio 97
battaglia di Algeri, La (The Battle of Algiers, 1966) 375

Belfagor 298
Belle ma povere (Pretty but Poor, 1957) 200
Bellino, Luca 229
Bellocchio, Piergiorgio 97
Bencivenga, Eduardo 27
Benda, Julien 280–1
Benjamin, Walter 25, 32, 219, 403
Berardinelli, Alfonso 323
Berlin: Symphony of a Great City (1927) 34
Bernardi, Alessandro 377, 379
Bernari, Carlo 10, 36–7, 178
Bertini, Francesca 27
Bertini, Valerio 240
Bertolucci, Bernardo 446, 452
Betti, Eloisa 222
Bettoia, Franca 383
Bevilacqua, Alberto 55, 180, 188–90
Bianciardi, Luciano 2, 16, 47, 100, 169, 179–80, 194–5, 205, 286–7, 295–305
Bible, The (1966) 457
Bigger Than Life (1956) 389
Bilenchi, Romano 10, 37
biopolitics 135, 138, 144–8
Bíos: Biopolitics and Philosophy (2008) 145
Blanchot, Maurice 177
Blasetti, Alessandro 35–6, 374, 421
Bo, Carlo 322
Bocca, Giorgio 289, 292
Boccaccio, Giovanni 9, 167
Boccioni, Umberto 30
Bolognini, Mauro 55
Bonifazio, Paola 4, 13, 368–9
Bontempelli, Massimo 10, 36
Bordwell, David 401–3
Borgnetto, Romano Luigi 28
Bosio, Aristide 64
Bouchard, Norma 3

Bourdieu, Pierre 96
bourgeoisie 7, 18, 25, 49, 75, 101, 110, 122, 140, 142, 149, 154, 155, 172, 185, 190, 208, 248, 256, 267, 269, 324, 351, 352–3, 376, 423, 434, 436, 459, 465–7, 482, 485
Bourneuf, Ronald 180, 187, 191
Bovay, Gilbert 452, 455
Branca, Remo 66, 68
Brand, Peter 3
Braudel, Fernand 404
Brecht, Bertolt 372
Brero, Caterina 262
breve vacanza, Una (A Brief Vacation, 1974) 55, 494
Briani, Giulio 72
Brief Encounter (1945) 383
Brigate Rosse (Red Brigades) 140, 149
Brunetta, Gian Piero 3
Bruni, Attila 225
Bruni, Francesco 231
Brutti, sporchi e cattivi (Down and Dirty, 1974) 480
Buccheri, Vincenzo 49
Buell, Lawrence 165
Bigatti, Giorgio 178
Buonarroti, Michelangelo 454
Busi, Aldo 208
Buzzanca, Lando 54
Buzzati, Dino 91
Buzzi, Giancarlo 16, 131, 273–82

Cabiria (1914) 28, 32
Cabrini, Carlo 47
Caccia tragica (Tragic Hunt, 1947) 42
Cacciari, Massimo 138, 141–2, 146–8
Caesar, Michael 3
Caino, Mario 373
Calandrone, Maria Grazia 160
califfa, La (1964 novel) 55, 188–91, 491
califfa, La (1970 film) 55, 493

Call center (2005) 215
Calvino, Italo 1, 77–9, 81, 88, 91, 98, 131, 135, 166, 169, 179–80, 184, 239–41, 245, 248, 253, 256, 262, 274, 283–4, 286–7, 290
calzolaio di Vigevano, Il (The Shoemaker from Vigevano, 1962) 100, 284, 492
Camerini, Mario 38, 411
cammino della speranza, Il (Path of Hope, 1950) 42
Camon, Ferdinando 91, 323
canale degli angeli, Il (The Canal of the Angels, 1934) 38
Cancellieri, Edmondo 68
Cani dietro le sbarre (Dogs Behind Bars, 1954) 375
Cantieri dell'Adriatico (Adriatic Construction Sites, 1932–1933) 38
Cantù, Cesare 10, 26
canzone dell'amore, La (The Song of Love, 1930) 33
Canzoniere (14 C) 167
Capital (1859) 105
Capofabbrica, Il (The Foreman, 1935) 37, 491
"Il capolavoro" (The Masterpiece, 1961) 239, 245–8, 492
Carducci, Giosuè 30
Carrà, Raffaella 436
Cartier, Max 48, 394
Casalini, Maria 38
caso Mattei, Il (The Mattei Affair, 1972) 11, 494
Cassola, Carlo 97
Catholicism 45, 56, 79, 267, 302, 405, 428, 482
Cavalli, Silvia 16, 81
Cavarero, Adriana 141
Ceccarelli, Giuseppe 38

Cecchi, Emilio 34–5
censorship 10, 12, 35–9, 193
Ceraso, Angela 215
Cerchio, Fernando 67
Ceserani, Remo 9
chant du styrène, Le (The Song of the Styrene, 1958) 446
Checchi, Andrea 43
Chemello, Adriana 10
Cherchi, Grazia 97
Chéroux, Clément 441
Chi si aiuta Dio l'aiuta (God Helps Those Who Help Themselves, 1865) 26
chiave a stella, La (The Wrench, 1978) 17, 98, 102, 137, 150, 208, 337–47, 352, 492
Chiodi e rose (Nails and Roses) 349
Chiti, Virgilio 73
Christian Democracy *see* Democrazia Cristiana
ciminiere di Casale, Le (Farmhouse Smokestacks, 1962) 160
Cinema Nuovo 386, 405
Cinemasessanta 405
Citati, Pietro 322
Città invisibili (Invisible Cities, 1972) 1
Civiltà delle macchine (Machine Civilization) 91–2, 97, 173
Clair, René 39
class consciousness 7, 37, 44, 110, 115, 120, 134, 156, 195, 205, 211, 331, 334, 373, 386
class struggle 13–4, 18, 20, 44–6, 102, 105–18, 137–50, 364, 376, 474, 479–89
Classe operaia 114, 139, 195
classe operaia va in paradiso, La (Lulù the Tool, 1972) 20, 52, 13, 137, 459–68, 494
Cobweb, The (1955) 389
Cochran, Steve 45

Col ferro e col fuoco (With Iron and Fire, 1926) 38
Cold War 65, 70, 81, 193, 205
Colloquii coi personaggi (Conversations with Characters, 1915) 276
Colombo, Furio 182
Comand, Mariapia 435, 437
Come tu mi vuoi (As You Desire Me, 1930) 33
Comencini, Francesca 228
Comencini, Luigi 55, 56, 431–2
Coming Community, The (1990) 148
commedia all'italiana (comedy Italian style) 50, 193, 435, 437, 460, 470–1, 488
Commedia delle Ninfe fiorentine (Comedy of the Florentine Nymphs, 14 C) 167
communism *see also* Partito Comunista Italiano 7, 30, 37, 43, 45, 70, 80, 105, 110, 138, 151, 154, 193, 195, 263–6, 341, 353, 373, 385, 428, 463, 465–6, 472, 474, 478, 481
Communist Manifesto, The (1848) 105, 110
compagni, I (The Organizer, 1963) 19, 232, 427–37, 494
Con gli occhi chiusi (1919) 284
condition ouvrière, La (1934) 156, 252
Conquest of Happiness, The (1958) 345
Consiglio, Stefano 226
consumerism 280, 282, 303, 321, 325, 374, 393, 459–61, 463, 465
Contemporaneo 295
Coppi, Fausto 288
Cordiali saluti (Kind Regards, 2005) 214
Corona, Gabriella 179–80
Corporale (Corporal, 1974) 307, 310–3
Corti, Maria 284
Cosa vuoi che sia (What's the Big Deal, 2016) 226

Cremaschi, Inisero 168–75
Crematorio di Vienna (Vienna Crematory, 1969) 325
Crispi, Francesco 429
Cristaldi, Franco 381–2, 431
Cristo non si è fermato a Eboli (Christ Did Not Stop at Eboli, 1949) 71–2
Cristo si è fermato a Ebodi (Christ Stopped at Eboli, 1945) 72
Croce, Benedetto 92, 138
Crowd, The (1928) 408
Culicchia, Giuseppe 208
Cuore (Heart, 1886) 26

D'Angeli, Concetta 156
D'Annunzio, Gabriele 30–2, 167
Da Vinci, Leonardo 454
Dalla lana al tessuto (From Wool to Fabric, 1950s) 68
Damicelli, Mario 452
Darwin, Charles 316
Das Lied der Strome (The Song of the Rivers, 1954) 371
Davì, Luigi 15, 17, 80, 88, 98, 178, 239–49, 286
De Amicis, Edmondo 10, 26, 436
De Carlo, Giancarlo 281
de Caro, Ciro 226
De Filippo, Eduardo 11, 18, 196, 361–69
De Filippo, Peppino 196, 369
De Gennaro, Riccardo 117
De Laurentiis, Dino 457
de Lauretis, Teresa 477
De Martino, Ernesto 395
De Negri, Giuliano 372
De Pascalis, Ilaria 20, 220
De Santis, Giuseppe 42, 193, 195, 372, 376, 460
De Seta, Vittorio 73
De Sica, Vittorio 38, 42, 55, 193–5, 362, 383, 431, 460

Debenedetti, Giacomo 321
Decamerone (14 C) 9
decima vittima, La (The 10th Victim, 1965) 459
Del Colle, Ubaldo Maria 29
Delitto d'amore (Somewhere Beyond Love, 1974) 55–6
delitto della piccina, Il (The Child's Crime, 1920) 29
Dell'arte della Guerra (The Art of War, 2012) 229
Della Giovanna, Ettore 449
Della Noce, Luisa 382–3
Delon, Alain 48
Democrazia Cristiana (Christian Democrats, DC) 262, 428, 459
Depero, Fortunato 30
Deserto rosso (Red Desert, 1964) 3, 19, 75, 439–48, 493
Desiati, Mario 215
Detto, Loredana 412
Dezio, Francesco 210, 212
Di Ciaula, Tommaso 17, 117–8, 208, 349–57
Di Lecce, Nicola 226
di Silvio, Anna 436
Die Windrose (The Wind Rose, 1957) 371
diga del ghiacciaio, La (The Dam of the Glacier, 1955) 63, 73
dipendente, Il (The Employee, 1994) 208, 213–4
dismissione, La (The Dismantling, 2002) 210
Divorzio all'italiana (Divorce, Italian style, 1961) 471
documentaries *see also* sponsored films 5, 11, 13, 34, 38, 47, 59–76, 227, 401, 433, 441
Dodi, Franco 73
Dolce Vita, La (Dolce Vita, 1960) 15, 193–206

Dolci, Danilo 333
domani della coscienza, Il (Consciousness' Future, 1914) 27
Domenichelli, Mario 9
Donnarumma all'assalto (The Men at the Gate, 1959) 15, 100, 130, 133, 172, 173–4, 251–9, 493
Dorfles, Gillo 91
Dramma della gelosia (The Pizza Triangle, 1970) 479
Duggan, Christopher 68
Durand, Gilbert 177

Eco, Umberto 91, 304
economic boom 2–4, 6, 11–3, 15–7, 20, 44, 46–52, 61, 81, 84, 88, 91, 96, 105, 111–2, 122, 151, 162, 168, 170, 182, 188–9, 206, 245, 266, 268, 278, 283–93, 296, 301, 303–5, 328, 373–4, 392–5, 399, 415, 432–3, 454, 457, 459–60, 462, 479, 483
Egidi, Carlo 382
Eliot, T.S. 383
Elsaesser, Thomas 402–3
Emmer, Luciano 19, 47, 374, 415, 423
Empire (2000) 146
Engels, Frederick 105
environment *see also* landscape *and* pollution 44–5, 55, 63, 165–76, 179–80, 190, 356
Esposito, Roberto 138, 145, 148
Essais critiques (Critical Essays, 1964) 275
Essence of Christianity, The (1841) 106
Essere donne (1965) 380
Europa '51 (Europe '51, 1952) 45, 494
Europa di notte (European Nights, 1959) 421
European Recovery Program *see* Marshall Plan
exploitation *see also* alienation 7, 13, 16, 51, 102, 109, 116, 125, 129, 133, 135, 138, 143, 189, 219, 223–4, 227–8, 232, 235, 251–9, 331, 335, 398, 416, 429

fabbrica e il suo ambiente, Una (A Factory and Its Environment, 1957) 64
Falco, Giorgio 215–6
famiglia, La (The Family, 1987) 480
family 5, 7, 16, 19, 29, 44, 48, 55, 61, 64, 68, 83, 152, 160, 162, 178, 180, 197–8, 200, 202, 213, 227, 278, 312, 316, 318, 320, 324–5, 331, 334–5, 349, 363, 368–9, 372, 377, 383–4, 386–9, 391–7, 408–9, 434–7, 459, 461, 472–4, 476–7, 480
Fantozzi (1975) 57
Fasano, Pino 9
Fasano, Ugo 449
fascino della violenza, Il (The Seduction of Violence, 1912) 27
Fascism *see also* Partito Nazionale Fascista 3, 5–6, 10–2, 31–2, 35–9, 42–3, 60–1, 65–9, 74, 92, 121, 308, 324, 361, 366, 368, 374, 459, 461
Fellini, Federico 2, 196–7, 199, 203–6, 401, 432
female workers 14, 18, 20, 29, 55, 100, 151–63, 227, 229–35, 241, 290, 371–80, 413–4, 463, 465, 472, 476–8
feminism 12, 20, 141, 148, 159, 163, 355, 379–80, 462, 465, 470, 472, 477
Fenoglio, Beppe 97
ferie di un operaio, Le (A Workers' Vacation, 1974) 117
Ferme, Valerio 3
Ferranti, Gastone 451
Ferreri, Marco 434
Ferretti, Gian Carlo 291
Ferroni, Giorgio 64, 67

ferroviere, Il (The Railroad Man, 1956) 381–2, 385, 389
Festa a Castelluccio (Celebration at Castelluccio, 1955) 375
Feuerbach, Ludwig 106
fiammella si è accesa, Una (A Flame is On, 1960) 73
fidanzamento, Il (The Engagement, 1956) 324
fidanzati, I (1963) 47, 401, 405, 408, 414, 494
Figini, Luigi 281
figli di nessuno, I (Nobody's Children, 1921) 29
figli di nessuno, I (Nobody's Children, 1951) 43, 494
Filmcritica 405
Filumena Marturano (1951) 363
Fina, Giuseppe 11, 48–9
Fioretti, Daniele 17, 343
firings *see also* unemployment 26–7, 29, 53, 93, 100, 232, 254, 263, 309, 327, 364, 366, 373, 378
First World War 28–9, 36, 120, 138, 151
fischio della sirena, Il (The Siren's Call to Duty, 1912) 27
Flaiano, Ennio 197
Fofi, Goffredo 488
Fontana, Eugenio 38
Foot, John 392
Fordism 92, 101–2, 112, 115, 138–9, 143, 219, 222, 224, 233, 345, 462–4
Forti, Marco 88, 296
Fortini, Franco 64, 93, 94–5, 97, 130, 135, 180, 280, 307
Fortunati, Leopoldina 141
Foucault, Michel 128, 134, 144, 477
Franck, Joseph 177
Franklin, Benjamin 26
Fresson, Bernard 415
Freud, Sigmund 311

Frusta, Arrigo 27
Futurism 10, 30–1, 36, 446

Gadda, Carlo Emilio 99, 101, 316, 323
Galileo Galilei (1942) 67
Gandin, Michele 64, 71–2, 368
Garbuglia, Mario 433
Garzanti, Livio 315, 324–5
Gassman, Vittorio 201
Gela 1959: Pozzi a mare (Gela 1959: Drilling at Sea, 1960) 73
Gemelli, Agostino 121
Gemma, Giuliano 55
Generazione 1000 euro (The 1000 Euros Generation, 2009) 227, 234
Gente di Vigevano (People from Vigevano, 1977) 285
Gentili, Dario 148–50
Germi, Pietro 18, 42, 381–90, 431, 471
Gerusalemme liberata (Jerusalem Delivered, 1581) 167, 172
Gettoni, I 80–1, 98, 239–40, 261
Gherardini, Oreste 27
Giacomelli, Enrico 202
Gianassi, Armida 376–7
Giannetti, Alfredo 382, 386, 388
Giannini, Giancarlo 55, 471
Ginsborg, Paul 122, 366
Gioca, Pietro! (Play, Pietro!, 1953) 34
Giomini, Pino 73
giornata d'uno scrutatore, La (The Watcher, 1963) 262
giornata particolare, Una (A Special Day, 1976) 480
Giorni e nuvole (Days and Clouds, 2007) 227
Giovanna (1955) 18, 371–80, 494
Gioventù senza sole (Dreary Youth, 1938) 151–2, 163
Giraldi, Franco 373, 376
Girardot, Annie 436

Girotti, Massimo 54
Giudici, Giovanni 88
Giuliani, Alfredo 329
giustizia dell'abisso, La (The Justice of the Abyss, 1912) 27
Gobetti, Piero 31
Godard, Jean-Luc 401, 443, 445
Gramsci, Antonio 30–1, 112, 137–9, 142, 157, 364, 463, 473–4, 476
Grande Rivolta, La (The Great Revolution, 1999) 333
grande vacanza, La (1953) 324
Grassilli, Raoul 48
Gregoretti, Ugo 51–2
Gregotti, Vittorio 304
grido, Il (The Outcry, 1957) 45–6, 493
Grignani, Maria Antonietta 286
Grillandi, Massimo 322
Gruppo 63 *see* neo-avantgarde
Gualino, Renato 382
Guerrazzi, Vincenzo 117–8, 351–2
Guglielmi, Angelo 131
Gymkhana-Cross (1957) 98, 239–49, 492

Hardt, Michael 145–6
Hediger, Vinzenz 64
Hegel, George Wilhelm Frederick 106, 141
Hemingway, Ernest 241, 243
History and Class Consciousness (1923) 108
Ho camminato nel mondo con l'anima aperta (I Walked the World with an Open Soul, 2018) 160
Hollow Men, The (1925) 384
Homo Sacer (1995) 144, 147
hot autumn 8, 12, 17, 52, 114, 328, 462
Huston, John 457

Iacoli, Giulio 180
Ieri oggi e domani (Yesterday, Today and Tomorrow, 1963) 362

Iguana, L' (The Iguana, 1965) 154–5
illness 37, 55, 101, 115, 122–3, 127, 149, 152, 158–9, 186, 268, 286, 308–10
In bici senza sella (On a Bike with No Saddle, 2016) 227
Incanto e verità (Enchantment and Truth, 1956) 261
Incontro alla Olivetti (Welcome to Olivetti, 1950) 64
Indagine su un cittadino al di sopra di ogni sospetto (Investigation of a Citizen Above Suspicion, 459 1970)
industrialization *see also* modernization 2, 5, 70, 75, 88, 95, 110, 122, 135, 153, 179, 180, 256, 282, 346, 362, 368, 405, 407, 434, 442, 455
Infermeria di fabbrica (The Factory Infirmary, 1951) 64
Inferno (13 C) 8
integration 18–9, 47, 56, 266, 269, 296, 305, 318, 332, 369, 391–99, 474
Integrazione, L' (The Integration, 1960) 29–7, 304, 491
Into Paradiso (2010) 226
intrepido, L' (Intrepido: A Lonely Hero, 2013) 227
Invernizio, Carolina 25
Invisibili (The Invisibles, 2003) 226
invisibili, Gli (The Unseen, 1987) 333
Io venditore di elefanti (I Was an Elephant Salesman, 1990) 208
iron *see* steel
Italian Theory (2012) 149
Italiani nel mondo (Italians the World Over, 1965) 20, 449–58
Italiani nel Venezuela (Italians in Venezuela, 1963–1965) 452
Ivens, Joris 371

jeune fille à l'usine, La (The Girl at the Factory, 1978) 160

Kafka, Franz 274–6
Kazan, Elia 49
Khouma, Pap 208
Khrushchev, Nikita 80, 139
Kovács, András Bálint 431
Kracauer, Siegfried 403, 409–11
Krisis (1976) 141–2
Kubrick, Stanley 50
Kushner, Rachel 330

Labate, Wilma 228
labor unions 2, 7, 17, 232, 254, 300, 314, 322, 328, 355–6, 366, 466, 468, 472
Ladri di biciclette (Bicycle Thieves, 1948) 42, 193–5, 383, 460
Lamina, Rossella 226
landscape *see also* environment *and* pollution 6, 7, 14, 41–6, 47, 56, 70, 75, 122, 165–76, 178, 181, 184–5, 187–9, 191–2, 282, 368, 416, 432, 439, 445, 473, 483
Landy, Marcia 434, 436
Lang, Fritz 39
Lattuada, Alberto 49, 457
lavoro culturale, Il (Cultural Labor, 1957) 194, 491
"Il lavoro del traduttore" (The Job of the Translator, 1961) 299
layoffs *see* firings
Lazzarato, Maurizio 140
Lazzarin, Stefano 277
Le Corbusier 281
Lean, David 383
legge truffa (swindle law) 262
Lento, Mattia 20–1, 469
Leo, Edoardo 227
Leonetti, Francesco 98
Lessona, Michele 26
Levi, Carlo 71–2, 333
Levi, Primo 17, 98, 102, 137, 147, 150, 208, 337–47, 352

linea gotica, La (1962) 130, 133, 168–9, 181–2, 493
Lizzani, Carlo 2, 42–3, 46–7
Lo chiameremo Andrea (1972) 55, 494
Lonzi, Carla 141
Loren, Sofia 363
Lotman, Jurij 177
Lukács, György 108, 110, 114
Lumière brothers 27, 35, 371
Luperini, Romano 278, 310
Lupo, Giuseppe 126–7, 178, 274
Luraghi, Giuseppe Eugenio 91
Luxembourg, Rosa 468
Luzi, Alfredo 185
Luzi, Silvia 229

Macasoli, Antonio 49
macchina mondiale, La (The Worldwide Machine, 1965) 310, 493
Maciste innamorato (Maciste in Love, 1919) 28
maestro di Vigevano, Il (The Teacher from Vigevano, 1962 novel) 20, 100, 284, 287, 289, 492
maestro di Vigevano, Il (The Teacher from Vigevano, 1963 film) 459–60, 465, 467, 494
mafia 211, 459, 471–4, 476, 478
Mafioso (1962) 49, 457, 494
Maggiorani, Lamberto 42
magliari, I (The Magliari, 1959) 202–3, 205
Magnaghi, Ubaldo 73
Magnani, Anna 376
Maia (1903) 30
Malavoglia, I (The House by the Medlar Tree, 1881) 279, 285
Malvarosa (2005) 210
Mammut (Mammoth, 1994) 208, 210–1
Manfredi, Nino 55
Mangini, Cecilia 380
"Le mani" (These Hands, 1968) 158, 492

maniera di farsi ricco, La (The Way to Wealth, 1758) 26
Manifesto del Futurismo (Manifesto of Futurism, 1909) 10, 30
manifesto, Il (The Manifesto, 1969) 158–9
Manzoni, Alessandro 10, 26
Maraini, Dacia 14, 97, 152, 158–9, 163
Marazzi, Christian 140
Marcuse, Herbert 108–9
mare non bagna Napoli, Il (Neapolitan Chronicles, 1953) 152
Marin, Luciano 386
Marinetti, Filippo Tommaso 10–1, 31, 446
Marino, Giovan Battista 167
Maritain, Jacques 281
Marito e moglie (Husband and Wife, 1952) 363
Marshall Plan 6, 62, 67, 71, 450
Martinelli, Elsa 49
Marx, Karl 13, 16, 105–10, 112–3, 131, 182, 251–2, 356, 463
Marxism 12, 15, 17, 42, 79–80, 93, 108, 112, 114, 137, 140–1, 146, 193–5, 258, 268, 281, 333, 339, 343, 345, 405
Mastandrea, Valerio 232
Mastriani, Luigi 25
Mastrocinque, Camillo 196
Mastroianni, Marcello 201, 204, 206, 232, 363, 437, 480
Mastronardi, Lucio 16, 20, 97, 100–1, 178, 283–93, 460
Matarazzo, Raffaello 43
Matrimonio all'italiana (Marriage Italian Style, 1964) 362
Mattei, Enrico 74
Mattioda, Enrico 344
Mauro, Walter 256
Mayakovsky, Vladimir 269

mechanization *see also* technology 5, 15–6, 31, 111–2, 251–9, 301, 421, 442–3, 476
Melato, Mariangela 55, 465, 472
melodrama 9, 11, 18–9, 29, 43–4, 48, 53–6, 205, 386–90, 395, 397, 399
Memoriale (My Troubles Began, 1962) 93, 100–1, 103, 112, 131–2, 137, 155, 174–6, 185–6, 248–9, 207–10, 350, 493
Menabò di letteratura, Il 13, 77–89, 94–5, 98, 165, 240, 245, 248, 253, 280, 284, 296
Meneghello, Luigi 97
meridionale di Vigevano, Il (The Southerner from Vigevano, 1964) 100, 284, 289–90
Metello (1970) 55, 493
Metropolis (1927) 39
Metropolis and Mental Life, The (1903) 404
Metz, Christian 401, 403
Mi piace lavorare (Mobbing) (I Like to Work: (Mobbing), 2004) 228
Miccichè, Lino 405–6, 427
middle class 6–7, 57, 65, 75, 214, 300, 383, 395, 401, 406–8, 413
migration *see also* southern Italy 6, 12, 14, 18, 20, 42, 46–8, 203, 205, 208, 284, 331, 365, 392, 452–4, 456–7, 479–89
Milani, Riccardo 227–8
Milano, Paolo 322
millesimo di millimetro, Un (A Thousandth of a Meter, 1949) 66
Mimì metallurgico ferito nell'onore (The Seduction of Mimì, 1972) 20, 55, 469–78, 494
Minardi, Mario 64
mining 416–21, 473

Minnelli, Vincente 389
mio paese, Il (My Country, 2006) 229
Missione Timirazev (Mission Timirazev, 1953) 375
"The Modern Cinema and Narrativity" (1966) 401
modernism 16, 45, 98–102, 373, 389, 402–3
modernity 2, 4, 17, 19, 21, 30, 44, 48, 50, 56, 61, 83, 84, 102, 139, 155, 170, 179, 184, 187, 205–6, 268, 277, 319, 368, 395, 396, 399, 401–14, 416, 434, 471
"Modernity: The Troubled Trope" (2011) 402
modernization *see also* industrialization 5, 37, 50, 53, 71, 75–6, 100, 179–80, 297, 364–5, 368, 395, 402–3, 434–5, 474
Modigliani, Amedeo 453
Momigliano, Franco 93
mondo deve sapere, Il (The World Must Know, 2006) 214–5, 231
Monicelli, Mario 19, 200, 202, 232, 427–37, 471
Montagnani, Renzo 54
Montaldi, Danilo 139
Montaldo, Giuliano 373
Montale, Eugenio 91, 261, 322
Morandi, Giorgio 160
Morante, Elsa 14, 152, 155–7, 163, 311, 323
Moravia, Alberto 97, 206, 323, 487
Morire di lavoro (Dying of Work, 2008) 229
Moro, Aldo 337, 428
Morricone, Ennio 464
mosche del capitale, Le (The Flies of Capital, 1989) 98, 102–3, 208, 314
Mounier, Emmanuel 281
Movimento Comunità (Community Movement) 64, 278

Multitude (2004) 145
Mulvey, Laura 411
Muraro, Luisa 141
Murgia, Michela 214, 229, 231
Musatti, Cesare 92, 126–7
Mussolini, Benito 32, 34, 37–9, 367

Nacache, Jacqueline 376
Naldini, Nico 325
Napoletani a Milano (Neapolitans in Milan, 1953) 11, 18, 196, 361–9, 493
Napoli milionaria! (Millionaires' Naples!, 1950) 363
Narration in the Fiction Film (1985) 402
Nata, Sebastiano 208, 213–4
Natella, Alfonso 115, 330, 333
Nazism 146, 239
Nazzari, Amedeo 43
Negri, Ada 30, 162
Negri, Antonio 138–9, 143–6, 148, 162
Nenni, Pietro 427–8
neo-avantgarde 3, 17, 92, 97–9, 115, 216, 290, 328–9, 350
neoliberalism *see also* precarity 14, 102, 143, 146, 149, 208, 209, 212, 217, 219, 222–4, 233
neorealism 3, 5, 11–2, 18–9, 35–6, 38, 41–4, 49, 69, 82, 100, 193–6, 369, 373, 375–6, 379–80, 383, 386, 405, 430–35, 460, 473, 486
Nevola, Edoardo 382–3
Niccolai, Giulia 328
Nicola Rubino è entrato in fabbrica (Nicola Rubino Entered the Factory, 2004) 210, 212
Nigro, Raffaele 210
Ninfale fiesolano (The Tale of the Fiesole Nymph, 14 C) 167
Nissim, Luciana 93
Nizzoli, Marcello 281
Nobili, Nella 14, 152, 160–3

Noce, Teresa 14, 151–2, 163
Non c'è pace tra gli ulivi (No Peace Under the Olive Tree, 1950) 42, 195
Nonostante Platone (In Spite of Plato, 1990) 141
Nord e Sud uniti nella lotta (North and South United in Struggle, 1974) 351, 492
Novelli, Diego 481, 484
Novissimi, I (The Very New Ones, 1961) 329
Nuovi argomenti 253
nuvola d'ira, Una (A Cloud of Rage, 1962) 16, 37, 261–71, 492
nuvola di smog, La (Smog, 1958) 166, 274

O'Leary, Alan 434
O'Rawe, Catherine 434
Obino, Stefano 226
Officina (Workshop) 98
Oggi (Today) 389
Olivetti, Adriano 17, 63, 92–4, 119–20, 123–6, 174, 249, 278, 280–1, 307–8, 310, 312–4
Olmi, Ermanno 3, 19, 47–8, 401–14, 446, 494
Ombres, Rossana 160
Omicron (1963) 51, 494
On the Origin of Species (1859) 316
onorevole Angelina, L' (Angelina, 1947) 376
Operai e capitale (1966) 139
operaismo (workerism) *see also* autonomism 17, 93, 114–5, 138–40, 142–3, 195, 333, 473
ordine simbolico della madre, L' (The Symbolic Order of the Mother, 1991) 141
Orfeo (Orpheus, 1607) 167
Ortese, Anna Maria 14, 152–5, 163, 492
Ossola, Carlo 10

Ottieri, Ottiero 3, 15–6, 21, 80, 87–8, 93, 98, 100, 111–3, 117, 130–1, 133, 168–9, 172, 174–75, 178–85, 251–9, 286, 307, 493
Ouellet, Réal 180, 187, 191

Pace, Maria 184–5
padrone delle ferriere, Il (The Owner of the Ironworks, 1919) 27–8
padrone e l'operaio, Il (The Boss and the Worker, 1975) 495
padrone, Il (The Boss, 1964) 17, 100, 113–4, 315–25
Pagano, Bartolomeo 28
Pagato per tacere (Paid to Keep Quiet, 1962) 169
Pagliarani, Elio 98, 178, 329
Pagni, Silvia 372
Paisà (Paisan, 1946) 375, 460
Pane e zolfo (Bread and Sulfur, 1956) 375
Pane, amore e fantasia (Bread, Love and Dreams, 1953) 432
Panseri, Sandro 410–1
Panzieri, Raniero 93, 139
Paolucci, Giovanni 67
Parise, Goffredo 17, 100, 111, 113–4, 315–25, 493
Parker, Ian 121–2, 129
Partito Comunista Italiano (Italian Communist Party, PCI) *see also* communism 7, 13, 16, 20, 30, 43, 79–80, 114, 117, 137–40, 194–5, 240, 262, 266, 308, 373, 428–9, 471–2, 476, 480–3, 485
Partito Nazionale Fascista (National Fascist Party, PNF) *see also* Fascism 5
Partito Socialista di Unità Proletaria (Italian Socialist Party of Proletarian Unity, PSIUP) *see also* socialism 429

Partito Socialista Italiano (Italian Socialist Party, PSI) *see also* socialism 13, 114, 117, 427–9
Parzen, Jeremy 3
Pascoli, Giovanni 30
Pasinetti, Francesco 38
Pasolini, Pier Paolo 54, 97, 168–9, 256, 266, 395, 401, 444–5
paternalism 26–7, 38, 93, 100
Paul-Lévy, Francoise 184
Pausa caffè (Coffee Break, 2004) 215–6
Pautasso, Sergio 285, 292
Peccato che sia una canaglia (Too Bad She's Bad, 1954) 374
Pedroni, Tania 226
Pelle viva (Scorched Skin, 1962) 11, 48–9, 494
Pellizza da Volpedo, Giuseppe 230
Pennacchi, Antonio 208, 210
Per immagini (Through Images, 2009) 451
Perego, Eugenio 27
Peretti, Luca 4, 20
Perilli, Ivo 39
Permettete? Rocco Papaleo (My Name is Rocco Papaleo, 1971) 479
Personaggi (Characters, 1906) 276
Pertile, Lino 3
Petrarca, Francesco 167
Petri, Elio 11, 20, 52, 131, 137, 284, 459–68, 475, 495
Phenomenology of the Spirit (1807) 106
Piacere, Il (The Child of Pleasure, 1889) 30
Piccoli calabresi sul Lago Maggiore: Nuovi ospiti alla colonia di Suna (Little Calabrians on Lake Maggiore: New Guests at Suna's Summer Camp, 1951) 63
Pietrangeli, Antonio 373–4, 431
Pignotti, Lamberto 88

Pinelli, Tullio 197
Pinkus, Karen 442
Piovene, Guido 321–2
Pirandello, Luigi 10, 31–5, 99, 276
Pirandello, Stefano 34
Pirella, Agostino 88
Pisacane, Carlo 200–1
Pivetta, Oreste 208
Placido, Beniamino 258
Placido, Michele 229
Poe, Edgar Allan 277
police 26, 202, 328, 332, 366–7, 459, 464, 466
Polidoro, Gian Luigi 202
Politecnico, Il 79–80
political film 11, 20
Poliziano, Angelo 167
Pollini, Gino 281
pollution *see also* environment *and* landscape 55, 167, 286
ponte della Ghisolfa, Il (Ghisolfa Bridge, 1958) 391, 493
Pontecorvo, Gillo 18, 371–80, 431, 495
Porta Portese (1954) 375
Porta, Antonio 328–9
Portafoglio d'un operaio (Workers' Wallet, 1871) 26
post-Fordism *see* neoliberalism
posto dell'anima, Il (The Soul's Place, 2003) 228
posto, Il (1961) 3, 19, 47, 401–14, 494
Potere operaio (group) 328, 333
Potere operaio (journal) 473
Poveri ma belli (Poor but Handsome, 1957) 199, 201
Poveri milionari (Poor Millionaires, 1958) 200
Poverty of Philosophy, The (1847) 109–10
Pozzo 18: Profondità 1650 (Well Number 18: Depth 1750, 1955) 74
Pravadelli, Veronica 19, 48, 395

precarity *see also* neoliberalism 137, 149, 219–35
prete bello, Il (Don Gastone and the Ladies, 1954) 315, 324
prigionieri del sottosuolo, I (The Prisoners of the Underground, 1956) 73
Primo Maggio (May First, 1980) 26
Pro o contro la bomba atomica (For or Against the Atomic Bomb, 1965) 311
proletarians *see* working class
promessi sposi, I (The Betrothed, 1827) 26
proprietà non è più un furto, La (Property Is no Longer a Theft, 1973) 459
protests *see also* hot autumn *and* strikes 8, 29, 54, 97, 114, 139, 152, 265, 304–5, 327–8, 343, 376, 378, 462, 479
psychology and psychoanalysis 13–4, 16, 31, 92–4, 107, 110–1, 115, 119–35, 180, 182, 185, 212, 257, 299, 307, 308, 319, 329, 334, 338, 419, 432, 442, 461–2, 467
Pupino, Angelo R. 276

Quaderni di Serafino Gubbio operatore (The Notebooks of Serafino Gubbio, Cinematograph Operator, 1925) 31
Quaderni piacentini 97
Quaderni rossi 114, 139, 195
Quaranta, Bruno 266
Quaroni, Ludovico 281
Quarto stato, Il (The Fourth Estate, 1898–1901) 230
Quattro passi fra le nuvole (A Walk in the Clouds, 1942) 36
ragazza con la pistola, La (The Girl with the Pistol, 1968) 471
ragazza in vetrina, La (Girl in the Window, 1961) 19, 47, 415–5, 494

Ragazze da marito (Girls to be Married, 1952) 363
ragazze di Piazza di Spagna, Le (Three Girls from Rome, 1952) 374
Ragazzo (1934) 39
ragazzo morto e le comete, Il (The Dead Boy and the Comets, 1951) 323–4
Ragonese, Isabella 233
Randi, Paola 226
Ray, Nicholas 389
Rea, Ermanno 210
Regina di cuoi (Queen of Leather, 1948–1953) 261
Resnais, Alain 446
Revelli, Nuto 333
ricerche del metano e del petrolio, Le (Researching in Gas and Oil, 1951) 73
Riis, Jacob 433
Risi, Dino 196, 199–200
Riso amaro (Bitter Rice, 1949) 42, 193, 374
Robert, Marthe 275
Rocco e i suoi fratelli (Rocco and His Brothers, 1960) 18, 48, 205, 391–9, 465, 495
Rodriguez Bradford, Ximena 160
Roma città aperta (Rome, Open City, 1945) 43, 457
Roma ore 11 (Rome 11:00, 1952) 376
Romanzo popolare (1974) 494
Rondini, Andrea 346–7
Rosi, Francesco 11, 202, 431, 495
Rossellini, Roberto 43, 45, 195, 373, 375, 432, 495
Rossi, Alessandro 26
Rotaie (Rails, 1930) 38
Roth, Philip 346
Rotunno, Giuseppe 433
Rousseau, Jean-Jacques 105–6, 279
Roversi, Roberto 97–8

Rozzi, Renato 128–9
Rubino, Gianfranco 184
Russell, Bertrand 345
Rustichelli, Carlo 49, 382
Ruttmann, Walter 11, 33–5

Sabel, Virgilio 66, 72–3
Salaried Masses, The (1930) 409–10
Salce, Luciano 54, 57, 495
Salinari, Carlo 266, 322
Salvatori, Renato 48, 51, 199, 201, 203
Samuels, Charles 441–2
Sandokan (2004) 333
Sandrelli, Stefania 55–6
Sanguineti, Edoardo 97, 329
Sannazaro, Jacopo 9
Scaffai, Niccolò 166, 323
Scalia, Gianni 82, 84–5, 88
Schooling in Modernity (2014) 4, 368
Sciascia, Leonardo 459
science fiction 48, 51, 459
Scola, Ettore 20–1, 53, 465, 469–70, 479–89, 495
Scotellaro, Rocco 333
Scrivano, Fabrizio 187
Scuola allievi Giovanni Agnelli (Fiat Vocational School, 1962) 73
Scusate se esisto (Do You See Me?, 2014) 227, 234
Se questo è un uomo (If This is a Man, 1947) 147, 150
Second World War 2, 5–6, 13, 30–1, 37, 39, 42, 66–7, 69, 75, 77, 79, 81, 92, 112, 121, 137–8, 162, 247, 285, 308, 323, 361, 366, 374–5, 455, 457–8, 469
Segaud, Marion 184
Segre, Andrea 229
Segre, Davide 155–7, 163
Sei personaggi in cerca d'autore (Six Characters in Search of an Author, 1921) 276–7

Sei stato felice, Giovanni (You Were a Happy One, Giovanni, 1952) 261
Selmi, Giulia 225
Seltzer, Mark 464
senatore, Il (The Senator, 1958) 16, 273–8, 491
Sereni, Vittorio 85–7
Servizio nelle stazioni di rifornimento (Service at Gas Stations, 1955) 73
Sette canne, un vestito (Seven Reeds, One Suit, 1949) 446–7
Si gira... (Shoot!, 1915) 31
Sibilia, Sydney 226
sickness *see* illness
Signorinaeffe (Miss F, 2007) 228
Silenzio a Milano (Silence in Milan, 1958) 152–4, 492
Simmel, Georg 404–5, 413
sindacalista, Il (1972) 54, 495
Sinisgalli, Leonardo 91, 155, 179, 274, 307
Sitney, P. Adams 3, 31
Slovic, Scott 167
Smetto quando voglio (I Can Quite Whenever I Want, 2014, 2017) 226–7
Smiles, Samuel 26
socialism *see also* Partito Socialista Italiano 19, 26–7, 35, 37, 80, 87–8, 117, 152, 194–5, 217, 258, 266, 314, 353, 372, 405, 427–9, 436, 466, 474
Soldati, Mario 34–5, 97
Soldini, Silvio 227
Sole (Sun, 1929) 36
Sole cuore amore (Sun, Heart, Love, 2016) 227, 234
sole negli occhi, Il (Empty Eyes, 1953) 373
sole sorge ancora, Il (Outcry, 1946) 42, 375
Solinas, Franco 372–5
soliti ignoti, I (Big Deal on Madonna Street, 1958) 200–2

sommersi e i salvati, I (The Drowned and the Saved, 1986) 147
Sordi, Alberto 50–1, 196, 198, 203, 284, 460–1
southern Italy *see also* migration *and* Southern Question 6–7, 18–9, 26, 36–7, 42, 47–9, 53, 55–6, 63, 70–3, 77, 81, 87, 100, 115, 117–8, 152, 179, 205, 211, 256–8, 284, 290, 330–5, 349, 351, 356, 361–9, 391–2, 395–6, 416, 462, 470, 473, 479, 481–3, 485–6
Southern Question *see also* southern Italy 70, 256, 365
Spaghetti Story (2013) 226
Spinazzola, Vittorio 199–200, 205
sponsored films *see also* documentaries 4, 11, 13, 18–9, 44, 47, 59–76, 362, 367–9, 446–7, 449, 451, 455
Spracklen, Karl 303
Sputiamo su Hegel (Let's Spit on Hegel, 1970) 141
Stalin, Joseph 80, 195
Statuto dei Lavoratori (Workers' Charter) 8, 217
steel 6, 11, 18, 28, 32–4, 38, 49, 153, 210, 357, 362, 367
Storia, La (History: A Novel, 1974) 155–7, 492
strikes *see also* hot autumn *and* protest 2, 18, 27–9, 35, 37, 45, 114, 151–2, 158, 230, 232, 246, 309–10, 314, 334, 373, 430, 437, 462, 466, 468
students 4, 8, 53, 97, 108, 116, 243–4, 317, 328, 334, 372, 466–7, 482, 485
sub-proletarians 364–6, 369, 487
suora giovane, La (The Novice, 1959) 261
svedesi, Le (The Swedes, 1960) 202
Svevo, Italo 99, 101, 289

Tagliaferri, Aldo 350
Tamburelli, Armando 452
Tamburini, Dolores 382
Tasso, Torquato 167
tavola dei poveri, La (The Table of the Poor, 1932) 35–6
technology *see also* mechanization 5, 10–1, 30, 49, 68, 84–5, 91–2, 95, 99, 108, 212, 216, 255, 268, 304, 328, 344, 347, 403, 421, 439, 441–3, 447, 477
Tempi stretti (Tight Times, 1957) 15, 98, 100, 111, 113, 130, 169, 251–9, 493
tempo si è fermato, Il (Time Stood Still, 1959) 47, 405
Teorema (1968) 54
Terra madre (Mother Earth, 1931) 36
terra trema, La (1948) 42, 193, 195
Terrosi, Mario 297
Tesio, Giovanni 290
Testori, Giovanni 169, 178–9, 286, 391, 493
textiles 18, 26, 68, 162, 229, 232, 262–3, 280, 376, 429, 476
tigre domestica, La (The Domestic Tiger, 1964) 280
Todo Modo (1976) 459
Todorov, Tzvetan 277
Togliatti, Palmiro 69, 79–80, 137–40, 264, 266
Tonelli, Elvira 436
Toracca, Tiziano 16, 132
Tosi, Piero 433
Totò 196, 201
Totò, Peppino e la... malafemmina (Totò, Peppino and the Hussy, 1956) 196
Tozzi, Federigo 284
trade unions *see* labor unions
tragedia d'un personaggio, La (The Tragedy of a Character, 1911) 276
Trahison des clercs, La (The Betrayal of the Intellectuals, 1927) 280

Tramuta, Marie-José 160
Tre operai (Three Workers, 1934) 36–7
Trevico- Torino: Viaggio nel Fiat-Nam (Trevico-Turin: Voyage in Fiatnam, 1973) 20, 53, 465, 469, 479–89, 495
Tronti, Mario 137–40, 143, 146, 149, 466
Trovatelli, Enzo 73
Truffaut, François 401
Turco, Paolo 53
Turri, Eugenio 180, 183
Tuta blu. Ire, ricordi e sogni di un operaio del Sud (Blue Overalls: Rages, Memories and Dreams of a Worker from the South, 1978) 17, 117, 208, 349–57, 492
Tutta la vita davanti (Your Whole Life Ahead of You, 2008) 227, 230–1, 233
Tutti giù per terra (We All Fall Down, 1994) 208
Twain, Mark 243

Umberto D (1952) 193, 431
unemployment *see also* firings 33, 42, 115, 117, 128, 158, 189, 193, 195, 226, 229, 241, 257, 310, 364, 366, 369, 392, 415, 460, 462
Unità, L' 153, 240, 373–4, 481
Uno mandato da un tale (He Who Was Sent By a Guy, 1959) 245, 492
uomini che mascalzoni..., Gli (What Scoundrels Men Are!, 1932) 411
Uomini del marmo (Men of Marble, 1955) 375
uomini del petrolio, Gli (The Oil Men, 1965) 452, 455
uomo di paglia, L' (A Man of Straw, 1958) 18, 381–90, 494
uomo flessibile, L' (The Flexible Man, 2003) 226

Urzì, Saro 382, 384

Vaillant-Courturier, Marie Claude 371–2
vangelo secondo Precario - Storie di ordinaria flessibilità, Il (The Gospel According to Precarious – Stories of Ordinary Flexibility, 2005) 226–7
vedovo, Il (The Widower, 1959) 196
Vele e prore (Sails and Bows, 1939) 67–8
vello d'oro, Il (The Golden Fleece, 1965) 239
Venier, Massimo 227
Ventura, Lino 420
Verga, Giovanni 10, 34, 82, 167, 279, 285
Vergano, Aldo 42, 375
Verri, Alessandro 9
Verri, Il 92, 328–9
via del petrolio, La (The Oil Route, 1967) 446, 452
Vicari, Daniele 227, 229
Vicolo dell'acciaio (The Alley of Steel, 2010) 210
Vidor, King 408
vie del metano, Le (The Methane Way, 1951) 73
Viganò, Renata 160
villaggio modello, Un (A Model Town, 1941) 368
violenza illustrata, La (Violence Illustrated, 1976) 333
Virdia, Ferdinando 257
Virzì, Paolo 227, 229–31, 233
Visconti, Luchino 18, 38, 42, 48, 193, 195, 205, 391–401, 431, 465, 495
Visentini, Bruno 311–12
vita agra, La (It's a Hard Life, 1962 novel) 100, 205, 298–9, 301–2, 304, 491
vita agra, La (It's a Hard Life, 1964 film) 47, 494

Vita precaria e amore eterno (Precarious Life and Eternal Love, 2006) 215
Vita standard di un venditore provvisorio di collant (The Standard Life of a Temporary Pantyhose Salesman, 1985) 208
Vite flessibili (The Flexible Lives, 2003) 226–7
vitelloni, I (1953) 15, 193, 196–200, 204, 206
Vitti, Monica 440
Vittorini, Elio 13, 77, 79–86, 88, 91, 94–6, 98–9, 165–6, 176, 239–41, 243–6, 248, 253, 256, 261, 284
Viva il call center (Long Live the Call Center, 2005) 215
Vladimir Ilyich Lenin (1924) 269
Vlady, Marina 415, 425
Vogliamo tutto (We Want Everything, 1971) 17, 115, 117, 137, 217, 327–35, 491
Voice center (2007) 215
Volere è potere (Will is Power, 1869) 26
Volonté, Gian Maria 52, 464, 466
Volponi, Paolo 3, 17, 92–3, 97–8, 100–2, 111–3, 117, 131–3, 137, 155, 169, 174–5, 178, 180, 185, 208, 248–9, 286, 307–14, 350, 493
Vonderau, Patrick 64

Wahl, François 322
Wasson, Haidee 59
Weigel, Milene 372
Weil, Simone 16, 156, 251–3
Wertmüller, Lina 20, 55, 465, 469–78, 495
white collar *see* middle class
William Wilson (1839) 277
women workers *see* female workers
workerism *see* operaismo
Workers Leaving the Lumière Factory (1895) 10, 27, 371
working class 7, 12, 14–5, 17, 21, 30–1, 36–9, 45, 53, 55, 61, 75, 100–3, 105, 109–10, 114, 117, 120, 122, 130, 135, 142, 149, 153–7, 159–61, 182, 193–206, 211–2, 232, 234, 239–49, 252, 254, 256, 262, 266, 269–70, 298–300, 303, 308, 314, 324, 338, 342, 344, 349–57, 365–7, 382, 385–6, 391, 407, 427–37, 462, 464–7, 474, 479, 482, 484–5
World War I *see* First World War
World War II *see* Second World War

Yesenin, Sergei 262

Zafred, Mario 373
Zampa, Luigi 376
Zanardo, Monica 156
Zavattini, Cesare 36, 42, 405, 486
Zeta, Zelda 215
Zinato, Emanuele 13, 77
Zveteremich, Renato 281

PANORAMAS • ITALIAN MODERNITIES

Edited by
Pierpaolo Antonello and Robert Gordon,
University of Cambridge

Panoramas is a new strand of books within the Italian Modernities series. These volumes aim to provide accessible, wide-ranging, research-led accounts of significant new trends, emerging fields of study and new methodologies within work on modern Italian culture, history, and related disciplines.

Proposals are welcome for edited collections in English. Please provide a detailed outline, including abstracts for each proposed chapter, and a CV for each volume editor. For further information, contact the series editors, Pierpaolo Antonello (paa25@cam.ac.uk) and Robert Gordon (rscg1@cam.ac.uk).

Vol. 1 Giancarlo Lombardi and Christian Uva (eds): *Italian Political Cinema: Public Life, Imaginary, and Identity in Contemporary Italian Film*. 456 pages, 2016.
ISBN 978-3-0343-2217-1

Vol. 2 Carlo Baghetti, Jim Carter and Lorenzo Marmo: *Italian Industrial Literature and Film: Perspectives on the Representation of Postwar Labor*. 568 pages, 2021.
ISBN 978-1-78874-598-7

ITALIAN MODERNITIES

Edited by
Pierpaolo Antonello and Robert Gordon,
University of Cambridge

The series aims to publish innovative research on the written, material and visual cultures and intellectual history of modern Italy, from the nineteenth century to the present day. It is open to a wide variety of different approaches and methodologies, disciplines and interdisciplinary fields: from literary criticism and comparative literature to archival history, from cultural studies to material culture, from film and media studies to art history. It is especially interested in work which articulates aspects of Italy's particular, and in many respects, peculiar, interactions with notions of modernity and postmodernity, broadly understood. It also aims to encourage critical dialogue between new developments in scholarship in Italy and in the English-speaking world.

Proposals are welcome for either single-author monographs or edited collections (in English and/or Italian). Please provide a detailed outline, a sample chapter, and a CV. For further information, contact the series editors, Pierpaolo Antonello (paa25@cam.ac.uk) and Robert Gordon (rscg1@cam.ac.uk).

Vol. 1 Olivia Santovetti: *Digression: A Narrative Strategy in the Italian Novel*. 260 pages, 2007.
ISBN 978-3-03910-550-2

Vol. 2 Julie Dashwood and Margherita Ganeri (eds):
The Risorgimento of Federico De Roberto. 339 pages, 2009.
ISBN 978-3-03911-858-8

Vol. 3 Pierluigi Barrotta and Laura Lepschy with Emma Bond (eds):
Freud and Italian Culture. 252 pages, 2009.
ISBN 978-3-03911-847-2

Vol. 4 Pierpaolo Antonello and Florian Mussgnug (eds): *Postmodern Impegno: Ethics and Commitment in Contemporary Italian Culture*. 354 pages, 2009.
ISBN 978-3-0343-0125-1

Vol. 5 Florian Mussgnug: *The Eloquence of Ghosts: Giorgio Manganelli and the Afterlife of the Avant-Garde*.
257 pages, 2010.
ISBN 978-3-03911-835-9

Vol. 6 Christopher Rundle: *Publishing Translations in Fascist Italy*.
268 pages, 2010.
ISBN 978-3-03911-831-1

Vol. 7 Jacqueline Andall and Derek Duncan (eds): *National Belongings: Hybridity in Italian Colonial and Postcolonial Cultures*. 251 pages, 2010.
ISBN 978-3-03911-965-3

Vol. 8 Emiliano Perra: *Conflicts of Memory: The Reception of Holocaust Films and TV Programmes in Italy, 1945 to the Present*. 299 pages, 2010.
ISBN 978-3-03911-880-9

Vol. 9 Alan O'Leary: *Tragedia all'italiana: Italian Cinema and Italian Terrorisms, 1970–2010*. 300 pages, 2011.
ISBN 978-3-03911-574-7

Vol. 10 Robert Lumley: *Entering the Frame: Cinema and History in the Films of Yervant Gianikian and Angela Ricci Lucchi*.
228 pages. 2011.
ISBN 978-3-0343-0113-8

Vol. 11 Enrica Maria Ferrara: *Calvino e il teatro: storia di una passione rimossa*. 284 pages, 2011.
ISBN 978-3-0343-0176-3

Vol. 12 Niamh Cullen: *Piero Gobetti's Turin: Modernity, Myth and Memory*. 343 pages, 2011.
ISBN 978-3-0343-0262-3

Vol. 13 Jeffrey T. Schnapp: *Modernitalia*. 338 pages, 2012.
ISBN 978-3-0343-0762-8

Vol. 14 Eleanor Canright Chiari: *Undoing Time: The Cultural Memory of an Italian Prison*. 275 pages, 2012.
ISBN 978-3-0343-0256-2

Vol. 15 Alvise Sforza Tarabochia: *Psychiatry, Subjectivity, Community: Franco Basaglia and Biopolitics*. 226 pages, 2013.
ISBN 978-3-0343-0893-9

Vol. 16 Katharine Mitchell and Helena Sanson (eds): *Women and Gender in Post-Unification Italy: Between Private and Public Spheres*. 282 pages, 2013.
ISBN 978-3-0343-0996-7

Vol. 17 Enrico Cesaretti: *Fictions of Appetite: Alimentary Discourses in Italian Modernist Literature*. 280 pages, 2013.
ISBN 978-30343-0971-4

Vol. 18 Jennifer Burns: *Migrant Imaginaries: Figures in Italian Migration Literature*. 228 pages, 2013.
ISBN 978-3-0343-0986-8

Vol. 19 Donatella Maraschin: *Pasolini: cinema e antropologia*. 306 pages, 2014.
ISBN 978-3-0343-0255-5

Vol. 20 Danielle Hipkins and Roger Pitt (eds): *New Visions of the Child in Italian Cinema*. 356 pages, 2014.
ISBN 978-3-0343-0269-2

Vol. 21 Emma Bond, Guido Bonsaver and Federico Faloppa (eds): *Destination Italy: Representing Migration in Contemporary Media and Narrative*. 479 pages, 2015.
ISBN 978-3-0343-0961-5

Vol. 22 Charlotte Ross: *Eccentricity and Sameness: Discourses on Lesbianism and Desire between Women in Italy, 1860s–1930s*. 318 pages, 2015.
ISBN 978-3-0343-1820-4

Vol. 23 Fabio A. Camilletti and Paola Cori (eds): *Ten Steps: Critical Inquiries on Leopardi*. 330 pages, 2015.
ISBN 978-3-0343-1925-6

Vol. 24 Charles Burdett: *Italy, Islam and the Islamic World: Representations and Reflections, from 9/11 to the Arab Uprisings*. 232 pages, 2016.
ISBN 978-3-0343-1976-8

Vol. 25 Danielle Hipkins: *Italy's Other Women: Gender and Prostitution in Italian Cinema, 1940–1965*. 451 pages, 2016.
ISBN 978-3-0343-1934-8

Vol. 26 Luigi Petrella: *Staging the Fascist War: The Ministry of Popular Culture and Italian Propaganda on the Home Front, 1938–1943*. 266 pages, 2016.
ISBN 978-1-906165-70-3

Vol. 27 Marina Spunta and Jacopo Benci (eds): *Luigi Ghirri and the Photography of Place: Interdisciplinary Perspectives*.
364 pages, 2017.
ISBN 978-3-0343-2226-3

Vol. 28 Pierpaolo Antonello, Matilde Nardelli and Margherita Zanoletti (eds): *Bruno Munari: The Lightness of Art*.
434 pages, 2017.
ISBN 978-3-0343-1937-9

Vol. 29 Fabio Camilletti: *Italia lunare: gli anni Sessanta e l'occulto*.
258 pages, 2018.
ISBN 978-1-78707-462-0

Vol. 30 Sciltian Gastaldi and David Ward (eds): *Era mio padre: Italian Terrorism of the Anni di Piombo in the Postmemorials of Victims' Relatives*. 284 pages, 2018.
ISBN 978-1-78874-326-6

Vol. 31 Patrick McGauley: *Matera 1945-1960: The History of a 'National Disgrace'.*
254 pages, 2018.
ISBN 978-1-78874-357-0

Vol. 32 Federica Mazzara: *Reframing Migration: Lampedusa, Border Spectacle and Aesthetics of Subversion.*
268 pages, 2019.
ISBN 978-3-0343-1884-6

Vol. 33 Fabrizio De Donno: *Italian Orientalism: Nationhood, Cosmopolitanism and the Cultural Politics of Identity.*
376 pages, 2019.
ISBN 978-1-78874-018-0

Vol. 34 John Champagne: *Queer Ventennio: Italian Fascism, Homoerotic Art, and the Nonmodern in the Modern.*
320 pages, 2019.
ISBN 978-1-78997-224-5

Vol. 35 Maria Morelli: *Queer(ing) Gender in Italian Women's Writing: Maraini, Sapienza, Morante.*
314 pages, 2021.
ISBN 978-1-78874-175-0

Vol. 36 Gianluca Cinelli and Robert S. C. Gordon (eds): *Innesti: Primo Levi e i libri altrui.* 416 pages, 2020.
ISBN 978-1-78997-450-8

Vol. 37 Meriel Tulante: *Italian Chimeras: Narrating Italy through the Writing of Sebastiano Vassalli.* 320 pages, 2020.
ISBN 978-1-78997-702-8

Vol. 38 Giancarlo Lombardi and Christian Uva (eds): *Italian Political Cinema: Public Life, Imaginary, and Identity in Contemporary Italian Film.* 427 pages, 2016.
ISBN 978-3-0343-2217-1 (Vol. 1 in *Panoramas*)

Vol. 39 Emanuela Patti, *Opera Aperta: Italian Electronic Literature from the 1960s to the Present*. Forthcoming 2021.
ISBN 978-1-78997-859-9

Vol. 40 Carlo Baghetti, Jim Carter and Lorenzo Marmo: *Italian Industrial Literature and Film: Perspectives on the Representation of Postwar Labor*. 568 pages, 2021.
ISBN 978-1-78874-598-7 (Vol. 2 in *Panoramas*)

www.ingramcontent.com/pod-product-compliance
Lightning Source LLC
Chambersburg PA
CBHW051551230426
43668CB00013B/1819